ALSO BY THE EDITORS AT AMERICA'S TEST KITCHEN

The America's Test Kitchen Family Baking Book
The America's Test Kitchen Family Cookbook
The Best of America's Test Kitchen 2007, 2008, 2009
America's Test Kitchen Cooking for Two Volume One

THE COOK'S COUNTRY SERIES:
America's Best Lost Recipes
The Cook's Country Cookbook
Cook's Country Best Grilling Recipes

THE BEST RECIPE SERIES:
The Best Slow & Easy Recipes
The Best Chicken Recipes
The Best International Recipe
The Best Make-Ahead Recipe
The Best 30-Minute Recipe
The Best Light Recipe
The Cook's Illustrated Guide to Grilling & Barbecue
Best American Side Dishes
The New Best Recipe
The Best Cover & Bake Recipes
The Best Meat Recipes
Baking Illustrated
Restaurant Favorites at Home
The Best Vegetable Recipes
The Best Italian Classics
The Best American Classics
The Best Soups & Stews

THE TV COMPANION SERIES:
America's Test Kitchen: The TV Companion Cookbook 2009
Behind the Scenes with America's Test Kitchen
Test Kitchen Favorites
Cooking at Home with America's Test Kitchen
America's Test Kitchen Live!
Inside America's Test Kitchen
Here in America's Test Kitchen
The America's Test Kitchen Cookbook

834 Kitchen Quick Tips

To order any of our books, visit us at
http://www.cooksillustrated.com
http://www.americastestkitchen.com
or call 800-611-0759

WELCOME TO
AMERICA'S TEST KITCHEN

THIS BOOK HAS BEEN TESTED, WRITTEN, AND edited by the folks at America's Test Kitchen, a very real 2,500-square-foot kitchen located just outside of Boston. It is the home of *Cook's Illustrated* magazine and *Cook's Country* magazine and is the Monday-through-Friday destination for more than three dozen test cooks, editors, food scientists, tasters, and cookware specialists. Our mission is to test recipes over and over again until we understand how and why they work and until we arrive at the "best" version.

We start the process of testing a recipe with a complete lack of conviction, which means that we accept no claim, no theory, no technique, and no recipe at face value. We simply assemble as many variations as possible, test a half dozen of the most promising, and taste the results blind. We then construct our own hybrid recipe and continue to test it, varying ingredients, techniques, and cooking times until we reach a consensus. The result, we hope, is the best version of a particular recipe, but we realize that only you can be the final judge of our success (or failure). As we like to say in the test kitchen, "We make the mistakes, so you don't have to."

All of this would not be possible without a belief that good cooking, much like good music, is indeed based on a foundation of objective technique. Some people like spicy foods and others don't, but there is a right way to sauté, there is a best way to cook a pot roast, and there are measurable scientific principles involved in producing perfectly beaten, stable egg whites. This is our ultimate goal: to investigate the fundamental principles of cooking so that you become a better cook. It is as simple as that.

You can watch us work (in our actual test kitchen) by tuning in to *America's Test Kitchen* (www.americastestkitchen.com) or *Cook's Country from America's Test Kitchen* (www.cookscountrytv.com) on public television, or by subscribing to *Cook's Illustrated* magazine (www.cooksillustrated.com) or *Cook's Country* magazine (www.cookscountry.com). We welcome you into our kitchen, where you can stand by our side as we test our way to the "best" recipes in America.

THE BEST SKILLET RECIPES

A BEST RECIPE CLASSIC

THE
BEST
SKILLET
RECIPES

A BEST RECIPE CLASSIC

BY THE EDITORS OF

COOK'S ILLUSTRATED

PHOTOGRAPHY

KELLER + KELLER, CARL TREMBLAY, AND DANIEL J. VAN ACKERE

ILLUSTRATIONS

JOHN BURGOYNE

America's
TEST KITCHEN

BROOKLINE, MASSACHUSETTS

America's Test Kitchen
17 Station Street
Brookline, MA 02445

ISBN-13: 978-1-933615-41-7
ISBN-10: 1-933615-41-9

Library of Congress Cataloging-in-Publication Data
The Editors of *Cook's Illustrated*

The Best Skillet Recipes: What's the best way to make lasagna with rich, meaty flavor, chunks of tomato, and gooey cheese, without ever turning on the oven or boiling a pot of water? In a skillet. Here are more than 250 foolproof recipes for both skillet standbys and easy new classics.

1st Edition
ISBN-13: 978-1-933615-41-7
ISBN-10: 1-933615-41-9
(hardcover): U.S. $35 CAN $45
I. Cooking. I. Title
2009

Manufactured in the United States of America

10 9 8 7 6 5 4 3 2 1

Distributed by America's Test Kitchen, 17 Station Street, Brookline, MA 02445

Editorial Director: Jack Bishop
Executive Editor: Elizabeth Carduff
Senior Food Editor: Julia Collin Davison
Associate Editors: Louise Flaig, Kate Hartke, and Rachel Toomey
Editorial Assistant: Elizabeth Pohm
Test Cooks: Suzannah McFerran, Bryan Roof, and Megan Wycoff
Assistant Test Cook: Adelaide Parker
Design Director: Amy Klee
Art Director: Greg Galvan
Designers: Tiffani Beckwith and Erica Lee
Staff Photographer: Daniel J. van Ackere
Additional Photography: Keller+Keller and Carl Tremblay
Food Styling: Marie Piraino and Mary Jane Sawyer
Illustrator: John Burgoyne
Production Director: Guy Rochford
Senior Production Manager: Jessica Lindheimer Quirk
Traffic and Project Manager: Alice Carpenter
Color and Imaging Specialist: Andrew Mannone
Production and Imaging Specialist: Judy Blomquist and Lauren Pettapiece
Copyeditor: Cheryl Redmond
Proofreader: Debra Hudak
Indexer: Elizabeth Parson

Pictured on front of jacket: Meaty Lasagna (page 98)

Pictured on back of jacket: Pan-Roasted Chicken with Sage-Vermouth Sauce (page 52), Classic Beef Pot Pie (page 193), Ricotta, Bacon, and Scallion Pizza (page 222), Baked Ziti with Sausage (page 100), and Lemon Soufflé (page 332)

Contents

PREFACE

MARION HARLAND WAS A CONTEMPORARY of Fannie Farmer and wrote a number of cookbooks. In 1875, Harland published *Breakfast, Luncheon and Tea* and in it extolled the virtues of the Dover eggbeater, saying, "But if I could not get another, I would not sell mine for fifty dollars—nor a hundred." Now, this was nothing more than the first hand-cranked rotary eggbeater. Before this time, cooks used a whisk and egg whites were often whipped up on a plate, the effort required to do the job being considerable.

So, yes, many cookware items do evolve over time, making existing designs seem instantly obsolete. My lifetime has seen the advent of the Cuisinart, the Chef's Choice Electric Knife Sharpener, and the Thermapen instant-read digital thermometer. I might be a bit less inclined to jump up and down about the electric wine bottle opener, the "Shrimp Butler" that slits shrimp shells in just seconds, or the Vacu-Vin Pineapple Slicer, which actually does a nice job (but a chef's knife ain't bad either).

But the skillet stands apart as a steady, reliable fixture in the kitchen virtually unchanged since the early days of cast iron. Sure, there are nonstick skillets and enameled cast-iron skillets; there are $20 skillets and $200 skillets; there are ovensafe skillets and those with handles that will melt at high temperatures, but the basic design has held up through the centuries.

This is a good thing. It demonstrates the essential value of this central piece of cookware and its flexibility down through the ages, serving as a dripping pan under roasts, as an all-purpose fryer, and as the everyday pan to cook bacon and eggs.

The question now was, what else could we do with it? That was what our test cooks asked a couple of years ago when we sat down to begin work on this book. Like finding 1,001 uses for duct tape, we wondered if the skillet had unrealized potential.

We began our investigations with the notion of browning meat or poultry in a skillet and then finishing it in the oven—you produce great flavor and then slow down the cooking in the oven so the meat ends up perfectly cooked and juicy. Next we turned to pasta. Could we make a quick and easy lasagna in a skillet and entirely on the stovetop? Yup. (I vastly prefer this version to the baked variety.) How about skillet suppers made with penne, chicken, sausage, broccoli, or beans? No problem.

Then we moved on to variations on pot pies, casseroles, shepherd's pie, pizzas, stir-fries, curries, frittatas, omelets, hash, strata, all sorts of vegetable dishes including glazed carrots, fritters, rösti, and ratatouille, and then we finished off with desserts: skillet cobblers, crisps, apple pancakes, and pudding cakes.

Not bad for a simple piece of cookware. And that's the point. Take something simple, something useful, and through the application of experience and skill, transform it into an extraordinary tool.

I will never forget the first time I looked into Charlie Bentley's toolbox on his 1949 Farmall tractor. It held nothing more than baling twine, a hammer, a pair of pliers, one screwdriver, wire, and assorted nuts and bolts. Yet he always managed to fix the tractor, the baler, or the hay wagon. You wouldn't believe what I have seen farmers do with whatever tools were at hand, even if it was just a crowbar or a flat rock.

Cooking isn't about expensive tools, imported knives, or the latest electrical bit of wizardry—it's about confidence and experience. That's what this book can provide. Start with something useful—a skillet—and then slowly build on that beginning with recipes that work, that are well-tested, but that also teach a wide range of possibilities from sautéing to stewing, braising, glazing, roasting, baking, and simmering. There is a whole world, right there, in the simplest of kitchen tools, the skillet. Not bad for something that has been around a lot longer than Fannie Farmer.

Christopher Kimball
Founder and Editor,
Cook's Illustrated and *Cook's Country*
Host, *America's Test Kitchen* and
Cook's Country from America's Test Kitchen

1

SKILLET BASICS

SKILLET BASICS

A GOOD SKILLET IS UNDOUBTEDLY THE MOST versatile pan in every cook's arsenal—it can be used to cook everything from the simplest pan-seared hamburger to a stir-fry or cherry cobbler.

Before you even get started, you have to select the right pan. For most of the recipes in this book, we recommend a traditional skillet, but we'll indicate when a nonstick skillet is necessary. A sturdy, heavy traditional skillet is great for cooking meat, poultry, pork, and pan sauces. To cook eggs, fish, or stir-fries, we prefer to use a nonstick skillet. (See pages 12 and 14 for our favorite traditional and nonstick skillets.)

For this first chapter, we went back to the basics and focused on the conventional uses for a skillet: sautéing, pan-searing, and pan-frying. We selected recipes that are cooked entirely on the stovetop, where mastering the fundamentals of heat level and technique and choosing the right cut of meat or fish are absolutely essential. When it comes to these elements, a little control and attention to detail go a long way. After all, when it's just you, a skillet, and a boneless, skinless chicken breast, there is no hiding from poor execution—an anemic-looking chicken breast cannot be saved (or disguised).

First, we tackled the cornerstones of skillet cookery: sautéing and pan-searing. Both rely on high heat and a small amount of fat to cook foods quickly, although pan-searing differs in that the cuts of meat and fish being sautéed are thicker, and the ultimate goal is a deeper-than-golden brown crust. Once you know how to sauté and pan-sear properly, and build a sauce from the fond (the browned bits left behind from sautéing or searing meat, fish, shellfish, or poultry), you will have mastered a culinary basic that you will use your entire life. Pan-frying, browning coated foods for a crispy exterior, is another excellent use for the skillet—its sloped sides make it easy to maneuver the food and facilitate evaporation, which enables browning.

Sticking with the basics, we developed a recipe for hamburgers (see page 35) cooked the old-fashioned way: in a skillet, with a crispy, deep brown exterior and tender, juicy interior. In addition, for those of us who love a burger but want a lighter option, we created a Pan-Seared Turkey Burger (page 34). Ricotta cheese makes for a turkey burger

that just might make you add burger night back to the weekly rotation.

In this chapter you'll also find recipes that build on the fundamentals to create dishes that are a bit more complex or go beyond the norm. To achieve crisp skin, flavorful meat, and a thick, glossy sauce in our Chicken Teriyaki (page 32), we had to get creative—we cooked the chicken thighs in the skillet, skin side down and weighted with a Dutch oven, and added the sauce at the end. We took a similar approach in our Steak au Poivre with Brandied Cream Sauce (page 37) so that the peppercorns didn't fall off into the pan—we resorted to pressing the peppercorns into the steaks with a cake pan as the steaks cooked. For our Crispy Tofu with Sweet Soy-Garlic Sauce (page 46), we revisited the standard cornstarch coating for tofu and added cornmeal—and came up with a tofu dish that really lives up to its name.

The recipes and basic techniques in this chapter will serve you well. After you learn how to sear and sauté like a pro, you can cook a variety of recipes, whether you want to make simple sautéed chicken cutlets, pan-seared shrimp accented with butter and parsley, or just a good hamburger.

SAUTÉED AND PAN-SEARED MEAT AND FISH

THE BEDROCK OF ALL COOKING, SAUTÉING may seem simple, but it actually takes some practice to get it right. Who hasn't thrown a chicken breast into a hot skillet only to have it stick firmly to the bottom of the pan, or charred the outside of a pork chop before the center was cooked through? Don't fret; there are tips to help you sauté properly.

The principles of sautéing and pan-searing are pretty straightforward, but they're not one-size-fits-all methods. Meat, fish, and shellfish cook differently; think of delicate thin fish fillets, or the cooking time of chicken as compared to steak. They all require slightly different handling. While the technique may vary, the ultimate goals are the same: a well-seared crust and a moist, juicy interior.

In most cases, we prefer to sauté in a traditional skillet, which provides even browning and allows for the creation of fond for making a pan sauce. Cooking fish is the exception—it is so delicate and prone to sticking and falling apart that using a non-stick skillet makes cooking it more foolproof. When it comes to the skillet, size matters; using a large, heavy skillet is key for even heat distribution.

In general, sautéing and pan-searing are suited to cuts of meat and fish that are tender—boneless chicken breasts, steaks, pork chops, fish fillets, shrimp, and scallops—and therefore can be cooked quickly. The first thing to consider is the size of the meat or fish. Be sure to select breasts, steaks, chops, and fillets of equal size, so they will cook at the same rate. To achieve the perfect crust, make sure that the meat, fish, or shellfish is patted dry (excess moisture on the surface prevents a flavorful golden brown exterior from forming), heat the fat or oil in the skillet to just smoking before you add anything to it, and don't crowd the skillet. If your pan is not hot enough, the meat will stick. And if the steaks or chops are jammed too tightly together, they will cool the pan down and stew, not sear.

Once the meat or fish has a brown crust on the first side, flip it over and continue to cook it on the second side. For thicker pieces of meat or fish, we lower the heat after turning them over to prevent the pan from scorching and the exterior from getting leathery and stringy. Resist the temptation to move the food while it cooks, as this will prohibit browning. And since thick cuts will continue to cook a little after you remove them from the pan, always undercook them a bit to allow for this. With these basics down, you can sauté or pan-sear pretty much anything; however, there are some details to keep in mind depending upon what you are cooking.

When it comes to chicken breasts (mainly boneless and skinless), we find that the thin tip of the breast and the opposite end, which is more plump, cook at different rates. To remedy this problem, we pound the chicken breasts gently to an even ½-inch thickness with a meat pounder or the bottom of a small saucepan. We also recommend trimming the fat and removing the tenderloin from each breast—the tenderloin tends to fall off when cooking and dramatically affect the cooking

REMOVING THE TENDERLOINS FROM CHICKEN BREASTS

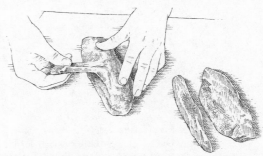

The tenderloin (the long, narrow piece of meat attached to each chicken breast) tends to fall off during pounding, so it is best removed and reserved for another use, such as a stir-fry. To remove, simply pull it off.

time (you can reserve it for another use such as a stir-fry). For cutlets, we suggest cutting your own (see page 7); store-bought cutlets are ragged and uneven. Whether cooking breasts or cutlets, we find that flouring the chicken prior to sautéing protects the meat from drying out and prevents it from sticking to the skillet.

With skillet cooking, it's a little easier (and quicker) to get a great steak-house meal in your own home. A great pan-seared steak has a deeply colored, crisp brown crust and a rosy, juicy interior. First, you have to choose the right steaks. The thickness, shape, and size of the steaks is important because this will determine how well they fit into the skillet and how evenly they will cook. If they are too large for your skillet or oddly shaped, you may need to cut them in half in order to make them fit. Depending on your steak, cooking time may vary widely, due to both thickness and size (see page 11 for recommended steaks for pan-searing).

Pan-searing pork chops is similar to pan-searing steak—choosing the right chops makes a difference. For simple pan-searing, bone-in chops have better flavor. Rib chops are juicier than the leaner center-cut chops, and don't forget that the thickness of the chops is important too. They should be about ½ to 1 inch thick, so that you can get a good sear, giving the chop a flavorful browned crust while still allowing a moist, pink interior. If you're not using enhanced pork (see page 40 for more information) and you have the time, we recommend brining the

TRIMMING CHICKEN BREASTS

Most chicken breasts have a little yellow or white fat still attached to the breast meat. Lay each breast tenderloin side down and smooth the top with your fingers. Any fat will slide to the edge of the breast, where it can be trimmed with a knife.

chops (soaking them in a solution of water, salt, and sometimes sugar; see page 56 for more information) to keep them moist and juicy.

Pork medallions, which are cut from the tenderloin, pose more of a challenge. Because medallions are boneless and relatively small, they can easily overcook by the time the exterior has seared. It's best to trim away the tapered end of the tenderloin (therefore limiting the number of oddly and unevenly shaped pieces), then cut the tenderloin into whopping 1½-inch-thick medallions, tying each medallion around the middle with twine to help it keep its shape during cooking (see the illustrations on page 13). Also, rather than leaving the sides of the medallions unbrowned, we stand them on their sides (using tongs) during the searing process, so they are evenly browned all over.

Fish fillets take well to sautéing. Preventing the fish from sticking to the skillet (and falling apart) is the big challenge. A nonstick skillet helps, as does using a wide, thin spatula to turn the fillets—in some cases, using two spatulas is helpful (see the illustration on page 13). Because fish cooks so quickly, overcooking can easily occur. For thin fillets, we flour them, lightly brown them on the first side, then flip them over and let them cook through, about 30 seconds longer. For thicker fillets, we slightly undercook the fish, as we would with meat, and then let it rest before serving; the residual heat will gently finish cooking the fish.

Like thin fillets, shrimp and scallops are delicate and cook quickly; the challenge lies in getting the outside brown before the inside overcooks.

When they're properly seared, the plumpness and sweetness of these shellfish will shine through. We recommend using peeled shrimp—they're easier to eat and unpeeled shrimp fail to pick up the delicious caramelized flavor that pan-searing provides. And just a pinch of sugar sprinkled over the shrimp before searing boosts the flavor and encourages browning. Scallops are a bit more finicky in the pan than the shrimp—they have to be perfectly dry to develop a good crust before being overcooked. We patted ours down with paper towels and cooked them in two batches so they would sear, not steam.

An added bonus to sautéing and pan-searing is the fond left behind in the skillet. It's the perfect starting point for making a quick, delicious pan sauce. Pan sauces provide endless variety, turning a simple sautéed piece of meat or fish into something truly special. But there are other options as well. In addition to pan sauces, we've included recipes for compound butters (butters flavored with aromatics, herbs, and sometimes cheese) and relish-type sauces. Mix and match the meat and fish recipes in this chapter with the pan sauces, compound butters, and relishes, and dinner will never be boring again.

Sautéed Chicken Breasts
SERVES 4

If you like, serve the chicken with a pan sauce (see pages 18–19), compound butter (see pages 22–24), or relish (see pages 20–22).

4   (5- to 6-ounce) boneless, skinless chicken breasts, tenderloins removed and breasts trimmed (see the illustrations on page 5 and above)
½   cup unbleached all-purpose flour
    Salt and ground black pepper
2   tablespoons vegetable oil

1. Following the illustration on page 7, pound each chicken breast between two sheets of plastic wrap to a uniform ½-inch thickness.

2. Place the flour in a shallow dish. Pat the chicken breasts dry with paper towels and season with salt and pepper. Working with 1 chicken breast

POUNDING CHICKEN BREASTS AND CUTLETS

To ensure that chicken breasts and cutlets are of even thickness (and so will cook evenly), you may need to pound them. Place the breasts or cutlets, smooth side down, on a large sheet of plastic wrap. Cover with a second sheet of plastic wrap and pound gently to make sure that each breast or cutlet has the same thickness from end to end.

at a time, dredge in the flour, shaking off the excess.

3. Heat the oil in a 12-inch skillet over medium-high heat until just smoking. Carefully lay the chicken breasts in the skillet and cook until well browned on the first side, 6 to 8 minutes.

4. Flip the chicken breasts over, reduce the heat to medium, and continue to cook until the thickest part of the chicken breasts register 160 to 165 degrees on an instant-read thermometer, 6 to 8 minutes longer.

5. Transfer the chicken breasts to a plate, tent loosely with foil, and let rest for 5 minutes, or while making a pan sauce. Serve.

Sautéed Chicken Cutlets

SERVES 4

Be careful not to overcook the cutlets—they really do cook through in just 4 minutes. Because these cutlets are so thin, they do not require a 5-minute resting time before serving. If you like, serve the chicken with a pan sauce (see pages 18–19), compound butter (see pages 22–24), or relish (see pages 20–22).

4	(5- to 6-ounce) boneless, skinless chicken breasts, tenderloins removed and breasts trimmed (see the illustrations on pages 5 and 6)
½	cup unbleached all-purpose flour
	Salt and ground black pepper
¼	cup vegetable oil

1. Following the illustrations below, slice each chicken breast in half horizontally into cutlets. Pound each cutlet between two sheets of plastic wrap to a uniform ¼-inch thickness.

2. Place the flour in a shallow dish. Pat the chicken cutlets dry with paper towels and season with salt and pepper. Working with 1 chicken cutlet at a time, dredge in the flour, shaking off the excess.

3. Heat 2 tablespoons of the oil in a 12-inch skillet over medium-high heat until just smoking. Carefully lay 4 of the chicken cutlets in the skillet and cook until lightly browned on both sides, about 4 minutes. Transfer the chicken cutlets to a plate and tent loosely with foil.

4. Add the remaining 2 tablespoons oil to the skillet and repeat with the remaining chicken cutlets. Transfer to the plate and tent loosely with foil if making a pan sauce or serve immediately.

SLICING CHICKEN BREASTS INTO CUTLETS

Cutlets are about half the thickness of boneless, skinless breasts and are called for in many recipes. Rather than buy them already cut, we prefer to make them ourselves—store-bought cutlets are often ragged, and they vary widely in size and thickness.

1. Lay the chicken breast flat on a cutting board, smooth side facing up. Rest one hand on top of the chicken and, using a sharp chef's knife, carefully slice the chicken in half horizontally.

2. This will yield two thin cutlets between ¼ and ½ inch thick.

Pan-Searing and Sautéing 101

Sautéing and pan-searing are not difficult but they do require some know-how for successful results. Follow our equipment recommendations and these tips for preparing browned, juicy breasts and cutlets, well-seared steaks and chops, and golden fish fillets.

EQUIPMENT

COOKWARE

Pans designed for sautéing come in two distinct styles: straight-sided and slope-sided. Through testing, we have found that straight sides inhibit moisture evaporation, allowing foods to "stew." Depending on the manufacturer, a sloped-sided pan may be called everything from an omelet pan to a skillet to a fry pan. For the sake of standardization, we refer to any slope-sided shallow pan as a skillet. For our favorite traditional and nonstick skillets, see pages 12 and 14, respectively.

ILL-SUITED FOR SAUTÉING
Straight-sided pans inhibit evaporation. They are best used for pan-frying and shallow braising.

PERFECT FOR SAUTÉING
Sloped sides allow for quick evaporation of moisture, preventing foods from stewing in exuded juices.

MEASURING A SKILLET
The industry may not agree on what to call a slope-sided pan, but there is agreement on sizing conventions. All skillets are measured outer lip to outer lip.

THE RIGHT TOOLS

To maneuver food in a skillet as it sautés, you need the following tools:

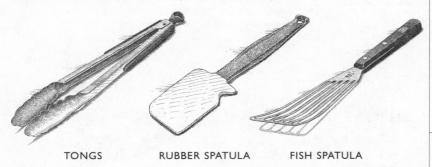

TONGS   RUBBER SPATULA   FISH SPATULA

TONGS are a heatproof extension of your hand and are invaluable whether moving cutlets or stirring vegetables (when closed, they work like a spoon or spatula). After testing a variety of brands and styles, we found models from OXO and Edlund to be our favorites because they opened wide, had a firm yet comfortable spring tension, and had scalloped—not serrated—tips that gripped securely without damaging food. Medium-length (12-inch) tongs are the most versatile size.

HEATPROOF RUBBER SPATULAS do a great job of scraping up stuck-on bits of food. After testing 10 popular brands of heatproof spatulas (through baking tasks, general scraping chores, and an abuse test), we found Rubbermaid's Professional 13½-Inch Heat Resistant Scraper and Tovolo's Silicone Spatula to be the best of the bunch (see page 275 for more information).

FISH SPATULAS maneuver delicate foods with ease. Wüsthof's Gourmet 7½-Inch Slotted Turner/Fish Spatula was our favorite in a recent test.

4 KEY STEPS TO SUCCESSFUL SAUTÉING

1. PAT THE MEAT DRY

Always pat the meat or fish dry with paper towels just before cooking. If you bypass this step, the excess moisture on the surface of the meat will prevent a flavorful brown crust from forming.

2. GET THE SKILLET HOT

To determine when a skillet is ready for sautéing, we use the term "just smoking." When wisps of smoke begin to rise from the oil in the skillet, that is when you should add your meat or fish. If the pan is not hot enough, food will stick and not brown as well.

3. DON'T TOUCH!

Leave the food undisturbed while it cooks, flipping it just once in order to brown the second side. If you constantly flip it or move it around the pan as it cooks, you will both inhibit the meat from browning and mar any crust that is forming.

4. LET CARRYOVER COOKING FINISH THE JOB

Don't cook the food through completely in the pan, or the residual heat will render it overcooked and dried out by the time you serve it. By slightly undercooking everything and letting it rest for 5 to 10 minutes before serving, you will ensure properly cooked and juicy meat every time. (The exceptions to this rule are chicken cutlets and thin fish fillets, which are thin enough to cook through in the pan.) See "Two Ways to Determine Doneness" on page 9 for more information.

OIL

BEST CHOICE: After sautéing chicken (as well as meat and fish) in a variety of different oils, from $48-per-liter extra-virgin olive oil to cheap canola oil, we found flavor differences to be virtually imperceptible. That said, we avoid unrefined oils such as extra-virgin olive oil because they have a low smoke point and are thus an inaccurate guide to the skillet's temperature. Butter, too, burns fairly easily unless mixed with oil.

SAUTÉ TROUBLESHOOTING

Over the years, we've found that the following problems are most likely to cause poor results when sautéing:

WARPED SKILLET: It's nearly impossible to brown meat or fish evenly in a skillet with an uneven, warped bottom. If you are unsure of your skillet's evenness, rest the pan on a flat surface. Does it rock to and fro? Does water pool in a particular spot? Adding extra oil to the skillet will help "level" the pan and can improve browning, but it's no guarantee. Warped pans, however, are fine for sautéing vegetables because they are moved frequently.

UNEVEN HEATING: Make sure your pan is properly sized to the burner. If the skillet is too big for the burner, only the center will fully heat; if it's too small, the pan may become excessively hot.

THIN PANS: Thin, inexpensive pans heat and cool more rapidly than thicker, heavy-bottomed pans and thus demand more attention. Gauge the browning speed and adjust the burner temperature accordingly.

OVERCROWDING: Avoid overcrowding the pan, which will cause food to steam and thereby affect flavor, color, and texture. Choose the right pan size and allow some space between the food (as shown at right).

STUCK-ON FOODS: If your meat or fish fuses to the skillet, try this tip for freeing it: Dip a flexible spatula into cold water and slide the spatula blade underneath the piece of meat. The cool, wet spatula blade breaks the bond between skillet and meat.

TWO WAYS TO DETERMINE DONENESS

Knowing when to pull the food out of the skillet is one of the most important keys to sautéing. An instant-read thermometer is the most reliable method for checking the doneness of chicken, beef, and pork (below left), while a simple nick-and-peek test (below right)—making a small nick at the center of the meat or fish and judging its color—works best for thick pieces of fish. That said, you can, in a pinch, use the nick-and-peek method for meat and poultry. Cutlets, thin fish fillets, shrimp, and scallops all cook too quickly for an actual doneness test and you should rely more on the visual cues and cooking times.

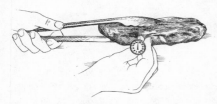

A. Insert an instant-read thermometer through the side of a chicken breast, steak, or pork chop for the most accurate reading. Refer to the chart below for the temperatures at which the meat should be removed from the pan (the temperature of the meat will continue to climb between 5 and 10 degrees as it rests before serving).

B. When you think the food is nearing doneness, make a small nick halfway through the meat with a paring knife and examine the color of the interior. If there is a bone, nick next to the bone for an accurate reading (the area along the bone takes the longest to cook).

MEAT	COOK UNTIL IT REGISTERS	SERVING TEMPERATURE
CHICKEN AND TURKEY BREASTS	160 to 165 degrees	160 to 165 degrees
CHICKEN THIGHS	175 degrees	175 degrees
PORK	140 to 145 degrees	150 degrees
BEEF AND LAMB		
Rare	115 to 120 degrees	125 degrees
Medium-Rare	120 to 125 degrees	130 degrees
Medium	130 to 135 degrees	140 degrees
Medium-Well	140 to 145 degrees	150 degrees
Well-Done	150 to 155 degrees	160 degrees

Pan-Seared Steaks

SERVES 4

See page 11 to help you choose a steak to your liking. Bigger steaks will take a longer time to cook and will be on the higher end of the range of cooking times in steps 1 and 2. If you like, serve the steaks with a pan sauce (see pages 18–19), compound butter (see pages 22–24), or relish (see pages 20–22).

2	pounds boneless beef steaks, 1 to 1¼ inches thick, trimmed
	Salt and ground black pepper
1	tablespoon vegetable oil

1. Pat the steaks dry with paper towels and season with salt and pepper. Heat the oil in a 12-inch skillet over medium-high heat until just smoking. Carefully lay the steaks in the skillet and cook until well browned on the first side, 3 to 5 minutes.

2. Flip the steaks over, reduce the heat to medium, and continue to cook to the desired doneness (see page 9), 5 to 20 minutes longer.

3. Transfer the steaks to a plate, tent loosely with foil, and let rest for 5 minutes, or while making a pan sauce. Serve.

Pan-Seared Pork Chops

SERVES 4

If the pork is enhanced (see page 40 for more information), do not brine. If brining the pork, do not season with salt in step 1. If you like, serve the pork chops with a pan sauce (see pages 18–19), compound butter (see pages 22–24), or relish (see pages 20–22).

4	(8- to 10-ounce) bone-in pork rib chops, ¾ to 1 inch thick, trimmed and brined if desired (see page 56)
	Salt and ground black pepper
1	tablespoon vegetable oil

1. Following the illustration at right, slit the sides of the pork chops. Pat the pork chops dry with paper towels and season with salt and pepper. Heat the oil in a 12-inch skillet over medium-high heat until just smoking. Carefully arrange the pork chops in the skillet and cook until well browned on the first side, about 4 minutes.

2. Flip the pork chops over, reduce the heat to medium, and continue to cook until the centers of the pork chops register 140 to 145 degrees on an instant-read thermometer, 5 to 10 minutes longer.

3. Transfer the pork chops to a plate, tent loosely with foil, and let rest until the centers of the pork chops register 150 degrees on an instant-read thermometer, about 5 minutes, or while making a pan sauce. Serve.

COOKING PORK CHOPS

Getting pork chops to lie flat and cook evenly requires two simple techniques.

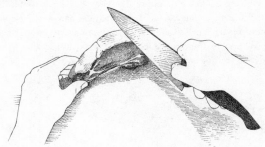

1. Pork chops buckle during cooking. To prevent this from happening, cut two slits about 2 inches apart through the fat and connective tissue.

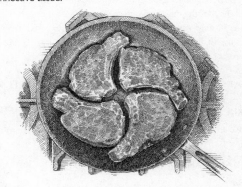

2. Arrange the pork chops in a pinwheel pattern with the tips of the ribs pointing toward the edge of the skillet in order to fit them evenly in the skillet.

Choosing a Steak

The array of steaks at the supermarket can be overwhelming, and the steak you choose can make all the difference in terms of cost, flavor, and texture. When choosing steak, look for meat that has a bright, lively color. Beef normally ranges in color from pink to red, but dark meat probably indicates an older, tougher animal. The external fat as well as the fat that runs through the meat (called intramuscular fat or marbling) should be as white as possible. The marbling should be smooth and fine, running all through the meat, rather than showing up in clumps; smooth marbling melts into the meat during cooking, while clumps remain as fat pockets. Stay away from packages that show a lot of red juice, known as purge. The purge may indicate a bad job of freezing; as a result, the steak will be dry and cottony.

Below we've listed the boneless steaks we recommend for pan-searing. Boneless steaks will rest flush against the pan and are easier to pan-sear than bone-in steaks. Steaks sport different names depending on locale. We've used industry names that we feel best describe where the steaks lie on the animal; you'll find some other common names also listed. We also provide a brief description of flavor and tenderness. And, as the price of steak varies widely depending on the cut, we provide an indication of cost ($$$$ being the most expensive).

RIB-EYE STEAK

ALTERNATE NAMES:
Spencer Steak or Delmonico Steak

COST: $$$

Rib-eye steaks have a rich, smooth texture and contain large pockets of fat.

TOP LOIN STEAK

ALTERNATE NAMES: Strip Steak, Sirloin Strip Steak, Hotel Steak, Kansas City Strip, or New York Strip

COST: $$$

The top loin steak has a rich, smooth flavor, but has a noticeable grain and is slightly chewy.

TENDERLOIN STEAK

ALTERNATE NAMES: Filet Mignon, Châteaubriand, or Tournedo

COST: $$$$

Tenderloin steaks are extremely tender and, since Americans prize tenderness above all else in their steaks, they are very expensive. Unfortunately, tenderloin steaks are not known for having much beefy flavor.

TOP SIRLOIN STEAK

ALTERNATE NAMES:
Shell Sirloin, New York Sirloin, Boneless Sirloin Butt Steak, or Top Sirloin Butt Center-Cut Steak

COST: $

Not to be confused with the superior top loin steak, the top sirloin steak has a strong, moderately rich flavor and an extremely chewy texture. This steak needs to be sliced thin against the grain before serving.

FLANK STEAK

ALTERNATE NAMES:
Jiffy Steak

COST: $$$

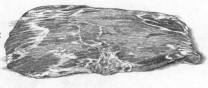

Flank steak has a clean, beefy flavor and a distinct longitudinal grain that is very chewy. To minimize the stringy, chewy nature of flank steak, it should not be cooked past medium and should always be sliced thin against the grain.

TOP BLADE STEAK

ALTERNATE NAMES:
Flat-Iron Steak, Blade Steak

COST: $

Top blade steaks are moderately tender with decent beef flavor, but they have a line of tough gristle running down the center that needs to be removed before cooking or serving. Also, we've found that the overall quality of blade steaks can vary dramatically, so check for excessive gristle before purchasing.

Pan-Seared Pork Tenderloin Medallions

SERVES 4 TO 6

We prefer natural pork to enhanced pork (see page 40 for more information), though both will work in this recipe. Begin checking the doneness of smaller medallions 1 or 2 minutes early; they may need to be taken out of the skillet a little sooner than the time specified. Serve with a pan sauce (see pages 18–19) or relish (see pages 20–22).

2	(1- to 1¼-pound) pork tenderloins
	Salt and ground black pepper
2	tablespoons vegetable oil

1. Following the illustrations on page 13, trim and discard the thin, tapered ends of the pork tenderloins, then cut the tenderloins crosswise into 1½-inch-thick medallions. Tie each pork medallion around the perimeter with kitchen twine and tie the thinner end pieces together. Pat the pork medallions dry with paper towels and season with salt and pepper.

2. Heat the oil in a 12-inch skillet over medium-high heat until just smoking. Carefully lay the pork medallions in the skillet and cook until well browned on the first side, 3 to 5 minutes.

3. Flip the pork medallions over, reduce the heat to medium, and continue to cook until well browned on the second side, 3 to 5 minutes longer. Using tongs, stand each pork medallion on its side and cook, turning the pieces as necessary, until the sides are well browned and the centers of the pork medallions register 140 to 145 degrees on an instant-read thermometer, 8 to 12 minutes.

4. Transfer the pork medallions to a plate, tent

EQUIPMENT: Traditional Skillets

We use traditional skillets all the time, whether we're making steaks, chops, or chicken. A traditional skillet is a smart investment; purchase a high quality, sturdy skillet, and you'll be rewarded with good food that is cooked well. We determined from earlier tests that a lightweight $10 skillet from a discount store was not the way to go. But how much do you need to spend? We looked at 12-inch pans from well-known manufacturers, ranging in price from $60 to twice that amount. (While we prefer 12-inch pans, there are some recipes in this book where we specify a smaller skillet.)

All of the pans we tested had flared sides, which makes it easier to flip foods in the pan. Also, all of the pans we tested fall into a category we refer to as traditional—that is, none of the pans were nonstick. Most had uncoated stainless-steel cooking surfaces, which we prize for promoting a fond—the browned, sticky bits that cling to the interior of the pan when food is sautéed and help flavor sauces.

The pans tested measured 12 inches in diameter (across the top) or as close to that as we could get. This large size is the most versatile because it can accommodate a big steak or all of the pieces of a cut-up 3-pound chicken. However, the cooking surface in a pan can measure considerably less than the top diameter measurement, meaning the pan has a smaller surface area and less room for the food to brown.

Another important factor that we uncovered when testing our skillets was weight. In our tests, a lightweight (about a pound) aluminum budget pan was the quickest to reach 361 degrees, at just under three minutes, but the lightweight pan performed poorly in kitchen tests. We concluded that the ideal weight for a 12-inch skillet is 3 to 4 pounds. Pans in this weight range brown foods beautifully and have enough heft for heat retention and structural integrity, but not so much that they are difficult to lift or manipulate.

Which skillet should you buy? For its combination of excellent performance, optimum weight and balance, and overall ease of use, our hands-down winner is the All-Clad Stainless 12-Inch Frypan ($135).

THE BEST TRADITIONAL SKILLET

ALL-CLAD

The All-Clad Stainless 12-Inch Frypan ($135) browns food perfectly and is spacious and easy to handle.

loosely with foil, and let rest until the centers of the pork medallions register 150 degrees on an instant-read thermometer, about 5 minutes, or while making a pan sauce. Serve.

➤ VARIATION

Pan-Seared Bacon-Wrapped Pork Tenderloin Medallions

Some brands of bacon have a tendency to burn, so be ready to reduce the heat if necessary.

Place 12 to 14 slices bacon (1 slice for each pork medallion), slightly overlapping, in a microwave-safe pie plate and cover. Cook in the microwave on high power until the slices shrink and release about ½ cup fat but are neither browned nor crisp, 1 to 3 minutes. Transfer the bacon to a paper towel–lined plate until cool, about 3 minutes. Follow the recipe for Pan-Seared Pork Tenderloin Medallions, omitting the kitchen twine in step 1 and wrapping 1 piece of bacon around the perimeter of each pork medallion, securing the overlapping ends of bacon with 2 toothpicks. Season the pork medallions with pepper (do not salt) and cook as directed.

MAKING PORK MEDALLIONS

1. Trim and discard the thin, tapered ends of the tenderloin, then cut the tenderloin crosswise into 1½-inch-wide pieces.

2. Tie each pork tenderloin medallion once around the middle with kitchen twine.

Pan-Seared Thick Fish Fillets

SERVES 4

Be sure to use a nonstick skillet here. For information about choosing fish fillets, see page 15. Be sure to check the fish for any pinbones and remove them before cooking (see the illustrations on page 14). If you like, serve the fish fillets with a simple wedge of lemon, a pan sauce (see pages 18–19), compound butter (see pages 22–24), or relish (see pages 20–22).

> 4   (6-ounce) fish fillets, 1 to 1½ inches thick
>   Salt and ground black pepper
> 1   tablespoon vegetable oil

1. Pat the fish fillets dry with paper towels and season with salt and pepper. Heat the oil in a 12-inch nonstick skillet over medium-high heat until just smoking. Carefully lay the fish fillets in the skillet (skin or skinned side facing up) and cook until well browned on the first side, about 5 minutes.

2. Flip the fish fillets over, reduce the heat to medium, and continue to cook until all but the very centers of the fish fillets have turned from translucent to opaque, about 3 minutes longer.

3. Transfer the fish fillets to a plate, tent loosely with foil, and let rest for 5 minutes, or while making a pan sauce. Serve.

FLIPPING FISH FILLETS

To easily turn fish fillets over without breaking them, use two spatulas. Use one spatula to get underneath the fish, while using the other both to hold the fish in place and "catch" the fish after it's been flipped over. An extra-wide spatula especially designed for fish works well on the "catching" end.

EQUIPMENT: Nonstick Skillets

A good, nonstick skillet is a given when cooking thin fish fillets, searing scallops, or scrambling eggs. The trouble is that the coating can wear away after a good amount of use. In our tests, we checked out both pricey and more cost-effective pans to see if they could stand the heat in our kitchen. While we find 12-inch skillets to be the most versatile and the most practical purchase, we do call for a smaller skillet in some recipes in this book.

Our tests included sautéing onions and carrots, cooking thin fillets of sole, and making omelets in each pan. Fish is delicate and tends to stick and break apart during cooking, making it especially well-suited to being cooked in a nonstick skillet. The same holds true for eggs, which can stick. All pans did an acceptable job cooking these foods.

As with our traditional skillets, we tested nonstick skillets measuring 12 inches from lip to lip, but we found plenty of differences in the usable cooking space. The actual flat cooking surface ranged from 9 inches to 10½ inches, which can make all the difference when you need room to sear an extra fish fillet. Unless the pans were too heavy for some users, we figured bigger was better. And, also harkening back to our traditional skillet tests, we preferred pans with flared sides, which made maneuvering food easier.

To gauge durability, we tested things that manufacturers specifically forbid in each pan: cutting with a sharp knife, removing frittata slices with a metal pie server, and washing with an abrasive metal scrubber.

Our favorites, which survived our beating and stood out for design and performance, are the pricey but worth it All-Clad Stainless Steel Nonstick 12-Inch Frypan ($135) and the more economic Wearever Premium Hard-Anodized 12-Inch Nonstick Sauté Pan ($28).

THE BEST NONSTICK SKILLETS

ALL-CLAD   WEAREVER

The All-Clad Stainless Steel Nonstick 12-Inch Frypan ($135) was the top performer in our kitchen tests, but the Wearever Premium Hard-Anodized 12-Inch Nonstick Sauté Pan ($28) is a great bargain that handles comfortably.

Sautéed Thin Fish Fillets

SERVES 4

Flounder and sole work well in this recipe. Do not use fillets thinner than ¼ inch or they will fall apart while cooking. For more information about choosing fish fillets, see page 15. Serve with a simple wedge of lemon, a compound butter (pages 22–24), or relish (see pages 20–22). If you'd like to serve the fish with a pan sauce, we recommend the variation on page 15 (instead of the sauces on pages 18–19) because it is very quick and the delicate fish won't have time to cool off before serving.

½	cup unbleached all-purpose flour
6–8	(3- to 4-ounce) boneless, skinless fish fillets, ¼ to ½ inch thick
	Salt and ground black pepper
¼	cup vegetable oil

TWO WAYS TO REMOVE PINBONES FROM FISH

Pinbones are small white bones that run through the center of a side of fish or a thick fish fillet (often salmon). Most fish is sold with the pinbones already removed, but it never hurts to check one more time.

A. For fish fillets, run your fingers firmly over the fish to feel for any bones, and use a clean pair of needle-nose pliers or tweezers to grab and remove.

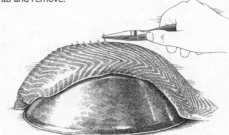

B. For a large piece of fish, drape it over an inverted bowl and use a clean pair of needle-nose pliers or tweezers to remove the pinbones. The curve of the bowl forces the pinbones to stick up and out, so they are easier to spot and remove.

1. Place the flour in a shallow dish. Pat the fish fillets dry with paper towels and season with salt and pepper. Working with 1 fish fillet at a time, dredge in the flour, shaking off the excess.

2. Heat 2 tablespoons of the oil in a 12-inch nonstick skillet over medium-high heat until shimmering. Carefully lay half of the fish fillets in the skillet and cook until lightly browned on the first side, 2 to 3 minutes.

3. Following the illustration on page 13, use two spatulas to gently flip the fish fillets over. Continue to cook on the second side until the thickest part of the fish fillets is firm to the touch and the fish flakes easily, 30 to 60 seconds longer. Transfer the fillets to a platter and tent loosely with foil.

4. Wipe out the skillet with a wad of paper towels. Add the remaining 2 tablespoons oil and repeat with the remaining fish fillets. Serve.

➤ VARIATION

Sautéed Thin Fish Fillets with Browned Butter and Parsley Sauce

Follow the recipe for Sautéed Thin Fish Fillets, transferring the second batch of cooked fish fillets to the platter with the first batch and tenting loosely with foil. Wipe out the skillet with a wad of paper towels. Add 4 tablespoons unsalted butter to the skillet and return to medium-high heat. Cook, swirling the skillet constantly, until the butter has melted and turned golden brown with a nutty aroma, 2 to 3 minutes. Off the heat, add 1½ tablespoons juice from 1 lemon and 1 tablespoon minced fresh parsley leaves. Season with salt and pepper to taste and spoon over the fish fillets before serving.

PATTING DRY MEAT AND FISH

To ensure even cooking, limit splatter, and promote a crisp crust, make sure that meat and fish are thoroughly patted dry between paper towels before sautéing or pan-searing.

INGREDIENTS:
Choosing Fish Fillets

Fish cooks well in the skillet, but getting the fish you want may not be an easy task. Fish can be sold in small pieces called "fillets," or they may be sold by the whole side and still be referred to as "fillets." Armed with a little knowledge, you can pick out the right catch of the day with ease. Here are tips for buying and cooking the fish that you are likely to encounter at the market.

THE CUT: If possible, have the fishmonger cut out the fillets from the whole side. Usually, the center part of the side will yield at least 4 fillets. Most markets will cut and weigh fillets to your specifications.

THE THICKNESS: To ensure evenly cooked fillets, order and buy fillets that are the same thickness. A skillet full of thin fillets will cook more evenly than a skillet containing a mix of thick and thin.

ABOUT THIN FILLETS: If the fish selection is limited, you can "cheat" by folding paper-thin fish fillets (often flounder or sole) in half lengthwise or by tucking the smaller part of the fillet under the larger part to form a symmetrical fillet. The adjusted fillets will cook more evenly alongside thicker fillets.

FLAVOR KEY

Flavor can run from mild to downright fishy. Here's how to buy fish that matches your preference:

FISH	THICKNESS	FLAVOR
CATFISH	1–1½"	Assertive
COD	¾–1½"	Medium
FLOUNDER	¼–½"	Mild
GROUPER	¾–1¼"	Medium
HADDOCK	¾–1½"	Medium
HAKE	¾–1½"	Medium
HALIBUT	1–1½"	Medium
ORANGE ROUGHY	¾–1½"	Assertive
RED SNAPPER	¾–1"	Assertive
SALMON	1–1½"	Assertive
SEA BASS	¾–1½"	Assertive
SOLE	¼–½"	Mild
TILAPIA	¾–1"	Assertive

Pan Sauces 101

THE SETUP

Because pan sauces cook quickly, before you begin to cook it is essential to complete your *mise en place*—that is, have all necessary ingredients and utensils collected and ready to use.

JUST-SEARED MEAT

After searing the meat or fish (thick fillets), transfer it to a plate and tent it loosely with foil while making the sauce. Keeping the foil loose will keep any crust that has formed from turning soggy.

SMALL BOWL

Have ready a small empty bowl or container to catch excess fat that might have to be poured off before you begin the sauce.

AROMATICS

Aromatics include garlic and onions, but are most often shallots—their flavor is mild, sweet, and complex. If "minced" is specified, make sure they are fine and even; this will allow them to release maximum flavor, and their texture will be less obtrusive in the finished sauce.

LIQUIDS

Leave liquid ingredients (such as wine, broth, or juices) in a measuring cup. Once emptied, keep the measuring cup close at hand; the reduced liquid can be poured back into the measuring cup toward the end of simmering to assess its final volume and to gauge if it is adequately reduced.

WOODEN UTENSIL

A squared-off wooden utensil (or heatproof rubber spatula, see page 8) works best to scrape up the fond while deglazing because it is rigid and does not scratch (like metal on metal). Either one is ideal because it can cover more of the surface area of the pan than the rounded tip of a spoon.

HERBS AND FLAVORINGS

Herbs are sometimes used in sprig form and removed from the sauce before serving. Delicate herbs such as parsley and tarragon are usually chopped and added to the sauce at the end so they do not discolor. Other flavorings such as mustard, lemon juice, and capers are often added at the end for maximum flavor impact.

WHISK

For maximum efficiency and easy maneuverability, use a medium-size whisk with flexible wires that can get into the rounded sides of the skillet.

BUTTER

Cut the butter into tablespoon-sized chunks so that it will melt quickly into the sauce. Cold butter is easier to incorporate into a sauce than softened butter, and it makes a sturdier emulsion that is more resistant to separation. Butter can be omitted, but the sauce will be thinner, with little silkiness.

SALT AND PEPPER

Tasting for and correcting seasoning is the last step before serving. Keep salt in a ramekin so that it is easy to measure out in small amounts.

THE EXECUTION

Here's how to make a pan sauce step by step:

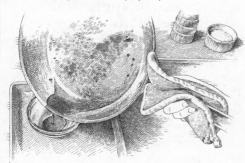

1. DISCARD EXCESS FAT

Sometimes seared meat will leave behind too much fat. After removing the seared or sautéed items from the skillet, discard excess fat, leaving just enough (several teaspoons) to cook the aromatics. With most steaks and chicken, this step is not necessary, but with fatty chops, it probably is.

2. SAUTÉ THE AROMATICS

Add the aromatics to the skillet and cook them until they soften slightly, usually no more than a couple of minutes, adjusting the heat if necessary. Be sure not to let the fond scorch, or the finished sauce will taste burnt and bitter.

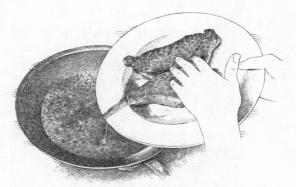

3. DEGLAZE AND THICKEN

Add the liquid to the skillet—it will sizzle and steam on contact—and scrape up the fond on the bottom of the skillet. Simmer to thicken the sauce.

4. RETURN THE JUICES TO THE SKILLET

As the meat rests, it will likely release juices; add these juices back to the skillet. If the juices should thin the sauce, allow it to simmer an additional minute or two to restore the proper consistency.

5. WHISK IN THE BUTTER

Whisk in the cold butter. Grab hold of the butter with the whisk and swirl it around in the skillet until it is melted and incorporated into the sauce. Taste for seasoning before serving.

Whisks come in all shapes and sizes. Is there one particular style that's best for making pan sauces? To find out, we rounded up 12 models, from balloon whisks (super skinny to large) to square-headed models and coil whisks. We ended up settling on the skinnier balloon whisk as having the best shape for pan sauces. When tilted on its side, this whisk covers a wide swath for efficient deglazing. Its relatively straight sides and flexible tines also come in handy when scraping a sauce from the sides of the pan. Of the models we tried, our favorite brand was the Best Manufacturers 12-Inch Standard French Whip.

BEST WHISK FOR PAN SAUCES

The Best Manufacturers 12-inch Standard French Whip ($9.95) boasts an ideal shape and agile set of tines that are perfect for preparing pan sauces.

QUICK PAN SAUCES

THE BASE OF A PAN SAUCE IS THE FOND that clings to the skillet after sautéing meat or fish. Once the protein is removed from the skillet, aromatics such as minced shallots can be sautéed. Then, in a process called deglazing, liquid—usually wine, broth, cream, or a combination—is added to help dissolve the fond into a flavorful sauce, which is simmered to concentrate its flavors and thicken. We also add in any juices released by the resting cooked meat or fish; these act to reinforce and deepen the flavor profile of the sauce. We found that the addition of 1 teaspoon of flour reduced the simmering time by helping to thicken the sauce. All of these sauces make enough for four servings of meat or fish.

Vermouth, Leek, and Tarragon Pan Sauce

MAKES ABOUT ¾ CUP

This sauce is great with poultry, pork, or fish.

2 teaspoons vegetable oil
1 medium leek, white part only, halved lengthwise and sliced ¼ inch thick
1 teaspoon unbleached all-purpose flour
¾ cup low-sodium chicken broth
½ cup dry vermouth or white wine
1 tablespoon unsalted butter, chilled
2 teaspoons minced fresh tarragon leaves
1 teaspoon whole grain mustard
Salt and ground black pepper

1. After removing the meat or fish from the skillet, pour off any fat left in the pan. Add the oil and leek and cook over medium-high heat until softened, about 2 minutes. Stir in the flour and cook for 30 seconds.

2. Stir in the broth and vermouth, scraping up any browned bits. Bring to a simmer and cook until the sauce measures ¾ cup, 3 to 5 minutes. Stir in any accumulated meat or fish juices, return to a simmer, and cook for 30 seconds.

3. Off the heat, whisk in the butter, tarragon, and mustard. Season with salt and pepper to taste. Spoon the sauce over the meat or fish before serving.

Lemon, Caper, and Parsley Pan Sauce

MAKES ABOUT ¾ CUP

Serve this sauce with poultry, pork, or fish.

2 teaspoons vegetable oil
1 medium shallot, minced (about 3 tablespoons)
1 teaspoon unbleached all-purpose flour
¾ cup low-sodium chicken broth
½ cup dry white wine
1 tablespoon unsalted butter, chilled
1 tablespoon capers, rinsed and chopped
1 tablespoon minced fresh parsley leaves
2 teaspoons juice from 1 lemon
Salt and ground black pepper

1. After removing the meat or fish from the skillet, pour off any fat left in the pan. Add the oil and shallot and cook over medium-high heat until softened, about 2 minutes. Stir in the flour and cook for 30 seconds.

2. Stir in the broth and wine, scraping up any browned bits. Bring to a simmer and cook until the sauce measures ¾ cup, 3 to 5 minutes. Stir in any accumulated meat or fish juices, return to a simmer, and cook for 30 seconds.

3. Off the heat, whisk in the butter, capers, parsley, and lemon juice. Season with salt and pepper to taste. Spoon the sauce over the meat or fish before serving.

Sweet-Tart Red Wine Sauce

MAKES ABOUT ¾ CUP

This sauce tastes best with beef.

2 teaspoons vegetable oil
1 medium shallot, minced (about 3 tablespoons)
1 teaspoon unbleached all-purpose flour
¾ cup low-sodium chicken broth
½ cup dry red wine
1 tablespoon unsalted butter, chilled

1 tablespoon light brown sugar

1 teaspoon minced fresh thyme leaves

1 teaspoon red wine vinegar

Salt and ground black pepper

1. After removing the meat from the skillet, pour off any fat left in the pan. Add the oil and shallot and cook over medium-high heat until softened, about 2 minutes. Stir in the flour and cook for 30 seconds.

2. Stir in the broth and wine, scraping up any browned bits. Bring to a simmer and cook until the sauce measures ¾ cup, 3 to 5 minutes. Stir in any accumulated meat juices, return to a simmer, and cook for 30 seconds.

3. Off the heat, whisk in the butter, sugar, thyme, and vinegar. Season with salt and pepper to taste. Spoon the sauce over the meat before serving.

Chipotle Chile and Orange Sauce

MAKES ABOUT ¾ CUP

This sauce is best with poultry, pork, or fish.

2 teaspoons vegetable oil

1 medium shallot, minced (about 3 tablespoons)

1 teaspoon unbleached all-purpose flour

¾ cup orange juice

½ cup low-sodium chicken broth

1 tablespoon unsalted butter, chilled

1 tablespoon minced fresh cilantro leaves

1 teaspoon minced chipotle chile in adobo sauce

Salt and ground black pepper

1. After removing the meat or fish from the skillet, pour off any fat left in the pan. Add the oil and shallot and cook over medium-high heat until softened, about 2 minutes. Stir in the flour and cook for 30 seconds.

2. Stir in the orange juice and broth, scraping up any browned bits. Bring to a simmer and cook until the sauce measures ¾ cup, 3 to 5 minutes. Stir in any accumulated meat or fish juices, return to a simmer, and cook for 30 seconds.

3. Off the heat, whisk in the butter, cilantro, and chipotle. Season with salt and pepper to taste. Spoon the sauce over the meat or fish before serving.

Mustard–Cream Sauce

MAKES ABOUT ¾ CUP

We prefer the texture and flavor of whole grain mustard here; however, regular Dijon mustard can be substituted. The heavy cream and mustard are used to thicken this sauce instead of flour. Serve with beef or pork.

2 teaspoons vegetable oil

1 medium shallot, minced (about 3 tablespoons)

½ cup low-sodium chicken broth

2 tablespoons dry white wine

6 tablespoons heavy cream

3 tablespoons whole grain Dijon mustard

1 tablespoon minced fresh tarragon leaves

Salt and ground black pepper

EQUIPMENT: Chef's Knives

We ask a lot of our chef's knives in the test kitchen. They have to be versatile enough to handle almost any cutting task, whether cutting tomatoes for salsa or slicing through meat and bones. The blade has to be sharp and slice easily with minimal force behind it, and the handle has to be comfortable and not get slippery when wet. We've tested many knives in recent years, and we keep coming back to the Victorinox Fibrox Chef's Knife. This knife always performs well in kitchen tests and gets points for handle comfort, blade sharpness, and edge retention. And, at $22.95, it's a great buy. It's the sharpest knife in the drawer on all fronts.

THE BEST CHEF'S KNIFE

VICTORINOX

Victorinox Fibrox 8-Inch Chef's Knife ($24.95) has a comfortable grip and sharp blade.

1. After removing the meat from the skillet, pour off any fat left in the pan. Add the oil and shallot and cook over medium-high heat until softened, about 2 minutes.

2. Stir in the broth and wine, scraping up any browned bits. Bring to a simmer and cook until the sauce measures ¼ cup, 3 to 5 minutes. Stir in the cream and any accumulated meat juices, return to a simmer, and cook for 30 seconds.

3. Off the heat, whisk in the mustard and tarragon. Season with salt and pepper to taste. Spoon the sauce over the meat before serving.

Relishes

THESE CONDIMENT-LIKE SALSAS, RELISHES, and sauces can be served with many of our recipes. Simply pass them at the table so diners can dollop on as much or as little as desired. Most of these quick recipes are made with raw ingredients and can be made in advance, refrigerated for several days, and then brought to room temperature before serving.

Tomato Salsa
MAKES ABOUT 3 CUPS

For more heat, include the jalapeño seeds and ribs when mincing. The amount of sugar and lime juice to use depends on the ripeness of the tomatoes. The salsa can be made 2 to 3 hours in advance, but hold off adding the salt, lime juice, and sugar until just before serving. This salsa is a nice accompaniment to poultry, pork, or fish.

1½	pounds firm, ripe tomatoes, cut into ½-inch dice (about 3 cups)
½	medium red onion, minced (about ½ cup)
1	large jalapeño chile, seeds and ribs removed, chile minced (see note)
¼	cup minced fresh cilantro leaves
1	small garlic clove, minced or pressed through a garlic press (about ½ teaspoon)
2	teaspoons juice from 1 lime, plus extra as needed
½	teaspoon salt
	Ground black pepper
	Sugar

CUTTING TOMATOES FOR SALSA

1. Cut each cored tomato in half through the equator.

2. Cut each half into ½-inch-thick slices.

3. Stack two slices; cut them into ½-inch strips, then into ½-inch dice.

1. Set a large colander inside a large bowl (or the sink). Place the tomatoes in the colander and let drain for 30 minutes. As the tomatoes drain, layer the onion, jalapeño, cilantro, and garlic on top.

2. Shake the colander to drain off the excess tomato juice, then transfer the vegetables to a serving bowl. Add the lime juice and salt and toss to combine. Season with pepper, sugar, and additional lime juice to taste and serve with meat or fish.

Salsa Verde
MAKES ABOUT ¾ CUP

A slice of sandwich bread pureed into the sauce keeps the flavors balanced and gives the sauce body. Toasting the bread rids it of excess moisture that might otherwise make for a gummy sauce. This sauce can be made 2 to 3 hours in advance. It makes a nice accompaniment to poultry, beef, or pork.

1   slice high-quality white sandwich bread
½   cup extra-virgin olive oil
2   tablespoons juice from 1 lemon
2   cups lightly packed fresh parsley leaves
2   medium anchovy fillets
2   tablespoons drained capers
1   small garlic clove, minced or pressed through
    a garlic press (about ½ teaspoon)
⅛   teaspoon salt

1. Toast the bread in a toaster at the lowest setting until the surface is dry but not browned, about 15 seconds. Remove and discard the crust and cut the bread into rough ½-inch pieces (you should have about ½ cup).

2. Process the bread pieces, oil, and lemon juice together in a food processor until smooth, about 10 seconds. Add the parsley, anchovies, capers, garlic, and salt. Pulse until the mixture is finely chopped (the mixture should not be smooth), about 5 pulses, scraping down the sides of the bowl as necessary. Transfer the sauce to a serving bowl and serve with meat or poultry.

Mango Relish
MAKES ABOUT 2 CUPS

For more heat, include the jalapeño seeds and ribs when mincing. This relish is excellent served with poultry, pork, or fish. It can be made 2 to 3 hours in advance.

2   medium mangos, peeled, pitted, and cut into
    ¼-inch cubes (see the illustrations at right)
1   medium shallot, minced (about
    3 tablespoons)
2   scallions, sliced thin
½   medium jalapeño chile, seeds and ribs
    removed, chile minced (see note)
2   tablespoons minced fresh cilantro leaves
1   tablespoon juice from 1 lime
    Salt and ground black pepper

Combine all of the ingredients in a serving bowl, season with salt and pepper to taste, and let sit at room temperature until the flavors meld, about 30 minutes. Serve with meat or fish.

PREPARING A MANGO

Because of their odd shape and slippery texture, mangos are notoriously difficult to peel and pit. Here's how we handle this task.

1. Remove a thin slice from one end of the mango so that it sits flat on a work surface.

2. Hold the mango cut side down and remove the skin in thin strips using a sharp paring knife, working from top to bottom.

3. Cut down along the side of the flat pit to remove the flesh from one side of the mango. Do the same on the other side of the pit.

4. Trim around the pit to remove any remaining flesh. The mango flesh can now be chopped or sliced as desired.

Cilantro Sauce

MAKES ABOUT 1½ CUPS

This sauce is wonderful served with poultry, pork, or fish. It can be made 2 to 3 hours in advance.

¼ cup walnuts
2 medium cloves garlic, unpeeled
2½ cups packed cilantro leaves and stems, tough ends trimmed (about 2 bunches)
½ cup olive oil
4 teaspoons juice from 1 lemon
1 scallion, sliced thin
 Salt and ground black pepper

1. Toast the walnuts in a small dry skillet over medium heat, stirring frequently, until just golden and fragrant, about 5 minutes; set aside. Add the garlic to the empty skillet and toast over medium heat, shaking the skillet occasionally, until fragrant and the color of the cloves deepens slightly, about 7 minutes. Let the garlic cool slightly, then peel and chop.

2. Process the walnuts, garlic, cilantro, oil, lemon juice, scallion, ½ teaspoon salt, and ⅛ teaspoon pepper together in a food processor until smooth, about 1 minute, scraping down the sides of the bowl as necessary. Season with salt and pepper to taste. Transfer the sauce to a serving bowl and serve with meat or fish.

Romesco Sauce

MAKES ABOUT 2 CUPS

Serve this Spanish sauce with poultry, beef, pork, or fish. It can be refrigerated in an airtight container for up to 2 days; return it to room temperature before serving.

2 slices high-quality white sandwich bread
3 tablespoons slivered almonds, toasted
1 (12-ounce) jar roasted red peppers, drained (about 1¾ cups)
1 small ripe tomato, cored, seeded, and chopped medium
2 tablespoons extra-virgin olive oil
1½ tablespoons sherry vinegar
1 large garlic clove, minced or pressed through a garlic press (about 1½ teaspoons)
¼ teaspoon cayenne pepper
 Salt

1. Toast the bread in a toaster at the lowest setting until the surface is dry but not browned, about 15 seconds. Remove and discard the crusts and cut the bread into rough ½-inch pieces (you should have about 1 cup).

2. Process the bread pieces and almonds together in a food processor until the nuts are finely ground, 10 to 15 seconds. Add the red peppers, tomato, oil, vinegar, garlic, cayenne, and ½ teaspoon salt and continue to process until the mixture has a mayonnaise-like texture, 20 to 30 seconds, scraping down the sides of the bowl as necessary. Season with salt to taste. Transfer the sauce to a serving bowl and serve with meat or fish.

COMPOUND BUTTERS

COMPOUND BUTTERS ARE BOTH VERSATILE and easy—simply mix the ingredients together and add a dollop to melt on your meat, chicken, or fish. These butters are also a zippy way to add flavor to vegetables, rice, and couscous. They can be prepared in advance and frozen for future use (see the illustrations on page 23).

Garlic-Herb Butter

MAKES ENOUGH FOR 8 SERVINGS
OF MEAT OR FISH

See instructions on page 23 on how to store any extra butter in the freezer.

8 tablespoons (1 stick) unsalted butter, softened
2 medium garlic cloves, minced or pressed through a garlic press (about 2 teaspoons)
2 tablespoons minced fresh sage leaves
1 tablespoon minced fresh parsley leaves
1 tablespoon minced fresh thyme leaves
 Salt and ground black pepper

Beat the butter with a large fork in a medium bowl until light and fluffy. Mix in the garlic and herbs until combined. Season with salt and pepper to taste. Wrap in plastic wrap and let rest to blend the flavors, about 10 minutes. Dollop 1 tablespoon butter on each portion of meat or fish before serving.

Parsley-Caper Butter

MAKES ENOUGH FOR 8 SERVINGS
OF MEAT OR FISH

See instructions at right on how to store any extra butter in the freezer.

- 8 tablespoons (1 stick) unsalted butter, softened
- ¼ cup minced fresh parsley leaves
- 4 teaspoons grated zest from 1 lemon
- 4 teaspoons capers, rinsed and minced
  Salt and ground black pepper

Beat the butter with a large fork in a medium bowl until light and fluffy. Mix in the parsley, lemon zest, and capers. Season with salt and pepper to taste. Wrap in plastic wrap and let rest to blend the flavors, about 10 minutes. Dollop 1 tablespoon butter on each portion of meat or fish before serving.

Blue Cheese Butter

MAKES ENOUGH FOR 8 SERVINGS
OF MEAT OR FISH

See instructions at right on how to store any extra butter in the freezer.

- 8 tablespoons (1 stick) unsalted butter, softened
- 2 ounces blue cheese, crumbled (½ cup)
- 2 teaspoons brandy
  Salt and ground black pepper

Beat the butter with a large fork in a medium bowl until light and fluffy. Mix in the cheese and brandy until combined. Season with salt and pepper to taste. Wrap in plastic wrap and let rest to blend the flavors, about 10 minutes. Dollop 1 tablespoon butter on each portion of meat or fish before serving.

Chipotle-Cilantro Butter

MAKES ENOUGH FOR 8 SERVINGS
OF MEAT OR FISH

See instructions below on how to store any extra butter in the freezer.

- 8 tablespoons (1 stick) unsalted butter, softened
- 5 teaspoons minced chipotle chile in adobo sauce
- 4 teaspoons minced fresh cilantro leaves
- 2 medium garlic cloves, minced or pressed through a garlic press (about 2 teaspoons)
- 2 teaspoons honey
- 2 teaspoons grated zest from 1 lime
  Salt and ground black pepper

PREPARING COMPOUND BUTTER FOR THE FREEZER

1. Place the compound butter on top of a piece of waxed paper, parchment paper, or plastic wrap.

2. Roll the butter into a long, narrow cylinder. Transfer the wrapped cylinder to a zipper-lock bag and freeze.

3. When you need it, take the butter out of the freezer, unwrap it, and cut off rounds about ½ inch thick. Place the rounds on top of freshly cooked hot foods and let them melt as you carry plates to the table.

Beat the butter with a large fork in a medium bowl until light and fluffy. Mix in the chipotles, cilantro, garlic, honey, and lime zest until combined. Season with salt and pepper to taste. Wrap in plastic wrap and let rest to blend the flavors, about 10 minutes. Dollop 1 tablespoon butter on each portion of meat or fish before serving.

Tarragon-Lime Butter

MAKES ENOUGH FOR 8 SERVINGS
OF MEAT OR FISH

See instructions on page 23 on how to store any extra butter in the freezer.

- 8 tablespoons (1 stick) unsalted butter, softened
- 2 scallions, minced
- 2 tablespoons minced fresh tarragon leaves
- 4 teaspoons juice from 1 lime
    Salt and ground black pepper

Beat the butter with a large fork in a medium bowl until light and fluffy. Mix in the scallions, tarragon, and lime juice until combined. Season with salt and pepper to taste. Wrap in plastic wrap and let rest to blend the flavors, about 10 minutes. Dollop 1 tablespoon butter on each portion of meat or fish before serving.

PAN-SEARED SHRIMP

PAN-SEARING IS A WONDERFUL WAY TO prepare shrimp—it produces the ultimate combination of a well-caramelized exterior and a moist, tender interior. If executed properly, this cooking method also preserves the shrimp's plumpness and trademark briny sweetness. That said, a good recipe for pan-seared shrimp is hard to find. We've seen many that result in dry, pale, tough, or gummy shrimp—hardly appetizing. It was time to take a closer look at how to pan-sear this popular crustacean.

We quickly uncovered a few basic principles for our recipe. First, tasters unanimously favored shrimp that were peeled before being cooked. Peeled shrimp are easier to eat, and unpeeled shrimp fail to pick up the delicious caramelized flavor that pan-searing provides. Second, oil was the ideal cooking medium, favored over both a dry pan (which made the shrimp leathery and metallic-tasting) and butter (which tended to burn). And last, we usually like to brine shrimp before grilling them, so we thought this step would be the natural starting point for our pan-seared shrimp.

In a fortuitous turn, our brining tests yielded an unexpected benefit. We had been adding sugar to the brining solution with the hope of improving the shrimp's browning characteristics. While the sugar did not promote browning in the brined shrimp, it did accentuate their natural sweetness and nicely set off their inherent sea-saltiness. Capitalizing on this discovery, we added a pinch of sugar to some unbrined shrimp along with the requisite salt and pepper. This did indeed boost the flavor, as we had expected, and, absent the water from the brine, the sugar also encouraged browning. We could skip the brining step and move right to the skillet.

Even in a 12-inch skillet, 1½ pounds of shrimp must be cooked in two batches, or they will steam instead of sear. The trick was to develop a technique that neither overcooked the shrimp nor let half of them turn cold while the other half finished cooking. To prevent overcooking, we tried searing the shrimp on one side, removing the pan from the flame, and then allowing the residual heat to finish cooking the other side of the shrimp. This worked like a charm. Better yet, the residual heat solved the cold shrimp problem. As soon as the second batch finished cooking (the first batch was now near room temperature), we tossed the first batch back into the pan, covered it, and let the residual heat work its magic once again. After about a minute, all of the shrimp were perfectly cooked and piping hot.

Now all we needed were a few quick sauces. A parsley-lemon butter perfectly complemented the sweet, briny shrimp. We also came up with two glazes made with assertive ingredients: one made with ginger and hoisin and another with chipotle chiles and lime. Each are a perfect foil to the shrimp's richness.

Pan-Seared Shrimp with Parsley-Lemon Butter
SERVES 4

The parsley and lemon are a natural counterpoint to the sweet, briny shrimp.

2	tablespoons unsalted butter, softened
1	tablespoon juice from 1 lemon
1	tablespoon minced fresh parsley leaves
1½	pounds extra-large shrimp (21 to 25 per pound), peeled and deveined (see the illustration on page 235)
	Salt and ground black pepper
⅛	teaspoon sugar
2	tablespoons vegetable oil

1. Mix the butter, lemon juice, and parsley together and set aside. Pat the shrimp dry with paper towels and season with ¼ teaspoon salt, ¼ teaspoon pepper, and the sugar.

2. Heat 1 tablespoon of the oil in a 12-inch nonstick skillet over high heat until just smoking. Carefully add half of the shrimp to the skillet in a single layer and cook until spotty brown and just pink around the edges, about 1 minute. Remove the skillet from the heat, use tongs to quickly flip each shrimp over, and let sit off the heat until all but the very center is opaque, about 30 seconds. Transfer the shrimp to a plate and cover with foil. Add the remaining 1 tablespoon oil to the skillet and repeat with the remaining shrimp.

3. After the second batch has stood off the heat, return the first batch to the skillet and toss to combine. Add the butter mixture, cover, and let sit off the heat until the butter melts, about 1 minute. Toss the shrimp to coat and serve.

➤ VARIATIONS
Pan-Seared Shrimp with Ginger-Hoisin Glaze
Combine 2 tablespoons hoisin sauce, 1 tablespoon rice vinegar, 2 teaspoons minced or grated fresh ginger, 2 teaspoons water, 2 scallions, sliced thin, 1½ teaspoons soy sauce, and a pinch red pepper flakes in a small bowl. Follow the recipe for Pan-Seared Shrimp with Parsley-Lemon Butter, substituting the ginger-hoisin glaze for the butter mixture in step 3.

Pan-Seared Shrimp with Chipotle-Lime Glaze
Combine 2 tablespoons juice from 1 lime, 2 tablespoons minced fresh cilantro leaves, 4 teaspoons brown sugar, and 1 tablespoon minced chipotle chile in adobo sauce in a small bowl. Follow the recipe for Pan-Seared Shrimp with Parsley-Lemon Butter, substituting the chipotle-lime glaze for the butter mixture in step 3.

PAN-SEARED SCALLOPS
SCALLOPS CAN BE PREPARED MYRIAD WAYS, though pan-searing is our favorite method. Cooking them over high heat caramelizes the exterior, forming a nutty-flavored crust that enhances their natural sweetness.

The biggest challenge when cooking scallops is getting a good crust before the scallops overcook and toughen. We have pan-seared everything from chicken to pork to salmon, so we know from experience that moisture is the enemy of a crusty brown exterior. Most scallops are processed—dipped in a phosphate and water mixture that turns them bright white—to extend shelf life. Unprocessed, or dry, scallops will be closer to an ivory or pinkish tan color and are our preference of the two (if unsure, ask your fishmonger what's available). The extra water in processed scallops makes them more difficult to cook because they shed so much of this liquid in a skillet that they steam rather than brown.

Whether using processed or unprocessed scallops, we had to make sure that they were perfectly dry going into the hot pan, so we laid them out in a single layer on a dish towel–lined plate. The towel absorbed any moisture that the scallops released and, as an extra precaution, we pressed paper towels onto the tops of the scallops just before they went into the pan. No drop of moisture was going to prevent our crust from forming. Or was it?

Although the scallops were bone-dry going into the pan, they still wouldn't brown. It seemed that they were so close together when cooked in one batch that they released moisture and steamed rather than sautéed. We decided to cook the scallops in two batches—once the first batch was browned on one side, but still rare, we transferred them to a plate (browned side up) while the second batch seared. We kept the second batch in the skillet, then lowered the heat and returned the first batch to the pan to cook through. It's critical for the formation of a good crust to leave the scallops alone once they hit the pan. The scallops should be placed in the pan one at a time, with a flat side down for maximum contact with the hot pan.

This solved the crust dilemma, but what about the interior of the scallops? As a scallop cooks, the soft flesh firms and you can see an opaqueness that starts at the bottom of the scallop, where it sits in the pan, and slowly creeps up toward the center. To preserve the creamy texture of our pan-seared scallops, we cooked them to medium-rare, so they were hot all the way through but the center still retained some translucence.

Typically, scallops are sautéed with at least 2 tablespoons of fat. We tried butter, olive oil, vegetable oil, and a combination of butter and oil. To achieve a golden exterior without overcooking the scallops, we had to crank the heat to high, which burned the butter before the scallops had a chance to form a crust. The scallops browned best in the olive and vegetable oils. Since tasters didn't detect a flavor difference between the two, we decided to use the vegetable oil, which has a slightly higher smoke point.

As for accompaniments, tasters agreed that they wanted some sort of sauce to drizzle over the scallops. Rich and creamy sauces were quickly nudged aside—the scallops themselves already exhibit these characteristics—in favor of a fresh-tasting sauce with a smooth texture.

Using a restaurant technique that involves simmering fruit juice until it has reduced to a syrup, we were able to create a bold fruit-flavored sauce. We tried a variety of flavors, but tangerine and pomegranate reductions were singled out as favorites with the scallops. The syrup, which we found achieved the perfect silky-smooth drizzling viscosity when thickened with a little cornstarch, just needed a touch of honey to temper its acidity, as

well as some shallot and thyme to round out its rich fruit flavor. We made the sauce in the skillet before cooking the scallops, so once the delicate scallops were done cooking, the sauce could be drizzled over the top and the dish served.

Pan-Seared Sea Scallops with Citrus Sauce

SERVES 4

Be sure to zest the tangerines before juicing them; if tangerines are unavailable, you can substitute 5 oranges. If desired, skip the tangerine sauce and serve the scallops with a relish (see pages 20–22). Be ready to serve the scallops right away because they will cool off quickly.

2	cups fresh juice from 6 to 8 tangerines
½	teaspoon cornstarch
3	sprigs fresh thyme
1	medium shallot, minced (about 3 tablespoons)
½	teaspoon grated tangerine zest
½	teaspoon honey
1½	pounds large sea scallops (16 to 20 scallops), tendons removed (see the illustration on page 179)
	Salt and ground black pepper
¼	cup vegetable oil

1. Whisk 1 tablespoon of the tangerine juice with the cornstarch and set aside. Simmer the remaining tangerine juice, the thyme, and shallot together in a 12-inch nonstick skillet over medium-high heat until the mixture measures about ½ cup, 10 to 12 minutes. Whisk the cornstarch mixture into the sauce and continue to cook until thickened, about 1 minute. Strain the mixture into a small bowl, discarding the solids. Stir in the zest and honey and set aside.

2. Wipe out the skillet with a wad of paper towels. Lay the scallops out on a dish towel–lined plate and season with salt and pepper. Press a single layer of paper towels onto the surface of the scallops and set aside.

3. Heat 2 tablespoons of the oil in the skillet over high heat until just smoking. Carefully add half of the scallops to the skillet and cook until

well browned on one side, 1 to 2 minutes (when the last scallop is added to the skillet, the first few scallops will be close to done). Transfer the scallops to a plate, browned side up, and set aside.

4. Wipe out the skillet with a wad of paper towels. Add the remaining 2 tablespoons oil to the skillet and return to high heat until just smoking. Add the remaining scallops and cook until well browned on one side, 1 to 2 minutes.

5. Reduce the heat to medium. Flip the second batch of scallops over and return the first batch of scallops to the skillet, browned side up. Continue to cook until the sides of the scallops have firmed up and all but the middle third of each scallop is opaque, 30 to 60 seconds longer. Transfer all the scallops to individual plates or a platter. Drizzle some of the sauce over the scallops and serve, passing the remaining sauce separately.

➤ VARIATION

Pan-Seared Sea Scallops with Pomegranate Sauce

Be sure to purchase straight pomegranate juice, which is sweet and slightly tart, not a flavored variety. If desired, add additional honey to taste.

Follow the recipe for Pan-Seared Sea Scallops with Citrus Sauce, substituting 2 cups pomegranate juice for the tangerine juice and omitting the tangerine zest.

INGREDIENTS: Scallops

There are three main varieties of scallops—sea, bay, and calico. Sea scallops are available year-round throughout the country and are normally the best choice. They are usually at least an inch in diameter and resemble squat marshmallows. Sometimes they are sold cut up, but we found that they can lose moisture when handled this way and are best purchased whole. Small, cork-shaped bay scallops (about half an inch in diameter) are harvested in a small area from Cape Cod to Long Island. Bay scallops are available from late fall through midwinter, and are delicious but nearly impossible to find outside of top restaurants. Calico scallops are a small species (less than half an inch across) that are inexpensive but generally not terribly good. Our recommendation is to stick with sea scallops, unless you have access to bay scallops.

BREADED CHICKEN BREASTS

A TENDER BONELESS CHICKEN BREAST, PAN-fried in a skillet with a cloak of mild-flavored crumbs, has universal appeal. Though simple, this dish can fall prey to a host of problems: rubbery or tasteless chicken, coatings that won't stay on, or coatings that, unfortunately, do stay on and become greasy or burnt. In a perfect world, our breading would be crisp, not greasy, and would actually adhere to the chicken breasts.

To explore our options, we pan-fried breasts coated with fresh bread crumbs (made from fresh sliced white sandwich bread ground in the food processor) and with dry bread crumbs. The dry bread crumbs had a disappointingly stale flavor. The fresh bread crumbs, however, swept the taste test with their mild, subtly sweet flavor and light, crisp texture. We then tested crumbs made from different styles of white bread, pitting the high-quality white sandwich bread used in our first test against Italian, French, and country-style breads. The sandwich bread was the sweetest and our tasters' clear favorite. That said, fresh crumbs made from any of these breads were good.

Our standard breading method is to dredge the breasts in flour, dip them in beaten egg, and then, finally, coat them with bread crumbs. During our breading tests, we made several important observations that helped us improve this process. We learned that the breasts had to be thoroughly dry before we began. If they were even slightly moist, the breading would peel off the cooked chicken in sheets. Dry breasts also encouraged the thinnest possible coating of flour, preventing any gumminess in the finished dish. We also confirmed that coating the chicken with flour first was essential—otherwise, the breading just didn't stick on the chicken during the cooking process.

After the breasts are lightly floured, they're quickly dipped in beaten egg. But the beaten egg is typically thick and viscous and has a tendency to stick to the meat in clumps, giving the breading an overly thick, indelicate texture. Thinning the egg with oil, water, or both is a common practice that allows any excess to slide off the meat more easily,

BREADING CHICKEN BREASTS

1. Dredge the breasts lightly but thoroughly in the flour mixture, shaking off the excess.

2. Using tongs, dip both sides of the breasts in the egg mixture, taking care to coat them thoroughly and allowing the excess to drip back into the dish to ensure a very thin coating. Tongs keep the egg from coating your fingers.

3. Dredge both sides of the breasts in the bread crumbs, pressing the crumbs in place with your fingers to form an even, cohesive coat.

4. Place the breaded breasts in a single layer on a wire rack set over a baking sheet and allow the coating to dry for about 5 minutes. This drying time stabilizes the breading so that it can be sautéed without sticking to the skillet or falling off.

leaving a thinner, more delicate coating. We tested all three practices and honestly couldn't detect much difference in the flavor or texture of the finished breading. We did notice, however, that the breading made with oil-thinned egg wash seemed to brown a little more deeply than that made with water-thinned wash, so we added a tablespoon of oil to our two beaten eggs and moved on.

As for the bread crumbs, we found that it was essential to press the crumbs onto the breasts to ensure an even, thorough coat. Once breaded, the breasts should rest for about five minutes before frying. This short rest period helps further bind the breading to the meat.

With our chicken ready to pan-fry, we got out the skillet. First we had to figure out how much oil we'd need to use for thorough browning. We discovered that adding enough oil to reach a third of the way up the pan would be sufficient. As for the heat level, to ensure that the breading doesn't overbrown or burn before the meat is done, the oil should be heated just until shimmering (but not smoking). And as with all pan-searing, it is important to make sure the chicken is not crowded in the pan, or it will steam and turn soggy rather than crisp. For this reason, we cook our chicken breasts in two batches, holding the first batch in a 200-degree oven to keep warm. The result is chicken with a crisp, well-browned crust every time.

Crispy Breaded Chicken Breasts
SERVES 4

When coating the breasts with the bread-crumb mixture, use your hands to pat a thorough, even coating onto the chicken to make sure the crumbs adhere. While homemade bread crumbs taste best, you can substitute 2 cups panko (ultra-crisp Japanese-style bread crumbs).

- 4 (5- to 6-ounce) boneless, skinless chicken breasts, tenderloins removed and breasts trimmed (see the illustrations on pages 5 and 6)
- ¾ cup unbleached all-purpose flour
  Salt and ground black pepper
- 2 large eggs

¾ cup plus 1 tablespoon vegetable oil

3 slices high-quality white sandwich bread, torn into quarters

1 lemon, cut into wedges, for serving

1. Adjust an oven rack to the middle position and heat the oven to 200 degrees. Following the illustration on page 7, pound each chicken breast between two sheets of plastic wrap to a uniform ½-inch thickness.

2. Combine the flour, ½ teaspoon salt, and ¼ teaspoon pepper in a shallow dish. Whisk the eggs and 1 tablespoon of the oil in a second shallow dish. Pulse the bread in a food processor to coarse crumbs, about 16 pulses, then transfer to a third dish.

3. Pat the chicken breasts dry with paper towels and season with salt and pepper. Working with 1 chicken breast at a time, dredge in the flour mixture, shaking off the excess, following the illustrations on page 28. Coat the chicken with the egg mixture, allowing the excess to drip off. Finally, coat with the bread crumbs, pressing gently to help the crumbs adhere. Place the breaded chicken breasts in a single layer on a wire rack set over a large rimmed baking sheet and let sit for 5 minutes.

4. Meanwhile, heat 6 tablespoons of the remaining oil in a 12-inch nonstick skillet over medium-high heat until shimmering. Carefully lay 2 of the chicken breasts in the skillet and cook until deep golden brown on the first side, 4 to 6 minutes. Flip the chicken breasts over and continue to cook until deep golden brown on the second side, 4 to 6 minutes longer. Drain the chicken breasts briefly on paper towels, then transfer to a clean wire rack set in a rimmed baking sheet and keep warm in the oven.

5. Pour off all of the fat from the skillet and wipe out the skillet with a wad of paper towels. Repeat with the remaining 6 tablespoons oil and 2 chicken breasts. Serve with the lemon wedges.

➤ VARIATIONS

Chicken Milanese

Follow the recipe for Crispy Breaded Chicken Breasts, replacing ¼ cup of the bread crumbs with ½ ounce Parmesan cheese, grated (about ¼ cup).

Crispy Chicken with Garlic and Oregano

Follow the recipe for Crispy Breaded Chicken Breasts, whisking 3 tablespoons minced fresh oregano leaves and 6 medium garlic cloves, minced or pressed through a garlic press (about 2 tablespoons), into the egg mixture in step 2.

Crispy Deviled Chicken

Follow the recipe for Crispy Breaded Chicken Breasts, whisking 3 tablespoons Dijon mustard, 1 tablespoon Worcestershire sauce, and 2 teaspoons minced fresh thyme leaves into the egg mixture in step 2, and seasoning the chicken with ⅛–¼ teaspoon cayenne pepper in addition to the salt and ground black pepper in step 3.

Crispy Chicken Fingers

Homemade chicken fingers are much tastier (and cheaper) than the frozen versions you can buy at the supermarket. For convenience, try making a big batch all at once, then freeze them in single-serving zipper-lock freezer bags, where they will keep for up to a month. Simply reheat them in a 425-degree oven until hot and crisp, about 15 minutes, flipping them once halfway through.

Follow the recipe for Crispy Breaded Chicken Breasts, using chicken breasts cut into strips, then breading and frying as directed in steps 2 through 5.

CHICKEN SALTIMBOCCA

SALTIMBOCCA, A SIMPLE VARIATION ON A basic sautéed veal scaloppine, hails from Rome. The traditional version has long been a standard menu item in the trattorias of Italy as well as Italian restaurants in this country. Made by sautéing veal cutlets with prosciutto and sage, this simple but elegant dish promises, literally, to "jump in your mouth" with its distinctive blend of flavors. Yet many saltimbocca dishes we've seen hardly do that, with unnecessary elements, like stuffing or breading, or proportions that are way off, allowing a thick slab of prosciutto to outshine the chicken and knock the balance of flavors out of whack. Saltimbocca seemed like a perfect candidate for a makeover—especially since it's already prepared in a skillet. We intended to keep the dish simple, while still giving each of the three original elements—chicken, prosciutto, and sage—its due.

Most of the chicken saltimbocca recipes we came across followed the traditional practice of threading a toothpick through the prosciutto and a whole sage leaf to attach them to the cutlet, then dredging the entire package in flour before sautéing it on both sides. When we started cooking, we had a few problems with this method. Flour got trapped in the small gaps where the ham bunched up around the toothpick, leaving sticky, uncooked spots. When we tried sautéing the chicken and prosciutto without any coating of flour, the ham crisped nicely, but the chicken browned unevenly and stuck to the pan. Surprisingly, flouring only the cutlet—taking a cue from our Sautéed Chicken Cutlets on page 7—before attaching the ham proved to be the solution. And by sautéing the cutlet prosciutto side down first, we were able to keep the flour under the prosciutto from turning gummy.

With our flouring method under control, it was time to look at the prosciutto. We liked imported prosciutto for the rich flavor it added to the overall dish, but we needed to figure out the right slice thickness. If the prosciutto was too thick, it had trouble staying put and the taste was overwhelming; if it was too thin, it fell apart easily. The ideal slice was just thick enough to hold its shape—about the thickness of two or three sheets of paper. Then we trimmed the ham to the size of the cutlet to make it fit.

While the prosciutto needed to be tamed, the sage flavor needed a boost. In the traditional dish, each cutlet features a single sage leaf—fried in oil before being attached—so that the herbal flavor imparted is very subtle. Tethering a leaf to the cutlet with a toothpick, however, was cumbersome and resulted in adding flavor only to bites that actually contained sage. We wanted a more even distribution of flavor. To infuse the cooking oil with sage, we tossed a handful of leaves into the oil before sautéing the cutlets, removing the herbs before they burned. Tasters, however, detected only a very slight flavor boost in the finished dish. The way to more intense and evenly distributed sage

flavor turned out to be as simple as chopping the leaves and sprinkling them over the floured cutlet before adding the ham. The only thing missing was the pretty look of the fried sage leaf. While not necessary, frying enough sage leaves to place on the cooked cutlets is easy enough and adds an elegant finishing touch.

The only aspect of the dish we had not yet examined was the toothpick. After skewering prosciutto to more than 100 cutlets in the course of our testing, we decided enough was enough. What would happen if we just dropped the toothpick altogether? After flouring the cutlet, sprinkling it with sage, and placing the prosciutto on top, we carefully lifted the bundle and placed it as we had been doing, prosciutto side down, in the hot oil. Once the edges of the chicken on the bottom had browned, we flipped the cutlet, revealing ham that seemed almost hermetically sealed to the chicken—no toothpick needed.

A quick pan sauce made from vermouth, lemon juice, butter, and parsley was all we needed to accentuate the perfect balance of flavors. We had taken our Chicken Saltimbocca to a new level, and it was both incredibly simple and elegant.

Chicken Saltimbocca

SERVES 4

Although whole sage leaves make a beautiful presentation, they are optional and can be left out of step 3. Make sure to buy prosciutto that is thinly sliced, not shaved; also avoid slices that are too thick, as they won't stick to the chicken. The prosciutto slices should be large enough to fully cover one side of each cutlet; if the slices are too large, simply cut them down to size. Feel free to substitute 8 veal, turkey, or even pork cutlets for the chicken—just make sure that they are about 3 ounces each.

CHICKEN

4 (5- to 6-ounce) boneless, skinless chicken breasts, tenderloins removed and breasts trimmed (see the illustrations on pages 5 and 6)

½ cup unbleached all-purpose flour
   Ground black pepper

1   tablespoon minced fresh sage leaves, plus 8 large whole leaves (optional)

8   thin prosciutto slices (about 3 ounces; see note)

¼   cup olive oil

SAUCE

2   teaspoons olive oil

1   medium shallot, minced (about 3 tablespoons)

1   teaspoon unbleached all-purpose flour

¾   cup low-sodium chicken broth

½   cup dry vermouth or white wine

1   tablespoon unsalted butter, chilled

1   tablespoon minced fresh parsley leaves

2   teaspoons juice from 1 lemon
    Salt and ground black pepper

1. FOR THE CHICKEN: Following the illustrations on page 7, slice each chicken breast in half horizontally into cutlets. Pound each cutlet between two sheets of plastic wrap to a uniform ¼-inch thickness.

2. Place the flour in a shallow dish. Pat the chicken cutlets dry with paper towels and season with pepper. Working with 1 chicken cutlet at a time, dredge in the flour, shaking off the excess, and lay the cutlets flat on a work surface. Sprinkle the minced sage evenly over the top of each cutlet. Place 1 prosciutto slice on top of each chicken cutlet, covering the sage, and press lightly to help it adhere.

3. Heat 2 tablespoons of the oil in a 12-inch skillet over medium-high heat until shimmering. Add the whole sage leaves (if using) and cook until the leaves begin to change color and are fragrant, 15 to 20 seconds. Using a slotted spoon, transfer the sage leaves to a paper towel–lined plate and set aside.

4. Carefully lay 4 of the chicken cutlets in the skillet, prosciutto side down, and cook until lightly browned on the first side, about 2 minutes. Flip the chicken cutlets over and continue to cook until no longer pink, 30 seconds to 1 minute longer. Transfer the chicken cutlets to a plate and tent loosely with foil.

5. Add the remaining 2 tablespoons oil to the skillet and repeat with the remaining cutlets. Transfer to the plate and tent loosely with foil while making the sauce.

6. FOR THE SAUCE: Pour off any fat left in the pan. Add the oil and shallot and cook over medium-high heat until softened, about 2 minutes. Stir in the flour and cook for 30 seconds. Stir in the broth and vermouth, scraping up any browned bits. Bring to a simmer and cook until the sauce measures ¾ cup, 3 to 5 minutes. Stir in any accumulated chicken juices, return to a simmer, and cook for 30 seconds.

7. Off the heat, whisk in the butter, parsley, and lemon juice. Season with salt and pepper to taste. Spoon the sauce over the chicken cutlets, sprinkle with the fried sage leaves (if using), and serve.

INGREDIENTS: **Dry Vermouth**

Though it's often used in cooking, and even more often in martinis, dry vermouth is a potable that is paid very little attention. Its base is a white wine, presumably not of particularly high quality, as evidenced by the relatively low prices of most vermouths. The wine is fortified with neutral grape spirits that up the alcohol level to 16 to 18 percent, and it is "aromatized," or infused, with "botanicals" such as herbs, spices, and fruits. Dry vermouth, also called extra-dry vermouth, is imported from France and Italy and is made domestically in California. We tasted several brands of vermouth straight (chilled) and in simple pan sauces for chicken; our favorites were Gallo Extra Dry and Noilly Prat Original French Dry.

THE BEST DRY VERMOUTHS

GALLO   NOILLY PRAT

Gallo Extra Dry ($5 for a 750-ml bottle) is floral and fruity, creating a balanced, complex, and smooth pan sauce. Noilly Prat Original French Dry ($6.79 for a 750-ml bottle) is herbaceous, with faint anise notes, which resulted in a balanced and fresh-tasting pan sauce.

CHICKEN TERIYAKI

WHEN THE FISH ISN'T SO FRESH AND THE soba's just so-so, you can usually count on chicken teriyaki as a reliable standby at most Japanese restaurants. But with so many lackluster Americanized adaptations out there—including everything from skewered chicken chunks in a corn-syrup sauce to over-marinated, preformed chicken breast patties—what's the real deal?

Traditionally, chicken teriyaki is pan-seared, grilled, or broiled, with the sauce added during the last stages of cooking. The sauce itself—unlike most bottled versions—consists of just three basic ingredients: soy sauce, sugar, and either mirin (a sweet Japanese rice wine) or sake. For our recipe, we wanted to make the teriyaki in a skillet, so pan-searing was our go-to method.

For the chicken, we chose thighs for a couple reasons. Tasters preferred them; also, boneless, skinless breasts—whether marinated and seared or left plain and sauced at the end—seemed to end up a bit dry and bland compared with the thigh meat. Now the questions of bone-in or bone-out, skin-on or skin-off, begged to be answered. The skin seemed to create a protective barrier against the heat source, keeping the meat moist, so it would have to be left on. Most skin-on chicken thighs are sold with the bone attached, so we would have to bone them ourselves if we wanted them deboned. We decided against the extra step—and extra work.

Because most of the recipes we came across in our research called for marinating the meat to infuse it with as much flavor as possible, all of our initial efforts began with this step. But whether we pricked the skin with a fork or slashed it with a knife, marinating the thighs in the teriyaki sauce caused the skin to become unattractively flabby. A combination of searing the thighs and finishing them under the broiler yielded the most promising results, but once the meat received its final cover of sauce to get that glazy shine, the skin always slipped back into sogginess.

After numerous tests, we tried one last thing that we had come across in our research. We browned unmarinated thighs skin side down in a nonstick skillet, while weighting them with a Dutch oven. The Dutch oven pressed the skin in direct contact with the hot pan, and the nonstick surface prevented the skin from sticking and tearing while it browned. We then simmered the thighs skin side up in the reducing sauce. This was the perfect compromise—the skin stayed crisp, while the meat was moist and flavorful. We had gotten so caught up with trying to infuse the meat with flavor that we had forgotten about one main technique of traditional teriyaki: applying the sauce at the end.

With the chicken taken care of, it was time to concentrate on the sauce. Working with various amounts of soy sauce, sugar, and mirin (which tasters preferred to sake), we found that the best balance of sweetness and saltiness was achieved with equal amounts of soy sauce and sugar (½ cup) and with a smaller amount of mirin (2 tablespoons), which added a slightly sweet wine flavor.

Giving the sauce a glaze-like consistency (neither as thick as molasses nor as thin as water) was difficult. We kept a close eye on the simmering sauce, but it either stayed too thin or became tacky while the soy sauce burned. A minimal amount of cornstarch (½ teaspoon) quickly solved this problem. Although the sauce was now clean and balanced, it needed more depth, which we provided by adding some minced fresh ginger and garlic. With crisp and moist, sweet and salty glazed chicken now available at home, we would never have to eat food-court teriyaki again.

Chicken Teriyaki

SERVES 4

Small thighs work best here. If the thighs are large, you may need to extend the browning time in step 2. A splatter screen (or a large, inverted strainer/colander) is helpful for reducing the mess when browning the second side of the chicken. There is a fair amount of soy sauce used in this dish, so there is no need to season it with extra salt. Serve with Simple White Rice (page 228).

½	cup soy sauce
½	cup sugar
2	tablespoons mirin
2	teaspoons minced or grated fresh ginger
I	medium garlic clove, minced or pressed through a garlic press (about I teaspoon)

½ teaspoon cornstarch
⅛ teaspoon red pepper flakes
8 small bone-in, skin-on chicken thighs, trimmed
Ground black pepper
1 tablespoon vegetable oil
2 scallions, sliced thin

1. Whisk the soy sauce, sugar, mirin, ginger, garlic, cornstarch, and red pepper flakes together in a small bowl and set aside.

2. Pat the chicken thighs dry with paper towels and season with pepper. Heat the oil in a 12-inch nonstick skillet over medium-high heat until shimmering. Carefully lay the chicken thighs, skin side down, in the skillet. Following the illustration below, weight the chicken thighs with a heavy pot and cook until the skin is well browned and very crisp, about 15 minutes. (The chicken thighs should be moderately brown after 10 minutes. Reduce the heat if they are very brown, or increase the heat if they are pale.)

3. Flip the chicken thighs over and continue to cook, without replacing the weight, until the thickest part of the chicken thighs registers 170 to 175 degrees on an instant-read thermometer, 5 to 10 minutes longer. Transfer the chicken thighs to a plate, tent loosely with foil, and let rest while making the sauce.

4. Pour off all the fat from the skillet. Whisk the soy mixture to recombine, then add it to the skillet and bring to a simmer over medium heat. Nestle the chicken thighs into the sauce,

WEIGHTING THE CHICKEN

Place a Dutch oven or heavy pot on top of the chicken as it cooks to weight the chicken and ensure crisp skin.

skin side up, and spoon some of the sauce over the top. Continue to simmer until the sauce is thick and glossy, about 2 minutes longer. Transfer the chicken thighs and sauce to a platter, sprinkle with the scallions, and serve.

TURKEY BURGERS

SUCCULENT, JUICY, AND MEATY—THESE ARE just a few attributes that come to mind when we think of big, beefy burgers. But what about the hamburger's leaner next of kin, the turkey burger? It can be all of these things too, plus it provides a good, healthy alternative at the neighborhood cookout. But, unfortunately, we've had turkey burgers that were dry, tasteless, and colorless. We set out to improve this underdog, and make a health-conscious indoor turkey burger with beef burger qualities—one pan-seared in a skillet until dark and crusty on the outside and full-flavored and juicy on the inside.

Finding the right meat was crucial to developing the best turkey burger. We had a few options: white meat (with 1 to 2 percent fat), dark meat (over 15 percent fat), and a blend of the two (ranging from 7 to 15 percent fat). At the grocery store, we found multiple variations on the white meat/dark meat theme, including higher-fat ground fresh turkey on Styrofoam trays, frozen turkey packaged in tubes like bulk sausage, and lower-fat ground turkey breasts. We also found individual turkey parts that we could grind up ourselves. We brought them all back to the test kitchen and fired up a skillet.

The higher-fat ground turkey turned out to be flavorful and reasonably juicy, but with a fat content close to that of a great beef burger, it impeded our goal of keeping a certain leanness in our turkey burger. We moved on to the ground turkey breast, which, with only 1 or 2 percent fat, needed extra fat to keep these burgers from being dessicated and bland. Lean ground turkey, with 7 percent fat, was the most popular style at all the grocery stores we visited. Burgers made from this mix were dry and mild-flavored. With a little help, however, these leaner patties would have real burger potential.

To improve texture and juiciness, we started with the obvious—milk-soaked bread. For comparison, we also made burgers with buttermilk- and yogurt-soaked bread. All these additions made the burgers feel too much like meatloaf and destroyed whatever meaty flavor there had been in the mild turkey meat. We tried other fillers to improve the texture, such as mashed pinto beans, but their flavors were too distinct. Rehydrated dried mushrooms helped the texture, but added a unique, mushroom flavor that seemed out of place. The winner—for flavor, texture, and availability—was ricotta cheese, which gave our burgers the moist, chewy texture of a beef burger.

Next, we decided the taste needed some work and decided to experiment a bit with added flavorings. We wanted only those which would enhance the burger's taste without drawing attention to themselves. We tried more than 25 different flavorings—from olive paste to teriyaki marinade—and found only two that we liked: Worcestershire sauce and Dijon mustard.

Finally, we turned to the cooking method. Since turkey burgers must be well-done for safety reasons, cooking them can be a bit tricky—too high a heat and they burn before they're done, too low and they look pale and steamed. For our Pan-Seared Hamburgers (page 35), adding a well in the middle of the shaped patty helps prevent the center of the burger from rising when it cooks, but we found this step unnecessary with our turkey burger. We tried several cooking methods, but nothing compared in quality and ease with browning the burgers in our skillet over medium heat, then cooking them partially covered (to ensure they were evenly and quickly cooked) over low heat until they registered 160 to 165 degrees on an instant-read thermometer.

As we sampled our skillet turkey burgers, we found that they were moist, with a nice crust, and still relatively healthy—unless, of course, we had seconds.

Pan-Seared Turkey Burgers

SERVES 4

The ricotta cheese can burn easily, so keep a close watch on the burgers as they cook. A well-seasoned cast-iron skillet is a great choice for this recipe, but any heavy-bottomed skillet can be used.

1¼	pounds 93 percent lean ground turkey
½	cup whole milk ricotta cheese
2	teaspoons Worcestershire sauce
2	teaspoons Dijon mustard
½	teaspoon salt
½	teaspoon ground black pepper
1	tablespoon vegetable oil
	Buns and desired toppings

1. Mix the turkey, ricotta, Worcestershire sauce, mustard, salt, and pepper together in a large bowl with your hands until uniformly combined. Divide the meat into 4 equal portions. Toss 1 portion of meat back and forth with cupped hands to form a loose ball. Pat lightly to flatten the meat into a 1-inch-thick burger. Repeat with the remaining portions of meat.

2. Heat the oil in a 12-inch skillet over medium heat until just smoking. Carefully lay the burgers in the skillet and cook until light brown and crusted on the first side, 3 to 4 minutes. Flip the burgers over and continue to cook until the second side is light brown, 3 to 4 minutes longer.

3. Reduce the heat to low, partially cover, and continue to cook until the thickest part of the burgers register 160 to 165 degrees on an instant-read thermometer, 8 to 10 minutes longer, flipping once more if necessary for even browning. Serve in the buns with desired toppings.

HAMBURGERS

AMERICANS PROBABLY EAT MORE HAMBURGERS than any other food. We should be experts at making them, as well as eating them, but many hamburgers seem merely to satisfy hunger rather than give pleasure. It's too bad, because making an exceptional hamburger isn't that hard or time-consuming. If you have the right ground beef and a heavy skillet, the perfect hamburger can be ready in less than 15 minutes, assuming you season, form, and cook it properly. The biggest difficulty for many cooks, though, may be finding the right beef.

To test which cut or cuts of beef would cook up into the best burgers, we ordered chuck, round, rump, and sirloin, all ground to order. After a side-by-side taste test, we quickly concluded that

SHAPING HAMBURGERS

1. With cupped hands, toss 1 portion of meat back and forth from hand to hand to shape it into a loose ball.

2. Pat lightly to flatten the meat into a ¾-inch-thick burger that measures 4½ inches across. Press the center of the patty down with your fingertips until it is ½ inch thick, creating a well in the center. Repeat with the remaining portions of meat.

most cuts of ground beef are pleasant but bland when compared with robust, beefy-flavored ground chuck. Pricier ground sirloin, for example, cooked up into a particularly boring burger. Pure ground chuck, the clear winner, is the cut of beef that starts where the ribs end and travels up to the shoulder and neck, ending at the foreshank. A test of burgers with various fat percentages helped us decide that 20 percent fat was good for burgers. Any more fat and the burgers are too greasy; any less starts to compromise the beef's juicy, moist texture.

When to season the meat with salt and pepper may seem an insignificant detail, but when making a dish as simple as a hamburger, little things matter. We tried seasoning the meat at four different points in the process. Our first burger was seasoned before the meat was shaped, the second burger was seasoned right before cooking, the third after each side was seared, and the fourth after the burger had been fully cooked. Predictably, the burger that had been seasoned throughout was our preference and had an

even saltiness. Our fresh-ground chuck would have to be seasoned at the beginning.

We now moved on to shaping and cooking. To test the validity of the overhandling warning you see in many recipes, we thoroughly worked a portion of ground beef before cooking it. The well-done exterior of the burger was nearly as dense as pâté, and the less well-done interior was compact and pasty. That said, it's actually pretty hard to overhandle a beef patty, especially if you're trying not to. Once the meat has been divided into portions—6 ounces of meat create a nicely sized burger—we found that tossing each portion from one hand to the other helped bring the meat together into a ball without overworking it (see the illustration at left).

Now nearly done with our testing, we needed only to perfect our skillet cooking method. Burgers require a real blast of heat if they are to form a crunchy, flavorful crust before the interior overcooks. We found that a heavy skillet heated over medium-high heat with a minimal amount of oil formed a crust quickly, without causing the burgers to stick to the skillet. In order to nail the perfect doneness, we reduced the heat to medium when cooking the second side (much like we would to sauté steaks). To prevent puffy tennis-ball burgers, we pressed a well into the center of each burger to ensure that they came out of the pan with an even thickness. Also, we avoided pressing down on the burgers as they cooked. Rather than speeding their cooking, pressing on the patties serves only to squeeze out their juices and make the burgers dry.

Our burgers were now done—juicy and delicious—and it was time to get out the ketchup and mustard.

Pan-Seared Hamburgers
SERVES 4
A well-seasoned cast-iron skillet is a great choice for this recipe, but any heavy-bottomed skillet can be used.

1½	pounds 80 percent lean ground beef chuck
¾	teaspoon salt
½	teaspoon ground black pepper
1	tablespoon oil
	Buns and desired toppings

1. Spread the meat out on a large plate, sprinkle the salt and pepper over the top, and toss lightly with your hands to distribute the seasonings. Divide the meat into 4 equal portions. Following the illustrations on page 35, toss 1 portion of meat back and forth with cupped hands to form a loose ball. Pat lightly to flatten the meat into a ¾-inch-thick burger. Make a ½-inch-thick well in the center of the burger by pressing down with your fingertips. Repeat with the remaining portions of meat.

2. Heat the oil in a 12-inch skillet over medium-high heat until just smoking. Add the patties, well side up, and cook until well-browned, about 3 minutes. Flip the burgers, reduce the heat to medium, and continue to cook to the desired doneness (see page 9), 3 to 5 minutes longer. Serve in the buns with desired toppings.

➤ VARIATION

Pan-Seared Cheeseburgers
Any type of cheese will work here—cheddar, Muenster, Swiss, and American cheeses are some of our favorites.

Follow the recipe for Pan-Seared Hamburgers, topping each burger with 1 slice cheese during the last minute of cooking and covering the skillet to let the cheese melt.

STEAK AU POIVRE
THERE'S NOTHING COMPLICATED ABOUT steak au poivre. When well executed, the slightly sweet, smooth sauce has more than a hint of shallot and brandy, the steak is well browned on the outside and cherry red on the interior, and the crust of cracked peppercorns provides a pungent, slow burn, adding fire and depth to an otherwise simple steak. A third-rate steak au poivre, however, has peppercorns that fall off the steak only to reveal underbrowned meat. What's more, the peppercorn coating prevents the steak from forming drippings in the skillet that form the base of a rich sauce. Because most steak au poivre recipes make no attempt to solve these problems, the home cook is left with tasteless steaks covered by an insipid sauce.

Our first tests were useful in determining the best cut of steak for au poivre. Filets are tender but too mild-flavored. Rib-eye steaks, always a favorite of ours, have abundant fat pockets and pronounced veins of gristle that separate two differently textured muscles. A peppercorn crust obscures these imperfections, requiring scrutiny and maneuvering on the part of the diner to eat around these parts. Strip steaks, however, have external lines of gristle that are easily trimmed before cooking, and their neat, tight, even grain makes them particularly well suited to steak au poivre.

We quickly decided what type of peppercorns to use. Among black, white, and a blend of green, pink, black, and white, plain old black peppercorns were the favorite in the test kitchen. Tasters extolled their sharp bite, rich and intense flavor, and elusive smokiness.

Next, we had to determine the amount of peppercorns—we first cooked the steaks with a crust of just a teaspoon of peppercorns on each side. Loose pepper fell off the steaks and scorched pitifully in the skillet. The pepper that did stick shielded the surface of the steaks, preventing browning and thereby the formation of a fond on which to build the sauce. In addition, most tasters thought we were far too liberal in our peppercorn allotment—the heat was vicious. Our first thought was to cut back on the peppercorns, but then a light bulb went on. What if the steaks were coated on one side only? We placed the skillet over medium-high heat until the oil was just smoking and cooked the steaks on the first side, unpeppered side down. This gave the steaks a few minutes to brown on the first side and form a fond. Then the steaks were flipped onto their peppered side and given only five to 10 minutes (depending on desired doneness) to complete their cooking at medium heat, this time without scorching the pepper. Our method worked like a charm. We found that pressing down on the steaks with the bottom of a cake pan while they cooked made for even browning and also helped the peppercorns to adhere.

The steak was done, so we turned our attention to the sauce. This pan sauce was no different than the others in this chapter, except for the fact that all steak au poivre sauces contain brandy, and most contain cream (though some achieve richness from butter only). After removing the steaks from the skillet, we sautéed a shallot and stirred in 1 teaspoon flour to give our sauce body without having to reduce it for too long. We then added broth and brandy, but we quickly found out that introducing brandy to the sauce was no trivial matter. We tried reducing it with the broth mixture to concentrate its flavor. This worked, but the resulting sauce lacked the spirited brandy bite. Our solution was to reduce ¼ cup of brandy with the broth, which relieved it of its alcoholic harshness and helped it meld with the broth. Before serving, we stirred 1 tablespoon raw brandy into the sauce to give the sauce a nice bite and fresh brandy flavor.

Lastly, we enriched the sauce with a bit of cream, which brought a luxurious and sophisticated tone. The cream was stirred in and the sauce was allowed to simmer again. To finish our Steak au Poivre, we added mustard and lemon juice along with the brandy to brighten things up, and chives for a touch of color.

CRUSHING PEPPERCORNS

If your pepper mill can't produce coarsely crushed peppercorns, you have two alternatives.

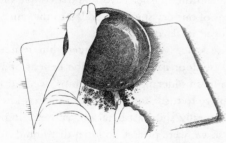

A. Use the bottom of a heavy pan and a rocking motion to crush peppercorns.

B. Spread the peppercorns in an even layer in a zipper-lock bag and whack them with a rolling pin or meat pounder.

Steak au Poivre with Brandied Cream Sauce

SERVES 4

Many pepper mills do not have a sufficiently coarse setting to produce crushed or cracked peppercorns. In that case, crush the peppercorns with a skillet or rolling pin (see the illustrations at left). Do not substitute finely ground pepper for the crushed peppercorns here.

STEAKS

4	(8- to 10-ounce) strip steaks, ¾ to 1 inch thick, trimmed
	Salt
4	teaspoons black peppercorns, crushed (see note)
1	tablespoon vegetable oil

SAUCE

2	teaspoons vegetable oil
1	medium shallot, minced (about 3 tablespoons)
1	teaspoon unbleached all-purpose flour
¾	cup low-sodium chicken broth
5	tablespoons brandy
2	tablespoons heavy cream
2	tablespoons minced fresh chives
2	teaspoons juice from 1 lemon
1	teaspoon Dijon mustard
	Salt

1. FOR THE STEAKS: Pat the steaks dry with paper towels and season with salt. Sprinkle one side of each steak with 1 teaspoon crushed peppercorns and press them into the steaks with your fingers to adhere.

2. Heat the oil in a 12-inch skillet over medium-high heat until just smoking. Carefully lay the steaks in the skillet, peppered side up. Press on the steaks with the bottom of a cake pan and cook until well browned on the first side, 3 to 5 minutes.

3. Flip the steaks over, reduce the heat to medium, and continue to cook, pressing again with the cake pan, to the desired doneness (see page 9), 5 to 10 minutes. Transfer the steaks to a plate, tent loosely with foil, and let rest while making the sauce.

4. FOR THE SAUCE: Pour off any fat left in the pan and remove any stray peppercorns. Add the oil and shallot and cook over medium-high heat until softened, about 2 minutes. Stir in the flour and cook for 30 seconds. Stir in the broth and ¼ cup of the brandy, scraping up any browned bits. Bring to a simmer and cook until the sauce measures ½ cup, 3 to 5 minutes. Stir in the cream and any accumulated meat juices, return to a simmer, and cook for 30 seconds.

5. Off the heat, whisk in the remaining 1 tablespoon brandy, the chives, lemon juice, and mustard. Season with salt to taste. Spoon the sauce over the steaks and serve.

BARBECUED PORK CHOPS

ONE OF OUR FAVORITE FLAVORS IN THE summer is that of charred, salty-sweet grilled pork chops coated with spicy barbecue sauce. Would we be able to move this dish inside, armed with only a skillet, and replicate that smoky flavor? We suspected it could be done.

We started with the pork chops, and picked bone-in rib chops—our preference because they are juicier and more flavorful than others due to a bit more fat. We made sure they were the same thickness, between ¾ and 1 inch; much thinner than that, and the chops have a tendency to overcook. We scored the fat around the edge of the chops, at 2-inch intervals, with a paring knife to prevent them from buckling or curling when we heated them in the skillet (see the illustration on page 10). While it's not necessary, we brined the chops (soaked them in a solution of water and salt) to help ensure even cooking later on from the bone all the way to the outer rim of the chop. (If your pork chops are enhanced, there's no need to brine them; see page 40 for more information.)

The next order of business was to find a way of giving the pork a nice, evenly charred surface without overcooking the interior. Pork chops are leaner than other meats, such as steaks and lamb chops, and therefore more prone to drying out. We

knew that, even though we had brined the chops, searing them in a blazing hot skillet to form a good crust before lowering the heat would overcook the meat before it could brown properly. In the pan, as opposed to on a grill, the chops would simmer in their own juices, lowering the temperature of the cooking surface, which is why the outside wouldn't brown as quickly as we needed it to. To get our pork to char, we added another outdoor element to the mix—the dry spice rub.

Though standard fare for a grill, a spice rub can cause trouble in a hot skillet. The rub, which darkens more readily than the pork proteins, doesn't just char, it blackens. But by starting with medium heat rather than high, we found we could let the spice rub char while the pork cooked at a gentler pace, resulting in chops that cooked perfectly inside and out.

Now we turned to the barbecue sauce. Starting with the requisite ketchup and molasses, we ran through a battery of taste tests. Worcestershire sauce and Dijon mustard gave the sauce complexity and heat, and onions and cider vinegar added a pungent kick. Brown sugar helped mellow out and blend the sharper flavors, and a couple of teaspoons of our dry spice rub added to the sauce also improved its flavor.

The sauce was now balanced, but it needed more outdoor flavor. Without the benefit of a live fire and smoldering hickory chips, we had only one place to turn: liquid smoke. In the test kitchen, we generally shun artificial or synthetic ingredients, so we were pleased to learn that liquid smoke is a completely natural product. All suspicions were laid to rest when a batch of sauce to which we had secretly added a teaspoon of liquid smoke swept the next blind tasting. The key to keeping liquid smoke palatable is moderation.

Now we had our charred pork and smoky sauce, but they were two distinct elements rather than parts of the same entity. On an outdoor grill, the sauce caramelizes and intensifies, lacquering the chops in a sticky glaze. Could we re-create this fusion on the stovetop without ruining our pans? Brushing the sauce directly onto the chops while they were still in the pan produced a sticky, burnt mess and a dirty stovetop. What if we brought the pork to the sauce instead? We cooked up a new batch of chops, this time removing them from the pan a few minutes early. After transferring the pork chops to a plate, we brushed them with a thin coat of barbecue sauce and wiped out the skillet so we could finish cooking with a clean, hot surface. When the pork chops sizzled as they went back into the hot pan, our hopes were high.

We flipped the chops and saw that the sauce had reduced to a sticky, smoky, caramelized glaze that firmly adhered to the meat. Served with the remaining reduced sauce, these skillet-barbecued pork chops finally tasted like the real deal.

Barbecued Pork Chops

SERVES 4

We prefer natural pork to enhanced pork (see page 40 for more information). If the pork is enhanced, do not brine. If brining the pork, omit the salt in the spice mixture in step 1. In step 3, check your chops after 3 minutes; if you don't hear a definite sizzle and the chops have not started to brown on the underside, increase the heat to medium-high and continue cooking as directed (follow the indicated temperatures for the remainder of the recipe).

PORK CHOPS
I	tablespoon paprika
I	tablespoon brown sugar
2	teaspoons ground coriander
I	teaspoon ground cumin
I	teaspoon ground black pepper
½	teaspoon salt
4	(8- to 10-ounce) bone-in pork rib chops, ¾ to 1 inch thick, trimmed and brined if desired (see page 56)
4	teaspoons vegetable oil

SAUCE
½	cup ketchup
3	tablespoons light or mild molasses
2	tablespoons grated onion
2	tablespoons Worcestershire sauce
2	tablespoons Dijon mustard
I	tablespoon cider vinegar
I	tablespoon brown sugar
I	teaspoon liquid smoke

1. FOR THE PORK CHOPS: Combine the paprika, brown sugar, coriander, cumin, pepper, and salt in a small bowl. Measure out and reserve 2 teaspoons of the spice mixture separately for the sauce.

2. Following the illustration on page 10, slit the sides of the pork chops. Pat the pork chops dry with paper towels and coat with the spice rub, pressing gently so the rub adheres. Shake off the excess rub.

3. Heat 1 tablespoon of the oil in a 12-inch nonstick skillet over medium heat until just smoking. Carefully arrange the pork chops in the skillet and cook until charred in spots on the first side, 5 to 8 minutes. Flip the pork chops over and continue to cook until well browned and charred on the second side and the center of the pork chops registers 130 degrees on an instant-read thermometer, 4 to 8 minutes longer. Transfer the pork chops to a plate.

4. FOR THE SAUCE: Meanwhile, whisk the sauce ingredients into the bowl with the reserved 2 teaspoons spice mixture. Lightly brush the top side of each pork chop with 2 teaspoons of the sauce.

5. Wipe out the skillet with a wad of paper towels. Add the remaining 1 teaspoon oil to the skillet and return to medium heat until just smoking. Add the pork chops to the skillet, sauce side down, and cook until the sauce has caramelized and is charred in spots, about 1 minute. While the pork chops are cooking, lightly brush the top side of each pork chop with 2 more teaspoons sauce. Flip the pork chops over and cook until the second side is charred and caramelized and the center of the pork chops registers 140 to 145 degrees on an instant-read thermometer, 1 to 2 minutes.

6. Transfer the pork chops back to the plate, tent loosely with foil, and let rest until the center of the pork chops registers 150 degrees on an instant-read thermometer, about 5 minutes.

7. Meanwhile, add the remaining sauce to the skillet and cook, scraping up any browned bits, until thickened and measures about ⅔ cup, about 3 minutes. Brush each pork chop with 1 tablespoon of the reduced sauce and serve, passing the remaining sauce separately.

SMOTHERED PORK CHOPS

SMOTHERED PORK CHOPS, A HOMEY SKILLET dish of chops braised in onion gravy, are folksy, not fancy. The cooking process is straightforward: You brown the chops, remove them from the pan, brown the onions, return the chops to the pan, cover them with the onions and gravy—hence the term smothered—and braise them until tender. To get this skillet dish just right, we knew we'd have to cook our chops perfectly and make the gravy its equal partner in the finished dish.

Some of our research recipes specified sirloin chops, which are cut from the rear end of the loin, but these cooked up dry. Of the remaining types of chops, blade chops, center-cut loin, and rib, we prefer rib chops because they are juicier and more flavorful. We tried rib chops as thick as 1½ inches and as thin as ½ inch (any thinner than that and the chops have a tendency to overcook) and were shocked when tasters unanimously chose the ½-inch chops for this recipe. Thick chops overwhelmed the gravy and didn't pick up as much onion flavor during cooking as the thin chops did.

INGREDIENTS:
Enhanced or Unenhanced Pork?

Because modern pork is remarkably lean and therefore somewhat bland and prone to dryness if overcooked, a product called "enhanced" pork has overtaken the market. In fact, it can be hard to find unenhanced pork in some areas. Enhanced pork has been injected with a solution of water, salt, sodium phosphate, sodium lactate, potassium lactate, sodium diacetate, and varying flavor agents to bolster flavor and juiciness, with the total amount of enhancing ingredients adding 7 to 15 percent extra weight. Pork containing additives must be so labeled, with a list of the ingredients. After several taste tests, we have concluded that while enhanced pork is indeed juicier and more tender than unenhanced pork, the latter has more genuine pork flavor. Some tasters picked up unappealingly artificial, salty flavors in enhanced pork. Enhanced pork can also leach juices that, once reduced, will result in overly salty pan sauces. In the test kitchen, we prefer natural pork, but the choice is up to you.

We usually recommend brining pork chops, unless they are enhanced (see below for more information) but decided against it because these chops would cook in a moist environment provided by the gravy. Also, the salt-infused meat caused our gravy to become intolerably salty.

We now had to determine the optimum amount of cooking time. Although we prefer to slightly undercook pork to ensure tenderness, this is one application where further cooking was necessary to infuse the meat with the flavor of the gravy and onions. After their initial browning, the chops registered a rosy 140 degrees on an instant-read thermometer. They were cooked through and tender, but had no flavor. Fifteen minutes of braising in gravy boosted the flavor but toughened the chops, which now registered almost 200 degrees. At that temperature, the meat fibers have contracted and expelled moisture, but the fat and connective tissue between the fibers, called collagen, have not had a chance to melt fully and turn into gelatin. This gelatin is what makes braised meats especially rich and tender. Another 15 minutes of braising time solved the problem—the chops registered 210 degrees and the meat was tender and succulent from the melted fat and collagen, and oniony from the gravy.

To pick the right kind and cut for the onions, we tried them minced, chopped, and sliced both thick and thin. The most important onion test was trying different types, including standard-issue supermarket yellow onions, red onions, and sweet Vidalia onions. The yellow onions, sliced thin, triumphed for their natural sweetness and balanced flavor. To make sure they released enough moisture to deglaze the fond, we salted them lightly. The heat and salt worked together to jump-start the breakdown of the onions' cell walls, which set their juices flowing. We also added 2 tablespoons of water to the pan for insurance.

Finally, we turned to the flavors and consistency of our gravy. Water produced a weak, thin gravy, but chicken broth improved the picture, adding much-needed flavor. To thicken the gravy, we added cornstarch, but this resulted in a gelatinous, translucent sauce that looked like it came from a roadside diner. Instead, we tried adding flour and made a roux, a mixture of flour and fat (in this case, vegetable oil) cooked together. The results were fantastic—the sauce thickened and gave the gravy both a smooth finish and a slightly nutty flavor.

The roux was good, but we improved it with two oft-used refinements. First, we fried three slices of bacon and substituted the rendered fat for the vegetable oil in the roux. It was a hit—the sweet, salty, and smoky bacon flavor underscored and deepened all of the other flavors in the dish. Beyond that, we followed in the footsteps of many a gravy master who has eked out even more flavor from a roux by browning it for five minutes to the shade of peanut butter. Cooking the flour this way unlocks a rich, toasty flavor that builds as the shade deepens.

Our Smothered Pork Chops were now well-seasoned with naturally salty bacon and chicken broth. We used garlic, thyme, and bay leaves to build extra flavor in the gravy. All we had to do now was garnish our chops with the crisped bacon pieces and pick up a fork.

Smothered Pork Chops

SERVES 4

We prefer natural pork to enhanced pork (see page 40 for more information), though either will work in this recipe. Serve smothered chops with egg noodles, rice, or mashed potatoes.

4	(7-ounce) bone-in pork rib chops, ½ to ¾ inch thick, trimmed
	Ground black pepper
2	tablespoons vegetable oil, plus extra as needed
2	medium onions, halved and sliced thin
	Salt
2	medium garlic cloves, minced or pressed through a garlic press (about 2 teaspoons)
1	teaspoon minced fresh thyme leaves
2	tablespoons water
3	ounces (about 3 slices) bacon, cut into ¼-inch pieces
2	tablespoons unbleached all-purpose flour
1¾	cups low-sodium chicken broth
2	bay leaves
1	tablespoon minced fresh parsley leaves

1. Following the illustration on page 10, slit the sides of the pork chops. Pat the pork chops dry with paper towels and season with pepper. Heat 1 tablespoon of the oil in a 12-inch skillet over medium-high heat until just smoking. Carefully arrange the pork chops in the skillet and cook until browned on the first side, about 3 minutes. Flip the pork chops over and continue to cook until browned on the second side, about 3 minutes longer. Transfer the pork chops to a plate and set aside.

2. Add the remaining 1 tablespoon oil to the skillet and return to medium heat until shimmering. Add the onions and ½ teaspoon salt, scraping up any browned bits, and cook until lightly browned, about 7 minutes. Stir in the garlic and thyme and cook until fragrant, about 30 seconds. Stir in the water, scraping up any browned bits, then transfer the onions to a bowl.

3. Add the bacon to the skillet, return to medium heat, and cook until crisp, about 8 minutes. Using a slotted spoon, transfer the bacon to a paper towel–lined plate, leaving the fat in the skillet (you should have at least 2 tablespoons, but if not, substitute vegetable oil as needed).

4. Whisk the flour into the fat left in the skillet and cook over medium-low heat until golden, about 5 minutes. Whisk in the broth, scraping up any browned bits. Return the pork chops to the skillet and cover with the onions. Add the bay leaves, cover, and simmer over low heat until the pork chops are tender and a fork meets little resistance when poked in the center of the pork chops, about 30 minutes.

5. Transfer the pork chops to a platter and tent loosely with foil. Continue to simmer the sauce, uncovered, until thickened, about 5 minutes. Discard the bay leaves, stir in the parsley, and season with salt and pepper to taste. Spoon the sauce over the pork chops, sprinkle with the reserved bacon, and serve.

➤ VARIATION

Smothered Pork Chops with Cider and Apples

Follow the recipe for Smothered Pork Chops, substituting 1¾ cups apple cider for the chicken broth and 1 large Granny Smith apple, peeled, cored, and cut into ½-inch wedges, for 1 of the onions.

GLAZED PORK CHOPS

BIG BONE-IN PORK CHOPS ARE OUR USUAL choice for just about any pork chop dish—they're hard to overcook, good candidates for brining (which keeps them moist), and have a meaty flavor from the bone. That said, for this book, we felt we should consider what we could do with the small, inexpensive boneless chops that seem to dominate our local supermarket meat case. Given their size, we'd have to be careful about overcooking them and wondered if a quick sear and a flavorful glaze might do the trick.

The perfect counterpart for chops is a sweet, sticky, and saucy glaze, as we saw with the flavors of our Barbecued Pork Chops (page 39). And glazing, in fact, is well suited to skillet cookery, since only one pan is required to cook both the protein and sauce. We also had a hunch that a generous coating of glaze could be used in lieu of a brine, and therefore turn this into a weeknight recipe.

First, we turned to the chops themselves and our traditional searing method: medium-high heat, smoking pan, even color on both sides of the meat. Unfortunately, the meat curled in the pan and took on a spotty, light golden sear by the time it was cooked through. The problem, which we had encountered with our bone-in pork chops, was easily solved when we slashed through the fat and the connective tissue, which creates a bowing effect as it contracts (see the illustration on page 10).

The second problem we came upon was the lack of a rich sear. We had thought we could get away with searing one side of the chop pretty heavily and putting a quick sear on the second side. Although this method worked, the timing was critical: A few extra seconds were all the pan's high heat needed to take the chops from perfectly tender to dry and tough. We put the cooking method on hold while we experimented with the glaze.

We started by whipping up a few simple glazes, but they were thick, sweet, and one-dimensional. While honey added a distinct depth of flavor, it tended to crystallize and become grainy. Instead, we settled on brown sugar. We tempered this sweet base with soy sauce, vinegar, Dijon mustard, and cayenne. Apple cider was added for depth of flavor

and the juices from the resting pork brought the final touch. Our glaze was sweet and savory, but the texture was inconsistent—at times too thick, at other times too thin. By adjusting the cooking time, we finally arrived at the point where the glaze both adhered well to the chops and was plentiful enough to spoon over them once they were plated.

Now we returned to our chops; we seared them on the first side until well browned and turned them over to finish on the other side. We came up with the idea of adding the glaze to the pan at this point, helping us to get a head start on its reduction, save time, and keep the fond from burning.

Not only did this trick work, but it gave us the insurance we'd been missing in our cooking method. Finishing the chops over moderate heat (rather than high heat) slowed things down just enough to give us a better chance of getting them out of the pan while they were still juicy; the precise cooking time became much less critical. What's more, unlike the high, relatively dry heat of searing, gently simmering the chops in the wet glaze over moderate heat helped them retain their moisture. Once the meat reached 140 degrees, a five-minute rest on a platter let the temperature rise a bit and let the juices redistribute throughout the meat, keeping it tender. Then we let the glaze reduce and returned the chops to the skillet to be coated by the glaze.

Finally, with a master recipe for glazed pork chops nailed down, we could develop a couple of interesting variations. Adding herbs, toasted seeds, beer, and various seasonings enhanced the baseline flavor in the glaze without disturbing its texture. Now we had three recipes for easy, foolproof pork that could make it from supermarket to weeknight dinner table in record time and with just one pan.

Glazed Pork Chops
SERVES 4

We prefer natural pork to enhanced pork (see page 40 for more information), though either will work in this recipe. If your chops are on the thinner side, check their internal temperature after the initial sear. If they are already at the 140-degree mark, remove them from the skillet and allow them to rest, tented loosely with foil, for 5 minutes, then add the accumulated juices and glaze ingredients to the skillet and proceed with step 4. If your chops are closer to 1 inch thick, you may need to increase the simmering time in step 3.

GLAZE

½   cup distilled white vinegar or cider vinegar
⅓   cup light brown sugar
⅓   cup apple cider or apple juice
2   tablespoons Dijon mustard
1   tablespoon soy sauce
     Pinch cayenne pepper

PORK CHOPS

4   (5- to 7-ounce) boneless pork center-cut or loin chops, ½ to ¾ inch thick, trimmed
     Salt and ground black pepper
1   tablespoon vegetable oil

1. FOR THE GLAZE: Combine all of the glaze ingredients in a medium bowl and set aside.

2. FOR THE PORK CHOPS: Following the illustration on page 10, slit the sides of the pork chops. Pat the pork chops dry with paper towels and season with salt and pepper. Heat the oil in a 12-inch skillet over medium-high heat until just smoking. Carefully lay the pork chops in the skillet and cook until well browned on the first side, 4 to 6 minutes. Flip the pork chops over and continue to cook for 1 minute longer. Transfer the pork chops to a plate and pour off all of the fat from the skillet. (Check the internal temperature of the thinner pork chops; see note.)

3. Return the pork chops to the skillet, browned side up, and add the glaze mixture. Cook over medium heat until the center of the pork chops registers 140 to 145 degrees on an instant-read thermometer, 5 to 8 minutes. Transfer the pork chops to a platter, tent loosely with foil, and let rest until the center of the pork chops registers 150 degrees on an instant-read thermometer, about 5 minutes.

4. Stir any accumulated meat juices into the glaze left in the skillet and simmer, whisking constantly, over medium heat until the glaze has thickened, 2 to 6 minutes. Return the pork chops to the skillet and turn to coat both sides with the

glaze. Transfer the pork chops back to the platter, browned side up, spread the remaining glaze over the top, and serve.

➤ VARIATIONS

Glazed Pork Chops with German Flavors

Toast ¾ teaspoon caraway seeds in a small dry skillet over medium heat, stirring frequently, until fragrant, 3 to 5 minutes. Roughly chop the seeds and set aside. Follow the recipe for Glazed Pork Chops, substituting ⅓ cup beer for the apple cider, reducing the amount of soy sauce to 2 teaspoons, and adding 3 tablespoons whole grain mustard (along with the Dijon mustard), 1 tablespoon minced fresh thyme leaves, and the reserved caraway seeds to the glaze. Omit the cayenne pepper.

Glazed Pork Chops with Asian Flavors

Toast 1 teaspoon sesame seeds in a small dry skillet over medium heat, stirring frequently, until lightly browned and fragrant, 3 to 5 minutes; set aside. Follow the recipe for Glazed Pork Chops, substituting ½ cup rice vinegar for the white vinegar, 3 tablespoons each orange juice and mirin for the apple cider, and adding 1 teaspoon minced or grated fresh ginger to the glaze ingredients. In step 4, stir an additional 2 teaspoons rice vinegar into the glaze before returning the chops to the skillet. Before serving, sprinkle the chops with the reserved sesame seeds and 1 teaspoon toasted sesame oil.

SPANISH-STYLE GARLIC SHRIMP

ON A RECENT VISIT TO A SPANISH REST-aurant, one thing caught our attention immediately—the heady aroma wafting up from a neighboring table's *gambas al ajillo*, shrimp sizzling in a pool of olive oil and garlic. Seeing this dish, we thought we could take some cues from our Pan-Seared Shrimp with Parsley-Lemon Butter (page 25) to help create our own gambas al ajillo made entirely in the skillet—not the *cazuela* (an earthenware ramekin) it's usually made and served in.

SHRIMP SIZES

Shrimp are sold by size (small, medium, large, and extra-large), as well as by the number needed to make a pound, usually given in a range. Choosing shrimp by the numerical rating is more accurate than choosing by a size label, which varies from store to store. Here's how the two sizing systems generally line up.

SMALL
51 to 60 per pound

MEDIUM
41 to 50 per pound

LARGE
31 to 40 per pound

EXTRA-LARGE
21 to 25 per pound

Traditional recipes call for using small shrimp, the perfect size for a shared appetizer. We decided to make our dish more substantial, and settled on a pound of large shrimp as the ideal portion size for a light dinner for three to four people. To cook the shrimp, recipes we found completely submerged the shrimp in oil, where they can be heated evenly and gently at a low temperature. But to fully submerge a pound of large shrimp, we'd need 2 cups of oil—a heavy amount for dinner for four. We wanted to find a way to reduce the amount but still maintain the juiciness of this dish. Thinking back to our pan-seared shrimp, we reduced the layer of oil in the pan so it would provide only a thin coating beneath the shrimp. The pan couldn't be kept at the same heat level as was needed to heat 2 cups of oil, so now we had to figure out how to adjust this element of our recipe.

We knew that we would have to turn the shrimp halfway through cooking, but we worried the first shrimp would be overcooked by the time we had turned the last ones. Keeping the heat at medium-low gave us plenty of time to turn each shrimp individually, so we managed to cook them as evenly and gently as if they had been covered by oil. We now had tender shrimp, but we were missing the great garlic flavor.

The key to achieving this flavor is the oil. We knew that allicin, the chemical responsible for garlic's flavor, is highly soluble in oil—so we could use the oil as a vehicle to deliver more flavor. Allicin is not formed until the garlic's cells are ruptured, so we smashed four garlic cloves before heating them in a fresh batch of olive oil. We allowed them to brown and impart a sweet roasted flavor to the oil, then we discarded the smashed cloves and added the shrimp. We also added several cloves of thinly sliced garlic, but the slices were acting more like a garnish than a fully integrated part of the dish. To our frustration, the shrimp were still not as garlicky as they could be. Surely a marinade would help.

We minced two garlic cloves and combined them with salt and 2 tablespoons of oil. After 30 minutes in the marinade, we cooked the shrimp and thinly sliced garlic in the oil in which we had previously browned the smashed cloves. It was a resounding success. Finally, we had juicy shrimp that were deeply flavored with garlic, which we had added in three different forms with three distinct effects: minced raw garlic provided pungency in the marinade, crushed and browned garlic infused sweetness into the oil, and slow-cooked sliced garlic added mild garlic flavor.

The traditional flavors of bay leaf and red chile were deemed essential, so we heated them with the sliced garlic, giving the finished dish a sweet, herbal aroma. Sherry vinegar and chopped parsley helped round out the flavors, providing a jolt of brightness that cut through the richness of the olive oil.

Spanish-Style Garlic Shrimp
SERVES 3 TO 4

If desired, substitute ¼ teaspoon sweet paprika for the dried chile. These shrimp can be served as a light dinner with salad and crusty bread for dipping in the richly flavored olive oil, or as an appetizer (serving 6) with baguette slices. The dish can be served directly from the skillet (make sure to use a trivet) or, for a dramatic sizzling effect, transferred to an 8-inch cast-iron skillet that's been heated for 2 minutes over medium-high heat.

14	medium garlic cloves, peeled
1	pound large shrimp (31 to 40 per pound), peeled, deveined, and tails removed (see the illustration on page 235)
½	cup olive oil
½	teaspoon salt
1	bay leaf
1	(2-inch) piece mild dried chile, such as New Mexico, roughly broken with some seeds
1	tablespoon minced fresh parsley leaves
1½	teaspoons sherry vinegar

1. Mince 2 of the garlic cloves (or press them through a garlic press). Toss the minced garlic, shrimp, 2 tablespoons of the olive oil, and salt together in a medium bowl. Let the shrimp marinate at room temperature for 30 minutes.

2. Meanwhile, smash 4 more garlic cloves. Heat the smashed garlic with the remaining 6 tablespoons olive oil in a 12-inch skillet over medium-low heat, stirring occasionally, until the garlic is light golden brown, 4 to 7 minutes. Remove the skillet from the heat and let the oil cool to room temperature. Remove and discard the smashed garlic.

3. Thinly slice the remaining 8 garlic cloves. Return the skillet to low heat, add the sliced garlic, bay leaf, and chile with seeds and cook, stirring occasionally, until the garlic is tender but not browned, 4 to 7 minutes. (If the garlic has not begun to sizzle after 3 minutes, increase the heat to medium-low.)

4. Increase the heat to medium-low, then carefully add the shrimp with the marinade to the oil in a single layer. Cook the shrimp until the oil starts to gently bubble, about 2 minutes. Flip the shrimp over and continue to cook until pink, slightly curled, and almost cooked through, about 2 minutes longer. Increase the heat to high, stir in the parsley and vinegar, and cook, stirring constantly, until the shrimp are cooked through and oil is bubbling vigorously, 15 to 20 seconds. Serve.

CRISPY TOFU

A CLASSIC ON CHINESE MENUS EVERYWHERE, crispy tofu features chunks of tofu, creamy on the inside and crunchy and brown on the outside, in a spicy-sweet sauce that provides a flavor contrast. We've seen this dish done lots of ways—and when it was soggy, slimy, or bland, we wanted to send it back. When done right, crispy tofu delivers an irresistible combination of textures and flavors. Could we re-create this deceptively simple dish without a deep fryer or a wok, and using only our trusty nonstick skillet?

Heading into the test kitchen, we knew our first task would be to sort out the myriad tofu options. Tofu, or fresh bean curd, is a natural candidate for stir-frying, but it's also perfect for pan-frying in a skillet. We guessed that extra-firm tofu, our preferred choice for stir-frying because it holds its shape, would be the winner here, but, taking nothing for granted, we tested extra-firm, firm, medium-firm, and soft tofu. They were all pan-fried with a coating of pure cornstarch, our usual approach when stir-frying tofu because of the way it clings to the tofu during cooking, creating a protective sheath. We were surprised to hear tasters say that the extra-firm tofu was their least favorite of the bunch. In fact, tasters unanimously preferred the medium-firm and soft tofu for their creamy, custard-like texture.

For most recipes using firm or extra-firm tofu, the tofu is generally pressed under a weighted plate to expel excess moisture. But because we would be using a softer and more delicate tofu, and we didn't want it to lose its shape, we decided to skip this step. Instead, we gently cut the tofu into planks and then placed them on multiple layers of paper towels to drain. Once the drained tofu was encased in a coating, a little excess water only helped the tofu stay moist in the pan.

We turned back to the coating. The cornstarch we used in our preliminary tests yielded a thin, crispy coating that barely browned, but held up well in the pan. Yet we sought more crispness than this could provide. In our library of Chinese cookbooks, we had stumbled across a couple of recipes where cornmeal is added to the coating. We started experimenting with an equal ratio of 1 cup cornmeal to 1 cup cornstarch, but tasters complained of an unappealingly gritty texture. We cut the cornmeal back to ⅓ cup, which proved just the right proportion, giving our tofu a hefty coating without any grit. This tofu had a crispy, golden coating with a creamy interior.

Up to this point we'd been cutting the tofu blocks into planks about 1 inch thick, but tasters started to complain that they wanted more coating. Cutting each plank in half to make "fingers" quickly solved the problem. Now we had a greater coating-to-tofu ratio that everyone thought gave the right balance of crispy to creamy.

With our tofu now perfectly fried, we shifted our attention to the sauce—we wanted a pungent sauce that would add pizzazz to the mild-tasting tofu. The most common sauce we came across in our research was a sweet soy-garlic sauce. We made our version of this sauce by combining sugar, soy sauce, water, and garlic in a saucepan and reducing it to a glaze. We balanced the sauce with a splash of rice vinegar and a shot of spicy chili-garlic paste. Now we just had to stack our crispy tofu on a plate, dip the pieces in sauce, and start eating.

Crispy Tofu with Sweet Soy-Garlic Sauce
SERVES 4

We prefer the softer, creamier texture of medium-firm or soft tofu here. Firm or extra-firm tofu will also work; however, they will taste drier. Be sure to handle the tofu gently and pat it dry thoroughly before seasoning and coating. Look for chili-garlic paste in the international aisle of the supermarket next to the other Asian ingredients; do not confuse the chili-garlic paste with Asian chili sauce, which is milder in flavor.

SAUCE
½   cup sugar
¼   cup soy sauce
¼   cup water
3   medium garlic cloves, minced or pressed through a garlic press (about 1 tablespoon)
1   tablespoon rice vinegar
1   teaspoon Asian chili-garlic paste
1   scallion, sliced thin
1   tablespoon minced fresh cilantro leaves

TOFU
2   (14-ounce) blocks medium-firm or soft tofu (see note), sliced crosswise into 1-inch-thick slabs, each slab sliced into two 1-inch-wide fingers
1   cup cornstarch
⅓   cup cornmeal
     Salt and ground black pepper
¾   cup vegetable oil

1. FOR THE SAUCE: Simmer the sugar, soy sauce, water, garlic, vinegar, and chili paste together in a small saucepan over medium heat until syrupy, 5 to 6 minutes. Stir in the scallion and cilantro, cover, and set aside to keep warm until needed.

2. FOR THE TOFU: Meanwhile, spread the tofu out over several layers of paper towels and let sit to drain slightly, about 20 minutes. Adjust an oven rack to the middle position, place a paper towel–lined platter on the rack, and heat the oven to 200 degrees.

3. Place a wire rack over a baking sheet and set aside. Toss the cornstarch and cornmeal together in a shallow dish. Season the tofu with salt and pepper. Working with a few pieces of tofu at a time, coat them thoroughly with the cornstarch mixture, pressing on the coating to adhere, then transfer to the wire rack.

4. Heat the oil in a 12-inch nonstick skillet over medium-high heat until shimmering. Carefully lay half of the tofu in the skillet and cook, turning the pieces occasionally with a spatula, until crisp and lightly golden on all sides, about 4 minutes. Using a spatula, gently lift the tofu from the oil, letting any excess oil drip back into the skillet, and transfer to the prepared platter in the oven.

5. Repeat with the remaining tofu pieces and let them drain briefly on the prepared platter. Serve, passing the sauce separately.

2

FROM STOVETOP TO OVEN

FROM STOVETOP TO OVEN

COOKING ON THE STOVETOP IS IDEAL FOR attaining a flavorful, browned crust on meat, poultry, or fish. But some foods, particularly those that are sizeable or thick, can't be cooked exclusively on the stovetop without scorching their exteriors. In these cases, roasting in the steady heat of the oven is usually considered the best method. The oven offers more even cooking, and because the temperature of an oven is more moderate and thus cooks the food more slowly, you have a larger window of time to make sure your meal is perfectly done. But there is another, perhaps less thought of option: pan-roasting. This restaurant technique browns food on the stovetop in a skillet and then moves it to the oven to allow the food to finish cooking through. This method combines the advantages of both stovetop and oven methods—in short, flavorful browning and even cooking. Additionally, this method allows for some walk-away time while the food is in the oven, but it also shortens the cooking time overall because of the jump-start made on the stovetop. Flavor and convenience make pan-roasting an all-around winner.

In this chapter, we have developed recipes that we think gain the most from pan-roasting. They include chicken, pork, even turkey and fish, and range from a simple weeknight meal (see our recipe for Indoor-Barbecued Chicken, page 60) to a dinner worthy of your most important guests (see Pan-Roasted Racks of Lamb with Mint Relish, page 67).

Pan-Roasted Chicken with Sage-Vermouth Sauce (page 52) is a perfect example of what this technique can do. With the help of our skillet, we were able to attain an evenly cooked, juicy chicken with crackling-crisp skin in a surprisingly short amount of time, and we used the fond, or caramelized drippings left in the skillet after browning, along with minimal ingredients to whip up a savory sauce. This triple use of the skillet (browning on the stovetop, cooking in the oven, and sauce-making) is the ultimate in economy: it keeps the flavor in the pan (and in the food) and minimizes dishes to wash. This simple, flavorful, and efficient recipe is indicative of what you will find throughout this chapter.

Pan-roasting is the key to simplifying the preparation of otherwise intimidating meals. Consider the dynamic duo of turkey and gravy. We used our skillet to prove you don't need to make a full-sized roast turkey to enjoy a flavorful bird with Thanksgiving-caliber gravy (see page 63). With the fond from browning a boneless turkey breast (and a few other tricks), we made a rich gravy with deep-roasted, meaty flavor to pair with juicy, golden brown turkey.

Reevaluating the size of what we were cooking came into play for other recipes beyond the turkey. Who would have thought you could make meatloaf after work and eat before 7 pm? Our answer was to divide and conquer. We made mini meatloaves that are started in a skillet to get the characteristic browned crust and then finished in a hot oven to caramelize the sweet glaze.

Pan-roasting isn't just for meats. Thick halibut steaks, a great option for a special occasion meal, are an ideal candidate for the technique. Adding a nice sear to these fish steaks lends enormous flavor, but too much of a good thing will lead to dry, overcooked steaks. We found that searing the halibut on just one side before slipping it into the oven to cook through gave us flavorful, perfectly cooked halibut. This is a technique that can work equally well for other meaty types of fish.

On matters of safety, please take note: Obviously, the skillet will be scorching hot when it comes out of the oven. Reaching for a potholder to remove a skillet (or any pan) from the oven may be second nature, but you might forget where that skillet has been once it's back on the stovetop and you've turned your attention elsewhere. We like to wrap (or hang) a potholder or dishtowel over the handle of the pan to remind us of the hot handle—just in case.

PAN-ROASTED CHICKEN

TO MAKE EVEN THE MOST BASIC VERSION of roast chicken, you not only have to plan ahead and do some prep work, but when it's time to cook, you have to devote a solid hour-plus to tending the bird while it roasts. Not to mention the tricks and techniques required to achieve perfectly cooked meat—brining the meat, air-drying the skin overnight, coordinating the doneness of the thighs and breast, flipping the bird as it roasts. If you've done everything right, the chicken emerges golden brown from the oven along with flavorful drippings that can be made into a rich gravy or sauce.

There is no denying that the flavor of roast chicken is unbeatable, but getting there is a lot of work. However, once we took a step back and looked at the end goal, we realized employing the restaurant practice of pan-roasting could be the answer to getting there in a much simpler way. This technique, in which food is browned on the stovetop and then moved to the oven to cook through, offers the benefits from both cooking techniques and can be a great help at speeding up otherwise time-intensive recipes. We set out for the kitchen, skillet in hand, ready to perfect our pan-roasted chicken.

Our plan was fairly simple: To make handling the meat easier we would cut up the chicken, then brown the meat on both sides on the stovetop, and, finally, slide the chicken, skillet and all, into a hot oven to finish cooking. Pan-roasting this way would mean no beautiful, whole roast chicken to bring to the table, but we were hoping superior skin, shorter preparation time, and a rich, savory pan sauce would outweigh that one shortcoming. The question was whether this technique was as simple as it seemed.

Chicken first. We settled on cutting a 3½- to 4-pound chicken into eight pieces—two each of drumsticks and thighs, and each breast cut in half to make four breast pieces. This arrangement meant that each serving could consist of a portion of both white and dark meat. We initially planned on keeping the wings, but since our 12-inch skillet was already full and they are the least favorite section, we decided to reserve them for another use.

With the chicken cut up, we were ready for browning. We started with high heat, hoping it would lead to more quickly and ideally crisped

---

Cutting Up a Whole Chicken 101

Cutting up a whole chicken may seem like an intimidating process, but it's a handy technique to learn. For one thing, cutting up a chicken yourself is economical. For another, you may have difficulty finding packages of chicken parts that are the right size, properly butchered, and of high quality.

1. With a sharp chef's knife, cut through the skin around the leg where it attaches to the breast.

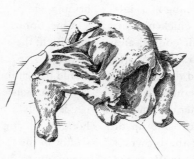

2. Using both hands, pop the leg joint out of its socket.

3. Use a chef's knife to cut through the flesh and skin to detach the leg from the body.

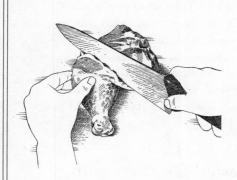

4. A line of fat separates the thigh and drumstick. Cut through the joint at this point. Repeat steps 1 through 4 with the other leg.

5. Bend the wing out from the breast and use a boning knife to cut through the joint. Repeat with the other wing.

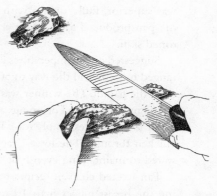

6. Cut through the cartilage around the wingtip to remove it. Discard the tip. Cut through the joint to split it. Repeat with the other wing. Reserve wings for another use.

7. Using kitchen shears, cut along the ribs to completely separate the back from the breast. Discard the backbone.

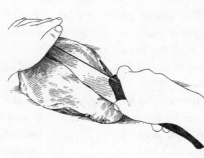

8. Place the knife on the breastbone, then apply pressure to cut through and separate the breast into halves.

9. Cut each breast half crosswise into two pieces.

skin, but this temperature sometimes resulted in burnt drippings, which we wanted to preserve for our gravy. Using medium-high heat felt much more in control; we got even browning and avoided the burnt drippings issue. We tried browning in a skillet without any oil, and while the chicken's skin had sufficient fat that rendered as it cooked and prevented sticking, the browning was spotty and not ideal. A tablespoon of oil evened things out.

After browning the chicken parts on both sides, the burning question became whether the chicken pieces should go into the oven skin side up or skin side down. We wanted to get the brownest skin possible while avoiding sogginess. We tested both options. Skin side up chicken did indeed brown, but the skin was mottled and crisped in some spots, soft in others. Skin side down chicken was superior. Full contact with the hot metal of the pan produced a crackling crisp, darker russet-toned skin.

Suggested oven temperatures in recipes we found ranged from 375 all the way to 500 degrees, and we tried the gamut. The winner was 450 degrees—we ended up with singed drippings at 500 degrees, and lower temperatures simply took longer to cook the chicken through. The lowest rack setting was best suited to maintaining even heat.

Pan-roasted chicken recipes recommend removing the breast pieces 5 to 10 minutes before the thigh pieces since the latter take longer to cook—the breast is done when it reaches 160 to 165 degrees and the thigh 175 degrees (the identical problem that plagues whole roasted poultry). However, in test after test the digital thermometer told us that the breast meat (despite being cut into four pieces) and the thigh pieces were finishing at about the same time. It appeared that the thickness of the breast pieces made them cook more slowly than the flat, thin thigh pieces and slim drumsticks.

We addressed a few last details for our chicken before moving on to our pan sauce. To brine or not to brine? When we pitted pan-roasted chickens that had been brined against those that had not, tasters preferred the brined birds for their moistness (the effects of the saltwater soak can act as a cushion against overcooking). However, the non-brined birds were also good; we leave the decision up to

you. If you do choose to brine, it won't take you too much longer. We found that because we were using a cut-up chicken, brining was expedited—as few as 30 minutes did the trick. (For more on brining, see page 56.)

One bonus of pan-roasting goes beyond the bird itself: the skillet is left with tasty caramelized drippings, or fond. Letting this fond go to waste would be criminal; it is ideal for making a rich, flavorful pan sauce for pairing with the chicken. We needed only a handful of ingredients to make an honest and simple sauce. We began by sautéing a shallot in the fond, then adding chicken broth and vermouth to deglaze the pan. Sage, always a good match for chicken, lent an herbaceous note, and the addition of the accumulated chicken juices and a few tablespoons of butter provided the finishing touch of flavor. We found that other simple combinations, like garlic with sherry and onion with ale, also paired well with our chicken.

Judging from the enthusiasm that met platefuls of our crisp-skinned, pan-roasted chicken and flavorful sauce, it was clear the dish was worthy of high marks. Who knew roasted chicken could be this easy?

Pan-Roasted Chicken with Sage-Vermouth Sauce
SERVES 4

If using kosher chicken, do not brine. If brining the chicken, do not season with salt in step 1. Four bone-in, skin-on split chicken breasts (10 to 12 ounces each) can be substituted for the whole cut-up chicken if desired; don't cut the breasts in half, and increase the roasting time to 15 to 20 minutes in step 3.

CHICKEN
I (3½- to 4-pound) chicken cut into 8 pieces (see the illustrations on page 51) and brined if desired (see page 56)
  Salt and ground black pepper
I tablespoon vegetable oil

SAUCE
I large shallot, minced (about 4 tablespoons)
¾ cup low-sodium chicken broth

½ cup dry vermouth or dry white wine
4 fresh sage leaves, torn in half
3 tablespoons unsalted butter, cut
    into 3 pieces and chilled
    Salt and ground black pepper

1. FOR THE CHICKEN: Adjust an oven rack to the middle position and heat the oven to 450 degrees. Pat the chicken dry with paper towels and season with salt and pepper.

2. Heat the oil in a 12-inch ovensafe skillet over medium-high heat until just smoking. Carefully lay the chicken pieces, skin side down, in the skillet and cook until well browned, 6 to 8 minutes. Flip the chicken and continue to brown lightly on the second side, about 3 minutes.

3. Flip the chicken skin side down and transfer the skillet to the oven. Roast the chicken until the thickest part of the breasts register 160 to 165 degrees and the thighs register 175 degrees on an instant-read thermometer, about 10 minutes.

4. Using a potholder (the skillet handle will be hot), remove the skillet from the oven. Transfer the chicken to a serving platter and let rest while making the sauce.

5. FOR THE SAUCE: Being careful of the hot skillet handle, pour off all but 1 teaspoon of the fat in the pan, add the shallot, and cook over medium-high heat until softened, about 2 minutes. Stir in the broth, vermouth, and sage, scraping up any browned bits. Bring to a simmer and cook until slightly thickened and measures about ¾ cup, about 5 minutes. Stir in any accumulated chicken juices, return to a simmer, and cook for 30 seconds.

6. Off the heat, remove the sage leaves and whisk in the butter, 1 piece at a time. Season with salt and pepper to taste, spoon the sauce over the chicken and serve.

➤ VARIATIONS
Pan-Roasted Chicken with Garlic-Sherry Sauce

Follow the recipe for Pan-Roasted Chicken with Sage-Vermouth Sauce, substituting 7 medium garlic cloves, peeled and sliced thin, for the shallots; cook until lightly golden, about 1½ minutes. Substitute ½ cup dry sherry for the vermouth and 2 sprigs

fresh thyme for the sage. Add ½ teaspoon lemon juice to the sauce after whisking in the butter.

Pan-Roasted Chicken with Onion-Ale Sauce

Brown ale gives this sauce a nutty, toasty, bittersweet flavor. Newcastle Brown Ale and Samuel Smith Nut Brown Ale are good choices.

Follow the recipe for Pan-Roasted Chicken with Sage-Vermouth Sauce, substituting ½ medium onion, sliced very thin, for the shallot; cook until softened, about 3 minutes. Substitute ½ cup brown ale for the vermouth and 1 sprig fresh thyme for the sage. Add 1 bay leaf and 1 teaspoon brown sugar to the skillet with the chicken broth and add ½ teaspoon cider vinegar after whisking in the butter.

GLAZED CHICKEN BREASTS

GLAZED CHICKEN IS TYPICALLY A HUMDRUM affair—dry meat with flabby skin and a cloyingly sweet sauce. But our fine-dining experiences with similar dishes, like duck à l'orange, impressively prepared with crisp-skinned slices of meat clad in a perfectly balanced sauce, gave us hope that there was room for improvement with glazed chicken. So we set out to develop a recipe for moist chicken and perfectly rendered skin sufficiently coated with a complexly flavored glaze: a main course worthy of fine china, but still something we could make in our skillet after work on a Tuesday night.

Most of the recipes for glazed chicken breasts uncovered in our research were simple "dump-and-bake" versions: Pour a jar of fruit preserves over raw chicken breasts and bake. We knew from experience that this technique, while attractive in its simplicity, inevitably results in flabby, pale skin. For our recipe, browning the chicken first on the stovetop over high heat would be the answer to achieving appealing, browned skin; only afterward would we add the glaze to the skillet and transfer the whole thing to the oven to finish cooking.

Before even considering the chicken (which we felt would be fairly straightforward), we needed to fix the glaze. Every recipe we dug up in our research used sticky, sweet ingredients for the base: fruit preserves, molasses, maple syrup, and brown sugar. Then one of our colleagues described a perfect duck à l'orange sauce he had had in Paris recently as "glazey yet not cloying"—this balance sounded like our goal, and we wondered how exactly it was achieved. Our hunch was that it was some sort of reduction sauce. Flipping through French cookbooks, we found our answer: reduced orange juice. Orange juice is sticky, but its acidity helps balance the sugar—another key ingredient in duck sauce. We were not interested in creating a recipe for chicken à l'orange, but using orange juice in our glaze seemed like a good place to start.

We decided it was time for a test run. After browning some chicken breasts, we transferred the meat to a plate while we reduced a mixture of orange juice and sugar until glazey. We then returned the chicken breasts to the skillet, rolled them in the glaze, and cooked them through in the oven. But tasters complained that the glaze was "too thin" and "unbearably sweet," and that it did not adhere to the chicken. Sugar would have been the ideal solution to the textural issue, but it was an inappropriate choice for a glaze that was already too sweet.

Then we remembered a technique a test kitchen colleague used for her cake-frosting recipe. She had mixed in a small amount of light corn syrup to add luster and body but, curiously, the addition did not contribute noticeable sweetness. We had always assumed corn syrup was super-sweet, but when we tasted a lineup of sugar, brown sugar, maple syrup, and honey against corn syrup, we discovered just the opposite. Nutrition labels on the sweeteners confirmed our finding: Corn syrup contains half (and sometimes less than half) as much sugar as the others.

Excited by the prospect that corn syrup might help our cause, we immediately trimmed some chicken breasts, heated a skillet and browned the meat, then whipped up a new batch of glaze. Not only did this corn syrup–enhanced glaze cook up perfectly, but the meat seemed juicier—especially surprising since the glaze without the corn syrup had already been keeping our chicken breasts quite moist. A quick call to our science editor revealed that the concentrated glucose in corn syrup has a high affinity for water, which means it helps to hold moisture in the glaze, making the overall dish seem juicier. That same glucose also thickened and added a gloss to our glaze.

However, as much as tasters liked the glaze's clean flavor, they now thought it wasn't sweet enough. A little honey gave the glaze just the right level of sweetness, and minced shallot, vinegar, Dijon mustard, and a pinch of red pepper flakes created complexity.

Despite these improvements, one complaint remained: The glaze still didn't cling to the chicken enough. From past work in the test kitchen, we knew that adding cornstarch or flour to the sauce would only make it gloppy. Maybe the problem wasn't with the glaze but with the chicken. What if we added a thin layer of flour to the outside of the meat before browning it? In the test kitchen we don't typically coat bone-in chicken with flour before browning or roasting, but in this case doing so served us well, giving the chicken breasts a thin, crispy crust that made a good grip for the glaze. To make sure we covered all our bases, we also tried coating the chicken in cornstarch. This also worked to hold the glaze, but it turned the skin a bit slimy. To ensure that the flour didn't brown too much before the chicken skin adequately rendered, we found it necessary to lower the flame to medium-high. As for oven temperature, we knew our glaze would have a tendency to burn because of its sugar content, so we settled on a moderate 350-degree oven. The chicken came out just cooked through and perfectly juicy, but our glaze still wasn't quite thick enough. While we let the chicken rest, we reduced the glaze over high heat. One minute was all it took to get it to just the right consistency.

We added a small amount of orange juice just before serving to brighten the flavors even further. With that, we had elevated glazed chicken to a new height.

Orange-Honey Glazed Chicken Breasts

SERVES 4

If the glaze begins to look dry during baking, add up to 2 tablespoons more orange juice to the skillet.

1½	cups plus 2 tablespoons orange juice
⅓	cup light corn syrup
3	tablespoons honey
I	tablespoon Dijon mustard
I	tablespoon distilled white vinegar
⅛	teaspoon red pepper flakes
	Salt and ground black pepper
½	cup unbleached all-purpose flour
4	(10- to 12-ounce) bone-in, skin-on split chicken breasts, trimmed (see the illustration below)
2	tablespoons vegetable oil
I	medium shallot, minced (about 3 tablespoons)

1. Adjust an oven rack to the middle position and heat the oven to 350 degrees. Whisk 1½ cups of the orange juice, the corn syrup, honey, mustard, vinegar, red pepper flakes, ⅛ teaspoon salt, and ⅛ teaspoon pepper together in a medium bowl and set aside.

2. Place the flour in a shallow dish. Pat the chicken dry with paper towels and season with salt and pepper. Working with 1 chicken breast at a time, dredge in the flour, shaking off the excess.

3. Heat the oil in a 12-inch ovensafe skillet over medium-high heat until just smoking. Carefully lay the chicken breasts skin side down in the skillet, and cook until well browned, 6 to 8 minutes. Flip the chicken and continue to brown lightly on the second side, about 3 minutes. Transfer the chicken to a plate.

4. Pour off all but 1 teaspoon of the fat in the pan, add the shallot, and cook over medium-high heat until softened, about 2 minutes. Increase the heat to high, add the orange juice mixture, and simmer, stirring occasionally, until syrupy and measures about 1 cup, 6 to 10 minutes.

5. Remove the skillet from the heat and tilt it to one side so that the glaze pools in the corner of the pan. Using tongs, roll each chicken breast in the pooled glaze to coat, then lay in the skillet, skin side down.

6. Transfer the skillet to the oven and bake the glazed chicken until the thickest part of the breasts register 160 to 165 degrees on an instant-read thermometer, 25 to 30 minutes, flipping the chicken over halfway through cooking.

7. Using a potholder (the skillet handle will be hot), remove the skillet from the oven. Transfer the chicken to a platter and let rest for 5 minutes. Meanwhile, being careful of the hot skillet handle, return the glaze to high heat and simmer, stirring constantly, until thick and syrupy, about 1 minute. Off the heat, whisk in the remaining 2 tablespoons orange juice. Spoon some of the glaze evenly over the chicken and serve with the remaining glaze.

➤ VARIATIONS

Apple-Maple Glazed Chicken Breasts

Follow the recipe for Orange-Honey Glazed Chicken Breasts, substituting 1½ cups plus 2 tablespoons apple cider for the orange juice and 2 tablespoons maple syrup for the honey.

Pineapple–Brown Sugar Glazed Chicken Breasts

Follow the recipe for Orange-Honey Glazed Chicken Breasts, substituting 1½ cups plus 2 tablespoons pineapple juice for the orange juice and 2 tablespoons brown sugar for the honey.

TRIMMING SPLIT CHICKEN BREASTS

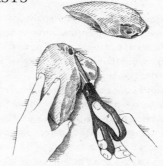

Using kitchen shears, trim off the rib sections from each breast following the vertical line of fat from the tapered end of the breast up to the socket where the wing was attached.

Brining 101

The process of brining (soaking meat in a solution of water and salt before cooking) can improve the flavor and tenderness of chicken, turkey, and pork. As it soaks, the meat absorbs the brine and then retains the solution during cooking. The result? Juicier, better-tasting poultry or pork. Best of all, brining is easy; all you need is some refrigerator space, a little time, and a container big enough to submerge the meat fully in the brine. Brining isn't essential, but we highly recommend it in simple pan-seared or pan-roasted recipes.

Do not brine kosher poultry, frozen injected turkey (such as Butterball), or enhanced pork (for more information on enhanced pork, see page 40). Before they make it to supermarket shelves, these products are treated with salt in one form or another. We have made this mistake before; brining any of these products only intensifies the saltiness, resulting in virtually inedible meat. If in doubt, check labels, which always indicate if salt has been added during processing.

BRINING DIRECTIONS

In a container or bowl large enough to hold the brine and meat, dissolve the salt in the water following the amounts in the chart below. Make sure to submerge the meat completely in the brine. Cover and refrigerate, following the times in the chart (do not overbrine or the meat will taste too salty). Remove the meat from the brine, rinse, and pat dry with paper towels. The meat is now ready to be cooked.

	COLD WATER	SALT	TIME
POULTRY			
4 (10- to 12-ounce) bone-in, split chicken breasts	2 quarts	½ cup	30 minutes to 1 hour
4 pounds bone-in chicken pieces (split breasts, thighs, and/or drumsticks)	2 quarts	½ cup	30 minutes to 1 hour
1 (3- to 4-pound) whole chicken	2 quarts	½ cup	1 hour
2 (2- to 2½-pound) boneless turkey breast halves (or one 4- to 4½-pound breast half)	2 quarts	½ cup	1 hour
PORK			
4 (8-ounce) boneless pork chops	2 quarts	¼ cup	30 minutes to 1 hour
4 (10- to 12-ounce) bone-in chops	2 quarts	¼ cup	30 minutes to 1 hour
2 (1- to 1¼-pound) pork tenderloins	2 quarts	¼ cup	30 minutes to 1 hour
1 (2½- to 3-pound) boneless pork loin roast	2 quarts	½ cup	1 hour

SCIENCE: WHY BRINING WORKS

Many have attributed the added juiciness of brined meat to osmosis—the flow of water across a barrier from a place with higher water concentration (the brine) to a place with lower (the chicken). We decided to test this explanation. If osmosis is the source of the added juiciness of brined meat, we reasoned, then a bucket of pure unsalted water should add moisture at least as well as a brine. After soaking one chicken in brine and another in water for the same amount of time, we found that both had gained moisture, about 6 percent by weight. We then roasted the two birds, along with a third chicken straight out of the package. We learned that osmosis, though partially responsible, was not the only reason brined meat cooked up juicy.

During roasting, the chicken taken straight from the package lost 18 percent of its original weight, and the chicken soaked in water lost 12 percent of its presoak weight. The brined bird shed a mere 7 percent. We realized that the benefit of brining could not be explained by osmosis alone; salt was playing a crucial role by aiding in water retention.

Salt is made up of two ions that are oppositely charged. Proteins, such as those in meat, are large molecules that contain a mosaic of charges, negative and positive. When proteins are placed in a solution containing salt, they readjust their shape to accommodate the opposing charges. This rearrangement compromises the structural integrity of the meat, reducing its overall toughness. It also creates gaps that fill up with water. The added salt makes the water less likely to evaporate during cooking, and the result is meat that is both juicy and tender.

TWO TYPES OF SALT FOR BRINING

You can use either kosher or regular table salt for brining. Kosher salt is ideal because its large, airy crystals dissolve so quickly in water. Unfortunately, the salt crystals of the two major brands of kosher salt—Morton and Diamond Crystal—are not equally airy, and therefore measure differently. This inconsistency between the two brands makes precise recipe writing a challenge. Because there's no way to tell which brand of kosher salt you might have on hand, we call for table salt in our brines. If you use kosher salt in your brine, keep the following in mind:

¼ cup table salt =
½ cup Diamond Crystal Kosher Salt
—or—
¼ cup plus 2 tablespoons Morton Kosher Salt

KOSHER SALT   **TABLE SALT**

CHICKEN UNDER A BRICK

THE POINT OF COOKING A CHICKEN UNDER a brick is not simply to impress your friends and neighbors (although it does look cool) but rather to achieve a stunningly crisp skin. The method generally used is simple. After the chicken is marinated (most often with garlic and rosemary), it is butterflied and pounded flat and pressed into a hot skillet under the weight of a brick (which, for reasons of hygiene, is usually wrapped in foil). The brick helps keep the chicken flat as it cooks, forcing all of the skin to make contact with the pan. Despite the seeming simplicity of chicken cooked under a brick, after trying a few recipes we noted two big problems. First, the skin that had become beautiful and crisp in the first half of cooking often turned soggy or greasy by the time the chicken finished. Second, the marinade burned in the hot pan, making the chicken taste scorched.

During our initial testing, we found we got more even weight distribution by using two bricks, rather than just one, and by placing the bricks in a Dutch oven or cast-iron skillet before weighting the chicken. We also found that chickens much larger than 4 pounds were difficult to fit into a 12-inch skillet. We kept these two key points in mind as we moved forward.

Using two unmarinated butterflied chickens, we tested the difference between pounding the chicken to an even thickness using a mallet versus simply pressing the chicken flat by hand. We would have preferred not dealing with another tool, but when pounded with a mallet, the super-flat chicken cooked evenly, and more of the skin was able to make contact with the pan and turn crisp. By comparison, only portions of the skin on the chicken flattened by hand were nicely browned.

Then we focused on cooking method. In these first tests, we cooked our chickens according to the directions found in most recipes we came across: skin side down first in a little vegetable oil with bricks on top, then flipping it over to cook the underside, again using the bricks to help keep the chicken flat. We found that this method didn't work. After the chickens were flipped and the weight was replaced on top, the skin, which had become crisp and delicate, tore in places and began to steam, turning shaggy and flaccid. We tried not replacing the bricks after the chicken was flipped, but the skin still turned rubbery from the steam and splattering oil.

So we tried reversing the order, cooking the underside of the chicken first and finishing with the skin side down. But this didn't work either; by the time the chicken was ready to flip, the pan was loaded with so much grease and nasty burnt bits that the skin ended up greasy, spotty, and slightly bitter. We then decided to try a different approach

BUTTERFLYING A CHICKEN

1. With the breast side down and the tail of the chicken facing you, use poultry shears to cut along the entire length of one side of the backbone.

2. With the breast side still down, turn the neck end to face you and cut along the other side of the backbone and remove it.

3. Turn the chicken breast side up. Open the chicken out on the work surface. Use the palm of your hand to flatten the chicken, then pound it with the flat side of a mallet to a fairly even thickness.

altogether. We cooked the chicken skin side down, underneath the weights, until it had a beautiful, roasty color. We then flipped the bird over in the skillet, and finished it in a hot oven without replacing the bricks. This was the answer to our problem. The hot, dry air of the oven ensured that the skin remained crisp as it finished cooking through. Like in our pan-roasted chicken recipes (pages 52–53), a 450-degree oven proved best, cooking the chicken quickly without singeing the drippings.

With the method nailed down, we moved our attention to flavor. Tasters preferred a simple olive oil–based marinade and, in addition to the usual garlic and rosemary, we added hot red pepper flakes and black pepper for bite. We tested substituting oregano for the rosemary, and the herb's flavor went over equally well with tasters. As for the issue of burning the marinade, we found we could include the flavors of the marinade without the risk of burning by waiting to brush our mixture onto the chicken until it went into the oven. The flavors remained fresh and potent during the brief cooking time, while the heat of the oven fused the mixture to the skin instantly without ruining the skin's crisp texture.

Chicken Under a Brick

SERVES 3 TO 4

If using kosher chicken, do not brine. If brining the chicken, do not season with salt in step 1. You can substitute any of the compound butters on pages 22–24 for the olive oil mixture prepared in step 3.

I	(3- to 4-pound) whole chicken, butterflied (see the illustrations on page 57), and brined if desired (see page 56)
	Salt and ground black pepper
I	tablespoon vegetable oil
¼	cup extra-virgin olive oil
I	medium garlic clove, minced or pressed through a garlic press (about I teaspoon)
½	teaspoon minced fresh rosemary or oregano leaves
	Pinch red pepper flakes
I	lemon, cut into wedges, for serving

CARVING A BUTTERFLIED CHICKEN

1. Place the chicken skin side down and use kitchen shears to cut through the breastbone. (Because the breastbone is broken and the meat is flattened during pounding, this should be easy.)

2. Once the breast has been split, only the skin holds the portions together. Cut the skin to separate each leg and thigh from each breast and wing.

1. Adjust an oven rack to the lowest position and heat the oven to 450 degrees. Pat the chicken dry with paper towels and season with salt and pepper.

2. Heat the vegetable oil in a 12-inch ovensafe skillet over medium-high heat until just smoking. Reduce the heat to medium and carefully lay the chicken skin side down in the skillet. Place a Dutch oven loaded with two bricks or heavy cans on top of the chicken and cook, checking every 5 minutes, until evenly browned, about 25 minutes. (After 20 minutes, the chicken should be fairly crisp and golden; if it is not, turn the heat up to medium-high and continue to cook until well browned.)

3. Meanwhile, mix the olive oil, garlic, rosemary, red pepper flakes, ⅛ teaspoon salt, and ⅛ teaspoon black pepper together.

4. Remove the skillet from the heat and remove the Dutch oven and weights. Using tongs, flip the

chicken skin side up. (If more than 3 tablespoons fat have collected in the skillet, transfer the chicken to a clean plate and pour most of the fat out of the skillet. Return the chicken to the skillet skin side up and continue.)

5. Brush the chicken with the olive oil mixture and transfer the skillet to the oven. Roast the chicken until the thickest part of the breast registers 160 to 165 and the thighs register 175 degrees on an instant-read thermometer, 8 to 15 minutes.

6. Using a potholder (the skillet handle will be hot), remove the skillet from the oven. Transfer the chicken to a carving board and let rest for 10 minutes. Carve the chicken following the illustrations on page 58 and serve with the lemon wedges.

INDOOR-BARBECUED CHICKEN

CHICKEN BARBECUED INDOORS IS RARELY as well flavored as the grilled version. In most recipes we found for it, chicken parts are slathered with barbecue sauce and baked, and the results are more often than not dismal: flabby skin, burnt sauce, flavorless chicken. The effort is minimal, but who cares if the results are so poor? We decided it was time to try turning this dull recipe around. Could we come up with a way to get juicy, tender, and well-seasoned indoor-barbecued chicken with a fresh, tangy sauce? We had already found success bringing barbecue inside with pork chops (see page 39) and in creating a similarly sauced recipe for glazed chicken breasts (see page 55), so as we grabbed our skillet and headed to the kitchen, we felt confident it could be done.

We began our testing with skin-on chicken parts, which we opted not to brine since they were being cooked with a sauce that would keep them moist. We browned the chicken in the skillet, slathered it with barbecue sauce and transferred the whole thing to the oven, where the chicken could finish cooking and the sauce could concentrate into a tasty, clingy coating. But no matter how crispy the skin was when the chicken came out

of the skillet, it turned flabby once the barbecue sauce had been added and the chicken had baked. Dealing with the skin was quickly becoming too fussy, so we decided to abandon skin-on chicken parts and go with the more convenient boneless, skinless chicken breasts.

The first attempt with boneless, skinless breasts showed promise, but it wasn't perfect: The exteriors of the breasts were drying out from the pan-searing. The solution was to scale things back and sear the chicken breasts very lightly, just until they began to color and develop a slightly rough surface to which the sauce could adhere.

At this point, we switched gears to focus on the sauce. To get the most flavor into our sauce, we removed the chicken from the skillet, setting it aside so we could make the sauce incorporating the browned bits, or fond. We wanted to keep things simple and rely strictly on pantry ingredients. After dozens of tests using all the typical barbecue sauce ingredients, we learned that a balanced combination of ketchup, molasses, grated onion, Worcestershire, and Dijon mustard were absolutes, as was the inclusion of maple syrup for its smoky sweetness and cider vinegar for its tang. A touch of cayenne pepper and chili powder added the right amount of spice. We whisked together the ingredients and added the mixture to the skillet with the fond to simmer and thicken. We then returned the chicken to the skillet, coated it with the sauce, and moved it to the oven to bake through.

From our earlier glazed chicken tests, we knew a moderate oven temperature would be key in allowing the flavors to meld while avoiding a scorched sauce. At 325 degrees, we found that the chicken had enough time to really simmer in the sauce and soak up the rich barbecue flavor. We finished the dish off using one last trick. Once the chicken reached 130 degrees, we switched the oven to broil to mimic the intense heat of the grill. Under the high heat of the broiler, the sugars in the barbecue sauce caramelized, giving us that slightly charred exterior characteristic of perfectly barbecued chicken. When the chicken reached 160 to 165 degrees, it was done—as moist and flavorful as we could have hoped, and no grill required.

Indoor–Barbecued Chicken

SERVES 4

We prefer the flavor of mild or original molasses in the sauce; the flavor of dark, robust, or blackstrap molasses is overpowering. Broiling times may vary from one oven to another so we recommend that you begin checking the chicken after 3 minutes of broiling.

BARBECUE SAUCE

1	cup ketchup
3	tablespoons cider vinegar
3	tablespoons mild molasses (see note)
2	tablespoons finely grated onion
2	tablespoons Worcestershire sauce
2	tablespoons Dijon mustard
2	tablespoons maple syrup
1	teaspoon chili powder
¼	teaspoon cayenne pepper

CHICKEN

4	(6- to 7-ounce) boneless, skinless chicken breasts, trimmed (see the illustration on page 6)
	Salt and ground black pepper
1	tablespoon vegetable oil

1. **FOR THE BARBECUE SAUCE:** Whisk all of the sauce ingredients together a small bowl.

2. **FOR THE CHICKEN:** Adjust an oven rack to the upper-middle position and heat the oven to 325 degrees. Pat the chicken dry with paper towels and season with salt and pepper.

3. Heat the oil in a 12-inch ovensafe skillet over medium-high heat until just smoking. Carefully lay the chicken breasts in the skillet and cook until very lightly browned on the first side, 1 to 2 minutes. Flip the chicken and continue to cook until very lightly browned on the second side, 1 to 2 minutes. Transfer the chicken to a plate.

4. Pour off all the fat in the pan and add the barbecue sauce, scraping up any browned bits. Return the pan to medium heat and simmer the sauce, stirring often, until the sauce is thick, glossy, and a wooden spoon or spatula leaves a clear trail when dragged across the skillet, about 4 minutes.

5. Off the heat, return the chicken to the skillet and coat well with the sauce. Turn the chicken pieces skinned side up and spoon the sauce over the top to create a thick coating. Transfer the skillet to the oven and bake the chicken until the thickest part of the breasts registers 130 degrees on an instant-read thermometer, 10 to 14 minutes.

INGREDIENTS: Boneless, Skinless Chicken Breasts

In a world of low-fat fanaticism, it's not a surprise that boneless, skinless chicken breasts are a standard in many home kitchens. And while we've come up with countless recipes to add zip to the chicken, we realized we had never stopped to look at the chicken itself. Is there a difference in flavor among the popular brands? To find out, we gathered six brands of boneless, skinless chicken breasts, broiled them without seasoning, and had 20 tasters sample the chickens side by side. Among the contenders were one kosher bird, two "natural," and one "free-range." The remaining two were just plain old "chicken."

The koshering process involves coating the chicken with salt to draw out any impurities; this process, similar to brining, results in moist, salty meat (for this reason, we do not recommend brining kosher birds). Natural—in the case of chicken—simply means there are no antibiotics or hormones, and the birds are fed a vegetarian diet. "Free-range" means exactly what it says: The birds are not confined to small cages but are allowed to roam freely.

Last place finishers (and lowest priced) Perdue and White Gem (our local store brand) were downgraded for poor texture and unnatural flavor. Tasters were also put off by the brash yellow color of the birds. Springer Farms All-Natural and Eberly's Free-Range chickens scored well, but the tie for first place went to Empire Kosher and the all-natural Bell & Evans. As the only kosher bird, Empire won points with tasters for its superior flavor, namely salt.

6. Adjust the oven rack 5 inches from the broiler element, and heat the broiler. Move the skillet to the broiler and broil the chicken until the thickest part of the breasts registers 160 to 165 degrees, 5 to 10 minutes longer.

7. Using a potholder (the skillet handle will be hot), remove the skillet from the broiler. Transfer the chicken to a platter and let rest 5 minutes. Meanwhile, being careful of the hot skillet handle, stir the sauce left in the skillet to combine and transfer to a small serving bowl. Serve the chicken with the extra sauce.

Boneless Turkey Breast with Gravy

TURKEY MAKES A GREAT DINNER YEAR-round, not just on Thanksgiving. But tackling the whole bird can be a bit much for an everyday meal. Turkey breast, meanwhile, is an ideal, often overlooked alternative. For one thing, many people prefer the white meat of a breast to the dark meat of legs and thighs, so there's not much waste. It's also much easier to handle than the whole bird, yet a turkey breast still provides a substantial amount of meat. On the downside, turkey breast often ends up dry and chalky. We wanted to develop a turkey breast recipe that had moist meat and that we could make any night of the week, and for added flavor we also wanted to end up with a rich gravy.

At the supermarket, we had a choice between bone-in and boneless turkey breast. Although bone-in meat generally stays more moist, we were drawn to the smaller size of a boneless turkey breast because it would cook more quickly and be easier to slice and serve. Boneless turkey breast is usually sold in a few varieties—natural (untreated), self-basted (injected with a brine solution), and kosher (salted and rinsed). Although the test kitchen prefers the taste of natural turkey, which we most often brine ourselves, we found after a few basic test recipes that any of

ROLLING AND TYING A TURKEY BREAST

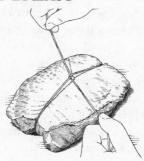

1. Tuck the tapered end of the turkey underneath and loosely tie the breast lengthwise to secure.

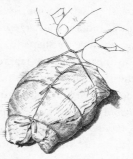

2. Tie the turkey breast securely crosswise at 1½-inch intervals to make a tidy, even roast.

the options would work here, and that brining is optional. (Kosher and self-basting birds should not be brined since they have already been salted.)

Just as the size of a whole turkey can range dramatically (from 10 to 24 pounds or larger), boneless turkey breasts can also range in size. Pitting a smaller, 2- to 2½-pound breast half against a larger, 4- to 5-pound breast half in a cook-off, we found the smaller breast to be a bit juicier and more tender. Although a 2-pound breast would probably feed four people for dinner, the prospect of having extra turkey around was just too appealing to overlook, so we scaled the recipe up and cooked two smaller breasts in a skillet at the same time. (Larger breasts, however, still produced decent results, and you may be forced to buy a large breast depending on what's in stock at your local market.)

Unlike boneless chicken breasts, boneless turkey breasts are always sold with their skin intact, making pan-roasting the perfect approach for cooking them. By starting them off on the stovetop, we would be able to quickly achieve a crisp, golden skin, while finishing the cooking in the oven would ensure tender, juicy meat. And because the meat gets a jump start on the stovetop before heading into the hot oven, the whole process would be much quicker than traditional roasting.

But before we could even start cooking, we ran into a problem as soon as we got back to the kitchen with our purchased turkey breasts. Boneless turkey breast halves are usually sold wrapped in elastic netting, and after unwrapping the turkey, we noticed how unevenly shaped boneless turkey breasts are. This meant that the tapered end would dry out by the time the thicker end was cooked through, especially with no bone to help protect the thinner, more delicate tail-end piece of meat. Tucking the tapered end underneath and tying the breast with twine made it more uniform in shape and thickness, and thus, easier to cook (see the illustrations on page 61). After browning the tied breast for about 10 minutes on the stovetop, we began experimenting with oven temperatures. After numerous tests, we found that a 325-degree oven produced the juiciest turkey breast.

Since pan-roasting a boneless turkey breast doesn't yield much in the way of drippings, we knew making a classic pan gravy was not an option. But we didn't let that stop us from creating a flavorful gravy; after all, the test kitchen has experience in making something out of nothing. In the past we have made gravy by doing nothing more than a using a roux (flour browned in fat) and adding canned broth to a few aromatics that we sautéed in the fond left from browning the meat. The combination of browned aromatics and roux had given us the toasted, meaty flavor that is key to a good gravy, and the roux also thickened the gravy to the right consistency. We felt we could apply this technique here. After browning the turkey breasts, we set them aside so we could sauté a few aromatics in the skillet. We opted for the simple combination of celery, onion, and carrot.

Rather than making our gravy start to finish at this point, we figured that cooking the vegetables a little longer along with the turkey couldn't hurt them—in fact, we thought it would help them.

INGREDIENTS:
Supermarket Chicken Broth

Which chicken broth should you reach for when you haven't the time to make your own? We recommend choosing a mass-produced, lower-sodium brand and checking the label for evidence of mirepoix ingredients (carrots, celery, onion, and herbs). In a taste test of all the widely available brands, Swanson Certified Organic Free Range Chicken Broth proved to be the winner, though if you don't mind adding water, Better Than Bouillon Chicken Base was the favorite of several tasters and came in a very close second. Swanson's less-expensive Natural Goodness Chicken Broth was almost as good, though some tasters thought it tasted "overly roasted."

THE BEST CHICKEN BROTHS

SWANSON CERTIFIED ORGANIC FREE RANGE CHICKEN BROTH
Swanson's newest broth won tasters over with "very chickeny, straightforward, and honest flavors," a hearty aroma, and restrained "hints of roastiness."

BETTER THAN BOUILLON CHICKEN BASE
We're not ready to switch to a concentrated base for all our broth needs (you have to add water), but the 18-month refrigerator shelf life means it's a good replacement for dehydrated bouillon.

SWANSON NATURAL GOODNESS CHICKEN BROTH
Swanson's standard low-sodium broth was full of chicken flavor, but several tasters noted an out-of-place, overly roasted flavor.

They would only become more caramelized and develop more flavor. So we threw the turkey on top of the vegetables in the skillet and put the whole thing in the oven. When the internal temperature of the turkey had reached 160 degrees, we knew it was time to take it out of the oven. Now there were also deep mahogany juices in the pan, and the vegetables had gone from a light golden to a deep brown. It was the perfect foundation for our gravy. We set the turkey aside to rest and finished our sauce. We browned flour in the skillet with the vegetables, fat, and juices, then slowly whisked in chicken broth. This first attempt at gravy tasted too lean, so we tried using all beef broth. This gravy proved to be too acidic, with a metallic aftertaste. The ideal combination was a mixture of equal parts chicken broth and beef broth.

While the turkey rested, we simmered the gravy until it was thickened to the proper consistency before straining it. We tried pushing the vegetables through the strainer with the liquid, but this produced gravy with an unappealing texture; we had better results when we left the vegetables out altogether and did not make them a part of the final gravy. Tasters were impressed with our rich, meaty gravy, but it still needed an extra boost. The trio of minced garlic, fresh thyme, and a bay leaf, added to the skillet before putting the turkey and vegetables in the oven, did the trick. The result was a deeply flavored gravy reminiscent of a Thanksgiving dinner, the perfect accompaniment to our moist turkey breast.

Pan-Roasted Boneless Turkey Breast with Gravy

SERVES ABOUT 8

If using a kosher or self-basting turkey, do not brine. If brining the turkey, do not season with salt in step 1. Often, boneless turkey breast halves are sold in elastic netting; be sure to remove the netting before brining or cooking. You can substitute one 4- to 4½-pound boneless turkey breast here, but you will need to increase the roasting time to about 1½ hours.

| 2 | (2- to 2½-pound) boneless turkey breast halves, trimmed, tied (see the illustrations on page 61) and brined if desired (see page 56) |

2   (2- to 2½-pound) boneless turkey breast halves, trimmed, tied (see the illustrations on page 61) and brined if desired (see page 56)
    Salt and ground black pepper
¼   cup vegetable oil
1   medium onion, chopped coarse
1   medium carrot, chopped coarse
1   celery rib, chopped coarse
6   medium garlic cloves, peeled and minced or pressed through a garlic press (about 2 tablespoons)
2   sprigs fresh thyme
1   bay leaf
¼   cup unbleached all-purpose flour
2   cups low-sodium chicken broth
2   cups low-sodium beef broth

1. Adjust an oven rack to the middle position and heat the oven to 325 degrees. Pat the turkey dry with paper towels and season with salt and pepper. Heat 2 tablespoons of the oil in a 12-inch ovensafe skillet over medium-high heat until just smoking. Brown the turkey breasts well on all sides, about 10 minutes. Transfer the turkey to a plate.

2. Add the remaining 2 tablespoons oil to the skillet and heat over medium heat until just shimmering. Add the onion, carrot, and celery and cook, stirring often, until the vegetables begin to soften and brown lightly, 4 to 6 minutes. Stir in the garlic, thyme, and bay leaf and cook until fragrant, about 30 seconds.

3. Lay the turkey breasts skin side up on top of the vegetables in the skillet and transfer the skillet to the oven. Roast the turkey until the thickest part of the breast registers 160 to 165 degrees on an instant-read thermometer, 50 to 60 minutes.

4. Using a potholder (the skillet handle will be hot), remove the skillet from the oven. Transfer the turkey to a carving board, tent loosely with foil, and let rest while making the gravy.

5. Place the skillet with the juices and vegetables over medium-high heat. Stir in the flour and cook, stirring constantly, until well browned, about

5 minutes. Slowly whisk in the chicken and beef broths, bring to a simmer, and cook, stirring often, until the gravy is thickened and measures about 2½ cups, 10 to 15 minutes.

6. Strain the gravy through a fine-mesh strainer and season with salt and pepper to taste. Remove the twine, slice the turkey crosswise into ¼-inch slices, and serve with the gravy.

MEATLOAF

A GREAT MEATLOAF IS ABOUT AS CLOSE AS you can get to the definition of down-home comfort food. But not all meatloaves are created equal. We have come across a multitude of recipes with too much (or the wrong) fillers, causing the texture to suffer and making the meatloaf overly dry. Not to mention the gloppy, cloyingly sweet glazes and offbeat additions we found: canned pineapple, cranberry sauce, raisins, prepared taco mix, even goat cheese. We wanted to take this dish back to the classic meatloaf like our mothers used to serve. But doing so means making a monstrous loaf (on average around two pounds), and waiting an hour for it to cook. Who has the time to get their mother's Sunday meatloaf on the table for a mid-week dinner? This American classic was a prime candidate for a shortcut skillet version.

In terms of ingredients, we were set on sticking with the tried and true for our master recipe. To determine which ground meat or meat mix makes the best loaf, we followed a very basic meatloaf recipe and made loaves using ground beef chuck, pork, veal, bacon, and ham in numerous proportions and combinations. We found out that meat markets haven't been selling meatloaf mix (a mix of beef, pork, and veal, usually in equal proportions) all these years for nothing. Not only did buying the mix keep things simple, but the loaves made with it were well balanced, tender, and nicely textured. We found that if you can't get your hands on a meatloaf mix, a half-and-half combination of 90 percent lean ground beef and ground pork also works well.

For the binding and filling, we again went through the gamut of options, including bread crumbs, oatmeal, and a panoply of cereals. In the end, we preferred crushed saltines for their mild flavor. Just ¼ cup of milk and a single egg were enough to help bind together the meat and add richness, moisture, and tenderness. We also tried tomato sauce, but this just made the loaf taste like a meatball with sauce, and while we liked the flavor of ketchup, we ultimately decided to save it for our glaze. After trying out numerous other classic additions, we settled on sautéed onion, garlic, Worcestershire sauce, Dijon mustard, thyme, and fresh parsley as the best combination for a well-seasoned loaf.

Once we had cooked the onion with the garlic and thyme in our skillet, we combined all the ingredients in a bowl and set out to shape the loaf. To scale things down to a quick-cooking size, we ditched the loaf pan traditionally used and instead

MAKING MINI MEATLOAVES

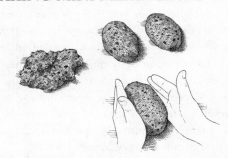

1. Divide the meatloaf mixture into four portions. Cup each portion with your hands to form four oval loaves.

2. While browning the second side of the loaves in the skillet, use a spatula to tidy up the edges so they maintain their oval shape.

made several smaller loaves. We found that four loaves made generous portions, and they all fit together comfortably in a 12-inch skillet. Searing the loaves in the skillet before transferring them to the oven significantly shortened the traditionally lengthy cooking time (down to 18 to 25 minutes total), while still achieving the brown crust that is the hallmark of any respectable meatloaf.

To get the familiar tangy-sweet top crust, we made a ketchup–brown sugar mixture, adding a few teaspoons of cider vinegar for tang and to keep the glaze from becoming overly sweet. After brushing the glaze on our loaves, we slipped them in the oven to roast at 350 degrees. These were terrific meatloaves with great flavor made in short order; tasters were surprised how much they tasted like the down-home classic.

With this version nailed down, we felt compelled to come up with a variation that offered a little kick but didn't stray too far from the original. We settled on meatloaves with Southwestern flavors, adding smoky chipotle chiles in adobo sauce and canned green chiles, and swapping fresh cilantro for the parsley.

All-American Mini Meatloaves

SERVES 4

If you can't find meatloaf mix, substitute 12 ounces each ground pork and 90 percent lean ground beef.

GLAZE
¼   cup ketchup
2   tablespoons light brown sugar
2   teaspoons cider vinegar

MEATLOAVES
4   teaspoons vegetable oil
1   small onion, minced (about ½ cup)
1   medium clove garlic, minced or pressed through a garlic press (about 1 teaspoon)
1   teaspoon fresh minced thyme leaves
17   saltines, crushed fine (about ⅔ cup)
⅓   cup minced fresh parsley leaves
¼   cup whole milk

3   tablespoons Worcestershire sauce
1   large egg
1½   tablespoons Dijon mustard
1   teaspoon salt
½   teaspoon ground black pepper
1½   pounds meatloaf mix (see note)

1. FOR THE GLAZE: Whisk all of the glaze ingredients together in a medium bowl.

2. FOR THE MEATLOAVES: Adjust an oven rack to the middle position and heat the oven to 350 degrees. Heat 2 teaspoons of the oil in a 12-inch ovensafe nonstick skillet over medium heat until shimmering. Add the onion and cook until softened, about 5 minutes. Stir in the garlic and thyme and cook until fragrant, about 30 seconds. Transfer the mixture to a large bowl. Wipe out the skillet with a wad of paper towels.

3. Stir the cracker crumbs, parsley, milk, Worcestershire sauce, egg, mustard, salt, and pepper into the cooked onion mixture. Add the meatloaf mix and thoroughly combine. Following the illustrations on page 64, press the mixture into 4 small oval loaves.

4. Heat the remaining 2 teaspoons oil in the skillet over medium-high heat until just smoking. Brown the meatloaves well on the first side, 3 to 5 minutes. Carefully flip the meatloaves, tidy up the edges with a spatula, and cook until lightly browned, about 2 minutes.

5. Brush the meatloaves with the glaze and transfer the skillet to the oven. Bake the meatloaves until the center of the loaves registers 160 degrees on an instant-read thermometer, about 15 to 20 minutes. Remove the skillet from the oven, transfer the meatloaves to a serving platter, and let rest for 5 minutes before serving.

➤ VARIATION

Southwestern Mini Meatloaves
Follow the recipe for All-American Mini Meatloaves, substituting ⅓ cup minced fresh cilantro leaves for the parsley and adding 1 (7-ounce) can chopped green chiles, drained, and 1 tablespoon minced chipotle chile in adobo sauce, to the meatloaf mixture in step 3.

Pan-Roasted Racks of Lamb

THE WORD "MOUTHWATERING" MUST HAVE been coined to describe rack of lamb—the meat is ultra-tender and incomparably luscious. But with a price of around $20 a pound, this is one expensive cut of meat—and there is nothing worse than investing in a rack and inviting company over to join in the extravagance, only to find you've improperly cooked it. Like other simple but fabulous dishes (roast chicken comes to mind), there's really not much to cooking it—except that there's no disguising imperfection. You want the meat to be perfectly pink and juicy, the outside intensely browned to boost flavor and provide contrasting texture, and the fat to be well enough rendered to encase the meat in a thin, crisp, brittle shell. Pan-roasting stood out as an ideal cooking method to get the crust we wanted and an evenly cooked interior, and to help make preparing this favorite cut foolproof.

We started with a rack of lamb that had been trimmed and frenched (the rib bones were cleaned of meat and fat for an attractive presentation). First,

---

INGREDIENTS: Rack of Lamb

Consumers typically have three choices when shopping for lamb: domestic meat, meat imported from Australia, or meat imported from New Zealand. Lambs in both Australia and New Zealand are pasture-fed on mixed grasses, which leads to their gamier, more pronounced flavor. Lambs raised in the U.S. begin on a diet of grass but finish with grain, resulting in the milder-tasting meat that our tasters preferred. Diet also accounts for the larger size of American lamb. On average, the domestic racks we used to develop our recipe were about 1½ pounds each, whereas the imported racks typically weighed in at just over a pound.

DOMESTIC RACK   **IMPORTED RACK**

American-raised lamb boasts bigger racks and a sweet, mild flavor. Racks from Australia (as well as New Zealand) come smaller with a stronger, gamier flavor.

---

we seared the fat side of the rack in a little vegetable oil in a skillet on top of the stove. It looked terrific; the crust was deep brown and crispy. The only refinement we saw a need for was finding a way to brown the strip of eye meat that lies below the bones on the bony side of the rack. After some experimentation we came up with the system of leaning two racks upright, one against the other, in the pan; this allowed us to brown all parts of the meat before moving it to the oven to roast.

Next, we needed to address oven temperature. We tried roasting the meat at temperatures as low as 200 degrees as well as moderate to high temperatures up to 500 degrees. The slow-roast technique was a bust: the meat had a funny, murky taste and mushy texture that we didn't like, and it took much too long to cook. Meanwhile, at the high end of the spectrum the flavor was better but there was too much risk of error. We ended up taking the middle road at 425 degrees: The meat lost the murky taste and the temperature felt more in control.

But now we were running into another problem: The racks we were cooking were too fatty and tasted greasy. In addition to the chop's exterior layer of fat, some chops also have a second layer of internal fat, separated by a thin piece of meat called the cap. We tried removing all of the cap, but that wasn't the solution; these racks ended up dry with very little of the distinctive lamb flavor—a lot of its trademark flavor comes from the fat. And given how expensive lamb chops are we didn't want to sacrifice the meat from the cap anyway. The compromise was to trim most of the fat between the bones but leave a thin layer over the loin (see the illustrations on page 68). With that, the meat browned perfectly and tasted great—full lamb flavor without being greasy.

Satisfied with our roasting technique, we were ready to work on a sauce. We wanted a quick sauce that we could prepare ahead of time so it would be ready to go as soon as the lamb was done. Mint is a classic pairing with lamb, but we were after something more interesting than just a ho-hum mint jam. Inspired by the parsley and garlic–based chimichurri recently made by a colleague in the test kitchen, we decided to incorporate its flavors into a mint relish. After experimenting with substituting different quantities of mint for some of the parsley, we settled on a 50-50 combination of the two herbs. A heavy hand with garlic as well as some minced shallot gave the sauce bite. Extra-virgin olive oil was favored over both regular olive oil and vegetable oil, since it stood up best to the boldness of the other ingredients. For the acid, we opted for red wine vinegar, which was smooth but not overshadowed by other ingredients. Adding a few tablespoons of water kept things balanced. After sitting for half an hour, the flavors of the sauce had melded into a bold but balanced whole—an ideal match for our perfectly cooked lamb.

Pan-Roasted Racks of Lamb with Mint Relish

SERVES 4 TO 6

We prefer the milder taste and bigger size of American lamb for this recipe (see page 66 for more information). If using imported lamb, note that the racks will probably be much smaller and will therefore cook through more quickly in the oven. Often, the racks of lamb you buy at the store have already been frenched (that is, the bones have been cleaned of excess fat and meat), but inevitably, they will still need some cleaning up.

MINT RELISH

½   cup minced fresh parsley leaves

½   cup minced fresh mint leaves

½   cup extra-virgin olive oil

¼   cup red wine vinegar

1   medium shallot, minced (about 3 tablespoons)

2   tablespoons water

5   medium garlic cloves, minced or pressed through a garlic press (about 5 teaspoons)

1   teaspoon salt

LAMB

2   (1½-pound) racks of lamb, trimmed and frenched (see the illustrations on page 68) Salt and ground black pepper

2   tablespoons vegetable oil

1. For the mint relish: Combine all of the relish ingredients in a medium bowl and let stand at room temperature for the flavors to meld, about 30 minutes.

2. For the lamb: Adjust an oven rack to the lower-middle position and heat the oven to 425 degrees. Pat the lamb with paper towels and season with salt and pepper.

3. Heat the oil in a 12-inch ovensafe skillet over high heat until shimmering. Following the illustrations below, place the racks in the skillet, fat side down with the ribs facing outwards, and cook until well browned, about 5 minutes. Using tongs, stand the racks up in the skillet, leaning them against each other, and brown the bottoms, about 2 minutes longer. (If the skillet contains more than 2 tablespoons of fat, carefully drain off the excess.)

4. Transfer the skillet to the oven, with the racks still standing up, and roast the lamb to the desired doneness (see page 9), 10 to 20 minutes.

5. Using a potholder (the skillet handle will be hot), remove the skillet from the oven. Transfer the lamb to a carving board, tent loosely with foil, and let rest for 10 minutes. Carve the lamb, slicing between each rib into individual chops, and serve with the mint relish.

BROWNING RACKS OF LAMB

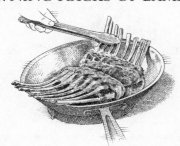

1. Browning a rack of lamb on both sides on top of the stove before placing it in the oven will produce a good crust. Start by placing two racks in a hot pan with the meat in the center and the ribs facing outward.

2. After the meat is browned, stand the racks up in the pan and lean them against each other to brown the bottoms.

TRIMMING FAT FROM THE RACK

1. With your hands, peel back the thick outer layer of fat from the racks, along with the thin flap of meat underneath it. Use a boning or paring knife to cut any tissue connecting the fat cap to the rack. (Not all lamb racks will have this cap of fat attached.)

2. Using a sharp boning or paring knife, trim the remaining thin layer of fat that covers the loin, leaving the strip of fat that separates the loin and small eye of meat directly above it.

3. Make a straight cut along the top side of the bones, an inch up from the small eye of meat.

4. Remove any fat above this line and scrape any remaining meat or fat from the exposed bones.

PAN-ROASTED PORK LOIN

THE UNASSUMING BONELESS PORK LOIN roast is hearty weeknight fare for a casual family feast. The practical advantages of this supermarket cut are many: It is affordable and widely available; the mild, sweet flavor of roast pork pairs well with most any side dish; and leftovers make great sandwiches. We wanted to develop a foolproof weeknight pan-roasted recipe for pork loin that would produce juicy, well-browned, and flavorful meat.

First off, we tried brining the pork loin to see if doing so would help to season the meat and boost juiciness, and it did indeed yield tender, juicy, well-seasoned pork. The unbrined pork wasn't bad, however, so while we recommend brining for this recipe it's not a necessity.

Innumerable tests proved that roasts with a deep brown, caramelized crust both look and taste better than those without, and searing the meat in the skillet allowed for great browning as well as good control over the process. Tying a roast may seem fussy to some, but we discovered that this small investment of time is amply rewarded. The uniform shape of a tied roast ensures that it fits well in the skillet, promotes even cooking, and yields attractive, round slices. After browning the exterior, we slid the pork loin into the oven to finish cooking through. We tested varying temperatures and found that at higher temperatures our roasts were dried out near the edges before the center was done. In the end, a moderate temperature of 325 degrees proved best.

Today's leaner pork may be pleasing to health-conscious carnivores, but its low fat content makes it exceptionally prone to overcooking. While older recipes recommend serving pork at 160 degrees (or higher), we have found it is best served at a temperature of 150 degrees. If, however, you wait to take the roast out of the oven until it has reached this temperature, it will be overcooked—the temperature of the roast will continue to rise, by as much as 10 degrees, once it has been taken out of the oven. To reach the ideal temperature at serving time, we found it was best to remove the roast from the oven when it registers 140 to 145 degrees and let it rest on the carving board for 15 to 20 minutes before slicing.

With our basic cooking method squared away, it was time to focus on the flavors. We considered pulling together numerous combinations of herbs before realizing herbes de Provence could be the simple answer we were hoping for. This mixture of dried herbs, frequently used in the south of France, typically includes basil, fennel seed, lavender, marjoram, rosemary, sage, summer savory, and thyme. So we tried seasoning the pork with the herbs along with pepper before browning it. Tasters enjoyed the subtle flavors that the herbs lent the finished dish; as the herbs simmered in

the juices released as the pork cooked, their flavors bloomed and intensified. But still, tasters felt the herbs alone weren't delivering enough flavor.

Since fruit is a traditional pairing with pork, we decided to try adding apples to the mix. Raw apples, added to the skillet with the browned pork before it went into the oven, didn't fully cook by the time the pork was done and didn't have much flavor. The solution was to remove the pork to a plate after browning and cook the apples separately on the stovetop. We then added the pork back to the skillet to let them finish together in the oven and let the flavors meld.

The results were surprising, but in a good way. Our apples had cooked down to a rustic, chunky applesauce. Tasters loved the idea of the fruit relish

EQUIPMENT: Instant-Read Thermometers

Of the many types of thermometers on the market, the digital instant-read thermometer is the least specialized and the most useful to the home cook. In the test kitchen we rely on instant-read thermometers for a number of jobs: to tell us when meat and poultry are optimally cooked, to check the temperature of bread, caramel sauce, and candy, and to test the temperature of oil when frying. Our favorite instant-read thermometer is the ThermoWorks Super-Fast Thermapen, a test kitchen workhorse that quickly provides accurate readings across a broad range of temperatures. But at $89, the Thermapen isn't cheap. We wondered, could a more inexpensive model approach the performance of our trusty Thermapen? We purchased 11 digital instant-read thermometers, all priced under $30, and put them through their paces in the kitchen.

The best models featured a broad temperature range; a stem long enough to reach the interior of a large cut of meat; a clear display; a way to recalibrate slips in accuracy; and, above all, speed, so you don't have to keep the oven door open too long. Readability and response time were particularly important to us; if these two characteristics are up to snuff, you'll be able to get in and out of any temperature-taking operation quickly—perhaps even instantly. We also looked at less-obvious concerns raised by our test cooks based on years of thermometer use: issues such as performance in shallow liquids and in thin foods, and user-friendly design details such as auto shutoff.

Though no model out-performed the Thermapen for speed or temperature range, our testing did reveal a worthy stand-in: The CDN ProAccurate Quick Tip Digital Cooking Thermometer DTQ450. Not only did it register accurately every time, sport a nearly 5-inch stem and clear display, and fit easily in our drawer, it further impressed us with a temperature range of -40 to 450 degrees, and it registered temperatures in only 10 seconds—all for roughly one-fifth the price of the Thermapen.

THE BEST INSTANT-READ THERMOMETERS

THERMOWORKS   CDN PROACCURATE

The ThermoWorks Super-Fast Thermapen 211-476 is fast, accurate, and easy to use. The Thermapen also has the widest temperature range (−58 to 572 degrees), but note its hefty price tag—$89. The CDN ProAccurate Quick Tip Digital Cooking Thermometer DTQ450 was not quite as fast as the mighty Thermapen, but fast enough, and its low price ($17.95) puts it in reach of most cooks.

to accompany our pork, but they wanted more fruit flavor. Dried cranberries, which we plumped in apple cider, added a bright fruity tang, and including the cider in the final dish reinforced the apple flavor. For more complexity, we added a few shallots when sautéing the apples. Not only did they help offset the sweetness of the dish but they also gave the mixture an appealing texture. Some brown sugar and butter rounded out the relish.

We not only had a flavorful dinner before us, but enough leftover pork loin for great sandwiches the next day.

Pan-Roasted Pork Loin with Apples and Cranberries

SERVES 4 TO 6

If the pork is enhanced (see page 40 for more information), do not brine. If brining the pork, omit the salt in step 2. We left a ¼-inch-thick layer of fat on top of the roast; if your roast has a thicker fat cap, trim it back to be about ¼ inch thick.

I	cup dried cranberries (4 ounces)
½	cup apple cider
I	(2½- to 3-pound) boneless pork loin roast, trimmed, tied at 1-inch intervals, and brined if desired (see page 56)
I	tablespoon dried herbes de Provence
	Salt and ground black pepper
3	tablespoons vegetable oil
4	medium shallots, peeled and quartered
I	pound Golden Delicious or Granny Smith apples (2 to 3 medium), peeled, cored, and cut into ½-inch-thick wedges
I	tablespoon brown sugar
I	tablespoon unsalted butter

1. Adjust an oven rack to the lowest position and heat the oven to 325 degrees. Combine the cranberries and cider in a small microwave-safe bowl. Cover and microwave on high until bubbling, about 30 seconds; keep covered and set aside until needed.

2. Pat the pork dry with paper towels and season with the herbes de Provence, salt, and pepper. Heat 2 tablespoons of the oil in a 12-inch ovensafe skillet over medium-high heat until just smoking. Brown the pork well on all sides, 7 to 10 minutes. Transfer the pork to a large plate.

3. Add the remaining tablespoon oil to the skillet and return to medium heat until shimmering. Add the shallots and cook until golden, about 3 minutes. Stir in the apples and cook, stirring often, until lightly golden, 5 to 7 minutes. Stir in the brown sugar and microwaved cranberry-cider mixture and cook until the sugar has dissolved, about 1 minute.

4. Off the heat, nestle the pork into the skillet, along with any accumulated juices. Transfer the skillet to the oven and roast the pork until the center of the roast registers 140 to 145 degrees on an instant-read thermometer, 35 to 55 minutes.

5. Using a potholder (the skillet handle will be hot), remove the skillet from the oven. Transfer the pork to a carving board, tent loosely with foil, and let rest until the center of the roast registers 150 degrees on an instant-read thermometer, 15 to 20 minutes.

6. Meanwhile, being careful of the hot skillet handle, stir the butter into the apple-shallot mixture left in the skillet, season with salt and pepper to taste, and cover to keep warm. Remove the twine from the pork, slice into ½-inch-thick slices, and transfer to a serving platter. Spoon the apple-shallot mixture over the pork and serve.

➤ VARIATION

Pan-Roasted Pork Loin with Sweet and Sour Apples and Cranberries

Follow the recipe for Pan-Roasted Pork Loin with Apples and Cranberries, substituting ¼ cup cider vinegar for ¼ cup of the cider in step 1. Omit the herbes de Provence and increase the amount of brown sugar to ¼ cup. Add 1 tablespoon mustard seeds and 1 teaspoon minced fresh thyme leaves to the skillet with the sugar in step 3.

Pan-Roasted Glazed Pork Tenderloins

NEW ENGLANDERS WILL SLATHER MAPLE syrup on just about anything, from pancakes to pineapple. Among the multitude of dishes done right with a dash of maple, classic New England maple-glazed pork tenderloin is one of our favorites. Sweet maple, with its delicate flavor notes of smoke, caramel, and vanilla, makes an ideal complement to pork, which has a faint sweetness of its own. The result of this marriage is a glistening maple-glazed pork roast, which, when sliced, combines the juices from tender, well-seasoned pork with a rich maple glaze to create complex flavor in every bite.

When we tested a few different recipes, however, we found that this dish often falls short of its savory-sweet promise. Many of the glazes were too thin to coat the pork properly, some were so sweet that they required a hotline to the dentist's office, and none of them had a pronounced maple flavor. Furthermore, many recipes required continual basting of the loin in a hot oven, as well as multiple pans: a skillet to brown the pork, a saucepan to cook the glaze, and a roasting pan to finish cooking the pork in the oven. We set out to achieve a flavorful, clingy glaze and moist pork—all in one skillet.

First we addressed the meat itself. As was the case with our Glazed Pork Chops recipe (page 42), we found that the excess moisture exuded from a brined pork tenderloin prevented the glaze from properly coating the surface, so we opted to forgo brining.

We wanted a flavorful crust on our pork, so we began by searing the pork in the skillet. We found that we could brown two 1-pound tenderloins at the same time in a 12-inch skillet. And instead of immediately transferring the tenderloins to the oven, we decided to set them aside and make use of the flavorful fond and our hot skillet to build our glaze. Tasters found that maple syrup alone was too sweet; the addition of whole grain mustard cut the syrup's sweetness and gave the glaze a tangy, pungent undertone. A little balsamic vinegar heightened this effect and added depth. After removing the tenderloins from the pan, we poured off the excess fat and added the glaze ingredients. Though the flavors were spot on, the glaze overall tasted weak and didn't seem thick enough to coat the meat. A quick 30-second simmer was the answer, and this step boosted the glaze flavor in two ways: It took advantage of the drippings that had been created when the meat seared, and it concentrated the maple flavor of the syrup.

We then returned the seared tenderloins to the skillet with the syrup glaze, twirled the pork around in the glaze a couple of times with tongs to coat it, and popped the whole thing into the oven. Instead of brushing or basting to keep the pork coated, halfway through cooking we simply twirled the pork again in the glaze with our tongs—it turned out that rotating the meat in this way also ensured even cooking. The pork emerged juicy, flavorful, and bathed in a glistening coat of glaze. While the pork rested, we briefly simmered the glaze left behind in the skillet until it was thick and syrupy.

Our maple glaze was simple and only required a few ingredients, so it was easy to substitute and add ingredients to come up with new flavor variations. We made an apricot-orange glaze with lemon juice, as well as a Southwestern version with smoky chipotles, honey, and lime juice. All are equally elegant, use only one pan, and take less than 45 minutes, start to finish.

REMOVING THE SILVER SKIN FROM A PORK TENDERLOIN

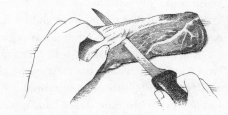

Slip a knife under the silver skin, angle it slightly upward, and use a gentle back and forth motion to remove the silver skin. Discard the skin. You can also use this method to remove the silver skin from beef tenderloin.

Pan-Roasted Maple Glazed Pork Tenderloins

SERVES 4 TO 6

Pork tenderloins are often sold two to a package that weighs 1½ to 2 pounds. To ensure that the tenderloins don't curl during cooking, remove the silver skin from the meat (see the illustration on page 71).

MAPLE GLAZE
¾   cup maple syrup
⅓   cup whole grain mustard
2   tablespoons balsamic vinegar

PORK TENDERLOINS
2   (12- to 16-ounce) pork tenderloins, trimmed
    Salt and ground black pepper
1   tablespoon vegetable oil

1. FOR THE MAPLE GLAZE: Whisk all of the glaze ingredients together in a medium bowl.

2. FOR THE PORK TENDERLOINS: Adjust an oven rack to the middle position and heat the oven to 325 degrees. Pat the tenderloins dry with paper towels and season with salt and pepper. Heat the oil in a 12-inch ovensafe skillet over medium-high heat until just smoking. Brown the tenderloins well on all sides, 7 to 10 minutes. Transfer the tenderloins to a plate.

3. Add the glaze to the pan, scraping up any browned bits, and simmer over medium heat until slightly thickened and fragrant, about 30 seconds. Return the tenderloins to the skillet, turning to coat them thoroughly with the glaze.

4. Transfer the skillet to the oven and roast the pork until the center of the tenderloins registers 140 to 145 degrees on an instant-read thermometer, 10 to 15 minutes, turning the meat in the glaze to coat halfway through the cooking time.

5. Using a potholder (the skillet handle will be hot), remove the skillet from the oven. Transfer the tenderloins to a carving board, tent loosely with foil, and let rest until the center of the tenderloins registers 150 degrees on an instant-read thermometer, about 10 minutes.

6. Meanwhile, being careful of the hot skillet handle, return the glaze to high heat and simmer, stirring constantly, until thick and syrupy, about 1 minute. Slice the pork, drizzle with the glaze, and serve.

VARIATIONS

Pan-Roasted Spicy Honey Glazed Pork Tenderloins

Whisk ¾ cup honey, ⅓ cup fresh lime juice from 3 limes, 2 teaspoons minced chipotle chile in adobo sauce, and 1½ teaspoons ground cumin together in a medium bowl. Follow the recipe for Pan-Roasted Maple Glazed Pork Tenderloins, substituting the honey mixture for the maple glaze.

Pan-Roasted Apricot-Orange Glazed Pork Tenderloins

Whisk 1 cup apricot preserves, ½ cup orange juice, and 3 tablespoons fresh lemon juice from 1 lemon together in a medium bowl. Follow the recipe for Pan-Roasted Maple Glazed Pork Tenderloins, substituting the apricot-orange mixture for the maple glaze.

PAN-ROASTED HALIBUT

TUNA, SALMON, AND SWORDFISH ARE THE fish steaks most American home cooks know best, but halibut also deserves its share of the limelight, particularly as a change of pace for special occasion meals. With its naturally lean, firm texture and clean, mild flavor, halibut is often preferred braised, rather than roasted or sautéed, because this moist-heat cooking technique keeps the fish from drying out. The downside, however, is that braising does not develop as much flavor as the other methods and produces fish the test kitchen considers lackluster. We hoped with pan-roasting we could achieve the intense flavor of a skillet-sear as well as a moist and tender piece of fish.

Before addressing the questions of technique and sauce, we took to the supermarkets and fishmongers to find the best cut of halibut for our recipe. We had already settled on steaks rather than fillets based on availability, but steaks vary considerably in size depending on the weight of the particular fish. A halibut's weight typically ranges anywhere from 15 to 50 pounds, but can reach up to 300 pounds. After buying more than 40 pounds of halibut, our advice is this: Inspect the steaks in the fish case and choose the two that are closest in size. This approach ensures that the steaks will cook at the same rate, thus avoiding the problem of overcooking the smaller one. (See below for more information on types of halibut steaks.) We found the best size steak for the home cook to be between 10 and 12 inches in length and roughly 1¼ inches thick. We did test thinner and thicker steaks, adjusting the cooking time as necessary, and had success with both. We also tried halibut steaks that we purchased frozen. While the flavor matched that of the fresh fish, tasters were disappointed in the mushy texture, so we crossed it off our list.

The first detail to tackle was skillet choice. As most home cooks know, fish is notorious for sticking, so a nonstick skillet was essential. Since we would be moving our skillet to the oven after searing the steaks, making sure our skillet was ovensafe was also key. Next, we turned to cooking technique. After a few simplified tests of browning the steaks and moving them to the oven to finish up, we knew our pan-roasting approach was a huge improvement from other cooking techniques—the flavor contributed by browning the fish was outstanding and the steaks were evenly cooked. But the process wasn't perfect. More often than not, our steaks were coming out overcooked.

After much additional testing, we finally hit on the solution. Instead of sautéing the steaks on both sides, we seared them on one side only, then flipped them seared side up and moved the skillet to the oven. After testing a range of oven temperatures, we opted for 325 degrees because it cooked the halibut in under 10 minutes but still allowed for a reasonable margin for error. (The lower the temperature, the slower the fish cooks and therefore the longer the window of time for doneness.) This worked beautifully, combining the enhanced flavor of browned fish with the moist interior that comes from finishing in the oven's even heat. Finally, we had moist fish with great sautéed flavor.

With the fish seared and roasted properly, we needed to develop a sauce to accompany it. We wanted something that was quick and easy to put together and had bold, bright flavors. Chermoula came to mind immediately. Chermoula is a traditional Moroccan sauce or paste that is usually used as a marinade for fish. It typically consists of generous amounts of cilantro, lemon, garlic, and olive oil, with spices such as cumin and paprika. Using it as a sauce rather than a marinade worked perfectly with our halibut—and it took no time to prepare.

THREE KINDS OF HALIBUT STEAK

FULL STEAK
4 Sections

BELLY CUT
2 Sections

BONELESS STEAK
I Section

Most halibut steaks consist of four pieces of meat attached to a central bone (left). It is not uncommon, however, to encounter a steak with just two pieces, both located on the same side of the center bone (center). These steaks were cut from the center of the halibut, adjacent to the belly cavity. The belly, in effect, separates the two halves. We slightly preferred full steaks with four meat sections; each full steak serves two or three people. If you can find only the belly steaks, you will have to purchase four steaks instead of two to make our pan-roasted halibut recipe. Avoid very small, boneless steaks (right) cut entirely free from the bone and each other. Most boneless steaks won't serve even one person.

Pan-Roasted Halibut with Chermoula

SERVES 4

This recipe will work with salmon and swordfish steaks as well; however, the cooking times might vary slightly depending on their thickness. Any of the relishes on pages 20–22 can be substituted for the chermoula.

CHERMOULA

¾	cup packed fresh cilantro leaves
½	cup extra-virgin olive oil
3	tablespoons juice from 1 lemon
4	medium garlic cloves, minced or pressed through a garlic press (about 4 teaspoons)
1	teaspoon ground cumin
1	teaspoon paprika
¼	teaspoon cayenne pepper
¼	teaspoon salt

HALIBUT

2	(1¼-pound) full halibut steaks, about 1¼ inches thick and 10 to 12 inches long, trimmed (see the illustration below) Salt and ground black pepper
2	tablespoons vegetable oil

TRIMMING HALIBUT

Cutting off the cartilage at the ends of the steaks ensures that they will fit neatly in the pan and diminishes the likelihood that the small bones located there will end up on your dinner plate.

SERVING HALIBUT STEAKS

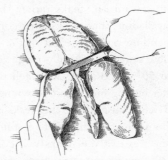

Remove the skin from the cooked steaks and separate each quadrant of meat from the bones by slipping a knife or spatula gently between them. Transfer the pieces of meat to a warm serving platter.

1. FOR THE CHERMOULA: Process all of the chermoula ingredients together in a food processor until smooth, about 20 seconds, stopping to scrape down the sides of the bowl as needed. Transfer to a serving bowl and set aside.

2. FOR THE HALIBUT: Adjust an oven rack to the middle position and heat the oven to 325 degrees. Pat the fish dry with paper towels and season with salt and pepper.

3. Heat the oil in a 12-inch ovensafe nonstick skillet over medium-high heat until just smoking. Carefully lay the fish steaks in the skillet and cook until well browned on one side, about 5 minutes.

4. Off the heat, gently flip the steaks over. Transfer the skillet to the oven and roast the halibut until the flesh is opaque and the fish flakes apart when gently prodded with a paring knife, 6 to 9 minutes.

5. Using a potholder (the skillet handle will be hot), remove the skillet from the oven. Transfer the steaks to a carving board, tent loosely with foil, and let rest for 5 minutes. Following the illustration above, separate the skin and bones from the fish with a spatula or knife. Transfer the fish to a platter and serve with the chermoula.

3

SKILLET PASTA

SKILLET PASTA

EVERY STEP COUNTS WHEN YOU'RE RUSH-ing to get dinner on the table. Even pasta dishes, many of which are quick-cooking by nature, can become labor intensive, especially when you cook the pasta in one pot, prepare a sauce in another, and, sometimes, transfer the mixture to a third container to bake in the oven. We wanted to create simple, tasty dinners with tender—not mushy—pasta, fresh vegetables, and juicy meat, all with satisfying sauces. And we wanted to do so using just one pan—a skillet.

Our most important breakthrough in developing skillet pasta recipes occurred when we found that we could eliminate the step of boiling pasta in a separate pot. Small amounts of pasta (12 ounces or less) cook very well in a 12-inch nonstick skillet with a brothy, creamy, or diluted tomato sauce. If the pasta is cooked at a vigorous simmer, it absorbs the cooking liquid and becomes tender in a reasonable amount of time. And because the pasta is cooked in the same skillet used to cook the meat, vegetables, and sauce, the pasta absorbs maximum flavor.

The right pasta-to-liquid ratio is crucial when making skillet pasta. If you use more pasta than required, there won't be enough liquid to cook it through; if you use less, the resulting sauce will be too thin. For the most accurate measurement, we weighed our pasta when developing these recipes. If you do not have a scale, use a dry measuring cup—tightly packed—to measure small to medium-sized pasta. To measure strand pasta, such as thin spaghetti or vermicelli, bunch it together into a tight circle; when the diameter of the pasta measures 1¾ inches, you have 12 ounces of pasta (or measure your pasta against the 1¾-inch-circle diagram on page 83). Pasta shape is important too—use the shape specified (or the alternative that is sometimes given) for best results. See the chart on page 83 for a list of pasta shapes, weights, and measurements.

Some recipes require a lid for simmering the pasta, while others are better cooked with the lid off. Tomato-based sauces fared better covered as this prevented the tomatoes from reducing too much and creating a thick, pasty sauce. Sauces made with broth or cream, however, were best cooked uncovered—most of the liquid was absorbed by the pasta and the remainder reduced down to a nice, silky sauce.

With so many recipe possibilities, where did we start? With the basics—spaghetti with a simple tomato sauce. Canned whole peeled tomatoes, pulsed briefly in a food processor with their juice, proved to be our favorite tomato product for the sauce. We stuck with the essential flavors—olive oil, onion, garlic, and basil—and cooked the pasta in our sauce. Our one-pan pasta was ready in just minutes, without any fuss. With our simple tomato sauce in place, we layered in olives, anchovies, capers, and red pepper flakes for our Pasta Puttanesca (page 82), and vodka, red pepper flakes, and cream for our Penne alla Vodka (page 86). We also made an easy spaghetti and meatballs (see page 80), which we cooked in the oven on a baking sheet for efficiency's sake, with our simple red sauce.

Some of our other dishes may surprise you. Who knew you could cook lasagna all in one skillet? We revisited the individual elements of this baked, layered pasta and created our own version (see page 98). To fit bulky lasagna noodles into the skillet, we broke them into pieces. For a rich meat sauce, we added browned meatloaf mix to canned tomatoes. With dollops of ricotta cheese melted on top (another reason to have a lid—the trapped heat helped our cheese melt), this lasagna holds a fresher appeal than its baked counterpart.

We also reinvented pasta alla carbonara for the skillet (see page 89), and we think it's better than the traditional recipe, in which the elements are prepared separately, then tossed together as quickly as possible before they can cool off and the resulting sauce clumps up. For our version, we simmered the pasta in broth, then added the sauce and served the dish piping hot directly from the skillet. This way, the sauce remains silky and smooth.

Don't think we limited our suppers to Italian-style pastas; we used instant ramen noodles to inspire our Asian-style dishes. Having ditched the dusty seasoning packets, we simmered the noodles in simply flavored broths to create our tender and tasty Kung Pao–Style Shrimp with Ramen (page 114) and Ramen with Beef, Shiitakes, and Spinach (page 112).

One final word about equipment: A 12-inch nonstick skillet worked best for these recipes, and a few recipes require an ovensafe skillet (see page 14 for our recommended nonstick skillet). If you do not have an ovensafe skillet and the recipe requires one, transfer the pasta mixture into a shallow 2-quart casserole dish before baking. Similarly, if a recipe calls for a lid and you don't have one, simply lay a sheet of aluminum foil over the skillet and crimp it around the edges to seal.

SPAGHETTI WITH TOMATO SAUCE

THE TASK AT HAND SEEMED EASY ENOUGH—build a simple tomato sauce in a skillet and then cook the pasta right in the sauce. But as we headed into the kitchen to do this, we quickly realized that we had more questions than answers. What key elements would we use to create the flavor base of our sauce? Which tomatoes would give us the freshest taste, even after being used to cook the pasta? We wanted to use the fewest ingredients possible, so we selected only the essential players—tomatoes, oil, garlic, onion, and salt—and eliminated non-essentials such as carrots, meat, and wine.

Our first hurdle was to determine which of the many canned tomato products would provide the desired results. We added a 28-ounce can of crushed tomatoes and a 14.5-ounce can of diced tomatoes to our sautéed onion and garlic. After simmering for 20 minutes, we added water (2½ cups) and our thin spaghetti. The finished dish was certainly lacking: a thick, one-dimensional sauce soaked the pasta with chunks of diced tomato. Another test, in which we crushed the diced tomatoes in the bottom of our skillet and added more water, also flopped.

It became apparent that to cook the pasta *in* the sauce, we had to build a lighter sauce. We turned our attention to the possibilities of whole peeled tomatoes. To obtain the near-smooth consistency we were looking for as the base of our sauce, we processed the tomatoes and their juice briefly in a food processor. We found the fresh taste of the whole peeled tomatoes to be the best choice—they were far superior to the canned crushed tomatoes in this dish.

Next we had to determine the right balance of flavors. Four cloves of garlic had not given us enough garlicky flavor, but six cloves was just right. For a better balance between sweet and tart, we added ¼ teaspoon of sugar. We also noted that long cooking times dulled the tomato flavor and resulted in too thick a sauce. Another question that came up was when to add the olive oil—at the beginning of cooking or at the end of cooking, which would provide a burst of fresh flavor. As we suspected, it was best to use 2 tablespoons of olive oil for cooking and a third tablespoon at the end to enhance the sauce.

With the flavor refined, we simmered our master recipe for a mere 10 minutes, building the perfect base on which to add the water and pasta. We added 2 cups of water to our skillet along with the thin spaghetti, broken in half. We found that 1 pound of pasta was too much volume for our skillet; 12 ounces of pasta provided four ample servings and a good ratio of sauce to pasta. Additional tests were done using angel hair pasta and regular spaghetti, but tasters were unanimous in their dislike of the thicker spaghetti, with many saying it was reminiscent of canned spaghetti, and the angel hair was too thin to hold onto any sauce.

We now had a finished skillet pasta that was perfectly sauced; it was neither thick and pasty nor runny on the plate. Topped with fresh chopped basil, it was pasta perfection.

Having come this far, we wondered if we could incorporate meatballs into the dish. First, we created a simple meatball mixture made with a combination of ground beef (we prefer 85 percent lean), sweet Italian sausage, moistened bread, and Parmesan cheese. Since this wouldn't be a long-simmering sauce that we could cook the meatballs in, we browned them in the skillet, which had the added benefit of creating a flavorful base for our sauce. While we proceeded with our sauce, we simply moved the meatballs to a baking sheet to finish cooking in the oven and then married sauce and meatballs in the skillet just before serving.

Spaghetti with Simple Tomato Sauce

SERVES 4

See page 83 for how to measure out long strands of pasta without using a scale. Be sure to simmer the tomatoes gently in step 2 or the sauce will become too thick.

3	(14.5-ounce) cans whole peeled tomatoes
3	tablespoons extra-virgin olive oil
1	medium onion, minced
	Salt
6	medium garlic cloves, minced or pressed through a garlic press (about 2 tablespoons)
¼	teaspoon sugar
2	cups water
12	ounces thin spaghetti or spaghettini, broken in half (see note)
	Ground black pepper
3	tablespoons chopped fresh basil leaves
	Freshly grated Parmesan cheese, for serving

SHREDDING BASIL

For larger herb leaves such as basil or mint, a cut called a chiffonade can be more attractive than a simple chop, and it also helps prevent the leaves from bruising.

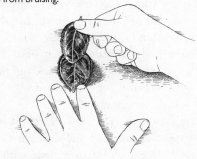

1. Stack 3 or 4 clean dry leaves.

2. Roll the leaves tightly like a cigar and then slice thin.

1. Pulse the tomatoes with their juice in a food processor until coarsely ground and no large pieces remain, about 12 pulses.

2. Heat 2 tablespoons of the oil in a 12-inch nonstick skillet over medium heat until shimmering. Add the onion and ½ teaspoon salt and cook, stirring often, until softened, 5 to 7 minutes. Stir in the garlic and cook until fragrant, about 30 seconds. Stir in the processed tomatoes and sugar. Reduce the heat to medium-low and simmer gently, stirring occasionally, until the tomatoes no longer taste raw, about 10 minutes.

3. Stir in the water, then add the pasta. Cover, increase the heat to medium-high, and cook, stirring often and adjusting the heat to maintain a vigorous simmer, until the pasta is tender, 12 to 15 minutes.

4. Stir in the remaining 1 tablespoon oil and season with salt and pepper to taste. Sprinkle with the basil and serve, passing the Parmesan separately.

➤ VARIATION
Spaghetti and Meatballs

See page 83 for how to measure out long strands of pasta without using a scale. Be sure to simmer the tomatoes gently in step 4 or the sauce will become too thick. The meatballs can be assembled ahead of time and refrigerated for up to 24 hours before cooking; do not cook the meatballs until you are ready to make the sauce.

	MEATBALLS
3	slices high-quality white sandwich bread, torn into quarters
5	tablespoons milk
½	pound 85 percent lean ground beef
½	pound sweet Italian sausage, casings removed
2	ounces Parmesan cheese, grated (1 cup)
3	tablespoons minced fresh parsley leaves
1	large egg
2	medium garlic cloves, minced or pressed through a garlic press (about 2 teaspoons)
½	teaspoon dried oregano
½	teaspoon salt
¼	teaspoon ground black pepper
2	tablespoons extra-virgin olive oil

SAUCE AND PASTA

3   (14.5-ounce) cans whole peeled tomatoes
3   tablespoons extra-virgin olive oil
1   medium onion, minced
    Salt
6   medium garlic cloves, minced or
    pressed through a garlic press
    (about 2 tablespoons)
¼   teaspoon sugar
2   cups water
12 ounces thin spaghetti or spaghettini,
    broken in half (see note)
    Ground black pepper
3   tablespoons chopped fresh basil leaves
    Freshly grated Parmesan cheese, for serving

1. FOR THE MEATBALLS: Adjust an oven rack to the middle position and heat the oven to 350 degrees. Mash the bread and milk to a paste in a large bowl. Add the beef, sausage, Parmesan, parsley, egg, garlic, oregano, salt, and pepper and mix thoroughly to combine. Pinch off 2-tablespoon-sized pieces of meat mixture and roll firmly into balls; you should have 16 meatballs.

2. Heat the oil in a 12-inch nonstick skillet over medium-high heat until shimmering. Add the meatballs and brown well on all sides, 6 to 8 minutes. Transfer the meatballs to a rimmed baking sheet and bake until cooked through, 8 to 10 minutes. Remove the meatballs from the oven, cover to keep warm, and set aside.

3. FOR THE SAUCE AND PASTA: Meanwhile, pulse the tomatoes with their juice in a food processor until coarsely ground and no large pieces remain, about 12 pulses.

4. Pour off any fat left in the skillet, add 2 tablespoons of the oil to the skillet, and heat over medium heat until shimmering. Add the onion and ½ teaspoon salt and cook, stirring often, until softened, 5 to 7 minutes. Stir in the garlic and cook until fragrant, about 30 seconds. Stir in the processed tomatoes and sugar. Reduce the heat to medium-low and simmer gently, stirring occasionally, until the tomatoes no longer taste raw, about 10 minutes.

5. Stir in the water, then add the pasta. Cover, increase the heat to medium-high, and cook,

INGREDIENTS: Canned Tomatoes

A ripe, fresh tomato should balance elements of sweetness and tangy acidity. Its texture should be somewhere between firm and pliant—certainly not mushy. Ideally, canned tomatoes, which are a better option than fresh for much of the year because they are packed at the height of ripeness, should reflect the same combination of characteristics. But with so many brands of canned tomatoes available, which one tastes best? We sampled several brands of canned whole and diced tomatoes to find out.

Whole tomatoes are steamed to remove their skins and then packed in tomato juice or puree. We prefer tomatoes packed in juice; they generally have a fresher, livelier flavor than tomatoes packed in puree, which has a cooked tomato flavor that imparts a slightly stale, tired taste to the whole can. We tasted whole tomatoes both straight from the can and in a simple tomato sauce. Progresso Whole Peeled Tomatoes with Basil finished at the head of the pack, with a bright flavor and firm texture. Be sure to buy the tomatoes packed in juice; Progresso has another, similar-looking can of whole peeled tomatoes packed in puree.

Diced tomatoes are simply whole tomatoes that have been roughly chopped during processing and then packed in juice. Tasters indicated that excessive sweetness or saltiness (from the salt added during processing), along with undesirable texture qualities, could make or break a can of tomatoes. Among the brands we tested, Muir Glen Organic Diced Tomatoes came out on top. They have a fresh, lively flavor (they are packed in juice, not puree) and are recipe-ready.

THE BEST CANNED WHOLE TOMATOES
Progresso Whole Peeled Tomatoes with Basil packed in juice have a bright flavor and firm texture.

PROGRESSO

THE BEST CANNED DICED TOMATOES
Muir Glen Organic Diced Tomatoes, also packed in juice, have a lively flavor.

MUIR GLEN

stirring often and adjusting the heat to maintain a vigorous simmer, until the pasta is tender, 12 to 15 minutes.

6. Stir in the remaining 1 tablespoon oil and season with salt and pepper to taste. Add the meatballs, coat them with sauce, and let them warm through, about 1 minute. Sprinkle with the basil and serve, passing the Parmesan separately.

Pasta Puttanesca

SAID TO HAVE BEEN CREATED BY NEAPOLITAN ladies of the night, puttanesca is a zesty sauce with an attitude. Many home cooks buy this lusty sauce by the jar, which can be disappointing. Even restaurant versions sometimes fall short, overpowered by one flavor, whether it's too fishy, too garlicky, too briny, or just plain too salty. It can also be unduly heavy or dull and monochromatic. We were searching for a satisfying sauce with aggressive but well-balanced flavors, and it had to fit the bill as a handy one-skillet supper.

We already had a good start, having created a fresh and appealing skillet tomato sauce (see page 80). Now all we had to do was incorporate the pungent ingredients that make puttanesca distinct. In our first test, we tried tossing all of the ingredients—minced garlic, minced olives, whole capers, chopped anchovies, and hot red pepper flakes—in with the tomatoes and simmering them. The result was a dull sauce with underdeveloped flavors. Clearly, we needed to rethink our method.

A technique we often use to develop a deeper flavor is to sauté the ingredients in oil, or bloom them, so that they permeate the oil. We decided to see if this method would improve our dish. First up were the anchovies. Not wanting bits of anchovy creating an uneven, fishy taste, we rinsed, minced, and sautéed them together with oil, garlic, and red pepper flakes. In two to three minutes, the anchovies melted into the oil and we had a full, rich flavor base to build on. Anchovies can be intimidating, but here they served to bring together all the other assertive ingredients in the sauce. We found that 4 teaspoons of minced anchovy (eight anchovies) was ideal and did not create a fishy sauce.

The next question we faced was how hot the sauce should be. We started testing with a full teaspoon of red pepper flakes. Our tasters were unanimous—the finished dish had way too much heat. We determined that a mere ½ teaspoon of red pepper flakes provided just the right heat level. At this point we added canned whole peeled tomatoes that we had processed briefly in a food processor, and simmered the mixture for 10 minutes to concentrate the flavors. To cook the pasta in our sauce, we had to add water (2 cups) to provide enough cooking liquid.

Finally, we had to incorporate the olives. We determined that it was best to coarsely chop them and toss them into the sauce at the very last minute, allowing the residual heat of the tomatoes to warm them. This preserved their flavor and texture and prevented them from disappearing into the sauce. The capers, rinsed thoroughly, were added along with the olives. Finished with fresh parsley, our one-skillet puttanesca was bright, boldly flavored, and perfectly balanced.

Pasta Puttanesca
SERVES 4

See page 83 for how to measure out long strands of pasta without using a scale. Be sure to simmer the tomatoes gently in step 2 or the sauce will become too thick.

3	(14.5-ounce) cans whole peeled tomatoes
3	tablespoons extra-virgin olive oil
8	anchovy fillets, rinsed and minced
6	medium garlic cloves, minced or pressed through a garlic press (about 2 tablespoons)
½	teaspoon red pepper flakes
	Salt
2	cups water
12	ounces thin spaghetti or spaghettini, broken in half (see note)
½	cup pitted kalamata olives, chopped coarse
¼	cup minced fresh parsley leaves
3	tablespoons capers, rinsed
	Ground black pepper
	Freshly grated Parmesan cheese, for serving

MEASURING PASTA

IN OUR SKILLET PASTA RECIPES, THE RATIO OF PASTA TO COOKING LIQUID IS CRITICAL to success. As the pasta cooks at a vigorous simmer, it absorbs the majority of the liquid and the rest reduces to a nice saucy consistency. Therefore, if you use more pasta than required, there won't be enough liquid to cook it through. Conversely, if you use less, the resulting sauce will be too thin or soupy. Also, pay close attention to the shape of pasta called for in each recipe, because different pasta shapes and sizes have slightly different cooking times and, therefore, not all shapes are interchangeable.

Measuring Pasta Shapes

The best method for measuring pasta is to weigh it using a scale. However, if you do not own a scale, we have provided the equivalent cup measurements for various shapes. Use dry measuring cups for the most accurate measurements, and pack them full.

PASTA TYPE	8 OUNCES	12 OUNCES
PENNE	2½ cups	3¾ cups
ZITI	2½ cups	3¾ cups
ORECCHIETTE	2½ cups	3½ cups
CAMPANELLE	3 cups	4½ cups
FARFALLE (BOW TIES)	3 cups	4½ cups
MEDIUM SHELLS	3 cups	4½ cups
SMALL SHELLS	2½ cups	3½ cups
ELBOW MACARONI	2 cups	3 cups

Measuring Strand Pasta

The best method for measuring strand pasta is to weigh it using a scale, but here's a nifty way to measure it when a scale isn't handy. When 12 ounces of uncooked thin spaghetti, spaghettini, or vermicelli are bunched together into a tight circle, the diameter measures about 1¾ inches. Either use a ruler to measure the diameter of the pasta bunch, or place the bunch inside the circle below—when the diameter for your bunch matches the diameter of the circle, it weighs 12 ounces.

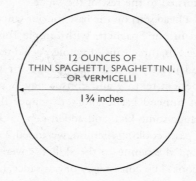

12 OUNCES OF THIN SPAGHETTI, SPAGHETTINI, OR VERMICELLI

1¾ inches

1. Pulse the tomatoes with their juice in a food processor until coarsely ground and no large pieces remain, about 12 pulses.

2. Cook 2 tablespoons of the oil, the anchovies, garlic, and red pepper flakes together in a 12-inch nonstick skillet over medium-low heat, stirring constantly, until the garlic is fragrant but not browned, 1 to 2 minutes. Stir in the processed tomatoes and ½ teaspoon salt. Simmer gently, stirring occasionally, until the tomatoes no longer taste raw, about 10 minutes.

3. Stir in the water, then add the pasta. Cover, increase the heat to medium-high, and cook, stirring often and adjusting the heat to maintain a vigorous simmer, until the pasta is tender, 12 to 15 minutes.

4. Stir in the remaining 1 tablespoon oil, the olives, parsley, and capers, season with salt and pepper to taste, and serve, passing the Parmesan separately.

PASTA ALLA NORMA

THIS TRADITIONAL SICILIAN DISH, REPORTedly named to honor Vincenzo Bellini's opera *Norma*, features a short tubular pasta, like penne, tossed with a gutsy yet simple tomato sauce studded with chunks of eggplant. Hefty amounts of garlic, red pepper flakes, and basil give this sauce its moxie, and some ricotta salata (ricotta that has been aged and hardened) adds a counterpoint of pungent creaminess. This is not your typical vegetable pasta sauce; the eggplant takes on a meaty quality, making this dish a rich and hearty vegetarian meal. Our goal was to turn this classic Italian dish into a one-pan pasta dinner, without compromising the texture of the eggplant.

With simple sauces like this one, building a good base of flavor is key. We began with the eggplant and focused on extracting as much flavor from it as possible in a short amount of time. Many people complain that their eggplant dishes are tough, pithy, and astringently bitter; or oil-soaked, slimy, and tasteless. This *is* preventable. Eggplant can—and should—be firm and meaty, with a rich, sweet, nutty flavor. We find that eggplants, as long as they are not huge, are rarely bitter. We didn't want to bother with salting the eggplant (salting extracts some of the juices and helps promote browning), because of the time involved. Instead we found that a sauté in a generous amount of olive oil brought out the robust quality we were after. One word of caution: Do not stir the eggplant too much as it cooks. This will cause the eggplant to break down and not brown properly. After browning the eggplant, we turned to the rest of the sauce.

We had a head start on the base for our sauce. As we learned in our Spaghetti with Simple Tomato Sauce (page 80), three cans of whole peeled tomatoes pulsed briefly in the food processor provide the perfect texture and consistency. A good amount of minced garlic and red pepper flakes gave the sauce some kick and added depth. Using our skillet pasta cooking method, we added 2 cups of water and the penne to the skillet, covered it, and let it cook. The consistency of our sauce, however, had a detrimental effect on the texture of the eggplant. By the time the sauce was done and the pasta finished cooking (about 25 minutes of total simmering time), the eggplant was mushy. We quickly realized there was good reason to stir the sautéed eggplant in at the very end.

In our next attempt, we sautéed the eggplant first, then transferred it to a bowl and set it aside. We built the tomato sauce in the same skillet, cooked the pasta in the sauce, and finally stirred the eggplant back in for a brief simmer. The eggplant was warmed through and retained its shape, giving the sauce a pleasantly chunky texture with meaty cubes of eggplant.

With shaved ricotta salata and a handful of fresh basil mixed in at the last minute, this skillet dish was every bit as good as the Sicilian classic.

Pasta alla Norma
SERVES 4

You can substitute ziti, medium shells, farfalle, campanelle, or orecchiette for the penne; however, the cup measurements will vary. See page 83 for more information on measuring pasta. If you cannot find ricotta salata cheese, substitute shaved Parmesan or Pecorino Romano; see page 86 for an illustration on how to shave cheese. It is important to stir the eggplant as little as possible when browning it in step 1, or it will turn mushy and not brown well. Be sure to simmer the tomatoes gently in step 3 or the sauce will become too thick.

5	tablespoons extra-virgin olive oil
2	medium eggplants (about 2 pounds), ends trimmed, cut into ½-inch cubes
	Salt
3	(14.5-ounce) cans whole peeled tomatoes
3	medium garlic cloves, minced or pressed through a garlic press (about 1 tablespoon)
¼–½	teaspoon red pepper flakes
2	cups water
12	ounces (about 3¾ cups) penne (see note)
4	ounces ricotta salata cheese, shaved (about 1 cup; see note)
¼	cup minced fresh basil leaves
	Ground black pepper
	Freshly grated Parmesan cheese, for serving

1. Heat 4 tablespoons of the oil in a 12-inch nonstick skillet over medium-high heat until shimmering. Add the eggplant and ¼ teaspoon salt and cook until it begins to brown, about 4 minutes. Reduce the heat to medium-low and continue to cook, stirring occasionally, until the eggplant is fully tender and lightly browned, 10 to 15 minutes longer. Transfer the eggplant to a bowl, cover to keep warm, and set aside.

2. Meanwhile, pulse the tomatoes with their juice in a food processor until coarsely ground and no large pieces remain, about 12 pulses.

3. Add the remaining 1 tablespoon oil, the garlic, and red pepper flakes to the skillet and cook over medium heat until fragrant, about 30 seconds. Stir in the processed tomatoes and ¼ teaspoon salt. Reduce

the heat to medium-low and simmer gently, stirring occasionally, until the tomatoes no longer taste raw, about 10 minutes.

4. Stir in the water, then add the pasta. Cover, increase the heat to medium-high, and cook, stirring often and adjusting the heat to maintain a vigorous simmer, until the pasta is tender, 15 to 18 minutes.

5. Stir in the eggplant and ricotta salata and cook until warmed through, about 1 minute. Stir in the basil, season with salt and pepper to taste, and serve, passing the Parmesan separately.

PENNE ALLA VODKA

PENNE ALLA VODKA QUICKLY BECAME A featured item at trendy restaurants when it won first place in a 1970s recipe contest promoting vodka. This dish relies on a few simple ingredients—cream, red pepper flakes, and vodka—to emphasize the pure flavor of tomatoes. Our goal was to fine-tune this modern classic to strike the right balance of sweet, tangy, spicy, and creamy, all in one skillet.

Most recipes for penne alla vodka begin with a basic tomato sauce (canned tomatoes, garlic, and red pepper flakes sautéed in olive oil), but the textures run the gamut from thick-and-chunky to ultra-smooth. Tasters preferred a middle-of-the-road texture, so we pulsed whole peeled tomatoes in the food processor, which provided the desired consistency and helped the sauce cling to the pasta. In 10 minutes, our simmering sauce was just right; now we had to bring the flavors together.

First, we sautéed some minced onion in the skillet, before simmering the tomatoes, to underscore the tomatoes' sweetness. We found that this sweetness, which was essential to the balanced flavor profile we sought, faded when we added the cream and vodka later on. We stirred in a tablespoon of tomato paste, which both reinforced the sweetness and provided depth to the overall flavor of the sauce. Also, we noticed that when we added the vodka near the end of the recipe, as many recipes do, its flavor dominated the finished dish. We looked more closely at the role alcohol was playing in our penne alla vodka.

Besides cutting through the richness of the cream, vodka contributes another nuance to the sauce, which tasters identified as "zinginess." Raw alcohol is an irritant, creating a stinging sensation on the tongue and in the throat. When cooked, alcohol doesn't entirely evaporate, and a mild burning sensation (aka zinginess) is left behind. It was this sensation we wanted in our dish, not an overly boozy flavor. We realized we'd have to add the vodka to the skillet earlier in the process (with the pasta and water), so that the alcohol mostly—but not completely—cooked off. Following our skillet pasta method, we stirred a small amount of vodka into the sauce when we added 2 cups of water and 12 ounces of pasta. Then we covered the skillet and let the sauce and pasta cook together at a vigorous simmer. Fifteen minutes later, the pasta was just tender and had absorbed maximum flavor.

It was time for the finishing touches: We swirled in ½ cup of heavy cream for a rich but not over-the-top consistency, then we garnished the pasta with chopped basil and grated Parmesan. Finally, we had a quick and delicious penne alla vodka that struck the flavor balance we'd been looking for.

INGREDIENTS: Tomato Paste

Canned tomato products are pantry staples, and one of our favorites is tomato paste. It's great for adding a slightly deeper, rounder flavor and color to soups, stews, and sauces.

Our favorite tomato paste—which comes in a tube, not a can—is Amore Tomato Paste, which we liked better than the six other brands we tested (including Hunt's). This tomato paste has a fresher, fuller tomato flavor. And because it's packaged in a tube, Amore lacks the tinny aftertaste that plagues many canned tomato pastes. One note: the label marks this as a "double concentrated" tomato paste, but in our testing, we found no differences between this and other tomato pastes. There's no need to use half as much Amore when tomato paste is called for in a recipe, just use the amount called for.

THE BEST TOMATO PASTE
Amore Tomato Paste has a fresher tomato flavor than its canned competitors.

AMORE

Penne alla Vodka
SERVES 4

You can substitute ziti, medium shells, farfalle, campanelle, or orecchiette for the penne; however, the cup measurements will vary. See page 83 for more information on measuring pasta. If possible, use premium vodka; inexpensive brands will taste harsh in this sauce. Pepper vodka imparts a pleasant flavor and can be substituted for plain. Be sure to simmer the tomatoes gently in step 2 or the sauce will become too thick.

3	(14.5-ounce) cans whole peeled tomatoes
2	tablespoons extra-virgin olive oil
¼	cup minced onion
I	tablespoon tomato paste
	Salt
2	medium garlic cloves, minced or pressed through a garlic press (about 2 teaspoons)
¼–½	teaspoon red pepper flakes
2	cups water
⅓	cup vodka
12	ounces (about 3¾ cups) penne (see note)
½	cup heavy cream
2	tablespoons minced fresh basil leaves
	Ground black pepper
	Freshly grated Parmesan cheese, for serving

1. Pulse the tomatoes with their juice in a food processor until coarsely ground and no large pieces remain, about 12 pulses.

SHAVING CHEESE

Sometimes thin shavings of cheese are nicer than just using grated cheese, and can quickly dress up an otherwise simple bowl of pasta. To quickly achieve paper-thin slices of a hard cheese, such as Parmesan, Pecorino Romano, or ricotta salata, simply run your vegetable peeler over a block of cheese using a light touch.

2. Heat the oil in a 12-inch nonstick skillet over medium heat until shimmering. Add the onion, tomato paste, and ½ teaspoon salt and cook, stirring often, until softened, 5 to 7 minutes. Stir in the garlic and red pepper flakes and cook until fragrant, about 30 seconds. Stir in the processed tomatoes. Reduce the heat to medium-low and simmer gently, stirring occasionally, until the tomatoes no longer taste raw, about 10 minutes.

3. Stir in the water and vodka, then add the pasta. Cover, increase the heat to medium-high, and cook, stirring often and adjusting the heat to maintain a vigorous simmer, until the pasta is tender, 15 to 18 minutes.

4. Stir in the cream and cook until hot, about 1 minute. Stir in the basil and season with salt and pepper to taste. Serve, passing the Parmesan separately.

PASTA QUATTRO FORMAGGI

WE LOVE MAC AND CHEESE, ESPECIALLY OUR skillet adaptation (see page 101), but sometimes we get a hankering for the Italian version, *pasta quattro formaggi*. This hearty dish is a rich and sophisticated blend of pasta and four cheeses. Our goal was to turn this recipe into a skillet pasta without losing the hallmark silkiness of the sauce.

The first issue we encountered—in terms of both flavor and texture—was, naturally, the cheese. The recipes we found called for varying combinations and amounts of Italian cheeses. Recipes contained anywhere from 1 cup to 6½ cups of cheese for 1 pound of pasta, and the selection of cheeses that turned up in our research was just as dizzying: Asiago, fontina, Taleggio, Pecorino Romano, mascarpone, mozzarella, Gorgonzola, Parmesan, and ricotta. Some initial testing reduced the scope quickly: Mascarpone and ricotta added neither flavor nor texture, and Asiago was bland. Pasta tossed with mozzarella was gooey and greasy, whereas Taleggio was not only difficult to obtain but also made the pasta too rich and gluey. Tasters favored a combination of Italian fontina (which is creamier and better-tasting than other versions of this cheese), Gorgonzola, Pecorino Romano, and Parmesan. For our skillet adaptation, we found that 5 ounces of cheese total (just under 2 cups) was the right amount for 12 ounces of pasta.

With our winning cheese combination selected, we turned our attention to incorporating it into the dish. Using our skillet pasta cooking method, we knew this would be a tricky proposition. Heating the cheeses and cream together, then adding the pasta and water to the sauce to cook through, produced an ugly mess with curdled or separated cheese that had lost its flavor. The cheese would need to wait until the end.

Instead, we began by sautéing shallots in butter until softened, then added wine to deglaze the pan and cut through the richness of the sauce. Water, heavy cream, and penne were added to the skillet and simmered until the pasta was tender. After cooking our way through dozens of batches of pasta quattro formaggi with varying amounts of water and cream, we settled on 4¾ cups water combined with 1¼ cups cream. This provided just the right amount of sauce for the cheese to melt into after the pasta was finished cooking.

We had learned that to create the best flavor, the cheeses had to be added off the heat. Then a quick toss melted the cheeses without cooking them. Our authentically flavored dish was simplified and ready to go, and we didn't have to sacrifice any flavor or texture.

Pasta Quattro Formaggi
SERVES 4

You can substitute ziti, medium shells, farfalle, campanelle, or orecchiette for the penne; however, the cup measurements will vary. See page 83 for more information on measuring pasta.

2	tablespoons unsalted butter
2	medium shallots, minced (about 6 tablespoons)
	Salt
¾	cup dry white wine
4¾	cups water
1¼	cups heavy cream
12	ounces (about 3¾ cups) penne (see note)
2	ounces Gorgonzola cheese, crumbled (½ cup)
1½	ounces Italian fontina cheese, shredded (¾ cup)
¾	ounce Pecorino Romano cheese, grated (⅓ cup)
¾	ounce Parmesan cheese, grated (⅓ cup)
	Ground black pepper

1. Melt the butter in a 12-inch nonstick skillet over medium heat. Add the shallots and ½ teaspoon salt and cook until softened, about 1 minute. Stir in the wine and simmer until nearly evaporated, 2 to 4 minutes.

2. Stir in the water and cream, then add the pasta. Increase the heat to high, and cook at a vigorous simmer, stirring often, until the pasta is tender and the liquid has thickened, 15 to 18 minutes.

3. Off the heat, stir in the Gorgonzola, fontina, Pecorino, and Parmesan, one at a time, until melted and combined. Season with salt and pepper to taste and serve.

PASTA ALLA CARBONARA

CARBONARA, A POPULAR ROMAN DISH, features a creamy egg sauce that cooks into a velvety consistency from the heat of just-drained pasta. Shards of bacon punctuate the dish and hot garlic gives it a kick. This is no diet food, but the indulgent nature of carbonara is one reason it is offered on every trattoria menu.

All too often, though, carbonara is a just a boring dish of spaghetti smothered in a dull, heavy sauce that makes you wonder if you ordered Alfredo by mistake. And even well-made carbonara can be destroyed by a waitperson; if the dish is not brought to the table immediately, the sauce congeals and the pasta strands get sticky and rubbery. Our goal was to adapt this Roman classic for the skillet, with a rich, creamy sauce that coated the pasta well.

BREAKING LONG-STRAND PASTA IN HALF

Though we don't normally recommend breaking pasta strands in half, this step makes it easier to cook thin spaghetti or toast vermicelli in a skillet.

1. To keep the pasta from flying every which way in the kitchen, roll up the bundle of pasta in a kitchen towel that overlaps the pasta by 3 or 4 inches at both ends.

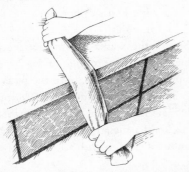

2. Holding both ends firmly, center the rolled bundle over the edge of a table or counter. Push down with both hands to break the pasta in the middle of the bundle.

Pasta alla carbonara is not only quick to prepare, but it relies on ingredients most cooks almost always have on hand—pasta, bacon, and eggs. We knew from prior testing that thin spaghetti is the best type of spaghetti to cook in a skillet because it cooks through more evenly than regular spaghetti, which is thicker.

Next up was the bacon. It is difficult to find the traditionally used *guanciale* (salt-cured pork jowl) in the United States, so we centered our tests on available options: bacon and pancetta (which is similar to American bacon but is cured rather than smoked). The pancetta gave the carbonara a substantial pork flavor, but tasters weren't crazy about its texture, which became chewy in the sauce even after being thinly sliced and fried. The bacon—thick-cut style to mimic the guanciale—managed to retain much of its crisp texture and added a pleasantly sweet and smoky flavor to the dish that tasters preferred. Eggs form the base of the sauce that binds the other ingredients to the slender strands of pasta. Basing our recipe on 12 ounces of pasta, we started out with one egg, but this sauce was thick and clumped when introduced to the hot pasta. Three eggs made a sauce too soupy and wet; two eggs were just right. The sauce was silky in texture, had the fortitude to cling to the spaghetti, and was moist and rich.

The last two variables were wine and cream. We tried multiple variations—a dry red wine (common in authentic recipes), vermouth (which appeared in only one recipe but piqued our interest), and a dry white wine (which was favored by the majority of the recipes we found). White wine created the most impact and resonance. It was full-flavored, and its acidic nature cut through the taste of the bacon, brightening the flavor of the dish. To bring the wine's full presence to the table, we needed to use ¾ cup. By reducing the wine in the skillet, before adding the broth, water, and spaghetti, we were able to develop the overall flavor of the dish to its potential.

With our ingredients largely in place, we turned our attention to the cooking method. In a traditional carbonara, cooked and drained pasta is tossed with eggs and cheese to make the sauce, which can quickly congeal and make a mess. The secret to our recipe was to simmer the pasta in a mixture of chicken broth and water until cooked, remove the skillet from the heat, then stir the eggs right into the skillet with the heavy cream and cheese (we preferred Pecorino Romano to Parmesan). The cream, which we had cut down from the usual ½ cup to ⅓ cup for a slightly lighter sauce, helped to loosen the sauce to the perfect consistency and prevented the eggs from scrambling. The heat from the pan melted the cheese to thicken the sauce. Now we just had to sprinkle the crisp bacon on top and dig in.

Our finished dish was so rich and creamy, and the pasta so evenly coated, that it seemed like pasta alla carbonara was destined to be a skillet superstar from the very beginning.

Pasta alla Carbonara

SERVES 4

See page 83 for how to measure out long strands of pasta without using a scale. Adding the eggs and cream to the skillet in step 5 as soon as the pasta has finished cooking is crucial because the heat from the pasta will cook the eggs and cream into a thick sauce. The sauce will dry out quickly, so serve the pasta immediately.

6	slices thick-cut bacon, cut into ½-inch pieces
5	medium garlic cloves, minced or pressed through a garlic press (about 5 teaspoons)
	Ground black pepper
¾	cup dry white wine
3	cups water
3	cups low-sodium chicken broth
	Salt
12	ounces thin spaghetti or spaghettini, broken in half (see note) (see the illustrations on page 88)
⅓	cup heavy cream
2	large eggs
1½	ounces Pecorino Romano cheese, grated (¾ cup)

1. Cook the bacon in a 12-inch skillet over medium-high heat until lightly browned and crisp, about 8 minutes. Transfer the bacon to a paper towel–lined plate and set aside. Pour off all but 1 tablespoon of the bacon fat.

2. Add the garlic and ½ teaspoon pepper to the bacon fat left in the skillet and cook over medium heat until fragrant, about 30 seconds. Stir in the wine and simmer until nearly evaporated, 2 to 4 minutes.

3. Stir in the water, broth, and ½ teaspoon salt, then add the pasta. Increase the heat to high and cook at a vigorous simmer, stirring often, until the pasta is tender and the liquid has thickened, 12 to 15 minutes.

4. Meanwhile, whisk the cream, eggs, and Pecorino together in a small bowl.

5. Off the heat, pour the egg mixture over the pasta and toss to combine. Add the bacon, season with salt and pepper to taste, and serve immediately.

SHRIMP SCAMPI WITH CAMPANELLE

NEARLY EVERY ITALIAN RESTAURANT IN THE United States features a shrimp scampi dish, and for good reason. It's a simply prepared dish, full of tender shrimp in a garlicky, lemony sauce. The linguine, with the full flavors of garlic and olive oil, slips and slides under succulent shrimp before it's wrapped around a fork and disappears from the plate. It's the kind of meal we never get tired of eating.

We set out to transform this dish from seafood heaven into a quick skillet pasta meal, and realized our main concern was the star ingredient—we've seen too many scampi dishes ruined with overcooked, rubbery shrimp. Our established skillet pasta method, which relies on building a sauce and cooking the pasta in it, presented a serious issue for our scampi. A typical scampi-style sauce is based on olive oil and garlic, so we had to devise a way to combine all of these elements and still retain the individual bright flavors, while also making sure the shrimp stayed plump and tender.

To prevent the shrimp from becoming tough, we knew they would have to be cooked quickly and at a high heat. We sautéed them in a single layer, without moving them, just long enough for the shrimp to become spotty brown on one side. This allowed us to develop a strong shrimp flavor in the skillet without overcooking the shrimp. We also amplified the flavor—and enhanced the browning—by revisiting a trick we used in our Pan-Seared Shrimp with Parsley-Lemon Butter (page 25): We tossed

PEELING GARLIC

Unless whole cloves are needed, we crush garlic cloves with the side of a large chef's knife to loosen the skins and make them easier to remove.

the shrimp with a little sugar prior to cooking. The shrimp were then stirred and cooked for an additional 30 seconds until almost, but not quite, done. We put them aside while we built the sauce, planning to finish them up in the skillet, where they could absorb the flavor of a garlicky sauce.

For the sauce, we began our tests with clam broth and water, thinking that the clam juice would naturally reinforce the shellfish flavor. Much to our surprise, the clam broth made a sauce that was so strongly flavored it masked the subtle complexity of the shrimp. Chicken broth turned out to be a much better choice, in spite of our initial reservations (it seemed a bit unusual to use chicken broth in a seafood dish).

We were now ready to incorporate the garlic and lemon flavors so essential to scampi. The garlic was too bitter if simply sautéed in olive oil, so we returned to a technique that we had used in other recipes—sautéing the garlic over very low heat until golden brown and mellow to develop a nutty flavor. For further flavor, we added spicy red pepper flakes. We were closing in on our sauce but it still lacked the garlicky punch our tasters craved. Was there a way to add raw garlic to this dish without it being too pungent? We made a paste with salt and two cloves of raw garlic, which we combined with 2 tablespoons of extra virgin olive oil. Added to our skillet after the pasta was done, this mixture did the trick.

The last element to be determined was the pasta shape. We began our testing with thin spaghetti, because it closely approximated the linguine pasta that we tend to find in scampi. After many batches of scampi, each using a different amount of liquid, we were still unhappy with the consistency of the sauce—it just felt too slick for the long strands of pasta and ended up being either too heavy or too loose. Campanelle, a shorter pasta shape, worked better; the smaller pasta offered many nooks and crannies to trap the sauce and afforded the dish a better balance overall.

We were now able to return the sautéed shrimp to the skillet to finish. With a little fresh lemon juice, lemon zest, and minced parsley added at the very end, this shrimp scampi had bright flavors and was full of tender shrimp.

Shrimp Scampi with Campanelle
SERVES 4

Be sure not to cook the shrimp through completely in step 2 or they will overcook when returned to the skillet in step 5. If you use larger or smaller shrimp than called for below, change the cooking times accordingly. You can substitute penne, ziti, medium shells, farfalle, or orecchiette for the campanelle; however, the cup measurements will vary. See page 83 for more information on measuring pasta.

2	medium garlic cloves, minced to a paste (see the illustration below)
5	tablespoons extra-virgin olive oil
1	pound extra-large shrimp (21 to 25 per pound), peeled and deveined (see the illustration on page 235)
	Salt and ground black pepper
1/8	teaspoon sugar
9	medium garlic cloves, minced or pressed through a garlic press (about 3 tablespoons)
1/4	teaspoon red pepper flakes
1/2	cup dry white wine
3	cups water
2	cups low-sodium chicken broth
12	ounces (about 4 1/2 cups) campanelle (see note)
3	tablespoons minced fresh parsley leaves
3	tablespoons juice from 1 lemon
1/2	teaspoon grated zest from 1 lemon

MINCING GARLIC TO A PASTE

To create garlic paste for our Shrimp Scampi with Campanelle, you can use salt crystals to break down the garlic. Start by mincing the garlic as fine as you can. Sprinkle the minced garlic with salt, then drag the side of the knife over the garlic-salt mixture to form a fine puree. Continue to mince and drag the knife as necessary to get to this texture. If possible, use kosher or coarse salt for this job; the larger crystals do a better job than fine table salt of breaking down the garlic.

1. Combine the garlic paste and 2 tablespoons of the oil in a small bowl; set aside. In a medium bowl, toss the shrimp with ¼ teaspoon salt, ⅛ teaspoon pepper, and the sugar.

2. Heat 1 tablespoon more oil in a 12-inch nonstick skillet over high heat until just smoking. Add the shrimp in a single layer and cook without stirring until beginning to brown, about 1 minute. Stir the shrimp and continue to cook until they are light pink and all but the very center is opaque, about 30 seconds. Transfer the shrimp to a bowl, cover to keep warm, and set aside.

3. Let the skillet cool slightly for about 1 minute. Add the remaining 2 tablespoons oil, the minced garlic, and red pepper flakes and cook over low heat, stirring constantly, until the garlic is sticky and golden, about 4 minutes. Stir in the wine, increase the heat to medium-high, and simmer until the liquid has nearly evaporated, 1 to 2 minutes.

4. Stir in the water, broth, and ½ teaspoon salt, then add the pasta. Increase the heat to high, and cook at a vigorous simmer, stirring often, until the pasta is tender and the liquid has thickened, 15 to 18 minutes.

5. Return the shrimp, along with any accumulated juices, to the skillet and cook until warmed through, about 30 seconds. Off the heat, stir in the garlic-oil mixture, parsley, lemon juice, and lemon zest. Season with salt and pepper to taste and serve.

PASTA PRIMAVERA

DESPITE THE NAME, PASTA PRIMAVERA ORIGInated in the United States, not Italy. This fresh-flavored dish, full of crisp vegetables, was created in the 1970s by the owner of Le Cirque, New York's famed French restaurant. It was dubbed spaghetti primavera—primavera is Italian for "spring"—and became a sensation in a New York minute.

This dish is a sure winner with guests, but for the cook, it's a labor of love. For one thing, it calls for blanching the green vegetables separately to retain their individual character; if the same pot is used for each vegetable, this step can take almost an hour. As if that weren't enough, once the vegetables

are blanched, you need five more pots: one to cook the vegetables in garlicky olive oil, one to sauté mushrooms, one to make a fresh tomato sauce flavored with basil, one to make a cream sauce with butter and Parmesan, and one to cook the pasta. While these steps aren't difficult, the timing is complicated—this dish is better suited to a professional kitchen with several cooks. But we love pasta primavera, so we wanted to see if we could simplify the process enough so it would require just one skillet and still keep the fresh flavors that are the hallmark of this recipe.

The first issue was to decide which vegetables were essential. Many of the ingredients in the original dish, such as broccoli, green beans, and zucchini, are not actually spring vegetables. We began testing spring vegetables not traditionally used in primavera and soon realized why they were not included. Artichokes were way too much work to prepare. The sweet, anise flavor of fennel overwhelmed the flavors of the other vegetables, and snow peas seemed superfluous, as the original recipe uses shelled peas. Asparagus, on the other hand, was a hit, so we included it along with peas (we liked the convenience and quality of frozen peas), zucchini, and mushrooms.

The next step was cooking and incorporating the vegetables into the dish. Knowing we didn't want to spend extra time blanching each vegetable individually, we searched for a different method. Sautéing the vegetables individually in the skillet worked, but tasters felt that the expected fresh and crisp qualities were now missing. We then tried pan-steaming the green vegetables briefly in a splash of water and a pat of butter until they were crisp, tender, and bright green. Now we were on the right track—this dish was clean and fresh tasting. We also discovered that we could skip pan-steaming the peas; they only needed a brief stint in the skillet when finishing the dish to shake off their frost, leaving their fresh flavor and vibrant color intact. The mushrooms, however, would still need to be browned to cook off their moisture and bring out their flavor. As for the fresh tomato sauce, we took a hint from other streamlined primavera recipes and skipped this ingredient. Instead, we focused on the cream sauce.

To build flavor in the sauce, garlic and butter proved essential. Tasters preferred the sweet, rich flavor of the butter to the flavor of olive oil. Using our skillet pasta method, we added a combination of vegetable broth and water (4 cups total) and our pasta to the skillet. Because we would be bulking up our dish by adding vegetables to the skillet, we used less pasta (8 ounces) than called for in our other skillet pasta recipes. We chose the trumpet-shaped campanelle, which stands up well to bites of vegetables; it absorbed most of the liquid as it simmered, and the remainder of the liquid reduced to a nice saucy consistency. We added the reserved vegetables and ½ cup cream and let the cream reduce for just a minute before stirring in a generous amount of Parmesan cheese and a handful of fresh chopped basil. The sauce was silky and creamy, but some tasters found it a tad too rich. A healthy dose of fresh lemon juice cut through the rich flavor and gave the dish a bright acidity that reminded us of spring.

Our recipe was just as delicious as the more laborious original, and we had just one pan to clean, not six. We had also reduced total preparation and cooking time by more than half. Our Pasta Primavera is a perfect weeknight meal when you are craving fresh vegetables and pasta.

TRIMMING TOUGH ENDS FROM ASPARAGUS

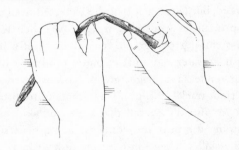

In our tests, we found that the tough, woody part of the stem will break off in just the right place if you hold the spear the right way. With one hand, hold the asparagus about halfway down the stalk; with the thumb and index fingers of the other hand, hold the spear about an inch up from the bottom. Bend the stalk until it snaps.

Pasta Primavera

SERVES 4

Fresh flavors are the key to success in this classic dish. We prefer the lighter flavor of vegetable broth here, but low-sodium chicken broth can be used instead. You can substitute penne, ziti, medium shells, farfalle, or orecchiette for the campanelle; however, the cup measurements will vary. See page 83 for more information on measuring pasta.

3	tablespoons unsalted butter
½	pound asparagus (½ bunch), tough ends trimmed (see the illustration at left) and sliced on the bias into 1-inch lengths
1	large zucchini (about 12 ounces), quartered lengthwise and cut into ½-inch chunks
2¼	cups water
	Salt
4	ounces white mushrooms, wiped clean and quartered
	Ground black pepper
3	medium garlic cloves, minced or pressed through a garlic press (about 1 tablespoon)
2	cups low-sodium vegetable broth
8	ounces (about 3 cups) campanelle (see note)
½	cup heavy cream
1	cup frozen peas
1	ounce Parmesan cheese, grated (½ cup), plus extra for serving
¼	cup minced fresh basil leaves
1	tablespoon juice from 1 lemon

1. Melt 1 tablespoon of the butter in a 12-inch nonstick skillet over medium heat. Add the asparagus, zucchini, ¼ cup of the water, and a pinch of salt. Cover and cook until the vegetables are crisp-tender, 3 to 4 minutes. Uncover and continue to cook until the vegetables are just tender and the liquid has nearly evaporated, 1 to 2 minutes longer. Transfer the vegetables to a bowl, cover to keep warm, and set aside.

2. Add 1 tablespoon more butter to the skillet and melt over medium heat. Add the mushrooms and a pinch of salt and cook until they have released

their moisture and are golden brown, about 5 minutes. Transfer the mushrooms to the bowl with the asparagus and zucchini, season with salt and pepper to taste, and cover to keep warm.

3. Wipe out the skillet with paper towels, add the remaining 1 tablespoon butter, and melt over medium heat. Stir in the garlic and cook until fragrant, about 30 seconds. Stir in the remaining 2 cups water, the broth, and ½ teaspoon salt, then add the pasta. Increase the heat to high and cook at a vigorous simmer, stirring often, until the pasta is tender and the liquid has thickened, 15 to 18 minutes.

4. Stir in the cream, peas, and cooked vegetables and cook until the cream has thickened and the vegetables are warmed through, about 1 minute. Off the heat, stir in the Parmesan, basil, and lemon juice and season with salt and pepper to taste. Serve, passing the extra Parmesan separately.

PASTA WITH PEAS AND PROSCIUTTO

WE COMBED THOUGH PILES OF COOKBOOKS for a new skillet pasta idea and found quite a few recipes for pasta with peas and prosciutto. Peas and pork (in some manifestation) taste delicious together, but the textural contrast of the two is what really steals the show; the subtle pop of the pea's shell and its starchy flesh are juxtaposed with the crisp yet chewy strands of sautéed prosciutto. Add to that pasta and a rich sauce, and you have something to talk about. With the three ingredients of pasta, prosciutto, and peas well established, we set out to incorporate them into a flavorful skillet pasta dinner that was quick and easy.

We started at the very beginning, by deciding what our base would be—a red sauce or a creamy white sauce? Tasters unanimously favored the idea of a creamy white sauce—they felt a red sauce would compete with the peas and prosciutto, while a creamy sauce would add a subtle richness. We

sautéed onion and garlic for flavor, then added 2 cups of cream along with some water, stirred in the pasta, and simmered it uncovered over high heat until the pasta was tender. The resulting sauce was bland and too thick. We replaced some water with vegetable broth to add flavor, and reduced the cream to 1 cup. The texture of the sauce was much improved, but tasters wanted something to bring out the meaty flavor of the prosciutto in the finished dish. Finally, we came up with the winning combination of chicken broth, water, and cream. We found that 5 cups of liquid (2 cups each of chicken broth and water and 1 cup cream) was the right amount for 12 ounces of pasta. The pasta— we chose medium shells, although many similar-sized shapes would also work well to capture the sauce—absorbed most of the liquid as is it cooked, and the remainder of the liquid reduced to a nice saucy consistency.

Next we moved on to the peas. While we normally avoid frozen vegetables, peas are an exception. Peas are so delicate that their flavor is compromised as soon as they are picked; like corn, their sugars instantly begin converting to starch after harvesting. Fortunately, frozen peas are processed within hours of being picked, when their flavor is at its peak. We knew they would need just a minute of cooking—after the pasta was done— to warm through and maintain their fresh, vibrant flavor.

We turned our attention to the prosciutto and how best to incorporate it into the sauce. Prosciutto is an uncooked, unsmoked ham that is salted and cured for anywhere from eight months to two years, depending on the manufacturer. One of the secrets of traditional prosciutto-making is that the pigs are fed on the leftover whey from the production of Parmesan cheese, which imparts its characteristic nuttiness to the meat. While prosciutto can be eaten raw, and generally is, we sautéed it briefly in olive oil to crisp it up, then set it aside until the end, when we sprinkled it over the pasta. Tasters favored this approach because it provided a textural contrast with the peas.

Our dish was good, but tasters wanted a bit more creaminess. Looking back at our research, we remembered that fresh ricotta had been used in some recipes. Ricotta, with its hint of sweetness, pairs particularly well with peas, but its grainy texture can be distracting when stirred into a hot sauce. To combat this, we placed heaping tablespoons of ricotta over the pasta (as we do in our Meaty Lasagna, page 98) just as it finished cooking, covered the dish, and let it stand off the heat so the ricotta would melt slightly. The sauce was at once silky and creamy. We added Parmesan and a touch of lemon zest to the ricotta, which perked things up and complemented the prosciutto. For an even fresher flavor reminiscent of spring, we finished our dish with a handful of fresh mint.

Pasta with Peas and Prosciutto

SERVES 4

We recommend using either whole milk or part-skim ricotta here, but do not use fat-free ricotta, which has a very dry texture and bland flavor. You can substitute ziti, farfalle, campanelle, or orecchiette for the shells; however, the cup measurements will vary. See page 83 for more information on measuring pasta.

1	cup ricotta cheese (see note)
1	ounce Parmesan cheese, grated (½ cup)
1	teaspoon grated zest from 1 lemon
	Salt and ground black pepper
1	tablespoon extra-virgin olive oil
4	ounces thinly sliced prosciutto, cut into ¼-inch pieces
1	medium onion, minced
2	medium garlic cloves, minced or pressed through a garlic press, (about 2 teaspoons)
2	cups low-sodium chicken broth
2	cups water
1	cup heavy cream
12	ounces (about 4½ cups) medium pasta shells (see note)
2	cups frozen peas
2	tablespoons unsalted butter, cut into 8 pieces
1	tablespoon juice from 1 lemon
2	tablespoons minced fresh mint leaves

1. Combine the ricotta, Parmesan, lemon zest, ¼ teaspoon salt, and ¼ teaspoon pepper in a medium bowl and set aside.

2. Heat the oil in a 12-inch nonstick skillet over medium-high heat until shimmering. Add the prosciutto and cook until well browned and crisp, 2 to 3 minutes. Transfer the prosciutto to a paper towel–lined plate, leaving the oil in the skillet.

3. Add the onion and ½ teaspoon salt to the oil left in the skillet and cook over medium heat, stirring often, until softened, 5 to 7 minutes. Stir in the garlic and cook until fragrant, about 30 seconds.

4. Stir in the broth, water, and cream, then add the pasta. Increase the heat to high and cook at a vigorous simmer, stirring often, until the pasta is tender and the liquid has thickened, 15 to 18 minutes.

5. Stir in the peas, butter, and lemon juice and cook until the peas are hot, about 1 minute. Season with salt and pepper to taste. Dot heaping tablespoons of the ricotta mixture over the noodles. Cover and let stand off the heat until the cheese warms and softens, 2 to 4 minutes. Sprinkle with the crisp prosciutto and mint and serve.

PENNE SKILLET SUPPERS

HAVING MASTERED SKILLET VERSIONS OF classic Italian pasta dishes, we turned our attention to developing lighter-sauced skillet pasta dishes that were still hearty enough to be complete meals. For the pasta, penne was our favorite (though other shapes worked as well) because it cooked to a perfect al dente in a mixture of broth and water, cream, and/or wine, and the sauce clung to the pasta and coated the inside. We found that since we were simmering the pasta in a brothy sauce, and then adding other elements after the pasta was cooked, we needed to use a smaller amount of pasta (8 ounces). And because we were cooking the pasta in the same skillet used to cook these other elements—chicken, sausage, beans, and vegetables—it absorbed maximum flavor.

We began our testing with the timeless pairing of chicken and broccoli—a perfect weeknight dinner. Unfortunately, this simple pairing often produces disappointing results—tough meat, bland pasta, and drab-looking vegetables blanketed by a flavorless cream sauce. We knew we could do better. We wanted to develop a foolproof method, which we could then use to create recipe variations. And we wanted to do this in just one skillet.

Right off the bat, we decided that boneless, skinless chicken breasts were the best choice; they're easy to prepare and ideal for quick weeknight meals. We tested various cooking methods, including microwaving, poaching, and sautéing. Not surprisingly, microwaving produced bland chicken with a steamed taste. Poaching the chicken in the simmering sauce produced meat that was tender and juicy, but the flavor was washed out. The best results came with sautéing; the meat was flavorful and the chicken was nicely browned. We turned to our basic stir-fry method, where the chicken is sliced thin and cooked in a skillet over high heat for a short period of time. This was the clear winner. When the chicken was just cooked through, we set it aside until the sauce and pasta were done, then stirred it back in to warm it.

As for the liquid component, we started with a simple chicken broth–based sauce, in which the pasta could simmer. We found it necessary to crank the heat to high so that the pasta really absorbed the liquid and became tender, and so the remaining liquid would reduce to a nice saucy consistency. We added wine to the skillet before stirring in the broth and water to bring some acidic notes to the dish. As for the cream, it would have to sit this one out—tasters favored a lighter, cleaner sauce.

After lots of testing, we found that the broccoli was best stirred in during the last five minutes of pasta cooking. This timing allowed the broccoli to cook up crisp-tender while also maintaining its vibrant color and flavor. A generous amount of garlic, a touch of red pepper flakes, and a handful of Parmesan rounded out the flavors and left tasters asking for more.

We then moved on to the classic combination of penne with sausage and spinach. To avoid having to drain the fat, as we would with pork

EQUIPMENT: Garlic Presses

A defiantly sticky and undeniably stinky job, hand mincing garlic is a chore many cooks avoid by pressing the cloves through a garlic press. The question for us was not whether garlic presses work, but which of the many available models works best. After squeezing our way through 12 different models, the unanimous winner was Kuhn Rikon's 2315 Epicurean Garlic Press. Solidly constructed of stainless steel, it has an almost luxurious feel, with ergonomically curved handles that are comfortable to squeeze and a hopper that smoothly and automatically lifts out for cleaning as you open the handles. It passed all our kitchen tests with flying colors. At $35 however, it is also quite expensive. Also doing well in our tests was the Trudeau Garlic Press—with a solid construction, it is sturdy and easy to use, and is our best buy at a reasonable $11.99.

THE BEST GARLIC PRESSES

KUHN RIKON

TRUDEAU

The Kuhn Rikon 2315 Epicurean Garlic Press ($35) produces a very fine mince, good yield, and great paste consistency, making it the all-around winner. The Trudeau Garlic Press ($11.99) is a solid choice for those looking to spend a little less money.

sausage, we used less greasy sausage made from turkey (chicken sausage works too). We browned the sausage, then added garlic, chicken broth, water, sun-dried tomatoes, and penne. Once the pasta was done cooking, we stirred in handfuls of spinach and cooked the mixture briefly until the spinach wilted. To finish the dish, we stirred in grated Parmesan, which not only added flavor, but also helped create a light sauce that perfectly coated the pasta. Toasted pine nuts provided the final touch to this hearty skillet supper.

For a couple of vegetarian options, we created one recipe with olives, cherry tomatoes, and white beans. We also came up with an asparagus and mushroom variation, in which we enriched the sauce with heavy cream and a splash of white wine to give the dish a sophisticated, complex flavor in little time.

Penne with Chicken and Broccoli

SERVES 4

You can substitute ziti, medium shells, farfalle, campanelle, or orecchiette for the penne; however, the cup measurements will vary. See page 83 for more information on measuring pasta.

¼	cup olive oil
1	pound boneless, skinless chicken breasts, (about 3 medium), trimmed and sliced thin (see the illustrations on page 228)
1	medium onion, minced
	Salt
6	medium garlic cloves, minced or pressed through a garlic press (about 2 tablespoons)
¼	teaspoon red pepper flakes
¼	teaspoon dried oregano
½	cup dry white wine
2½	cups water
2	cups low-sodium chicken broth
8	ounces (about 2½ cups) penne (see note)
8	ounces broccoli florets, cut into bite-sized pieces (about 3 cups)
2	ounces Parmesan cheese, grated (1 cup), plus extra for serving
	Ground black pepper

1. Heat 1 tablespoon of the oil in a 12-inch nonstick skillet over high heat until just smoking. Add the chicken, break up any clumps, and cook, without stirring, until beginning to brown, about 1 minute. Stir the chicken and continue to cook until cooked through, 2 to 3 minutes longer. Transfer the chicken to a bowl, cover to keep warm, and set aside.

2. Add 1 tablespoon more oil to the skillet and heat over medium heat until shimmering. Add the onion and ½ teaspoon salt and cook, stirring often, until softened, 5 to 7 minutes. Stir in the garlic, red pepper flakes, and oregano and cook until fragrant, about 30 seconds. Stir in the wine and simmer until nearly evaporated, 1 to 2 minutes.

3. Stir in the water and broth, then add the pasta. Increase the heat to high and cook at a vigorous simmer, stirring often, for 12 minutes.

4. Stir in the broccoli and continue to simmer, stirring often, until the pasta and broccoli are tender and the liquid has thickened, 3 to 5 minutes.

5. Return the chicken, along with any accumulated juices, to the skillet and cook until warmed through, about 1 minute. Off the heat, stir in the remaining 2 tablespoons olive oil, Parmesan, and season with salt and pepper to taste. Serve, passing the extra Parmesan separately.

Penne with Sausage and Spinach

SERVES 4

Use either hot or sweet Italian-style turkey (or chicken) sausage here. Pork sausage can be substituted, but you will have to drain off the extra fat before adding the garlic in step 1. You can substitute ziti, medium shells, farfalle, campanelle, or orecchiette for the penne; however, the cup measurements will vary. See page 83 for more information on measuring pasta. The spinach may seem like a lot at first, but it wilts down substantially.

1	tablespoon olive oil
1	pound Italian-style turkey sausage, casings removed
3	medium garlic cloves, minced or pressed through a garlic press (about 1 tablespoon)
2½	cups water
2	cups low-sodium chicken broth
½	cup oil-packed sun-dried tomatoes, rinsed and chopped fine
	Salt
8	ounces (about 2½ cups) penne (see note)
1	(6-ounce) bag baby spinach
1	ounce Parmesan cheese, grated (½ cup)
¼	cup pine nuts, toasted
	Ground black pepper

1. Heat the oil in a 12-inch nonstick skillet over medium-high heat until just smoking. Add

the sausage and cook, breaking apart the meat, until lightly browned and no longer pink, 3 to 5 minutes. Stir in the garlic and cook until fragrant, about 30 seconds.

2. Stir in the water, broth, sun-dried tomatoes, and ½ teaspoon salt, then add the pasta. Increase the heat to high and cook at a vigorous simmer, stirring often, until the pasta is tender and the liquid has thickened, 15 to 18 minutes.

3. Stir in the spinach, a handful at a time, and cook until wilted. Off the heat, stir in the Parmesan and pine nuts. Season with salt and pepper to taste and serve.

Penne with Cherry Tomatoes, White Beans, and Olives
SERVES 4

Although we prefer the lighter flavor of vegetable broth here, low-sodium chicken broth can be used instead. You can substitute ziti, medium shells, farfalle, campanelle, or orecchiette for the penne; however, the cup measurements will vary. See page 83 for more information on measuring pasta.

2½	cups water
2	cups low-sodium vegetable broth (see note)
8	ounces (about 2½ cups) penne (see note)
	Salt
1	pint cherry tomatoes, halved
1	(15-ounce) can cannellini beans, rinsed
½	cup pitted kalamata olives, chopped
1	ounce Parmesan cheese, grated (½ cup)
½	cup chopped fresh basil leaves
2	tablespoons extra-virgin olive oil
1	tablespoon juice from 1 lemon
	Ground black pepper

1. Bring the water, broth, pasta, and ½ teaspoon salt to a simmer in a 12-inch nonstick skillet over high heat. Cook at a vigorous simmer, stirring often, until the pasta is tender and the liquid has thickened, 15 to 18 minutes.

2. Stir in the tomatoes, beans, and olives and continue to cook until warmed through, about

1 minute. Off the heat, stir in the Parmesan, basil, oil, and lemon juice. Season with salt and pepper to taste and serve.

Creamy Penne with Mushrooms and Asparagus
SERVES 4

You can substitute ziti, medium shells, farfalle, campanelle, or orecchiette for the penne; however, the cup measurements will vary. See page 83 for more information on measuring pasta.

1	tablespoon olive oil
10	ounces white mushrooms, wiped clean and sliced thin
1	medium shallot, minced (about 3 tablespoons)
6	medium garlic cloves, minced or pressed through a garlic press (about 2 tablespoons)
½	ounce dried porcini mushrooms, rinsed and minced
1	teaspoon minced fresh thyme leaves, or ¼ teaspoon dried
	Salt
½	cup dry white wine
3½	cups water
1	cup heavy cream
8	ounces (about 2½ cups) penne (see note)
1	pound asparagus (about 1 bunch), tough ends trimmed (see the illustration on page 92) and sliced on the bias into 1-inch lengths
1	ounce Parmesan cheese, grated (½ cup)
	Ground black pepper

1. Heat the oil in a 12-inch nonstick skillet over medium-high heat until shimmering. Add the white mushrooms and cook until they have released their moisture and are golden brown, 7 to 10 minutes.

2. Stir in the shallot, garlic, porcini, thyme, and ½ teaspoon salt and cook until the shallot has softened, about 1 minute. Stir in the wine and simmer until nearly evaporated, 1 to 2 minutes.

3. Stir in the water and cream, then add the pasta. Increase the heat to high and cook at a vigorous simmer, stirring often, for 12 minutes.

4. Stir in the asparagus and continue to simmer, stirring often, until the pasta and asparagus are tender and the liquid has thickened, 3 to 5 minutes. Off the heat, stir in the Parmesan, season with salt and pepper to taste, and serve.

LASAGNA

LASAGNA IS A CROWD-PLEASER THAT NEVER goes out of style, and second helpings are almost always mandatory. But lasagna is not a dish you can throw together at the last minute. Even with the invention of no-boil noodles, it can still take a good amount of time to make the components and assemble and bake the casserole.

While lasagna is traditionally made with fully or partially cooked elements that meld together during baking, we wondered if it would be possible to take the same components and cook them on the stovetop in a skillet, to result in the same flavors and textures. Our plan was simple: We would first brown the meat, then build a thin but flavorful sauce in which to cook the pasta (regular lasagna noodles broken into 2-inch lengths). We would finish the dish by adding ricotta cheese, Parmesan, mozzarella, and any other flavors we thought were necessary.

Most lasagna sauces simmer for hours, giving the ingredients and flavors a chance to blend, but since speed is a key to weeknight dinner success, we wanted to forgo this step. We limited the time that it took to simmer the sauce to the time that it took to cook the pasta. To rein in the ingredient list, we started with onions and garlic, which gave the sauce its depth. Our lasagna was meant to be a complete meal, so we added some protein. Ground beef was good, but we thought meatloaf mix (a combination of ground beef, pork, and veal sold in one package at most supermarkets) was even better. For a flavor variation, tasters liked a combination of Italian sausage and sweet red pepper.

We next turned to the type of tomatoes we would use in the sauce. We started our tests with tomato puree, but this made a sauce that was a tad too heavy; the pasta sat on top of the sauce and cooked unevenly. Adding a little water created a better medium in which to cook the pasta, but the resulting lasagna was bland. Abandoning tomato puree, we revisited our previous tomato-based skillet pasta recipes, and added whole peeled tomatoes pulsed briefly in a food processor. This gave the sauce a slightly chunky and substantial texture—and there was just enough liquid to cook the pasta.

To replicate the cheesiness of traditional lasagna, we stirred in ricotta, shredded mozzarella, and grated Parmesan, but this didn't quite give us the results we were looking for. Once mixed in, the sweet creaminess of the ricotta was lost and the sauce turned into a grainy, pink mess. We had success when we stirred in the mozzarella and Parmesan first, then placed dollops of ricotta on top of the lasagna and covered the pan, allowing the mozzarella to melt and the ricotta to heat through but still remain a distinct element. The ricotta also created an attractive pattern over the top of the dish. A sprinkling of freshly chopped basil further enhanced the look and flavor of our skillet lasagna.

Meaty Lasagna
SERVES 4

Do not substitute no-boil lasagna noodles for the traditional, curly-edged lasagna noodles here. Meatloaf mix is a combination of ground beef, pork, and veal, sold prepackaged in many supermarkets. If it's unavailable, use ½ pound each ground pork and 85 percent ground beef. We recommend using either whole milk or part-skim ricotta here, but do not use fat-free ricotta, which has a very dry texture and bland flavor.

    3   (14.5-ounce) cans whole peeled tomatoes
    1   tablespoon olive oil
    1   medium onion, minced
        Salt

3 medium garlic cloves, minced or pressed
   through a garlic press (about 1 tablespoon)
⅛ teaspoon red pepper flakes
1 pound meatloaf mix
10 curly-edged lasagna noodles
   (about 8½ ounces), broken into
   2-inch lengths
2 ounces mozzarella cheese, shredded (½ cup)
½ ounce Parmesan cheese, grated (¼ cup)
   Ground black pepper
¾ cup ricotta cheese (see note)
3 tablespoons chopped fresh basil leaves

1. Pulse the tomatoes with their juice in a food processor until coarsely ground and no large pieces remain, about 12 pulses.

2. Heat the oil in a 12-inch nonstick skillet over medium heat until shimmering. Add the onion and ½ teaspoon salt and cook, stirring often, until softened, 5 to 7 minutes. Stir in the garlic and red pepper flakes and cook until fragrant, about 30 seconds. Add the ground meat and cook, breaking apart the meat, until lightly browned and no longer pink, 3 to 5 minutes.

3. Scatter the pasta over the meat, then pour the processed tomatoes over the pasta. Cover, increase the heat to medium-high, and cook, stirring often and adjusting the heat to maintain a vigorous simmer, until the pasta is tender, about 20 minutes.

4. Off the heat, stir in half of the mozzarella and half of the Parmesan. Season with salt and pepper to taste. Dot heaping tablespoons of the ricotta over the noodles, then sprinkle with the remaining mozzarella and Parmesan. Cover and let stand off the heat until the cheese melts, 2 to 4 minutes. Sprinkle with the basil and serve.

➤ VARIATION

Lasagna with Sausage and Peppers
Follow the recipe for Meaty Lasagna, substituting 1 pound Italian sausage, removed from its casing, for the meatloaf mix. Add 1 red bell pepper, stemmed, seeded, and chopped coarse, to the skillet with the onion in step 2.

BAKED ZITI

THIS ITALIAN-AMERICAN CLASSIC CAN BE found at many a church supper and potluck dinner, as well as in many home kitchens. Although the dish is simple enough, requiring only cheese, sauce, and pasta, the result is often dry and bland or overly heavy and gooey. We knew it was possible to get a good baked ziti on the table; we just had to figure out how to do it in a skillet.

Tomato sauce was the first ingredient we considered. Keeping in mind that we wanted to streamline the recipe, the sauce would have to be easy to prepare as well. We felt the sauce should be smooth, with a fresh tomato flavor that would lighten the dish. In the first test, we tried canned crushed tomatoes but found that they coated the ziti too heavily for our skillet cooking method. We returned to our skillet standby, canned whole peeled tomatoes, which provided a fresher taste, and briefly processed them in a food processor to help smooth out the final consistency. The flavor base of the sauce was provided by sautéing garlic with extra virgin olive oil and red pepper flakes. To this, we added the processed tomatoes and simmered for 10 minutes. Because we were looking for a smoother, creamier sauce, we added more water (3 cups) than we had in our other tomato-based pasta recipes, along with the ziti, which absorbed the flavors of the sauce as it cooked.

Traditionally, mozzarella cheese is used in baked ziti to bind the pasta together and make the casserole rich. Because the pasta would be cooked in the sauce, we had to find another way to make the dish creamy. We found that adding ½ cup of heavy cream to the sauce—after the pasta cooked—gave us the desired consistency. We also added grated Parmesan cheese and chopped fresh basil to brighten the flavor. To ensure that the cheese and cream would be evenly distributed throughout the casserole, we stirred them thoroughly into the pasta before placing the skillet in the oven. Topped off with shredded mozzarella, our pasta required only 10 to 15 minutes at 475 degrees (not the hour called for in many recipes) to finish cooking the ziti and brown the top.

Baked Ziti

SERVES 4

You can substitute penne, campanelle, medium shells, farfalle, or orecchiette for the ziti; however, the cup measurements will vary. See page 83 for more information on measuring pasta. Be sure to simmer the tomatoes gently in step 2 or the sauce will become too thick.

1	(28-ounce) can whole peeled tomatoes
1	tablespoon olive oil
6	medium garlic cloves, minced
	or pressed through a garlic press
	(about 2 tablespoons)
¼	teaspoon red pepper flakes
	Salt
3	cups water
12	ounces (about 3¾ cups) ziti (see note)
½	cup heavy cream
1	ounce Parmesan cheese, grated (½ cup)
¼	cup chopped fresh basil leaves
	Ground black pepper
4	ounces mozzarella cheese, shredded (1 cup)

1. Adjust an oven rack to the middle position and heat the oven to 475 degrees. Pulse the tomatoes with their juice in a food processor until coarsely ground and no large pieces remain, about 12 pulses.

2. Cook the oil, garlic, and red pepper flakes together in a 12-inch ovensafe nonstick skillet over medium-high heat until fragrant, about 1 minute. Stir in the processed tomatoes and ½ teaspoon salt. Reduce the heat to medium-low and simmer gently, stirring occasionally, until the tomatoes no longer taste raw, about 10 minutes.

3. Stir in the water, then add the pasta. Cover, increase the heat to medium-high, and cook, stirring often and adjusting the heat to maintain a vigorous simmer, until the pasta is tender, 15 to 18 minutes.

4. Stir in the cream, Parmesan, and basil and season with salt and pepper to taste. Sprinkle the mozzarella evenly over the top. Transfer the skillet to the oven and bake until the cheese has melted and browned, 10 to 15 minutes. Serve.

➤ VARIATION

Baked Ziti with Sausage

You can use either sweet or hot Italian sausage here.

Follow the recipe for Baked Ziti, omitting the oil and cooking 1 pound Italian sausage, casings removed, in the skillet over medium-high heat, breaking apart the meat, until lightly browned and no longer pink, 3 to 5 minutes. Stir in the garlic and red pepper flakes and continue to cook as directed in step 2.

MACARONI AND CHEESE

WHILE SUPERMARKET MAC AND CHEESE MIXES are certainly convenient and a kid favorite, this meal-in-a-box just doesn't hold the same allure for adults. And many "quick" homemade macaroni and cheese recipes are just as lackluster, involving a tasteless mix of shredded cheese and evaporated milk. When done right, macaroni and cheese is a wonderfully satisfying dish, with a smooth silky sauce and real cheese flavor that coats the macaroni inside and out. Our goal was to develop a skillet macaroni and cheese that the whole family could enjoy.

There are two styles of macaroni and cheese. The more common one features a béchamel sauce that blankets the macaroni, which is then topped with bread crumbs and baked. The other variety is custard-based, also topped with bread crumbs and baked. For this style, a mixture of egg and milk is poured over layers of grated cheese and noodles. As the dish bakes, the eggs, milk, and cheese set into a custard. Since we wanted to confine our recipe to the stovetop, we opted for the béchamel approach and headed into the kitchen.

Working with our skillet pasta method, we brought a mixture of water and evaporated milk (which many recipes suggest over whole milk, half-and-half, and heavy cream) to a simmer in a 12-inch nonstick skillet, stirred in the macaroni, and cooked it until tender. As it cooked, we wondered if the dish really needed evaporated milk and why. After testing the recipe with whole milk, low-fat milk, half-and-half, and cream, we realized that evaporated milk was indeed an important ingredient. The macaroni and cheese dishes we made with fresh milk curdled a bit, and the one we made with cream was simply too rich once all the cheese had been stirred in. When we used evaporated milk, however, the sauce remained silky smooth. Playing with varying amounts of liquid in which to cook 12 ounces of macaroni, we settled on 3½ cups of water combined with 1 cup of evaporated milk.

By the time the macaroni was tender, there was just enough liquid left in the pan to make a quick sauce. In lieu of making a béchamel—which seemed a bit fussy for our skillet version—we mixed an additional ½ cup evaporated milk with cornstarch to thicken it, and for flavor we added dry mustard and hot sauce. We stirred this into the skillet, brought it to a simmer, and let it thicken briefly.

Now it was time for the cheese. Up to this point, we had been adding 1 pound of shredded cheddar cheese to the sauce, but wondered if less would be more. Testing varying amounts of cheese from 8 ounces all the way up to 20 ounces, we determined that 12 ounces (about 3 cups) was the winning number—this amount provided maximum creaminess and good cheese flavor. More than that and the dish was simply too glutinous; when we added less than that, the dish suffered from a lack of true cheese flavor. One problem that had annoyed us from the beginning, however, was now impossible to ignore—the grainy texture of the cooked cheddar cheese. To avoid this, many recipes mix cheddar with other types of cheese. We tried replacing some of the cheddar with Gruyère, but its strong flavor did not sit well with testers. Gouda, Havarti, and fontina were all given a shot, but none tasted just right. We hit the jackpot with Monterey Jack—it helped smooth out the sauce and created that silky texture we were after. Trying various ratios of cheddar to Monterey Jack, we found that the best balance was equal parts cheddar for flavor and Monterey Jack for meltability.

Finally, a little butter enriched the dish, making it smooth and silky. In addition, we came up with a host of flavor variations—one with spicy chipotle chiles, one with ham and peas, another with garlic and broccoli, and a fourth with kielbasa and mustard.

Macaroni and Cheese
SERVES 4

You can substitute small shells (about 3½ cups) for the macaroni.

3½	cups water, plus extra as needed
1	(12-ounce) can evaporated milk
12	ounces (about 3 cups) elbow macaroni (see note)
	Salt
1	teaspoon cornstarch
½	teaspoon dry mustard
¼	teaspoon hot sauce
6	ounces cheddar cheese, shredded (1½ cups)
6	ounces Monterey Jack cheese, shredded (1½ cups)
3	tablespoons unsalted butter
	Ground black pepper

1. Bring 3½ cups water, 1 cup of the evaporated milk, the macaroni, and ½ teaspoon salt to a simmer in a 12-inch nonstick skillet over high heat. Cook at a vigorous simmer, stirring often, until the macaroni is tender and the liquid has thickened, 9 to 12 minutes.

2. Whisk the remaining ½ cup evaporated milk, the cornstarch, mustard, and hot sauce together in a small bowl, then stir into the skillet. Continue to simmer until slightly thickened, about 1 minute.

3. Off the heat, stir in the cheddar and Monterey Jack, one handful at a time, adding water as needed to adjust the consistency of the sauce. Stir in the butter, season with salt and pepper to taste, and serve.

➤ VARIATIONS

Spicy Macaroni and Cheese
Ro-Tel brand tomatoes are diced tomatoes with green chiles and seasonings added.

Follow the recipe for Macaroni and Cheese, adding 2 teaspoons minced chipotle chile in adobo sauce and 1 (10-ounce) can Ro-Tel tomatoes, drained, to the skillet with the cornstarch mixture in step 2.

Macaroni and Cheese with Ham and Peas

Follow the recipe for Macaroni and Cheese, adding 4 ounces deli-style baked ham, diced medium, and ½ cup frozen peas to the skillet with the cornstarch mixture in step 2.

Macaroni and Cheese with Broccoli and Garlic

Follow the recipe for Macaroni and Cheese, cooking 1 tablespoon olive oil, 3 garlic cloves, minced, and ¼ teaspoon red pepper flakes in the skillet over medium-high heat until fragrant, about 1 minute, before adding the water, evaporated milk, and macaroni in step 1. Stir in 1 (10-ounce) package frozen broccoli florets, thawed and squeezed dry, after the cheese has been incorporated in step 3.

Macaroni and Cheese with Kielbasa and Mustard

Heat 1 tablespoon vegetable oil in a 12-inch nonstick skillet over medium-high heat until just smoking. Add 8 ounces kielbasa, halved lengthwise and sliced thin, and cook until lightly browned, 3 to 5 minutes. Transfer the kielbasa to a paper towel–lined plate and set aside. Follow the recipe for Macaroni and Cheese, adding the browned kielbasa and 1 tablespoon whole grain mustard to the skillet with the cornstarch mixture in step 2.

CHILI MAC

SYNONYMOUS WITH SIMPLER TIMES—AND simpler food—chili mac is a favorite childhood comfort food whose appeal, for many of us, extends well into adulthood. Initial tests divided our kitchen—which version of chili mac was best? For some, it was a macaroni-and-cheese-like version with a bit of chili stirred in. For others, it was predominantly chili with a little macaroni. Others insisted (after tasting the previous examples) that there could be only one way to make the best chili mac: spicy chili, with elbows stirred in (no other pasta would do), and lots of gooey, melted cheese on top. Many recipes we came across in our research were a sorry mixture of canned chili and jarred salsa stirred into packaged macaroni and cheese—not an appetizing dinner. Our goal was to create a quick skillet version that would combine the best spicy beef chili, real cheese, and perfectly cooked macaroni.

Our first challenges were finding the correct heat level for the chili and determining the ideal proportion of chili to macaroni. We focused on the chili first, and started by sautéing onion and garlic with chili powder (jalapeños added too much heat) and cumin. This step helped to bloom the flavors of the chili and reduce its harshness. We added lean ground beef to the skillet and now had a "taco seasoned" mixture that was waiting for the tomato component to transform it into chili.

We added a can of tomato sauce, which tasters preferred in chili mac to diced or whole peeled tomatoes, then sprinkled in the macaroni and poured in the water, which thickened and bound the dish together as it simmered and the pasta cooked. A small amount of brown sugar was added to help tame the acidity of the tomato. Thanks to the chili powder and cumin, the spiciness level of the chili was perfect without being overbearing. Eight ounces of macaroni proved the ideal amount of pasta—just the right balance of chili to macaroni. We added 2 cups of water for 8 ounces of macaroni to cook properly. Now our sauce was spoonable and thick.

At this point, we needed to put the cheese component into play. When we used all cheddar, the flavor was good but the texture was a bit grainy. We then stirred in shredded Monterey Jack; this cheese lent a nice creaminess but not enough flavor. The winner ended up being a shredded Mexican cheese blend, widely available in supermarkets, which is a combination of cheddar, Monterey Jack, asadero, and queso blanco cheeses. The cheeses help bind the mixture together and infuse the chili mac with cheesy flavor. For an even spicier chili mac, we created a variation with green chiles, sweet corn, and cilantro.

Cheesy Chili Mac

SERVES 4

If you can't find shredded Mexican cheese blend, substitute 1 cup each shredded Monterey Jack cheese and shredded cheddar cheese. To make the dish spicier, add ½ teaspoon red pepper flakes along with the chili powder. You can substitute small shells (about 2½ cups) for the macaroni.

1	tablespoon vegetable oil
1	medium onion, minced
1	tablespoon chili powder
1	tablespoon ground cumin
	Salt
3	medium garlic cloves, minced or pressed through a garlic press (about 1 tablespoon)
1	tablespoon brown sugar
1	pound 90 percent lean ground beef
2	cups water
1	(15-ounce) can tomato sauce
8	ounces (about 2 cups) elbow macaroni (see note)
1	(8-ounce) package shredded Mexican cheese blend (2 cups) (see note)
	Ground black pepper

1. Heat the oil in a 12-inch nonstick skillet over medium heat until shimmering. Add the onion, chili powder, cumin, and ½ teaspoon salt and cook, stirring often, until softened, 5 to 7 minutes. Stir in the garlic and brown sugar and cook until fragrant, about 30 seconds. Add the beef and cook, breaking apart the meat, until lightly browned and no longer pink, 3 to 5 minutes.

2. Stir in the water and tomato sauce, then add the pasta. Cover, increase the heat to medium-high, and cook, stirring often and adjusting the heat to maintain a vigorous simmer, until the pasta is tender, 9 to 12 minutes.

3. Off the heat, stir in 1 cup of the cheese and season with salt and pepper to taste. Sprinkle the remaining 1 cup cheese over top, cover, and let stand off the heat until the cheese melts, 2 to 4 minutes. Serve.

➤ VARIATION

Chili Mac with Corn and Green Chiles

Follow the recipe for Cheesy Chili Mac, stirring 1 cup frozen corn, 1 (4.5-ounce) can chopped green chiles, drained, and 2 tablespoons minced fresh cilantro into the skillet with the cheese in step 3.

AMERICAN CHOP SUEY

DESPITE ITS CHINESE NAME, CHOP SUEY IS not a Chinese dish. In fact, it's probably the furthest thing from it. A combination of ground beef, vegetables, and macaroni all cooked in a tomato sauce, chop suey actually conjures up images of grade-school cafeteria food. Unfortunately, many of the existing chop suey recipes—often nothing more than ground beef mixed with canned spaghetti—do nothing to dispel the negative associations many of us have with American chop suey. Looking past these dreadful recipes, we could imagine a really good chop suey, one with plenty of beefy flavor, fresh vegetables, and a bright tomato sauce. We also wanted our dish to be prepared neatly from start to finish in one pan.

We started with the ground beef. Most recipes we consulted, quick and traditional, tended to be overly greasy. We rectified the problem by using 90 percent lean ground beef, which we cooked just until no longer pink. When it came to the vegetables, we kept things simple, as is the style of this dish. Onions and garlic provided the sauce with deep flavor, celery gave the dish much-needed texture, and a red pepper lent both texture and a touch of sweetness. Once the ground beef and vegetables were cooked, we turned to the sauce.

Our main task was to avoid making a sauce that would be too thick and pasty. We tried using two cans of diced tomatoes and their juice, but in an effort to build a light sauce, we made one that was too thin. Next we tried using a combination of diced tomatoes and tomato sauce—a can of each struck a good balance. The tomato sauce gave the dish some body and an even tomato flavor, while the diced tomatoes and their juice added freshness. To provide the sauce with a richer flavor and prevent it from tasting like an Italian meat sauce for pasta, we added ½ cup of chicken broth.

The chicken broth also played a key role in cooking the pasta. When we first stirred in the macaroni to simmer—and let the flavors in the skillet develop and meld—we found that there wasn't enough liquid for the pasta to absorb, and we soon had a mass of uncooked pasta on our hands. We steadily increased the chicken broth until we had added a total of 1½ cups. When the pasta had fully cooked and released its starches, the sauce was the perfect consistency.

American Chop Suey

SERVES 4

You can substitute small shells (about 2½ cups) for the macaroni.

2	tablespoons vegetable oil
1	medium onion, minced
1	red bell pepper, stemmed, seeded, and chopped medium
1	celery rib, chopped medium
	Salt
2	medium garlic cloves, minced or pressed through a garlic press (about 2 teaspoons)
1	pound 90 percent lean ground beef
1	(15-ounce) can tomato sauce
1	(14.5-ounce) can diced tomatoes
1½	cups low-sodium chicken broth
8	ounces (about 2 cups) elbow macaroni (see note)
	Ground black pepper

1. Heat the oil in a 12-inch nonstick skillet over medium heat until shimmering. Add the onion, bell pepper, celery, and ½ teaspoon salt and cook, stirring often, until softened, 5 to 7 minutes. Stir in the garlic and cook until fragrant, about 30 seconds. Add the beef and cook, breaking apart the meat, until lightly browned and no longer pink, 3 to 5 minutes.

2. Stir in the tomato sauce, diced tomatoes with their juice, and chicken broth, then add the pasta. Cover, increase the heat to medium-high, and cook, stirring often and adjusting the heat to maintain a vigorous simmer, until the pasta is tender, 9 to 12 minutes. Season with salt and pepper to taste and serve.

PASTITSIO

EVERY GREEK COOKBOOK HAS A RECIPE FOR *pastitsio*, a layered casserole consisting of ground meat, tomato sauce, pasta, a creamy béchamel, and a sprinkling of cheese. When well prepared, it is comfort food at its finest, but often recipes for pastitsio yield a mishmash of overseasoned lamb filling, soggy pasta, and thick, gluey béchamel. And then there's the fact that pastitsio is not at all cut out for quick weeknight dining—the pasta, meat sauce, and béchamel are cooked in separate pots, then layered in a casserole and baked. We set out to turn this classic Greek dish into an easy and quick skillet supper worthy of serving to our friends from Greece.

We began by selecting the meat. Some of the recipes called for ground beef or veal, while more traditional recipes called for ground lamb. Not surprisingly, those made with beef didn't taste terribly authentic, and those made with veal lacked depth of flavor. Lamb, on the other hand, was rich and contributed a gaminess that we have come to associate with Greek cuisine. We have learned over the years that ground lamb can be incredibly fat laden, making a dish greasy. To remedy this potential problem, we cooked the ground lamb until it was just cooked through and then drained the excess fat before adding the other ingredients.

With the meat chosen and its cooking technique established, we turned to our aromatics. Onion and garlic were a given, but getting the spices set proved to be more of a puzzle. Several recipes called for a whole array of spices, including cumin, coriander, cardamom, cinnamon, nutmeg, and cloves, but tasters found this abundance overpowering. We aimed for a lighter touch, and the simple combination of cinnamon, oregano, and nutmeg did the trick.

Next, we had to decide which tomato product to use. Diced tomatoes were acceptable, but tasters did not care for the overly assertive chunks of tomato, which stood out in the sauce. We then tried crushed tomatoes, but again tasters were not happy—they wanted a deeper flavor with less tomato product. We turned to tomato paste, which provided the perfect backbone of flavor. It helped thicken the meat sauce slightly and rounded out the flavors.

It was time to add the pasta to the skillet, along with chicken broth and heavy cream for more liquid, to simmer until tender. We tried spaghetti, because many recipes call for long pasta such as perciatelli, which is similar to bucatini but hard to find. However, tasters complained that the long strands were difficult to eat in this dish. So we turned to more manageable pasta shapes, and tested large and small elbow macaroni, penne, and ziti. The penne and ziti bulked up the size of the dish unnecessarily and produced a pasta-heavy casserole that didn't have the creaminess we wanted. Large macaroni was a definite improvement, but we wanted each bite to combine all three elements of the dish evenly. The smaller elbow macaroni gave tasters multi-flavored bites with every spoonful.

In lieu of preparing the béchamel sauce separately, we decided to simply finish the dish with a quick replication: more heavy cream thickened with cornstarch. The addition of 1 cup of Pecorino Romano (a substitute for the traditional Greek cheese *kefalotyri*, which is hard to find) enriched the sauce while intensifying the flavor of the lamb. We stirred half into the sauce; the remaining half we sprinkled on top for the finishing touch.

We then slid the skillet into a hot oven to briefly brown the top—and once it came out, no one could tell that this typically time-consuming Greek classic took us just minutes to prepare.

Pastitsio

SERVES 4

Ground lamb is traditional in this dish and we like the flavor, but you can substitute 90 percent lean ground beef if you prefer. If using 90 percent lean ground beef, do not drain the meat in step 1. You can substitute small shells (about 2½ cups) for the macaroni.

1	pound ground lamb
1	medium onion, minced
¼	teaspoon ground cinnamon
⅛	teaspoon fresh grated nutmeg
6	medium garlic cloves, minced or pressed through a garlic press (about 2 tablespoons)
2	tablespoons tomato paste
2	teaspoons minced fresh oregano leaves, or ¾ teaspoon dried
3	cups low-sodium chicken broth
1	cup heavy cream
	Salt
8	ounces (about 2 cups) elbow macaroni (see note)
1	teaspoon cornstarch
2	ounces Pecorino Romano cheese, grated (1 cup)
	Ground black pepper

1. Adjust an oven rack to the middle position and heat the oven to 475 degrees. Cook the lamb in a 12-inch ovensafe nonstick skillet over medium-high heat, breaking apart the meat, until no longer pink and the fat has rendered, 3 to 5 minutes. Transfer the lamb to a strainer set over a medium bowl and let drain, reserving 1 tablespoon of the fat.

2. Add the reserved tablespoon fat to the skillet and return to medium heat until shimmering. Add the onion, cinnamon, and nutmeg and cook, stirring often, until softened, 5 to 7 minutes. Stir in the garlic, tomato paste, and oregano and cook until fragrant, about 30 seconds.

3. Stir in the broth, ½ cup of the cream, and ½ teaspoon salt, then add the pasta and drained lamb. Increase the heat to high and cook at a vigorous simmer, stirring often, until the pasta is tender, 9 to 12 minutes.

4. Whisk the remaining ½ cup cream and cornstarch together in a small bowl, then stir into the skillet and continue to simmer until slightly thickened, about 1 minute. Off the heat, stir in ½ cup of the Pecorino and season with salt and pepper to taste. Sprinkle the remaining ½ cup Pecorino over the top and bake until lightly browned, 5 to 10 minutes. Serve.

NOODLE CASSEROLES

TUNA NOODLE CASSEROLE WAS ONCE A family favorite. Unfortunately, as processed convenience foods became more widespread and people's devotion to spending time in the kitchen faded, this casserole took a turn for the worse and went from being a satisfying mix of egg noodles and tuna in a creamy sauce to a lackluster dish with no distinct flavor. We decided to revamp this classic into a gooey dish with fresh flavors and perfect pasta—and we would get rid of the baking dish in favor of the skillet, simplifying an already easy-to-make entrée. There would be no army of pots and pans to clean; this would be a true one-pan dish.

Many recipes we found were made from a canned-soup base—cream of mushroom and cream of celery are the usual choices—mixed with soggy noodles, canned tuna, and a few stray vegetables. To give this classic a well-deserved makeover, we began by shutting the cupboard door to all canned soups and focused on making a sauce from scratch. Fortunately, our skillet method was ideally suited to this task.

We knew that a mushroom-flavored sauce was essential. The key, we discovered, to an intense mushroom flavor was to start out by sautéing thinly sliced white mushrooms until they released all their liquid and began to brown. We then added a mixture of chicken broth and heavy cream, which would provide the right basic flavor and consistency to our finished dish. A total of 4½ cups liquid created enough sauce to cook 8 ounces of noodles without being either too soupy or too thick. To

round out the flavor of the sauce, we stirred in grated Parmesan cheese and minced fresh parsley just before baking.

Moving on to the vegetables, we noted that many recipes use a lot of celery, which adds crunch but almost no flavor. Interestingly enough, our tasters preferred no celery at all. Frozen peas were the only vegetable given the thumbs-up by the test kitchen staff. To keep them from turning mushy, we added them along with the tuna—solid white tuna packed in water was our first choice for this dish—right before baking.

Finally, we chose our noodles. Elbow macaroni was called for in several recipes we researched, but we found that elbows resulted in a starchy, thick consistency in our finished dish. We preferred wide egg noodles for both their delicate texture and the way they held onto the other components in the casserole. As for the topping, we decided that store-bought bread crumbs had an unappealing, sandy texture. We tested a topping made of cracker crumbs but found they burned too easily at our

INGREDIENTS: Egg Noodles

In dishes like our Tuna Noodle Casserole and Beef Stroganoff, egg noodles can make or break a meal. Classic egg noodles are thick, wide ribbons of pasta with a fat content that's slightly higher than that of other kinds of pasta because of their high percentage of eggs. Their firm, sturdy texture is what makes them so appealing in casseroles or stews.

We tasted several brands, cooked and tossed in a small amount of oil to prevent clumping. The winner, Light 'n Fluffy, was praised for its clean, slightly buttery flavor and a firm yet yielding texture.

THE BEST EGG NOODLES

LIGHT 'N FLUFFY

With a buttery flavor and firm texture, Light 'n Fluffy Wide Egg Noodles won tasters over.

high (475-degree) baking temperature. In the end, lightly toasted fresh bread crumbs produced a perfectly toasty and browned topping.

The finished casserole reminded us of another favorite casserole, turkey tetrazzini. We decided we could easily build a variation on our tuna casserole by cooking thinly sliced turkey cutlets in butter at the beginning of the process, then adding them back to the dish with the peas and cheese to finish in the oven. A splash of sherry added with the broth, cream, and noodles enhanced the flavor of this satisfying casserole.

Tuna Noodle Casserole

SERVES 4

Do not substitute other types of noodles for the wide egg noodles here. Solid white tuna packed in water has the best flavor and texture for this dish.

2	slices high-quality white sandwich bread, torn into quarters
3	tablespoons unsalted butter
10	ounces white mushrooms, wiped clean and sliced thin
1	medium onion, minced
	Salt
3½	cups low-sodium chicken broth
1	cup heavy cream
8	ounces (about 3 cups) wide egg noodles
2	(6-ounce) cans water-packed solid white tuna, drained well and flaked
1	cup frozen peas
2	ounces Parmesan cheese, grated (1 cup)
2	tablespoons minced fresh parsley leaves
	Ground black pepper

1. Adjust an oven rack to the middle position and heat the oven to 475 degrees. Pulse the bread in a food processor to coarse crumbs, about 6 pulses. Melt 1 tablespoon of the butter in a 12-inch ovensafe nonstick skillet over medium-high heat. Add the bread crumbs and toast until just golden brown, 3 to 5 minutes. Transfer the crumbs to a small bowl and set aside.

2. Wipe the skillet clean with paper towels. Melt the remaining 2 tablespoons butter in the skillet over medium-high heat. Add the mushrooms, onion, and ½ teaspoon salt and cook, stirring often, until the mushrooms have released their moisture and are golden brown, 7 to 10 minutes.

3. Stir in the broth and cream, then add the noodles. Increase the heat to high and cook at a vigorous simmer, stirring often, until the noodles are nearly tender and the sauce is slightly thickened, about 8 minutes.

4. Off the heat, stir in the tuna, peas, Parmesan, and parsley and season with salt and pepper

INGREDIENTS: Canned Tuna

In recent years, pouched tuna has appeared in supermarkets, promising a fresher, less-processed, better-tasting alternative to canned tuna. But is pouched tuna really better than its canned cousin?

A preliminary tasting showed that tasters had a strong preference for solid white albacore tuna packed in water, which is the mildest variety of processed tuna; chunk light tuna had unappealing strong flavors, and albacore packed in oil was too mushy. Given the minimal flavor differences in the mild white albacore tunas, our tasters focused on texture—and here's where the canned tunas won the race.

Because the cans are about three times as wide as the pouches (1½ inches versus about half an inch), the tuna must be broken down to get it into the pouch; the cans hold larger pieces of fish. Larger pieces mean that canned tuna has larger flakes than pouched tuna. In the end, we found texture to be more variable than flavor, and meaty canned tuna was preferable to mushier pouched tuna. After tasting several brands, our top pick is Chicken of the Sea Solid White Albacore Tuna in Water.

THE BEST CANNED TUNA

CHICKEN OF THE SEA

Chicken of the Sea Solid White Albacore Tuna in Water boasts large, meaty flakes of tuna.

to taste. Sprinkle the crumbs over the top, transfer the skillet to the oven, and bake until the topping is crisp and the casserole is bubbling lightly around the edges, about 8 minutes. Serve.

➤ VARIATION
Turkey Tetrazzini
Do not substitute other types of noodles for the wide egg noodles here.

2	slices high-quality white sandwich bread, torn into quarters
4	tablespoons (½ stick) unsalted butter
I	pound fresh turkey cutlets, trimmed and sliced thin
10	ounces white mushrooms, wiped clean and sliced thin
I	medium onion, minced
	Salt
3½	cups low-sodium chicken broth
I	cup heavy cream
2	tablespoons dry sherry
8	ounces (about 3 cups) wide egg noodles
I	cup frozen peas
4	ounces Gruyère cheese, shredded (about I cup)
2	tablespoons minced fresh parsley leaves
	Ground black pepper

1. Adjust an oven rack to the middle position and heat the oven to 475 degrees. Pulse the bread in a food processor to coarse crumbs, about 6 pulses. Melt 1 tablespoon of the butter in a 12-inch ovensafe nonstick skillet over medium-high heat. Add the bread crumbs and toast until just golden brown, 3 to 5 minutes. Transfer the crumbs to a small bowl and set aside.

2. Wipe the skillet clean with paper towels. Melt 1 tablespoon more butter in the skillet over high heat. Add the turkey, break up any clumps, and cook, without stirring, until lightly browned, about 1 minute. Stir the turkey and continue to cook until cooked through, 2 to 3 minutes longer. Transfer the turkey to a bowl, cover to keep warm, and set aside.

3. Melt the remaining 2 tablespoons butter in the skillet over medium-high heat. Add the mushrooms, onion, and ½ teaspoon salt and cook, stirring often, until the mushrooms have released their moisture and are golden brown, 7 to 10 minutes.

4. Stir in the broth, cream, and sherry, then add the noodles. Increase the heat to high and cook at a vigorous simmer, stirring often, until the noodles are nearly tender and the sauce is slightly thickened, about 8 minutes.

5. Off the heat, return the turkey, along with any accumulated juices, to the skillet. Stir in the peas, cheese, and parsley and season with salt and pepper to taste. Sprinkle the crumbs over the top, transfer the skillet to the oven, and bake until the topping is crisp and the casserole is bubbling lightly around the edges, about 8 minutes. Serve.

BEEF STROGANOFF

BEEF STROGANOFF IS A DECEPTIVE DISH. While most people think of it as a long-simmering braise, like beef stew or beef Burgundy, it is in fact a simple sauté of beef and mushrooms finished with a creamy pan sauce. But no matter how it's cooked, stroganoff is invariably overseasoned, weighty with the addition of sour cream, and muddled in flavor from too many ingredients. With an eye toward avoiding these pitfalls, we set out to remake this classic Russian dish as an easy, inexpensive skillet meal.

We started with the beef, which, along with mushrooms, onions, and sour cream, is a classic ingredient in stroganoff. The meat is usually a tender cut, like tenderloin, rather than a braising cut such as chuck or brisket, which need a lot of cooking time and patience. Though we knew beef tenderloin was traditional in stroganoff, as we sliced up this incredibly tender and expensive cut of meat, we wondered why. If you spend a lot of money on filet, you probably don't want to smother it in gravy.

We decided to try some cheaper cuts of beef. Because these cuts are generally tough, we knew we would have to move from a quick sauté to a short braise, so the moist heat could break down the fibers and collagen in the meat, making it tender. We had success with sirloin steak tips (aka flap meat); they were tender, but they also took on an accordion shape as they cooked. We found that pounding the tips before cutting them into strips compressed the fibers of the meat and helped keep the strips neat and uniform as they cooked. Tasters were happy with the meat choice and were willing to put up with a slightly longer cooking time for a cheaper, but flavorful, cut of beef. And by browning the meat, we could develop a rich fond on the bottom of the pan, which would then form the base of our sauce.

Mushrooms are another essential ingredient in stroganoff. We were after a strong mushroom presence and found that using 10 ounces of mushrooms brought their flavor to the forefront. But just simmering the mushrooms in the sauce, like many recipes suggested, gave the mushrooms a slimy exterior and added little flavor. Instead, we tried sautéing the mushrooms first, after cooking the meat, until their edges had browned. This made them silky and intensified their earthy flavor—a vast improvement.

As for flavoring the dish, a little restraint helped. An onion provided the base notes of the sauce. We abandoned seasonings like prepared mustard, paprika, and Worcestershire, feeling that they did nothing but cover up the flavor of the beef and mushrooms. We also tried adding spirits such as brandy, sherry, and red wine. Brandy was the winner and gave the stroganoff some brightness and depth. Small amounts of tomato paste and brown sugar improved the sauce's appearance and balanced the other flavors, and 2 tablespoons of flour helped thicken the sauce. To finish, we used just ⅔ cup of sour cream, which provided just enough of that tangy richness we were after. (So the sour cream wouldn't curdle, we tempered it with a few tablespoons of the hot liquid before adding it to the skillet.)

With the flavors settled, we turned our attention to the noodles. We already knew we'd have to depart from our usual skillet pasta method of simmering the pasta and sauce vigorously to cook the pasta. To prevent the meat from overcooking and becoming tough, we would have to keep the skillet on low heat, which meant we had to slightly rejigger the pasta cooking method. We decided to cover the skillet, which would keep enough additional heat and liquid in the skillet to cook the noodles, after the beef had already simmered for 30 minutes. This led us to question just how much liquid and pasta we should use.

We began playing with the amounts of chicken and beef broth (which were preferred over either one used alone) that we were using as the base for the dish. After a couple of trials using 8 ounces of pasta, we realized we would have to use less pasta based on the amount of liquid (3 cups) we needed to braise the beef. We settled on 6 ounces of pasta as the right amount to add after the half hour of braising—this amount prevented the dish from becoming too soupy or, on the flip side, from becoming dried-out egg noodles and beef without sauce. The combination of 6 ounces pasta and 3 cups liquid also helped the sauce reduce to a nice consistency and kept the beef and mushroom flavors intact.

With a touch of lemon juice and a handful of parsley, this dish was at last stroganoff, recognizably retro, quite affordable, and pretty irresistible.

Beef Stroganoff

SERVES 4

Steak tips can be cut from a half-dozen muscles; make sure you are buying what butchers refer to as flap meat sirloin tips, which are the most flavorful. Do not substitute other types of noodles for the wide egg noodles here. Be sure to add the brandy to the skillet after stirring in the broth in step 4, or else the brandy may ignite. Simmering the noodles gently over low heat in step 5 is important in order to prevent the beef from turning tough and chewy.

1½	pounds sirloin steak tips (see note)
	Salt and ground black pepper
¼	cup vegetable oil
10	ounces white mushrooms, wiped clean and sliced thin
1	medium onion, minced
2	tablespoons all-purpose flour
1	teaspoon tomato paste
1½	cups low-sodium chicken broth
1½	cups low-sodium beef broth
⅓	cup brandy
1½	teaspoons dark brown sugar
6	ounces (about 3 cups) wide egg noodles
⅔	cup sour cream
2	teaspoons juice from 1 lemon
1	tablespoon minced fresh parsley leaves

1. Using a meat pounder, pound the beef to an even ½-inch thickness. Slicing with the grain of the meat, slice the meat into 2-inch-wide strips, then slice each strip crosswise into ½-inch-wide pieces.

2. Pat the beef dry with paper towels and season with salt and pepper. Heat 1 tablespoon of the oil in a 12-inch nonstick skillet over medium-high heat until just smoking. Brown half of the beef until well browned on both sides, 6 to 8 minutes; transfer the beef to a bowl. Repeat with 1 tablespoon more oil and the remaining beef; transfer to the bowl.

3. Add the remaining 2 tablespoons oil to the skillet and return to medium-high heat until shimmering. Add the mushrooms, onion, and ½ teaspoon salt and cook, stirring often, until the mushrooms have released their moisture and are golden brown, 7 to 10 minutes.

4. Stir in the flour and tomato paste and cook for 30 seconds. Gradually whisk in the broths. Stir in the brandy, sugar, and beef with any accumulated juices. Bring to a simmer, cover, and cook over low heat until the beef is tender, 30 to 35 minutes.

5. Stir the noodles into the skillet. Cover and continue to cook over low heat, stirring often, until the noodles are tender, 10 to 12 minutes.

6. Off the heat, stir a few tablespoons of the sauce into the sour cream to temper it, then stir the sour cream mixture back into the skillet. Stir in the lemon juice and season with salt and pepper to taste. Sprinkle with the parsley and serve.

VERMICELLI WITH CHICKEN AND CHORIZO

THIS SKILLET SUPPER IS BASED ON THE traditional Mexican dish *sopa seca,* which translates literally as "dry soup." It begins with an aromatic broth built in a skillet (the soup part), which is poured over thin strands of pasta in a baking dish and baked until the liquid is absorbed and the pasta is tender (the dry part). It's not a difficult dish to make, nor is it time-consuming, but we wanted to get rid of the baking time and cook the entire dish in our skillet on the stovetop. We also wanted a dish that, unlike the original version, relied on easily accessible ingredients and was substantial enough to serve as a weeknight dinner.

Traditionally, the pasta used in this dish is *fideos,* thin strands of coiled, toasted noodles, which lend a distinctive background flavor. These noodles are great, but they are often unavailable at our local market. We found that vermicelli, toasted uncooked in a skillet until golden brown, was the closest match in terms of texture and depth of flavor. After toasting the vermicelli, we browned thinly sliced boneless, skinless chicken breasts—our first addition to bulk up the dish for dinnertime—and then transferred the chicken to a bowl while we built the sauce.

Jalapeño chiles are a given in authentic sopa seca, so we started our broth by sautéing an onion and a jalapeño. We found that the fresh jalapeño gave this stovetop interpretation just too much of a raw chile flavor. Instead, we used canned chipotle chiles in adobo, which are smoked jalapeños in a vinegary sauce; they brought exactly the level of spice we sought. Garlic and chorizo, a popular and easy-to-find Mexican sausage, were also added to the skillet to enhance the flavor. We then added canned diced tomatoes with their juice, along with chicken broth, to make a rich base. To bring additional heft to the dish, canned black beans went into the skillet.

Lastly, we added the vermicelli back in and simmered the mixture, covered, until most of the liquid was absorbed and the pasta was tender. We returned the chicken to the pan and sprinkled shredded Monterey Jack cheese over the noodles; the cheese melted to form a gooey layer. A little minced cilantro added freshness, color, and authenticity to our skillet version of sopa seca.

Vermicelli with Chicken and Chorizo

SERVES 4

To make the dish spicier, increase the amount of chipotle chiles to 1 tablespoon. Serve with sour cream, diced avocado, and thinly sliced scallions.

8	ounces vermicelli, broken in half (see the illustrations on page 88)
3	tablespoons vegetable oil
I	pound boneless, skinless chicken breasts (about 3 medium), trimmed and sliced thin (see the illustrations on page 228)
I	medium onion, minced
	Salt
4	ounces chorizo, halved lengthwise and sliced ¼ inch thick
2	medium garlic cloves, minced or pressed through a garlic press (about 2 teaspoons)
2	teaspoons minced chipotle chile in adobo sauce (see note)
2	cups low-sodium chicken broth
I	(15-ounce) can black beans, drained and rinsed
I	(14.5-ounce) can diced tomatoes
	Ground black pepper
2	ounces Monterey Jack cheese, shredded (½ cup)
¼	cup minced fresh cilantro leaves

1. Toast the vermicelli in 1 tablespoon of the oil in a 12-inch nonstick skillet over medium-high heat, tossing frequently with tongs, until golden, about 4 minutes. Transfer to a paper towel–lined plate and set aside.

2. Add 1 tablespoon more oil to the skillet and place over high heat until shimmering. Add the chicken, break up any clumps, and cook, without stirring, until lightly browned, about 1 minute. Stir the chicken and continue to cook until cooked through, 2 to 3 minutes longer. Transfer the chicken to a bowl, cover to keep warm, and set aside.

3. Add the remaining 1 tablespoon oil to the skillet and place over medium heat until shimmering. Add the onion and ½ teaspoon salt and cook, stirring often, until softened, 5 to 7 minutes. Stir in the chorizo, garlic, and chipotles and cook until fragrant, about 30 seconds.

4. Stir in the broth, beans, and tomatoes with their juice, then add the toasted vermicelli. Cover, increase the heat to medium-high, and cook, stirring often and adjusting the heat to maintain a vigorous simmer, until the vermicelli is tender, about 10 minutes.

5. Off the heat, return the chicken, along with any accumulated juices, to the skillet. Season with salt and pepper to taste and sprinkle the cheese over the top. Cover and let stand off the heat until the cheese melts, 2 to 4 minutes. Sprinkle with the cilantro and serve.

RAMEN NOODLE SUPPERS

INSTANT RAMEN NOODLES HAVE THE reputation of being a mainstay on college campuses across the country. They are cheap (under $1 a package) and they cook quickly (in about 10 minutes), making them a convenient dinner for the thrifty, time-crunched cook. However, in Japan, ramen (or ramen soup) is a much more serious endeavor, with ramen shops on almost every street corner and noodles served in a variety of richly flavored broths. We wanted to take a second look at these quick-cooking noodles and see if we could give them a fresh, new flavor.

We started by pitching the seasoning packets that come in packages of ramen—they're loaded with a day's worth of sodium, not to mention stale, dehydrated ingredients that we can't even pronounce.

To create our own broth in which to simmer the noodles, we sautéed fresh garlic and ginger; to that we added chicken broth and a splash of soy sauce, which provided a nice base for our broth. It took us a few tries to get the correct ratio of broth to noodles, so the noodles would have enough liquid in which to cook. If we used too much broth, the flavors were diluted and the noodles turned mushy. In the end we settled on 3½ cups of broth and 12 ounces of noodles.

To turn our ramen dish into a substantial meal, we decided to add some beef. Tasters approved of thinly sliced flank steak, to which we added shiitake mushrooms and spinach for a classic Asian combination. Before cooking the beef, we sliced it thin and tossed it with a little soy sauce for flavor and to promote browning. We sautéed it briefly over high heat until it was just cooked through, and then set it aside, to be returned to the skillet when the noodles were done simmering in the broth.

Finally, we focused on the noodles. We were a little hesitant to use the dried ramen noodles that flood grocery store shelves. For comparison, we sought out dried ramen from an Asian market (although they seemed indistinguishable from their supermarket counterpart), along with high-end *chuka soba* noodles (noodles made from all wheat flour or a combination of wheat and buckwheat flours) and fresh Chinese egg noodles. Chuka soba noodles were much thinner and, frankly, didn't have as much flavor as the more common dried ramen noodles. That might be because dried ramen noodles are actually fried as part of the drying process. This frying instills a richer flavor, which in our tests gave them an advantage over fresh noodles. Plus, the ramen noodles instantly soaked up our rich broth when they hit the skillet.

With our basic recipe down, we created a few spin-offs. Thinly sliced pork tenderloin, shredded cabbage, and sliced scallions gave us another dish, while seared shrimp, red bell pepper, roasted peanuts, and hoisin sauce added richness and heft to a kung pao–style shrimp dish. And a vegetarian version with tofu features an interpretation of the flavors found in hot and sour soup.

Ramen with Beef, Shiitakes, and Spinach
SERVES 4

Do not substitute other types of noodles for the ramen noodles here. The sauce in this dish will seem a bit brothy when finished, but the liquid will be absorbed quickly by the noodles when serving.

1	pound flank steak, trimmed and sliced thin across the grain on the bias (see the illustrations on page 228)
8	teaspoons soy sauce
2	tablespoons vegetable oil
8	ounces shiitake mushrooms, wiped clean, stemmed, and sliced thin
3	medium garlic cloves, minced or pressed through a garlic press (about 1 tablespoon)
1	tablespoon minced or grated fresh ginger
3½	cups low-sodium chicken broth
4	(3-ounce) packages ramen noodles, seasoning packets discarded

INGREDIENTS: Soy Sauce

Most of us rarely give a second thought when it comes to soy sauce. There are many brands to choose from at the supermarket, so we sought to narrow the field.

We tasted 12 soy sauces three different ways: plain, drizzled over warm rice, and cooked in a simple teriyaki glaze over chicken thighs. The brands varied in origin—some were domestic, while imports hailed from China and Japan—and cost, with $6.49 being the highest price. Fortunately, our overall winner, Lee Kum Kee Tabletop Soy Sauce, came in at a much lower price ($1.99 for a 5.1-ounce bottle). Tasters praised Lee Kum Kee for a "salty, sweet, pleasant" flavor with a "great aroma." Lee Kum Kee is our top pick for cooking, but the pricey $6.49 soy sauce, Ohsawa Nama Shoyu Organic Unpasteurized Soy Sauce, is a great choice for dipping sauces.

THE BEST SOY SAUCE
Lee Kum Kee Tabletop Soy Sauce is our favorite, with depth and balance.

LEE KUM KEE

3   tablespoons dry sherry

2   teaspoons sugar

1   (6-ounce) bag baby spinach

1. Pat the beef dry with paper towels and toss with 2 teaspoons of the soy sauce. Heat 1 tablespoon of the oil in a 12-inch nonstick skillet over high heat until just smoking. Add the beef, break up any clumps, and cook without stirring until beginning to brown, about 1 minute. Stir the beef and continue to cook until it is nearly cooked though, 1 minute longer. Transfer the beef to a bowl, cover to keep warm, and set aside.

2. Wipe out the skillet with paper towels. Add the remaining 1 tablespoon oil to the skillet and return to medium-high heat until shimmering. Add the mushrooms and cook until browned, about 4 minutes. Stir in the garlic and ginger and cook until fragrant, about 30 seconds.

3. Stir in the broth. Break the bricks of ramen into small chunks and add to the skillet. Bring to a simmer and cook, tossing the ramen constantly with tongs to separate, until the ramen is just tender but there is still liquid in the pan, about 2 minutes.

4. Stir in the remaining 2 tablespoons soy sauce, the sherry, and sugar. Stir in the spinach, one handful at a time, until it is wilted and the sauce is thickened. Return the beef, along with any accumulated juices, to the skillet and cook until warmed through, about 30 seconds. Serve.

Ramen with Pork, Scallions, and Cabbage

SERVES 4

Do not substitute other types of noodles for the ramen noodles here. We found it best to use low-sodium soy sauce here because the oyster-flavored sauce is quite salty. The sauce in this dish will seem a bit brothy when finished, but the liquid will be absorbed quickly by the noodles when serving.

1   pound pork tenderloin (about 1 medium tenderloin), trimmed and sliced into thin strips (see the illustrations on page 228)

8   teaspoons low-sodium soy sauce (see note)

2   tablespoons vegetable oil

12   medium scallions, white and green parts separated, both parts sliced on the bias into 1-inch lengths

6   medium garlic cloves, minced or pressed through a garlic press (about 2 tablespoons)

1   tablespoon minced or grated fresh ginger

1/8   teaspoon red pepper flakes

3 1/2   cups low-sodium chicken broth

4   (3-ounce) packages ramen noodles, seasoning packets discarded

2   tablespoons oyster-flavored sauce

2   teaspoons toasted sesame oil

1/2   pound green cabbage (about 1/4 medium head), cored and sliced thin (see the illustrations on page 114)

1. Pat the pork dry with paper towels and toss with 2 teaspoons of the soy sauce. Heat 1 tablespoon of the oil in a 12-inch nonstick skillet over high heat until just smoking. Add the pork, break up any clumps, and cook without stirring until beginning to brown, about 1 minute. Stir the pork and continue to cook until cooked through, 1 minute longer. Transfer the pork to a bowl, cover to keep warm, and set aside.

2. Add the remaining 1 tablespoon oil to the skillet and return to medium-high heat until shimmering. Add the scallion whites and cook until lightly browned and softened, about 3 minutes. Stir in the garlic, ginger, and red pepper flakes and cook until fragrant, about 30 seconds.

3. Stir in the broth. Break the bricks of ramen into small chunks and add to the skillet. Bring to a simmer and cook, tossing the ramen constantly with tongs to separate, until the ramen is just tender but there is still liquid in the pan, about 2 minutes.

4. Stir in the remaining 2 tablespoons soy sauce, the oyster-flavored sauce, and sesame oil. Stir in the scallion greens and cabbage and cook until the cabbage is wilted and the sauce is thickened, about 1 minute. Return the pork, along with any accumulated juices, to the skillet and cook until warmed through, about 30 seconds. Serve.

SHREDDING CABBAGE

1. Cut the cabbage into quarters and cut away the hard piece of core attached to each quarter.

2. Separate the cored cabbage into stacks of leaves that flatten when pressed lightly.

3a. Use a chef's knife to cut each stack diagonally (this ensures long pieces) into thin shreds.

3b. Or roll the stacked leaves crosswise to fit them into the feed tube of a food processor fitted with the shredding disk.

Kung Pao–Style Shrimp with Ramen
SERVES 4

Do not substitute other types of noodles for the ramen noodles here. Be sure not to cook the shrimp through completely in step 1 or they will overcook and turn rubbery when returned to the skillet to heat through in step 4. If the shrimp are larger or smaller than called for below, the cooking times may change accordingly. The sauce in this dish will seem a bit brothy when finished, but the liquid will be absorbed quickly by the noodles when serving.

1	pound extra-large shrimp (21 to 25 per pound), peeled and deveined (see the illustration on page 235)
¼	teaspoon salt
⅛	teaspoon ground black pepper
	Pinch sugar
2	tablespoons vegetable oil
1	red bell pepper, stemmed, seeded, and sliced thin
½	cup roasted unsalted peanuts
3	medium garlic cloves, minced or pressed through a garlic press (about 1 tablespoon)
1	tablespoon minced or grated fresh ginger
1	teaspoon red pepper flakes
3½	cups low-sodium chicken broth
4	(3-ounce) packages ramen noodles, seasoning packets discarded
2	tablespoons hoisin sauce
1	tablespoon rice vinegar
2	teaspoons toasted sesame oil
3	scallions, sliced thin on the bias (see the illustration on page 231)

1. Toss the shrimp, salt, pepper, and sugar together in a medium bowl. Heat 1 tablespoon of the oil in a 12-inch nonstick skillet over high heat until just smoking. Add the shrimp in a single layer and cook without stirring until beginning to brown, about 1 minute. Stir the shrimp and continue to cook until they are light pink and all but the very centers are opaque, about 30 seconds. Transfer the shrimp to a bowl, cover to keep warm, and set aside.

2. Add the remaining 1 tablespoon oil to the skillet and return to medium-high heat until shimmering. Add the bell pepper and peanuts and cook until the pepper is softened, 2 to 3 minutes. Transfer to the bowl with the shrimp.

3. Add the garlic, ginger, and red pepper flakes to the oil left in the skillet and return to medium-high heat until fragrant, about 30 seconds. Stir in the broth. Break the bricks of ramen into small chunks and add to the skillet. Bring to a simmer and cook, tossing the ramen constantly with tongs to separate, until the ramen is just tender but there is still liquid in the pan, about 2 minutes.

4. Stir in the hoisin, vinegar, and sesame oil and continue to simmer until the sauce is thickened, about 1 minute. Return the shrimp-pepper mixture to the skillet and cook until heated through, about 30 seconds. Sprinkle with the scallions and serve.

Hot and Sour Ramen with Tofu, Shiitakes, and Spinach

SERVES 4

Do not substitute other types of noodles for the ramen noodles here. We prefer the lighter flavor of vegetable broth here; however, low-sodium chicken broth can be substituted. To make the dish spicier, add extra Asian chili sauce (for more information on Asian chili sauce, see page 239). The sauce in this dish will seem a bit brothy when finished, but the liquid will be absorbed quickly by the noodles when serving.

I	(14-ounce) package extra-firm tofu, cut into I-inch cubes
8	teaspoons soy sauce
2	tablespoons vegetable oil
8	ounces shiitake mushrooms, wiped clean, stemmed, and sliced thin
2	teaspoons Asian chili sauce
3	medium garlic cloves, minced or pressed through a garlic press (about I tablespoon)
I	tablespoon minced or grated fresh ginger
3½	cups low-sodium vegetable broth (see note)
4	(3-ounce) packages ramen noodles, seasoning packets discarded
3	tablespoons cider vinegar
2	teaspoons sugar
I	(6-ounce) bag baby spinach

1. Pat the tofu dry with paper towels and toss with 2 teaspoons of the soy sauce. Heat 1 tablespoon of the oil in a 12-inch nonstick skillet over high heat until just smoking. Add the tofu and cook, turning every few minutes, until all sides are crisp and browned, 8 to 10 minutes. Transfer the tofu to a bowl, cover to keep warm, and set aside.

2. Add the remaining 1 tablespoon oil to the skillet and return to medium-high heat until shimmering. Add the mushrooms and cook until browned, about 4 minutes. Stir in the chili sauce, garlic, and ginger and cook until fragrant, about 30 seconds.

3. Stir in the broth. Break the bricks of ramen into small chunks and add to the skillet. Bring to a simmer and cook, tossing the ramen constantly with tongs to separate, until the ramen is just tender but there is still liquid in the pan, about 2 minutes.

4. Stir in the remaining 2 tablespoons soy sauce, vinegar, and sugar. Stir in the spinach, one handful at a time, until the spinach is wilted and the sauce is thickened. Return the tofu, along with any accumulated juices, to the skillet and cook until warmed through, about 30 seconds. Serve.

PAD THAI

PAD THAI IS THE PERFECT REMEDY FOR A dulled palate. Hot, sweet, and pungent Thai flavors are sure to wake up the senses. We have downed numerous platefuls of pad thai, many from an excellent Thai restaurant only a few blocks away from our test kitchen. What we noticed was that from one order to the next, pad thai prepared in the same reliable restaurant kitchen was inconsistent. If it was perfect, it was a symphony of flavors, but sometimes it fell flat and was weakly seasoned. We have attempted it several times in the test kitchen with only moderate success, and that we attribute to luck.

We have found recipes that were unclear, ingredient lists that were daunting, and steps that led to dry, undercooked noodles and unbalanced flavors. Our goal was to build on our experience and produce a consistently superlative pad thai. We took solace in the fact that at least this dish has always been made in a skillet.

Flat rice noodles, or rice sticks, the type of noodles used in pad thai, are often only partially cooked, particularly when used in stir-fries. We found three different methods of preparing them: soaking them in room-temperature water, soaking them in hot tap water, and boiling them. We began with boiling and quickly realized this was a bad move. Drained and waiting in the colander, the noodles glued themselves together, then wound up soggy and overdone in the finished dish. Noodles soaked in room-temperature water remained fairly stiff. After lengthy stir-frying, they became tender, but longer cooking made this pad thai drier and stickier. We finally tried soaking the noodles in water that had been brought to a boil and then removed them from the heat. They softened, turning limp and pliant, but were not fully tender. Drained, they were loose and separate and they cooked through easily with stir-frying. The result? Noodles that were at once pleasantly tender and resilient. With our noodles ready to go, we focused on creating the right flavor profile.

Sweet, salty, sour, and spicy are the flavor characteristics of pad thai, and they should be equally balanced. Although the cooking time is short, the ingredient list isn't. Fish sauce supplies a salty-sweet pungency, sugar gives sweetness, heat comes from ground chiles, rice vinegar provides acidity, and tamarind rounds out the dish with its fruity, earthy, sweet-tart molasses-tinged flavor. Garlic and sometimes shallots contribute their heady, robust flavors. Some recipes call for ketchup, and some require soy sauce.

With our basic ingredients in hand, we set off to find out which ones—and what amounts—were key to success. For 8 ounces of rice noodles, 3 tablespoons of fish sauce and the same amount of sugar were ideal. Three-quarters of a teaspoon of cayenne (many recipes call for Thai chiles, but for the sake of simplicity, we opted not to use them) brought a low, even heat—not a searing burn—and 1 tablespoon of rice vinegar (preferred in pad thai for its mild acidity and relatively complex fermented-grain flavor) greatly boosted the flavors. We tried adding a little ketchup, but its vinegary tomato flavor was out of place; soy sauce, even just a tablespoon, acted as a big bully—its assertive flavor didn't play nicely with the others. As for the garlic, 1 tablespoon minced was our tasters' preference. Shallots had a surprising impact on flavor—just one medium shallot produced a round, full sweetness and depth of flavor. To coax the right character out of these two aromatics, we found that browning them was critical; they tasted mellow, sweet, and mildly toasty. Tamarind was the most enigmatic ingredient on our list.

Tamarind is a fruit that grows as a round brown pod about five inches long and is often sold as a paste (a hard, flat brick) or as a sticky concentrate. (For more information, see page 118.) It is central—if not essential—to the unique flavor of pad thai. Tests showed that tamarind paste has a fresher, brighter, fruitier flavor than concentrate, which tasted dull by comparison. For those who cannot obtain either tamarind paste or concentrate, we worked out a formula of equal parts lime juice and water as a stand-in (see page 118). This mixture produces a less interesting and less authentic dish, but we polished off several such platefuls of pad thai made with this substitution with no qualms whatsoever.

The other ingredients in pad thai are sautéed shrimp (we used medium-sized shrimp to keep with tradition and to keep balance in the dish), scrambled eggs, chopped peanuts, bean sprouts, and scallions, all of which would definitely stay. A few obscure ingredients, such as dried shrimp and Thai salted preserved radish, fell by the wayside in an effort to cut back on the ingredient list. Tasters felt that they were worthy embellishments, but not essential.

Oddly, after consuming dozens of servings of pad thai, we weren't tired of it—we were addicted to it. Nowadays, if we order it in a restaurant, we prepare ourselves for disappointment.

Pad Thai

SERVES 4

Do not substitute other types of noodles for the flat rice noodles here. Be sure not to cook the shrimp through completely in step 3 or they will overcook and turn rubbery when returned to the skillet to heat through in step 6. If the shrimp are larger or smaller than called for below, the cooking times may change accordingly. This dish cooks very quickly, so be sure to have all of the ingredients prepared and within easy reach at the stovetop before you begin cooking.

SAUCE

- 2 tablespoons tamarind paste plus ¾ cup boiling water, or tamarind substitute (see page 118)
- 3 tablespoons fish sauce
- 3 tablespoons sugar
- 2 tablespoons vegetable oil
- 1 tablespoon rice vinegar
- ¾ teaspoon cayenne pepper

NOODLES AND SHRIMP

- 8 ounces (¼-inch-wide) dried flat rice noodles (see sidebar at right)
- 12 ounces medium shrimp (41 to 50 per pound), peeled and deveined (see the illustration on page 235) Salt
- ⅛ teaspoon ground black pepper Pinch sugar
- 2 tablespoons vegetable oil
- 1 medium shallot, minced (about 3 tablespoons)
- 3 medium garlic cloves, minced or pressed through a garlic press (about 1 tablespoon)
- 2 large eggs, lightly beaten
- 3 cups bean sprouts (about 6 ounces)

- ¼ cup chopped unsalted roasted peanuts, plus extra for garnish
- 3 scallions, sliced thin on the bias (see the illustration on page 231)
- ¼ cup loosely packed fresh cilantro leaves (optional)
- 1 lime, cut into wedges, for serving

1. **FOR THE SAUCE:** Following the instructions on page 118, soak and rehydrate the tamarind paste in boiling water until softened, about 10 minutes. Push the tamarind mixture through a fine-mesh strainer into a medium bowl to remove the seeds and fibers and extract as much pulp as possible. Stir in the remaining sauce ingredients and set aside.

2. **FOR THE NOODLES AND SHRIMP:** Bring 4 quarts water to a boil in a large pot. Remove the boiling water from the heat, add the rice noodles,

INGREDIENTS: Rice Noodles

In Southeast Asia and southern regions of China, a delicate pasta made from rice flour and water is used in an array of dishes including soups, stir-fries, and salads. Unlike other pasta, these delicate noodles should not be boiled because they have a tendency to overcook very quickly, resulting in a mushy, sticky mess. Instead, it is best to bring a pot of water to a boil, then remove the pot from the heat and steep the noodles gently in the hot water.

Flat rice noodles come in several different widths from extra small to extra large. We use a medium-width noodle, similar to linguine in size (about ¼ inch wide) for our Pad Thai.

FLAT RICE NOODLES

Flat rice noodles, made from rice flour, are essential for an authentic homemade pad thai.

and let stand off the heat, stirring occasionally, until the noodles are softened, pliable, and just tender, about 10 minutes. Drain the noodles and set aside.

3. Toss the shrimp, ⅛ teaspoon salt, pepper, and sugar together in a medium bowl. Heat 1 tablespoon of the oil in a 12-inch nonstick skillet over high heat until just smoking. Add the shrimp in a single layer and cook without stirring until beginning to brown, about 1 minute. Stir the shrimp and continue to cook until they are light pink and all but the very centers are opaque, about 30 seconds. Transfer the shrimp to a bowl, cover to keep warm, and set aside.

4. Add the remaining 1 tablespoon oil, the shallot, garlic, and ⅛ teaspoon salt to the skillet, return to medium heat, and cook, stirring constantly, until light golden brown, about 1½ minutes. Stir in the eggs and cook, stirring constantly, until scrambled and barely moist, about 20 seconds.

5. Add the drained rice noodles and toss to combine. Add the sauce, increase the heat to high, and cook, tossing constantly, until the noodles are evenly coated, about 1 minute. Add the bean sprouts, peanuts, and all but ¼ cup of the scallions and continue to cook, tossing constantly, until the noodles are tender, about 2 minutes.

6. Return the shrimp, along with any accumulated juices, to the skillet and cook until heated through, about 30 seconds. Transfer the noodles to a serving platter, sprinkle with the reserved ¼ cup scallions, cilantro (if using), and additional peanuts. Serve with the lime wedges.

➤ VARIATION
Pad Thai with Tofu
Tofu is a good and common addition to pad thai.

Follow the recipe for Pad Thai, adding 4 ounces extra-firm tofu, cut into ½-inch cubes (about 1 cup), to the skillet with the cooked shrimp in step 6.

INGREDIENTS: Tamarind

Sweet-tart, brownish red tamarind is a necessary ingredient for authentic pad thai. Tamarind is commonly sold in paste (also called pulp) and in concentrate form. But don't fret if neither is available—you can still make a very good pad thai using lime juice and water.

Tamarind paste, or pulp, is firm, sticky, and filled with seeds and fibers. We favor this product because it has the freshest, brightest flavor. To rehydrate the tamarind, soak it in boiling water until softened and mushy, 10 to 30 minutes (depending on the amount of tamarind). Mash the softened tamarind to break it up, then push it through a mesh strainer to remove the seeds and fibers and extract as much pulp as possible. This pulp can now be used in a recipe.

Tamarind concentrate is black, thick, and shiny. It tastes less fruity and more "cooked" than tamarind paste, and it colors the noodles a shade too dark, but it still works fine. To use in the Pad Thai recipe, mix 1 tablespoon with ⅔ cup hot water.

If tamarind is out of the question, replace it with a combination of ⅓ cup lime juice and ⅓ cup water; use light brown sugar instead of granulated to give the noodles some color and a faint molasses flavor. Because it will already have a good bite from the lime, do not serve this version of Pad Thai with lime wedges.

TAMARIND PASTE OR PULP

TAMARIND CONCENTRATE

LIME JUICE AND WATER SUBSTITUTE

Both tamarind paste and concentrate will work in our Pad Thai recipe. In a pinch, lime juice and water can be used instead.

BAKED ZITI WITH SAUSAGE **PAGE 100**

SPANISH-STYLE GARLIC SHRIMP **PAGE 45**

WARM CABBAGE SALAD WITH CRISPY TOFU **PAGE 183**

SPINACH AND GOUDA STRATA   **PAGE 274**

CHICKEN SALTIMBOCCA **PAGE 30**

STEAK TACOS **PAGE 161**

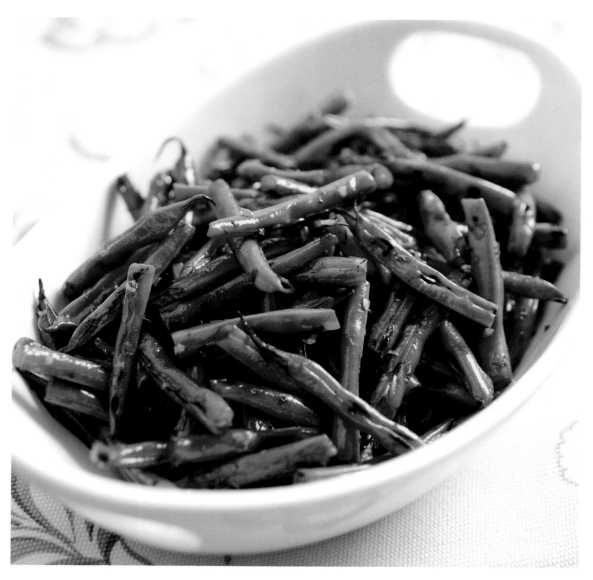

SAUTÉED GREEN BEANS WITH GARLIC AND HERBS **PAGE 291**

125

BEEF STROGANOFF **PAGE 109**

126

SAUTÉED CHERRY TOMATOES WITH CAPERS AND ANCHOVIES **PAGE 301**

ORANGE-HONEY GLAZED CHICKEN BREASTS **PAGE 55**

RICOTTA, BACON, AND SCALLION PIZZA **PAGE 222**

PAN-ROASTED CHICKEN BREASTS WITH POTATOES **PAGE 148**

PAN-ROASTED ASPARAGUS WITH TOASTED GARLIC AND PARMESAN **PAGE 281**

TUSCAN-STYLE STEAK WITH GARLICKY SPINACH **PAGE 155**

132

CHERRY COBBLER **PAGE 313**

LEMON SOUFFLÉ   **PAGE 332**

134

4
SKILLET SUPPERS

SKILLET SUPPERS

MAKING A WELL-ROUNDED MEAL OFTEN means pulling out one pan for the meat, at least one for the vegetables, another for the starch, and so on. That's a lot of steps, and a lot of dishes, for one meal—not something you want to deal with for a quick weeknight dinner. For this chapter, we wanted to make complete meals while reducing the number of pans used to the bare essentials—to just a skillet in almost every case. However, in a few instances, for our bone-in chicken recipes (see pages 148–149) and pork tenderloin recipe (see page 172), it was necessary to utilize a two-track approach, pan-searing the meat in the skillet before transferring it to another dish to finish cooking in the oven. But even here, the skillet is the key to success, enabling us to brown the meat for flavor and color, speed up cooking time, and prepare sides accented with the flavorful fond in the skillet. This approach also ensured everything was ready at the same time. The microwave also came in handy in a few recipes; a short spell in the microwave before finishing on the stovetop gave long-cooking foods such as potatoes a head start.

Simplicity aside, skillet suppers do pose particular challenges. Needing to include a protein, a starch, and vegetables meant that we were often faced with ingredients that had very different cooking times. Orchestrating these different ingredients in and out of the skillet so that they were all hot and properly cooked when finished proved to be quite difficult. For example, when developing a recipe for paella, we had to figure out how to cook the rice, shrimp, and peas (ingredients with very disparate cooking times) in the same skillet while avoiding sticky rice, rubbery shrimp, and mushy peas. After much trial and error, we learned not only how to narrow down original recipes to a list of workable ingredients for our skillet adaptations, but also the order in which they should be added to the skillet. In this chapter, the recipes aim to choreograph the cooking into a streamlined process and deliver flavorful one-skillet meals.

While we simply updated skillet classics like Sloppy Joes (see page 166), for our new skillet-based recipes we found that, rather than limiting us, having to rotate ingredients in and out of the skillet actually allowed us to be quite inventive.

We were able to create dishes like Chicken and Couscous with Fennel and Orange (page 144), and Cornmeal Fried Fish and Succotash (page 175).

The recipes in this chapter require a 12-inch skillet, and many also require a cover. In most cases, you can use a traditional skillet, but a few recipes do require a nonstick skillet for best results. See page 12 for the results of our traditional skillets test and page 14 for the nonstick skillets results.

CHICKEN AND RICE

MOST SKILLET RECIPES FOR CHICKEN AND rice rely on boneless chicken breasts, instant rice, canned soup, and a smattering of peas. Predictably, the chicken comes out dry, the rice mushy, and the sauce tastes, well, canned. Not to mention the peas, which come out a less-than-appealing shade of army green. We knew we could do better on all fronts. We wanted fresh-tasting chicken and rice that resembled the traditional, well-flavored version, and we wanted it all done in the skillet.

Because chicken breasts are so lean, they require special treatment to prevent the meat from drying out. We tried cooking them with the skin on to avoid the dryness issue, but this left us with pale, flabby skin. Even if they had been incredibly juicy, we were after the deep flavor that only comes from a nicely browned piece of chicken. We found that dredging skinless chicken breasts in flour before browning protected their exterior and gave the chicken a golden crust, ensuring juicy meat and deep flavor. After browning, we just set them aside until it was time to finish cooking them through over the rice.

Our research into skillet chicken and rice made it clear that quick-cooking instant rice is the key to most recipes. Wanting to avoid the texture and flavor issues that tend to accompany instant rice, we opted instead for long-grain rice, which offers more flavor and is far better at withstanding cooking without fear of turning to mush. To boost the flavor, we sautéed it first in butter with onion and garlic and then added the cooking liquid to the skillet. This step not only gave the rice a deeper flavor, but it kept the grains distinct and creamy without turning mushy.

As for the canned soup, forget it. There are some convenience products we find acceptable in certain applications (chicken broth, for one), but canned soup just doesn't make the cut. We chose to sauté our aromatics along with the browned bits (called fond) left in the pan from searing the chicken, then added chicken broth. It was a flavorful liquid, perfect for cooking our rice and chicken. To ensure that the chicken did not dry out, we cooked it with the rice until just done, then set it aside while the rice finished.

For the peas, we immediately settled on the frozen variety—fresh peas are available for only a short time each year, and the labor involved in shucking them almost negates any flavor benefits. Frozen peas are picked at the height of the season, ensuring their sweetness, and are convenient to use. We tried adding them at the onset of cooking, but they turned soft and became an unappealing shade of green. After a few attempts at preserving their bright green color and sweet flavor, we found it best to add them to the skillet off the heat when they were still frozen, letting the residual heat cook them through without turning them mushy or drab.

To boost the flavors even further, we added red pepper flakes when sautéing the aromatics and we stirred lemon juice and scallions into the rice before serving. The result was a greatly improved, and twice as flavorful, rendition of the canned soup and instant rice version. We also created a number of variations with both familiar and unique flavor combinations—broccoli and cheddar, coconut milk and pistachios, curry and raisins, and a Spanish-style dish with saffron and chorizo—that were just as easy to make.

INGREDIENTS: Frozen Peas

For bright green, sweet peas in our chicken and rice recipes, we depend on the frozen variety. Not only are they more convenient than their fresh, in-the-pod comrades, but they taste better. While this may seem counterintuitive, there is good reason behind it.

Green peas are one of the oldest vegetables known to humankind, but despite their long history, they are actually relatively delicate; fresh peas have little stamina. Green peas lose a substantial portion of their nutrients within 24 hours of being picked. This rapid deterioration is the reason for the starchy, bland flavor of most "fresh" peas found at the grocery store. These not-so-fresh peas might be several days old, depending on where they came from and how long they were kept in the cooler. Frozen peas, on the other hand, are picked, cleaned, sorted, and frozen within several hours of harvest, which helps to preserve their delicate sugars and flavors. When commercially frozen vegetables began to appear in the 1920s and 1930s, green peas were one of the first among them.

Finding good frozen peas is not hard. After tasting peas from the two major national frozen food purveyors, Birdseye and Green Giant, along with some from a smaller organic company, Cascadian Farm, tasters found little difference between them. All of the peas were sweet and fresh, with a bright green color. So unless you grow your own or can stop by your local farm stand for fresh picked, you're better off cruising up the frozen food aisle for a bag of frozen peas.

Chicken and Rice with Peas and Scallions
SERVES 4

Be sure to use chicken breasts that are roughly the same size to ensure even cooking.

4	(5- to 6-ounce) boneless, skinless chicken breasts, tenderloins removed and breasts trimmed (see the illustrations on pages 5 and 6)
½	cup unbleached all-purpose flour
	Salt and ground black pepper
2	tablespoons vegetable oil
2	tablespoons unsalted butter
I	medium onion, minced
I ½	cups long-grain white rice
3	medium garlic cloves, minced or pressed through a garlic press (about I tablespoon)
	Pinch red pepper flakes
4 ½	cups low-sodium chicken broth
I	cup frozen peas
5	scallions, sliced thin
2	tablespoons juice from I lemon

1. Following the illustration on page 7, pound each chicken breast between two sheets of plastic wrap to a uniform ½-inch thickness. Place the flour in a shallow dish. Pat the chicken breasts dry with

INGREDIENTS: Long-Grain Rice

The beauty of white rice resides in its neutral flavor, which makes it good at carrying other flavors. But is all long-grain white rice created equal? We set up a taste test to find out.

We rounded up a converted rice, three standard supermarket options, and an organic white rice available in bulk from a natural foods store. The most noticeable difference was an unpredictable variance in cooking time. According to the U.S. Rice Producers Association, the age of the rice, its moisture content, and the variety used can affect the rate of water uptake. Inconsistent cooking times are barely noticeable in plain rice, but they can become more apparent when other ingredients—such as aromatics and vegetables—are added to the pot.

All rices but one were noted for being "clean" and "like rice should be." The exception was Uncle Ben's, a converted rice that failed to meet our standards on all fronts. Converted rice is processed in a way that ensures separate grains, a firm texture, and more pronounced flavor. Those "round," "rubbery" grains and the telltale yellowish tint immediately brought back not-so-fond memories of "dining hall rice." Tasters agreed that some "stickiness" and minor "clumping" make for more natural-looking and better-tasting rice. The recommended brands were universally liked and are listed here alphabetically.

THE BEST LONG-GRAIN RICE

CANILLA

CAROLINA

SEM-CHI

The flavor of Canilla Extra Long was likened to that of jasmine rice, and tasters found Carolina Extra Long Grain Enriched Rice to be a good, clean slate on which to add flavor. Sem-Chi Organically Grown Florida Long Grain Rice was rated the chewiest, with roasted and nutty flavors.

paper towels and season with salt and pepper. Working with 1 chicken breast at a time, dredge in the flour, shaking off the excess.

2. Heat the oil in a 12-inch nonstick skillet over medium-high heat until just smoking. Carefully lay the chicken breasts in the skillet and cook until lightly browned on both sides, 6 to 8 minutes. Transfer the chicken to a plate and pour off any fat left in the pan.

3. Add the butter to the skillet and melt over medium heat. Add the onion and ½ teaspoon salt and cook until the onion is softened, about 5 minutes. Stir in the rice, garlic, and red pepper flakes and cook until fragrant, about 30 seconds.

4. Stir in the broth, scraping up any browned bits. Nestle the chicken into the rice and bring to a simmer. Cover, reduce the heat to medium-low, and cook until the thickest part of the chicken registers 160 to 165 degrees on an instant-read thermometer, about 10 minutes.

5. Transfer the chicken to a clean plate, brushing any rice that sticks to the chicken back into the skillet, and tent the chicken loosely with foil to keep warm. Cover and continue to cook the rice over medium-low heat, stirring occasionally, until the liquid has been absorbed and the rice is tender, about 10 minutes.

6. Off the heat, sprinkle the peas over the rice, cover, and let warm through, about 2 minutes. Add the scallions and lemon juice and gently fold into the rice. Season the rice with salt and pepper to taste and serve with the chicken.

➤ VARIATIONS

Chicken and Rice with Broccoli and Cheddar

Be sure to use chicken breasts that are roughly the same size to ensure even cooking.

4	(5- to 6-ounce) boneless, skinless chicken breasts, tenderloins removed and breasts trimmed (see the illustrations on pages 5 and 6)
½	cup unbleached all-purpose flour
	Salt and ground black pepper
3	tablespoons vegetable oil
1	medium onion, minced

1½ cups long-grain white rice
3 medium garlic cloves, minced or pressed
through a garlic press (about 1 tablespoon)
4½ cups low-sodium chicken broth
1 (10-ounce) package frozen broccoli florets,
thawed
4 ounces cheddar cheese, shredded (1 cup)
1 teaspoon hot sauce

1. Following the illustration on page 7, pound each chicken breast between two sheets of plastic wrap to a uniform ½-inch thickness. Place the flour in a shallow dish. Pat the chicken breasts dry with paper towels and season with salt and pepper. Working with 1 chicken breast at a time, dredge in the flour, shaking off the excess.

2. Heat 2 tablespoons of the oil in a 12-inch nonstick skillet over medium-high heat until just smoking. Carefully lay the chicken breasts in the skillet and cook until lightly browned on both sides, 6 to 8 minutes. Transfer the chicken to a plate.

3. Add the remaining 1 tablespoon oil to the skillet and return to medium-high heat until shimmering. Add the onion and ½ teaspoon salt and cook until softened, about 5 minutes. Stir in the rice and garlic and cook until fragrant, about 30 seconds.

4. Stir in the broth, scraping up any browned bits. Nestle the chicken into the rice and bring to a simmer. Cover, reduce the heat to medium-low, and cook until the thickest part of the chicken registers 160 to 165 degrees on an instant-read thermometer, about 10 minutes.

5. Transfer the chicken to a clean plate, brushing any rice that sticks to the chicken back into the skillet, and tent the chicken loosely with foil to keep warm. Cover and continue to cook the rice over medium-low heat, stirring occasionally, until the liquid has been absorbed and the rice is tender, about 10 minutes.

6. Off the heat, gently fold the broccoli, ½ cup of the cheddar, and the hot sauce into the rice and season with salt and pepper to taste. Sprinkle the remaining ½ cup cheddar over the top, cover, and let sit until the cheese melts, about 2 minutes. Serve with the chicken.

Chicken and Rice with Coconut Milk and Pistachios

Be sure to use chicken breasts that are roughly the same size to ensure even cooking. Garam masala is an Indian spice blend that can be found in well-stocked supermarkets and Indian markets. We use light coconut milk here; full-fat coconut milk is simply too rich for this dish.

4 (5- to 6-ounce) boneless, skinless chicken
breasts, tenderloins removed and breasts
trimmed (see the illustrations on pages 5 and 6)
½ cup unbleached all-purpose flour
Salt and ground black pepper
3 tablespoons vegetable oil
1 medium onion, minced
1½ teaspoons garam masala (see note)
1½ cups long-grain white rice
3 medium garlic cloves, minced or pressed
through a garlic press (about 1 tablespoon)
2¾ cups low-sodium chicken broth
1 (13.5-ounce) can light coconut milk
(see note)
1 cup frozen peas
½ cup chopped pistachios, toasted
½ cup minced fresh cilantro leaves

1. Following the illustration on page 7, pound each chicken breast between two sheets of plastic wrap to a uniform ½-inch thickness. Place the flour in a shallow dish. Pat the chicken breasts dry with paper towels and season with salt and pepper. Working with 1 chicken breast at a time, dredge in the flour, shaking off the excess.

2. Heat 2 tablespoons of the oil in a 12-inch nonstick skillet over medium-high heat until just smoking. Carefully lay the chicken breasts in the skillet and cook until lightly browned on both sides, 6 to 8 minutes. Transfer the chicken to a plate.

3. Add the remaining 1 tablespoon oil to the skillet and return to medium-high heat until shimmering. Add the onion, garam masala, and ½ teaspoon salt and cook until the onion is softened, about 5 minutes. Stir in the rice and garlic and cook until fragrant, about 30 seconds.

4. Stir in the chicken broth and coconut milk, scraping up any browned bits. Nestle the chicken

into the rice and bring to a simmer. Cover, reduce the heat to medium-low, and cook until the thickest part of the chicken registers 160 to 165 degrees on an instant-read thermometer, about 10 minutes.

5. Transfer the chicken to a clean plate, brushing any rice that sticks to the chicken back into the skillet, and tent the chicken loosely with foil to keep warm. Cover and continue to cook the rice over medium-low heat, stirring occasionally, until the liquid has been absorbed and the rice is tender, about 10 minutes.

6. Off the heat, sprinkle the peas over the rice, cover, and let warm through, about 2 minutes. Add the pistachios and cilantro and gently fold into the rice. Season with salt and pepper to taste and serve with the chicken.

Curried Chicken and Rice

Be sure to use chicken breasts that are roughly the same size to ensure even cooking. The spice level of curry varies from brand to brand. If your curry powder is very spicy, you may need to reduce the amount listed.

4	(5- to 6-ounce) boneless, skinless chicken breasts, tenderloins removed and breasts trimmed (see the illustrations on pages 5 and 6)
½	cup unbleached all-purpose flour
	Salt and ground black pepper
3	tablespoons vegetable oil
1	medium onion, minced
1	tablespoon curry powder
1½	cups long-grain white rice
3	medium garlic cloves, minced or pressed through a garlic press (about 1 tablespoon)
4½	cups low-sodium chicken broth
1	cup frozen peas
¼	cup raisins
¼	cup minced fresh cilantro

1. Following the illustration on page 7, pound each chicken breast between two sheets of plastic wrap to a uniform ½-inch thickness. Place the flour in a shallow dish. Pat the chicken breasts dry with paper towels and season with salt and pepper. Working with 1 chicken breast at a time, dredge in the flour, shaking off the excess.

2. Heat 2 tablespoons of the oil in a 12-inch nonstick skillet over medium-high heat until just smoking. Carefully lay the chicken breasts in the skillet and cook until lightly browned on both sides, 6 to 8 minutes. Transfer the chicken to a plate.

3. Add the remaining 1 tablespoon oil to the skillet and return to medium-high heat until shimmering. Add the onion, curry powder, and ½ teaspoon salt and cook until softened, about 5 minutes. Stir in the rice and garlic and cook until fragrant, about 30 seconds.

4. Stir in the broth, scraping up any browned bits. Nestle the chicken into the rice and bring to a simmer. Cover, reduce the heat to medium-low, and cook until the thickest part of the chicken registers 160 to 165 degrees on an instant-read thermometer, about 10 minutes.

5. Transfer the chicken to a clean plate, brushing any rice that sticks to the chicken back into the skillet, and tent the chicken loosely with foil to keep warm. Cover and continue to cook the rice over medium-low heat, stirring occasionally, until the liquid has been absorbed and the rice is tender, about 10 minutes.

6. Off the heat, sprinkle the peas and raisins over the rice, cover, and let warm through, about 2 minutes. Add the cilantro and gently fold into the rice. Season with salt and pepper to taste and serve with the chicken.

Spanish-Style Chicken and Rice

Be sure to use chicken breasts that are roughly the same size to ensure even cooking. If you can't find chorizo, use tasso, andouille, or linguiça sausage.

4	(5- to 6-ounce) boneless, skinless chicken breasts, tenderloins removed and breasts trimmed (see the illustrations on pages 5 and 6)
½	cup unbleached all-purpose flour
	Salt and ground black pepper
3	tablespoons vegetable oil
6	ounces chorizo sausage, quartered lengthwise and sliced ¼ inch thick
1	medium onion, minced

1   red bell pepper, stemmed, seeded, and
      chopped fine
      Pinch saffron threads, crumbled, or pinch
      saffron powder

1½   cups long-grain white rice

3   medium garlic cloves, minced or pressed
      through a garlic press (about 1 tablespoon)

4½   cups low-sodium chicken broth

1   cup frozen peas

1. Following the illustration on page 7, pound each chicken breast between two sheets of plastic wrap to a uniform ½-inch thickness. Place the flour in a shallow dish. Pat the chicken breasts dry with paper towels and season with salt and pepper. Working with 1 chicken breast at a time, dredge in the flour, shaking off the excess.

2. Heat 2 tablespoons of the oil in a 12-inch nonstick skillet over medium-high heat until just smoking. Carefully lay the chicken breasts in the skillet and cook until lightly browned on both sides, 6 to 8 minutes. Transfer the chicken to a plate.

3. Add the remaining 1 tablespoon oil to the skillet and return to medium-high heat until shimmering. Add the chorizo, onion, bell pepper, saffron, and ½ teaspoon salt and cook until the onion is softened, about 5 minutes. Stir in the rice and garlic and cook until fragrant, about 30 seconds.

4. Stir in the broth, scraping up any browned bits. Nestle the chicken into the rice and bring to a simmer. Cover, reduce the heat to medium-low heat, and cook until the thickest part of the chicken registers 160 to 165 degrees on an instant-read thermometer, about 10 minutes.

5. Transfer the chicken to a clean plate, brushing any rice that sticks to the chicken back into the skillet, and tent the chicken loosely with foil to keep warm. Cover and continue to cook the rice over medium-low heat, stirring occasionally, until the liquid has been absorbed and the rice is tender, about 10 minutes.

6. Off the heat, sprinkle the peas over the rice, cover, and let warm through, about 2 minutes. Season with salt and pepper to taste and serve with the chicken.

CHICKEN AND COUSCOUS

COUSCOUS, GRANULAR SEMOLINA THAT IS usually cooked in water, is a mainstay on North African tables and has become increasingly popular around the globe in recent years. Offering a change from the same old chicken and rice dinner, it seemed like a perfect option for an unusual and flavorful skillet supper for a busy weeknight. We wanted a one-dish chicken and couscous meal where the couscous was light and fluffy, the chicken was lightly browned and moist, and the flavors were bright.

The real trick with this dish would be deciding the best way to cook the chicken and couscous in the same skillet without compromising the flavor or integrity of either. After searching through dozens of chicken and couscous recipes with various flavor combinations, we settled on a simple yet tasty rendition spiked with fennel, red onion, orange, and cilantro.

First, we tackled how our chicken would be cooked. We kept things simple by following our basic Sautéed Chicken Breasts recipe (page 6), first browning the chicken over medium-high heat, then reducing the heat and cooking it through. From our previous testing, we had learned when sautéing boneless, skinless chicken breasts (our cut of choice here since they are the least fussy), there are a few keys to moist, tender meat. Pounding the chicken to an even half-inch thickness allows it to cook more evenly, and removing the tenderloin, which has a tendency to fall off during cooking, exposes more of the breast to the skillet. This ensures even browning, which in turn is key to sealing in the juices. We knew that lightly dredging the chicken in flour also encourages the browning further without drying out the surface of the chicken. With these techniques in place, we were well on our way to perfectly cooked chicken to pair with our couscous.

Once the chicken had cooked, we set it aside and moved on to our couscous. We began with our vegetables, a pairing of red onion and fennel. They would provide the dish with body, texture, and a clean vegetal sweetness. We added both to the skillet and cooked them until the onion began to soften and the fennel was crisp-tender.

Next, we stirred the couscous into the vegetables along with garlic and a pinch of cayenne for heat. Toasting the couscous with the oil and aromatics served two purposes: It added a nutty flavor, and it helped keep the grains separate and prevent clumping throughout the cooking process.

We then considered the cooking liquid. Most recipes employ either water or broth to hydrate the couscous. Cooking in water resulted in bland couscous, even with our assortment of aromatics and fennel, so we opted for the more flavorful choice of chicken broth. To incorporate the orange, we found recipes that added orange segments, but this technique was tedious and failed to provide the ample orange flavor we wanted. Instead, we supplemented our chicken broth with orange juice, which was sweet and slightly acidic and helped to bring out more of the fennel's flavor and brighten the entire dish. We brought our mixture to a simmer, then let it sit off the heat until the couscous absorbed the liquid and was evenly plump and tender—which took a mere five minutes.

For our final touches, we folded in a few tablespoons of cilantro and then drizzled both the chicken and the couscous with a fragrant oil accented with orange juice, cayenne, and cilantro—all ingredients we had already used in the recipe—before serving.

Our variation with chickpeas, dried apricots, and cinnamon offers a pleasant sweetness and contrasting touch of spice, and it is a dish that is as fragrant and flavorful as the original.

Chicken and Couscous with Fennel and Orange

SERVES 4

Be sure to use regular (or fine-grain) couscous; large-grain couscous, often labeled Israeli-style, takes much longer to cook and won't work in this recipe.

4	(5- to 6-ounce) boneless, skinless chicken breasts, tenderloins removed and breasts trimmed (see the illustrations on pages 5 and 6)
½	cup unbleached all-purpose flour
	Salt and ground black pepper
½	cup olive oil
I	medium red onion, sliced thin
I	fennel bulb, trimmed, cored, and sliced thin (see the illustrations on page 307)
I	cup couscous (see note)
3	medium garlic cloves, minced or pressed through a garlic press (about I tablespoon)
	Cayenne pepper
I	cup orange juice
¾	cup low-sodium chicken broth
¼	cup minced fresh cilantro leaves

1. Following the illustration on page 7, pound each chicken breast between 2 sheets of plastic wrap to a uniform ½-inch thickness. Place the flour in a shallow dish. Pat the chicken breasts dry with paper towels and season with salt and pepper. Working with 1 chicken breast at a time, dredge in the flour, shaking off the excess.

2. Heat 2 tablespoons of the oil in a 12-inch nonstick skillet over medium-high heat until just smoking. Carefully lay the chicken breasts in the skillet and cook until well browned on the first side, 6 to 8 minutes.

3. Flip the chicken breasts over, reduce the heat to medium, and continue to cook until the thickest part of the chicken registers 160 to 165 degrees on an instant-read thermometer, 6 to 8 minutes longer. Transfer the chicken breasts to a plate, tent loosely with foil, and let rest while cooking the vegetables and couscous.

4. Add 1 tablespoon more oil to the skillet and return to medium-high heat until shimmering. Add the onion, fennel, and ½ teaspoon salt and cook until the onion is softened, 5 to 7 minutes. Stir in the couscous, garlic, and a pinch cayenne and cook until fragrant, about 30 seconds. Stir in ¾ cup of the orange juice and broth, scraping up any browned bits. Bring to a simmer, cover, and let sit off the heat until the liquid is absorbed, about 5 minutes.

5. Whisk the remaining 5 tablespoons oil, remaining ¼ cup orange juice, 2 tablespoons of the cilantro, and a pinch cayenne together in a small bowl.

6. Gently fold the remaining 2 tablespoons cilantro into the couscous with a fork and season

with salt and pepper to taste. Drizzle the oil–orange juice mixture over the chicken and couscous before serving.

➤ VARIATION

Chicken and Couscous with Chickpeas and Apricots

Follow the recipe for Chicken and Couscous with Fennel and Orange, omitting the fennel. Substitute ½ teaspoon ground cinnamon for the cayenne in step 4, and a pinch ground cinnamon for the cayenne in step 5. Add 1 (15-ounce) can chickpeas, drained and rinsed, and 1 cup dried apricots, coarsely chopped, with the orange juice in step 4.

SAUTÉED CHICKEN WITH CHERRY TOMATOES

KNOWING WELL HOW TO AVOID THE problems with sautéed chicken breasts (see page 5)—mainly dry, leathery meat—and having mastered some basic pan sauces (see pages 18–19), we wanted to find new ways to transform plain sautéed chicken breasts into a quick weeknight meal that was flavorful and bright. We came across a magazine photo of perfectly browned boneless, skinless breasts paired with a mixture of tomatoes, olives, and feta cheese. This dish was colorful and inviting, and we thought it would make the perfect simple meal for a hot summer night.

Preparing the chicken was easy. We followed our basic recipe for Sautéed Chicken Breasts (page 6), trimming and pounding the chicken to an even thickness, seasoning it with salt and pepper, dredging it in flour before browning it in the skillet, and then lowering the heat and cooking it through. This time we included a sprinkling of ground coriander when we seasoned each chicken breast to brighten the flavor and complement the fresh tomatoes.

After cooking the chicken, we set it aside so we could whip together the side dish in our skillet. We knew the key ingredients would be fresh cherry tomatoes, rich kalamata olives, and tangy feta, so it was a matter of nailing down the quantities of each, the method of cooking, and finally fine-tuning the flavors.

Garlic and olive oil are a natural pairing with tomatoes, so we started there. Tossing a few cloves of minced garlic, some olive oil, and fresh cherry tomatoes straight into the pan all at once left us with a harsh garlic flavor. Cooking the garlic first over low heat helped, but we had better results from cooking it in hot olive oil over moderately high heat for about 30 seconds. This was enough time to flavor the oil and mellow any harshness.

Next into the skillet went the cherry tomatoes. We first tried adding them whole, but by the time the skins were adequately wilted, they had begun to burst, which added more liquid to the pan than we had hoped for. For our next attempt, we halved the tomatoes. This simple step, combined with the high heat of the pan, allowed for some release of the tomatoes' liquid while keeping the skin relatively taut. The tomato juices mingled with the fond in the pan and created a mixture that was part sauce, part side dish.

Thinking we were done at this point, we tossed in the remaining ingredients (olives and feta) and gave the dish a taste. To our surprise, tasters' comments focused on the briny bite of the olives; they wanted a mellower flavor to allow the sweetness of the tomatoes to shine through. Reducing the amount of olives left the mixture too bland, and rinsing them was even worse. Our solution was to add the olives to the skillet along with the tomatoes. The heat calmed the olives' brininess and lent saltiness to the tomatoes. The final result was a salty-sweet combination that tasters loved.

Instead of adding the feta cheese to the hot pan, where it would melt, we poured the tomato-olive mixture onto a serving platter, and then sprinkled the cheese over the top. The cool, tangy cheese was the perfect contrast to the warm, sweet tomatoes and briny olives. As our chicken finished up in the oven, we added the final touch, a sprinkling of shredded mint leaves for color and freshness, to our side dish.

Tasters liked this dish so much that we came up with slightly heartier variations, one using chili powder and corn and another with herbes de Provence and squash.

Sautéed Chicken with Cherry Tomatoes, Olives, Feta, and Mint

SERVES 4

If desired, basil can be substituted for the mint.

4	(5- to 6-ounce) boneless, skinless chicken breasts, tenderloins removed and breasts trimmed (see the illustrations on pages 5 and 6)
½	cup unbleached all-purpose flour
1	teaspoon ground coriander
	Salt and ground black pepper
3	tablespoons plus 2 teaspoons olive oil
2	medium garlic cloves, minced or pressed through a garlic press (about 2 teaspoons)
2	pints cherry tomatoes, halved
½	cup kalamata olives, pitted and halved
2	ounces feta cheese, crumbled (about ½ cup)
¼	cup shredded fresh mint leaves

1. Following the illustration on page 7, pound each chicken breast between 2 sheets of plastic wrap to a uniform ½-inch thickness. Place the flour in a shallow dish. Pat the chicken breasts dry with paper towels and season with the coriander, salt, and pepper. Working with 1 chicken breast at a time, dredge in the flour, shaking off the excess.

2. Heat 2 tablespoons of the oil in a 12-inch nonstick skillet over medium-high heat until just smoking. Carefully lay the chicken breasts in the skillet and cook until well browned on the first side, 6 to 8 minutes.

3. Flip the chicken breasts over, reduce the heat to medium, and continue to cook until the thickest part of the chicken registers 160 to 165 degrees on an instant-read thermometer, 6 to 8 minutes longer. Transfer the chicken breasts to a plate, tent loosely with foil, and let rest while cooking the vegetables.

4. Add 2 teaspoons more oil and garlic to the skillet and return to medium-high heat until fragrant, 30 to 60 seconds. Stir in the tomatoes and olives, scraping up any browned bits, and cook until the tomatoes are just softened, about 2 minutes.

5. Off the heat, stir in the remaining tablespoon oil, transfer to a large serving platter, and sprinkle with the feta and mint. Serve with the chicken.

➤ VARIATIONS

Sautéed Chicken with Cherry Tomatoes and Toasted Corn

Be sure not to stir the corn when cooking in step 4 or it will not brown well.

4	(5- to 6-ounce) boneless, skinless chicken breasts, tenderloins removed and breasts trimmed (see the illustrations on pages 5 and 6)
½	cup unbleached all-purpose flour
1	teaspoon chili powder
	Salt and ground black pepper
3	tablespoons plus 2 teaspoons olive oil
4	ears corn, husk and silk removed, kernels cut from the cob (about 3 cups; see the illustration on page 289), or 3 cups frozen corn, thawed
1	medium shallot, minced (about 3 tablespoons)
2	medium garlic cloves, minced or pressed through a garlic press (about 2 teaspoons)
1	pint cherry tomatoes, halved
¼	cup minced fresh cilantro leaves
2	tablespoons juice from 1 lime

1. Following the illustration on page 7, pound each chicken breast between 2 sheets of plastic wrap to a uniform ½-inch thickness. Place the flour in a shallow dish. Pat the chicken breasts dry with paper towels and season with the chili powder, salt, and pepper. Working with 1 chicken breast at a time, dredge in the flour, shaking off the excess.

2. Heat 2 tablespoons of the oil in a 12-inch nonstick skillet over medium-high heat until just smoking. Carefully lay the chicken breasts in the skillet and cook until well browned on the first side, 6 to 8 minutes.

3. Flip the chicken breasts over, reduce the heat to medium, and continue to cook until the thickest part of the chicken registers 160 to 165 degrees on an instant-read thermometer, 6 to 8 minutes longer. Transfer the chicken breasts to a plate, tent

loosely with foil, and let rest while cooking the vegetables.

4. Add 2 teaspoons more oil to the skillet and return to medium-high heat until shimmering. Add the corn and cook, without stirring, until well browned and roasted, 8 to 10 minutes. Stir in the shallot and garlic and cook until fragrant, about 30 seconds. Stir in the tomatoes, scraping up any browned bits, and cook until the tomatoes are just softened, about 2 minutes.

5. Off the heat, stir in the remaining tablespoon oil, cilantro, and lime juice and season with salt and pepper to taste. Transfer to a large serving platter and serve with the chicken.

Sautéed Chicken with Cherry Tomatoes, Zucchini, and Yellow Squash

If desired, mint can be used instead of the basil.

4	(5- to 6-ounce) boneless, skinless chicken breasts, tenderloins removed and breasts trimmed (see the illustrations on pages 5 and 6)
½	cup unbleached all-purpose flour
1	teaspoon herbes de Provence
	Salt and ground black pepper
3	tablespoons plus 2 teaspoons olive oil
2	medium zucchini, quartered lengthwise, then cut into ½-inch pieces
2	medium yellow squash, quartered lengthwise, then cut into ½-inch pieces
2	medium garlic cloves, minced or pressed through a garlic press (about 2 teaspoons)
1	pint cherry tomatoes, halved
2	tablespoons capers, rinsed
¼	cup shredded fresh basil leaves

1. Following the illustration on page 7, pound each chicken breast between 2 sheets of plastic wrap to a uniform ½-inch thickness. Place the flour in a shallow dish. Pat the chicken breasts dry with paper towels and season with the herbes de Provence, salt, and pepper. Working with 1 chicken breast at a time, dredge in the flour, shaking off the excess.

2. Heat 2 tablespoons of the oil in a 12-inch nonstick skillet over medium-high heat until just smoking. Carefully lay the chicken breasts in the skillet and cook until well browned on the first side, 6 to 8 minutes.

3. Flip the chicken breasts over, reduce the heat to medium, and continue to cook until the thickest part of the chicken registers 160 to 165 degrees on an instant-read thermometer, 6 to 8 minutes longer. Transfer the chicken breasts to a plate, tent loosely with foil, and let rest while cooking the vegetables.

4. Add 2 teaspoons more oil to the skillet and return to medium-high heat until shimmering. Add the zucchini and squash and cook until well browned, about 10 minutes. Stir in the garlic and cook until fragrant, about 30 seconds. Stir in the tomatoes and capers and cook until the tomatoes are just softened, about 2 minutes.

5. Off the heat, stir in the remaining 1 tablespoon oil, basil, and season with salt and pepper to taste. Transfer to a large serving platter and serve with the chicken.

PAN-ROASTED CHICKEN AND VEGETABLES

ROASTED CHICKEN AND POTATOES IS A classic combination, and while roasting the pair in the oven is a reliable method, pan-roasting lends the dish several unique benefits. The chicken achieves a perfectly roasted hue and crispy skin from cooking first in the skillet, and by moving the chicken to another dish to finish cooking in the oven (a must for bone-in chicken breasts to cook evenly), the skillet is left with a savory fond that is ideal for either making a rich pan sauce (see pages 18–19) or flavoring pan-roasted vegetables—in this case, potatoes. We were determined to turn a dinner of roasted potatoes and chicken into a simple yet flavorful skillet standby.

We began with the chicken. Bone-in chicken breasts are difficult to sauté or cook through entirely on the stovetop due to their great girth on one end and thin, tapered point on the other, and if overcooked, they become dry and have the texture of over-chewed bubble gum. However, pan-roasting produces evenly cooked chicken with the help of the steady heat of the oven, while sautéing helps to create a crispy-skinned exterior and shortens the oven time so the interior stays juicy.

First, we employed the test kitchen's simple technique for pan-roasted chicken breasts. We heated 1 tablespoon oil in the skillet until it was smoking and browned both sides of the chicken, which helped develop flavor on the exterior and gave the chicken a beautiful roasted hue with perfectly crispy skin.

To free up our skillet for the potatoes, we then transferred the chicken to a baking dish to finish cooking in the oven. We tested oven temperatures ranging from 375 to 500 degrees. The highest temperatures caused profuse smoking and in some cases singed drippings, while temperatures on the lower end meant protracted cooking times, defeating our goal for a quick weeknight supper. At 450 degrees, however, the skin was handsomely browned and crackling crisp, and the chicken cooked swiftly (about 18 minutes for 12-ounce breasts) to an internal temperature of 160 degrees.

With the chicken issues settled and our skillet free, we moved on to the potatoes. We opted for Red Bliss potatoes because their tender skin doesn't require peeling, saving us some prep time. In our initial tests we had trouble getting the potatoes simultaneously golden-crisp on the outside and tender on the inside; they were either burnt on the outside and raw in the middle, or pale and completely blown out. The solution to our potato problem was to use the microwave to parcook them. While the chicken browned, we popped the potatoes in the microwave to give them a head start, and by the time the chicken was ready for the oven, the potatoes were ready to finish up in the skillet with the flavorful fond. They only needed 10 minutes in the skillet, and placing the potatoes in a single layer ensured deeply caramelized exteriors and creamy, moist interiors.

As a final touch, we mimicked the tasty pan juices of a traditional roast chicken by infusing olive oil with lemon juice, garlic, red pepper flakes, and thyme. Drizzled over the chicken and potatoes just before serving, it lent the same moistness and bright flavors of traditional pan juices.

This recipe was so successful we decided to apply our technique to other combinations, pan-roasted chicken with baby carrots and pan-roasted chicken with cherry tomatoes and artichokes.

Pan-Roasted Chicken Breasts with Potatoes
SERVES 4

If using kosher chicken, do not brine. If brining the chicken, do not season with salt in step 3. We prefer to use small or medium potatoes (1½ to 3 inches in diameter) because they are easier to cut into uniform pieces. Regardless of what size potatoes you use, however, be sure to cut them into uniform wedges to ensure even cooking and browning.

1½	pounds small or medium Red Bliss potatoes (5 to 9 potatoes), scrubbed, and cut into 1-inch wedges (see note)
6	tablespoons olive oil
	Salt and ground black pepper
4	(10- to 12-ounce) bone-in, split chicken breasts, trimmed, and brined if desired (see pages 55 and 56)
2	tablespoons juice from 1 lemon
1	medium garlic clove, minced or pressed through a garlic press (about 1 teaspoon)
1	teaspoon minced fresh thyme leaves
	Pinch red pepper flakes

1. Adjust an oven rack to the middle position and heat the oven to 450 degrees.

2. Toss the potatoes with 1 tablespoon of the oil, ¼ teaspoon salt, and a pinch pepper in a microwave-safe bowl. Microwave on high, uncovered, until the potatoes soften but still hold their shape, about 10 minutes, gently stirring twice during cooking.

3. While the potatoes microwave, pat the chicken dry with paper towels and season with salt and pepper. Heat 1 tablespoon more oil in a 12-inch nonstick skillet over medium-high heat until just smoking. Carefully lay the chicken breasts, skin side down, in the skillet and cook until well browned, 6 to 8 minutes. Flip the chicken and continue to brown lightly on the second side, about 3 minutes.

4. Transfer the chicken, skin side up, to a baking dish and bake until the thickest part of the chicken registers 160 to 165 degrees on an instant-read thermometer, 15 to 20 minutes.

5. While the chicken bakes, drain the microwaved potatoes well. Add 1 tablespoon more oil to the skillet and return to medium-high heat until shimmering. Add the drained potatoes, cut side down, in a single layer and cook until golden brown on one side, 5 to 7 minutes. Gently stir the potatoes, rearrange in a single layer, and cook until tender and deep golden brown on the second side, 5 to 7 minutes longer.

6. Transfer the potatoes and chicken to a large serving platter. Whisk the remaining 3 tablespoons oil, the lemon juice, garlic, thyme, and red pepper flakes together in a small bowl. Drizzle the oil-lemon mixture over the chicken and potatoes before serving.

➤ VARIATIONS
Pan-Roasted Chicken Breasts with Baby Carrots

If using kosher chicken, do not brine. If brining the chicken, do not season with salt in step 3. Regular carrots, peeled and cut into ½-inch pieces, can be substituted for the baby carrots.

1½	pounds baby carrots
	Salt and ground black pepper
4	(10- to 12-ounce) bone-in, split chicken breasts, trimmed, and brined if desired (see pages 55 and 56)
1	tablespoon vegetable oil
6	tablespoons (¾ stick) unsalted butter
1	teaspoon sugar
1	medium shallot, minced (about 3 tablespoons)
2	teaspoons minced fresh tarragon

1. Adjust an oven rack to the middle position and heat the oven to 450 degrees.

2. Toss the carrots with ¼ teaspoon salt and a pinch pepper in a microwave-safe bowl. Cover the bowl and microwave on high until the carrots begin to soften, 5 to 7 minutes, stirring the carrots halfway through cooking.

3. While the carrots microwave, pat the chicken dry with paper towels and season with salt and pepper. Heat the oil in a 12-inch nonstick skillet over medium-high heat until just smoking. Carefully lay the chicken breasts, skin side down, in the skillet and cook until well browned, 6 to 8 minutes. Flip the chicken and continue to brown lightly on the second side, about 3 minutes.

4. Transfer the chicken, skin side up, to a baking dish and bake until the thickest part of the chicken registers 160 to 165 degrees on an instant-read thermometer, 15 to 20 minutes.

5. While the chicken bakes, drain the microwaved carrots well. Pour off any fat left in the skillet, add 2 tablespoons of the butter, and melt over medium heat. Add the drained carrots to the skillet with the sugar and cook, stirring occasionally, until golden brown and tender, about 10 minutes.

6. Transfer the carrots and chicken to a large serving platter. Microwave the remaining 4 tablespoons butter with the shallot in a microwave-safe bowl on 50 percent power until the butter has melted and the shallot is softened, 30 to 60 seconds. Stir in the tarragon. Drizzle the butter-tarragon mixture over the chicken and carrots before serving.

Pan-Roasted Chicken Breasts with Artichokes and Cherry Tomatoes

If using kosher chicken, do not brine. If brining the chicken, do not season with salt in step 3. The artichokes will release a significant amount of water in the microwave as they defrost; be sure to drain them well before adding them to the skillet or they will not brown.

2	(9-ounce) packages frozen artichoke hearts
	Salt and ground black pepper
4	(10- to 12-ounce) bone-in, split chicken breasts, trimmed, and brined if desired (see pages 55 and 56)
5	tablespoons olive oil
1	pint cherry tomatoes, halved
2	tablespoons capers, rinsed
2	tablespoons juice from 1 lemon
1	medium garlic clove, minced or pressed through a garlic press (about 1 teaspoon)
1	teaspoon minced fresh oregano
	Pinch red pepper flakes

1. Adjust an oven rack to the middle position and heat the oven to 450 degrees.

2. Toss the artichokes with ¼ teaspoon salt and a pinch pepper in a microwave-safe bowl. Cover the bowl and microwave on high until the artichokes begin to soften, 5 to 7 minutes, stirring the artichokes halfway through cooking.

3. While the artichokes microwave, pat the chicken dry with paper towels and season with salt and pepper. Heat 1 tablespoon of the oil in a 12-inch nonstick skillet over medium-high heat until just smoking. Carefully lay the chicken breasts, skin side down, in the skillet and cook until well browned, 6 to 8 minutes. Flip the chicken and continue to brown lightly on the second side, about 3 minutes.

4. Transfer the chicken, skin side up, to a baking dish and bake until the thickest part of the chicken registers 160 to 165 degrees on an instant-read thermometer, 15 to 20 minutes.

5. While the chicken bakes, drain the microwaved artichokes well. Add 1 tablespoon more oil to the skillet and return to medium-high heat until shimmering. Add the drained artichokes and cook, stirring occasionally, until golden brown, about 8 minutes. Stir in the tomatoes and capers and cook until the tomatoes are lightly wilted, about 2 minutes.

6. Transfer the artichoke-tomato mixture and chicken to a large serving platter. Whisk the remaining 3 tablespoons oil, the lemon juice, garlic, oregano, and red pepper flakes together. Drizzle the oil-lemon mixture over the chicken and vegetables and serve.

PAN-SEARED STEAK WITH FRIES

WHILE STEAK AND FRIES MIGHT SEEM LIKE a mundane dinner, in American chophouses this pairing has been elevated to an art form. The steak is always perfectly cooked, nicely seared and juicy-tender, and the potato wedges are fluffy on the inside with perfectly crisped exteriors. But when the home cook attempts to re-create this dish in his or her own kitchen, all too often the steak is bland and flavorless, and the fries almost instantly turn soggy sitting among the steak's juices on the plate.

We set out to create chophouse-caliber pan-seared steak with steak fries in our own kitchen, relying, of course, on our skillet.

We started with the steak. For a perfectly seared steak, a large, heavy skillet is key for even heat distribution, as is the right level of heat. We quickly discovered that to achieve the perfect crust, it is necessary to make sure of two things: that the skillet is just smoking before adding the steaks and that the skillet is not overcrowded. If it's not hot enough, or if the steaks are jammed too tightly together, which will cause the pan to cool down, the steaks will end up stewing rather than searing. And because moving the steaks releases their liquid, once they were in the pan we made sure to let them be. Getting a deep brown crust on the first side took about five minutes, then we flipped them, reduced the heat to medium, and continued cooking until they were medium-rare (120 to 125 degrees), another five to 10 minutes. We found it best to always undercook the steaks a bit to allow for carryover cooking as the steaks rest.

Next we tackled the potatoes. Sautéing them not only allowed us to forgo the messy business of deep-frying, but the results were far less greasy. From past test kitchen experience, we knew that high-starch russet potatoes make the best steak fries, but simply dumping a handful of raw potato wedges into a hot skillet with a modicum of oil left us chewing on charred fries with raw centers. Upping the amount of oil to 4 tablespoons helped us achieve more evenly golden fries, but it did little to solve the undercooked middles. Then we realized we could borrow a technique from our Pan-Roasted Chicken Breasts with Potatoes (page 148), parcooking the potatoes in the microwave before adding them to the skillet. This meant we could get the potatoes started while the steaks seared, and then sauté them just long enough to finish cooking their interiors and crisp up their exteriors. The microwave also helped make the interior of the fries light and fluffy, as if they had been deep fried.

While purists won't want to adorn their steak with anything other than a sprinkling of salt and freshly ground pepper, here in the test kitchen many tasters appreciated a touch of Italian Salsa Verde (page 20), a rustic, pureed parsley and olive oil sauce flavored with capers and lemon juice.

Pan-Seared Strip Steak with Crispy Potatoes

SERVES 4

Though we like to serve Salsa Verde with this dish, you can also serve the steaks with a pan sauce (see pages 18–19) or a compound butter (see pages 22–24).

3   medium russet potatoes (about 1¾ pounds), scrubbed, each cut lengthwise into 6 wedges

6   tablespoons vegetable oil
      Salt and ground black pepper

2   (1-pound) boneless strip steaks, about 1½ inches thick, each steak cut in half crosswise

1   recipe Salsa Verde (optional, page 20)

1. Toss the potatoes with 1 tablespoon of the oil, ¼ teaspoon salt, and ⅛ teaspoon pepper in a microwave-safe bowl. Cover the bowl and microwave on high until the potatoes begin to soften, 7 to 10 minutes, stirring the potatoes halfway through cooking.

2. While the potatoes microwave, pat the steaks dry with paper towels and season with salt and pepper. Heat 1 tablespoon more oil in a 12-inch nonstick skillet over medium-high heat until just smoking. Carefully lay the steaks in the skillet and cook until well browned on the first side, 3 to 5 minutes.

3. Flip the steaks over, reduce the heat to medium, and continue to cook to the desired doneness (see page 9), 5 to 10 minutes longer. Transfer the steaks to a plate, tent loosely with foil, and let rest while finishing the potatoes.

4. Drain the microwaved potatoes well. Add the remaining 4 tablespoons oil to the skillet and return to medium-high heat until shimmering. Add the drained potatoes and cook, without stirring, until golden brown on one side, about 6 minutes. Flip the potatoes and continue to cook, without stirring, until golden brown on the second side, about 6 minutes longer. (If the potatoes are browning unevenly, use tongs and gently move them around as necessary.)

5. Transfer the potatoes to a platter and serve with the steak and Salsa Verde (if using).

Filet Mignon with Pan-Seared Asparagus

WHEN IT COMES TO PERFECTLY COOKED steak, Americans prize tenderness above all—and filet mignon is the most tender steak there is. Filets are thick (usually 1¼ to 2 inches), boneless steaks cut from the slender, incredibly tender and ultra-lean tenderloin muscle, which rests under the steer's spine. Traditionally, filet mignon (also referred to as tenderloin steak or simply filet) is served rare with a deeply seared crust and adorned with a rich, luxurious pan sauce or flavored butter.

For all its desirable qualities, the mildly flavored filet mignon is also expensive, giving it a long-standing reputation as a grand, celebratory restaurant meal. We felt there was no reason to limit the decadence to restaurants. After all, filets are available in any supermarket with a meat case. We wanted to replicate the best restaurant filets at home, which meant developing a deeply browned, rich crust on the steak's outside without overcooking the interior. We also wanted to pair our perfect filet with a classic steakhouse offering, asparagus.

We shopped for filets at six local supermarkets and were not satisfied with the butchering job from a single one. The steaks were usually cut unevenly, with one end noticeably thicker than the other. Beyond that, different steaks in the same package were different sizes and weights, far from acceptable given their cost and premium reputation. After all, consistency of size and thickness is important for even cooking of each steak, as well as from steak to steak in the pan. With this in mind, we took to purchasing a small, roughly 2-pound section of the tenderloin, called a tenderloin roast, and cut our own steaks from it. The process was easy, taking less than two minutes, and our hand-cut filets were perfectly uniform. Tenderloin roasts were available wherever we shopped, so if you can get them, we recommend going this route. Alternatively, ask the butcher to cut the steaks for you.

To determine the optimal thickness for filets, we tested steaks cut in ¼-inch intervals from 1 to

2 inches thick. Tasters preferred the 1½-inch cut, which made for a generous but not over-the-top portion.

Pan-searing is ideal for cooking meat, filet included, because it develops a deep brown, caramelized crust on the meat that is critical for lending deep flavor. So our next tests involved searing filets that we had dried well with paper towels in a dry pan and searing similarly dried filets in a pan filmed with oil. We knew that drying the steaks thoroughly would aid in developing a crust. Not surprisingly for such lean meat, the oil was necessary to produce a deep, dark, satisfying crust.

In our tests for cooking the filets at different heat levels, we found that higher heat produced a better-developed crust than did a lower flame. But when cooked over high heat for the entire time, the browned bits left in the pan after the steaks were cooked, known as the fond, were often scorched by the time the meat reached medium-rare, essentially ruining the pan for the asparagus to follow. We tried a couple of tactics to remedy the problem.

First, we made sure we used a heavy-bottomed skillet to avoid hot spots that have a tendency to scorch. Smaller or lighter pans, we found, overheat too easily. Second, we seared the first side of the steak over medium-high heat, then turned the heat down to medium when cooking the second side. This approach offered the double advantage of protecting the fond from the prolonged heat and giving us a few extra minutes to ensure preferred doneness, since steaks of this size can cook from medium-rare to medium-well in a matter of minutes. With the steaks perfectly cooked and off to the side resting (which allowed the juices and heat to redistribute, resulting in a better tasting steak), we returned the skillet to the stove to cook the asparagus.

Crisp, brown spears of asparagus usually come from the grill, but we wanted to duplicate these results in our skillet. We added a tablespoon of oil to our skillet, still hot on the stovetop, along with a tablespoon of butter for flavor. We then added the asparagus and waited for evenly cooked, crisp-tender stalks and lightly browned tips. That moment never came. The asparagus cooked unevenly, with some stalks becoming soggy and army-green while others remaining practically raw. The only good

that came from this test was that the fond from the bottom of the skillet flavored the asparagus. But there was something wrong with our technique; we needed to reevaluate.

In order for all the asparagus to cook at the same rate, the heat would have to be evenly distributed among the spears. This meant putting a lid on the skillet, at least for part of the cooking. We didn't want to steam them for too long because we'd only end up with limp spears. Covering the asparagus at the onset of cooking allowed it to steam and just start to become tender. Five minutes was all it took. Then we uncovered the asparagus and continued to cook until we had achieved sufficient browning, about five minutes longer.

With the filets and asparagus done, all we needed was a fresh garlic-herb butter to top it all off. We whipped some softened butter with minced fresh tarragon, parsley, and thyme, minced garlic, and a touch of salt and pepper. It was a flavorful combination that complemented both our filet and asparagus.

Filet Mignon with Pan-Seared Asparagus and Garlic-Herb Butter
SERVES 4

This recipe works best with asparagus that is at least ½ inch thick near the base. If using thinner spears, reduce the covered cooking time to 3 minutes and the uncovered cooking time to 3 to 5 minutes. Do not use pencil-thin asparagus because it overcooks too easily.

- 5 tablespoons unsalted butter, softened
- 1 tablespoon minced fresh tarragon leaves
- 1½ teaspoons minced fresh parsley leaves
- 1½ teaspoons minced fresh thyme leaves
- 1 medium garlic clove, minced or pressed through a garlic press (about 1 teaspoon) Salt and ground black pepper
- 4 (7- to 8-ounce) center-cut filets mignons, about 1½ inches thick
- 4 teaspoons plus 1 tablespoon vegetable oil
- 2 pounds thick asparagus (about 2 bunches), tough ends trimmed (see the illustration on page 92) (see note)

1. Beat 4 tablespoons of the butter with a large fork in a small bowl until light and fluffy. Mix in the tarragon, parsley, thyme, and garlic until combined. Season with salt and pepper to taste and set aside.

2. Pat the steaks dry with paper towels and season with salt and pepper. Heat 4 teaspoons of the oil in a 12-inch skillet over medium-high heat until just smoking. Carefully lay the steaks in the skillet and cook until well browned on the first side, 3 to 5 minutes. Flip the steaks over, reduce the heat to medium, and continue to cook to the desired doneness (see page 9), 5 to 10 minutes longer. Transfer the steaks to a plate, tent loosely with foil, and let rest while cooking the asparagus.

3. Add the remaining 1 tablespoon oil and remaining 1 tablespoon butter to the skillet and return to medium-high heat until the foaming subsides. Add half the asparagus to the skillet with the tips pointed in one direction, and the other half with the tips pointed in the opposite direction. Distribute the spears in an even layer. Cover and cook until the asparagus is bright green and still crisp, about 5 minutes.

4. Uncover the asparagus and season with salt and pepper to taste. Increase the heat to high and continue to cook, using tongs to occasionally move the asparagus around, until the spears are tender and well browned along one side, 5 to 7 minutes.

5. Transfer the asparagus to a serving platter and season with salt and pepper to taste. Spoon 1 tablespoon of the garlic-herb butter over each steak and serve with the asparagus.

TUSCAN-STYLE STEAK

WHEN AMERICANS GARNISH A STEAK, IT'S often with A.1. Steak Sauce. The French prefer a flavored compound butter. The Italians have their own favorite—olive oil and lemon. *Bistecca alla Fiorentina*, as it is called in Tuscany, couldn't be simpler: a thick juicy steak is grilled to rare, sliced, and served with a drizzle of extra-virgin olive oil and a squeeze of lemon. For many of us in the test kitchen, this unexpected combination was a revelation, and we expect that anyone who loves a good steak and tries it will become a convert too. Fruity, peppery olive oil amplifies the savory nature of the beef, while the lemon provides a bright counterpoint that cuts through the richness.

While the flavors quickly became a test kitchen favorite, we felt the problem with Tuscan-style steak was that it is traditionally grilled. Grilled steaks offer outstanding flavor, but grilling is not always the most accessible cooking method. We wanted to keep things simple, so we moved the testing inside, where we could put our skillet to work. To make a complete meal, we decided to pair our steaks with garlicky spinach. It sounded like the perfect combination. But could we pull it off using just one skillet and without performing a cumbersome juggling act? In a dish this direct, good technique can mean the difference between mediocre and magical.

When all was said and done, we had cooked our way through more than 30 pounds of steak before perfecting the technique and the details concerning the olive oil and lemon garnish—namely, when

SLICING T-BONE AND PORTERHOUSE STEAKS

1. Cut along the bone to remove the large top loin, or strip, section.

2. Cut the smaller tenderloin section off the bone.

3. Cut each large piece crosswise into ½-inch-thick slices for serving.

INGREDIENTS: Supermarket Extra-Virgin Olive Oil

On today's supermarket shelves you will find row upon row of different olive oils, with even the most ordinary of stores offering more than a dozen choices. But given the cost—an average of $18.99 per liter for the oils in our lineup—we wondered if we could just go with the cheapest supermarket variety or if we needed to forgo them all in favor of something better from a gourmet shop or online seller?

To find out if there were any extra-virgin olive oils truly worth bringing home from the supermarket, we chose 10 of the top-selling brands and conducted a blind taste test—first plain, and then warmed and tossed with pasta.

Here's the not-so-great news: Our highest average scores barely reached 5 out of a possible 10 points. While a few supermarket oils passed muster, most ranged from plain Jane to distinctly unpleasant, even tasting a bit old, though all were purchased only a few days before we tasted them.

However, we did find two acceptable products. Perhaps not surprisingly, origin did make a difference—both are made from all-Italian olives. Price was a factor, too: Our top picks were the two most expensive oils. Our front-runner was Lucini Italia Premium Select Extra Virgin Olive Oil ($39.98 per liter), which tasters described as "fruity, with a slightly peppery finish," and "buttery undertones." A close second was Colavita Extra Virgin

Olive Oil ($23.98 per liter). Tasters observed that it was "round and buttery," with a "light body" and a "briny and fruity" flavor.

But both were bested in a second tasting that included our favorite premium brand, Columela, available in better supermarkets. Tasters found it offered exceptionally fruity, well-balanced flavor, and at about $36 per liter, it's actually cheaper than Lucini.

THE BEST SUPERMARKET EXTRA-VIRGIN OLIVE OILS

LUCINI   COLAVITA   COLUMELA

Tasters described our winning supermarket brand Lucini as "aromatic, with a good balance." Our runner-up, Colavita, was noted as being "round and buttery," with a "light body." But both were beat out by our favorite premium brand, Columela. It took top honors for its fruity flavor and excellent balance.

---

and how to introduce it. And we certainly didn't ignore the spinach. We tested and retested the best way to avoid the all-too-common waterlogged plate of sautéed spinach before arriving at spinach worthy of partnering with our steak.

Thick T-bone and porterhouse are the steaks recommended most often for bistecca alla Fiorentina. Both feature a T-shaped bone with meat from the top loin (also known as the strip) on one side and from the tenderloin on the other. The primary difference between the two is the size of the tenderloin piece, which is larger on the porterhouse. We sampled both steaks and found them equally appealing—tender with robust, well-balanced flavor. There was no reason to test additional cuts.

To cook the steaks, we looked first to our established method for pan-searing boneless steaks (see page 10). We encouraged the flavor of Tuscany by rubbing each steak all over with the cut half of a garlic clove before seasoning liberally with

salt and pepper. This simple trick perfumed the meat without overpowering it with garlic flavor. We cooked the steaks for about seven minutes on each side to produce a well-browned crust and a medium-rare interior. The suggested thickness, around 1½ inches, also worked out well, allowing for an appealing textural contrast between the crispy crust and the tender interior. Given their rather large and unwieldy size, we could only fit two T-bones in our skillet at a time, but each was meaty enough to serve two people.

So while the steaks cooked, we started on the spinach. Usually we scoff at the notion of sautéing spinach. It releases an absurd amount of water when it hits the skillet and predictably turns into a slimy green mess. But we couldn't ignore sautéed spinach forever, especially when it can be such a perfect accompaniment to an entrée when done well. Obviously, we had to get around the water problem first.

We opted for fresh baby spinach because of its convenience. We first tried blanching, shocking, draining, and drying the spinach before sautéing, but this was such a long, drawn-out process that we had to find an alternative. Taking advice straight off the bag the spinach had come in, we tried microwaving it. To our surprise, the spinach began to wilt and release its water. We wanted to rid the spinach of as much water as possible, but we wondered if adding a splash of water before microwaving would actually coax more water out. We added ¼ cup water, and crossed our fingers. It worked!

We transferred the spinach to a colander to drain, then tossed it in a hot skillet for a test run. Despite our valiant effort, it was more of the same watery mess that we had struggled to get away from. After consulting fellow test cooks, someone suggested that after we microwaved and drained the spinach, we try coarsely chopping it and draining it again before sautéing. It turned out that while our first draining eliminated the spinach's surface moisture, plenty of water still resided within the cells of the leaves. A rough chop would presumably rupture some of these cells, releasing more of the spinach's water. It made sense, so we tried it. This time around the skillet remained considerably drier, well within an acceptable range.

With the method for cooking the spinach determined, we could move on to the final details of flavoring. To continue our Tuscan theme, we toasted sliced garlic and red pepper flakes in olive oil until lightly browned before adding our microwaved, chopped, twice-drained spinach. We only needed to sauté it for about two minutes to finish wilting it and allow it to pick up the garlic flavor. After another splash of olive oil, our spinach was ready to join its steak. We found that for timing, we could first prep our spinach for the skillet, then cook our steaks and set them aside. The time our steaks needed to rest gave us the few minutes we needed to finish up the spinach in the skillet.

Only a few simple steps remained. We sliced the meat off the T-bones and drizzled it with olive oil. A squeeze of lemon added a light acidic contrast to the sweet garlic and olive oil flavors. That was all that was needed.

Tuscan-Style Steak with Garlicky Spinach
SERVES 4

These large T-bone steaks are big enough to serve two. If you don't have a microwave-safe bowl large enough to accommodate the entire amount of spinach, cook it in a smaller bowl in two batches, reducing the amount of water to 2 tablespoons per batch and the cooking time for each batch to about 1½ minutes.

3	(6-ounce) bags baby spinach (about 16 cups)
¼	cup water
2	(28-ounce) T-bone or porterhouse steaks, 1½ inches thick
5	medium garlic cloves, 1 clove halved, 4 cloves sliced thin crosswise
	Salt and ground black pepper
5	tablespoons extra-virgin olive oil
¼	teaspoon red pepper flakes
1	lemon, cut into wedges, for serving

1. Place the spinach and water in a large microwave-safe bowl. Cover the bowl and microwave on high power until the spinach is wilted and has decreased in volume by half, 3 to 4 minutes.

2. Remove the bowl from the microwave and keep covered for 1 minute. Carefully uncover the spinach and transfer it to a colander set in the sink. Using the back of a rubber spatula, gently press the spinach against the colander to release the excess liquid. Transfer the spinach to a cutting board and roughly chop. Return the spinach to the colander and press a second time; set aside.

3. Pat the steaks dry with paper towels, rub the halved garlic clove over the bone and meat on each side of the steaks, and season with salt and pepper. Heat 1 tablespoon of the oil in a 12-inch skillet over medium-high heat until just smoking. Carefully lay the steaks in the pan and cook until well browned on the first side, 5 to 7 minutes. Flip the steaks over, reduce the heat to medium, and continue to cook to the desired doneness (see page 9), 5 to 12 minutes longer. Transfer the steaks to a carving board, tent loosely with foil, and let rest while finishing the spinach.

4. Heat 2 tablespoons more oil, the remaining 4 cloves sliced garlic, and red pepper flakes in the skillet over medium-high heat until golden brown, 2 to 3 minutes. Add the chopped, drained spinach, toss with tongs to coat with the oil, and cook until uniformly wilted and glossy green, about 2 minutes. Stir in 1 tablespoon more oil and season with salt and pepper to taste.

5. Transfer the spinach to a large serving platter. Following the illustrations on page 153, cut the steaks neatly away from the bones, then slice the steaks crosswise about ½ inch thick. Arrange the steak on the platter with the spinach, drizzle with the remaining 1 tablespoon oil, and serve with the lemon wedges.

LAMB PITA SANDWICHES

WHETHER YOU CALL IT *KEFTA, KIBBE, KOFTA,* or simply ground lamb patties, this staple appears all over the Middle East. Generally sold by street vendors, the patties are stuffed into pitas with any number of toppings, from incendiary sauces and exotic pickles to simply tahini or a yogurt-based sauce and lettuce and tomato. These sandwiches echo the flavors of their more labor-intensive, familiar cousin, the gyro, which relies on minced lamb that has been slow-roasted on a spit; we thought this simple version would be ideal for an unusual weeknight skillet dinner. A palette of Middle Eastern spices and subtly exotic lamb turns an otherwise prosaic meatball sandwich into something special.

We needed to determine the best recipe for the patties and an accompanying sauce, as well as how to handle the garnishes. The patty recipes we found ran the gamut with respect to both flavor and preparation technique. Some included a long list of ingredients that necessitated a great deal of effort, while others kept the flavors simple and prep work brief. The simplest versions tasted bland, while the fancy versions buried the meat under a mass of spices and took entirely too long to assemble. We would seek a comfortable medium.

After looking at numerous ingredient lists, we broke the patty down into three components: the meat, the binding, and the seasoning. Unlike ground beef, ground lamb is normally available in only one (unspecified) percentage of fat content. While surplus fat will render out, much of lamb's somewhat gamey flavor is located in the fat, and we found that leaner samples of meat tasted milder. If gaminess is a concern, you can request leaner lamb from a butcher who can grind it to order.

Next we looked at the binding for our patties. Taking a cue from our experience with meatball recipes, we incorporated a modified panade (a paste of fresh bread crumbs and milk) to make the meat juicier. But tasters found these patties a little too mushy. Skipping ahead, we realized our recipe called for pita pockets with the top quarters cut off so they could be filled. Since pita bread is fairly dry and we had no other use for the tops, we wondered if using pita crumbs would improve the texture of the patties. We gave it a shot and, indeed, the patties gained a sturdier structure along with a fuller, more savory flavor—and no waste.

As for the seasoning, many recipes we researched contained a vast selection. To reduce complexity, we added chopped onion, lemon juice, minced garlic, and some salt and pepper to the food processor with our pita when making the panade. We stirred this mixture into the lamb along with some cilantro before rolling the mixture into balls and flattening them into small disks. This simple flavoring combination complemented the meat without overpowering it.

While we warmed the pitas in the oven, we cooked the patties. Traditionally, the patties are grilled on skewers, but for the sake of convenience, we opted for pan-frying. Though broiling would have been the logical indoor replacement for grilling, we found pan-frying offered more control and the patties developed a crisper crust. All of the patties could fit into a large skillet at one time and were cooked through in less than 10 minutes.

Just because we had nicely warmed pitas and well-seasoned meat didn't mean we were finished. Yogurt-based sauces appear throughout the Middle East and are a perfect accompaniment in lamb recipes, as the sharpness of the yogurt cuts the lamb's richness. We stirred in cilantro for brightness and cayenne pepper for spiciness and, to add pungency and round out the yogurt's tang, we included minced garlic—just one clove so as not to overwhelm the other flavors.

With all of our components ready, all we had to do was put them together. We spread a quarter of the sauce on one side of each pita slice before adding three lamb patties and filling the rest of the space with lettuce and tomatoes. A single bite confirmed that this was a great alternative to a cold cut sandwich or burger any night of the week.

Middle Eastern–Style Lamb Pita Sandwiches

SERVES 4

Although we prefer the richness of plain, whole milk yogurt, low-fat yogurt can be substituted. You can substitute mint for the cilantro in both the yogurt sauce and the lamb mixture. Don't be concerned if the skillet appears crowded when cooking the patties; they will shrink slightly as they cook.

YOGURT SAUCE
- 1   cup plain whole milk yogurt (see note)
- 1   tablespoon minced fresh cilantro
- 1   small garlic clove, minced or pressed through a garlic press (about ½ teaspoon)
-      Salt
-      Cayenne pepper

SANDWICHES
- 4   (8-inch) pita breads
- ½   medium onion, chopped coarse (about ½ cup)
- 4   teaspoons juice from 1 lemon
- 2   medium garlic cloves, minced or pressed through a garlic press (about 2 teaspoons)
- ½   teaspoon salt
- ¼   teaspoon ground black pepper
- 1   pound ground lamb
- 2   tablespoons minced fresh cilantro leaves
- 2   teaspoons vegetable oil
- 1   large tomato, sliced thin
- 2   cups shredded iceberg lettuce

1. FOR THE YOGURT SAUCE: Combine all of the sauce ingredients in a small bowl and season with salt and cayenne to taste.

2. FOR THE SANDWICHES: Adjust an oven rack to the middle position and heat the oven to 350 degrees. Cut the top quarter off of each piece of pita, reserving the trimmed pieces, then stack the pitas and tightly wrap them with foil. Tear the reserved pita trimmings into ½-inch pieces; you should have about ¾ cup.

3. Process the torn pita pieces, onion, lemon juice, garlic, salt, and pepper together in a food processor to a smooth, uniform paste, about 30 seconds, scraping down the sides of the bowl as needed. Transfer the onion mixture to a large bowl, add the lamb and cilantro, and mix until evenly combined. Divide the mixture into 12 equal pieces (about ¼ cup each) and roll them into balls. Gently flatten the balls into round disks, about ½ inch thick and 2½ inches in diameter.

4. Place the foil-wrapped pitas directly on the oven rack and heat for 10 minutes. Meanwhile, heat the oil in a 12-inch nonstick skillet over medium-high heat until just smoking. Add the patties and cook until well browned and a crust forms on the first side, 3 to 4 minutes. Flip the patties, reduce the heat to medium, and cook until well browned and a crust forms on the second side, about 5 minutes longer. Transfer the patties to a paper towel–lined plate.

5. Spread ¼ cup of the sauce inside the warm pitas. Divide the patties evenly among the pitas and top with the tomato slices and shredded lettuce. Serve, passing the remaining sauce at the table.

CHICKEN FAJITAS

WHAT IS LABELED AS CHICKEN FAJITAS IN most restaurants these days is barely edible, with guacamole, sour cream, and salsa slathered on in a weak attempt to mask the blandness of the key ingredients. We wanted to go back to the basics and come up with a simple combination of smoky roasted vegetables and strips of chicken, wrapped up at the table in warm flour tortillas. That said, we wanted a fajita recipe that could be made without lugging out the grill; we would rely instead on our skillet.

While the skirt steak in classic beef fajitas could potentially get away with foregoing a marinade, boneless chicken breasts need all the help they can get. Starting with a mixture of lime juice, vegetable oil, garlic, salt, and pepper as our base, we tried several marinating methods. Soaking the chicken breasts in the marinade over an extended time left the chicken exuding too much liquid in the skillet and muted the seared flavor we were after. Also, marinating the chicken any longer than 15 minutes in our lime juice–heavy marinade meant that the meat actually started to "cook" in the acid, like a chicken ceviche of sorts. We also tried brining— soaking the chicken in a saltwater solution. This seasoned the chicken and kept it juicy, but tasters found the meat too moist—waterlogged, even.

INGREDIENTS: Flour Tortillas

It's no surprise that the best flour tortillas are those that are made fresh to order. But those of us without a local *tortilleria* must make do with the packaged offerings at the local supermarket. To find out which ones taste best, we rounded up every flour tortilla we could find. Tasters immediately zeroed in on texture, which varied dramatically from "doughy and stale" to "thin and flaky." Most brands had a mild, pleasantly wheaty flavor, but two of the doughier brands, Olé and La Banderita (both made by the same company), were panned for off, sour notes. The thinner brands were the hands-down winners, with tasters choosing thin, flaky Tyson Mexican Original Flour Tortillas, Fajita Style, above the rest.

THE BEST SUPERMARKET FLOUR TORTILLAS
Thin, flaky Tyson Mexican Original Flour Tortillas, Fajita Style, were tasters' clear favorite.

TYSON

"It might as well have been poached," said one. We even got so creative as to make a "brinerade," a cross between a brine and a marinade, by adding the marinade to a concentrated 2-cup brine, but this only weakened the final flavors. We settled on a post-marinade, sautéing the chicken plain and tossing the cooked strips in the marinade afterward. This method yielded the best results: tender browned chicken with bright, unadulterated tang.

Our post-marinade's high acid content (4 tablespoons lime juice to 2 tablespoons oil) added fresh citrus flavor notes to the chicken that tasters approved of, but it still lacked smokiness and depth. After trying numerous unsuccessful flavor additions, we finally hit upon Worcestershire sauce. Though an unlikely choice for chicken, Worcestershire sauce has a savory quality known as umami (a culinary term that refers to a fifth taste sensation beyond the familiar sweet, sour, bitter, and salty). It was just what our chicken fajita meat needed. A mere 2 teaspoons of Worcestershire added another layer of saltiness and smokiness. A bit of brown sugar helped round out the flavors of our marinade, and cilantro added freshness.

Both bell peppers and onion gave the fajitas some needed contrast, not just in terms of color but in their bitter and sweet flavors. While the chicken rested, we sautéed the peppers and onions in the same skillet, taking advantage of the flavorful fond left by the meat. A little water added to the pan helped the process along. Though the fond lent the vegetables a full flavor that needed minimal enhancement, we experimented with a variety of spices. We settled on chili powder, which added a characteristically Southwestern touch.

As for the flour tortillas, 8- to 10-inch rounds yielded too much excess tortilla; 6-inch tortillas were the perfect size. We warmed our tortillas (see page 160 for more information on warming tortillas) and pulled together our favorite toppings, which we could now use to complement—not cover up—our full-flavor fajitas. All that was left to do was build them and eat.

Chicken Fajitas

SERVES 4

If you like your fajitas spicy, add a sliced jalapeño to the skillet along with the bell pepper. Serve with salsa, sour cream, chopped avocado, shredded cheese, shredded lettuce, and lime wedges.

4	(5- to 6-ounce) boneless, skinless chicken breasts, tenderloins removed and breasts trimmed (see the illustrations on pages 5 and 6)
	Salt and ground black pepper
¼	cup vegetable oil
2	red, yellow, or orange bell peppers, stemmed, seeded, and sliced thin
I	medium red onion, halved and sliced thin
¼	cup water
1½	teaspoons chili powder
¼	cup juice from 2 limes
2	tablespoons minced fresh cilantro leaves
2	teaspoons Worcestershire sauce
½	teaspoon brown sugar
12	(6-inch) flour tortillas, warmed (see the illustration on page 160)

1. Following the illustration on page 7, pound each chicken breast between two sheets of plastic wrap to a uniform ½-inch thickness. Pat the chicken breasts dry with paper towels and season with salt and pepper.

2. Heat 2 tablespoons of the oil in a 12-inch skillet over medium-high heat until just smoking. Carefully lay the chicken breasts in the skillet and cook until well browned on the first side, 6 to 8 minutes. Flip the chicken breasts over, reduce the heat to medium, and continue to cook until the thickest part of the chicken registers 160 to 165 degrees on an instant-read thermometer, 6 to 8 minutes longer. Transfer the chicken to a carving board and tent loosely with foil to keep warm.

3. Add the bell peppers, onion, water, chili powder, and ½ teaspoon salt to the skillet and cook over medium-high heat, scraping up any browned bits, until the onion is softened, 5 to 7 minutes. Transfer to a serving bowl and tent loosely with foil.

4. Mix the lime juice, cilantro, Worcestershire sauce, brown sugar, remaining 2 tablespoons oil, and ¼ teaspoon salt together in a large bowl. Cut the chicken into ¼-inch-thick slices, toss with the lime juice mixture to combine, and serve with the vegetables and warm tortillas.

STEAK TACOS

BEEF TACOS MADE INDOORS ARE TYPICALLY the everyday ground-beef kind, while preparation of the more upscale steak tacos, modeled after authentic Mexican *carne asada*, is generally reserved for the grill. For this latter higher-end fare, a thin cut of beef, typically skirt or flank steak, is marinated, then grilled, cut into pieces, and served in a soft corn tortilla with simple garnishes. Done properly, the meat has a rich, smoky flavor. Given the choice, most people prefer the beefier flavors of a steak taco over a ground beef one, but what about those times when cooking outdoors isn't possible? We wanted to develop a method for cooking steak tacos indoors that would yield meat as tender, juicy, and rich tasting as tacos made with meat straight off the grill. We also wanted our indoor technique to have the same success rate as grilling, foolproofed against a common problem encountered when cooking indoors: pale, textureless meat that lacks a proper sear and is also overcooked.

Our first task was to choose the right cut of meat. We decided from the outset to shy away from steaks like rib eye and top loin—though both are exceptionally beefy and tender, paying high prices for meat that we were going to wrap up in tortillas seemed a waste. Traditional Mexican recipes typically call for skirt or flank steak for taco meat, both of which come from the belly of the cow. We also wanted to try two other inexpensive cuts: blade steak, which comes from the shoulder, and a particular cut of steak tips (which as a group can be cut from a half-dozen muscles) called flap meat sirloin tips. We pan-seared each type to determine which would work best. Tasters liked the well-marbled steak tips and skirt steak, but we found that availability of these cuts was spotty. While the flavor of the blade steak was great, it contained too much internal gristle. Flank steak proved to be the best choice all around. It had a nice beefy flavor and, when sliced thin against the grain, was very tender.

The flank steak was good, but we wondered if there was a technique we could employ to render the meat even juicier. Referring back to an old test kitchen recipe for grilled flank steak, we found that sprinkling the meat with a liberal dose of salt and allowing it to sit for an hour (a technique similar to brining) markedly boosted juiciness. We were able to reduce the resting time to just 30 minutes by poking holes into the steak with a fork, which allowed the salt to sink into the meat's interior more quickly.

Given that the grill is the foundation of traditional steak taco recipes, we felt it was critical to mimic the caramelized exterior and crisp, brittle edges of grilled meat as much as possible. Pan-searing proved to be a promising method; we achieved some caramelization, but we wanted more. We needed more of the meat to come in contact with the skillet's surface. We tried increasing the meat's surface area by laying the steak flat on the cutting board and slicing it in half, parallel to the board—a technique known as butterflying—but this was a tedious process that didn't yield significantly better results. Next, we experimented with cutting the steak lengthwise with the grain into four long strips about 2½ inches wide and around 1 inch thick. The results were impressive. Because the strips were relatively thick, we could brown them on four sides instead of two, which gave us even more exposed edges that could become crisp and flavorful. Two more test kitchen tricks helped us promote caramelization and boost flavor even further: We sprinkled the steak with a little sugar before browning, and we upped the cooking oil from 2 teaspoons to 2 tablespoons. We cooked the pieces of steak for just a few minutes

WARMING TORTILLAS

Our preferred way to warm tortillas is over the open flame of a gas burner. This technique gives them a nice roasted flavor. However, you can also toast them in a skillet one at a time over medium-high heat until soft and speckled with brown spots (20 to 30 seconds per side), or warm them in the microwave. To microwave, simply stack tortillas on a plate, cover with microwave-safe plastic wrap, and microwave on high power until warm and soft, 1 to 2 minutes.

Once warmed, keep the tortillas wrapped in foil or a kitchen towel until ready to use, or they will dry out. If your tortillas are very dry, pat each with a little water before warming.

To warm tortillas over the open flame of a gas burner, place each tortilla directly on the cooking grate over a medium flame. Heat until slightly charred around edges, about 30 seconds per side.

on each side, a short cooking time that, combined with the fact that we had salted the meat, ensured that the steak never dried out.

With a successful cooking method squared away, we now looked at adding some other flavor dimensions to the steak. Reviewing our recipe, our first thought was to incorporate a dry spice rub when we salted the meat, which would not only add flavor, but might also help with the surface texture of the meat. But after a couple of tests we found that the dry spice rubs just tasted dusty and raw. A wet rub or paste, provided it was removed before cooking so it wouldn't impede caramelization, seemed a better option. After looking into traditional marinades, we settled on a combination of cilantro, scallions, garlic, and jalapeño. Processed into a pesto-like paste with some oil, this mixture added fresh flavor to the steak, and when coupled with the salt soak, our oil-based paste was pulled into the steak, allowing it to flavor the meat throughout. The paste yielded one more benefit. Before we slathered it over the steak, we reserved 2 tablespoons and mixed it with some lime juice. After the steak had cooked and was sliced, we tossed it with this paste-based sauce. It not only lent an aspect of juiciness to the steak, but it also brightened the flavor and presentation.

When it comes to garnishing steak tacos, simplicity is customary. We opted for raw onion, cilantro leaves, and lime wedges—all of which echoed the flavors in our paste. Tasters also liked thinly sliced radishes and cucumbers for the contrasting texture they provided.

We finally had a flavorful, fresh-tasting alternative to the ubiquitous ground beef taco—no grill required.

Steak Tacos

SERVES 4 TO 6

We prefer cooking flank steak to medium-rare or medium; rare flank steak tends to be overly chewy, while well-done flank steak tastes very tough. For a less spicy dish, remove some or all of the ribs and seeds from the jalapeño before chopping it for the marinade. In addition to the toppings suggested below, you can serve the tacos with thinly sliced radish or cucumber, or salsa.

MARINADE

½ cup packed fresh cilantro leaves

3 medium scallions, chopped coarse

3 medium garlic cloves, chopped coarse

1 medium jalapeño chile, stemmed and chopped coarse (see note)

½ teaspoon ground cumin

¼ cup vegetable oil

1 tablespoon juice from 1 lime

STEAK AND TACOS

1 (1½- to 1¾-pound) flank steak, trimmed and cut lengthwise (with the grain) into 4 equal pieces
Salt

½ teaspoon sugar
Ground black pepper

2 tablespoons vegetable oil

12 (6-inch) corn tortillas, warmed (see the illustration on page 160)
Fresh cilantro leaves, for serving
Minced white onion, for serving

1 lime, cut into wedges, for serving

1. FOR THE MARINADE: Pulse the cilantro, scallions, garlic, jalapeño, and cumin together in the food processor until finely chopped, 10 to 12 pulses, scraping down the sides of the bowl as needed. Add the oil and process until the mixture is smooth and resembles pesto, about 15 seconds, scraping down the sides of the bowl as necessary. Transfer 2 tablespoons of the herb paste to a medium bowl, stir in the lime juice, and reserve separately until serving time.

2. FOR THE STEAK AND TACOS: Using a dinner fork, poke each piece of steak 10 to 12 times on each side. Place the steak in a large baking dish, rub all sides of the steak pieces evenly with 1½ teaspoons salt, and then coat with the cilantro paste. Wrap the steaks with plastic wrap and refrigerate for at least 30 minutes, or up to 1 hour.

3. Scrape the cilantro paste off the steak and sprinkle all sides of the pieces evenly with the sugar and ½ teaspoon black pepper. Heat the oil in 12-inch nonstick skillet over medium-high heat until just smoking. Carefully place the steak in the skillet and cook until well browned on the first side, about 3 minutes. Flip the steak and sear until well browned on the second side, about 3 minutes. Using tongs, stand each piece on a cut side and continue cook, turning as necessary to brown all sides well, to the desired doneness (see page 9), 3 to 10 minutes longer. Transfer the steak to a carving board, tent loosely with foil, and let rest for 5 minutes.

4. Slice each piece of steak against the grain into ⅛-inch-thick pieces. Transfer the sliced steak to the bowl with the reserved cilantro-lime mixture and toss to coat. Season the steak with salt and pepper to taste. Spoon a small amount of the sliced steak into the center of each warm tortilla and serve immediately, passing the cilantro, onion, and lime wedges separately.

GROUND BEEF TACOS

SO MAYBE THEY'RE NOT AUTHENTICALLY Mexican. They're more Tex-Mex…maybe even gringo. But ground beef tacos have earned a special place in the palates of at least a couple of generations of Americans. We can recall our mothers ripping open the seasoning packet, the colorful array of toppings in mismatched bowls that cluttered the tabletop, and, of course, the first bite that cracked the crispy corn taco shell and sent a trickle of orange grease running down our wrists. We remember a mix of spicy skillet-cooked ground beef, shredded cheese, sweet chopped tomatoes (or, as some would have it, jarred salsa), and cool iceberg lettuce. Those in favor of more toppings could always add chopped onions, diced avocado, and sour cream. Perhaps these tacos were somewhat pedestrian, but there was also something deliciously appealing about them. It seemed as though it would be simple enough to come up with a tasty recipe to help us relive our childhood.

Sadly, when we sampled a few tacos made from supermarket kits in the test kitchen, our happy memories faded. The fillings tasted flat and stale, and they reeked of dried oregano and onion powder. The store-bought shells tasted greasy and junky—too much like unwholesome snack food to be served at the dinner table. There's no denying that the seasoning packets, along with prefab taco shells, make taco-making ridiculously easy, but with only a little more effort we thought we could produce a fiery, flavorful filling and crisp, toasty taco shells. We wanted tacos that even adults could enjoy.

For burgers we prefer the relatively fatty 80 percent lean ground chuck, and we expected we would like the same for the taco filling. But after tasting a range, we were surprised to learn that our taste buds favored the leaner types. Anything fattier than 90 percent lean ground beef cooked into a slick, greasy mess, so we stopped there.

We then began making fillings according to the few cookbook recipes we had uncovered. There were two approaches. The first had us brown ground beef in a skillet, add spices, water, and sometimes chopped onion and garlic, and simmer. The second method had us sauté the onion and garlic before adding the beef to the pan, a technique we decidedly preferred. Sautéing the onion softened its texture and made it full and sweet, while only a minute of cooking the garlic helped bring out its flavor. For a pound of ground beef, a small chopped onion was enough; as for garlic, we liked the wallop of a tablespoonful of it minced.

We proceeded with determining our seasoning by looking at store-bought taco seasoning packets. They indicated a hodgepodge of ingredients, including dehydrated onion and garlic, MSG, mysterious "spices," and even soy sauce. They all included chili powder, however, so that's where we started to fashion our own mixture. We began with 1 tablespoon and quickly increased it to 2 tablespoons for a good amount of kick. A teaspoon each of ground cumin and ground coriander added savory, complex flavors. Dried oregano in a more modest amount—½ teaspoon—provided herbal notes. For a little heat, we added cayenne pepper.

The flavors were bold, but we wanted to make them fuller and rounder. From past experience we knew that heating spices on the stovetop in a dry skillet, as is often done in various types of ethnic cooking, makes their flavors bloom, so we tried this technique with our taco filling. For one batch, we simply sprinkled the spices over the beef as it simmered, and for the second we added the spices to the sautéed onion and garlic and gave them a minute to cook before adding the meat. The difference was marked. The second batch was richly and deeply flavored, and the spices permeated the beef, whereas the flavors in the first batch seemed to merely sit in the liquid that had cooked out, leaving the beef itself tasting rather dull.

The final flavor adjustments came in the form of sweet and sour. A teaspoon of brown sugar expanded and enriched the flavor of the spices, and 2 teaspoons of cider vinegar added just enough acidity to perk up everyone's taste buds.

We still needed a sauce to carry the flavors of the spices in our meat filling; with our lean meat

MAKING YOUR OWN TACO SHELLS

STORE-BOUGHT TACO SHELLS ARE FINE IF pressed for time, but we wanted something better. The convenience of the ready-to-eat shells is obviously a huge draw for many home cooks, but we wondered if it would be worth the trouble to purchase corn tortillas that could be fried at home, thereby producing a superior shell for our taco filling. The flavor of the first home-fried shells we tried, though not perfect, was a revelation, so we went on to perfect a technique.

Because corn tortillas are like thin pancakes—they will not hold a shape—the question was how to fry them into the traditional wedge shape used for tacos. The method we settled on was simple enough. We fried one half of the tortilla until it stiffened, holding onto the other half above the oil with tongs. Next, the other half was submerged in the oil while we kept the shell mouth open (about 2 inches wide), again using the tongs. Finally, we slipped the first half back into the oil to finish cooking. Each shell took about 2½ minutes, not an unreasonable investment of time given the huge improvement in taste and texture that home-made taco shells offer.

Home-Fried Taco Shells

MAKES 8 SHELLS

The taco shells can be fried before you make the filling and rewarmed in a 200-degree oven for about 10 minutes before serving.

¾   cup vegetable oil
8   (6-inch) corn tortillas

1. Heat the oil in an 8-inch heavy-bottomed skillet over medium heat to 350 degrees, about 5 minutes (the oil should bubble when a small piece of tortilla is dropped in, and the tortilla piece should rise to the surface in 2 seconds and be light golden brown in about 1½ minutes). Meanwhile, line a rimmed baking sheet with a double thickness of paper towels.

2. Following the illustrations below, shape and fry the tortillas until golden brown.

FRYING YOUR OWN TACO SHELLS

1. Using tongs to hold the tortilla, slip half the tortilla into the hot oil. With a metal spatula in the other hand, keep half the tortilla submerged in the oil. Fry until just set, but not brown, about 30 seconds.

2. Flip the tortilla and hold open about 2 inches while keeping the bottom submerged in the oil. Fry until golden brown, about 1½ minutes. Flip again and fry the other side until golden brown, about 30 seconds.

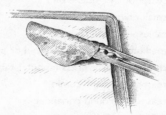

3. Transfer the shell upside down to the prepared baking sheet to drain. Repeat with the remaining tortillas, adjusting the heat as necessary to keep oil between 350 and 375 degrees.

not contributing much in the way of juices, we were going to have to add some liquid. Many recipes call only for water, but it produced a thin, hollow-tasting mixture. We then tried canned chicken broth, canned plain tomato sauce, and a combination of the two. The combination was best. With that, our taco filling was in the words of one taster, "perfect."

As for the tacos' toppings, it's largely a matter of choice. Shredded cheese, in our opinion, is required; Monterey Jack and cheddar were the obvious picks. We bypassed jarred salsa in favor of some simple chopped tomato and onions for their fresher, brighter flavors and textures. Shredded iceberg lettuce was preferred over romaine for its crispier crunch. Sour cream and diced avocado were also on the shortlist of toppings. Finally, chopped fresh cilantro—never an option on our mothers' tables—was also welcomed. It helped to pull the tacos out of the past and into the present. These were tacos that tasted better than we remembered.

Spicy Ground Beef Tacos

MAKES 8 TACOS, SERVING 4

Try making the homemade taco shells (see page 163) if you have time; they're worth the extra effort. They can be fried before you make the filling and rewarmed in a 200-degree oven for about 10 minutes before serving. Serve with shredded cheddar and/or Monterey Jack cheese, sour cream, shredded iceberg lettuce, chopped tomatoes, minced onion, diced avocado, and fresh cilantro leaves.

2	teaspoons vegetable oil
I	small onion, minced
2	tablespoons chili powder
3	medium garlic cloves, minced or pressed through a garlic press (about I tablespoon)
I	teaspoon ground cumin
I	teaspoon ground coriander
½	teaspoon dried oregano
¼	teaspoon cayenne pepper
	Salt
I	pound 90 percent lean ground beef
½	cup canned tomato sauce
½	cup low-sodium chicken broth
2	teaspoons cider vinegar

I	teaspoon brown sugar
	Ground black pepper
8	Home-Fried Taco Shells (page 163), or store-bought shells (warmed according to package instructions)

1. Heat the oil in a 12-inch skillet over medium heat until shimmering. Add the onion and cook, stirring occasionally, until softened, about 5 minutes. Add the chili powder, garlic, cumin, coriander, oregano, cayenne, and ½ teaspoon salt and cook, stirring constantly, until fragrant, about 1 minute.

2. Add the ground beef and cook, breaking the meat up with a wooden spoon, until the beef is no longer pink, about 5 minutes. Add the tomato sauce, chicken broth, vinegar, and brown sugar and bring to a simmer. Reduce the heat to medium-low and simmer, uncovered, stirring frequently and breaking the meat up so that no chunks remain, until the liquid has reduced and thickened (mixture should not be completely dry), about 10 minutes. Season with salt and pepper to taste.

3. Divide the filling evenly among the warm taco shells and serve.

FISH TACOS

BORN IN THE BAJA REGION OF MEXICO, FISH tacos have become a staple street snack throughout much of that country as well as Southern California. While they appear in many guises, the standard American version—made famous by a chain called Rubio's in San Diego—is composed of battered white fish tucked into a corn tortilla with shredded lettuce and a tangy white sauce. It may sound like an odd pairing to some, but those of us in the test kitchen who had tasted fish tacos knew it was a winning combination. With few components and little preparation needed, we knew we could pull a quick recipe together without compromising flavor. But we wanted something fresher—forget the heavy, beer-battered fish. Could we eliminate the deep-frying and still come out with a crispy, flavorful piece of fish? We headed into the kitchen to see if we could put our spin on this California classic.

The fish itself was the natural starting point. In Southern California, the favored choice is a sturdy white fish, like cod, halibut, or haddock. We experimented with the three, cutting skinned fillets into 1-inch-thick pieces about 4 to 5 inches long, just about the diameter of a small tortilla. In the end, we found all three varieties acceptable. To make sure we weren't missing anything, we went on to test some more unconventional choices as well. We tried salmon, but some tasters felt its flavor was too strong and departed too far from the original recipe. Tilapia appealed to us because it is widely available and usually fairly cheap, but we found it to be too delicate—it just broke apart into tiny, cat food–like shreds during cooking.

With our fish choices pinned down, we focused on perfecting the cooking method. We felt we could arrive at something that tasted much fresher than the traditional beer batter and that didn't waste so much oil. We dredged the fish in flour and tested cooking it in varying amounts of oil. We found that ¼ cup—a far cry from deep-frying—was the minimum amount of oil needed to get the nicely browned fish we were looking for. Any less and all we got were pieces of fish with caramelized edges. When we paired it with lettuce and a mayo-based sauce in a corn tortilla, we saw great promise. However, we all agreed that the fish needed a flavor boost. Aggressively seasoning the flour turned out to be the answer. A full tablespoon of chili powder, 1 teaspoon of salt, and ½ teaspoon of pepper added to ½ cup of flour did the trick.

The fish was now well seasoned, but there was still room for improvement for the next component on our list, the sauce. Rubio's sauce is nothing more than mayonnaise and yogurt spiked with lime juice. While it was deemed acceptable by tasters (and thousands of Californians approve of it daily), we wanted a sauce with a bit more character. Not wedded to the Rubio's recipe, we opted to exclude the yogurt and add minced chipotle chiles for both heat and flavor. The chipotles added smokiness, and we threw in some garlic, lime juice, and cilantro to round things out. This sauce added all the flavor we were looking for, so all that remained was the lettuce.

Adding cool, crisp lettuce to a hot taco usually results in warm, limp lettuce in a matter of seconds.

Shredded cabbage, however, is an alternate choice that many fish taco purveyors rely on because it is able to hold on to its crunch, even when pressed with a little heat. We added raw shredded cabbage to a batch of tacos and took a bite. While it was crispy, it was also a bit bland, so we decided to toss the cabbage with a few ingredients to bring its flavor up to the level of the fish and sauce. Keeping it light, we added some minced onion, cider vinegar, salt, and enough oil to barely coat the shredded leaves. We thought adding chili powder might work well, but it tasted raw and the flavor was overwhelming since we already had smoky chipotles in the sauce. Our final, simple cabbage was well seasoned and oniony, the perfect accompaniment for our fish tacos.

As for the tortillas, corn is the only option for fish tacos, with white preferable to yellow corn. The tortillas may be heated in a variety of ways, but we preferred toasting them over the open flame of a gas burner (for more on warming tortillas, see page 160).

These tacos had traveled a great distance from their original starting point, but they didn't leave flavor behind. With crispy sautéed fish, spicy chipotle mayonnaise, and a crunchy cabbage salad, these tacos weren't lacking much of anything in our

INGREDIENTS: Corn Tortillas

We tasted six brands of corn tortillas and found that thicker tortillas did not brown as well in the oven and became more chewy than crisp. Thin tortillas, either white or yellow, quickly became feather-light and crisp when oven-fried. The same applied to steaming, and the thicker varieties quickly became leathery as they cooled. Flavor differences between brands were slight, but locally made tortillas did pack a bit more corn flavor than national brands. Our advice? Purchase the thinnest tortillas you can find and choose a locally made brand, if possible.

THICK:
TOO CHEWY

THIN:
JUST RIGHT

mind. However, if you're one to embellish, cilantro leaves, avocado, and a splash of lime juice make a good thing even better.

Fish Tacos

SERVES 4

You can substitute haddock or halibut for the cod. In addition to the cabbage and spicy sauce, serve these tacos with fresh cilantro leaves, sliced scallion, diced avocado, or sliced radish.

CABBAGE AND SAUCE

¼   head green cabbage (about 12 ounces), shredded (about 4 cups) (see illustrations on page 114)

3   tablespoons minced onion

2   tablespoons cider vinegar

1   teaspoon vegetable oil

    Salt

¾   cup mayonnaise

1–3   teaspoons minced chipotle chile in adobo sauce

1   tablespoon minced cilantro leaves

1   tablespoon juice from 1 lime

1   medium garlic clove, minced or pressed through a garlic press (about 1 teaspoon)

    Ground black pepper

FISH AND TORTILLAS

½   cup unbleached all-purpose flour

1   tablespoon chili powder

    Salt and ground black pepper

1½   pounds skinless cod, cut into 1-inch-wide strips

¼   cup vegetable oil

1   lime, cut into wedges, for serving

12   (6-inch) corn tortillas, warmed (see the illustration on page 160)

1. FOR THE CABBAGE AND SAUCE: Toss the cabbage, onion, vinegar, oil, and ½ teaspoon salt together in a medium bowl and set aside. In a separate small bowl, whisk the mayonnaise, chipotles, cilantro, lime juice, and garlic together, season with salt and pepper to taste, and set aside.

2. FOR THE FISH AND TORTILLAS: Whisk the flour, chili powder, 1 teaspoon salt, and ½ teaspoon pepper together in a large shallow dish. Pat the fish dry with paper towels and toss gently in the flour mixture to coat. Transfer the fish to a strainer and shake gently, allowing the excess flour to fall back into the dish.

3. Heat the oil in a 12-inch nonstick skillet over medium-high heat until just smoking. Add the fish and cook, without moving, until lightly browned on the first side, about 5 minutes. Flip the fish over and continue to cook until the fish just begins to flake apart when prodded with a paring knife, about 2 minutes longer. Transfer the cooked fish to a paper towel–lined plate and let drain briefly, about 1 minute.

4. Smear each warm tortilla with the chipotle mayonnaise, then sprinkle with the cabbage salad. Lay 1 piece fish inside each tortilla and serve with the lime wedges.

SLOPPY JOES

SLOPPY JOES, WHILE POPULAR AND QUICK, are often little more than a can of sweet sauce dumped over greasy, third-rate burger meat that is brought to a simmer in a skillet. Though the base for Sloppy Joes is pretty constant among most published recipes—ground beef, onion, garlic, spices, something sweet, something sour, and something tomato—many of the recipes we tried were either greasy, dry, crumbly, bland, too sweet, too sour, or just too saucy. With a little research and a few tests, we felt that we could turn the ho-hum Sloppy Joe around; time well spent if we could come up with a quick, well-flavored skillet supper that would appeal to both adults and kids. The key would be in finding the right balance among the flavors.

Since the sauce is often so problematic, we started there. We stuck with the onion-garlic combination. Ketchup is a must, but too much made the sauce saccharine. Most recipes also called for excessive amounts of sugar, which just made things worse. In search of an alternative to "meat candy on a bun," we tested just about every tomato product we could get our hands on.

Heinz Chili Sauce was the right consistency, but it contained flecks of horseradish that turned the sauce bitter. Canned crushed tomatoes needed lengthy cooking, while tomato paste made the sauce dry and stiff. Tomato puree, however, added the strong tomato flavor we were looking for. When mixed with ketchup and just a teaspoon of brown sugar, it produced a sauce that was first and foremost about tomatoes, with a gentle sweetness that everyone (even the test kitchen's naysayers) liked.

Aside from being too sweet, most published recipes were also too greasy. After much trial and error, we found that, as we did for our Spicy Ground Beef Tacos recipe (page 164), we preferred 90 percent lean ground beef, which has just enough fat to yield tender but not slick meat.

We soon discovered that the way we cooked the meat was just as important as its fat content. Most recipes say to brown the meat completely before adding the liquid ingredients, but each time we did so, our Sloppy Joes turned out tough and crumbly. We eventually stumbled on the key to soft, tender meat: Cook it until just pink, no further, then add the remaining ingredients and finish cooking.

Because Sloppy Joes are made with kids in mind, we wanted to keep the spices to a minimum. Just ½ teaspoon of chili powder and a dash or two of hot sauce added subtle heat. Ten minutes of simmering was all this mixture needed to transform it from a runny meat sauce to a nicely thickened, saucy meat dish—ideal for sitting on a soft burger bun.

In the test kitchen, we are never content to leave well enough alone. Our colleagues liked this recipe so much that they wanted variations. We found we could substitute ground turkey for the beef as long as we followed the same cooking procedure—that is, cook the meat until just pink and no further before adding the sauce. And for Sloppy Joes with a wood-fired twist, we replaced the ketchup with barbecue sauce to create a smoky version of this family classic.

Sloppy Joes
SERVES 4

Serve this kid-friendly favorite with pickles.

2	tablespoons vegetable oil
1	medium onion, minced
½	teaspoon chili powder
	Salt
2	medium garlic cloves, minced
	or pressed through a garlic press
	(about 2 teaspoons)
1	pound 90 percent lean ground beef
1	cup tomato puree
½	cup ketchup
¼	cup water
1	teaspoon brown sugar
	Hot sauce
4	hamburger buns

1. Heat the oil in a 12-inch skillet over medium heat until shimmering. Add the onion, chili powder, and ½ teaspoon salt and cook until the onion is softened, about 5 minutes. Stir in the garlic and cook until fragrant, about 30 seconds.

2. Add the beef and cook, breaking up the meat with a wooden spoon, until almost cooked through but still slightly pink, about 3 minutes. Stir in the tomato puree, ketchup, water, brown sugar, and ¼ teaspoon hot sauce. Simmer until the sauce is slightly thicker than ketchup, 8 to 10 minutes.

3. Season with salt and hot sauce to taste. Spoon the meat mixture onto hamburger buns and serve.

➤ VARIATIONS
Skinny Joes
This is a slightly lower-fat version of the original.

Follow the recipe for Sloppy Joes, substituting 1 pound 93 percent lean ground turkey for the ground beef.

Smoky Joes
Try this sweet and smoky version on soft deli-style onion rolls instead of hamburger buns.

Follow the recipe for Sloppy Joes, substituting ½ cup barbecue sauce for the ketchup.

BRATWURST WITH SAUERKRAUT

SOME MIGHT CALL THE DISTINCT FLAVOR of sauerkraut an acquired taste, but it is a healthy and traditional foundation for several classic German and Alsatian meals, of which bratwurst and sauerkraut may be the best known. Well-browned, flavorful sausage nestled in meltingly soft sauerkraut—what's not to love? Unfortunately, the dish traditionally relies on a long list of ingredients and a slow simmer in the oven for its full flavor. Despite these challenges, we sensed the dish was ripe for a skillet makeover.

We were not out to reinvent the classic, just to find a way to cook it in a skillet without compromising its essential flavors. This meant examining the classic technique and flavors to identify the core ingredients and then employing our creative skills to come up with shortcuts. Our first realization was that a well-heated surface area was crucial to quickly cooking the sauerkraut, so we pulled out our 12-inch heavy-bottomed skillet with a lid; this offered plenty of surface area for both the sauerkraut and the sausage to cook. The fond that developed on the bottom of the pan when the sausage browned would, in turn, flavor the sauerkraut.

As for the meat, bratwurst is the classic choice, though knackwurst follows closely, and the two can be combined to mix things up. Authentic bratwurst is made from a combination of pork and veal seasoned with a variety of spices, including ginger, nutmeg, and caraway. Knackwurst is a combination of beef and pork flavored with cumin and garlic. While our local German butcher supplied the best-quality sausages, we were also able to find them in our local supermarket's deli department, next to bags of sauerkraut of course. Both bratwurst and knackwurst are fresh sausages and must be thoroughly cooked; browning starts the process and steaming the sausages in the sauerkraut finishes it. About five minutes of browning was enough to intensify the flavor of the sausages and develop a fond to season the sauerkraut.

At its simplest, sauerkraut is nothing but thinly sliced cabbage that has been tightly packed with salt and slowly fermented. Recipes for the dish actually date back to the Middle Ages. Depending on the temperature at which the cabbage is stored, fermentation may last a year before the sauerkraut is ready. But rarely does it go this long; one or two months is more conventional. Regardless, our aim was not to make our own; using store-bought sauerkraut as our starting point would suffice. Luckily, all the brands we tested were perfectly acceptable, especially when well rinsed to get rid of the potent brine.

To boost the flavor of the sauerkraut, we stuck to conventional additions like apple and onion. Coarsely grated on a box grater, the apple broke down to enrich the sauerkraut. We tried grating the onions also but found they did not brown as well as they did when sliced, and the resulting sauerkraut suffered, lacking depth.

Despite the sweetness provided by the onion and apple, tasters agreed that the sauerkraut needed more. White sugar worked adequately, but brown sugar lent a new dimension; 4 teaspoons did the job. Traditional seasonings in the recipes we found included sage, caraway seeds, garlic, cloves, bay leaves, and juniper berries. We tried most of them—solo and in various combinations—and tasters most enjoyed the woodsy, almost camphor-like flavor of the juniper, as it added complexity without competing with the assertive spiciness of the sausage. To give the sauerkraut smokiness, we added a couple of slices of bacon, which we removed before serving.

For a cooking liquid, everything from cider and beer to chicken broth and water appeared in the recipes we found. We tested cider, but it made the cabbage too sweet and fruity for most tasters, even when diluted with water. Beer added a malty note that some tasters enjoyed, but the majority felt it clashed with the sauerkraut's tang, so we skipped it. Water lent little, and in the end chicken broth was the best choice; it added richness and depth without altering the dish's balanced flavors.

Start to finish, this skillet dinner was simple and quick. We browned the brats, then set them aside while we browned the onion and simmered the sauerkraut with all its flavorings in the broth until tender, about 10 minutes. Then all we had to do was add the brats back to the pan and steam it all together until done.

One final, though crucial, lesson we learned was the importance of pricking the sausages prior to cooking. Without a liberal pricking, the sausages were prone to explode—an unsightly mess, to say the least.

Bratwurst with Sauerkraut

SERVES 4

Juniper berries can be found in the spice section of the supermarket. Although sauerkraut comes packed in cans and jars, we found sauerkraut packaged in plastic bags (which are found in the refrigerated section) to be superior in flavor and texture. Serve with toasted hoagie rolls and mustard.

2	tablespoons unsalted butter
1½	pounds bratwurst, cut into 3-inch lengths and pricked all over with a fork
1	medium onion, sliced thin
	Salt
2	pounds packaged sauerkraut, rinsed
1	cup low-sodium chicken broth
2	slices bacon
1	Granny Smith apple, peeled and grated
10	juniper berries
4	teaspoons brown sugar
2	bay leaves
	Ground black pepper

1. Melt the butter in a 12-inch skillet over medium-high heat. Brown the bratwurst on all sides, 5 to 7 minutes. Transfer to a plate and set aside.

2. Return the skillet to medium heat, add the onion and ½ teaspoon salt, and cook until the onion is softened, about 5 minutes. Stir in the sauerkraut, broth, bacon, apple, juniper berries, brown sugar, and bay leaves. Bring to a simmer and cook until tender, about 10 minutes.

3. Nestle the bratwurst into the sauerkraut, cover, and reduce the heat to medium-low. Cook until the sausages are no longer pink in the center, 10 to 15 minutes.

4. Off the heat, discard the bay leaves and bacon. Season with salt and pepper to taste and serve.

PORK WITH BRAISED RED CABBAGE

PORK AND CABBAGE ARE BY NO MEANS A new combination. We've come across dozens of recipes that combine the two in myriad ways, from simple homey fry-ups to fussy restaurant-style compositions. There's a good reason for the pairing's popularity: each ingredient balances the other well in both flavor and texture. But, despite all the recipes we found starring pork and cabbage, we failed to come across a simple skillet-braised preparation. We wondered what it would take to develop a no-fuss, one-skillet pork and cabbage dinner, one that didn't necessarily take it to the restaurant-style level but offered more flavor and punch than the often bland home-style dish.

We opted for boneless pork center-cut chops, which we chose for their convenience (they require little trimming). We pulled out our traditional rather than our nonstick skillet, to encourage browning, a step that would heighten the flavor of the chops and ensure we had a nice fond left in the pan that would in turn add flavor to our cabbage. We browned the chops for about five minutes on each side and then set them aside while we prepared the cabbage.

We chose red cabbage for its vibrant color and began building flavor for it by first sautéing an onion in our empty skillet. Along with onions, apples are often a component of this dish. We selected Granny Smith for its fruity tartness, and just one apple did the trick. Once the onion had softened, we added the apple, cabbage, and a shot of broth before returning the pork to the skillet, and we then simmered everything until the cabbage was tender.

What had sounded good in theory failed to come together in practice; the meat was tough and bland and the cabbage was pale and mushy. But on the upside, the cabbage was highly flavored from the meat juices and fond; it was the textural issues that needed the most work.

We needed to alter either the cut of meat or the cooking method, and we decided to tackle the latter. The low heat and moisture—an environment that is so beneficial to tougher, fattier cuts of meat—was turning the lean pork chops rubbery and bland. Evidently, pork center-cut chops are not ideal for a lengthy simmer, lacking both collagen-rich connective tissue and fat to keep the meat from drying out. Our solution was to cook the pork just long enough after searing to bring the meat between 140 and 145 degrees, since after that point it would begin to overcook. So we added the seared chops back to the skillet after the cabbage had simmered for 15 minutes, cooked them just until the ideal temperature had been reached, then pulled them from the skillet to rest while the cabbage finished cooking. This allowed ample time for the meat's juices to redistribute, leaving us with moist, tender pork chops.

With our method in hand, we could start tackling the auxiliary flavors. We noticed that as the apples broke down, they lost much of their sweetness. Looking to pump up the flavor, we decided to replace the chicken broth with apple cider, which added a fruity base we couldn't achieve using a piece of fresh fruit alone. A few bacon slices added smokiness and bulked up the pork flavor, while thyme and bay leaves added fresh floral notes.

There was still one nagging issue that we needed to solve. During the slow simmer, the once vibrant red cabbage turned an anemic bluish hue. It tasted fine, but the color was less than appetizing. With a little research, we found the answer to our problem. Red cabbage is high in anthocyanins, the pigment responsible for the vibrant reds of vegetables like cabbage, beets, and radishes. Anthocyanins are water-soluble and will leach from food into the liquid in which it is cooked; hence the cabbage's sickly shade. But there's a quick fix: acid. Adding a splash of vinegar brought the red right back and livened the taste of the final dish.

Pork Chops with Braised Red Cabbage
SERVES 4

If your pork chops are enhanced (see page 40 for more information), do not brine. If brining the chops, do not season with salt in step 1.

4	(8-ounce) boneless pork center-cut or loin chops, 1 inch thick, trimmed and brined if desired (see page 56)
	Salt and ground black pepper
2	tablespoons unsalted butter
1	medium onion, halved and sliced thin
1	small head red cabbage (about 1½ pounds), shredded fine (about 6 cups)
1	cup apple cider
2	slices bacon
1	Granny Smith apple, peeled and grated
1	tablespoon brown sugar
2	bay leaves
1½	teaspoons minced fresh thyme leaves
2	tablespoons cider vinegar

1. Following the illustration on page 10, slit the sides of the pork chops. Pat the pork chops dry with paper towels and season with salt and pepper. Melt the butter in a 12-inch skillet over medium-high heat until the foaming subsides. Brown the chops lightly on both sides, 5 to 7 minutes. Transfer the chops to a plate and set aside.

2. Return the skillet to medium heat, add the onion and ½ teaspoon salt, and cook until softened, about 5 minutes. Add the cabbage, cider, bacon, apple, brown sugar, bay leaves, and thyme and cook, covered, until the cabbage is softened, about 15 minutes.

3. Nestle the pork chops into the cabbage, cover, and cook until the center of the chops registers 140 to 145 degrees on an instant-read thermometer, 5 to 10 minutes.

4. Transfer the chops to a plate, tent with foil, and let rest until the center registers 150 degrees while finishing the cabbage. Return the cabbage to a simmer and cook, uncovered, until the liquid is slightly thickened, 5 to 7 minutes. Discard the bay leaves and bacon. Stir in the vinegar, season with salt and pepper to taste, and serve.

Spiced Pork Tenderloin with Potato Rösti

FOR A WEEKNIGHT SUPPER, NOTHING IS simpler or tastier than a juicy pork tenderloin dressed up with a flavorful spice rub and roasted to perfection. That is, unless you want to take it to the next level and pair it with a wedge of crispy potato *rösti*. The national potato dish of Switzerland, rösti is made of strands of grated potato cooked until crisp with salt, pepper, and a healthy dose of butter and pressed into a single skillet-sized pancake. When served with a pork tenderloin seasoned with warm, bold spices that represent Switzerland's German heritage, the pair evolves from uninspired pork and potatoes to a perfect flavor and texture combination. We sought to develop a recipe for warmly spiced pan-roasted pork tenderloin that would go perfectly with a crispy potato rösti. And again, we wanted to pull it all off by relying on our skillet.

We knew we would brown our tenderloin in the skillet to flavor not only the meat but also the potatoes, which we would cook in the skillet once we moved the tenderloin to the oven to finish up. Moving the tenderloin to the oven to finish would free up our skillet so we could get started on the rösti, ensuring our side dish would be ready to eat while the pork was still hot. We trimmed away the tenderloin's silver skin (a thin, very tough membrane found on the surface), then added some vegetable oil to our skillet, browned the pork all over, and transferred it to the oven to finish cooking. We started testing oven temperatures at 450 degrees and then tested intervals of 25 degrees above and below that mark. After numerous tests and a range of results, we found that about 15 minutes in a 425-degree oven produced the most evenly cooked, moist tenderloins.

Our meat was now perfectly cooked, but it needed flavor. Once pork tenderloins have been trimmed, they have very little fat. This leanness, while appealing to some, means that the flavor is also very neutral, making it a perfect candidate for a spice rub. We cobbled together a warm spice

mixture of caraway seeds, coriander, allspice, and nutmeg, rubbed it over a tenderloin, then commenced with cooking it. After pulling the tenderloin from the oven and taking a taste, we found we weren't far off the mark with our initial flavor concept. Slightly reducing the initial amounts of nutmeg and allspice mellowed their assertiveness, and switching from vegetable oil to butter gave the pork a nutty flavor as the butter browned. Now we could turn our attention to the rösti.

We really didn't anticipate the work involved in achieving a perfect rösti. Our initial test involved simply shredding potatoes, seasoning them with salt and pepper, then adding them to a hot skillet with some butter. This left us with a crispy, burnt exterior and raw, starchy strands of potato on the inside. Browning the outside wasn't going to be the challenge, it was cooking the inside while somehow removing the starchy gumminess. We had our work cut out for us.

We started by choosing our potato. We tested both Yukon Gold and russet potatoes, the two most popular choices used in our researched recipes, and tasters slightly favored the buttery flavor of the Yukon Golds. (In a pinch russets would work just fine.)

As it turns out, excess moisture and starch are your worst enemies when making rösti. Too much moisture prevents proper browning of the exterior, and too much starch leaves the potatoes gummy. We had to neutralize both of these factors if we wanted to be successful. Soaking the shredded potatoes in a bowl of water, in effect rinsing them, removed enough of the starch to banish gumminess, and drying them lessened the moisture. Drying evolved from laying the potato strands on paper towels to eventually squeezing them in a clean kitchen towel. The latter yielded the driest strands, and, in turn, produced the lightest, fluffiest rösti yet.

The only problem with our method was that starch was necessary to hold the rösti together, and now we had removed so much that our rösti was falling apart. Our solution was to add a teaspoon of cornstarch. This was enough to hold it all together without making things gummy again.

One final trick led us to rösti perfection: covering the rösti as it cooked. While we thought this would trap moisture and make the cake dense and gummy, just the opposite occurred. The gumminess had been due in part to undercooked potatoes and the cover addressed that problem. The batches of rösti that were cooked covered for a period were surprisingly light, as if the moist heat cooked the potatoes through more fully than dry heat alone. Further testing allowed us to zero in on a covered cooking time of six minutes, followed by two minutes uncovered to crisp and brown the bottom. Flipping the rösti, we continued cooking just long enough to brown the second side.

Served with a dollop of sour cream and applesauce, our spiced pork tenderloin and crispy potato rösti were a match made in heaven. Easy enough for a weeknight dinner but elegant enough for company, this skillet supper delivers big on flavor and small on labor.

Spiced Pork Tenderloin with Potato Rösti

SERVES 4

If the pork is enhanced (see page 40 for more information), do not brine. If brining the pork, omit the salt in the rub in step 2. We prefer to shred the potatoes using the large shredding disk of a food processor. You can use a box grater to shred the potatoes, but they should be shredded lengthwise, so you are left with long shreds. It is important to squeeze the potatoes as dry as possible in step 1 to ensure a crisp exterior. Serve with applesauce and sour cream.

1½	pounds Yukon Gold or russet potatoes (3 to 4 medium), peeled and shredded (see note above)
1	teaspoon cornstarch
	Salt and ground black pepper
1	teaspoon caraway seeds
½	teaspoon ground allspice
½	teaspoon ground coriander
¼	teaspoon ground nutmeg
2	(1- to 1¼-pound) pork tenderloins, trimmed (see the illustration on page 71) and brined if desired (see page 56)
6	tablespoons (¾ stick) unsalted butter

1. Adjust an oven rack to the middle position and heat the oven to 425 degrees. Place the potatoes in a large bowl, fill with cold water, and swirl to remove excess starch. Drain the potatoes into a strainer. Working in two batches, wrap the potatoes in a clean kitchen towel, squeeze out the excess liquid, and transfer the potatoes to a dry bowl. Sprinkle the cornstarch, ½ teaspoon salt, and ¼ teaspoon pepper over the potatoes and gently toss until thoroughly incorporated; set aside.

2. Mix the caraway, allspice, coriander, nutmeg, 1 teaspoon salt, and ½ teaspoon pepper together in a small bowl. Pat the tenderloins dry with paper towels and rub them with the spice mixture.

3. Melt 2 tablespoons of the butter in a 12-inch nonstick skillet over medium-high heat. Brown the tenderloins on all sides, reducing the heat if the pan begins to scorch, 6 to 8 minutes. Transfer the tenderloins to a 13 by 9-inch baking dish and roast in the oven until the thickest part of the tenderloins register 140 to 145 degrees on an instant-read thermometer, 15 to 18 minutes. Transfer the tenderloins to a carving board, tent loosely with foil, and let rest until the center registers 150 degrees.

4. Meanwhile, while the pork cooks in the oven, melt 2 tablespoons more butter in the skillet over medium heat. Add the potato mixture and spread it into an even layer. Cover and cook for 6 minutes.

5. Uncover and use a spatula to gently press the potatoes down to form a compact, round cake. Continue to cook, uncovered, occasionally pressing on the potatoes to shape into a uniform round cake, until the bottom is deep golden brown, about 2 minutes longer. Following the illustrations on page 295, slide the rösti onto a large plate.

6. Melt the remaining 2 tablespoons butter in the skillet. Invert the rösti onto a second plate and slide it back into the skillet, browned side facing up. Continue to cook, uncovered and occasionally pressing down on the cake, until the bottom is well browned, 5 to 7 minutes.

7. Remove the pan from the heat and allow the rösti to cool in the pan for 5 minutes. Slice the pork into ½-inch-thick slices. Slide the rösti onto a cutting board, cut into 4 wedges, and serve with the pork.

Pan-Seared Salmon with Lentils and Chard

SALMON WITH LENTILS HAS BEEN A CLASSIC pairing in homes and restaurants across France for centuries, putting to good use the country's famous *lentilles du Puy* and the salmon fished from their shores. For good reason, this match of earthy lentils and assertively flavored salmon has become something of a restaurant darling here in America in recent years, appearing on hundreds of menus in one variation or another. Our goal was to re-create the dish for the home cook, adding a leafy green used often in French cooking, Swiss chard, for a complete skillet dinner.

We started our testing with the lentils, looking for a way to cook them so that they were infused with flavor but not overpowered by any one ingredient. To begin with, we had trouble locating the French lentilles du Puy in most grocery stores. So instead, we opted for readily available brown lentils. We knew we'd want to build a flavor base in the skillet and then add the lentils and the braising liquid. Experimenting with a variety of aromatics, including shallots, scallions, and onion, we settled on the last choice for its sweetness and body. The other options proved too assertive. A couple cloves of garlic rounded out the flavors.

Much of the flavor in the lentils, however, was to come from an unexpected ingredient: chard stems. Chard is an unusual green in that the stems are as desirable as the leaves. Chard stems possess an earthy, beet-like flavor that betrays the fact that chard is, in fact, a relative of the beet. From the outset, we had decided that the stems would be braised with the lentils and the more delicate leaves would be cooked separately. Since chard stems are at their best sautéed in butter, that is how we prepared them, cooking them with the onions prior to adding the lentils and cooking liquid. Fresh thyme complemented the other flavors, and chicken broth provided a neutral yet rich

backdrop. A touch of lemon juice served two purposes. It added brightness, and, since lemon juice is an acid, it helped the lentils retain their shape while cooking. When the lentils were cooked through, we transferred them to a bowl to free up the skillet for our Swiss chard leaves.

Our intention with the chard leaves was to wilt them, much as we do spinach or any other leafy green, by putting the chopped greens in a hot pan with some butter and cooking them until tender. We normally favor the addition of garlic and lemon to sautéed greens, but in this case we let them stand alone, simply seasoned with salt and the butter in which they were cooked. Once wilted, they went into the bowl with the cooked lentils.

As we were adding the sautéed chard leaves to the lentils, we realized it would be just as easy to wilt the chard in the skillet with the cooked lentils, omitting one extra step. When folded into the braised lentils, the sliced leaves wilted perfectly. As a finishing touch, we stirred in 1 tablespoon of butter, which added just the right amount of richness.

Turning our attention to pan-searing the salmon, we gave the skillet a quick wipe with a wad of paper towels and patted the salmon dry before seasoning it liberally with salt and freshly ground black pepper. We found that a modest amount of oil—just 1 tablespoon—was enough to brown the fish and crisp the skin. The salmon was cooked in a matter of minutes, and things were really coming together.

With all the components cooked and ready to go, it was time to assemble the meal. This is certainly a time for restaurant-style plating—we like to place a few spoonfuls of lentils and chard in the center of the plate and top it with the salmon. Diners will be impressed that such a meal can be whipped up so quickly and without a sink full of dishes.

Inspired by our success, we decided to try another classic French pairing: lentils and sausage. Following the format of our salmon recipe, we simply swapped the sausage for the salmon—an easy substitution that created a very different dish. When ordered in France, this meal usually comes to the table with the sausage nestled in the lentils, but we found that cooking the sausage in the lentils made for a very greasy dish. Instead we browned the sausages separately in a sauté pan, then simply placed them on top of a few spoonfuls of lentils and chard. It proved easy, authentic, and delicious.

Pan-Seared Salmon with Braised Lentils and Chard

SERVES 4

You can use either skin-on or skinless salmon here; some tasters loved the crisp, cooked salmon skin. Lentils lose flavor with age, and because most packaged lentils do not have expiration dates, try to buy them from a store that specializes in natural foods and grains.

3   tablespoons unsalted butter

1   small onion, minced

1   bunch Swiss chard (10 to 12 ounces), stems and leaves separated (see the illustration on page 299), stems chopped medium and leaves cut into 1-inch pieces

2   medium garlic cloves, minced or pressed through a garlic press (about 2 teaspoons)

¼   teaspoon fresh minced thyme leaves
    Salt

3   cups low-sodium chicken broth

1   cup brown lentils (about 7 ounces), picked over and rinsed

1   teaspoon lemon juice
    Ground black pepper

4   (6-ounce) center-cut salmon fillets, pinbones removed (see the illustrations on page 14)

1   tablespoon vegetable oil

1   lemon, cut into wedges, for serving

1. Melt 2 tablespoons of the butter in a 12-inch nonstick skillet over medium-high heat. Add the onion, chard stems, garlic, thyme, and ¼ teaspoon salt and cook, stirring often, until the onion softens and begins to brown, about 5 minutes. Stir in the broth, lentils, and lemon juice and bring to a boil. Reduce the heat to low, cover, and cook until the lentils are tender, 25 to 30 minutes.

2. Uncover and continue to cook, stirring often, until most of the excess liquid has evaporated, about 2 minutes. Season with salt and pepper to taste, transfer to a bowl, and cover to keep warm.

3. Pat the salmon dry with paper towels and season with salt and pepper. Wipe out the skillet with a wad of paper towels, add the oil, and return it to medium-high heat until just smoking. Carefully lay the salmon in the skillet (skin or skinned side facing up) and cook until well browned on the first side, about 5 minutes.

4. Flip the salmon fillets over, reduce the heat to medium, and continue to cook until all but the very center of each fish fillet has turned from translucent to opaque, about 3 minutes longer. Transfer the fish to a clean plate, tent loosely with foil, and let rest while finishing the lentils.

5. While the salmon rests, return the skillet to medium-high heat, add the cooked lentils, and reheat until hot, about 4 minutes. Stir in the chard leaves and remaining 1 tablespoon butter and cook, stirring constantly, until the chard is wilted and incorporated, 2 to 3 minutes. Serve the lentils and salmon with the lemon wedges.

VARIATION

Sausage with Braised Lentils and Chard

Any kind of fresh pork sausage, such as Italian, works well here.

Follow the recipe for Pan-Seared Salmon with Braised Lentils and Chard, substituting 1½ pounds sausage links (about 6 links) for the salmon; brown the sausage on all sides in step 3, about 7 minutes. When browned, pour ½ cup water over the sausages in the skillet, cover, reduce the heat to medium, and cook until no longer pink in the center, 10 to 15 minutes. Transfer the cooked sausages to a carving board, tent loosely with foil, and let rest while cooking the chard leaves in step 4. Slice the sausages on the bias before serving.

CORNMEAL FRIED FISH AND SUCCOTASH

WE WANTED TO MAKE CORNMEAL FRIED FISH the center of a skillet meal; all we needed to find was an appropriate accompaniment. Succotash—the classic American vegetable blend of lima beans, corn, and red or green peppers—came to mind. Their sweet flavors and blend of textures—crisp, starchy, and soft—are ideal complements to fish. With the aid of frozen vegetables, we set out to make this classically Southern dish with bargain-priced ingredients, one that could be in and out of the skillet and ready to eat in about half an hour.

We started with the succotash. We began by briefly sautéing red bell pepper—green peppers tasted unpleasantly bitter—and onions in butter, which would add an element of sweetness and depth. From previous recipe development in the test kitchen, we knew that good succotash could be made, in part, with frozen corn and frozen lima beans. The lima beans benefited from a bit of sautéing to intensify their otherwise mild flavor, so after the onions had softened we added the lima beans to the skillet and cooked them until softened, about five minutes. The frozen corn was at its best when just warmed through, so we added it next and cooked it for only a minute.

The foundation for our succotash was there, we just needed to add a little extra flavor. Tasters favored a modest amount of tarragon; its mild anise flavor added depth to the succotash and we knew it would complement the fish. We transferred the succotash to a platter, dotted it with butter and covered it to keep it from drying out, and moved on to the fish.

We wanted fish with a crisp cornmeal coating that was easy to prepare—no three-step breading for this recipe. We chose catfish fillets, not only for their earthy flavor, which paired well with the succotash, but also because they are thin and cook quickly. However, any other thin-filleted fish, such as trout, flounder, or tilapia, will work here also.

We found that seasoning the fish with salt and pepper and letting it sit while we prepared the succotash drew out excess moisture, which was enough to allow our coating to stick without the need for dipping the fish in an egg mixture. After setting the succotash aside, we wiped out the skillet with paper towels to avoid burning any remaining vegetable debris, which would potentially give our fish an off-flavor. One cup of oil in our 12-inch skillet was enough to partially submerge the fillets and allow for even cooking. While the oil was heating, we dredged the fillets in a mixture of equal parts flour and cornmeal, which gave us the browning benefits of flour and the crunchy texture of cornmeal. The fillets browned beautifully and cooked through in only a matter of minutes. After draining the fish briefly on paper towels, we were ready to eat.

Cornmeal Fried Fish and Succotash

SERVES 4

Trout, flounder, or tilapia fillets make good alternatives to the catfish—if the fillets are small, buy four and do not cut them in half. Serve with lemon wedges or tartar sauce.

2	(12-ounce) skinless catfish fillets, cut in half lengthwise
	Salt and ground black pepper
½	cup unbleached all-purpose flour
½	cup fine-ground cornmeal
4	tablespoons (½ stick) unsalted butter
I	medium onion, minced
I	red bell pepper, steamed, seeded, and chopped fine
I	(10-ounce) package frozen lima beans
1½	cups frozen corn
I	tablespoon minced fresh tarragon
I	cup vegetable oil
I	lemon, cut into wedges, for serving

1. Season the fish with salt and pepper and set aside. Mix the flour and cornmeal together in a shallow dish and set aside.

2. Melt 2 tablespoons of the butter in a 12-inch nonstick skillet over medium heat until the foaming

subsides. Add the onion, bell pepper, and ½ teaspoon salt and cook until the onion is softened, about 5 minutes. Add the lima beans and cook until heated through and softened, about 5 minutes. Stir in the corn and cook until heated through, about 1 minute.

3. Off the heat, stir in the tarragon and season with salt and pepper to taste. Transfer the vegetables to a large serving platter, dot with the remaining 2 tablespoons butter, and cover to keep warm.

4. Wipe out the skillet with a wad of paper towels, add the oil, and return to medium-high heat until shimmering. Meanwhile, dredge the fish in the cornmeal mixture, 1 piece at a time, pressing gently to help the coating adhere.

5. Fry the fillets until golden on both sides, about 4 minutes total (if the fillets are large, you may need to fry them in two batches). Remove the fried fish from the oil and let it drain briefly on a paper towel–lined plate, about 1 minute (if necessary, keep the first batch warm in the oven). Transfer the fish to the platter with the succotash and serve with the lemon wedges.

Paella

SPAIN'S SAFFRON-INFUSED PAELLA IS A festive, flavorful rice dish incorporating an array of ingredients, and because it is traditionally prepared in a flat-bottomed pan (it is actually named after this two-handled piece of cookware), it struck us as a perfect candidate for a skillet makeover. Spanish agricultural workers first made paella with local, easy-to-find ingredients such as snails, rabbit, and green beans. It was a utilitarian dish and a far cry from today's big production piece with a commanding list of ingredients—artichokes, broad beans, bell peppers, peas, chorizo, pork, chicken, and numerous types of seafood, to start—and many complicated steps. We set out to create a less daunting recipe that could be made in a reasonable amount of time, with a manageable number of ingredients, and without a special paella pan.

There appeared to be five key steps: browning the sturdier proteins, sautéing the aromatics, toasting the rice, adding liquid to steam the rice,

and, last, cooking the seafood. As for proteins, we quickly ruled out lobster (too much work), diced pork (sausage would be enough), fish (flakes too easily and gets lost in the rice), and rabbit and snails (too unconventional). We settled on chorizo, chicken, shrimp, and mussels.

We began by browning the chicken and chorizo; this would give the meat a head start and lend necessary flavor to the rendered fat we would use to sauté the onion and garlic later on. Tasters preferred Spanish chorizo for having "more bite" than the larger refrigerated Mexican-style chorizo, and slicing it in half lengthwise and then into half moons increased the surface area for browning and made rendering the fat easier.

We browned the sausage for about five minutes, then set it aside and turned our attention to the chicken. While many recipes call for bone-in, skin-on chicken pieces, to save time we opted for boneless, skinless thighs, which are richer in flavor and less prone to drying out than breasts. We seared both sides of large chunks of chicken thighs in a tablespoon of olive oil, not cooking them all the way through to make sure they would be tender and juicy when added back to the rice to complete cooking.

With the browned meat set aside, it was time to add some flavoring and aromatics. The Spanish use a trio of onions, garlic, and tomatoes—called *sofrito*—as the building block for rice dishes. We began by sautéing one finely diced onion until soft along with one red bell pepper for added flavor and a large dose of minced garlic. Traditionally, the final ingredient, tomato, is added in seeded, grated form. To avoid the mess, we used a can of drained diced tomatoes, leaving the pieces whole for added texture and cooking the resulting mixture until thick and slightly darkened.

We could now focus on the rice. Long-grain rice seemed out of place (a paella is not supposed to be light and fluffy), and most medium-grain rice got a firm thumbs-down for its one-dimensional, blown-out texture. Of the short-grain varieties, we found that the more traditional Bomba rice of Calasparra, Spain, yielded grains that were too chewy and separate for most tasters. Valencia was preferred for its creamy but still distinct grains, and medium-grain Italian Arborio followed closely behind. To feed four, 1¼ cups of rice was just right. Once the rice was sautéed in the sofrito just long enough to become slightly toasted and coated with the flavorful base, it was time to add the liquid.

Most recipes use a liquid-to-rice ratio of 2 to 1, and we confirmed that 2½ cups of liquid to 1¼ cups of rice was ideal. For its clean, full-bodied flavor, tasters preferred rice cooked in chicken broth with a bit of white wine, which provided an additional layer of flavor.

Saffron gives paella its brilliant color and adds a distinctive earthy flavor. Most recipes call for steeping the saffron threads in a pot of simmering liquid. To save time and keep this a one-pot dish, we added ½ teaspoon of saffron to the rice along with cold chicken broth and wine, then added the browned chicken and chorizo and brought everything to a boil. After a few quick stirs to make sure the saffron was distributed evenly, we covered the pot and turned things down to a simmer, leaving the paella untouched until the rice had soaked up most of the liquid, about 15 minutes. Did it work? Yes!

With the rice nearly done, the quick-cooking seafood was ready to make its appearance. The mussels, placed in the skillet hinged end down so that they could open readily, cooked in about 10 minutes. The shrimp were not so easy. When added raw along with the mussels, the shrimp were juicy but bland. Briefly searing the shrimp in a hot skillet improved their flavor but turned them tough and rubbery. The solution? We marinated the raw shrimp briefly in olive oil, salt, pepper, and minced garlic to boost the flavor before adding them with the mussels.

Now all the paella lacked was a little green. Peas were the most vibrant, least fussy choice. Adding the peas while the rice and broth came to a boil resulted in shriveled, gray, cafeteria-style pebbles, but scattering them over the rice toward the end of cooking with the seafood allowed them to retain their bright green hue.

At this point we could easily have called it a day, but several people demanded *soccarat,* the crusty brown layer of rice that develops on the bottom of a perfectly cooked batch of paella. We waited until

the dish was completely cooked and then removed the lid and put the skillet back on the stove. After only about five minutes, a spoon inserted into the depths of the rice revealed nicely caramelized grains. After allowing the paella to rest, covered, for about five more minutes so the rice could continue to firm up and absorb excess moisture, we added garnishes of parsley and lemon and we were done.

Now that we didn't have to spend all day in the kitchen to make paella, we could even afford to hang out with our dinner guests. Sangria, anybody?

INGREDIENTS: Short-Grain Rice

When it comes down to it, a good paella is all about the rice; it's not just filler. Unfortunately, the rice you probably have in your pantry—the long-grain variety—just won't cut it. Long-grain rice is great for recipes in which light and fluffy grains are desirable (pilafs, for instance), but not for paella. We like short-grain rice, which retains distinct, individual grains while keeping the creamy-chewy texture that is so important in this dish. We tested three kinds of rice in our paella. Here's what we found.

Bomba rice, grown in the Calasparra region of Spain, is the traditional choice for paella. Its short, round, fairly translucent grains are prized for their ability to absorb up to three times their volume in liquid while retaining a separate, distinct texture. Tasters liked the "nutty" flavor of this rice.

Spanish Valencia rice has grains that are short and round like Bomba, though they are a bit larger. Tasters liked this rice best, praising its balance of textures: separate and chewy, but with a bit of creaminess. Use this rice if you can find it.

Italian Arborio rice (which is actually medium-grain rice) has larger, longer, and more opaque grains than Bomba and Valencia. Also creamier, more tender, and a bit stickier than either of the two Spanish grains, it is an acceptable choice for paella.

THE BEST SHORT-GRAIN RICE

VALENCIA

Tasters noted the winner as having "perfect texture" and as being "chewy but still creamy."

Paella

SERVES 4

If you can't find chorizo, use tasso, andouille, or linguiça. Soccarat, the traditional crusty brown layer of rice that develops on the bottom of a perfectly cooked batch of paella, is optional in step 7, but adds a nice roasted flavor to the paella.

¾   pound extra-large shrimp
     (21 to 25 per pound), peeled and deveined,
     (see the illustration on page 235)

9   medium garlic cloves, minced or pressed
     through a garlic press (about 3 tablespoons)

2   tablespoons olive oil
     Salt and ground black pepper

12   ounces boneless, skinless chicken thighs,
     trimmed and cut crosswise into thirds

8   ounces chorizo sausage, halved and sliced
     ¼ inch thick

1   red bell pepper, stemmed, seeded, and
     chopped fine

1   medium onion, minced

1   (14.5-ounce) can diced tomatoes, drained

1¼   cups Valencia or Arborio rice

2¼   cups low-sodium chicken broth

¼   cup dry white wine

½   teaspoon saffron threads

1   dozen mussels, scrubbed and debearded

½   cup frozen peas

1   lemon, cut into wedges, for serving

1. Toss the shrimp with 1 teaspoon of the garlic and 1 tablespoon of the oil and season with salt and pepper; set aside. Pat the chicken dry with paper towels and season with salt and pepper; set aside.

2. Heat the remaining 1 tablespoon oil in a 12-inch nonstick skillet over medium-high heat until shimmering. Add the chorizo and cook until deeply browned and the fat begins to render, about 5 minutes. Transfer the chorizo to a medium bowl and set aside.

3. Add the chicken pieces to the skillet in a single layer and cook over medium-high heat until browned on the first side, about 3 minutes. Flip the chicken over and brown on the second side, about 3 minutes longer. Transfer the chicken to the bowl with the chorizo.

4. Add the bell pepper and onion to the skillet and cook over medium heat until the onion is softened, about 5 minutes. Stir in the remaining 8 teaspoons garlic and cook until fragrant, about 30 seconds. Stir in the tomatoes and cook until the mixture begins to darken and thicken slightly, about 3 minutes. Stir in the rice and cook until the grains are well coated with the tomato mixture, 1 to 2 minutes.

5. Stir in the chicken broth, wine, saffron, and ¼ teaspoon salt. Return the chicken and chorizo to the skillet and bring to a boil, stirring occasionally. Cover the skillet, reduce the heat to medium-low, and cook until most of the liquid is absorbed, about 15 minutes.

6. Scatter the shrimp over the rice and insert the mussels hinged side down into the rice (so they stand upright). Continue to cook, covered, until the shrimp are opaque and the mussels have opened (discard any mussels that do not open), 6 to 8 minutes.

7. Scatter the peas over the seafood and rice and cook, covered, until the peas are warmed through, about 2 minutes longer. If soccarat is desired (see note), set the skillet, uncovered, over medium-high heat and continue to cook until the bottom layer of rice is golden and crisp, about 5 minutes, rotating halfway through cooking to ensure even browning.

8. Let the paella stand, covered, for about 5 minutes. Serve, passing the lemon wedges separately.

WILTED SPINACH SALAD

WILTED SALADS, SADLY, ARE OFTEN THE victims of unfair stereotyping. Thought of as complicated and difficult to execute, they are somehow perceived as an item you can enjoy only in a restaurant, and often they're only thought of as a first course. We would beg to differ with all these points. Warm spinach salads are quick enough to make for a midweek dinner, as they in fact require little time and effort, and when topped with quick-cooking scallops, they make an elegant meal. Our aim? To create a warm spinach salad hearty enough to qualify as a main course and keep it simple enough that it could be prepared start-to-finish in our skillet.

The easiest part would be taking care of the scallops. To let their briny flavor shine through, we simply seasoned them with salt and pepper and browned them in batches in the skillet. We then set them aside while we addressed the more complicated aspects of our recipe, the spinach and dressing.

Warm spinach salad at its finest is a pleasantly simple dish of tender spinach leaves slightly wilted by a warm aromatic dressing. But after several tests in the kitchen, we found this ideal is not so easily achieved. The salads we tried ran the gamut from tough leaves covered with bland, insipid dressing to overdressed piles of mushy greens standing in puddles of greasy vinaigrette. We knew we had to address two major factors: the type of spinach used and how to dress it.

There are two categories of spinach: curly leaf and flat leaf. Curly-leaf spinach is probably the variety most people are familiar with; it is usually packaged in cellophane bags and sold at the local supermarket. This type of spinach didn't do well in our tests. Tasters felt the leaves were too dry and chewy, and the remaining stems were fibrous. The leaves also didn't wilt when the warm vinaigrette was added.

When we tried flat-leaf spinach, our results were more encouraging. We tested two types of flat-leaf spinach commonly available at the market: baby spinach and the larger leaf spinach. The larger leaf spinach, which was sold in bundles, worked fine in our salad; its tender leaves were moist and wilted well under a warm vinaigrette. But the bunches we bought were full of dirt and required several washings to rid them of all the grit. Discouraged by the amount of time this consumed, we bought a bag of the baby spinach sold in the supermarket on the same aisle as the prepared salads-in-a-bag. Baby spinach worked perfectly. The small, tender leaves came washed and trimmed, and all we had to do was open the bag and place the spinach in a bowl. You can't get much quicker than that. To add an element of crunch, we tossed the spinach with toasted almonds, and then added some bite with sliced red onions. Both of these additions worked well with the sweetness of the scallops without overcomplicating the dish.

REMOVING TENDONS FROM SCALLOPS

The small, crescent-shaped muscle that is sometimes attached to the scallop becomes incredibly tough when cooked. Use your fingers to peel this muscle away from the side of each scallop before cooking.

With the base of our salad ironed out, we could focus on how to make a flavorful dressing that didn't overpower the greens or make them greasy. Our method for making the vinaigrette would be simple; we would sauté a small amount of aromatics in oil until soft, add the vinegar and other flavors, and cook it down to the desired strength and consistency. We knew that the flavors in our warm dressing should be based on the accompanying salad ingredients. Therefore, a scallop salad vinaigrette would need to be light, bright, and citrusy to complement the scallops' delicate briny flavor. For the acidic components, we found that tasters preferred a mixture of orange segments and sherry vinegar, especially when combined with the savory crispness of the onion and crunch of the almonds. We also noticed that if we added the sherry vinegar in the early stages of the cooking process, the flavors were muted. Instead, simmering the vinegar, and for that matter, the orange segments, at the end for only about 15 seconds retained the punch of the vinegar and sweetness of the orange and kept the vinaigrette bright. Two teaspoons of fresh thyme added with the orange contributed the right herbal note.

We then fine-tuned the oil component of the dressing. Too much olive oil in the vinaigrette bogged down the spinach, making it wet and slick. Too little made for an overly sharp vinaigrette that overpowered all of the other elements of the salad. Tasters felt 4 tablespoons of oil was most balanced; we used the full amount to sauté our aromatics before stirring in our vinegar, orange, and thyme.

Our warm vinaigrette wilted the spinach perfectly, and the leaves retained a satisfying crunch without becoming cooked and slimy. Topped with tender, perfectly browned scallops, we now had bright, fresh-tasting spinach salad that wasn't too greasy and was hearty enough to serve as a main course.

As one variation, we paired the scallops and spinach with bacon, natural matches, as well as apple and hazelnuts. We adjusted our first dressing recipe to suit these new ingredients, tossing the salad with a less acidic whole grain mustard vinaigrette. Using the rendered bacon fat in the vinaigrette helped spread a light smokiness throughout the salad. This dressing went well with all of the salad's components as well as the scallops, and tasters liked its autumnal theme.

Pairing shrimp with a spinach salad is another nice change from the ordinary, and because shrimp are slightly sweeter, with a more assertive flavor than scallops, we settled on a stronger, Asian-inspired dressing. Peppery radishes, pungent scallions, and a robust sesame vinaigrette were the perfect foil to the shrimp without being overpowering. Toasted sesame seeds lent their trademark toasty notes to the dressing, as well as visual appeal.

SEGMENTING AN ORANGE

1. Cut a thin slice off the top and bottom of the orange, then stand it on end and slice away the rind and white pith from the sides.

2. Cut the orange into sixths, from top to bottom. Trim away any stringy pith from the center of each piece. Slice each piece, crosswise, into ¼-inch pieces.

Warm Spinach Salad with Scallops, Almonds, and Oranges

SERVES 4

Tangerines can be substituted for the oranges.

8	ounces baby spinach (10 cups)
1	cup sliced almonds, toasted
½	red onion, sliced thin
1½	pounds sea scallops (16 to 24 large), tendons removed (see the illustration on page 179)
	Salt and ground black pepper
¼	cup vegetable oil
¼	cup extra-virgin olive oil
2	medium shallots, halved and sliced thin
2	oranges, peeled and pith removed, quartered, and sliced crosswise into ½-inch pieces (see the illustrations below)
2	tablespoons sherry vinegar
2	teaspoons minced fresh thyme leaves

1. Combine the spinach, almonds, and onion in a large bowl and set aside. Lay the scallops out over a dish towel–lined plate and season with salt and pepper. Press a single layer of paper towel flush to the surface of the scallops and set aside.

2. Heat 2 tablespoons of the vegetable oil in a 12-inch nonstick skillet over high heat until just smoking. Carefully add half of the scallops and cook until well browned on one side, 1 to 2 minutes (when the last scallop is added to the skillet, the first few scallops will be close to done). Transfer the scallops to a plate, browned side up, and set aside.

3. Wipe out the skillet with a wad of paper towels. Add the remaining 2 tablespoons vegetable oil to the skillet and return to high heat until just smoking. Add the remaining scallops and cook until well browned on one side, 1 to 2 minutes.

4. Reduce the heat to medium. Flip the second batch of scallops over and return the first batch of scallops to the skillet, browned side up. Continue to cook until the sides of the scallops have firmed up and all but the middle third of the scallop is opaque, 30 to 60 seconds longer. Transfer all of the scallops to a large plate, browned side up, and tent loosely with foil to keep warm.

5. Wipe out the skillet with a wad of paper towels. Add the olive oil to the skillet and return to medium heat until shimmering. Add the shallots and cook until the shallots are softened, about 2 minutes. Stir in the oranges, vinegar, and thyme and bring to a brief simmer, about 15 seconds.

6. Season the warm dressing with salt and pepper to taste, pour it over the spinach mixture, and gently toss to wilt. Divide the spinach between four plates, top with the scallops, and serve.

➤ VARIATIONS
Warm Spinach Salad with Scallops, Bacon, and Hazelnuts
A tart apple, such as a Granny Smith, adds a nice contrast to the sweet scallops, but any type of apple may be used. If after rendering the bacon you do not have 3 tablespoons of bacon fat, supplement it with vegetable oil.

8	ounces baby spinach (10 cups)
1	apple, cored and sliced into ¼-inch wedges
1	cup (5 ounces) hazelnuts, toasted and lightly crushed
½	medium red onion, sliced thin
1½	pounds sea scallops (16 to 24 large), tendons removed (see the illustration on page 179) Salt and ground black pepper
4	slices thick-cut bacon, cut into ½-inch pieces
¼	cup vegetable oil, plus extra as needed (see note)
1	medium shallot, minced (about 3 tablespoons)
2	medium garlic cloves, minced or pressed through a garlic press (about 2 teaspoons)
3	tablespoons cider vinegar
2	tablespoons apple cider
1	tablespoon whole grain mustard
2	teaspoons minced fresh thyme leaves

1. Combine the spinach, apple, hazelnuts, and red onion in a large bowl and set aside. Lay the scallops out over a dish towel–lined plate and season with salt and pepper. Press a single layer of paper towel flush to the surface of the scallops and set aside.

2. Cook the bacon in a 12-inch nonstick skillet over medium heat until crisp, about 8 minutes. Transfer the bacon to a paper towel–lined plate and set aside. Reserve the rendered bacon fat for the vinaigrette (you should have about 3 tablespoons).

3. Wipe out the skillet with a wad of paper towels. Heat 2 tablespoons of the oil in the skillet over high heat until just smoking. Carefully add half of the scallops and cook until well browned on one side, 1 to 2 minutes (when the last scallop is added to the skillet, the first few scallops will be close to done). Transfer the scallops to a plate, browned side up, and set aside.

4. Wipe out the skillet with a wad of paper towels. Add the remaining 2 tablespoons oil to the skillet and return to high heat until just smoking. Add the remaining scallops and cook until well browned on one side, 1 to 2 minutes.

5. Reduce the heat to medium. Flip the second batch of scallops over and return the first batch of scallops to the skillet, browned side up. Continue to cook until the sides of the scallops have firmed up and all but the middle third of the scallop is opaque, 30 to 60 seconds longer. Transfer all of the scallops to a large plate, browned side up, and tent loosely with foil to keep warm.

6. Wipe out the skillet with a wad of paper towels. Add the reserved bacon fat to the skillet and return to medium heat until shimmering. Add the shallot and cook until softened, about 2 minutes. Stir in the garlic and cook until fragrant, about 30 seconds. Whisk in the vinegar, apple cider, mustard, and thyme and bring to a brief simmer, about 15 seconds.

7. Season the warm dressing with salt and pepper to taste, pour it over the spinach mixture, and gently toss to wilt. Divide the spinach between four plates, top with the scallops, and serve.

Warm Spinach Salad with Shrimp and Sesame Vinaigrette
If the shrimp are larger or smaller than called for below, the cooking times will change accordingly.

8	ounces baby spinach (10 cups)
1	small cucumber, peeled and sliced thin
8	radishes, sliced thin

1 tablespoon sesame seeds, toasted

1½ pounds extra-large shrimp
(21 to 25 per pound), peeled and deveined
Salt and ground black pepper

⅛ teaspoon plus ½ teaspoon sugar

2 tablespoons plus 4 teaspoons vegetable oil

1 medium shallot, minced
(about 3 tablespoons)

1 teaspoon minced or grated fresh ginger

1 medium garlic clove, minced or pressed
through a garlic press (about 1 teaspoon)

3 tablespoons rice vinegar

2 tablespoons soy sauce

4 teaspoons toasted sesame oil

½ teaspoon dried mustard

1. Combine the spinach, cucumber, radishes, and sesame seeds in a large bowl and set aside. Pat the shrimp dry with paper towels and season with ¼ teaspoon salt, ¼ teaspoon pepper, and ⅛ teaspoon of the sugar.

2. Heat 1 tablespoon of the oil in 12-inch non-stick skillet over high heat until just smoking. Carefully add half of the shrimp in a single layer and cook until spotty brown and just pink around the edges, about 1 minute. Remove the skillet from the heat, use tongs to quickly flip each shrimp over, and let sit off heat until all but the very center is opaque, about 30 seconds. Transfer the shrimp to a plate and cover with foil. Add 1 tablespoon more oil to the skillet and repeat with the remaining shrimp (do not remove them from the skillet).

3. After the second batch has stood off the heat, return the first batch to the skillet and toss to combine. Transfer the shrimp to the bowl with the spinach mixture.

4. Wipe out the skillet with a wad of paper towels. Add the remaining 4 teaspoons vegetable oil to the skillet and heat over medium heat until shimmering. Add the shallot and cook until softened, about 2 minutes. Stir in the ginger and garlic and cook until fragrant, about 30 seconds. Whisk in the vinegar, soy sauce, sesame oil, mustard, and remaining ½ teaspoon sugar, and bring to a brief simmer, about 15 seconds.

5. Season the warm dressing with salt and pepper to taste, pour it over the spinach mixture, and gently toss to wilt. Divide the spinach between four plates, top with the shrimp, and serve.

NAPA CABBAGE WITH CRISPY TOFU

THOUGH OFTEN UNDERESTIMATED, CABBAGE makes a great salad—not just coleslaw or a picnic side dish but a crunchy, flavorful, dressed-up kind of salad. And when paired with crispy pan-fried tofu and a zesty dressing, this otherwise simple ingredient is transformed into an impressive entrée. Cabbage's natural spicy-sweetness and crunch and tofu's neutral flavor and custard-like texture are at their best when dressed with strong, unconventional flavor combinations—we were picturing a mixture of spicy chiles with a sweet element, tangy acids, and strong herbal or spice flavors. We wanted to come up with a cabbage and tofu skillet dinner that was simple yet flavorful, and avoided the common pitfalls encountered when preparing our two main ingredients. We knew all too well that cabbage salads commonly turn into watery, bland concoctions, and as for the tofu, we would need to find the right kind for the job, one that balanced the crispy cabbage. We would also need to settle on the best way to give the tofu a tasty, crispy exterior. We headed to the test kitchen to see what we could do.

First, how to avoid a watery mess of cabbage salad. This problem occurs because the cells of the cabbage are full of water that leaches out into the salad, diluting its consistency and flavor. We knew that salting the cabbage and setting it over a colander would draw out a good bit of this liquid, but because salting also makes the cabbage somewhat soft, we passed on this technique. We wanted the crispest salad possible, so we just kept in mind that our dressing would need a little extra punch to counterbalance any water that leached from the cabbage.

We chose napa cabbage over regular green cabbage because it is lighter in texture and its milder flavor blends better with an array of ingredients. In search of a light, crunchy salad, carrots were a logical addition, and tasters liked the bright flavors of fresh cilantro, scallions, and mint. The addition of peanuts lent a good earthiness.

To retain the crispness of our salad, we would need a light dressing—we wanted to get far away from the heavy mayonnaise-based variety. Since our salad had begun to take on a slightly Vietnamese feel with the peanuts, fresh mint, and cilantro leaves, we continued down this path and combined rice vinegar, garlic, and fish sauce with a few tablespoons of oil to make a quick, simple dressing. The addition of sugar balanced the pungency of the fish sauce, and chili sauce added some heat. Warmed through and poured over the cabbage, the dressing was crisp, clean, and, as some said, powerful—able to withstand any water that might leach from the cabbage—without overwhelming the vegetable's flavor.

With the salad component of our dish squared away, we were now able to turn our attention to the tofu. Based on what we had learned when creating Crispy Tofu with Sweet Soy-Garlic Sauce (page 46), we knew that tofu is an ideal candidate for pan-frying, with the crispy coating serving as a perfect foil to the creamy, mild interior. We decided to keep the flavors simple, knowing that our bracing Vietnamese vinaigrette would enliven the tofu's muted flavor.

During our crispy tofu tests, we had dredged each kind of tofu available in cornstarch (a technique the test kitchen utilizes when stir-frying to encourage browning) and pan-fried each for a tasting. We had found that tasters unanimously preferred the medium-firm and soft tofus for their creamy, custard-like texture, so we stuck with those findings for this recipe (the two worked equally well, so we leave the final choice up to you). We also knew that because we were using a softer tofu, we wouldn't press it in order to keep its shape. Instead, we simply placed the tofu on multiple layers of paper towels to drain prior to dredging in the coating. Past experience had also told us tasters

like a higher ratio of coating to tofu, so we cut our tofu into planks then again into four pieces to make "tofu fingers" prior to laying them on the towels to drain.

Next, our coating. Though we had had good luck with a pure cornstarch coating for stir-fries, we decided for this recipe, like our crispy tofu, we could be a bit more adventurous and develop a little more texture. We opted to again employ a mixture of cornstarch and cornmeal, which gave us the crispy golden coating and crunch we were after without being gritty. All we had to do was toss the tofu in the a mixture of 1 cup cornstarch and ⅓ cup cornmeal and fry it for a few minutes in vegetable oil.

Finally we hammered out the process of preparing our skillet meal. We first combined all the salad ingredients in a large bowl before frying our tofu. When the tofu was done, we set it aside, wiped out the skillet with a wad of paper towels, and made our dressing. Reserving some of our dressing to spoon over the tofu just before serving, we tossed the balance with the cabbage at the last possible moment, which helped ensure the crispest salad possible. Our final cabbage salad and tofu dish was colorful, flavorful, and achieved a perfect balance between creamy and crispy textures. It was eaten up as quickly as it was made.

Warm Cabbage Salad with Crispy Tofu
SERVES 4

We prefer the softer, creamier texture of medium-firm or soft tofu here. Firm or extra-firm tofu will also work, but they will taste drier. Be sure to handle the tofu gently and thoroughly pat it dry after draining on paper towels before seasoning and coating.

SALAD
1   medium head napa cabbage (about 1 pound), shredded (about 6 cups)
2   medium carrots, peeled and grated on the large holes of a box grater
¾   cup unsalted peanuts, toasted and crushed

4   scallions, sliced thin
½   cup whole fresh cilantro leaves
½   cup chopped fresh mint leaves

TOFU
2   (14-ounce) blocks medium-firm or soft tofu
    (see note), sliced crosswise into 1-inch-thick
    slabs, each slab sliced into two 1-inch-wide
    fingers
1   cup cornstarch
⅓   cup cornmeal
    Salt and ground black pepper
¾   cup vegetable oil

DRESSING
3   tablespoons vegetable oil
2   medium garlic cloves, minced or pressed
    through a garlic press (about 2 teaspoons)
5   tablespoons rice vinegar
2   tablespoons fish sauce
2   tablespoons sugar
1–2 teaspoons Asian chili sauce

1. FOR THE SALAD: Combine all of the salad ingredients in a large bowl and set aside.

2. FOR THE TOFU: Spread the tofu out over several layers of paper towels and let sit to drain slightly, about 20 minutes. Adjust an oven rack to the middle position, place a paper towel–lined platter on the rack, and heat the oven to 200 degrees.

3. Place a wire rack over a baking sheet and set aside. Toss the cornstarch and cornmeal together in a shallow dish. Season the tofu with salt and pepper. Working with a few pieces of tofu at a time, coat them thoroughly with the cornstarch mixture, pressing on the coating to adhere, then transfer to the wire rack.

4. Heat the oil in a 12-inch nonstick skillet over medium-high heat until shimmering. Carefully lay half of the tofu in the skillet and cook, turning the pieces occasionally with a spatula, until crisp and lightly golden on all sides, about 4 minutes. Using a spatula, gently lift the tofu from the oil, letting any excess oil drip back into the skillet, and transfer to the prepared platter in the oven. Repeat with the remaining tofu pieces and transfer to the platter in the oven. Discard any oil left in the skillet and wipe it out with a wad of paper towels.

5. FOR THE DRESSING: Add the oil to the skillet and return to medium heat until shimmering. Add the garlic and cook until fragrant, about 30 seconds. Whisk in the vinegar, fish sauce, sugar, and chili sauce, and bring to a brief simmer, about 15 seconds.

6. Off the heat, measure out and reserve 2 tablespoons of the dressing. Pour the remaining dressing over the cabbage mixture and toss to combine. Divide the cabbage between four plates and arrange the warm tofu over the top. Spoon the reserved dressing over the tofu before serving.

5

POT PIES, CASSEROLES, AND PIZZA

POT PIES, CASSEROLES, AND PIZZA

WITH A FLAKY CRUST AND TENDER CHUNKS of meat and vegetables, pot pie may just be the ultimate comfort food. In this chapter, we have simplified some all-American classics, like chicken pot pie and beef pot pie, while also looking at other celebrated dishes, including chicken divan and shrimp and grits, that we thought could be made in a skillet too. And we invented a few recipes we hope will become just as popular as these well-known classics, like Pork Tinga Tamale Pie (page 204), a new spin on tamale pie featuring pork and chorizo covered in corn bread, and Thanksgiving Turkey Bake (page 206), which provides all the holiday flavors, minus the visit to the relatives' house.

The challenges of making a great pot pie or casserole are numerous, and limiting ourselves to just one pan only upped the ante. We'd be cutting back on dirty dishes, a definite plus, but we would need a plan of action. The strategy we used was to rotate ingredients in and out of the skillet and cook proteins and vegetables in a sauce that was also built in the very same pan. Then we topped the pot pies and casseroles, popped them in the oven, and baked all of them right in the skillet.

We still had to look out for the usual pot pie disasters. If the sauce is too thin and watery, the topping will become soggy; if the filling is overcooked by even a moment before assembly, the meat will turn tough and sinewy, and the vegetables mushy and flavorless while in the oven. And we haven't even mentioned toppings—it took us days in the kitchen to identify and solve the myriad problems they pose. For example, we discovered that when we used a solid sheet of puff pastry to cover our Spring Vegetable Pot Pie (page 198), the delicate vegetables in the filling overcooked and turned unappetizing colors. The remedy was simple enough: We cut the pastry into rectangles so the entire dish wasn't covered, allowing some heat and steam to escape so our vegetables remained crisp. Our casserole dishes use different toppings—we have seen top layers made from everything from corn bread to Parmesan cheese—so we had to get creative. We covered our Tuscan Bean Casserole (page 215) with small chunks of baguette for a rustic feel and flavor.

While we revisited many traditional pot pies and casseroles, we also looked at one of our favorite foods—pizza. Pizza fits right in with our other recipes because it's built in one pan, and then layered and baked. We knew the skillet could help streamline this dish, as it did with the pot pies and casseroles. Developing our Cheese Pizza recipe (page 221), we found that we didn't even have to heat up the skillet in advance; we could build the whole pizza in a room-temperature skillet, then use heat from both the stovetop and the oven to cook it. We simply placed our dough in the skillet, covered it with no-cook sauce—a great time-saver—and shredded cheese, and set the skillet over high heat to get the crust baking. After 10 minutes in the oven, the pizza was ready, with a thin, crispy crust, and it was time for dinner.

Our pot pies, casseroles, and pizzas are fresh and tasty takes on family classics and provide lots of suppertime options, plus you won't need to spend all day laboring over a hot stove. Now you just have to figure out what to do with your free time.

CHICKEN POT PIE

EVERYONE LOVES A GOOD CHICKEN POT PIE —what's not to love about juicy chunks of chicken, vegetables, and a full-flavored sauce, all covered with a buttery crust? But, like a lot of satisfying dishes, traditional pot pie takes time. Before the pie even makes it to the oven, the cook must poach a chicken, take the meat off the bones and cut it up, prepare and blanch the vegetables, make a sauce, and make and roll out the pie dough. Given the many time-consuming steps it can take to make a pot pie, our goal was to make the best one we could, relatively quickly, using only one skillet. Pot pie, after all, is simple supper food.

We began with the chicken, and decided to use boneless, skinless chicken breasts since they cook quicker than both bone-in pieces and dark meat. To determine the best cooking method, we sautéed raw breast meat that had been cut into bite-sized pieces, sautéed whole breasts and shredded the meat when it had cooled, and poached whole breasts in broth, also shredding the meat when cool. The sautéed chicken pieces had too smooth a surface for the sauce to adhere to, and the sautéed breasts had formed a crusty outer layer, which we didn't like in the pie, although these breasts had the most flavor. The poached and shredded chicken was tender and mixed well with the vegetables, but we preferred the flavor of the sautéed breasts. We tried one more test, this time sautéing the chicken breasts briefly over moderate heat, then poaching them in the sauce and shredding them. This was the ideal combination—poaching ensured that the meat remained tender, while the short sauté time added good flavor without a crispy crust. Also, the flavor of the sauce was enhanced by the released chicken juices.

We turned our attention to the vegetables, which tend to overcook in pot pies. Starting with the classic combination of peas and carrots, we experimented with raw vegetables, frozen vegetables, and parboiled vegetables. We found that while the frozen vegetables held their color best and the peas tasted great, the carrots lacked flavor. The parboiled vegetables also kept their color but tasted bland, and the raw vegetables weren't fully cooked at the end of the baking time. We settled on fresh carrots and frozen peas. To ensure that the carrots would be fully cooked in the finished dish, we sautéed them in the skillet once the chicken came out, along with some celery and onion. The frozen peas, though, would have to wait their turn; we added them, still frozen, to the sauce just before the baking time. We knew that this would help preserve their fresh color and flavor.

Next, we wanted to develop a sauce that was flavorful and creamy, with the proper consistency. Traditionally, the sauce for chicken pot pie is broth-based and thickened with a roux (a mixture of flour and butter or other fat sautéed together briefly). To keep things simple, and in one skillet, we added the flour with the cooked vegetables before adding the chicken broth. Our sauce was very lean, so we chose to enrich it with cream, but how much would we need?

Because of the dish's inherent richness, we wanted to use a minimal amount of cream. We tried our sauce three different ways, using ¾ cup cream, 1¼ cups half-and-half, and 2 cups milk. Going into the oven, all the fillings had the right consistency and creaminess; when they came out, however, it was a different story. Vegetable and meat juices diluted

the consistency and creaminess of the milk and half-and-half sauces, making them watery. We decided to stick with cream and tested different amounts in the sauce: ¼ cup, ½ cup, and ¾ cup. The sauce made with ¼ cup wasn't rich enough, and the one with ¾ cup was too heavy and dominated by the flavor of the cream. The sauce made with ½ cup of cream was just right, with a silky consistency and a flavor that didn't overpower the other components of the dish.

Though our sauce was now the ideal consistency, it still tasted a little bland (even when we had poached our chicken in it). In another test, we added a splash of vermouth just before the broth and cream were added to the flour and vegetables. This worked perfectly—the vermouth gave the sauce the big flavor boost it needed.

To keep to one pan, we would top (and bake) the filling in the same skillet. Some recipes call for simply cutting out a few rounds of frozen puff pastry or rolling out biscuit dough. To that, we said no way—anything other than our homemade all-butter pie dough seemed to be missing the point. We rolled the dough out to ¼-inch thickness, then trimmed it to measure 12 inches across—the same size as the skillet. We then folded and crimped the dough around the edge, which not only looks pretty but supports the outer rim of crust so it doesn't melt into the filling during baking (it also gives some breathing room for the bubbling filling during baking). To make transferring the crust to the top of the skillet easy, we froze the shaped crust until stiff, then plopped it right onto the warm filling in the skillet.

We had trouble achieving a fully cooked crust; the underside was soggy. To find the right temperature, we baked six pot pies at six different temperatures, starting at 325 degrees and increasing by 25-degree increments. We found that using a 425-degree oven, and topping the pie while the ingredients were still piping hot, allowed the crust to bake through more evenly and thoroughly, preventing a soggy underside. We also noted that because the pie crust insulates the filling ingredients, we needed to let the pot pie rest for a full 20 minutes before serving (or else suffer the wrath of angry tasters with burnt mouths). The time elapsed, and we dug in. Mission accomplished—we had created a full-flavored yet simple chicken pot pie.

Classic Chicken Pot Pie

SERVES 4

We prefer the buttery flavor and flaky texture of homemade pie dough here; however, you can substitute store-bought pie dough if desired. If using store-bought pie dough, roll it into a 12-inch circle, crimp the edges, cut vent holes, and freeze as directed in the Skillet Pot Pie Crust recipe (page 192) before using, and reduce the pot pie baking time to 30 to 35 minutes in step 5. Make sure the filling is still hot when the frozen crust is placed on top.

1½	pounds boneless, skinless chicken breasts (about 4 medium), trimmed (see the illustration on page 6)
	Salt and ground black pepper
4	tablespoons (½ stick) unsalted butter
3	medium carrots, peeled and cut crosswise ½ inch thick
1	medium onion, minced
1	celery rib, sliced ¼ inch thick
¼	cup unbleached all-purpose flour
⅓	cup dry vermouth or dry white wine
2	cups low-sodium chicken broth
½	cup heavy cream
2	teaspoons minced fresh thyme leaves, or ½ teaspoon dried
1	cup frozen peas
1	recipe Skillet Pot Pie Crust (page 192), frozen for at least 30 minutes

1. Adjust an oven rack to the middle position and heat the oven to 425 degrees. Pat the chicken dry with paper towels and season with salt and pepper. Melt 2 tablespoons of the butter in a 12-inch ovenproof skillet over medium heat. Carefully lay the chicken breasts in the skillet and cook until lightly browned on both sides, 6 to 8 minutes. Transfer the chicken to a plate.

2. Add the remaining 2 tablespoons butter to the skillet and melt over medium heat. Add the carrots, onion, celery, and ½ teaspoon salt and cook until the vegetables are softened, 5 to 7 minutes.

3. Stir in the flour and cook, stirring constantly, until incorporated, about 1 minute. Slowly stir in the vermouth and cook until evaporated, about 30 seconds. Slowly stir in the broth, cream, and thyme and bring to a simmer. Nestle the browned chicken into the skillet, cover, and cook over medium-low heat until the thickest part of the breast registers 160 degrees on instant-read thermometer, about 10 minutes.

4. Off the heat, transfer the chicken to a plate. When the chicken is cool enough to handle, shred it into bite-sized pieces following the illustration below. Return the shredded chicken to the skillet, stir in the peas, and season with salt and pepper to taste.

5. Remove the frozen crust from the freezer, discard the parchment paper, and place the crust on top of the filling following the illustration on page 195. Bake the pot pie until the crust is golden brown and the filling is bubbling, 45 to 50 minutes. Let the pot pie cool for 20 minutes before serving.

➤ VARIATIONS

Chicken Pot Pie with Spring Vegetables
Follow the recipe for Classic Chicken Pot Pie, omitting the celery and onion. Add 1 medium leek, white and light green parts only, halved lengthwise, sliced ¼ inch thick, to the skillet with the carrots in step 2. Add ½ pound thin asparagus, tough ends trimmed and cut into 1-inch lengths, with the shredded chicken and peas in step 4.

SHREDDING CHICKEN

To shred chicken meat, hold a fork in each hand, with the tines facing down. Insert the tines into the chicken and gently pull the forks away from each other, breaking the meat apart and into long, thin strands.

Chicken Pot Pie with Artichokes

Follow the recipe for Classic Chicken Pot Pie, omitting the peas. Before starting step 2, melt 2 tablespoons more unsalted butter in the skillet over medium-high heat and cook 1 (16-ounce) package frozen artichokes (4 cups), thawed, until well browned, about 10 minutes; transfer to a bowl. Continue with step 2 as directed, adding ½ teaspoon dried tarragon to the skillet with the onion, carrots, and celery. Stir in the cooked artichokes and 1½ teaspoons grated lemon zest in step 4.

INGREDIENTS:
Store-Bought Pie Dough

A flaky, buttery homemade pie crust is the ultimate crown for chicken and beef pot pies, but it's also a fair amount of work. How much would we sacrifice by using a store-bought crust instead?

To find out, we tried several types and brands, including both dry mixes (just add water) and ready-made crusts, either frozen or refrigerated. The dry mixes, including Betty Crocker, Jiffy, Krusteaz, and Pillsbury, all had problems. Some were too salty, some were too sweet, and all required both mixing and rolling—not much work saved. Frozen crusts, including Mrs. Smith's (also sold as Oronoque Orchards) and Pillsbury Pet-Ritz, required zero prep, but tasters found them pasty and bland, and it was nearly impossible to pry them from the flimsy foil "pie plate" in which they are sold. The one refrigerated contender, Pillsbury Just Unroll! Pie Crusts, wasn't bad. Though the flavor was somewhat bland, the crust baked up to an impressive flakiness. Better yet, this fully prepared product comes rolled up and is ready to go when you are.

THE BEST STORE-BOUGHT PIE DOUGH

PILLSBURY

Pillsbury Just Unroll! Pie Crusts (one package includes two 9-inch crusts) bake up light and fluffy.

BEEF POT PIE

PLAINLY STATED, BEEF POT PIE IS BEEF STEW baked under a crusty topping. After hours of slow simmering, the stew is ladled into a baking dish, topped with biscuits or a pastry crust, and cooked even longer. It is an all-day affair, requiring hours of diligent attention. Certainly there's nothing wrong with such a labor of love, but we wanted a simpler, faster alternative. Could a richly flavored beef pot pie—with all the nuance of a slow-simmered beef stew—be made in a fraction of the time and entirely in one skillet?

We started the testing process with our primary concern: the choice of meat. Beef stew develops its rich flavor through the slow, deliberate simmering of inexpensive yet flavorful cuts of beef. But cooking these tougher cuts quickly and over high heat is disastrous—they turn as tough and bland as a tire. Clearly, if we wanted a quick-cooking cut of meat, we had to look elsewhere. Tender steaks were an obvious choice. Our first choice was blade steak, an underutilized, reasonably priced steak we have used for beef teriyaki and kebabs. Trimmed into small cubes, browned, and simmered in the oven underneath a crust, it was tender and flavorful. Pricey sirloin steaks treated in the same fashion yielded nearly identical results, but at a much higher cost. We would stick with blade steaks.

With the meat chosen, we could now work on finessing the pie's flavor. Sticking to the basics, we included onions, carrots, peas, and garlic. We sautéed the onions, carrots, and garlic directly in the skillet after the meat was removed. We had learned in our Classic Chicken Pot Pie (page 190) that adding the peas still frozen to the filling just before baking is best for preserving their color. But tasters wanted a heartier filling, so we upped the amount of onions and garlic to make a more flavorful stew. Then we added white mushrooms for their rich, meaty flavor and the texture they brought to the mixture.

For the sauce, we wanted more of a gravy than a heavy cream sauce, since this was a beef pot pie. We started by making a roux with the vegetables in the skillet, then thinning it with broth. Focusing on the broth, we tried both chicken and beef broth

Skillet Pot Pie Crust

MAKES 1 POT PIE CRUST

Don't substitute low-fat or nonfat sour cream, or the crust will be much less crisp and flaky.

2	tablespoons sour cream
4–6	tablespoons ice water
1⅔	cups (8¼ ounces) unbleached all-purpose flour
¾	teaspoon salt
10	tablespoons (1¼ sticks) cold unsalted butter, cut into ½-inch pieces and frozen for 10 minutes

1. Mix the sour cream and 4 tablespoons of the ice water together in a small bowl. Process the flour and salt together in a food processor until combined, about 3 seconds. Add the butter and pulse until the butter is the size of large peas, 6 to 8 pulses. Add half of the sour cream mixture and pulse to incorporate, about 3 pulses. Repeat with the remaining sour cream mixture.

2. Pinch the dough together between your fingers; if it feels floury, dry, and does not hold together, add the remaining 2 tablespoons water and pulse until the dough forms large clumps and no dry flour remains, 3 to 5 pulses.

3. Turn the dough onto a work surface. Shape into a ball and flatten to a 5-inch disk; wrap in plastic and refrigerate until firm, at least 1 hour, or up to 2 days.

4. If the dough is very firm, let it sit on the counter to soften slightly, about 10 minutes. Roll the dough out to a ¼-inch-thick round on a large piece of parchment paper.

5. With the dough still on the parchment, trim the dough into a tidy 12-inch circle following the illustrations at right. Fold back the outer ½-inch rim, then crimp the folded edge. Cut four oval-shaped vents, each about 3 inches long and ½ inch wide, in the center of the dough. Slide the parchment paper and dough onto a baking sheet, cover loosely with plastic wrap, and freeze until firm, at least 30 minutes, or up to 24 hours.

MAKING A SKILLET POT PIE CRUST

1. Roll the dough out to a ¼-inch-thick round on a large piece of parchment paper. Leaving the dough on the parchment, use a paring knife to trim the dough into a tidy 12-inch circle. If you don't have a ruler, use the rim of an overturned skillet (the same skillet that will be used to make the pot pie) as a guide.

2. Fold back the outer ½-inch rim of the dough.

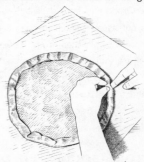

3. Using your knuckle and forefingers, crimp the folded edge of the dough to make an attractive fluted rim.

4. Using a paring knife, cut four oval-shaped vents, each about 3 inches long and ½ inch wide, in the center of the dough.

to build the sauce. Chicken broth yielded a weakly flavored stew; beef broth was richer in flavor but the resulting sauce lacked complexity. Our solution was to fortify the flavor of the beef broth by adding a substantial splash of red wine, a tablespoon of tomato paste, and some thyme.

With our filling perfected, it was time for a topping. We tried both biscuits and our Skillet Pot Pie Crust (page 192). While there were tasters in favor of each, the combination of our flaky crust with rich beef stew was hard to pass up. We stuck to the more traditional pastry topping. We found that a 425-degree oven allowed the crust to bake through evenly and thoroughly, preventing a soggy underside.

We had achieved our goal of making an easy beef pot pie entirely in a skillet. And not only was it convenient (and our kitchen wasn't piled high with dishes when we were done), but tasters weren't leaving a crumb behind.

Classic Beef Pot Pie

SERVES 4

We prefer the buttery flavor and flaky texture of homemade pie dough here; however, you can substitute store-bought pie dough if desired. If using store-bought pie dough, roll it into a 12-inch circle, crimp the edges, cut vent holes, and freeze as directed in the Skillet Pot Pie Crust recipe (page 192) before using, and reduce the pot pie baking time to 30 to 35 minutes in step 5. Make sure the filling is still hot when the frozen crust is placed on top. When trimming the steaks, be sure to remove the gristle that runs down the middle.

1½	pounds blade steaks, trimmed and cut into 1-inch pieces (see the illustrations on page 242) Salt and ground black pepper
2	tablespoons vegetable oil
1	medium onion, minced
2	medium carrots, peeled and cut crosswise ½ inch thick
8	ounces white mushrooms, wiped clean, and quartered
3	garlic cloves, minced or pressed through a garlic press (about 1 tablespoon)
¼	cup unbleached all-purpose flour
1	tablespoon tomato paste
⅓	cup dry red wine
2½	cups low-sodium beef broth
2	teaspoons minced fresh thyme leaves, or ½ teaspoon dried
1	cup frozen peas
1	recipe Skillet Pot Pie Crust (page 192), frozen for at least 30 minutes

1. Adjust an oven rack to the middle position and heat the oven to 425 degrees. Pat the beef dry with paper towels and season with salt and pepper. Heat 1 tablespoon of the oil in a 12-inch ovenproof skillet over medium-high heat until just smoking. Add the meat and cook, stirring occasionally, until well browned, 5 to 7 minutes. Transfer the meat to a plate and set aside.

2. Add the remaining 1 tablespoon oil to the skillet and heat over medium heat until shimmering. Add the onion, carrots, and ½ teaspoon salt and cook until the vegetables are softened, 5 to 7 minutes. Stir in the mushrooms and cook until softened, about 5 minutes.

3. Stir in the garlic and cook until fragrant, about 30 seconds. Stir in the flour and tomato paste and cook, stirring constantly, until the flour is incorporated, about 1 minute. Stir in the wine and cook until evaporated, about 30 seconds. Slowly stir in the broth and thyme and bring to a simmer.

4. Off the heat, season the sauce with salt and pepper to taste, then stir in the browned beef with any accumulated juices and the peas.

5. Remove the frozen crust from the freezer, discard the parchment paper, and place the crust on top of the filling following the illustration on page 195. Bake the pot pie until the crust is golden brown and the filling is bubbling, 45 to 50 minutes. Let the pot pie cool for 20 minutes before serving.

➤ VARIATIONS

Beef Pot Pie with Portobello Mushrooms, Sherry, and Rosemary

Follow the recipe for Classic Beef Pot Pie, substituting 1 teaspoon minced fresh rosemary for the thyme and 8 ounces portobello mushroom caps, brushed clean, gills removed, and cut into ½-inch pieces, for the white mushrooms; increase the mushroom cooking time to 8 minutes in step 2. Before adding the garlic in step 3, stir in ¼ cup dry sherry and cook until nearly evaporated, about 30 seconds.

Beef Pot Pie with Provençal Flavors

Follow the recipe for Classic Beef Pot Pie, omitting the peas, increasing the amount of tomato paste to 2 tablespoons, increasing the amount of red wine to 1 cup, and reducing the amount of beef broth to 1¾ cups. Add ¼ ounce dried porcini mushrooms, rinsed and minced, with the garlic in step 3. Add ½ teaspoon grated zest from one orange, ½ cup pitted niçoise olives, patted dry and chopped coarse, and 1 anchovy fillet, rinsed and minced, with the broth and thyme in step 3.

WINTER ROOT VEGETABLE POT PIE

A THICK, HEARTY VEGETABLE POT PIE SEEMS like just the thing for the darkening days of fall and winter. And most markets are packed with a broad range of choices to include in a filling, from vibrantly colored winter squashes like acorn and butternut to pale parsnips and turnips. But a good vegetable pot pie is easier said than done. Vegetable pot pies face hurdles that neither chicken nor beef pot pies do, the biggest being how to develop a full-flavored filling without tender chunks of beef or chicken. Even trickier, vegetable pies can take much longer to make than traditional meat pies, thanks to the tons of peeling and chopping involved, and the different cooking times for each vegetable. We wondered if we could develop a vegetable-based pot pie perfect for a vegetarian entrée, one that took no more time to make than our beef and chicken pot pies and could be made entirely in a skillet.

After assessing a wide range of recipes for vegetable pot pie, we realized we were looking forward to the challenge. Boiled or steamed vegetables buried in a bland sauce and topped with a cardboard-like crust? No thanks. Gravely disappointed in most of the recipes we tested, we decided to start from scratch. The basic pot pie vegetables—onions, celery, and carrots—would remain, of course; without them, the filling was doomed to blandness. Right away, we decided to increase the amount of each to help boost the flavor.

Next we looked to the selection of vegetables. Parsnips and turnips both added complexity and sweet flavors, but tasters favored parsnips; turnips were too strong. Next, we opted to trade out the celery stalks for celery root to bulk up the filling and flavor. Then we turned to mushrooms to achieve the meatiness that we felt the filling needed. White mushrooms were the right size and added a nice texture to the mix, but we wanted more depth of flavor. Adding dried porcini mushrooms gave our pot pie just the flavor boost it needed. We skipped over potatoes; they wouldn't add much flavor, plus this pot pie would have a pastry crust, so there was no need to introduce more starch into the dish. We looked at rutabagas, kohlrabi, and chayote—these were too esoteric. We were going to keep it simple.

To yield the best results, we needed to cook the vegetables in such a way as to maximize their flavor. Because mushrooms release a good amount of liquid, they would be cooked first on their own. For all of the vegetables, our goal was to sauté them in the skillet over medium heat (medium-high for the mushrooms) until beginning to brown. Caramelizing them maximized their flavors, which was just what our vegetable pot pie needed. To make room for building the sauce, we removed most of the vegetables from the skillet, setting them aside for the moment.

Now that we'd settled on the filling ingredients, we could finally tackle the sauce. We sautéed the onions with dried porcini mushrooms for flavor, then added vermouth, vegetable broth (instead of chicken broth), and cream. But the vegetable broth lacked flavor and needed to be bulked up with other flavorings. We went back and added a hearty five cloves of garlic, minced thyme, and 1 tablespoon of tomato paste before we added the liquids. These three ingredients brought the flavor up to par. To thicken the sauce, we added ¼ cup of flour, then stirred in the liquids and the vegetables. At this point, the flavor of our root vegetable pot pie was far superior to that of all the other recipes we had tested.

All that was left was to top (and bake) the filling right in the skillet. Since we were going for the ultimate vegetable pot pie, nothing other than our homemade buttery pie dough would do. We had already perfected the rolling and baking method for pot pie crust in our chicken and beef pot pie recipes, so all we had to do was roll out and trim the dough into a 12-inch circle with nicely crimped edges, cut a few vent holes, and freeze it until firm. When the pot pie filling was ready, we simply plopped the frozen crust into the skillet and headed for the oven. Then we baked the pot pie at 425 degrees—this temperature allowed the crust to bake through evenly and thoroughly, preventing a soggy underside—and let the pot pie cool for a full 20 minutes, as the filling was incredibly hot (the pastry crust acts as insulation and keeps in the heat). Finally, we had a root vegetable pot pie that could compete with its meaty cousins and thrill our vegetarian friends.

TOPPING A SKILLET POT PIE WITH PIE CRUST

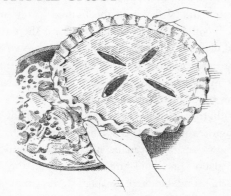

Gently lay the frozen Skillet Pot Pie Crust (page 192) on top of the filling in the pan.

Winter Root Vegetable Pot Pie
SERVES 4

We prefer the buttery flavor and flaky texture of homemade pie dough here; however, you can substitute store-bought pie dough if desired. If using store-bought pie dough, roll it into a 12-inch circle, crimp the edges, cut vent holes, and freeze as directed in the Skillet Pot Pie Crust recipe (page 192) before using, and reduce the pot pie baking time to 30 to 35 minutes in step 5. Make sure the filling is still hot when the frozen crust is placed on top.

6	tablespoons (¾ stick) unsalted butter
1	pound white mushrooms, wiped clean, and quartered
	Salt
3	medium carrots, peeled and cut crosswise ½ inch thick
3	medium parsnips, peeled and cut crosswise ½ inch thick
1	celery root, peeled and cut into ½-inch pieces
2	medium onions, minced
½	ounce dried porcini mushrooms, rinsed and minced
5	medium garlic cloves, minced or pressed through a garlic press (about 5 teaspoons)
2	teaspoons minced fresh thyme leaves, or ½ teaspoon dried
1	tablespoon tomato paste
¼	cup unbleached all-purpose flour
⅓	cup dry vermouth or dry white wine
2	cups low-sodium vegetable broth
½	cup heavy cream
	Ground black pepper
1	recipe Skillet Pot Pie Crust (page 192), frozen for at least 30 minutes

1. Adjust an oven rack to the middle position and heat the oven to 425 degrees. Melt 2 tablespoons of the butter in a 12-inch ovenproof skillet over medium-high heat. Add the mushrooms and a pinch salt and cook, stirring often, until the mushrooms release their liquid and begin to brown, about 10 minutes. Transfer the mushrooms to a bowl.

2. Melt 2 tablespoons more butter in the skillet over medium heat. Add the carrots, parsnips, celery root, and a pinch salt and cook, stirring often, until the vegetables begin to brown, about 15 minutes. Transfer to the bowl with the mushrooms.

3. Melt the remaining 2 tablespoons butter in the skillet. Add the onions, porcini mushrooms, and ½ teaspoon salt and cook until the onion is softened, 5 to 7 minutes. Stir in the garlic and thyme and cook until fragrant, about 30 seconds. Stir in the tomato paste and flour and cook, stirring constantly, until the flour is incorporated, about 1 minute. Slowly stir in the vermouth and cook until evaporated, about 30 seconds. Slowly stir in the broth and cream and bring to a simmer.

4. Off the heat, stir in the cooked vegetables and season with salt and pepper to taste.

5. Remove the frozen crust from the freezer, discard the parchment paper, and place the crust on top of the filling following the illustration on page 195. Bake the pot pie until the crust is golden brown and the filling is bubbling, 45 to 50 minutes. Let the pot pie cool for 20 minutes before serving.

INGREDIENTS: Puff Pastry

Puff pastry is a super-flaky dough with hundreds of buttery layers. It is made by wrapping a simple pastry dough around a stick of cold butter, rolling the dough, folding the dough over itself at least four times, and chilling the dough for at least one hour after each fold. When baked, the water in the butter creates steam, which causes the dough to puff into flaky, delicate layers.

For home cooks, there are usually just one or two commercial options in the freezer case. Pepperidge Farm Puff Pastry Sheets (made with vegetable oil, not butter) are available in almost every supermarket. Better supermarkets and gourmet shops might carry Classic Puff Pastry from Dufour Pastry Kitchens. When pitted in the test kitchen against Pepperidge Farm, the all-butter pastry was easy to pick out and was the clear favorite. That said, pot pies made with Pepperidge Farm pastry were still quite good. Our advice is to buy all-butter puff pastry if you can, but don't go without pot pie if Pepperidge Farm is your only option.

SPRING VEGETABLE POT PIE

RIDING HIGH ON THE SUCCESS OF OUR Winter Root Vegetable Pot Pie (page 195), we decided to try our luck on a vegetable pot pie filled with the lighter, brighter flavors of spring. Given the milder flavors of spring vegetables, we wondered if we could develop a spring vegetable pot pie just as flavorful as the root vegetable pie.

"Spring vegetables" can refer to any number of early season vegetables. As a general rule, they are mild and herbaceous in flavor, requiring a light hand with seasoning and careful cooking because they overcook easily, losing both color and flavor. Leeks, peas, and asparagus all fit the bill, as do spinach and artichokes. Identifying the best mix for a pot-pie filling was the crux of our testing.

Working with the root vegetable pot pie as our jumping-off point, we began finessing the vegetable list. We chose to replace the onions in the winter root vegetable pot pie with leeks and omit the celery altogether because of its pervasive flavor. The carrots, however, remained, lending sweetness and some color to the filling. We also decided to keep the white mushrooms in the mix for their mass and flavor. Frozen peas, which would be stirred in right before baking, were a given thanks to their pleasant, sweet flavor. Artichokes sounded appealing, but were just too troublesome, needing to be peeled and prepared. We considered canned or jarred artichokes, but found that they contributed an artificial flavor to the filling. Frozen artichokes would need to be browned on their own in a skillet; since we already needed to brown the mushrooms on their own to keep their meatiness intact in the finished dish, we put aside the artichokes to keep this pot pie simple.

With the artichokes ruled out, it looked like asparagus would be the spring vegetable star of the show. Asparagus can be fussy to cook and we worried how it would fare submerged in the filling. When undercooked, asparagus tastes grassy and bland; overcooked, it is close to cabbage in both smell and flavor. There's a small window in which to keep the asparagus crisp yet tender, and vibrantly colored. For our first attempt at cooking the stalks, we sautéed them with the other vegetables, but they were overcooked by the time the pot pie had finished baking. We tried blanching them (boiling briefly until tender, then plunging in ice water to stop the cooking and retain the color) before adding them to the filling, but this also resulted in overcooked, dingy asparagus. Surprisingly, the easiest method yielded the best flavor—simply stirring the raw sliced asparagus into the hot filling before topping it yielded perfectly cooked pieces.

For the sauce, we wanted a light and creamy white sauce. We sautéed our aromatics in butter, then added flour, which would help our sauce thicken up when we added the vegetable broth and vermouth. We also added ½ cup cream for a silky texture. To enhance and brighten the sauce, we stirred in lemon zest and minced fresh tarragon.

With the filling set, we were now ready to cover and bake it. With its light and delicate texture, frozen puff pastry seemed the perfect choice for our delicate spring vegetables. Readily available in most supermarkets, frozen puff pastry is a cinch to prepare: just defrost, roll out, and bake. In our first attempt, we rolled out sheets of the defrosted dough and trimmed them to fit snugly over the top of the skillet, sealing the filling beneath. Unfortunately, the tight seal of the pastry yielded overcooked, drab green asparagus. We suspected that the topping trapped escaping steam, thereby prompting the filling to boil. In addition, the puff

Puff-Pastry Rectangles for Skillet Pot Pie

MAKES ENOUGH FOR I POT PIE

This topping is partially baked and finished on top of the pot pie. If desired, cut the pastry into 12 large circles using a 3-inch round cookie cutter instead of cutting it into rectangles in step 1; don't twist the cutter when stamping out the pastry rounds, or the pastry will rise crookedly during baking.

> Unbleached all-purpose flour, for dusting the work surface
> I sheet (9½ by 9 inches) frozen commercial puff pastry, thawed at room temperature for 30 minutes
> I large egg, lightly beaten

1. Adjust an oven rack to the middle position and heat the oven to 425 degrees. Line a baking sheet with parchment paper. Dust a work surface lightly with flour and unfold the sheet of puff pastry. Following the illustration, use a pizza cutter or sharp paring knife to cut the dough into 12 rectangles.

2. Brush each square with beaten egg and transfer to the baking sheet. Chill the dough on the baking sheet in the freezer for 10 minutes. Remove the pan from the freezer and place it directly in the oven. Bake for 10 minutes or until the rectangles are puffed and lightly browned. Let the pastry cool on the baking sheet until needed.

MAKING PUFF-PASTRY RECTANGLES

Use a pizza cutter or sharp paring knife to cut the sheet of puff pastry into three pieces along the seams, then crosswise in fourths to make 12 rectangles.

pastry itself was more soggy than crisp. Clearly, a solid sheet would not do.

We shifted gears and experimented with cutting the pastry into smaller pieces, prebaking them before laying them on the filling. Parbaking helped crisp up the pastry before placing it over the wet filling, and using smaller pieces of pastry had the added benefit of allowing excess steam from the filling to evaporate in the oven, keeping our asparagus fresh and green. To make prepping the pastry easy, we simply cut it into rectangles (you can cut fancy circles, however, if desired) with a sharp knife. Because this pot pie was covered by pastry pieces, not a whole layer of pastry, it needed just 10 minutes to cool off. Before we knew it, we were enjoying the bright, fresh flavors of our new vegetable pot pie.

Spring Vegetable Pot Pie

SERVES 4

While we prefer the mild flavor of vegetable broth in this recipe, low-sodium chicken broth may be substituted.

6	tablespoons (¾ stick) unsalted butter
1	pound white mushrooms, wiped clean, and quartered
	Salt
3	medium carrots, peeled and cut crosswise ¼ inch thick
4	medium leeks, white and light green parts only, halved lengthwise, sliced crosswise ¼ inch thick, and rinsed thoroughly
5	medium garlic cloves, minced or pressed through a garlic press (about 5 teaspoons)
¼	cup unbleached all-purpose flour
⅓	cup dry vermouth or dry white wine
2	cups low-sodium vegetable broth
½	cup heavy cream
	Ground black pepper
1	pound asparagus (about 1 bunch), tough ends trimmed (see the illustration on page 92) and cut on the bias into ½-inch lengths
1	cup frozen peas
2	teaspoons minced fresh tarragon

1	teaspoon grated zest from 1 lemon
1	recipe Puff-Pastry Rectangles for Skillet Pot Pie (see page 197)

1. Adjust an oven rack to the middle position and heat the oven to 400 degrees. Melt 3 tablespoons of the butter in a 12-inch ovenproof skillet over medium-high heat. Add the mushrooms and a pinch salt and cook, stirring often, until the mushrooms release their liquid and begin to brown, about 10 minutes. Transfer the mushrooms to a bowl.

2. Melt the remaining 3 tablespoons butter in the skillet over medium heat. Add the carrots, leeks, and ½ teaspoon salt and cook, stirring often, until the leeks begin to soften, about 8 to 10 minutes. Stir in the garlic and cook until fragrant, about 30 seconds. Stir in the flour and cook, stirring constantly, until the flour is incorporated, about 1 minute.

3. Slowly stir in the vermouth and cook until evaporated, about 30 seconds. Slowly stir in the broth and cream, bring to a simmer, and cook until thickened, about 2 minutes.

4. Off the heat, stir in the cooked mushrooms, asparagus, peas, tarragon, and lemon zest and season with salt and pepper to taste.

5. Following the illustration below, place the baked puff-pastry rectangles on top of the filling. Bake the pot pie until the pastry is a deep golden brown and the filling is bubbling, 13 to 15 minutes. Let the pot pie cool for 10 minutes before serving.

TOPPING A SKILLET POT PIE WITH PUFF PASTRY

Carefully place nine of the baked rectangles around the edge of the skillet and fit three of the baked rectangles in the center of the skillet.

SALMON AND LEEK POT PIE

POT PIES COME IN ALL STRIPES—SOME classic, some not so classic. Fish pies fall into the former category, and we found recipes dating back hundreds of years. Unfortunately, for a dish with such a lengthy history, modern fish pie often tends to be no better than a use for leftover fish. We knew we could elevate this dish to a showstopping elegant entrée, especially since fish cooks so quickly, making it ideal for a pot pie and perfect for a weeknight supper.

The most common fish pies use either flaky white fish, such as cod, or firm-fleshed salmon. Since salmon is wildly popular and reasonably priced, we decided it would be just the thing for our first tests. We collected a variety of salmon pie recipes and prepared those that seemed the most promising. The best were reasonably light and simple, highlighting the fish's distinct flavor. Our favorites bound the fish and a complementary vegetable or two in a fairly light, milk-based sauce. As for toppings, flaky pastry and mashed-potato crusts were common, as was puff pastry—an option we favored because the pastry's elegance and light texture suited the salmon, and because it's so easy to use.

We learned a few important lessons from our initial tests. First, the salmon was overcooked in every single recipe we tried. The recipes required precooking the fish before mixing it into the sauce; this method resulted in a chalky texture and flavorless fish. It was pretty obvious to us that the fish could be added raw to the hot filling and would cook through by the time the pastry browned. Second, for the most part, the sauces were thin and bland, or thick and spicy; none of them were quite right. And, finally, the vegetables mostly disappeared in the finished dish.

We wanted to use vegetables that complemented the salmon but held their own ground in the sauce. Based on previous tests, we chose a simple combination of leeks and peas—both classic accompaniments to salmon because of their mild, sweet flavor. We included a good amount of leeks, cooking them in butter until they were soft and supple. As for the peas, we knew that frozen peas require little cooking—like the salmon, they would cook through in the oven.

Next, we tackled the sauce. It would need to be light so the flavors of the salmon and leeks could shine through, yet flavorful in its own right. Following the lead of our other pot pies, we made a sauce right in the skillet by stirring milk, bottled clam juice, and vermouth in with sautéed leeks, garlic, and flour. The brininess of the clam juice paired well with the salmon's sweet flesh; we also tried chicken broth, our usual choice, but it clashed with the flavor of the salmon.

Balanced but rather bland, our sauce needed some seasoning. A tablespoon each of Dijon mustard and lemon juice helped to cut through the richness. For herbs, we looked no further than dill—its light, almost tangy flavor is without parallel as a complement to salmon. Our sauce was now the perfect replacement for the canned soup that so many other recipes relied on.

We were almost ready to bake—we simply had to add our salmon and the pastry. For the salmon, we cut fillets into small (½-inch) cubes, seasoned them with salt and pepper, and tossed them in the sauce with the filling. Shielded from direct heat by the sauce and pastry, the salmon stayed moist and flavorful. We had decided on store-bought puff pastry for the topping and already knew the best method for preparing it, thanks to our Spring Vegetable Pot Pie (page 198). The puff pastry had to be parbaked and cut into smaller pieces to ensure crispness—otherwise it turned soggy and hardly puffed.

Our pot pie went into a 400-degree oven for 15 minutes, then rested for 10 minutes. Salmon and Leek Pot Pie is second to none for a sophisticated yet easy weeknight dinner; finally, we were giving fish pie its due.

Salmon and Leek Pot Pie

SERVES 4

Be sure to check the salmon for pinbones before cutting it into pieces (see illustrations on page 14). Do not substitute dried dill for the fresh dill here.

1½	pounds skinless salmon fillets, cut into ½-inch pieces
	Salt and ground black pepper
2	tablespoons unsalted butter
2	medium leeks, white and light green parts only, halved lengthwise, sliced crosswise ¼ inch thick, and rinsed thoroughly
1	medium garlic clove, minced or pressed through a garlic press (about 1 teaspoon)
¼	cup unbleached all-purpose flour
1	tablespoon Dijon mustard
⅓	cup dry vermouth or dry white wine
1½	cups whole milk
1	(8-ounce) bottle clam juice
1	cup frozen peas
¼	cup chopped fresh dill leaves
1	tablespoon juice from 1 lemon
1	recipe Puff-Pastry Rectangles for Skillet Pot Pie (see page 197)
1	lemon, cut into wedges, for serving

1. Adjust an oven rack to the middle position and heat the oven to 400 degrees. Season the salmon with salt and pepper and set aside.

2. Melt the butter in a 12-inch ovenproof skillet over medium heat. Add the leeks and ½ teaspoon salt and cook, stirring occasionally, until softened, about 5 minutes. Stir in the garlic and cook until fragrant, about 30 seconds. Stir in the flour and mustard and cook, stirring constantly, until incorporated, about 1 minute.

3. Slowly stir in the vermouth and cook until evaporated, about 30 seconds. Slowly stir in the milk and clam juice and bring to a simmer.

4. Off the heat, season with salt and pepper to taste, then stir in the salmon, peas, dill, and lemon juice.

5. Following the illustration on page 198, place the baked puff-pastry rectangles on top of the filling. Bake the pot pie until the pastry is a deep golden brown and the filling is bubbling, 13 to 15 minutes. Let the pot pie cool for 10 minutes and serve, passing the lemon wedges separately.

SHEPHERD'S PIE

A RICH LAMB STEW BLANKETED BY A MASHED potato crust, shepherd's pie is a hearty casserole from the cool climes of sheep-centric northern Britain. Best eaten on a blustery winter day, this lamb dish used to be a meal made on Monday with Sunday night's leftovers—the remnants of the roast, vegetables, and mashed potatoes. In this day and age, few of us have such delicious Sunday dinners, much less leftovers, so we aimed to create an assertively flavored shepherd's pie from scratch. We also wanted to put to work what we had learned about simplifying pot pies, with all of the ingredients for the pie being cooked in just one skillet.

Our first step was to figure out which cut of lamb worked best. We started our testing with ground lamb, which meant we wouldn't have to spend any time trimming the meat, and sautéed it until just cooked. Because lamb can be fatty, we removed the cooked ground meat from the skillet and drained all but 1 tablespoon of the rendered fat. We then used the rendered fat in place of oil, and sautéed our vegetables—carrots, onions, and garlic—in it. Peas, characteristic of many British-style meat stews, were added still frozen just before the dish went into the oven, bringing bright color and sweetness to an otherwise drab-looking dish. As for the liquid in the stew, we settled on chicken broth thickened with ¼ cup of flour. Chicken broth provided a neutral flavor that we liked; we did a few tests with beef broth, but tasters felt that the beef broth clashed with the lamb's earthy flavors. We were getting close now, but our pie was just a little bland.

For a stronger flavor profile, we added tomato paste, to bring out the sweeter meaty tones, and Worcestershire sauce, to bring forth the lamb's more subtle flavors. With the basic lamb flavors elevated, all the filling needed was a dose of minced thyme. At last, our shepherd's pie filling was meaty, robust, and fully flavored.

With the filling assembled and cooked, we were ready to top it off with a mashed-potato crust. We quickly found out that simple mashed potatoes would not do; they crumbled and broke down while baking. We started our adjustments by reducing the amount of butter and dairy we usually add to mashed potatoes, and added two egg yolks. The yolks gave the potatoes some structure, turning them into French-style duchess potatoes. This did the trick—the potatoes retained their shape and texture and picked up a little more richness in the bargain. Plus, the yolks gave the potatoes a slight golden hue that complemented the deep brown of the stew beneath. Given the added richness from the yolks, the crust would be too heavy if we added half-and-half, so we replaced it with whole milk, which tasters much preferred. We then placed dollops all over our pie, spreading them into an even layer, and popped the pan into the oven.

Because both the lamb and mashed potatoes were already cooked when the skillet went into the oven, the baking time was short—about 20 minutes. Once the potato crust turned golden brown, the shepherd's pie was done and ready to come out of the oven.

Shepherd's Pie
SERVES 4

We like the authentic flavor of ground lamb here, but you can substitute 90 percent lean ground beef if you prefer.

POTATO TOPPING

1½	pounds russet potatoes (about 3 medium), peeled and cut into 1-inch pieces
4	tablespoons (½ stick) unsalted butter, softened
½	cup whole milk, warmed
2	large egg yolks
	Salt and ground black pepper

FILLING

1½	pounds ground lamb
1	medium onion, minced
2	medium carrots, peeled and cut crosswise ½ inch thick
	Salt
2	medium garlic cloves, minced or pressed through a garlic press (about 2 teaspoons)
¼	cup unbleached all-purpose flour
1	tablespoon tomato paste
2	cups low-sodium chicken broth
1½	teaspoons minced fresh thyme, or ½ teaspoon dried
2	teaspoons Worcestershire sauce
1	cup frozen peas
	Ground black pepper

1. FOR THE TOPPING: Adjust an oven rack to the middle position and heat the oven to 400 degrees. Put the potatoes in a large saucepan, cover with water, and bring to a boil. Once the boiling reduces to a simmer, cook until the potatoes are tender and a fork inserted into the center meets little resistance, 15 to 20 minutes.

2. Drain the potatoes well and return them to the saucepan over low heat. Mash the potatoes thoroughly with a potato masher. Fold in the butter until melted, then stir in the warm milk and egg yolks. Season with salt and pepper to taste, cover, and set aside while preparing the filling.

3. FOR THE FILLING: Meanwhile, cook the lamb in a 12-inch ovenproof skillet over medium heat, breaking up the meat with a wooden spoon, until no longer pink and the fat has rendered, about 3 minutes. Drain the lamb through a fine-mesh strainer, discarding all but 1 tablespoon of the rendered fat.

4. Heat the 1 tablespoon reserved lamb fat in the skillet over medium heat until shimmering. Add the onion, carrots, and ½ teaspoon salt and cook until the vegetables are softened, 5 to 7 minutes. Stir in the garlic and cook until fragrant, about 30 seconds. Stir in the flour and tomato paste and cook, stirring constantly, until the flour is incorporated, about 1 minute.

5. Slowly stir in the broth, thyme, and Worcestershire sauce, scrape up the browned bits, and bring to a simmer. Reduce the heat to medium-low and cook until the sauce has thickened, 3 to 5 minutes.

6. Off the heat, stir in the drained lamb and peas, season with salt and pepper to taste, and smooth the filling into an even layer. Dollop the potato topping evenly over the filling, then spread it into an even

layer, covering the filling completely and anchoring the potatoes to the sides of the skillet. Bake the pie until the top is golden brown, 20 to 25 minutes. Let the pie cool for 10 minutes before serving.

TAMALE PIE

POPULAR TEX-MEX FARE, A GOOD TAMALE pie contains a juicy, spicy mixture of meat and vegetables encased in or topped with a cornmeal crust. Bad tamale pies, however, are dry and bland and usually have too much or too little filling. We wanted to develop a really good tamale pie—one with just the right proportion of filling to topping.

In our research, we found that most recipes use either ground beef or ground pork as the base. We tested both and the all-beef pie came out on top for being both richer and more flavorful than the tamale pie made with ground pork. We sautéed some onion and garlic first, then added our meat to brown. Next we looked at the traditional Southwestern ingredients, tomatoes and black beans—adding a can of each right in with our ground beef helped us keep to our simple-and-quick strategy and brought an authentic touch to the dish.

We had all the right ingredients in place, but we had to work on the Tex-Mex flavor a bit. For a spicy kick, we added some chili powder to the sautéed onion, then stirred in minced fresh cilantro right before the skillet went into the oven. We thought the mixture could use more substance so it wasn't just a bowl of ground beef, but what could we add? A cup of shredded cheddar cheese gave our dish some oomph, bringing the filling together so it was both thicker and more flavorful.

Now we turned to the traditional cornmeal topping. At first, we were torn—should it taste like the exterior of real tamales (made from masa)? Or should it be more like corn bread (as we'd seen in so many other recipes)? We tried both. The tamale-style topping didn't fly with our tasters; it was a bit bland. Not to mention the fact that we put some miles on our car driving around town to locate the masa. The slightly sweet, spongy corn bread topping—made with equal amounts of cornmeal and flour, along with leavening agents and some

fat—had a nice texture and just the right amount of corn flavor. Tasters also preferred the clean, simple flavor of corn bread in contrast with the spicy meat filling; it was the clear winner.

Putting together filling and topping was simple. We simply poured the corn bread batter over the filling in the skillet, and spread it in an even layer to the edges of the dish. A moderately high oven temperature of 450 degrees for just 15 minutes did the best job of getting a golden, light crust and heating the filling.

Tamale Pie
SERVES 4

We prefer to make our own corn bread topping, but you can substitute your favorite store-bought corn bread mix if desired; follow the package instructions to make the corn bread batter, then dollop the batter over the filling and bake as directed in step 4.

FILLING
- 2 tablespoons vegetable oil
- 1 medium onion, minced
- 2 tablespoons chili powder
-   Salt
- 2 medium garlic cloves, minced or pressed through a garlic press (about 2 teaspoons)
- 1 pound 90 percent lean ground beef
- 1 (15-ounce) can black beans, drained and rinsed
- 1 (14.5-ounce) can diced tomatoes, drained
- 4 ounces cheddar cheese, shredded (1 cup)
- 2 tablespoons minced fresh cilantro leaves
-   Ground black pepper

CORN BREAD TOPPING
- ¾ cup (3¾ ounces) unbleached all-purpose flour
- ¾ cup (3¾ ounces) yellow cornmeal
- 3 tablespoons sugar
- ¾ teaspoon baking powder
- ¼ teaspoon baking soda
- ¾ teaspoon salt
- ¾ cup buttermilk
- 1 large egg
- 3 tablespoons unsalted butter, melted and cooled

1. FOR THE FILLING: Adjust an oven rack to the middle position and heat the oven to 450 degrees. Heat the oil in a 12-inch ovenproof skillet over medium heat until shimmering. Add the onion, chili powder, and ½ teaspoon salt and cook until the onion is softened, 5 to 7 minutes. Stir in the garlic and cook until fragrant, about 30 seconds.

2. Stir in the ground beef, beans, and tomatoes and bring to a simmer, breaking up the meat with a wooden spoon, about 5 minutes. Off the heat, stir in the cheddar and cilantro and season with salt and pepper to taste. Set aside while preparing the topping.

3. FOR THE CORN BREAD TOPPING: Whisk the flour, cornmeal, sugar, baking powder, baking soda, and salt together in a large bowl. In a separate bowl, whisk the buttermilk and egg together. Stir the buttermilk mixture into the flour mixture until uniform, then stir in the butter until just combined.

4. Smooth the filling into an even layer in the skillet. Dollop the corn bread topping evenly over the filling, then spread it into an even layer, covering the filling completely. Bake the pie until the topping is golden and has baked through completely in the center, 15 to 20 minutes. Let the pie cool for 10 minutes before serving.

PORK TINGA TAMALE PIE

SPICED WITH CHORIZO SAUSAGE AND chipotle chiles, pork tinga is a stew-like dish from Mexico. We wondered if we could turn this stew into a sort of skillet tamale pie—a hearty, potent, and unusual one loaded with juicy pork instead of black beans and ground beef. We had been inspired by Tex-Mex flavors after creating our Tamale Pie (page 202) and were on a mission to pair our sweet corn bread topping with another spicy filling.

Taking a look at pork tinga recipes, we knew this dish of shredded stewed or braised pork shoulder and chorizo simmered in a tomato-based sauce was made for skillet cookery. It already had the one-dish aspect going for it. But closer research revealed that the texture of the cooked pork in the finished dish should be slightly dry, more like a

saucy stir-fry than a stew. A traditional braise using pork shoulder, of course, would not be possible with fewer than two hours of cooking, but thinly sliced and sautéed pork could fill its role—not authentic, but still a good stand-in.

We experimented with several cuts of pork, and tenderloin proved the easiest to prepare as well as the most flavorful. To cook the meat as quickly as possible, we sliced it into cutlets from the whole tenderloin and then cut those into thin strips. We browned the meat in just a couple of minutes in our skillet and set it aside until it was baking time.

While the pork was easy to figure out, the sauce took some effort. The best versions of pork tinga we tasted were finely balanced between hot and sweet, suffused with smoky heat from chorizo and chiles, and lightened with fresh oregano. Onions, tomatoes, and garlic rounded out the flavors.

The first step for the sauce, then, was to sauté the chorizo, which would provide some of the fat necessary to soften the onions and garlic. Chorizo is integral to both Mexican and Spanish cooking and is available in most markets. It browned quickly and rendered enough additional fat in which to cook the onion and garlic. We sautéed the onion until soft and added 4 cloves of garlic and a can of diced tomatoes (no prep work needed, save for a quick drain).

Chipotle chiles, the last addition to the sauce, are a spunky ingredient—searingly hot and smoky-tasting. Also known as smoked jalapeños, chipotle chiles are available dried or rehydrated and packed in an adobo sauce, which contains tomato, onion, oil, and herbs. Whereas dried chiles must be toasted and rehydrated, the canned chiles are ready to go, saving valuable preparation time. After trying multiple batches, tasters favored 2 teaspoons of chiles—this amount gave a pain-free spiciness to the dish, which already had a good bite from the chorizo.

We found that we needed to add more liquid for deeper flavor and a smoother texture; canned chicken broth fit the bill. For the most balanced flavor, we added some brown sugar to temper the spiciness and simmered the sauce for about 10 minutes, just long enough to blend the flavors, break down the tomatoes, and reduce the liquid. We reserved the pork until the final moments to prevent it from overcooking—always a risk when simmering thin pieces of meat—and tossed in some chopped fresh oregano with it.

We had already perfected corn bread topping with our Tamale Pie (page 202) and knew that the mildly sweet flavor of our corn bread would contrast perfectly with the smoky-spicy pork filling. We poured the batter over the filling and smoothed it out to the edges before baking in a 450-degree oven. There was no denying that our invention was a success—tasters inhaled this festive pie in record time.

Pork Tinga Tamale Pie
SERVES 4

If you can't find chorizo sausage, substitute either linguiça or kielbasa. If you like things spicy, use the higher amount of chipotle chiles. We prefer to make our own corn bread topping, but you can substitute your favorite store-bought corn bread mix if desired; follow the package instructions to make the corn bread batter, then dollop the batter over the filling and bake as directed in step 6.

FILLING

4	teaspoons vegetable oil
1	(1- to 1¼-pound) pork tenderloin, trimmed and sliced into thin strips (see the illustrations on page 228)
8	ounces chorizo, quartered lengthwise and then cut crosswise into ¼-inch-thick pieces
3	medium carrots, peeled and cut crosswise ¼ inch thick
1	medium onion, minced
	Salt
4	medium garlic cloves, minced or pressed through a garlic press (about 4 teaspoons)
1–2	teaspoons chipotle chile in adobo sauce, minced
1	(14.5-ounce) can diced tomatoes, drained
1¾	cups low-sodium chicken broth
1	tablespoon brown sugar
	Ground black pepper
1½	teaspoons coarsely chopped fresh oregano leaves

CORN BREAD TOPPING

¾	cup (3¾ ounces) unbleached all-purpose flour
¾	cup (3¾ ounces) yellow cornmeal
3	tablespoons sugar
¾	teaspoon baking powder
¼	teaspoon baking soda
¾	teaspoon salt
¾	cup buttermilk
1	large egg
3	tablespoons unsalted butter, melted and cooled

1. FOR THE FILLING: Adjust an oven rack to the middle position and heat the oven to 450 degrees. Heat 2 teaspoons of the oil in a 12-inch ovenproof skillet over medium-high heat until smoking. Add the pork in a single layer and cook without stirring until browned on one side, about 1 minute. Stir and continue to cook for 1 minute longer. Transfer the pork to a bowl and set aside.

2. Add the remaining 2 teaspoons oil and the chorizo to the skillet and cook over medium heat, stirring often, until lightly browned, about 2 minutes. Stir in the carrots, onion, and ¼ teaspoon salt and cook, stirring often, until the vegetables are softened, 8 to 10 minutes.

3. Stir in the garlic and chipotles and cook until fragrant, about 30 seconds. Stir in the tomatoes, broth, and sugar and bring to a simmer. Reduce the heat to medium-low and cook until the liquid has thickened slightly, and the mixture measures about 5 cups, about 10 minutes.

4. Off the heat, season with salt and pepper to taste. Stir in the cooked pork and oregano and set aside while preparing the topping.

5. FOR THE CORN BREAD TOPPING: Whisk the flour, cornmeal, sugar, baking powder, baking soda, and salt together in a large bowl. In a separate bowl, whisk the buttermilk and egg together. Stir the buttermilk mixture into the flour mixture until uniform, then stir in the butter until just combined.

6. Smooth the filling into an even layer in the skillet. Dollop the corn bread topping evenly over the filling, then spread it into an even layer, covering the filling completely. Bake the pie until the topping is golden and has baked through completely in the center, 15 to 20 minutes. Let the pie cool for 10 minutes before serving.

THANKSGIVING TURKEY BAKE

THE LABOR-INTENSIVE THANKSGIVING dinner comes only once a year, but what if you want to enjoy turkey and all that goes with it—rich gravy, savory stuffing, green beans, and sweet-tart cranberry sauce—more often? With this sentiment in mind, we set out to develop a skillet turkey casserole recipe that would offer up the soul of Thanksgiving year-round, but without all the fuss (and dirty dishes).

Although most people think of the bird first, we would be building this casserole from the bottom up, beginning with the gravy. Gravy, by definition, is a thickened sauce made of meat juices and pan drippings. Obviously, we would have to find our rich roasted flavor elsewhere. Right off the bat we decided to sauté chopped carrots, celery, and onion in the skillet to help create a flavor base and a fond from which we could build a sauce. We cooked the vegetables until they began to brown and then added flour, like we had in our pot pie recipes, but this time we went darker, toasting the flour for a rich, roasted flavor.

Next we tested our liquid options for the gravy. In the past we've found that canned low-sodium chicken broth provides a great gravy base. In this instance, gravy made with only chicken broth tasted flat. Gravy made with only beef broth tasted like beef stew broth—not very deep or rich. Equal amounts of chicken and beef broths gave us just the gravy flavor we were looking for—rich and meaty. Lastly, we seasoned it with thyme—a classic herb used in gravy.

Looking beyond the gravy, we pondered how to add other classic Thanksgiving flavors to our turkey bake. How might we incorporate cranberries and green beans? First we tested the cranberry options. We tried fresh, frozen, and dried. The fresh and frozen berries simply liquefied into the gravy, making it watery. The dried cranberries, on the other hand, plumped slightly and added just the right touch of tang and sweetness.

The green beans were more of a challenge. Overcooked green beans taste muddy and turn an unappealing brown-green. While undercooked green beans stay bright green, they would add an unwelcome crunch to our casserole. We sought the middle ground—bright green beans, with just a slight bite. We cut the green beans into bite-sized, 1-inch pieces and cooked them three different ways: we sautéed them before adding them to the gravy, we simmered them in the gravy for five minutes before baking, and we simply stirred them into the gravy right before baking. Two of our fears were realized—the sautéed beans turned army green, and those that were stirred in just before baking remained crunchy. The beans that had simmered in the gravy before baking were perfect—brightly colored and just the right texture.

With the gravy, cranberries, and green beans sorted out, it was time to look at the turkey options. We scanned our local supermarkets and immediately zeroed in on turkey cutlets (whole breasts or legs would take too long to cook.) Using whole cutlets seemed a little odd in a casserole, but we wanted something more elegant than shredded or cubed turkey pieces. Our solution was to cut the cutlets into 2-inch-wide strips—reminiscent of Thanksgiving turkey servings. Our cooking plan was to stir the turkey strips into the sauce right before adding the topping, poaching the turkey in the sauce while the casserole baked. We decided not to brown the turkey first because we wanted to avoid forming a crust on the small pieces, and we knew that simply poaching these strips would yield moist, tender turkey—flavoring the gravy as it cooked—while keeping the dish to just one pan.

With the filling ready, we moved on to the topping. We wanted a super simple stuffing, with just some herbs to flavor it. We chose white sandwich bread to make a classic-looking stuffing and dried it out in the oven. To add onion flavor without using a second pan to cook more onions (we already had them in the filling), we cooked some extra onions along with the ones for the filling and pulled out ¼ cup cooked onions for the stuffing topping. Then we tossed the dried bread with the onion, minced fresh sage—for classic stuffing flavor—two eggs, chicken broth, and butter for moisture.

With the details for our gravy, cranberries, beans, and turkey all figured out, we were ready to go. We prepared our gravy on the stovetop, tossed in the green beans, then added turkey and cranberries. Finally, we topped the filling with stuffing and slid the casserole in the oven to bake until golden brown. The top of the stuffing turned crisp, while the underside stayed moist—a great mop for the gravy and the perfect contrast to the cranberry-studded, turkey filling. We know this recipe will never take the place of a traditional Thanksgiving dinner, but it certainly is an excellent alternative and a viable option any day of the week, any time of the year.

Thanksgiving Turkey Bake
SERVES 4

Be sure to brown the flour well in step 3, as it contributes to both the flavor and color of the gravy-like sauce.

6	slices high-quality white sandwich bread, cut into 1-inch cubes (about 4 cups)
5	tablespoons unsalted butter
2	medium onions, minced
	Salt
2	medium carrots, peeled and cut crosswise ¼ inch thick
1	celery rib, sliced ¼ inch thick
¼	cup unbleached all-purpose flour
2	cups low-sodium chicken broth
1½	cups low-sodium beef broth
½	pound green beans, trimmed (see the illustration on page 235) and cut into 1-inch lengths
	Ground black pepper
1½	pounds turkey cutlets, sliced crosswise into 2-inch strips
¾	cup dried cranberries
1½	teaspoons minced fresh thyme leaves, or ½ teaspoon dried
1½	teaspoons minced fresh sage
2	large eggs, lightly beaten

1. Adjust an oven rack to the middle position and heat the oven to 350 degrees. Spread the bread cubes out over a baking sheet and bake until crisp and dry, but not browned, about 15 minutes, turning the pieces over and rotating the baking sheet halfway through baking. Set the bread aside to cool.

2. Increase the oven temperature to 450 degrees. Melt 2 tablespoons of the butter in a 12-inch oven-proof skillet over medium heat. Add the onions and ½ teaspoon salt and cook until softened, 5 to 7 minutes. Measure out and reserve ¼ cup of the cooked onion for the bread stuffing.

3. Stir in 1 tablespoon more butter, the carrots, and celery into the skillet with the remaining onions and cook over medium heat until the vegetables begin to brown, 8 to 10 minutes. Stir in the flour and cook, stirring constantly, until browned and fragrant, about 5 minutes.

4. Slowly stir in 1½ cups of the chicken broth and all the beef broth and bring to a simmer. Stir in the green beans and simmer until the sauce thickens, 3 to 5 minutes. Off the heat, season with salt and pepper to taste, then stir in the turkey, cranberries, and thyme.

5. Meanwhile, toss the bread cubes, reserved cooked onions, sage, ½ teaspoon salt, and ¼ teaspoon pepper together in a large bowl. Add the remaining ½ cup chicken broth and the eggs and toss gently to combine. Melt the remaining 2 tablespoons butter, add to the bread mixture, and toss to combine.

6. Smooth the turkey filling into an even layer in the skillet. Spoon the bread stuffing evenly over the filling, then spread it into an even layer, covering the filling completely. Bake the casserole until the topping is golden brown and the filling is bubbling, 15 to 20 minutes. Let the casserole cool for 10 minutes before serving.

CHICKEN DIVAN

DESPITE ITS CURRENT REPUTATION AS A cheesy chicken and broccoli casserole made with cream of chicken soup, chicken divan has a long and elegant history. The original recipe from New York's famed (but now defunct) Divan Parisien restaurant dates back almost 100 years and required a whole poached chicken, boiled broccoli, a béchamel sauce, and hollandaise sauce. The ingredients were combined at the last minute and broiled to perfection. Sounds good, but it requires at least a couple of pans and more time than we'd care to spend in the kitchen. No wonder most recipes rely on canned soup.

To speed up chicken divan without compromising the trademark flavors of the dish, we turned to the one pan we wanted to use—our dependable skillet. We thought we could cook all the elements in batches, and started out with the broccoli. It was easily sautéed and then steamed in a little chicken broth, emerging flavorful, tender, and emerald green. We set the broccoli aside and moved on to the chicken.

For convenience and speed, we chose to use boneless, skinless chicken breasts. We made sure the chicken breasts were dry, coated them with flour, and seared them until brown on each side. Then we pulled the chicken breasts out of the skillet so we could build our sauce.

Mimicking the original sauce took some kitchen trickery. For that rich, silky feel, we simmered 2 cups of chicken broth and 1 cup of heavy cream. At this point, we returned our chicken breasts to the skillet for 10 minutes to cook through in the broth-and-cream mixture, then put them back on the sidelines. The chicken had fortified the flavor of our sauce nicely, but it needed some work. To round out the flavors, we added sherry, Worcestershire sauce, and ½ cup of grated Parmesan.

Our sauce was good, but without the hollandaise—and its decadent egg yolks and butter and bright lemon juice—it wasn't exactly right. Instead of preparing a separate hollandaise, could we just add these ingredients to our existing sauce? We whisked three yolks and 1 tablespoon lemon juice together, then tempered the mixture with ¼ cup of the hot pan sauce. Once we returned this mixture to the pan—off the heat so as not to curdle the eggs—and added some butter, the sauce thickened to pure luxury.

We sliced the chicken breasts into medallions for a more elegant presentation, and nestled them and the broccoli into the sauce. We topped the whole dish with more Parmesan and moved the skillet into the oven to brown. After 10 minutes, our Chicken Divan was as opulent as the original but didn't require anywhere near the effort, and we used only one pan to do it.

Chicken Divan
SERVES 4

We like the delicate flavor of shallots here; however, a small minced onion can be substituted.

3	tablespoons plus 1 teaspoon vegetable oil
12	ounces broccoli florets, trimmed into 1-inch pieces (about 4 cups)
2½	cups low-sodium chicken broth
½	cup unbleached all-purpose flour
1½	pounds boneless, skinless chicken breasts (about 4 medium), trimmed (see the illustration on page 6)
	Salt and ground black pepper
2	medium shallots, minced (about 6 tablespoons)
1	cup heavy cream
½	cup dry sherry
2	teaspoons Worcestershire sauce
2	ounces Parmesan cheese, grated (1 cup)
3	large egg yolks
1	tablespoon juice from 1 lemon
3	tablespoons unsalted butter

1. Adjust an oven rack to the middle position and heat the oven to 450 degrees. Heat 1 tablespoon of the oil in a 12-inch ovenproof skillet over medium-high heat until just smoking. Add the broccoli and cook until spotty brown, about 3 minutes. Add ½ cup of the broth, cover, and steam until just tender, about 2 minutes. Remove the lid and continue to cook until the liquid has evaporated, about 1 minute. Transfer the broccoli to a paper towel–lined plate. Wipe out the skillet with a wad of paper towels.

2. Place the flour in a shallow dish. Pat the chicken breasts dry with paper towels and season with salt and pepper. Working with 1 chicken breast at a time, dredge in the flour, shaking off the excess. Heat 2 tablespoons more oil in the skillet over medium-high heat until just smoking. Carefully lay the chicken breasts in the skillet and cook until lightly browned on both sides, 6 to 8 minutes. Transfer the chicken to a plate.

3. Add the remaining 1 teaspoon oil and the shallots to the skillet and cook over medium-low heat

until softened, about 1 minute. Stir in the remaining 2 cups of broth and the cream, scraping up any browned bits. Return the chicken to the skillet, cover, and cook over medium-low heat until the thickest part of the breast registers 160 degrees on an instant-read thermometer, about 10 minutes.

4. Transfer the chicken to a plate and let cool slightly. Continue to simmer the sauce until it measures about 1 cup, about 10 minutes. Stir in the sherry and Worcestershire sauce and continue to simmer until it measures about 1½ cups, about 30 seconds.

5. Off the heat, stir in ½ cup of the Parmesan. Whisk the yolks and lemon juice together in a small bowl. Whisk about ¼ cup of the warm sauce into the egg yolks to temper, then stir the yolk mixture back into the sauce. Whisk in the butter until combined.

6. Slice the chicken crosswise into ½-inch-thick pieces and nestle them into the sauce. Scatter the cooked broccoli over the top and sprinkle with the remaining ½ cup Parmesan. Bake the casserole until the cheese is melted and golden, about 10 minutes. Let the casserole cool for 10 minutes before serving.

TORTILLA CASSEROLE

CHICKEN TORTILLA CASSEROLE, WITH CHILES, tomatoes, and layers of earthy corn tortillas, offers a refreshing change of pace from more traditional chicken casseroles. But when we started our research, we turned up countless recipes that, when made, left us with overcooked chicken bathed in canned cream soup and gobs of cheese—it seemed the tortilla casserole wasn't as far off from its Americanized relative as we thought. We wanted to breathe some life into this dish, and simplify it into a quick weeknight skillet dinner.

Using the technique we had perfected for cooking chicken breasts for our Classic Chicken Pot Pie (page 190), we started by browning boneless, skinless chicken breasts in a skillet, then set them aside and built the sauce that we would later poach them in.

We knew what *not* to put in our sauce—canned cream of chicken soup. But as for the rest of the ingredients, recipes varied widely. Tasters didn't care for olives, mushrooms, or green bell peppers, but did like the Tex-Mex options of chipotle peppers and Ro-Tel tomatoes (the Texas brand of spicy canned tomatoes). We cooked some onions and garlic with the chipotle chile in adobo sauce—which lent smokiness and heat—and then added chicken broth and a can of undrained Ro-Tel tomatoes to simmer. Ten minutes of kitchen work yielded a flavorful sauce that put sad canned soup to shame.

INGREDIENTS: Tortilla Chips

Our favorite Mexican restaurant chips are thick, crunchy, and terrifically "corny"; they're as good eaten alone as they are dunked into salsa. But now several "upscale" corn chip brands sold in supermarkets promise authentic Mexican restaurant–style texture and crunch. There are so many chips to choose from, how do you know whether these fancy brands are better than the generic bags? To find out, we held a blind taste test of several brands of tortilla chips.

We found that the boutique brands lived up to their promise of good flavor. Tasters liked an authentic taste, and consistently rated highly those they felt had the most corn flavor. Despite their corny flavor, some chips were ultimately rejected by tasters as being too thick—so thick they tasted stale, in fact. Coarse-textured, super-corny chips might be fine in a Mexican restaurant (where they can be freshly fried), but when bagged for sale at the supermarket, this style of chip can come off as stale, especially when compared with thinner chips. In contrast, the finer-textured chips (several of which are made with corn flour, not stone-ground corn) were described as "thin and crispy" and were perceived as being fresher. Our favorite from the tasting was Santitas Authentic Mexican Style White Corn Tortilla Chips, which had a sturdy, compelling texture and a crunch that topped the crispness charts.

THE BEST TORTILLA CHIPS

Santitas Authentic Mexican Style White Corn Tortilla Chips is our pick for a tortilla chip with a "mild and salty" flavor and satisfying, crisp texture.

SANTITAS

This sauce, we thought, would coat our tortillas perfectly. But by the time the casserole was done, our tortillas were a bland, soggy mess. Instead we turned to store-bought tortilla chips. We stirred a hefty 5 cups of tortilla chips into the sauce, nestled in the chicken breasts, and simmered the mixture until the chicken was cooked through and some of the tortilla chips broke down and thickened the sauce.

Now the only thing missing from the sauce was the silky, smooth texture. No tortilla casserole would be complete without cheese, so that was where we looked to add creaminess to our sauce. We tried Monterey Jack, cheddar, and sharp cheddar cheese. The Monterey Jack was a bit stringy, and its flavor got lost in the sauce. Cheddar was better, but the sharp cheddar proved our best option. With a silky sauce, and a cheese settled upon, it was time to look at the bulk of our casserole.

We shredded the cooked chicken and stirred it back into the sauce, along with 1 cup shredded cheddar cheese, minced cilantro, and lime juice. This made a creamy sauce, with bright flavor from the cilantro and lime juice. For some crunch in the finished dish, we added another 5 cups of tortilla chips. Lastly, we topped the casserole with more shredded cheese and broiled it briefly to melt the cheese. (If we cooked the casserole for too long, the chips turned to mush.) To bring a little color and bite of fresh flavor to the finished dish, we added a sprinkling of fresh cilantro before serving.

Tortilla Casserole

SERVES 4

Ro-Tel tomatoes are simply tomatoes canned with green chiles; you can find them at the market either next to other types of canned tomatoes or alongside other Latin American ingredients. If you like things spicy, use the higher amount of chipotle chiles. Tortilla chips tend to be quite salty, so be sure to season the chicken lightly with salt in step 2.

1½	pounds boneless, skinless chicken breasts (about 4 medium), trimmed (see the illustration on page 6) Salt and ground black pepper
¼	cup vegetable oil
1	medium onion, minced
6	medium garlic cloves, minced or pressed through a garlic press (about 2 tablespoons)
2–4	teaspoons minced chipotle chile in adobo sauce (see note)
3	cups low-sodium chicken broth
1	(10-ounce) can Ro-Tel tomatoes (see note)
8	ounces tortilla chips, broken into 1-inch pieces (about 10 cups)
8	ounces sharp cheddar cheese, shredded (2 cups)
¼	cup minced fresh cilantro leaves
1	tablespoon juice from 1 lime

1. Adjust an oven rack to 5 inches from the broiler element and heat the broiler.

2. Pat the chicken breasts dry with paper towels and season lightly with salt and pepper. Heat 2 tablespoons of the oil in the skillet over medium-high heat until just smoking. Carefully lay the chicken breasts in the skillet and cook until lightly browned on both sides, 6 to 8 minutes. Transfer the chicken to a plate.

3. Add the remaining 2 tablespoons oil to the skillet and return to medium heat until shimmering. Add the onion and ¼ teaspoon salt and cook until softened, 5 to 7 minutes. Stir in the garlic and chipotles and cook until fragrant, about 30 seconds. Stir in the broth and tomatoes with their juice, scraping up any browned bits, and bring to a simmer.

4. Stir in 5 cups of the tortilla chips. Nestle the browned chicken into the skillet, cover, and cook over medium-low heat until the thickest part of the breast registers 160 to 165 degrees on an instant-read thermometer, about 10 minutes. Transfer the chicken to a carving board. When the chicken is cool enough to handle, shred it into bite-sized pieces following the illustration on page 190.

5. Return the shredded chicken to the skillet and stir in 1 cup of the cheddar, 2 tablespoons of the cilantro, and the lime juice. Stir in the remaining 5 cups tortilla chips until moistened.

6. Sprinkle the remaining 1 cup cheddar over the top. Broil the casserole until the cheese is melted and golden, 5 to 10 minutes. Let the casserole cool for 10 minutes and sprinkle with the remaining 2 tablespoons cilantro before serving.

SHRIMP AND GRITS CASSEROLE

IN SOUTH CAROLINA, SHRIMP AND GRITS HAS long been a basic breakfast for coastal fishermen and families during the shrimp season. The dish consists of a pot of grits with shrimp that have been cooked in a little bacon fat. Over the years, this humble dish has taken on a whole new life as an anytime casserole, chock-full of shrimp, cheese, and grits. We wanted to develop a recipe for shrimp and grits casserole, with cheesy grits (not overcooked and pasty, which tends to be the trend) and tender, succulent shrimp. And we wanted to do it all in one skillet, as opposed to the usual skillet and the extra casserole dish used for baking.

We started by looking at the grits available in our local grocery store. There were two kinds: instant, which cook in five minutes; and old-fashioned, which cook in 15 minutes. In a side-by-side taste test, most tasters thought the instant grits were too creamy and tasted overprocessed. The old-fashioned grits were creamy yet retained a slightly coarse texture that tasters liked—these grits deserve their name.

After doing some research, we uncovered recipes that were simple, yet devoid of any kick of flavor. We began to look at the options that might add pizzazz to this usually plain dish. Sautéed minced onion and garlic got our juices flowing, but we wanted a stronger flavor to complement the other elements of the dish. Minced chipotle chile in adobo sauce provided a touch of smokiness and spice to the dish—just what we were looking for. Sliced scallions, stirred in just before baking, also perked up the casserole with their color and mild onion flavor. Now for the grits.

To add richness without relying solely on butter, as many recipes do, we decided to try cooking the grits in milk rather than water. They tasted good, but more like hot breakfast cereal—not the flavor we were hoping for. And the flavor of the grits disappeared behind the lactose-heavy milk flavor.

We then tried cooking them in a small amount of heavy cream and water mixed together. Everyone liked this batch—the grits were rich, but without an overwhelming dairy flavor. We were surprised to find that cooked cream does not develop the same strong "cooked" flavor as milk. This is because the extra fat in cream keeps the milk proteins from breaking down when heated. After a few more batches of varying proportions, we found that using just ½ cup of cream to 3½ cups of water for 1 cup of grits offered the best balance of richness and flavor.

Next we looked at cheese options. Monterey Jack made the grits taste bland, so it was out. Regular cheddar was also bland, but the flavor was getting there. As in our Tortilla Casserole (page 209), a cheddar with some sharpness proved to be the winner. The flavor was assertive and complemented the subtle corn flavor.

Our grits were good, but the texture wasn't quite what we wanted. We wanted a denser, heartier dish, one closer to baked polenta than custardy spoon bread. We decided to add a couple eggs to bind the grits and give the dish the dense texture we desired. Two eggs didn't change the texture of our grits much, and four eggs made them too heavy and imparted an eggy flavor. Three eggs, on the other hand, provided just enough structure without making the grits taste eggy.

It was time for the star of the show—the shrimp. We knew that we would have to be careful not to overcook them, as most of the recipes we had tested did just that. We thought the best option would be to simply nestle them into the fully cooked grits before transferring the skillet to the oven. When the grits were cooked, we stirred in half of the shredded cheddar cheese and the eggs, nestled in the shrimp, sprinkled the remaining cheese over the top, and baked the whole dish right in the skillet. The shrimp were perfectly cooked and the combination of flavors was in balance. This was the best shrimp and grits casserole any of us (including a few Southerners) had ever eaten.

Shrimp and Grits Casserole

SERVES 4

Do not substitute instant grits here. Be sure to remove the shrimp shells completely (including the tails) before nestling them into the grits in step 4. Feel free to substitute smoked cheddar or smoked Gouda for the extra-sharp cheddar.

2	tablespoons unsalted butter
1	medium onion, minced
1	teaspoon salt
2	medium garlic cloves, minced or pressed through a garlic press (about 2 teaspoons)
1	teaspoon minced chipotle chile in adobo sauce
3½	cups water
½	cup heavy cream
1	cup old-fashioned grits (see note)
6	ounces extra-sharp cheddar cheese, shredded (1½ cups)
3	large eggs, lightly beaten
4	scallions, thinly sliced
¼	teaspoon ground black pepper
1½	pounds extra-large shrimp (21 to 25 per pound), peeled and deveined (see the illustration on page 235)

1. Adjust an oven rack to the middle position and heat the oven to 450 degrees.

2. Melt the butter in a 12-inch ovenproof skillet over medium heat. Add the onion and salt and cook until softened, 8 to 10 minutes. Stir in the garlic and chipotles and cook until fragrant, about 30 seconds.

3. Stir in the water and cream and bring to a boil. Slowly whisk in the grits. Reduce the heat to low and cook, stirring frequently, until the grits are thick and creamy, about 15 minutes.

4. Off the heat, whisk in ¾ cup of the cheddar, the eggs, scallions, and pepper. Nestle the shrimp into the grits so that they are no longer visible. Smooth the grit-shrimp filling into an even layer in the skillet, then sprinkle the remaining ¾ cup cheddar over the top. Bake the casserole until the top is browned and the grits are hot, about 15 minutes. Let the casserole cool for 10 minutes before serving.

POLENTA BAKE

POLENTA IS DRIED GROUND CORN COOKED until silky-smooth and finished with butter and cheese. Most often served in its soft, velvety form, polenta is rarely thought of as the basis for a baked dish or casserole. Yet it makes perfect sense—polenta can withstand being chilled and reheated nicely, and is easy to fully cook in a skillet. We imagined our baked polenta to be a sophisticated dish, with a layer of soft polenta covered by savory toppings and a touch of tangy blue cheese. We also thought this would be a perfect vegetarian entrée for any night of the week, served with a simple green salad. Our mouths were already watering at the thought of this creamy dish, but first we had to focus on the recipe.

We knew that if we wanted to precook any of the topping ingredients, we would have to do it before making the polenta to keep our cooking to one skillet. We were immediately drawn to the idea of using mushrooms in some fashion because their woodsy flavor is a classic pairing with polenta, and mushrooms add a certain heft and meatiness to meatless dishes. After sautéing some sliced white mushrooms with a little onion, garlic, and fresh thyme, we realized the key to achieving good mushroom flavor would be to use several different varieties of mushrooms. Portobellos offer a hearty bite, while inexpensive white button mushrooms help to bulk up the yield without costing a fortune. Also, the intense flavor of dried porcini mushrooms (now widely available in supermarkets) really helped to drive home a serious mushroom flavor. We sautéed our new combination of mushrooms and set them aside while we focused on the polenta itself.

We knew that the polenta must be added very slowly to boiling salted water to prevent clumping. To give the flavor of the polenta a boost, we tried cooking it in boiling milk. The milk rounded out the flavor of the polenta nicely, but it also added an unwelcome, slimy texture. Using a combination of roughly 1 part milk to 3 parts water, we were able to add some flavor to the polenta without ruining its creamy texture. It took about 20 minutes over moderate heat to fully cook the polenta. We finished it with a little butter, which helped keep it

211

smooth and soft, and a bit of garlic—this polenta was just right.

With the polenta fully cooked, we smoothed it out, spread the cooked mushrooms over the top, and sprinkled on the Gorgonzola and walnuts—a classic pair in their own right. (Cheese mixed directly into the polenta caused it to stiffen up, a problem that would be compounded by the time in the oven.) After 15 minutes in a 450-degree oven, the cheese was melted and the nuts were toasty and flavorful. Garnished with a bit of fresh parsley, our polenta bake was not only elegant and modern, but delicious too.

Mildly flavored and easy to prepare, our baked polenta can serve as a great backdrop for many ingredients besides mushrooms. We also made a variation using sautéed sausage, Swiss chard, and Asiago cheese for yet another simple suppertime option.

Polenta Bake with Gorgonzola and Walnuts

SERVES 4

This recipe uses traditional dried polenta, often found alongside the rice and grains in the supermarket; do not substitute premade tubes of polenta or instant polenta. When stirring the polenta, make sure to scrape the sides and bottom of the skillet to ensure even cooking.

MUSHROOM TOPPING

¼	cup olive oil
1	medium onion, minced
	Salt
12	ounces portobello mushroom caps (about 8 medium caps), brushed clean and sliced ¼ inch thick
1¼	pounds white mushrooms, wiped clean and sliced ¼ inch thick
¼	ounce dried porcini mushrooms, rinsed and chopped coarse
6	medium garlic cloves, minced or pressed through a garlic press (about 2 tablespoons)
1	tablespoon minced fresh thyme leaves
	Ground black pepper

POLENTA

3¼	cups water
1	cup whole milk
	Salt
1	cup polenta (see note)
3	tablespoons unsalted butter
1	medium garlic clove, minced or pressed through a garlic press (about 1 teaspoon)
	Ground black pepper
8	ounces Gorgonzola cheese or other mild blue cheese, crumbled (2 cups)
¾	cup walnuts, coarsely chopped
2	tablespoons minced fresh parsley leaves

1. **FOR THE MUSHROOM TOPPING:** Adjust an oven rack to the middle position and heat the oven to 450 degrees. Heat the oil in a 12-inch ovenproof skillet over medium-high heat until shimmering. Add the onion and 1 teaspoon salt and cook until beginning to soften, about 2 minutes. Stir in the portobello, white, and porcini mushrooms and cook, stirring often, until the mushrooms have released their liquid and are well browned, about 20 minutes. Stir in the garlic and thyme and cook until fragrant, about 30 seconds. Season with salt and pepper to taste and transfer to a large bowl.

2. **FOR THE POLENTA:** Add the water and milk to the skillet and bring to a boil over medium-high heat. Stir in 1 teaspoon salt, then very slowly pour the polenta into the boiling liquid while stirring constantly in a circular motion with a wooden spoon.

3. Reduce the heat to low and simmer the polenta, stirring often, until all of the liquid has been absorbed, the mixture is uniformly smooth, and it no longer has a raw cornmeal flavor.

4. Off the heat, stir in the butter and garlic and season with salt and pepper to taste. Smooth the polenta into an even layer in the skillet. Spoon the

mushroom topping evenly over the polenta, then sprinkle with the Gorgonzola and walnuts. Bake the casserole until the cheese is melted and the walnuts have toasted, 15 to 20 minutes. Let the casserole cool for 10 minutes and sprinkle with the parsley before serving.

➤ VARIATION

Polenta Bake with Sausage and Chard

This recipe uses traditional dried polenta, often found alongside the rice and grains in the supermarket; do not substitute premade tubes of polenta or instant polenta. When stirring the polenta, make sure to scrape the sides and bottom of the skillet to ensure even cooking.

SAUSAGE AND CHARD TOPPING
1 tablespoon olive oil
1 pound sweet Italian sausage, removed from its casing
1 medium red bell pepper, stemmed, seeded, and sliced into ¼-inch-wide strips
1 medium onion, minced
1 small bunch Swiss chard (8 to 10 ounces), stems and leaves separated (see the illustration on page 299), stems chopped medium and leaves cut into 1-inch pieces
 Salt
6 medium garlic cloves, minced or pressed through a garlic press (about 2 tablespoons)
2 teaspoons minced fresh thyme leaves, or ¾ teaspoon dried
¼ teaspoon red pepper flakes
1 (14.5-ounce) can diced tomatoes
1 tablespoon red wine vinegar
 Ground black pepper

POLENTA
3¼ cups water
1 cup whole milk
 Salt
1 cup polenta (see note)
3 tablespoons unsalted butter

1 medium garlic clove, minced or pressed through a garlic press (about 1 teaspoon)
 Ground black pepper
4 ounces Asiago cheese, grated (2 cups)

1. FOR THE SAUSAGE AND CHARD TOPPING: Adjust an oven rack to the middle position and heat the oven to 450 degrees. Heat the oil in a 12-inch ovenproof skillet over medium-high heat until shimmering. Add the sausage and cook, breaking up the meat with a wooden spoon, until lightly browned, about 10 minutes.

2. Stir in the pepper, onion, chard stems, and ½ teaspoon salt and cook until the vegetables are softened, 8 to 10 minutes. Stir in the garlic, thyme, and red pepper flakes and cook until fragrant, about 30 seconds. Stir in the tomatoes with their juice and simmer until they are softened, about 3 minutes.

3. Stir in the chard leaves, a handful at a time, and cook until they are bright green and slightly wilted, about 2 minutes. Off the heat, stir in the vinegar and season with salt and pepper to taste. Transfer the mixture to a bowl and set aside.

4. FOR THE POLENTA: Add the water and milk to the skillet and bring a boil over medium-high heat. Stir in 1 teaspoon salt, then very slowly pour the polenta into the boiling liquid while stirring constantly in a circular motion with a wooden spoon.

5. Reduce the heat to low and simmer the polenta, stirring often, until all of the liquid has been absorbed, the mixture is uniformly smooth, and it no longer has a raw cornmeal flavor.

6. Off the heat, stir in the butter and garlic and season with salt and pepper to taste. Smooth the polenta into an even layer in the skillet. Spoon the sausage and chard topping evenly over the polenta, then sprinkle with the Asiago. Bake the casserole until the cheese is melted and golden, 15 to 20 minutes. Let the casserole cool for 10 minutes before serving.

TUSCAN BEAN CASSEROLE

CANNELLINI ALL'UCCELLETTO, OR "BEANS cooked like a little bird," is a traditional Tuscan dish as native to the region as baked beans are to Boston and cheese steaks are to Philadelphia. Essentially, they are white beans stewed for hours with tomatoes and garlic—also a common Italian method for preparing small game birds like quail, hence the bird reference. The flavors blend and sweeten, and the beans become creamy. We liked the concept and flavors of the dish, but not the time required to prepare it. We sought to rework this classic into a faster-to-the-table casserole—complete with a crisp, rustic bread topping—by making it entirely in a skillet.

Traditionally, the dish is prepared with dried cannellini beans, which accounts for much of the long cooking time. We generally prefer the superior flavor and texture of dried beans, but milder, softer canned beans are an acceptable substitute when time is tight. The trick, however, is infusing them with flavor before they become mushy. Canned beans simply cannot withstand an extended cooking time.

With that in mind, we knew we had to establish a base for this dish and develop much of its flavor prior to the beans' introduction. Following the lead of conventional recipes, we prepared a *soffrito* (the Italian term for a slow-cooked mixture of chopped vegetables) using sautéed onion, carrots, and celery. Cooked over moderate heat, the vegetables developed a sweet flavor base for the beans, which we enhanced with minced garlic and rosemary.

We next considered including tomatoes, another traditional ingredient. For convenience, we hoped that canned diced tomatoes would work. While tasters liked their flavor, they disliked the overly firm texture. We then tried adding the tomatoes to the cooked soffrito to soften and intensify in flavor before the beans and any liquid were added. This time the texture was right on, and the tomatoes added nice fruity and acidic notes.

Still in search of another hearty ingredient or two to play off the still-to-come beans in our one-skillet meal, we hit on earthy kale, also a Tuscan favorite, along with pancetta. We sautéed the pancetta in the skillet with the vegetables, which helped enrich our flavor base. To cook the kale, we added the tough stems with our soffrito, since they need more time to cook than the leaves. The leaves were simmered for just five minutes in the skillet once the liquid had been added.

To build the sauce, we tried adding 2 cups of water, but this flavorless base lacked any richness. When we tried half water, half chicken broth, the flavor of the dish was right on—the only complaint was that the

---

INGREDIENTS: Canned Cannellini Beans

While it is hard to beat the full flavor and firm texture of dried beans cooked from scratch, canned beans are perfectly acceptable in certain recipes, like our Tuscan Bean Casserole (page 215) and French-Style White Bean Casserole (page 216). These dishes are so richly flavored that the stronger flavor of the dried beans isn't missed, and the cooking time is short enough that the softer canned beans do not have a chance to overcook and turn mushy.

But are all canned cannellini beans of equal caliber? We looked for multiple brands of nationally distributed cannellini beans to taste against one another, and found so few that we decided to include both great Northern and navy beans in the tasting as well. From sweet to bland and chalky to mushy, the different brands ran the gamut in quality. Our favorite of the bunch was Westbrae Organic Great Northern Beans, which won accolades for their earthy flavor and creamy texture. In second place, tasters liked Progresso Cannellini Beans for their "plump shape" and "sweet, slightly salty" flavor.

THE BEST CANNED WHITE BEANS

WESTBRAE   PROGRESSO

Westbrae Organic Great Northern Beans are the best of the bunch, due to excellent flavor and texture. Progresso Cannellini Beans also scored points, thanks to their full shape and sweet-salty flavor.

sauce seemed too thin. We considered adding cream, but that seemed out of place in this olive oil–based Italian dish. More oil wasn't the answer either. We needed to thicken our casserole so it was more of a hearty stew, rather than a broth-based soup. Looking for a thickening agent that would keep with the tone of the dish, we realized there was an obvious solution—beans pureed with broth or water, a common thickener used in many soup and stew recipes. We pureed 1 cup of the beans with 2 cups chicken broth. This creamy mixture added just the right amount of texture to the dish, while another can of whole rinsed beans filled out the sauce.

Since the original dish is typically served with a crusty loaf of bread, we sought a topping that contributed a similar flavor and texture. Finely ground bread crumbs didn't quite cut it; they were too sandy in texture and tasted bland. We wanted heartier, more rustic texture and flavor—the crunchy crust and tough pull of a loaf, with a flavor to match. We opted to toss chunks of baguette in olive oil and Parmesan before scattering them over the beans. The baguette gave us a higher crust-to-crumb ratio, making for a textured topping. The croutons browned attractively in a 450-degree oven and had a flavorful combination of crisp crust and tender, sweet crumb.

A modern take on an old-world standby, our Tuscan Bean Casserole was still fully rustic, with buttery beans that contrasted nicely with the crisp, salty Parmesan croutons.

Tuscan Bean Casserole
SERVES 4

Canned navy or great Northern beans can be substituted for the cannellini beans. If pancetta is unavailable, substitute 4 ounces of bacon (about 4 slices). Any type of hearty rustic bread can be substituted for the baguette.

- 2 (15-ounce) cans cannellini beans, drained and rinsed
- 2 cups low-sodium chicken broth
- 4 ounces pancetta, cut into ¼-inch pieces (see note)
- 3 tablespoons extra-virgin olive oil
- 1 medium onion, minced
- 2 medium celery ribs, chopped medium
- 2 medium carrots, peeled and chopped medium
- ½ bunch kale or collard greens (about ½ pound), stems and leaves separated (see the illustration on page 299), stems chopped medium and leaves cut into 1-inch pieces
- 5 medium garlic cloves, minced or pressed through a garlic press (about 5 teaspoons)
- 1 teaspoon minced fresh rosemary
- 1 (14.5-ounce) can diced tomatoes, drained
- 1 cup water
- 2 bay leaves
   Salt and ground black pepper
- ½ rustic baguette, torn into 1-inch pieces (about 4 cups)
- 2 ounces Parmesan cheese, grated (1 cup)

1. Adjust an oven rack to the middle position and heat the oven to 450 degrees. Blend 1 cup of the beans with the chicken broth in a blender until smooth, about 30 seconds; set aside.

2. Cook the pancetta and 1 tablespoon of the oil in a 12-inch ovenproof skillet over medium heat, stirring occasionally, until the pancetta is lightly browned, 6 to 10 minutes. Stir in the onion, celery, carrots, and kale stems and cook, stirring occasionally, until the vegetables are softened and lightly browned, 8 to 10 minutes.

3. Stir in the garlic and rosemary and cook until fragrant, about 30 seconds. Stir in the tomatoes and cook until softened and dry, about 5 minutes. Stir in the blended bean-broth mixture, the remaining beans, water, and bay leaves. Increase the heat to high, bring to a simmer, and cook until the beans are heated through, about 5 minutes.

4. Stir in the kale leaves, a handful at a time, and continue to simmer until the liquid has thickened slightly and begins to fall below the level of the vegetables, and the mixture measures about 6 cups, about 5 minutes. Off the heat, discard the bay leaves and season with salt and pepper to taste.

5. Toss the bread with the remaining 2 tablespoons oil and Parmesan cheese and sprinkle over the stew. Bake the casserole until the cheese has melted and the croutons are golden brown, about 15 minutes. Let the casserole cool for 10 minutes before serving.

FRENCH-STYLE WHITE BEAN CASSEROLE

THIS HEARTY CASSEROLE IS BASED ON cassoulet, a rich French dish that's perfect anytime there's a chill in the air. Typically composed of garlicky white beans, pork sausage, duck confit (a separate dish made from duck legs), and a variety of other meats, and occasionally topped with buttery bread crumbs, cassoulet can take three days to make, and the ingredients can be both hard to find and difficult to prepare. We wanted to use the basic flavors from cassoulet to create a much simpler white bean casserole that could be made in a skillet in under an hour.

To start, we looked at the types of meat typically included—sausage, duck confit, and pork. We had to trim the ingredient list, and eliminated the duck confit entirely since it can only be found in very high-end grocers, and it takes an eternity to make at home. Instead, our white bean casserole would use a combination of pork and sausage. After ruling out hard-to-find French sausages, we found that both kielbasa and andouille sausages gave us the smokiness we desired. Kielbasa was a bit easier to find, so it got our vote. We then looked over the pork options in the meat case and finally settled on boneless country-style pork ribs. Unlike spareribs and baby-back ribs, country-style ribs are cut more towards the shoulder (where the pork butt comes from), so they have more fat and flavor.

To get the most flavor out of the ribs, we cut them into 1-inch pieces and browned them in our skillet; a minced onion and some garlic were then added to sauté with the pork. From the spice cabinet, we pulled out thyme, a bay leaf, and ground cloves, flavors that we thought would play off our beans, ribs, and kielbasa nicely. One tablespoon of tomato paste brought out the sweet notes. Now we were ready for the beans.

While cassoulet is prepared with kidney-shaped white beans that are difficult to find stateside, we thought that cannellini beans would work just fine in our casserole. Since we were aiming for a quick casserole we reached for canned beans—there would be enough flavorful ingredients in this dish that we suspected no one would miss the flavor of dried beans. Turning to our sauce, we added chicken broth and vermouth to the skillet; their flavors formed a bright base for our French-inspired dish. We then added two cans of beans—along with a can of diced tomatoes—to simmer for 20 minutes in the broth and vermouth with the ribs. This was just long enough for the beans and tomatoes to soften slightly, but not so long that the beans exploded.

For the bread topping, we wanted something rustic. We tore half a French baguette into 1-inch pieces and tossed it with olive oil. The sliced kielbasa was stirred in (since it was precooked sausage, it only had to be heated up), and the baguette pieces were scattered on top of the skillet.

With a quick finish in the oven, our tasty white bean casserole had a country-style feel and flavor, but was streamlined enough for modern-day, time-starved cooks.

French-Style White Bean Casserole

SERVES 4

Canned navy or great Northern beans can be substituted for the cannellini beans. Serve this casserole with a simple green salad.

1	pound boneless country-style pork ribs, cut into 1-inch pieces
	Salt and ground black pepper
¼	cup olive oil
1	medium onion, minced
1	tablespoon tomato paste
1	tablespoon minced fresh thyme leaves, or 1 teaspoon dried
2	medium garlic cloves, minced or pressed through a garlic press (about 2 teaspoons)
1	bay leaf
	Pinch ground cloves
1¾	cups low-sodium chicken broth
1	(14.5-ounce) can diced tomatoes, drained
1	cup dry vermouth or dry white wine
2	(15-ounce) cans cannellini beans, drained and rinsed

½ pound kielbasa, halved lengthwise
    and sliced ¼ inch thick
½ rustic baguette, torn into 1-inch pieces
    (about 4 cups)

1. Adjust an oven rack to the middle position and heat the oven to 450 degrees. Pat the pork dry with paper towels and season with salt and pepper. Heat 2 tablespoons of the oil in a 12-inch ovenproof skillet over medium-high heat until shimmering. Add the pork and cook, stirring occasionally, until lightly browned, about 5 minutes.

2. Stir in the onion and ½ teaspoon salt and cook, stirring occasionally, until the onion is softened, 5 to 7 minutes. Stir in the tomato paste, thyme, garlic, bay leaf, and ground cloves and cook until fragrant, about 1 minute. Stir in the chicken broth, tomatoes, and vermouth, scraping up any browned bits.

3. Stir in the beans, increase the heat to high, and bring to a simmer. Reduce the heat to medium-low, cover, and simmer until the pork is tender, 20 to 25 minutes. Off the heat, gently stir in the kielbasa.

4. Toss the bread with the remaining 2 tablespoons oil and sprinkle on top of the bean mixture to cover. Bake the casserole until the bread is toasted and golden, about 15 minutes. Let the casserole rest for 10 minutes before serving.

Phyllo Pie

MOST TAVERNS IN GREECE, AND CERTAINLY every Greek-American restaurant, offer some version of phyllo pie on the menu. The most common is spanakopita, which is filled with spinach and cheese. A less widely known alternative, called *kotopita*, replaces the spinach with chicken. Both varieties are made by layering sheets of phyllo dough with a filling of chicken or spinach and tangy feta cheese, spiked with garlic and herbs. The pies are then baked, resulting in the perfect marriage of crisp, flaky pastry and savory, satisfying filling.

But phyllo pie can be a tough dish to get right at home. The chicken can be dense and dry,

characteristics that are only amplified by thin, dried-out pastry. And random chunks of feta cheese don't do much to improve the dish. Add to that the difficulty of working with store-bought phyllo dough, and you might as well dine out. We knew we could improve upon this classic dish; we wanted a simpler version, with a moist chicken filling, bright flavors, and evenly spaced bites of feta that didn't dull after baking. We also wanted to build and bake the whole pie in our trusty skillet, and, to keep things simple, use the phyllo as the topping instead of layering it throughout the dish.

We focused first on perfecting the chicken and feta filling, which would form the base of our pie. Ground chicken was our first choice for the meat, since it's easy to find and easy to use for a weeknight meal. After a couple of tests, we determined that ground dark meat surpassed ground white meat both for its flavor and for remaining moist in the baked phyllo pie. It was crucial to break the chicken meat into small pieces as it cooked. If the meat remained in large clumps, it didn't create a uniform filling. We added some garlic for flavor and chicken broth to keep the meat moist. To avoid big chunks of feta in the filling and ensure that it was evenly distributed, we first crumbled it up, then mixed it with eggs. The eggs bound the filling ingredients together, adding richness and flavor, and lightened the layer of chicken that would otherwise be dense when baked in the oven.

Scallions and mint are traditional ingredients in phyllo pies, but they are usually added in such paltry amounts that the flavors disappear. We increased the quantities of each and mixed them in with the feta and eggs. Lemon juice and cayenne pepper are less commonly included, but tasters unanimously approved of both. In search of more punch, we added chopped kalamata olives, which gave a bold flavor to our ground chicken filling. With the flavors now bright and clean, we mixed the feta filling into the cooked ground chicken. It was time to move on to the phyllo.

The single most important thing to know when working with phyllo dough is that it needs to be at room temperature. Most problems arise when packages are hastily thawed; sheets that are still cold will crack along the folds or stick together at the corners. Frozen phyllo dough should be thawed slowly in the refrigerator for at least eight hours or overnight. (You can also thaw it on the counter for several hours.)

Phyllo is famous for its crisp, flaky layers, but it was this quality that gave us the most trouble once the pie hit the hot oven. In every test, the papery layers curled and separated from each other as they baked. Cutting into the baked dish sent shattered pieces of phyllo everywhere. Looking for a solution, we tried brushing each layer with olive oil, which helped the pastry layers stick together. One teaspoon of oil per sheet is adequate if spread carefully, but we preferred the added flavor and crispness of a slightly more generous amount of fat, about half a tablespoon per sheet. To fit our skillet, we placed the layers over each other in a pinwheel pattern, then folded the edges over the top to make a circle (see the illustrations below). We found it helpful to prepare the phyllo first and have it ready to go when our filling was done, so in subsequent tests, we assembled our stack of phyllo sheets first, then stored them in the freezer to keep them firm for the short amount of time it took to make the filling.

Lastly, we wondered about the lengthy baking times specified by most recipes—usually an hour in the oven at 350 degrees, until the phyllo is golden and crisp. But when the hour was up, our bright flavors were washed out and flat, and the phyllo topping was dried out and more prone to shattering. Increasing the temperature to 450 degrees and reducing the cooking time to about 15 minutes resulted in a filling and crust that were both done to perfection.

Since spanakopita is so popular, we used the same method to create a variation with frozen chopped spinach and ricotta cheese. A good amount of fresh dill enhances the dish, keeping the flavors bright and lively.

Phyllo Pie with Chicken
SERVES 4

Thaw the phyllo completely before using, either in the refrigerator overnight or on the counter for several hours; don't thaw the phyllo in the microwave. Do not substitute white chicken meat here, or the filling will taste very dry and bland.

PHYLLO CRUST

½ pound (14 by 9-inch) phyllo, thawed
   (see note)
⅓ cup olive oil

FILLING

8 ounces feta cheese, crumbled fine (2 cups)
3 large eggs, lightly beaten
1 bunch scallions, sliced thin
½ cup pitted kalamata olives, chopped coarse
⅓ cup minced fresh mint leaves

MAKING A PHYLLO TOP CRUST

1. Lay the first sheet of phyllo on a large piece of parchment paper and brush the pastry lightly, but thoroughly, with oil.

2. Lay the remaining sheets on top of the first, in a pinwheel fashion, to make a circle, brushing each sheet with more oil.

3. Fold the edges of phyllo over the top so the circle measures 11 inches across, then slide the parchment and phyllo onto a baking sheet and freeze until firm before using.

3 tablespoons juice from 1 lemon

½ teaspoon salt

¼ ground black pepper

¼ teaspoon cayenne pepper

1 tablespoon olive oil

2 pounds ground dark meat chicken (see note)

3 medium garlic cloves, minced or pressed through a garlic press (about 1 tablespoon)

½ cup low-sodium chicken broth

1. **FOR THE PHYLLO CRUST:** Adjust an oven rack to the middle position and heat the oven to 450 degrees. Following the illustrations on page 218, lay 1 phyllo sheet on a large sheet of parchment paper and brush the pastry lightly with oil. Repeat with 9 more phyllo sheets, placing them in a pinwheel pattern and brushing each sheet with oil. Fold the edges of the phyllo over so that the circle measures 11 inches. Slide the parchment and phyllo circle onto a baking sheet and freeze while making the filling.

2. **FOR THE FILLING:** Mix the feta, eggs, scallions, olives, mint, lemon juice, salt, pepper, and cayenne together in a large bowl.

3. Heat the oil in a 12-inch ovenproof skillet over medium heat until shimmering. Add the chicken and cook, breaking up the meat with a wooden spoon, until no longer pink, about 5 minutes. Stir in the garlic and cook until fragrant, about 30 seconds. Stir in the chicken broth, scraping up the browned bits. Off the heat, stir in the feta mixture until well combined.

4. Smooth the filling into an even layer in the skillet. Lay the frozen phyllo circle on top of the filling and press lightly to adhere. Bake the pie until the phyllo is golden and crisp, about 15 minutes. Let the pie cool for 10 minutes before serving.

➤ VARIATION

Phyllo Pie with Spinach and Ricotta

Thaw the phyllo completely before using, either in the refrigerator overnight or on the counter for several hours; don't thaw the phyllo in the microwave. Be sure to squeeze the spinach thoroughly of excess moisture before stirring it into the filling.

PHYLLO CRUST

½ pound (14 by 9-inch) phyllo, thawed (see note)

⅓ cup olive oil

FILLING

8 ounces feta cheese, crumbled fine (2 cups)

8 ounces whole milk ricotta cheese

3 (10-ounce) packages frozen chopped spinach, thawed and squeezed dry

3 large eggs, lightly beaten

1 bunch scallions, sliced thin

⅓ cup minced fresh dill leaves

3 tablespoons juice from 1 lemon

½ teaspoon salt

¼ ground black pepper

⅛ teaspoon cayenne pepper

2 tablespoons olive oil

1 medium onion, minced

3 medium garlic cloves, minced or pressed through a garlic press (about 1 tablespoon)

½ cup low-sodium chicken broth

1. **FOR THE PHYLLO CRUST:** Adjust an oven rack to the middle position and heat the oven to 450 degrees. Following the illustrations on page 218, lay 1 phyllo sheet on a large sheet of parchment paper and brush the pastry lightly with oil. Repeat with 9 more phyllo sheets, placing them in a pinwheel pattern and brushing each sheet with oil. Fold the edges of the phyllo over so that the circle measures 11 inches. Slide the parchment and phyllo circle onto a baking sheet and freeze while making the filling.

2. **FOR THE FILLING:** Mix the feta, ricotta, spinach, eggs, scallions, dill, lemon juice, salt, pepper, and cayenne together in a large bowl.

3. Heat the oil in a 12-inch ovenproof skillet over medium heat until shimmering. Add the onion and cook until softened, 5 to 7 minutes. Stir in the garlic and cook until fragrant, about 30 seconds. Stir in the chicken broth, scraping up the browned bits. Off the heat, stir in the feta mixture until well combined.

4. Smooth the filling into an even layer in the skillet. Lay the frozen phyllo circle on top of the filling and press lightly to adhere. Bake the pie until the phyllo is golden and crisp, about 15 minutes. Let the pie cool for 10 minutes before serving.

SKILLET PIZZA

A CRISP, THIN-YET-STURDY CRUST SIMPLY topped with fresh tomato sauce and melted cheese is pizza at its finest. But making good thin-crust pizza at home requires a pizza stone (which in turn requires plenty of time to get good and hot in the oven), not to mention the agility required to maneuver the dough onto the stone and the piping hot pizza off it, without burning fingers or arms. We wanted to ditch the stone and come up with an easier, quicker way to make pizza in a home oven.

We thought our handy skillet might help fill the role of a pizza stone. Our idea was to build the pizza in the skillet and give it a jump-start with heat from the stovetop before transferring it to the oven.

First, we'd have to perfect the crust—we wanted a thin, crispy crust, not the thick, doughy crust of a pan pizza. We already had a handful of great pizza dough recipes in our library, but would any of these translate to the thin skillet-based crust we were after? For our first attempt, we heated some oil in a skillet over medium-high heat, gently laid the pizza dough inside, and cooked it on the stovetop before piling on the toppings and baking it. The pizza looked perfect as it emerged from the oven, but once we cut into it, we could see that the crust was thick and gummy, not thin and crispy. Plus, dropping an 11-inch round of dough into a skillet full of hot oil was a bit challenging to say the least.

We would need to test a slew of methods to get the dough right. First, we scaled down the amount of dough our recipe made, so we would have a thinner layer in the skillet. Also, we used bread flour instead of all-purpose flour to increase the chewiness in the finished crust. As for the cooking technique, we tried the simplest possible method—putting the dough into a cold skillet. To kill two birds with one stone, we decided to test heat levels at the same time. We oiled three 12-inch skillets and placed the dough in them off the heat (removing the danger of burnt fingertips). We then put the skillets over three different heat levels on

---

Basic Skillet Pizza Dough

MAKES 1 POUND DOUGH,
ENOUGH FOR TWO 11-INCH PIZZAS

All-purpose flour can be substituted for the bread flour, but the resulting crust will be a little less chewy. If desired, you can slow down the dough's rising time by letting it rise in the refrigerator for 8 to 16 hours in step 2; let the refrigerated dough soften at room temperature for 30 minutes before using.

2 cups (11 ounces) bread flour, plus extra as needed
1⅛ teaspoons (about ½ envelope) instant or rapid-rise yeast
¾ teaspoon salt
1 tablespoon olive oil, plus extra for the bowl
¾ cup warm water (110 degrees)

1. Pulse the flour, yeast, and salt together in a food processor (fitted with a dough blade if possible) to combine. With the processor running, slowly pour the oil, then water through the feed tube and process until the dough forms a sticky ball that clears the sides of the workbowl, 1½ to 2 minutes. (If, after 1 minute, the dough is sticky and clings to the blade, add extra flour, 1 tablespoon at a time, as needed until it clears the side of the workbowl.)

2. Turn the dough out onto a lightly floured work surface and form it into a smooth, round ball. Place the dough in a lightly oiled large bowl and cover tightly with greased plastic wrap. Let rise in a warm place until doubled in size, 1 to 1½ hours. (Once risen, the dough can be sealed in a zipper-lock bag and frozen for up to 1 month; let thaw on the counter for 2 to 3 hours, or overnight in the refrigerator, before using.)

➤ VARIATION

Whole Wheat Skillet Pizza Dough
Follow the recipe for Basic Skillet Pizza Dough, substituting 1 cup whole wheat flour for 1 cup of the bread flour.

the stovetop: high, medium-high, and medium. The medium-heat pizza crust took six minutes to set and turn brown, and it was gummy when it was done. The pizza crust cooked over medium-high heat took four minutes to cook and was also a little gummy. The high-heat crust took three minutes, and it was crisp with a chewy center. A cold skillet and high heat was the right combination. As for oven temperature, we knew that with pizza, the hotter, the better, so we cranked the oven up to 500 degrees.

The crust was ready for toppings, but we weren't sure when to add them. Should they go on just before the pizza went into the oven or before the dough was cooked on the stovetop? We tested both methods, and found no difference between the two pizzas. For simplicity's sake, we decided to top the pizza before placing it on the stovetop.

Next, we tested cooked and no-cook pizza sauce. Much to our delight—since we are always in favor of simplifying—the no-cook pizza sauce was favored by tasters. This sauce was a simple mix of canned whole tomatoes, olive oil, garlic, and salt that we pureed in the food processor. For the cheese, we used traditional shredded mozzarella, with a sprinkling of fresh grated Parmesan for a nice saltiness.

Realizing that a pound of pizza dough was a bit much for one 11-inch pizza, we decided to cut the dough in half and make two pizzas. We divided the dough at the beginning and set half aside, building and baking one pizza. When the first one was done and the skillet had cooled for a few minutes, we simply wiped the skillet clean and started with the second ball of pizza dough.

For those nights when we want something more festive than cheese pizza, we came up with a few variations. In our first one, we replaced the mozzarella with fontina cheese, then topped the fully cooked pizzas with arugula and prosciutto, which add nice textural and heat-level variations. For a snazzy vegetarian option, we made a pizza with goat cheese, olives, and spicy garlic oil. Saving the best for last, we created a pizza with ricotta, bacon, and scallions—tasters couldn't get enough of this addictive combination. For even more variety, we've included a whole wheat spin on our basic pizza dough.

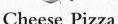

Cheese Pizza

MAKES TWO 11-INCH PIZZAS, SERVES 4

We like to use our Basic Skillet Pizza Dough (page 220) and No-Cook Pizza Sauce (page 222); however, you can substitute premade pizza dough or sauce (or both) from the supermarket. Feel free to sprinkle simple toppings over the pizza before baking, such as pepperoni, sautéed mushrooms, or browned sausage, but keep the toppings light or they may weigh down the thin crust and make it soggy.

¼	cup olive oil
1	pound pizza dough (see note)
1	cup pizza sauce (see note)
6	ounces mozzarella cheese, shredded (1½ cups)
½	ounce grated Parmesan cheese (¼ cup)

1. Adjust an oven rack to the upper-middle position and heat the oven to 500 degrees. Grease a 12-inch ovenproof skillet with 2 tablespoons of the oil.

2. Turn the dough out onto a lightly floured work surface, divide it into 2 equal pieces, and cover

EQUIPMENT: Pizza Cutter

A shoddy pizza cutter drags melted cheese out of place and fails to cut through crisp crust cleanly. A good pizza cutter gets the job done quickly, neatly, and safely (and also makes an excellent tool for trimming the edges of rolled-out pastry dough).

The basic wheel cutter is the most common variety, and we tested eight of them to find the best one. While all of them cut through thin-crust pizza without a problem, only a few could cleanly slice through deep-dish pies loaded with cheese and toppings. Our favorite pizza wheel is the OXO Good Grips 4-Inch Pizza Wheel. It has a large wheel that keeps our hands grease-free and features a comfortable rubber handle and angled neck for easy cutting.

THE BEST PIZZA CUTTER
The OXO Good Grips 4-Inch Pizza Wheel ($9.95) cuts through extra cheese easily and comfortably.

OXO

with greased plastic wrap. Working with 1 piece of dough at a time (keep the other piece covered), press and roll the dough into an 11-inch round on a lightly floured work surface. Transfer the dough to the prepared skillet.

3. Spread ½ cup of the pizza sauce over the dough, leaving a ½-inch border around the edge. Sprinkle ¾ cup of the mozzarella and 2 tablespoons of the Parmesan over the top. Set the skillet over high heat and cook until the outside edge of the dough is set, the pizza is lightly puffed, and the bottom crust is spotty brown when gently lifted with a spatula, about 3 minutes.

4. Transfer the pizza to the oven and bake until the edges are brown and the cheese is golden in spots, 7 to 10 minutes. Using pot holders (the skillet handle will be hot), transfer the pizza to a carving board, slice into wedges, and serve.

5. Wipe the skillet clean, let it cool slightly, then repeat with the remaining 2 tablespoons oil, remaining dough, remaining ½ cup pizza sauce, remaining ¾ cup mozzarella, and remaining 2 tablespoons Parmesan to make a second pizza.

➤ VARIATIONS
Fontina, Arugula, and Prosciutto Pizza
Follow the recipe for Cheese Pizza, omitting the Parmesan and substituting 6 ounces fontina cheese, shredded (1½ cups), for the mozzarella. Immediately after baking, sprinkle 2 ounces thinly sliced prosciutto, cut into 1-inch strips, and 1 cup fresh arugula over the top of each pizza before serving (you will need 4 ounces prosciutto and 2 cups arugula for both pizzas).

Goat Cheese, Olive, and Spicy Garlic Oil Pizza
If your olives are particularly salty, be sure to rinse them.
Follow the recipe for Cheese Pizza, omitting the Parmesan. Mix 2 tablespoons olive oil, 1 medium clove garlic, minced or pressed through a garlic press (about 1 teaspoon), and ¼ teaspoon red pepper flakes together in a small bowl. Brush half of the garlic-oil mixture over the top of each

pizza before adding the sauce in step 3. Sprinkle 5 ounces goat cheese, crumbled (⅓ cup), and ¼ cup pitted kalamata olives, halved, on top of the mozzarella on each pizza before baking (you will need 10 ounces goat cheese and ½ cup olives for both pizzas).

Ricotta, Bacon, and Scallion Pizza
Cook 4 ounces (4 slices) bacon, cut into ¼-inch pieces, in a small skillet over medium heat until browned and most of the fat has rendered, about 10 minutes; transfer to a paper towel–lined plate. Mix 7 ounces whole milk ricotta cheese (⅔ cup), 2 thinly sliced scallions, ¼ teaspoon salt, and a pinch ground pepper together. Follow the recipe for Cheese Pizza, omitting the Parmesan. Dollop half of the ricotta mixture, a tablespoon at a time, on top of the mozzarella on each pizza, then sprinkle with half of the bacon. Sprinkle each pizza with 1 more sliced scallion before serving.

No-Cook Pizza Sauce
MAKES 1 CUP
We prefer the softer texture of canned whole peeled tomatoes here; however, diced canned tomatoes can be substituted in a pinch.

- 1 (14.5-ounce) can whole peeled tomatoes, drained with juices reserved
- 1 tablespoon extra-virgin olive oil
- 1 medium garlic clove, minced, or pressed through a garlic press (about 1 teaspoon)
- ¼ teaspoon salt

Pulse the drained tomatoes, oil, garlic, and salt together in a food processor until coarsely ground and no large pieces remain, about 12 pulses. Transfer the mixture to a liquid measuring cup and add the reserved canned tomato juice until the sauce measures 1 cup.

6

STIR-FRIES AND CURRIES

STIR-FRIES AND CURRIES

THE STIR-FRIES OF ASIA AND THE CURRIES of both India and Thailand are their cultures' cornerstone dishes, and while they offer strikingly different flavors, all three share a similar foundation. In stir-fries, meat and vegetables are quickly seared in stages, then tossed with a simple yet flavorful sauce, and it is all done in a single piece of cookware. Curries, a broad term that literally means "sauce," are similarly efficient and use only one pot, in this case to simmer meat and/or vegetables in a highly spiced gravy.

The wok, the cookware traditionally used for stir-frying, and India's similarly broad, sloped pan called a *karahi* both rely on a similar technique—rapid, even heat transforms individual ingredients into a dish with unified flavor. This heat, combined with a combination of intense aromatics and spices, is how maximum flavor is drawn out. These dishes' efficiency and unique flavors make them attractive options for the American home cook, but to prepare them correctly, some adaptation must be done first.

Though woks and karahis may be the best choice for their respective country's kitchens, to re-create these dishes in an American home, we don't recommend you go wok shopping or seek out your local karahi vendor. Over a traditional pit-style Asian stove, a wok gets incredibly hot because these stoves have a recession that fits the curved piece of cookware perfectly, surrounding the pan in heat and letting little escape. American stoves, as we all know, are flat—even if one uses a "wok ring," which mimics the shape of a pit, the wok won't get appropriately hot. Karahis and other flat-bottomed woks are more stable and slightly better suited to a Western stove, but they are still not ideal. For our country's flat stoves, your best choice is our own kitchen workhorse: the skillet.

On Western stoves, the skillet successfully mimics the effects of the wok and karahi. Its large, flat surface maximizes direct contact with the heat source, so you get the largest and most even cooking surface possible. The direct contact with high heat ensures that for stir-fries, the meat and vegetables sear properly, rather than steam as they would at lower temperatures. When making curries, uniform heat is important for developing the flavor of the sauce. The skillet transforms the raw ingredients of a Thai curry's paste, the dish's core element that is heavy on aromatics (and lighter on dried spices than Indian curries), into a surprisingly rounded whole—the harmonious balance of bold flavors that is the hallmark of Thai cooking. For Indian curries, a hot skillet with a little oil allows us to "bloom" the spices, the trick that is key for getting the deep, explosive flavors Indian dishes are known for.

Keep in mind the tricks and tips we share here and you will have no problem creating quick, flavorful curries and stir-fries any night of the week.

STIR-FRIES

A STIR-FRY IS AN IDEAL QUICK-AND-EASY weeknight meal—both protein and vegetables, cut into small pieces, are cooked quickly over high heat, then tossed together with a flavorful sauce and served over rice. There is nothing overly complicated about stir-fries; the key is plenty of intense heat. The pan must be hot enough to caramelize sugars, deepen flavors, and evaporate unnecessary juices all in a matter of minutes. And with everything happening so quickly, it is critical to determine a process and get organized ahead of time. Because the heat is key, naturally the piece of cookware you use is critical to success. We recommend a large skillet, one that is 12 inches in diameter to maximize your heating surface, with a nonstick coating.

Most stir-fries start with some sort of protein—lean cuts of beef or pork (we generally prefer flank steak and pork tenderloin), chicken breasts, shrimp, or tofu. We found that freezing beef, chicken, or pork for at least 15 minutes made it easier to cut the meat into wide, flat slices that would cook quickly and brown nicely. For both the meat and shrimp, we determined that a simple yet flavorful marinade (we like a combination of soy sauce and Chinese rice cooking wine) was all that was necessary to give these ingredients another dimension without overwhelming the whole.

225

Because chicken tends to dry out when stir-fried, traditional recipes call for a technique called velveting to lock in moisture and create a golden crust. Velveting involves coating the chicken in a thin mixture of cornstarch and egg white or oil, then parcooking before stir-frying. We found we could get similar results by simply adding cornstarch, sesame oil, and a little flour right into our marinade, and we employed this trick in several recipes.

We also learned a good trick for prepping tofu that lent texture in the final dish. Cornstarch was again a key player; a quick coating ensured that the tofu would form a crispy crust. In fact, we skipped a wet marinade entirely when using this technique. Doing so kept things simple and the results pleased even the staunchest of tofu skeptics.

Next, we considered the cooking process, which we knew would be fairly universal no matter the protein. We cooked the meat, shrimp, or tofu over high heat in two batches. By adding just a small volume of food at a time, we were able to maintain the intense heat in the pan. We browned one side without stirring, then stirred once to quickly brown the second side. (Of course, cubed tofu was the exception, requiring a few extra flips to brown all sides.) Although choosing not to "stir-fry" seems counterintuitive and goes against the constant stirring suggested in many recipes, we found the continuous motion detracted from the browning.

After the protein was cooked, we removed it from the pan and added the vegetables in batches. To cook very tough vegetables that won't soften even after several minutes of stir-frying, we steamed them by adding a bit of water to the pan and covering with a lid; once the vegetables were crisp-tender, the cover came off so excess water could evaporate. This method works especially well with broccoli and green beans. Slow-cooking vegetables, such as onions and mushrooms, should go into the pan next, followed shortly after by quicker-cooking items such as celery and snow peas. Leafy greens and herbs should go in last. We found the combinations of vegetables to be limitless, from broccoli and red bell peppers to green beans and shiitake mushrooms. We even discovered the more exotic pairing of kimchi (a traditional Korean dish of pickled, fermented vegetables) and bean sprouts. Once you become comfortable with the techniques of stir-frying and learn how long each vegetable takes to cook, you can mix and match most any combination to your liking.

Most stir-fry recipes add the aromatics (typically garlic, ginger, and scallions) at the outset of the cooking process, when the pan is empty. But in batch after batch, by the time the stir-fry was done our aromatics had burnt and become harsh-tasting. We found we could avoid this problem by cooking the aromatics after the vegetables. When the vegetables were done, we pushed them to the sides of the pan, added the aromatics and some oil to the center, and cooked until they were fragrant but not colored, about 20 seconds. We then stirred the aromatics into the vegetables.

At this point, we were close to finished. We had only one final component: the sauce. We found that chicken broth (or orange or tangerine juice when appropriate—particularly good for sauces to be paired with shrimp stir-fries) makes the best base because it is not overpowering. Soy, hoisin, oyster, and black bean sauces, as well as sesame oil, are all excellent flavor enhancers, and we discovered various combinations that worked well. We involved as few ingredients as possible; keeping the sauce simple is not only easier for the cook but allows the vegetables and protein to take center stage.

While determining options for flavoring the sauce was fairly easy, the sauce consistency needed adjustment. Many of our stir-fry sauces were turning out too thin and would not adhere properly to the solids. Once again, cornstarch came into play. Adding a little bit to these sauces, adjusting the amount depending on the viscosity of the other ingredients, helped them to coat the meat and vegetables.

Our components and process were set: We made the sauce, cooked the protein, then the vegetables and aromatics, added the protein and sauce to the pan, and finally cooked the whole dish just until the sauce thickened, which took all of about 30 seconds. Incredibly quick and simple, any of these stir-fries makes a complete meal when served with Simple White Rice (page 228).

Stir-Fried Beef and Broccoli with Classic Stir-Fry Sauce

SERVES 4

To make slicing the steak easier, freeze it for 15 minutes first. Feel free to use 1 pound of broccoli florets and omit the stems if desired.

1	pound flank steak, trimmed and sliced thin across the grain on the bias (see the illustrations on page 228)
2	teaspoons soy sauce
2	teaspoons Chinese rice cooking wine or dry sherry
6	medium garlic cloves, minced or pressed through a garlic press (about 2 tablespoons)
1	tablespoon minced or grated fresh ginger (see the illustrations at right)
2	scallions, minced
2	tablespoons plus 1 teaspoon vegetable oil
1	medium bunch broccoli (about 1¼ pounds), florets and stems separated, florets cut into bite-sized pieces, stems trimmed, peeled, and sliced ⅛ inch thick on the bias (see the illustrations on page 284)
⅓	cup water
1	small red bell pepper, stemmed, seeded, and sliced into ¼-inch-wide strips
1	recipe Classic Stir-Fry Sauce (page 238)

1. Toss the beef with the soy sauce and rice wine in a medium bowl and let marinate for at least 10 minutes, or up to 1 hour. In a separate bowl, mix the garlic, ginger, scallions, and 1 teaspoon of the oil together.

2. Heat 1½ teaspoons more oil in a 12-inch nonstick skillet over high heat until just smoking. Add half of the beef, break up any clumps, and cook without stirring until the meat is browned at the edges, about 1 minute. Stir the meat and continue to cook until it is nearly cooked through, about 1 minute longer. Transfer the beef to a medium bowl and repeat with 1½ teaspoons more oil and the remaining beef; transfer to the bowl and cover to keep warm.

3. Add the remaining tablespoon oil to the skillet and heat over medium-high heat until shimmering. Add the broccoli florets, broccoli stems, and water,

cover, and steam until the broccoli is bright green and beginning to soften, about 2 minutes. Uncover and allow the water to evaporate, 30 to 60 seconds. Add the bell pepper and continue to cook until the vegetables are crisp-tender, about 2 minutes.

4. Clear the center of the skillet, add the garlic mixture, and cook, mashing the mixture into the pan, until fragrant, 15 to 30 seconds. Stir the garlic mixture into the vegetables.

5. Return the beef, along with any accumulated juices, to the skillet. Whisk the sauce to recombine, then add to the skillet and cook, tossing constantly, until the sauce is thickened, about 30 seconds. Transfer to a platter and serve.

PREPARING GINGER

You can prepare ginger for the recipes in this chapter in one of two ways: mincing or grating.

1a. To mince, slice the peeled knob of ginger into thin rounds using a sharp knife. Then fan the rounds out and cut them into thin, matchstick-like strips.

1b. Chop the matchsticks crosswise into a fine mince.

2. To grate, peel a small section of a large piece of ginger. Using the small holes of a box grater, grate the peeled portion, using the rest of the ginger as a handle to keep fingers safely away from the grater.

Stir-Frying 101

Stir-fries are naturally quick cooking. The key is to have all your meat and vegetables prepped before you begin cooking. They should be cut into even pieces so they all cook at the same rate.

SLICING MEAT FOR STIR-FRIES

It is better to take five minutes and cut up your own meat rather than to buy packages labeled "for stir-fry," since this can be any type or cut of meat, merely cut into small pieces. The right type of meat makes all the difference between tender bites and pieces that resemble shoe leather. To make it easier to cut meat thin, place it in the freezer for 15 minutes.

BEEF

We like to use flank steak because is easy to find, relatively lean, and has a big beefy flavor that can stand up to the potent flavors in a stir-fry.

1. Place the partially frozen steak on a clean, dry work surface. Using a sharp chef's knife, slice the steak lengthwise into 2-inch-wide pieces..

2. Cut each 2-inch piece of flank steak across the grain into very thin slices.

PORK

Although some stir-fry recipes call for ground pork or thinly sliced boneless chops, we find that strips cut from a pork tenderloin are the most tender and flavorful option.

1. Place the partially frozen pork tenderloin on a clean, dry work surface. Using a sharp chef's knife, slice the pork crosswise into ¼-inch-thick medallions.

2. Slice each medallion into ¼-inch-wide strips.

CHICKEN

Boneless, skinless breasts work best for stir-fries and are easy to cut into ½-inch-wide strips. In the world of stir-frying, chicken requires a fairly long time to cook through and brown slightly—at least three or four minutes.

1. To produce uniform pieces of chicken, separate the tenderloins from the partially frozen boneless, skinless breasts.

2. Slice the breasts across the grain into ½-inch-wide strips that are 1½ to 2 inches long. Center pieces need to be cut in half so they are approximately the same length as the end pieces.

3. Cut tenderloins on the diagonal to produce pieces about the same size as the strips of breast meat.

SIMPLE WHITE RICE
MAKES ABOUT 5 CUPS

To rinse the rice, you can either place it in a fine-mesh strainer and rinse under cool water or place it in a medium bowl and repeatedly fill the bowl with water while swishing the rice around, then carefully drain off the water.

2	cups long-grain or medium-grain white rice, rinsed
2½	cups water

1. Bring the rice and water to a boil in a large saucepan, then cover, reduce the heat to low, and cook until the water is just absorbed and there are small holes in the surface of the rice, about 10 minutes.

2. Remove the pot from the heat and let stand, covered, until the rice is tender, about 15 minutes longer. Serve.

STIR-FRYING STEP BY STEP

Here are the four key steps to making a stir-fry. (Be sure to use a 12-inch nonstick skillet and cook over high heat.)

1. Start by cooking the protein, but don't cook it through completely; instead, remove it from the pan when it is just shy of being done and cover with foil to keep warm. It will finish cooking with the sauce at the end.

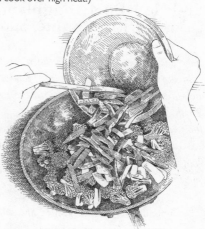

2. Next, cook the vegetables in batches, adding the tougher vegetables first and the more delicate vegetables later. This ensures that each vegetable will be perfectly cooked.

3. Push the vegetables to the edges of the skillet, clearing a spot in the middle. Add the garlic, ginger, and a little oil to the cleared spot and cook, mashing them into the hot pan using a wooden spoon until they are fragrant, about 30 seconds.

4. Return the cooked protein to the skillet, add the sauce, and toss to combine. Continue to cook until the sauce has thickened and the meat (if using) is fully cooked, 1 to 2 minutes.

ESSENTIAL TOOLS FOR STIR-FRYING SUCCESS

Stir-frying requires only a couple of pieces of basic equipment (you probably already own them). Woks are the traditional cooking vessel for stir-frying in China. Conically shaped, woks rest in cylindrical pits containing the fire. Flames lick the bottom and sides of the pan so that food cooks remarkably quickly. A wok, however, is not designed for stovetop cooking, where heat only comes from the bottom. Therefore, we prefer a 12-inch nonstick skillet for stir-frying. This pan requires a minimum of oil and prevents food from burning onto the surface as it stir-fries. We tested major brands of nonstick skillets (see page 14) and particularly liked pans that were sturdy, but not overly heavy, with a good nonstick performance.

Our second choice for stir-frying is a regular 12-inch traditional skillet. Without the nonstick coating, you will need to use slightly more oil. However, this pan will deliver satisfactory results. If you do not own a large skillet of any kind, do not substitute a smaller size. A 10-inch skillet is not large enough to accommodate all the ingredients in a stir-fry recipe for four. The ingredients will steam rather than stir-fry.

Chinese cooks use long-handled metal shovel-like spatulas to move food around woks. The same tool works well in a nonstick skillet, although to protect the pan's surface, you should use only plastic or wooden implements. We prefer a large shovel with a wide, thin blade and long, heat-resistant handle.

Stir-Fried Beef, Eggplant, and Basil with Sesame Sauce

SERVES 4

To make slicing the steak easier, freeze it for 15 minutes first. Small, firm eggplants, sometimes labeled Asian or Japanese eggplants, work great in stir-fries if you can find them. Substitute 2 of these smaller eggplants (about 8 ounces each), trimmed, cut in half lengthwise, and sliced crosswise into ½-inch-thick half-moons, for the regular eggplant and reduce the cooking time to about 3 minutes in step 3.

1	pound flank steak, trimmed and sliced thin across the grain on the bias (see the illustrations on page 228)
2	teaspoons soy sauce
2	teaspoons Chinese rice cooking wine or dry sherry
3	medium garlic cloves, minced or pressed through a garlic press (about 1 tablespoon)
1	tablespoon minced or grated fresh ginger (see the illustrations on page 227)
2	scallions, minced
2	tablespoons plus 1 teaspoon vegetable oil
1	medium eggplant (about 1 pound), peeled and cut into ¾-inch cubes
1	recipe Sesame Stir-Fry Sauce (page 239)
2	cups whole basil leaves
1	lime, cut into wedges, for serving

1. Toss the beef with the soy sauce and rice wine in a medium bowl and let marinate for at least 10 minutes, or up to 1 hour. In a separate bowl, mix the garlic, ginger, scallions, and 1 teaspoon of the oil together.

2. Heat 1½ teaspoons more oil in a 12-inch nonstick skillet over high heat until just smoking. Add half of the beef, break up any clumps, and cook without stirring until the meat is browned at the edges, about 1 minute. Stir the meat and continue to cook until it is nearly cooked through, about 1 minute longer. Transfer the beef to a medium bowl and repeat with 1½ teaspoons more oil and the remaining beef; transfer to the bowl and cover to keep warm.

3. Add the remaining tablespoon oil to the skillet and heat over high heat until shimmering. Add the eggplant and cook until beginning to brown and no longer spongy, about 4 minutes.

4. Clear the center of the skillet, add the garlic mixture, and cook, mashing the mixture into the pan, until fragrant, 15 to 30 seconds. Stir the garlic mixture into the eggplant.

5. Return the cooked beef, with any accumulated juices, to the skillet. Whisk the sauce to recombine, then add to the skillet with the basil leaves. Cook, tossing constantly, until the sauce is thickened, about 30 seconds. Transfer to a platter and serve with the lime wedges.

Stir-Fried Pork, Kimchi, and Bean Sprouts with Mild Sauce

SERVES 4

Kimchi is a spicy Korean pickled vegetable dish and commonly contains napa cabbage, scallions, garlic, and ground chiles in brine; you can find it in the refrigerated section at the supermarket. To make slicing the pork easier, freeze it for 15 minutes first.

1	pound pork tenderloin (about 1 medium tenderloin), trimmed and sliced into thin strips (see the illustrations on page 228)
2	teaspoons soy sauce
2	teaspoons Chinese rice cooking wine or dry sherry
3	medium garlic cloves, minced or pressed through a garlic press (about 1 tablespoon)
1	tablespoon minced or grated fresh ginger (see the illustrations on page 227)
2	tablespoons plus 1 teaspoon vegetable oil
1	cup kimchi, drained thoroughly (see note)
5	scallions, white and green parts separated, sliced on the bias into 1-inch lengths (see the illustration on page 231)
4	ounces mung bean sprouts (about 2 cups)
1	recipe Mild Stir-Fry Sauce (page 238)

1. Toss the pork with the soy sauce and rice wine in a medium bowl and let marinate for at least 10 minutes, or up to 1 hour. In a separate bowl, mix the garlic, ginger, and 1 teaspoon of the oil together.

2. Heat 1½ teaspoons more oil in a 12-inch nonstick skillet over high heat until just smoking. Add half of the pork, break up any clumps, and cook without stirring until the meat is browned at the edges, about 1 minute. Stir the meat and continue to cook until it is nearly cooked through, about 1 minute longer. Transfer the pork to a medium bowl and repeat with 1½ teaspoons more oil and the remaining pork; transfer to the bowl and cover to keep warm.

3. Add the remaining tablespoon oil to the skillet and heat over medium-high heat until shimmering. Add the kimchi and scallion whites and cook until the vegetables are softened, 2 to 3 minutes. Stir in the bean sprouts.

4. Clear the center of the skillet, add the garlic mixture, and cook, mashing the mixture into the pan, until fragrant, 15 to 30 seconds. Stir the garlic mixture into the vegetables.

5. Return the pork, along with any accumulated juices, to the skillet. Whisk the sauce to recombine, then add to the skillet with the scallion greens. Cook, tossing constantly, until the sauce is thickened, about 30 seconds. Transfer to a platter and serve.

Stir-Fried Pork, Scallions, and Bell Peppers with Classic Stir-Fry Sauce

SERVES 4

To make slicing the pork easier, freeze it for 15 minutes first. The scallions are used as a vegetable in this stir-fry, rather than simply as a garnish; you will need about 12 ounces (2 to 4 bunches) of scallions.

1	pound pork tenderloin (about 1 medium tenderloin), trimmed and sliced into thin strips (see the illustrations on page 228)
2	teaspoons soy sauce
2	teaspoons Chinese rice cooking wine or dry sherry
6	medium garlic cloves, minced or pressed through a garlic press (about 2 tablespoons)
1	tablespoon minced or grated fresh ginger (see the illustrations on page 227)
⅛	teaspoon red pepper flakes
2	tablespoons plus 1 teaspoon vegetable oil

12	scallions, white and green parts separated, sliced on the bias into 1-inch lengths (see the illustration below)
2	medium red bell peppers, stemmed, seeded, and sliced into ¼-inch-wide strips
1	recipe Classic Stir-Fry Sauce (page 238)

1. Toss the pork with the soy sauce and rice wine in a medium bowl and let marinate for at least 10 minutes, or up to 1 hour. In a separate bowl, mix the garlic, ginger, red pepper flakes and 1 teaspoon of the oil together.

2. Heat 1½ teaspoons more oil in a 12-inch nonstick skillet over high heat until just smoking. Add half of the pork, break up any clumps, and cook without stirring until the meat is browned at the edges, about 1 minute. Stir the meat and continue to cook until it is nearly cooked through, about 1 minute longer. Transfer the pork to a medium bowl and repeat with 1½ teaspoons more oil and the remaining pork; transfer to the bowl and cover to keep warm.

3. Add the remaining tablespoon oil to the skillet and heat over medium-high heat until shimmering. Add the scallion whites and cook until beginning to soften, about 1 minute. Add the bell peppers and cook, stirring occasionally, until crisp-tender, 2 to 3 minutes.

4. Clear the center of the skillet, add the garlic mixture, and cook, mashing the mixture into the pan, until fragrant, 15 to 30 seconds. Stir the garlic mixture into the vegetables.

5. Return the pork, along with any accumulated juices, to the skillet. Whisk the sauce to recombine,

SLICING SCALLIONS ON THE BIAS

Slicing the scallions on the bias makes for an attractive presentation. Simply hold the scallion at an angle, then slice the scallion thin.

then add to the skillet with the scallion greens. Cook, tossing constantly, until the sauce is thickened, about 30 seconds. Transfer to a platter and serve.

Stir-Fried Chicken and Bok Choy with Teriyaki Sauce
SERVES 4

To make slicing the chicken easier, freeze it for 15 minutes first. Washing the bok choy after prepping it is the best way to completely remove all the dirt and sand.

- 1   pound boneless, skinless chicken breasts (about 3 medium), trimmed and sliced thin (see the illustrations on pages 6 and 228)
- 2   tablespoons toasted sesame oil
- 1   tablespoon cornstarch
- 1   tablespoon unbleached all-purpose flour
- 2   teaspoons soy sauce
- 2   teaspoons Chinese rice cooking wine or dry sherry
- 3   medium garlic cloves, minced or pressed through a garlic press (about 1 tablespoon)
- 1   tablespoon minced or grated fresh ginger (see the illustrations on page 227)
- 2   scallions, minced
- 2   tablespoons plus 1 teaspoon vegetable oil
- 1   small head bok choy (about 1 pound), stalks and greens separated, stalks sliced crosswise into ¼-inch-wide pieces and greens cut into ½-inch-wide strips (see the illustrations at right)
- 1   recipe Teriyaki Stir-Fry Sauce (page 238)

1. Toss the chicken with the sesame oil, cornstarch, flour, soy sauce, and rice wine in a medium bowl and marinate for at least 10 minutes, or up to 1 hour. In a separate bowl, mix the garlic, ginger, scallions, and 1 teaspoon of the vegetable oil together.

2. Heat 1½ teaspoons more vegetable oil in a 12-inch nonstick skillet over high heat until just smoking. Add half of the chicken, break up any clumps, and cook without stirring until the chicken is browned at the edges, about 3 minutes. Stir the chicken and continue to cook until the chicken is cooked through, about 3 minutes longer. Transfer the chicken to a medium bowl and repeat with 1½ tea-

PREPARING BOK CHOY

1. Trim the bottom inch from the head of bok choy. Cut the leafy green portion away from either side of the white stalk.

2. Cut each stalk in half lengthwise and then crosswise into ¼-inch-wide pieces.

3. Stack the leafy greens and then slice them crosswise into ½-inch-wide strips.

spoons more vegetable oil and the remaining chicken; transfer to the bowl and cover to keep warm.

3. Add the remaining tablespoon vegetable oil to the skillet and heat over medium-high heat until shimmering. Add the bok choy stalks and cook until beginning to soften, 1 to 2 minutes. Clear the center of the skillet, add the garlic mixture and cook, mashing the mixture into the pan, until fragrant, 15 to 30 seconds. Stir the garlic mixture into the bok choy.

4. Return the chicken, along with any accumulated juices, to the skillet. Whisk the sauce to recombine, then add to the skillet with the bok choy greens. Cook, tossing constantly, until the sauce is thickened, about 30 seconds. Transfer to a platter and serve.

Stir-Fried Chicken, Pineapple, and Red Onion with Sweet and Sour Sauce

SERVES 4

To make slicing the chicken easier, freeze it for 15 minutes first. If necessary, you can substitute one 20-ounce can of pineapple chunks, drained, for the fresh pineapple.

1	pound boneless, skinless chicken breasts (about 3 medium), trimmed and sliced thin (see the illustrations on pages 6 and 228)
2	tablespoons toasted sesame oil
1	tablespoon cornstarch
1	tablespoon unbleached all-purpose flour
2	teaspoons soy sauce
2	teaspoons Chinese rice cooking wine or dry sherry
3	medium garlic cloves, minced or pressed through a garlic press (about 1 tablespoon)
1	tablespoon minced or grated fresh ginger (see the illustrations on page 227)
2	scallions, minced
2	tablespoons plus 1 teaspoon vegetable oil
1	large red onion, halved and sliced ½ inch thick
½	medium pineapple, peeled, cored, and cut into 1-inch chunks (about 2 cups)
1	recipe Sweet and Sour Stir-Fry Sauce (page 239)

1. Toss the chicken with the sesame oil, cornstarch, flour, soy sauce, and rice wine in a medium bowl and let marinate for 10 minutes, or up to 1 hour. In a separate bowl, mix the garlic, ginger, scallions, and 1 teaspoon of the vegetable oil together.

2. Heat 1½ teaspoons more vegetable oil in a 12-inch nonstick skillet over high heat until just smoking. Add half of the chicken, break up any clumps, and cook without stirring until the chicken is browned at the edges, about 3 minutes. Stir the chicken and continue to cook until the chicken is cooked through, about 3 minutes longer. Transfer the chicken to a medium bowl and repeat with 1½ teaspoons more vegetable oil and the remaining chicken; transfer to the bowl and cover to keep warm.

3. Add the remaining tablespoon vegetable oil to the skillet and heat over medium-high heat until shimmering. Add the onion and cook, stirring occasionally, until lightly browned, about 3 minutes. Add the pineapple and cook until heated through, about 1 minute.

4. Clear the center of the skillet, add the garlic mixture, and cook, mashing the mixture into the pan, until fragrant, 15 to 30 seconds. Stir the garlic mixture into the vegetables.

5. Return the chicken, along with any accumulated juices, to the skillet. Whisk the sauce to recombine, then add to the skillet and cook, tossing constantly, until the sauce is thickened, about 30 seconds. Transfer to a platter and serve.

Stir-Fried Shrimp, Asparagus, and Carrots with Tangerine Sauce

SERVES 4

If the asparagus spears are very thick, slice them in half lengthwise before cutting them into 2-inch lengths.

1	pound extra-large shrimp (21 to 25 per pound), peeled and deveined (see the illustration on page 235)
2	teaspoons soy sauce
2	teaspoons Chinese rice cooking wine or dry sherry
3	medium garlic cloves, minced or pressed through a garlic press (about 1 tablespoon)
1	tablespoon minced or grated fresh ginger (see the illustrations on page 227)
2	scallions, minced
2	tablespoons plus 1 teaspoon vegetable oil
1	pound asparagus (about 1 bunch), tough ends trimmed (see the illustration on page 92) and sliced on the bias into 2-inch lengths
2	carrots, peeled and cut into 2-inch-long matchsticks (see the illustrations on page 234)
1	recipe Tangerine Stir-Fry Sauce (page 239)

1. Toss the shrimp with the soy sauce and rice wine in a medium bowl and let marinate for at least

10 minutes, or up to 1 hour. In a separate bowl, mix the garlic, ginger, scallions, and 1 teaspoon of the oil together.

2. Heat 1½ teaspoons more oil in a 12-inch non-stick skillet over high heat until just smoking. Add half of the shrimp and cook, without stirring, until the shrimp are browned at the edges, about 1 minute. Stir the shrimp and continue to cook until they are nearly cooked through, about 30 seconds longer. Transfer the shrimp to a medium bowl and repeat with 1½ teaspoons more oil and the remaining shrimp; transfer to the bowl and cover to keep warm.

3. Add the remaining tablespoon oil to the skillet and heat over medium-high heat until shimmering. Add the asparagus and carrots and cook until crisp-tender, 3 to 4 minutes.

4. Clear the center of the skillet, add the garlic mixture, and cook, mashing the mixture into the pan, until fragrant, 15 to 30 seconds. Stir the garlic mixture into the vegetables.

5. Return the shrimp, along with any accumulated juices, to the skillet. Whisk the sauce to recombine, then add it to the skillet and cook, tossing constantly, until the sauce has thickened, about 30 seconds. Transfer to a platter and serve.

CUTTING CARROTS INTO MATCHSTICKS

1. Start by slicing the carrot on the bias into rounds.

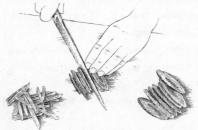

2. Fan the rounds and cut them into strips that measure about 2 inches long and ¼ inch thick.

Stir-Fried Shrimp, Snap Peas, and Bell Peppers with Sweet and Sour Sauce

SERVES 4

If using smaller or larger shrimp, the cooking times may vary accordingly.

1	pound extra-large shrimp (21 to 25 per pound), peeled and deveined (see the illustration on page 235)
2	teaspoons soy sauce
2	teaspoons Chinese rice cooking wine or dry sherry
3	medium garlic cloves, minced or pressed through a garlic press (about 1 tablespoon)
1	tablespoon minced or grated fresh ginger (see the illustrations on page 227)
2	scallions, minced
2	tablespoons plus 1 teaspoon vegetable oil
1	pound snap peas, stems and strings removed (see the illustration on page 236)
⅓	cup water
1	red bell pepper, stemmed, seeded, and sliced into ¼-inch-wide strips
1	recipe Sweet and Sour Stir-Fry Sauce (page 239)
2	tablespoons sesame seeds, toasted

1. Toss the shrimp with the soy sauce and rice wine in a medium bowl and let marinate for 10 minutes, or up to 1 hour. In a separate bowl, mix the garlic, ginger, scallions, and 1 teaspoon of the oil together.

2. Heat 1½ teaspoons more oil in a 12-inch nonstick skillet over high heat until just smoking. Add half of the shrimp and cook, without stirring, until the shrimp are browned at the edges, about 1 minute. Stir the shrimp and continue to cook until they are nearly cooked through, about 30 seconds longer. Transfer the shrimp to a medium bowl and repeat with 1½ teaspoons more oil and the remaining shrimp; transfer to the bowl and cover to keep warm.

3. Add the remaining tablespoon oil to the skillet and heat over medium-high heat until shimmering. Add the snap peas and water, cover, and steam until

DEVEINING SHRIMP

Hold the peeled shrimp between your thumb and forefinger and cut down the length of its back, about ⅛ to ¼ inch deep, with a sharp paring knife. If the shrimp has a vein, it will be exposed and can be pulled out easily. Once you have freed the vein with the tip of a paring knife, just touch the knife to a paper towel and the vein will slip off the knife and stick to the towel.

the peas are bright green and beginning to soften, about 2 minutes. Uncover and allow the water to evaporate, 30 to 60 seconds. Add the bell pepper and continue to cook until the vegetables are crisp-tender, about 2 minutes.

4. Clear the center of the skillet, add the garlic mixture, and cook, mashing the mixture into the pan, until fragrant, 15 to 30 seconds. Stir the garlic mixture into the vegetables.

5. Return the shrimp, along with any accumulated juices, to the skillet. Whisk the sauce to recombine, then add to the skillet and cook, tossing constantly, until the sauce is thickened, about 30 seconds. Transfer to a platter, sprinkle with sesame seeds, and serve.

Stir-Fried Tofu, Green Beans, and Shiitakes with Teriyaki Sauce

SERVES 4

Coat the tofu with cornstarch just before cooking, or the cornstarch coating will turn soggy as it sits and begin to clump.

- 3 medium garlic cloves, minced or pressed through a garlic press (about 1 tablespoon)
- 1 tablespoon minced or grated fresh ginger (see the illustrations on page 227)
- 2 scallions, minced
- 4 tablespoons plus 1 teaspoon vegetable oil
- ⅓ cup cornstarch
- 1 (14-ounce) block extra-firm tofu, patted dry and cut into 1-inch cubes
- 1 pound green beans, ends trimmed (see the illustration below) and cut on the bias into 1-inch pieces
- ⅓ cup water
- 8 ounces shiitake mushrooms, stems discarded, caps wiped clean and sliced ¼ inch thick
- 1 recipe Teriyaki Stir-Fry Sauce (page 238)

1. Mix the garlic, ginger, scallions, and 1 teaspoon of the oil together in a small bowl; set aside. Spread the cornstarch into a wide, shallow dish, then coat all sides of the tofu evenly with the cornstarch and transfer to a plate.

2. Heat 1½ tablespoons more oil in a 12-inch nonstick skillet over high heat until just smoking. Add half of the tofu and cook, turning every few minutes, until all sides are crisp and browned, about 8 minutes. Transfer the tofu to a medium bowl and repeat with 1½ tablespoons more oil and the remaining tofu; transfer to the bowl and cover to keep warm.

3. Add the remaining tablespoon oil to the skillet and heat over medium-high heat until shimmering. Add the green beans and water, cover, and steam until the beans are bright green and beginning to soften, about 2 minutes. Uncover and allow the water to evaporate, 30 to 60 seconds. Add the mushrooms and continue to cook until they are lightly browned, about 3 minutes.

TRIMMING ENDS FROM GREEN BEANS

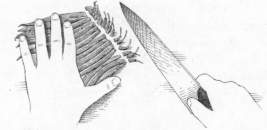

Instead of trimming the end from one green bean at a time, line up the beans on a cutting board and trim all the ends with just one slice.

4. Clear the center of the skillet, add the garlic mixture, and cook, mashing the mixture into the pan, until fragrant, 15 to 30 seconds. Stir the garlic mixture into the vegetables.

5. Return the tofu to the skillet. Whisk the sauce to recombine, then add to the skillet and cook, tossing constantly, until the sauce is thickened, about 30 seconds. Transfer to a platter and serve.

Stir-Fried Glazed Tofu, Snow Peas, and Cabbage with Sesame Sauce

SERVES 4

This recipe glazes the tofu in soy sauce, sugar, and vegetable broth for extra flavor. Low-sodium chicken broth can be substituted for the vegetable broth if desired.

¼   cup low-sodium vegetable broth

2   tablespoons soy sauce

2   tablespoons sugar

3   medium garlic cloves, minced or pressed through a garlic press (about 1 tablespoon)

1   tablespoon minced or grated fresh ginger (see the illustrations on page 227)

2   scallions, minced

4   tablespoons plus 1 teaspoon vegetable oil

⅓   cup cornstarch

1   (14-ounce) block extra-firm tofu, patted dry and cut into 1-inch cubes

1   pound green cabbage (about ½ medium head), cored and cut into 2-inch squares

⅓   cup water

1   cup snow peas, tips and strings removed (see the illustration at right)

1   recipe Sesame Stir-Fry Sauce (page 239)

1. Whisk the broth, soy sauce, and sugar together in a small bowl. In a separate bowl, mix the garlic, ginger, scallions, and 1 teaspoon of the oil together. Spread the cornstarch into a wide, shallow dish, then coat all sides of the tofu evenly with the cornstarch and transfer to a plate.

2. Heat 1½ tablespoons more oil in a 12-inch nonstick skillet over high heat until just smoking. Add half of the tofu and cook, turning every few minutes, until all sides are crisp and browned, about 8 minutes. Transfer the tofu to a medium bowl and repeat with 1½ tablespoons more oil and the remaining tofu. Return all of the tofu to the skillet, add the broth mixture, and cook until the tofu is nicely glazed, 1 to 2 minutes. Transfer the glazed tofu to a plate and cover to keep warm.

3. Wipe out the skillet with a wad of paper towels. Add the remaining tablespoon oil to the skillet and heat over medium-high heat until shimmering. Add the cabbage and water, cover, and steam until the cabbage is a beginning to soften and wilt, about 2 minutes. Uncover and allow the water to evaporate, 30 to 60 seconds. Add the snow peas and continue to cook until the vegetables are crisp-tender, about 45 seconds.

4. Clear the center of the skillet, add the garlic mixture, and cook, mashing the mixture into the pan, until fragrant, 15 to 30 seconds. Stir the garlic mixture into the vegetables.

5. Whisk the sauce to recombine, then add to the skillet and cook, tossing constantly, until the sauce is thickened, about 30 seconds. Return the glazed tofu to the skillet and toss to coat. Transfer to a platter and serve.

STRINGING SNOW PEAS AND SNAP PEAS

Snap off the tip of the snow pea or snap pea while pulling down along the flat side of the pod to remove the string.

Create-Your-Own Stir-Fry

SERVES 4

This recipe allows you to personalize your stir-fry. If using chicken, consider adding 1 tablespoon flour, 1 tablespoon cornstarch, and 2 tablespoons toasted sesame oil to the marinade in step 2 to give it a super-silky texture. If using tofu, consider substituting a dusting of cornstarch for the marinade in step 2, and cook it with a little extra oil to achieve a super-crisp crust.

1	pound beef flank steak, pork tenderloin, boneless skinless chicken breasts, extra-large shrimp (21 to 25 per pound), or 1 (14-ounce) block extra-firm tofu
2	teaspoons soy sauce
2	teaspoons Chinese rice cooking wine or dry sherry
3	garlic cloves, minced or pressed through a garlic press (about 1 tablespoon)
1	tablespoon minced or grated fresh ginger (see the illustrations on page 227)
2	scallions, minced
2	tablespoons plus 1 teaspoon vegetable oil
1½	pounds vegetables, cut into bite-sized pieces and divided into cooking groups following the Stir-Fry Vegetables chart below
⅓	cup water (optional, for very tough vegetables only)
1	recipe stir-fry sauce (pages 238–239)

1. If using beef, pork, or chicken, follow the illustrations on page 228 to trim the meat and slice it thin. If using shrimp, peel and devein them following the illustration on page 235. If using tofu, pat it dry and cut it into 1-inch cubes.

2. Toss the protein with the soy sauce and rice wine in a medium bowl and let marinate for at least 10 minutes, or up to 1 hour. (If using chicken or tofu, see the note above for alternate prep methods if desired.) In a separate bowl, mix the garlic, ginger, scallions, and 1 teaspoon of the oil together.

3. Heat 1½ teaspoons more oil in a 12-inch nonstick skillet over high heat until just smoking. Add half of the protein, break up any clumps, and cook, stirring occasionally until lightly browned on all sides, 1½ to 8 minutes. Transfer to a medium bowl and repeat with 1½ teaspoons more oil and the remaining protein; transfer to the bowl and cover to keep warm.

4. Add the remaining tablespoon oil to the skillet and heat over medium-high heat until shimmering. Add the tough vegetables and water (if using), cover, and steam until the vegetables are brightly colored and beginning to soften, about 2 minutes. Uncover and allow the water to evaporate, 30 to 60 seconds. Add the longer-cooking vegetables and cook, stirring occasionally, until crisp-tender, 1 to 3 minutes. Add the faster-cooking vegetables and cook until all of the vegetables are crisp-tender, 30 to 60 seconds.

5. Clear the center of the skillet, add the garlic mixture, and cook, mashing the mixture into the pan until fragrant, 15 to 30 seconds. Stir the garlic mixture into the vegetables.

STIR-FRY VEGETABLES

To ensure even cooking, cut each vegetable to make the pieces uniform in size, then stir-fry based on the chart below. For very tough vegetables, it is necessary to cook them in a covered skillet with some water (about ⅓ cup) to help them steam and soften.

VEGETABLE TYPE	COOKING TIME	VEGETABLE
TOUGH	3 to 7 minutes	Broccoli, Green Cabbage, Cauliflower, Green Beans, Snap Peas
LONGER-COOKING	1 to 4 minutes	Asparagus, Baby Corn, Bell Peppers, Bok Choy Stalks, Carrots, Frozen Shelled Edamame, Eggplant, Fennel, Kimchi, Mushrooms, Onions, Scallion Whites, Water Chestnuts
FASTER-COOKING	30 to 60 seconds	Bean Sprouts, Bok Choy Greens, Napa Cabbage, Celery, Scallion Greens, Frozen Peas, Snow Peas, Tender Greens, Tomatoes

6. Return the cooked protein, with any accumulated juices, to the skillet. Whisk the sauce to recombine, then add to the skillet and cook, tossing constantly, until the sauce is thickened, about 30 seconds. Transfer to a platter and serve.

Classic Stir-Fry Sauce

MAKES ENOUGH FOR I STIR-FRY RECIPE

This quintessential stir-fry sauce pairs well any combination of protein and vegetables.

½   cup low-sodium chicken broth
¼   cup Chinese rice cooking wine or dry sherry
3   tablespoons hoisin sauce or
     oyster-flavored sauce
I   tablespoon soy sauce
2   teaspoons cornstarch
I   teaspoon toasted sesame oil

Whisk all of the ingredients together in a medium bowl and use as directed in stir-fry recipes.

Mild Stir-Fry Sauce

MAKES ENOUGH FOR I STIR-FRY RECIPE

This simple, mild-flavored sauce is perfect for stir-fries with potent or uniquely flavored components, like the kimchi in the pork stir-fry on page 230.

¾   cup low-sodium chicken broth
3   tablespoons soy sauce
I   tablespoon sugar
2   teaspoons cornstarch
I   teaspoon toasted sesame oil

Whisk all of the ingredients together in a medium bowl and use as directed in stir-fry recipes.

INGREDIENTS: Hoisin Sauce

Hoisin sauce is a thick, reddish brown mixture of soybeans, sugar, vinegar, garlic, and chiles used in many classic Chinese dishes, so it is a natural ingredient for our Classic Stir-Fry Sauce (at left). Taste tests of six hoisin sauces indicated that no two brands of this staple condiment are identical; they vary dramatically, from gloppy and sweet, like plum sauce, to grainy and spicy, like Asian chili paste.

According to our tasters, the perfect hoisin sauce balances sweet, salty, pungent, and spicy elements so that no one flavor dominates. Kikkoman came closest to this ideal, with tasters praising its initial "burn" that mellowed into a harmonious blend of sweet and aromatic flavors. Two other brands also fared well in our tasting. Koon Chun was described as "fruity" (if a bit grainy), and Lee Kum Kee was deemed "plummy" but salty. Tasters were not impressed by the three remaining brands, Ka-Me, House of Tsang, or Sun Luck.

THE BEST HOISIN SAUCE

Kikkoman's Hoisin Sauce won praise for its balance of sweetness and salinity.

KIKKOMAN

Teriyaki Stir-Fry Sauce

MAKES ENOUGH FOR I STIR-FRY RECIPE

You can substitute 1 tablespoon white wine or sake mixed with 1 teaspoon sugar for the mirin. For a vegetarian stir-fry, such as the tofu stir-fry on page 236, substitute low-sodium vegetable broth for the chicken broth.

¾   cup low-sodium chicken broth
2   tablespoons soy sauce
2   tablespoons sugar
I   tablespoon mirin (see note)
2   teaspoons cornstarch
⅛   teaspoon red pepper flakes

Whisk all of the ingredients together in a medium bowl and use as directed in stir-fry recipes.

REMOVING LARGE STRIPS OF CITRUS ZEST

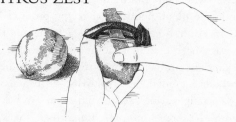

Run a vegetable peeler from pole to pole to remove long, wide strips of zest. Be sure to avoid the white, bitter-tasting pith that lies beneath the zest.

Tangerine Stir-Fry Sauce

MAKES ENOUGH FOR I STIR-FRY RECIPE

Orange juice can be used in place of the tangerine juice.

2   (2-inch-long) strips tangerine zest from
    I tangerine (see the illustration above)
¾   cup juice from 3 to 4 tangerines (see note)
2   tablespoons soy sauce
2   tablespoons Chinese black bean sauce
I   tablespoon sugar
I   teaspoon cornstarch
I   teaspoon toasted sesame oil
¼   teaspoon red pepper flakes

Whisk all of the ingredients together in a medium bowl and use as directed in stir-fry recipes.

Sweet and Sour Stir-Fry Sauce

MAKES ENOUGH FOR I STIR-FRY RECIPE

Pineapple juice can be used in place of the orange juice.

6   tablespoons red wine vinegar
6   tablespoons orange juice
6   tablespoons sugar
3   tablespoons ketchup

I   teaspoon cornstarch
½   teaspoon salt

Whisk all of the ingredients together in a medium bowl and use as directed in stir-fry recipes.

Sesame Stir-Fry Sauce

MAKES ENOUGH FOR I STIR-FRY RECIPE

Don't confuse Asian chili sauce with Asian chili-garlic paste, which has a stronger, spicier flavor (see below for more about Asian chili sauce). For a vegetarian stir-fry, such as the tofu stir-fry on page 236, substitute low-sodium vegetable broth for the chicken broth.

¾   cup low-sodium chicken broth
¼   cup soy sauce
2   tablespoons Chinese rice cooking wine
    or dry sherry
I   tablespoon cornstarch
I   tablespoon sugar
I   tablespoon sesame seeds, toasted
2   teaspoons toasted sesame oil
I   teaspoon Asian chili sauce

Whisk all of the ingredients together in a medium bowl and use as directed in stir-fry recipes.

INGREDIENTS: Asian Chili Sauce

Used both in cooking and as a condiment, this sauce comes in many different forms, each with varying degrees of heat. You'll find jars of chili sauce labeled "sambal oelek," "sriracha," and "chili garlic sauce" (not to be confused with chili garlic paste) in the international aisle of larger supermarkets. You can use them interchangeably whenever a recipe calls for Asian chili sauce—just remember, a little goes a long way with these fiery sauces. Consisting of chiles, sugar, vinegar, salt, and sometimes garlic, Asian chili sauce will keep indefinitely when refrigerated.

THAI CHILE BEEF

THE CUISINE OF THAILAND IS ONE THAT appeals to all the senses. Based on a sophisticated combination of four flavors—spicy, sweet, sour, and salty—it satisfies the palate in a way that no other foods can. Among the country's many well-known dishes, we were particularly captivated by Thai chile beef, a complex and unique dish, and we felt it would be a perfect addition to our assortment of stir-fry recipes. To our surprise, we found in our research that the dish is built on a foundation of just a few key ingredients: chiles, sugar, lime juice, and fish sauce. Creating our own skillet recipe seemed like a more than reasonable goal.

We set out with high hopes, rounding up and testing cookbook recipes and even ordering Thai chile beef from three neighborhood restaurants.

INGREDIENTS: Fish Sauce

Fish sauce, or *nam pla* or *nuoc cham*, is a salty amber-colored liquid made from salted, fermented fish. It is used both as an ingredient and a condiment in Southeast Asia. Used in very small amounts, it adds a well-rounded, salty flavor to sauces, soups, and marinades. We tasted six brands of fish sauce—one from Vietnam, one from the Philippines, and the rest from Thailand. Tasters had preferences among the sauces, but those preferences varied from taster to taster. With such a limited ingredient list—most of the brands contained some combination of fish extract, water, salt, and sugar—the differences among sauces were minimal. If you are a fan of fish sauce and plan to use it often, you might want to make a special trip to an Asian market to buy a rich, dark sauce, like Tiparos fish sauce, that is suitably pungent. Because most supermarkets don't carry a wide selection of fish sauce, we recommend buying whatever is available. That will most likely be Thai Kitchen, an Americanized brand found in most supermarkets, which was the lightest-colored (and flavored) brand we tasted.

THE BEST FISH SAUCES

Tiparos is a dark and pungent sauce, while Thai Kitchen has a milder flavor but is more widely available.

TIPAROS   THAI KITCHEN

The net result of all this tasting and testing, however, was disappointment—with one notable exception. One authentic Thai recipe produced a wonderful dish. It contained no vegetables and the meat was sauced in a thick, complex, well-balanced chile jam. The problem? For starters, the ingredient list, which included dried prawns, shrimp paste, tamarind pulp, galangal, and palm sugar. And then there was the three-hour prep time, which involved deep-frying many of the ingredients separately. We had tasted the ultimate Thai chile beef, but now we wanted to re-create it for an American home kitchen in a more approachable form.

We started with the centerpiece: the beef. Though we typically prefer to use flank steak in our stir-fry recipes, we decided to test a few other options since this dish would incorporate some unique, bold flavors. We stir-fried four easy-to-find cuts (filet, sirloin steak, strip steak, and blade steak) and compared them with our usual flank steak. As expected, the flank steak fared well. Mild filet, though the choice in several recipes, could not stand up to the assertive Thai flavors. Sirloin and strip steaks both fared poorly because stir-fried meats tend to end up thoroughly cooked, making these cuts chewy and dry. The cheapest cut of all, the blade steak, was the surprise winner of the tasting. Generally, beef with the biggest flavor is tough, but blade steak is an exception. Cut from the chuck—the forequarter of the animal—this inexpensive, well-marbled cut delivered more than enough flavor to stand up to its spicy coating.

Salty, fermented fish sauce is a traditional ingredient in Thai chile beef—it seasons and tenderizes the meat—so it played a key role in our marinade. Using fish sauce also simulated the briny flavors of the dried shrimp and shrimp paste listed in the original recipe, but something was still missing. We dug deeper into a few Thai cookbooks and discovered that white pepper is almost always included—and for good reason. It is deeply spicy and penetrating. We added a small amount to the marinade, along with some citrusy coriander. This was a huge hit with tasters and substantially boosted the complexity and sophistication of the dish, even though the meat was only marinated for 10 minutes.

We also added some of the sweet element in this dish to the marinade as a strategy for developing extra caramelization on the beef. Palm sugar is the traditional sweetener used in Thai cooking, but we found light brown sugar to be a perfectly acceptable substitute. A single teaspoon was just the right amount; any more caused scorching.

Thai chiles are the classic chile choice for this recipe, but they can be difficult to find. A taste test told us that moderately hot serranos or milder jalapeños are the best stand-ins. (Insanely hot habanero chiles were admired by some but panned by most, who found the heat level punishing.) Cooking shallots with our chiles added a balancing sweetness that tasters liked.

After settling on the type of chiles, a new problem emerged: wildly inconsistent heat levels. Even though we were using a constant number of jalapeños, some stir-fries were flaming hot, while others didn't even send up sparks. We came up with a straightforward solution that can be used in any recipe calling for chiles. The trick is to use not one but two sources of heat, one of which is easily controlled (by nature, fresh chiles vary in heat). We tested adding cayenne and hot red pepper flakes and both produced likeable results, but the winner was Asian chili sauce, which provided a complex mix of flavors—spicy, toasty, and garlicky. We decided it would serve us best in our sauce, the next item on our list.

The last step in a stir-fry is to deglaze the hot pan with sauce ingredients. After many trials, we realized the importance of reintroducing every member of the Thai quartet at this stage. Adding fish sauce and brown sugar to the marinade boosted flavor, but the inclusion of both in the sauce, along with the Asian chili sauce, really brought together the finished dish. For the sour component, both rice vinegar and tamarind paste fared better than lime juice since they are less acidic. We settled on rice vinegar since we usually keep it in our pantry.

The only remaining considerations were the fresh, raw ingredients added just before serving. Thai basil is traditional; it contributes freshness and a cooling counterpoint to the chiles. We also added chopped peanuts for crunch, and a squirt of fresh lime juice at the table was the final touch.

Thai Chile Beef

SERVES 4

If you cannot find blade steak, substitute 1¾ pounds of flank steak, trimmed and sliced thin across the grain on the bias (see the illustrations on page 228). To make slicing the steak easier, freeze it for 15 minutes first. If you can't find Thai basil leaves, substitute regular basil.

SAUCE

2 tablespoons fish sauce
2 tablespoons rice vinegar
2 tablespoons water
1 tablespoon light brown sugar
1 tablespoon Asian chili sauce

STIR-FRY

1 tablespoon fish sauce
1 teaspoon light brown sugar
¾ teaspoon ground coriander
⅛ teaspoon ground white pepper
2 pounds blade steaks, trimmed (see the illustrations on page 242), and sliced crosswise on the bias into ¼-inch-thick pieces
3 medium garlic cloves, minced or pressed through a garlic press (about 1 tablespoon)
3 tablespoons vegetable oil
3 Thai, serrano, or jalapeño chiles, halved lengthwise, seeds and ribs removed, and sliced crosswise ⅛ inch thick
3 medium shallots, ends trimmed, peeled, quartered lengthwise, and layers separated
½ cup loosely packed fresh Thai basil leaves (see note)
½ cup loosely packed fresh cilantro leaves
⅓ cup coarsely chopped roasted unsalted peanuts
1 lime, cut into wedges, for serving

1. FOR THE SAUCE: Whisk all of the ingredients together in a small bowl.

2. FOR THE STIR-FRY: Whisk the fish sauce, sugar, coriander, and pepper together in a large bowl. Add the beef, toss to coat, and let marinate for at least 10 minutes, or up to 1 hour. In a separate bowl, mix the garlic with 1 teaspoon of the oil.

3. Heat 2 teaspoons more oil in a 12-inch non-stick skillet over high heat until just smoking. Add one-third of the beef, breaking up any clumps, and cook, without stirring, until well browned, about 2 minutes. Stir the meat and continue to cook until it is nearly cooked through, about 30 seconds. Transfer the beef to a large bowl and repeat with 4 teaspoons more oil and the remaining beef in two batches; transfer to the bowl and cover to keep warm.

4. Add the remaining 2 teaspoons oil to the skillet and heat over medium heat until shimmering. Add the chiles and shallots and cook, stirring frequently, until beginning to soften, about 3 minutes. Clear the center of the skillet, add the garlic mixture, and cook, mashing the mixture into the pan, until fragrant, 15 to 30 seconds. Stir the garlic mixture into the chiles and shallots.

5. Return the beef, along with any accumulated juices, to the skillet. Add the sauce to the skillet and cook, tossing constantly, until the sauce is thickened, about 30 seconds. Stir in half of the basil and cilantro, then transfer to a serving platter. Garnish individual servings with the peanuts and remaining basil and cilantro. Serve with the lime wedges.

TRIMMING BLADE STEAKS

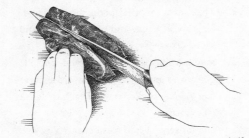

1. Halve each steak lengthwise, leaving the gristle on one half.

2. Cut away the gristle from the half to which it is still attached.

SPICY THAI CHICKEN WITH BASIL

THOUGH THIS DISH IS CONSIDERED PEASANT food in Thailand, spicy chicken with basil seemed to us as anything but. The dish consists of spicy, quickly cooked ground chicken and lots of fragrant Thai basil, served over white rice and sometimes topped with a fried egg. It is both flavorful and satisfying, and we felt we could come up with a recipe to make the dish simple enough to prepare in a skillet on any given weeknight.

To start, we noted that ground chicken is sold in a variety of textures, from finely ground to coarsely processed. We found that coarsely ground chicken developed an unappetizing wormlike texture as it cooked, so it fell to the bottom of our list. The finely ground chicken was easy to break into small, bite-sized pieces as it cooked; we recommend buying it if you can find it. We wondered if mincing the ground chicken further in the food processor or processing whole chicken breasts would result in a better texture. The processed chicken breasts cooked into dry little morsels, and the advantage of the processed ground chicken was insignificant. We stuck with our smashed ground chicken. We found it best to smash the raw chicken with the back of a spoon before cooking to ensure that it would break down into small pieces, and then continue to break it into small pieces as it cooked. Cooking it over a lower heat (compared to the high heat we had been using for our stir-fries) ensured that the ground meat wouldn't dry out.

Next, we moved on to flavorings. Most recipes we researched called for similar ingredients, including fish sauce, lime juice, garlic, shallots, and chiles. We decided to forgo mincing the individual dry ingredients and instead tossed the chiles, garlic, and shallots all together into the food processor. Next we cooked the mixture until fragrant before adding the chicken to the skillet to cook. We then considered the sauce's main component, fish sauce. We found that ⅓ cup for 2 pounds of meat was ideal. The fish sauce enhanced the flavor of the meat and was balanced nicely by 3 tablespoons of sugar and 3 cups of fragrant Thai basil.

INGREDIENTS: Thai Basil

As many Thai recipes call specifically for Thai basil, we wondered whether we could use Italian basil (also called sweet basil) and Thai basil interchangeably, or if using this special breed of basil would indeed make a difference. To find out, we pitted the Thai variety head to head against the more commonly found sweet basil in a basic Southeast Asian–style spring roll recipe.

The differences were as subtle as a sledgehammer. Thai basil has a distinctive flavor, with hints of mint, licorice, and cinnamon that tasters found "authentic," "clean," and "refreshing." The sweet basil was described as having a more mellow, grassy flavor, which tasters thought was "better suited to a tomato sauce."

If you can find Thai basil, by all means use it over the Italian variety. You will certainly appreciate the difference it makes in the final dish.

While this dish traditionally doesn't have more than a drizzle of liquid, some tasters wanted a bit more sauce for their rice. But when we raised the amount of fish sauce, the sauce became too salty and wasn't thick enough. So instead, we supplemented our ⅓ cup of fish sauce with an equal amount of low-sodium chicken broth, along with 1 teaspoon of cornstarch to thicken it. This gave us just enough sauce to flavor the rice without it dominating the overall dish. We tried adding a fried egg as a finishing touch, but tasters felt this was unnecessary for such a simple dish; a dash of lime juice added just before serving was all it needed.

Spicy Thai Chicken with Basil

SERVES 4

Do not overcook the chicken or it will taste very dry. Most packages of ground chicken include both light and dark meat; if given the choice, use all dark meat because it is much more flavorful and less prone to drying out. For more heat, include the chile ribs and seeds. If you can't find Thai basil, substitute regular basil.

10	Thai, serrano, or jalapeño chiles, seeds and ribs removed (see note)
8	medium garlic cloves, peeled
6	shallots, peeled
⅓	cup fish sauce
⅓	cup low-sodium chicken broth
3	tablespoons sugar
1	teaspoon cornstarch
2	pounds ground chicken (see note)
3	tablespoons vegetable oil
3	cups loosely packed fresh Thai basil leaves (see note)
3	tablespoons juice from 2 limes

1. Pulse the chiles, garlic, and shallots together in a food processor to a coarse paste, about 15 pulses, scraping down the bowl as needed. In a small bowl, whisk the fish sauce, chicken broth, sugar, and cornstarch together.

2. In a medium bowl, mash the ground chicken using the back of a spoon until smooth and no strand-like pieces of meat remain.

3. Heat the oil in a 12-inch nonstick skillet over medium heat until shimmering. Add the processed chile mixture and cook until fragrant and the moisture has evaporated, 3 to 5 minutes. Add the chicken and cook, breaking up the meat with a wooden spoon, until it is no longer pink, about 7 minutes.

4. Sprinkle the basil leaves evenly over the chicken. Whisk the fish sauce mixture to recombine, then add it to the skillet and cook, stirring constantly, until the sauce has thickened, 2 to 3 minutes. Stir in the lime juice, then transfer to a platter and serve.

THAI CURRIES

THAI CURRIES EMBRACE A DELICATE BALANCE of tastes, textures, temperatures, and colors that come together to create a harmonious whole. The balance in these dishes usually tilts toward the aromatics, while a coconut milk–based sauce blends and carries the flavors. The aromatics, added in the form of a paste, traditionally consist of garlic, ginger, shallots, lemon grass, kaffir lime leaves, shrimp paste, and chiles. Though the curries themselves come together rather quickly and must simmer gently for only a short amount of time before they are done, curry pastes can be quite involved, requiring an hour of preparation. Our goal was to simplify the curry paste and create a streamlined recipe for a couple of Thai curry dishes that could be cooked in our skillet.

First, we set out to explore the two most common types of Thai curries: green and red. We wanted to understand the basic structure of these dishes so that we could figure out ways they could be made more accessible to the American home cook. We hoped we could determine substitutes for some ingredients, such as kaffir lime leaves and shrimp paste, which are not readily available in most American supermarkets. Our work broke down into three neat areas: developing recipes for the pastes, cooking the pastes to draw out their flavor, and incorporating the chicken into the curry. We started with the pastes.

For the green curry paste, we noted that fresh green Thai chiles are most commonly called for. But they can be difficult to find, so we tested several substitutions and found that serranos and jalapeños are the best candidates. Meanwhile, red curry paste relies on dried red Thai chiles, though we confirmed that japonés and de árbol chiles work well too. The dried chiles are usually soaked in hot water until softened, but we found that we could get more flavor out of the chiles if we toasted them and then tossed them in the blender dry instead of soaking first. Because we would be including some liquid ingredient in the paste, the chiles would rehydrate right in the blender. Dried chiles lack body, so we supplemented them with fresh red jalapeños.

Chiles aside, red and green curry pastes rely on a similar assortment of ingredients. Shallots, garlic, cumin, and ginger are constants in most pastes, and so they went into our recipes. Toasted and ground coriander seeds, as well as fresh coriander root, are other common additions. Ground coriander was easy enough; we tested cilantro leaves (which are actually the leaves of the coriander plant) as a substitute for the difficult-to-find roots, but found that they were too moist and floral; cilantro stems worked fine.

Lemon grass is an ingredient essential to Thai curry, and we were happy to discover that it is relatively easy to find. We did find a substitute for galangal, a relative of ginger that's both peppery and sour: a combination of fresh ginger and lime juice. We found that adding the lime juice directly to the finished curry, rather than to the curry paste, best preserved its flavor.

The next ingredient on our list for the curry paste was kaffir lime leaves. They have a clean, floral aroma that many tasters compared to lemon verbena. Lime zest yielded a good approximation.

Shrimp paste—a puree of salted, fermented shrimp and other seasonings—lends a salty, fishy note to Thai curry pastes. Since this ingredient can be hard to find, we searched for substitutes. We tried anchovy paste and considered it a reasonable option, but in the end fish sauce, a more traditional ingredient, proved the better choice. Added directly to the curry, it provided the right kind of subtle fishy flavor we were after.

With the ingredients of our curry paste determined, we needed to figure out how to combine

MINCING LEMON GRASS

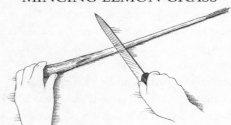  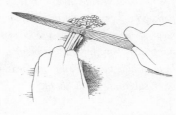

1. Trim and discard all but the bottom 5 inches of the lemon grass stalk.

2. Remove the tough outer sheath from the trimmed lemon grass. If the lemon grass is particularly thick or tough, you may need to remove several layers to reveal the tender inner portion of the stalk.

3. Cut the trimmed and peeled lemon grass in half lengthwise, then slice it thin crosswise.

them. To quickly and easily process them all together into a paste, we turned to a blender. To facilitate blending, we found that we had to add some liquid to the paste. Oil worked well—it didn't compete with the other curry flavors—but we had to use a fair amount to achieve a smooth paste. We realized that instead we could use some water, about ⅓ cup, and thus reduce the amount of oil to 2 tablespoons, giving us a less greasy sauce. With that, our paste was set.

Moving on to the other components of the dish—the meat and vegetables—we decided to use chicken for our master recipe and beef and shrimp in variations. Poaching the chicken was our approach of choice. After the paste mixture had been cooked in the skillet, we added water, along with a little fish sauce and brown sugar. We poached the chicken in this liquid, which in turn would become a flavorful component in our sauce. We tested cutting the chicken in strips and chunks, but tasters unanimously preferred shredded chicken. We removed the chicken once it was fully cooked and set it aside to cool before shredding it with two forks. Before returning the shredded chicken to the skillet, we stirred coconut milk into the sauce for a luxuriously smooth texture.

As far as vegetables go, common additions in Thai curries include pea eggplant, breadfruit, bamboo shoots, young jackfruit, banana blossoms, and pumpkin tendrils. The bamboo shoots were the only choice that was easy to find, but since we only found them canned, none of us were keen on their inclusion. We had noted that it wasn't unusual to have a curry with only protein, especially with such a hefty amount of fresh herbs added at the end, so we gave a no-vegetable recipe a test run. Indeed, tasters liked the simplicity of the chicken-only curries.

Final garnishes of fresh basil, cilantro, and lime juice completed the dish. Because Thai curries are saucy and hot, be sure to serve it over a nice cushion of rice.

Shrimp is a quick and easy substitute for the chicken, requiring just a few minutes of simmering time to cook through. For our beef variation, we found blade steak to be our best option—it lends itself well to the cooking method, which is essentially a braise, and it remains tender and flavorful.

Thai Green Curry with Chicken
SERVES 4 TO 6

We strongly prefer the flavor of Thai chiles here; however, serrano or jalapeño chiles can be substituted. For more heat, include the chile ribs and seeds when mincing. You can use light coconut milk in this dish instead of regular, but the flavor will not be as rich. If you can't find Thai basil leaves, substitute regular basil.

CURRY PASTE

⅓	cup water
12	Thai, serrano, or jalapeño chiles, seeds and ribs removed, chiles minced (see note)
8	medium garlic cloves, peeled
3	medium shallots, peeled and quartered
2	stalks lemon grass, bottom 5 inches only, trimmed and minced (see the illustrations on page 244)
2	tablespoons minced fresh cilantro stems
2	tablespoons grated zest from 2 limes
2	tablespoons vegetable oil
1	tablespoon minced or grated fresh ginger (see the illustrations on page 227)
2	teaspoons ground coriander
1	teaspoon ground cumin
1	teaspoon salt

CHICKEN

1¼	cups water
2	tablespoons fish sauce
1	tablespoon light brown sugar
1½	pounds boneless, skinless chicken breasts (about 4 medium), trimmed (see the illustration on page 6)
1	(14-ounce) can coconut milk (see note)
½	cup loosely packed fresh Thai basil leaves (see note)
½	cup loosely packed fresh cilantro leaves
2	tablespoons juice from 1 lime

1. FOR THE CURRY PASTE: Puree all of the ingredients together in a blender to a fine paste, about 3 minutes, scraping down the blender jar as needed. Add the curry paste to a 12-inch nonstick skillet and cook over medium-high heat, stirring

often, until it begins to sizzle and no longer smells raw, about 2 minutes.

2. FOR THE CHICKEN: Stir the water, fish sauce, and sugar into the curry paste in the skillet, then nestle the chicken into the mixture and bring to a simmer. Cover, reduce the heat to medium-low, and simmer until the thickest part of the breast registers 160 to 165 degrees on an instant-read thermometer, 12 to 18 minutes, flipping the breasts halfway through cooking.

3. Transfer the chicken to a carving board. Stir the coconut milk into the skillet and return to a simmer until the sauce has thickened slightly, 8 to 10 minutes. When the chicken is cool enough to handle, shred it into bite-sized pieces (see the illustration on page 190).

4. Return the shredded chicken to the sauce and continue to cook until heated through, about 2 minutes. Off the heat, stir in the basil, cilantro, and lime juice and serve.

VARIATIONS

Thai Green Curry with Beef

To make slicing the steak easier, freeze it for 15 minutes first.

Follow the recipe for Thai Green Curry with Chicken, substituting 1½ pounds beef blade steak, trimmed (see the illustrations on page 242), and sliced crosswise on the bias into ½-inch-thick pieces, for the chicken. Increase the amount of water to 2 cups and simmer the beef, covered, until tender, about 40 minutes. When the beef is tender, stir in the coconut milk and continue to simmer, uncovered, until the sauce is thick and creamy, 10 to 15 minutes. Stir in the herbs and lime juice as directed in step 4.

Thai Green Curry with Shrimp

Follow the recipe for Thai Green Curry with Chicken, omitting the chicken. Add the coconut milk with the water in step 2 and simmer the sauce, uncovered, until creamy and thickened, 10 to 15 minutes. Stir in 1½ pounds extra-large shrimp (21 to 25 per pound), peeled and deveined (see the illustration on page 235), and continue to simmer until the shrimp are fully cooked, 3 to 5 minutes. Stir in the herbs and lime juice as directed in step 4.

Thai Red Curry with Chicken
SERVES 4 TO 6

We recommend wearing gloves when handling the toasted chiles; they are very spicy and might burn your skin. If you can't find fresh red jalapeño chiles, you can substitute green jalapeño chiles, but the color of the sauce will be slightly muddy. For more heat, include the jalapeño ribs and seeds when mincing. We prefer the richer flavor of regular coconut milk here; however, light coconut milk can be substituted. If you can't find Thai basil leaves, substitute regular basil.

CURRY PASTE

8	small, dried red chiles, such as Thai, japónes, or de árbol, brushed clean
⅓	cup water
4	medium shallots, peeled and quartered
2	stalks lemon grass, bottom 5 inches only, trimmed and minced (see the illustrations on page 244)
6	medium garlic cloves, peeled
1	medium red jalapeño chile, seeds and ribs removed, chile minced (see note)
2	tablespoons minced fresh cilantro stems
2	tablespoons vegetable oil
1	tablespoon grated zest from 1 lime
2	teaspoons ground coriander
1	teaspoon ground cumin
1	teaspoon minced or grated fresh ginger (see the illustrations on page 227)
1	teaspoon tomato paste
1	teaspoon salt

CHICKEN

1¼	cups water
2	tablespoons fish sauce
1	tablespoon light brown sugar
1½	pounds boneless, skinless chicken breasts (about 4 medium), trimmed (see the illustration on page 6)
1	(14-ounce) can coconut milk
½	cup loosely packed fresh Thai basil leaves
½	cup loosely packed fresh cilantro leaves
2	tablespoons juice from 1 lime

1. FOR THE CURRY PASTE: Adjust an oven rack to the middle position and heat the oven to

350 degrees. Place the dried red chiles on a rimmed baking sheet and toast in the oven until fragrant and puffed, about 5 minutes. Remove the chiles from the oven and let cool. When cool enough to handle, seed and stem the chiles, then break into small pieces.

2. Puree the toasted chile pieces and remaining curry paste ingredients together in a blender to a fine paste, about 3 minutes, scraping down the blender jar as needed. Add the curry paste to a 12-inch nonstick skillet and cook over medium-high heat, stirring often, until it begins to sizzle and no longer smells raw, about 2 minutes.

INGREDIENTS: Coconut Milk

Coconut milk is not the thin liquid found inside the coconut itself; that is called coconut water. Coconut milk is a product made by steeping equal parts shredded coconut meat and either warm milk or water. The meat is pressed or mashed to release as much liquid as possible, the mixture is strained, and the result is coconut milk.

We tasted seven nationally available brands (five regular and two light) in coconut pudding, coconut rice, Thai-style chicken soup, and green chicken curry. Among the five regular brands, tasters gravitated to those with more solid cream at the top of the can (most cans recommend shaking before opening to redistribute the solids). These brands also had a much stronger coconut flavor.

In the soup and curry, tasters preferred Chaokoh because of its exceptionally low sugar content (less than 1 gram per ⅓ cup). By comparison, brands with more than twice as much sugar (Ka-Me, Goya, Thai Kitchen) tasted "saccharine." In the sweet recipes, tasters gave velvety Ka-Me top votes for its "fruity" and "complex" flavor. In these recipes, the extra sugar was an advantage. Meanwhile, the light coconut milks we tasted were not nearly as creamy.

THE BEST COCONUT MILK

By far the winner and best choice for savory dishes, this coconut milk lacked the complexity and sweetness of the runner up, Ka-Me, but made up for it with its superior smooth texture. It was also voted "the creamiest" brand.

CHAOKOH

3. FOR THE CHICKEN: Stir the water, fish sauce, and sugar into the curry paste in the skillet, then nestle the chicken into the mixture and bring to a simmer. Cover, turn the heat to medium-low, and simmer until the thickest part of the breast registers 160 to 165 degrees on an instant-read thermometer, 12 to 18 minutes, flipping the breasts halfway through cooking.

4. Transfer the chicken to a carving board. Stir the coconut milk into the skillet and return to a simmer until the sauce has thickened slightly, 8 to 10 minutes. When the chicken is cool enough to handle, shred into bite-sized pieces (see the illustration on page 190).

5. Return the shredded chicken to the sauce and continue to cook until heated through, about 2 minutes. Off the heat, stir in the basil, cilantro, and lime juice and serve.

➤ VARIATIONS

Thai Red Curry with Beef

To make slicing the steak easier, freeze it for 15 minutes first.

Follow the recipe for Thai Red Curry with Chicken, substituting 1½ pounds beef blade steak, trimmed (see the illustrations on page 242), and sliced crosswise on the bias into ½-inch-thick pieces, for the chicken. Increase the amount of water to 2 cups and simmer the beef, covered, until tender, about 40 minutes. When the beef is tender, stir in the coconut milk and continue to simmer, uncovered, until the sauce is thick and creamy, 10 to 15 minutes. Stir in the herbs and lime juice as directed in step 5.

Thai Red Curry with Shrimp

Follow the recipe for Thai Red Curry with Chicken, omitting the chicken. Add the coconut milk with the water in step 3 and simmer the sauce, uncovered, until creamy and thickened, 10 to 15 minutes. Stir in 1½ pounds extra-large shrimp (21 to 25 per pound), peeled and deveined (see the illustration on page 235), and continue to simmer until the shrimp are fully cooked, 3 to 5 minutes. Stir in the herbs and lime juice as directed in step 5.

INDIAN CURRIES

INDIAN CURRIES CAN BE COMPLICATED affairs, with lengthy ingredient lists and fussy techniques. We wanted to create an authentic chicken curry with perfectly cooked meat, vegetables, and a deep, flavorful sauce, but we wanted a curry we could cook in a skillet on a weeknight in less than an hour. Most streamlined recipes we tried, however, were uninspired, while others, overloaded with spices, were harsh and overpowering. We had our work cut out for us.

We first addressed what would go into our curry powder, which is in fact a mixture of as many as 20 different spices. Our instincts told us we would be better off creating our own rather than relying on store-bought. While some curries are made with exotic whole and ground spices (fenugreek, asafetida, dried rose petals, and so on), we decided to limit ourselves to everyday ground spices such as cumin, cloves, cardamom, cinnamon, and coriander. Our testing dragged on for days, and it was hard to reach consensus. Most of the homemade spice mixtures we tried were fine, but still, none proved themselves as the stand-out winner.

We had been reluctant to use store-bought curry powder, assuming its flavor would be inferior to a homemade blend, but at this point it seemed worth a try. We were surprised when tasters liked the store-bought curry powder nearly as well as our homemade versions. It turns out that store-bought curry powder contains some of the exotic spices we had dismissed at the outset.

To further improve the flavor of the curry powder, we tried cooking it in oil, a process known as "blooming," until its fragrance emerged. This simple step took less than a minute and turned commercial curry powder into a flavor powerhouse.

With the curry powder settled, we worked on building our sauce. Many classic curry recipes begin with a generous amount of sautéed onion, which adds depth and body, so we followed suit. Ghee (clarified butter), traditionally used to sauté the onions, added terrific richness, but we found that vegetable oil was a fine substitute and a more accessible option. Almost all curry recipes add equal amounts of garlic and ginger to the onions, and we found no reason to stray from this method. Wanting

to take our sauce to the next level, we stirred in a minced fresh jalapeño chile for heat and a spoonful of tomato paste for contrasting sweetness. Though decidedly inauthentic, we felt the latter ingredient was a must for the depth it created.

When testing the liquid component of the sauce, we were surprised to find that water and a can of whole tomatoes, which we pureed, did a fine job. Typically we would reach for chicken broth instead of water for a recipe like this, but given the complexity of our curry spices, chicken broth proved unnecessary (not to mention untraditional). Most authentic curry recipes we researched also include yogurt or coconut milk. Though we had trouble with both when adding them at the beginning of cooking, we found that if we added them at the end, we avoided curdling, and it was the perfect creamy finish to our curry. We liked the flavor of both, so we leave the decision of which to use up to you.

With the sauce set, it was time to focus on the chicken and vegetables. First, we investigated whether it was essential to sear the chicken before it was simmered in the sauce. In a side-by-side test of chicken curries made with seared and unseared chicken, we found that it was nearly impossible to distinguish between the two; searing added little noticeable flavor given the assertiveness of the spices.

As for the type of chicken, we preferred boneless, skinless chicken breasts because they required less than 20 minutes of simmering to cook through. After simmering, we removed them from the sauce and shredded the meat, stirring it back into the curry before serving. Cubed chicken pieces were not only less appealing visually, but they didn't soak up the sauce as well as the shredded chicken did.

For the vegetables, we settled on the classic pairing of cauliflower and peas. We added the cauliflower to the sauce when we added the chicken to cook through, and we waited to stir in the peas until the end so they would just heat through and hold their color. The combination of textures and colors was good, and both vegetables did a nice job of picking up flavor from the sauce.

Our curry tasted very good, but there was still something missing. We experimented with garam masala (literally "hot spice blend" in Hindi), which is often sprinkled onto Indian dishes before serving. Like curry powder, the ingredients of garam masala vary but usually include warm spices such as black pepper, cinnamon, coriander, and cardamom. Following our success with the curry powder, we decided to buy a jar of commercial garam masala, but when we added a few pinches to the curry at the end of cooking, the result was raw and harsh-tasting. What if we first bloomed the garam masala along with the curry powder? The garam masala mellowed into a second wave of flavor that helped the dish achieve even more complexity. We stirred in cilantro for our last touch of brightness. With that, we had created a robust, satisfying chicken and vegetable curry that was simple to prepare—no complicated homemade spices required.

Indian Chicken Curry with Cauliflower and Peas

SERVES 4 TO 6

We prefer the richer flavor of whole milk yogurt and regular coconut milk here; however, low-fat yogurt, nonfat yogurt, or light coconut milk can be substituted. For more heat, include the jalapeño seeds and ribs when mincing.

1	(14.5-ounce) can whole peeled tomatoes
¼	cup vegetable oil
1 ½	tablespoons sweet or mild curry powder
1	teaspoon garam masala
1	medium onion, minced
	Salt
3	medium garlic cloves, minced or pressed through a garlic press (about 1 tablespoon)
1	tablespoon minced or grated fresh ginger (see the illustrations on page 227)
1	jalapeño chile, seeds and ribs removed, chile minced (see note)
1	tablespoon tomato paste
1	cup water
1 ½	pounds boneless, skinless chicken breasts (about 4 medium), trimmed (see the illustration on page 6)
½	medium head cauliflower, trimmed, cored, and cut into 1-inch florets (about 4 cups)
1	cup frozen peas

½	cup coconut milk or plain whole milk yogurt
¼	cup minced fresh cilantro leaves

1. Pulse the tomatoes with their juice in a food processor until no large chunks remain, about 12 pulses.

2. Heat the oil in a 12-inch nonstick skillet over medium heat until shimmering. Add the curry powder and garam masala and cook, stirring constantly, until fragrant, about 30 seconds. Stir in the onion and 1 teaspoon salt and cook, stirring frequently, until the onion is softened and lightly browned, about 10 minutes. Stir in the garlic, ginger, jalapeño, and tomato paste and cook until fragrant, about 30 seconds.

3. Slowly stir in the water and processed tomatoes, stirring out any clumps with a wooden spoon. Nestle the chicken and cauliflower in the liquid and bring to a simmer. Cover, reduce the heat to medium-low, and simmer until the thickest part of the breast registers 160 to 165 degrees on an instant-read thermometer, 12 to 18 minutes, flipping the breasts halfway through cooking.

4. Transfer the chicken to a carving board to cool. When the chicken is cool enough to handle, shred into bite-sized pieces (see the illustration on page 190).

5. Return the chicken, along with any accumulated juices, to the skillet. Stir in the peas and coconut milk and reheat briefly over medium-low heat until hot, 1 to 2 minutes. Stir in the cilantro, season with salt to taste, and serve.

➤ VARIATIONS

Indian Shrimp Curry with Green Beans and Red Bell Peppers

We prefer the richer flavor of whole milk yogurt and regular coconut milk here; however, low-fat yogurt, nonfat yogurt, or light coconut milk can be substituted. For more heat, include the jalapeño seeds and ribs when mincing.

1	(14.5-ounce) can whole peeled tomatoes
¼	cup vegetable oil
1 ½	tablespoons sweet or mild curry powder
1	teaspoon garam masala
1	medium onion, minced
	Salt

3 medium garlic cloves, minced or pressed
through a garlic press (about 1 tablespoon)

1 tablespoon minced or grated fresh ginger
(see the illustrations on page 227)

1 jalapeño chile, seeds and ribs removed, chile
minced (see note)

1 tablespoon tomato paste

1 cup water

¾ pound green beans, ends trimmed (see the
illustration on page 235) and cut into 2-inch
pieces

1 red bell pepper, stemmed, seeded, and sliced
into ¼-inch-wide strips

1½ pounds extra-large shrimp (21 to 25 per
pound), peeled and deveined (see the
illustration on page 235)

½ cup coconut milk or plain whole milk yogurt

¼ cup minced fresh cilantro leaves

1. Pulse the tomatoes with their juice in a food processor until no large chunks remain, about 12 pulses.

2. Heat the oil in a 12-inch nonstick skillet over medium heat until shimmering. Add the curry powder and garam masala and cook, stirring constantly, until fragrant, about 30 seconds. Stir in the onion and 1 teaspoon salt and cook, stirring frequently, until the onion is softened and lightly browned, about 10 minutes. Stir in the garlic, ginger, jalapeño, and tomato paste and cook until fragrant, about 30 seconds.

3. Slowly stir in the water and processed tomatoes, stirring out any clumps with a wooden spoon. Stir in the green beans and bell pepper and bring to a simmer. Cover, reduce the heat to medium-low, and simmer until the vegetables are almost tender, 12 to 18 minutes.

4. Stir in the shrimp and coconut milk and continue to simmer gently until the shrimp are fully cooked, 3 to 5 minutes. Stir in the cilantro, season with salt to taste, and serve.

Indian Vegetable Curry with Cauliflower, Potatoes, Chickpeas, and Peas

In this curry variation, we much prefer the flavor and richness of regular coconut milk to light coconut milk (or yogurt). For more heat, include the jalapeño seeds and ribs when mincing.

1 (14.5-ounce) can whole peeled tomatoes

¼ cup vegetable oil

1½ tablespoons sweet or mild curry powder

1 teaspoon garam masala

12 ounces red potatoes (2 to 3 medium),
scrubbed and cut in ½-inch chunks

1 medium onion, minced
Salt

3 medium garlic cloves, minced or pressed
through a garlic press (about 1 tablespoon)

1 tablespoon minced or grated fresh ginger
(see the illustrations on page 227)

1 jalapeño chile, seeds and ribs removed, chile
minced (see note)

1 tablespoon tomato paste

1 cup water

1 (15-ounce) can chickpeas, drained and rinsed

½ medium head cauliflower, trimmed, cored,
and cut into 1-inch florets (about 4 cups)

1 cup frozen peas

½ cup coconut milk (see note)

¼ cup minced fresh cilantro leaves

1. Pulse the tomatoes with their juice in a food processor until no large chunks remain, about 12 pulses.

2. Heat the oil in a 12-inch nonstick skillet over medium heat until shimmering. Add the curry powder and garam masala and cook, stirring constantly, until fragrant, about 30 seconds. Stir in the potatoes and onion and 1 teaspoon salt and cook, stirring frequently, until the onion is softened and lightly browned, about 10 minutes. Stir in the garlic, ginger, jalapeño, and tomato paste and cook until fragrant, about 30 seconds.

3. Slowly stir in the water and processed tomatoes, stirring out any clumps with a wooden spoon. Stir in the chickpeas and cauliflower and bring to a simmer. Cover, reduce the heat to medium-low, and simmer until the cauliflower and potatoes are tender, 12 to 18 minutes.

4. Stir in the peas and coconut milk and continue to simmer over medium-low heat until hot, 1 to 2 minutes. Stir in the cilantro, season with salt to taste, and serve.

7

HEARTY EGGS

HEARTY EGGS

EGGS HAVE LONG BEEN A QUICK AND convenient meal. Who doesn't have a carton of eggs in their fridge most days of the week? But when you start cracking the eggs into the skillet, it's all too easy to get stuck in the rut of just scrambling and frying, losing sight of the fact that eggs can be and do so much more. Eggs pair well with a variety of ingredients and flavors, taking them far beyond a simple breakfast food. In this chapter, we wanted to create recipes that rely on a few extra ingredients and steps to elevate eggs from average start to your day to starring part of any meal: breakfast, brunch, lunch, or dinner. We achieved this with recipes like Chorizo and Bell Pepper Scrambled Eggs on Toast, accented with chipotle butter and cheddar cheese (page 255), a soufflé-like Spinach and Gouda Strata (page 274), and a velvety Spanish Egg and Potato Tortilla (page 266).

The flavor and spice combinations in this chapter prove that eggs are complemented by far more than just salt and pepper. Our Indian-Spiced Tortilla (page 267) incorporates both flavor and texture with curry powder and brown mustard seeds, which are mellowed in turn by the light, fresh touch of cilantro and scallions—tasters couldn't get enough of this dish. Our Egg, Sausage, and Pepper Supper (page 271), based on the popular egg dish *chackchouka* found in the Middle East and parts of North Africa, is a combination that offers a delicate spiciness in a tomato-based sauce countered by the cooling creaminess of softly cooked eggs. Our Tex-Mex Popover Casserole (page 276) pairs the kick from chorizo and pepper Jack cheese with sweet red bell pepper. We found that the combinations of flavors we could pair with the eggs were limitless.

During our testing, we discovered that avoiding excess moisture was one key to preparing eggs successfully—moisture leads inevitably to soggy results. Vegetables are a leading culprit for carrying a lot of water, so precooking vegetable add-ins proved essential in most cases. We kept things simple by sautéing most vegetables in the skillet before simply pouring the eggs over the top. For items like asparagus, a quick sauté of two to four minutes was all that was needed, while peppers and onions benefited from a lengthier stint in the pan, not only to remove enough moisture but also to draw out flavors. For potatoes, we had the best results from parcooking them in the microwave before adding them to the skillet. The microwave was an easy alternative to the traditional parboiling method (which would have actually added moisture back to the potatoes) that gave the interior of the potatoes a light, fluffy texture without breaking down the exterior.

However you prepare your eggs, there are a few tools to keep on hand. First, a good ovenproof, heavy-bottomed nonstick skillet is a necessity—it's as close to an insurance policy against stuck, scorched eggs as you can get. We utilized both 10- and 12-inch skillets, depending on the recipe. Ten-inch skillets were useful for making thick skillet casseroles and stratas, while a 12-inch skillet was more useful when we were seeking a well-browned crust, for recipes such as our Asparagus, Ham, and Gruyère Frittata (page 263) and Corned Beef Hash (page 269). For several of our recipes we move from the stovetop to the oven to finish cooking, so having an ovenproof skillet is essential. (See page 14 for the results of our nonstick skillet test.)

A heatproof rubber spatula is another key implement—not only does it loosen eggs easily from the skillet so they come out in one tidy round, but it also saves the nonstick surface of the skillet from scratches. (See page 275 for the results of our rubber spatula test.) A wooden spoon is an alternative; while it doesn't have quite the flexibility of a rubber spatula, it will get the job done. Employing these equipment choices will save you a lot of frustration.

One last bit of advice: Because eggs cook so quickly, in almost all cases it's a good idea to have all of your prep work done before you start cooking.

HEARTY SCRAMBLED EGGS ON TOAST

WHAT COULD POSSIBLY BE SO HARD ABOUT cooking scrambled eggs? They contain only a few ingredients, and the whole process—from walking into the kitchen to sitting down at the table—takes but a few minutes. But the simplest things are not always the easiest. Ideally, scrambled eggs should be a dreamy mound of airy, soft curds just shy of being undercooked. But all too often they end up heavy and hard, or unevenly cooked, with some spots browned and others undercooked or weepy. We wanted to perfect our scrambling technique and to elevate this breakfast staple to supper status by introducing hearty, sophisticated flavors. We would go beyond scrambled eggs with toast alongside— the entire meal would work together.

We first tested beating the eggs to varying degrees. Our advice is to stop muscling the raw eggs into a tight froth. Overbeating can cause premature coagulation of the eggs' protein, guaranteeing tough eggs before they even hit the pan. We whipped our eggs until we had a smooth, consistently yellow color and no streaks of white, making sure to stop while the bubbles were large.

Next we looked at the few basic ingredients often added before beating—salt and pepper, and either water or dairy. When we compared them side by side, we noted that scrambled eggs made with water are less flavorful, don't fluff as nicely, and aren't as soft as those made with dairy. Whole milk gave us better scrambled eggs than fat-free or low-fat milk; it had a pillowy effect and helped create large curds. The bigger the curds, the more steam you'll trap inside, and that translates to fluffier eggs.

For these early batches, we tried most of the pans in our kitchen and confirmed that those with a nonstick surface are best, and a heavy-bottomed skillet is preferable for even heating. Pan size is important, too: For 12 eggs and 6 tablespoons of liquid, nothing but a 12-inch skillet will do.

We tried making our scrambled eggs over low heat, but by the time the eggs were cooked through, they had become tough, dried out, and overcoagulated, like a badly made meringue that "weeps." We found that a very hot pan will begin to cook eggs instantaneously, which leads to the quickest coagulation and creates the steam essential for a light, fluffy texture. The problem with using high heat is that absolute vigilance is needed. To reduce our margin of error, we scaled back to medium heat, which gave us relatively quick coagulation without the constant fear of overcooking.

Technique is critical for getting the fluffiest scrambled eggs. A folding method, rather than constant stirring, yields the creamiest, softest scrambled eggs with large, airy curds. A rubber or wooden spatula works best; use the flat edge to snowplow a 2- to 3-inch swath of eggs across the pan in one pass. The idea is to push slowly, lift, and fold. Because they will continue to cook off the heat, the eggs should look almost underdone when you make that final fold and stir in the other ingredients.

Now we needed to decide how to make these scrambled eggs into a full-fledged supper. The duo of ham and cheese is a natural pairing with eggs; we cooked the eggs until they were just beginning to set but still soft, then off the heat we folded in some chopped ham and cheddar cheese. The residual heat from the eggs was enough to perfectly melt the cheese and warm the ham, but now a new problem cropped up: our eggs were weepy. The new ingredients were adding moisture; we needed to reduce the amount of liquid elsewhere. We knew some dairy was important for soft texture, but perhaps instead of milk we should be using half-and-half or cream, both of which contain less moisture and more fat than milk. Heavy cream was too heavy, but the half-and-half was perfect. These eggs were substantial, soft, and didn't weep when we added the ham and cheese.

To give another boost of flavor, we cooked our eggs in a compound butter. Maple butter, made by simply mashing maple syrup together with softened butter and a pinch of cayenne, accentuated the ham's salty-sweetness. For toast worthy of being topped by our perfectly scrambled eggs, we also slathered some of this butter onto thick slices of toasted rustic bread. After piling our fluffy scrambled eggs onto the maple-buttered toast, all that was left to do was dig in.

Ham and Cheese Scrambled Eggs on Toast

SERVES 4 TO 6

We prefer to use Maple Butter in this recipe, but any of the butters on page 257 will work.

1	recipe Maple Butter (page 257)
6	thick slices rustic white bread, toasted
12	large eggs
6	tablespoons half-and-half
¾	teaspoon salt
¼	teaspoon ground black pepper
8	ounces sliced deli ham, chopped coarse
2	ounces sharp cheddar cheese, shredded (½ cup)

1. Spread 4 tablespoons of the maple butter over the toast, place the toast on individual plates, and set aside. Whisk the eggs, half-and-half, salt, and pepper together until combined.

2. Melt the remaining tablespoon maple butter in a 12-inch nonstick skillet over medium heat. Following the illustrations at right, add the eggs and cook, using a rubber or wooden spatula to push them back and forth, until curds begin to form. Continue to cook, lifting and folding the curds from side to side, until they clump in a single mound but are still very moist, about 3 minutes.

3. Off the heat, gently fold in the ham and cheddar. Spoon the eggs on top of the toast and serve immediately.

➤ VARIATIONS

Chorizo and Bell Pepper Scrambled Eggs on Toast

Although we prefer chorizo, a Spanish-style pork sausage, andouille or linguiça can be substituted here.

1	recipe Chipotle Butter (page 257)
6	thick slices rustic white bread, toasted
12	large eggs
6	tablespoons half-and-half
¾	teaspoon salt
¼	teaspoon ground black pepper
1	teaspoon vegetable oil
8	ounces chorizo sausage, cut into ½-inch pieces
1	red bell pepper, stemmed, seeded, and cut into ½-inch pieces
3	scallions, white and green parts separated and sliced thin
2	ounces sharp cheddar cheese, shredded (½ cup)

1. Spread 4 tablespoons of the chipotle butter over the toast, place the toast on individual plates, and set aside. Whisk the eggs, half-and-half, salt, and pepper together until combined.

2. Heat the oil in a 12-inch nonstick skillet over medium heat until shimmering. Add the chorizo and cook until the fat begins to render, about 2 minutes. Add the bell pepper and scallion whites and continue to cook until the chorizo begins to

SCRAMBLING EGGS

We learned that a folding method yielded the creamiest, softest scrambled eggs. If you push the eggs to and fro with a spatula, instead of constantly stirring them (which is the more conventional method), you will end up with large, airy curds and very fluffy scrambled eggs.

1. Using a rubber or wooden spatula, push the eggs from one side of the pan to the other.

2. As the curds form, lift and fold the eggs until they are clumped in a single mound.

brown, about 3 minutes. Transfer the chorizo mixture to a small bowl and set aside. Wipe out the skillet with a wad of paper towels.

3. Melt the remaining tablespoon chipotle butter in the skillet over medium heat. Following the illustrations on page 255, add the eggs and cook, using a rubber or wooden spatula to push them back and forth, until curds begin to form. Continue to cook, lifting and folding the curds from side to side, until they clump in a single mound but are still very moist, about 3 minutes.

4. Off the heat, gently fold in the chorizo mixture, scallion greens, and cheddar. Spoon the eggs on top of the toast and serve immediately.

Smoked Salmon Scrambled Eggs on Toast

Since the flavor of the salmon plays a key role in this recipe, buy the best quality smoked salmon that you can afford.

1	recipe Chive Butter (page 257)
6	thick slices rustic white bread, toasted
12	large eggs
6	tablespoons half-and-half
¾	teaspoon salt
¼	teaspoon ground black pepper
2	ounces smoked salmon, minced

REHYDRATING PORCINI MUSHROOMS

Rinse the mushrooms of any grit and place in a small bowl. Pour 1 cup of boiling water over the mushrooms to cover and let stand until softened. Use a fork to lift the mushrooms from the liquid, leaving any additional grit behind. The mushrooms are ready to be minced and used as directed.

1. Spread 4 tablespoons of the chive butter over the toast, place the toast on individual plates, and set aside. Whisk the eggs, half-and-half, salt, and pepper together until combined.

2. Melt the remaining tablespoon chive butter in a 12-inch nonstick skillet over medium heat. Following the illustrations on page 255, add the eggs and cook, using a rubber or wooden spatula to push them back and forth, until curds begin to form. Continue to cook, lifting and folding the curds from side to side, until they clump in a single mound but are still very moist, about 3 minutes.

3. Off the heat, gently fold in the salmon. Spoon the eggs on top of the toast and serve immediately.

Prosciutto and Asparagus Scrambled Eggs on Toast

If you don't have prosciutto on hand, use any thinly sliced deli ham.

1	recipe Porcini Butter (page 257)
6	thick slices rustic white bread, toasted
12	large eggs
6	tablespoons half-and-half
¾	teaspoon salt
¼	teaspoon ground black pepper
1	teaspoon vegetable oil
½	pound asparagus (½ bunch), tough ends trimmed (see the illustration on page 92) and sliced thin on the bias
3	ounces thinly sliced prosciutto, chopped coarse
1	ounce Parmesan cheese, grated (½ cup)

1. Spread 4 tablespoons of the porcini butter over the toast, place the toast on individual plates, and set aside. Whisk the eggs, half-and-half, salt, and pepper together until combined.

2. Heat the oil in a 12-inch nonstick skillet over medium heat until shimmering. Add the asparagus and cook until lightly browned and crisp-tender, 2 to 4 minutes. Transfer the asparagus to a plate and set aside. Wipe out the skillet with a wad of paper towels.

3. Melt the remaining tablespoon porcini butter in the skillet over medium heat. Following the illustrations on page 255, add the eggs and cook, using a rubber or wooden spatula to push them back and forth, until curds begin to form. Continue to cook, lifting and folding the curds from side to side, until they clump in a single mound but are still very moist, about 3 minutes.

4. Off the heat, gently fold in the cooked asparagus, prosciutto, and Parmesan. Spoon the eggs on top of the toast and serve immediately.

Maple Butter
MAKES ABOUT 5 TABLESPOONS

This butter adds spicy sweetness to our ham and cheese scrambled eggs recipe; it's also great with pancakes.

4   tablespoons (½ stick) unsalted butter, softened
2   tablespoons maple syrup
    Pinch cayenne pepper
    Salt and ground black pepper

Beat the butter with a fork in a small bowl until light and fluffy. Mix in the maple syrup and cayenne until combined. Season with salt and pepper to taste.

Chipotle Butter
MAKES ABOUT 5 TABLESPOONS

This butter complements the flavors in our chorizo and bell pepper scrambled eggs recipe; it also spices up meat or chicken.

4   tablespoons (½ stick) unsalted butter, softened
2½ teaspoons minced chipotle chile in adobo sauce
1   small garlic clove, minced or pressed through a garlic press (about ½ teaspoon)
    Salt and ground black pepper

Beat the butter with a fork in a small bowl until light and fluffy. Mix in the chipotles and garlic until combined. Season with salt and pepper to taste.

Chive Butter
MAKES ABOUT 5 TABLESPOONS

This versatile butter livens up our smoked salmon scrambled eggs recipe; it also pairs particularly well with fish and vegetables.

4   tablespoons (½ stick) unsalted butter, softened
¼   cup minced fresh chives
    Salt and ground black pepper

Beat the butter with a fork in a small bowl until light and fluffy. Mix in the chives until combined. Season with salt and pepper to taste.

Porcini Butter
MAKES ABOUT 5 TABLESPOONS

This butter adds an earthy flavor to our prosciutto and asparagus scrambled eggs recipe; it also lends excellent flavor to steaks and even rice or couscous.

4   tablespoons (½ stick) unsalted butter, softened
¼   ounce dried porcini mushrooms, rehydrated (see the illustration on page 256) and minced
1   teaspoon minced shallot
    Salt and ground black pepper

Beat the butter with a fork in a small bowl until light and fluffy. Mix in the mushrooms and shallot until combined. Season with salt and pepper to taste.

FAMILY-SIZED OMELET

THE TRADITIONAL METHOD FOR COOKING omelets involves a number of tricks and techniques that require both practice and patience—stirring with a flat fork in a circular motion until the egg mixture has thickened, tapping the handle to dislodge the set eggs, and sliding the omelet up one side of the pan for the final tri-fold or roll before serving. So, not surprisingly, many people have been led to believe that you have to be a trained chef to turn out a well-made omelet. While this may have once been the case, nonstick skillets have made cooking omelets far more feasible. But the truth is, if you want to make more than one or two it's just not a very practical (or quick) meal.

Enter the family-sized omelet. One big omelet can be hearty enough to feed a family of four, and it can be made almost as quickly as a small one. The key is technique. Yes, a nonstick skillet definitely helps, but it won't make the omelet for you. Poor technique will leave you with runny eggs on top and burnt eggs underneath. While our initial tests were disastrous, we were determined to see if we could successfully make one big cheese omelet that would satisfy a hungry family.

Our first question was, how much should we beat the eggs? Most classic recipes merely dictate that the eggs be "completely incorporated," although some say "beat until frothy" and others "beat until barely combined." It was a question we had just visited in our scrambled eggs tests (see page 254), but we weren't sure if an omelet would require the eggs to be treated differently, so we started from scratch. We tried three methods of mixing our eggs: beating them lightly until the yolks and whites were barely combined, beating them more vigorously to mix them completely but stopping just shy of foamy, and beating them until they turned frothy. The best method proved to be beating the eggs until well mixed but not foamy. This technique gave the omelet a more uniform texture than those eggs that had been beaten less, and beating them more, until they were frothy, simply didn't improve the texture.

The next step was to determine the best heat level for cooking our omelet. Since many egg preparations call for gentle heat, we wondered if low heat would make a more tender omelet. On the contrary, we found that all it does is slow down the cooking process. So we jumped to the other end of the heat spectrum to see what would happen. Medium-high to high heat cooked the eggs too quickly, leaving them overly browned on the bottom. Medium heat was the way to go—the eggs cooked relatively quickly and had a nicely browned exterior without any burning.

Looking again to our scrambled eggs recipe, we wondered if adding liquid to the eggs would give us a fluffier, creamier omelet. We tested a scant tablespoon each of water, milk, and cream in three separate egg mixtures. Although liquid helped the omelet remain moist in the event of overcooking, it detracted from the flavor of the eggs. Water and milk merely lessened the purity of the eggs, while cream actually competed and even overwhelmed the flavor of the eggs. Though tasters were fine with liquid additions in our scrambled eggs, they felt that an omelet's beauty was in its true eggy flavor, so we opted to bench the liquid.

While nonstick skillets make most of the old, tricky techniques unnecessary, we still wondered about the stirring. The classic method is to stir until the eggs thicken, then pull in the edges to finish. We tested this technique, as well as a simplified version of pulling in the edges until the omelet was set, but never stirring the eggs. The results were clear: stirring was a must. Because stirring breaks up and integrates the cooked egg with the uncooked egg, our stirred omelet had a consistent texture and a smooth appearance. The omelet we had not stirred was less homogeneous texturally and had an uneven exterior. About a minute of stirring was all it took, and it provided the added benefit of a shorter cooking time.

We wanted to stick as close to tradition as possible, but obviously flipping a behemoth, eight-egg omelet was out of the question. That meant we had to figure out a way to cook the top of the omelet. We found it easiest to just reduce the heat and cover the skillet with a tight-fitting lid, thus trapping the steam and cooking the top layer of eggs. Once the eggs began to set on top, we removed the omelet from the heat, sprinkled on a few ounces of shredded cheese, and replaced the cover until the cheese began to melt. Shaping this supersized omelet was as simple as sliding it halfway out of the pan and then folding it over onto itself.

With our basic cheese omelet recipe set, it was easy to come up with a few variations that offered a bit more heft: one with tomato, bacon, and garlic and another with arugula, sun-dried tomato, and provolone.

Family-Sized Cheese Omelet

SERVES 4

Monterey Jack, Colby, or any good melting cheese can be substituted for the cheddar.

8	large eggs
½	teaspoon salt
⅛	teaspoon ground black pepper
2	tablespoons unsalted butter
3	ounces cheddar cheese, shredded (¾ cup)

1. Whisk the eggs, salt, and pepper together until combined. Melt the butter in a 12-inch nonstick skillet over medium heat.

2. Add the eggs and cook, stirring gently in a circular motion, until the mixture is slightly thickened, about 1 minute. Following the illustrations

---

INGREDIENTS: Supermarket Cheddar Cheese

Supermarket cheddars are certainly not on par with their artisanal brethren, but since they are easier to find and more affordable, we were interested in exploring their merits. We organized a blind tasting of eight common brands to find out which ones were best fresh out of the package and which fared best in a grilled cheese sandwich. We limited the tasting to sharp cheddars, which are aged from 60 days up to a year.

In the end, we settled on four supermarket cheddars that are worthy of recommending, with Cabot Sharp Vermont Cheddar Cheese coming out on top. This cheese came in first place in both the grilled cheese and raw cheese taste tests. It was described as "sharp," "clean," and "tangy," and in the sandwich, tasters noted it was "buttery" and "mellow" without being even the slightest bit greasy. Tillamook Sharp Cheddar Cheese stood out not only for its color (it was the only orange rather than white cheese in the tasting), but also for its "tangy" and "piquant" characteristics. Cracker Barrel, though not the overall winner, was perhaps the greatest surprise; this relatively inexpensive contender won over tasters with its "mellow," "clean"

flavor and outpolled the more costly Organic Valley Organic Raw Milk Sharp Cheddar (which we don't recommend). Grafton Village Cheese Company's cheddar earned good marks for its crumbly texture and pungent flavor (though some found it too "pungent" and "sour").

Those at the bottom of our list were described as "buttermilky" and "sour" (Organic Valley) and "completely one-dimensional," "tasteless," and "rubbery" (Heluva Good Sharp Cheddar Cheese).

THE BEST SUPERMARKET CHEDDAR

CABOT

Tasters liked this cheese's approachable favor, described as "sharp," "clean," and "tangy."

HOW TO MAKE A FAMILY-SIZED OMELET

1. To cook the omelet evenly, pull the cooked edges of the egg mixture toward the center of the pan and allow the raw egg to run to the edges.

2. When the omelet is set on the bottom but still very runny on the top, cover the skillet and reduce the heat to low.

3. After the top of the omelet begins to set, remove the cover and sprinkle with the cheese. Let the omelet rest off the heat, covered, until the cheese has partially melted.

4. Use a rubber spatula to slide half of the omelet out onto a platter, then tilt the skillet so that the omelet folds over onto itself to make the traditional half-moon shape.

at left, use a rubber spatula to pull the cooked edges of egg toward the center of the pan, tilting the pan so the uncooked egg runs to the cleared edge of the pan. Repeat until the bottom of the omelet is just set but the top is still runny, about 1 minute.

3. Cover the skillet, reduce the heat to low, and cook until the top of the omelet begins to set but is still moist, about 5 minutes. Remove the pan from the heat. Sprinkle the cheese evenly over the eggs, cover, and let sit until the cheese partially melts, about 1 minute.

4. Slide half of the omelet onto a serving platter or cutting board using a rubber spatula, then tilt the skillet so the remaining omelet flips over onto itself, forming a half-moon shape. Cut into wedges and serve immediately.

➤ VARIATIONS

Family-Sized Tomato, Bacon, and Garlic Omelet

Less-spicy Monterey Jack cheese can be used instead of pepper Jack if preferred.

8	ounces (about 8 slices) bacon, cut into ¼-inch pieces
1	large tomato, cored, seeded, and chopped fine
½	green bell pepper, stemmed, seeded, and chopped fine
4	medium garlic cloves, minced or pressed through a garlic press (about 4 teaspoons)
8	large eggs
½	teaspoon salt
⅛	teaspoon ground black pepper
2	tablespoons unsalted butter
3	ounces pepper Jack cheese, shredded (¾ cup)

1. Cook the bacon in a 12-inch nonstick skillet over medium-high heat until crisp, about 8 minutes. Transfer the bacon to a paper towel–lined plate and discard all but 2 teaspoons of the bacon fat. Stir in the tomato and bell pepper and cook until the vegetables are softened, about 6 minutes. Stir in the garlic and cook until fragrant, about 30 seconds.

Transfer the mixture to the plate with the bacon. Wipe out the skillet with a wad of paper towels.

2. Whisk the eggs, salt, and pepper together until combined. Add the butter to the skillet and melt over medium heat.

3. Add the eggs and bacon mixture to the skillet and cook, stirring gently in a circular motion, until the mixture is slightly thickened, about 1 minute. Following the illustrations on page 260, use a rubber spatula to pull the cooked edges of egg toward the center of the pan, tilting the pan so the uncooked egg runs to the cleared edge of the pan. Repeat until the bottom of the omelet is just set but the top is still runny, about 1 minute.

4. Cover the skillet, reduce the heat to low, and cook until the top of the omelet begins to set but is still moist, about 5 minutes. Remove the pan from the heat. Sprinkle the cheese evenly over the eggs, cover, and let sit until the cheese partially melts, about 1 minute.

5. Slide half of the omelet onto a serving platter or cutting board using a rubber spatula, then tilt the skillet so the remaining omelet flips over onto itself, forming a half-moon shape. Cut into wedges and serve immediately.

Family-Sized Arugula, Sun-Dried Tomato, and Provolone Omelet

Feel free to substitute the flavorful oil from the sun-dried tomatoes for the olive oil.

1	tablespoon olive oil
1	small onion, minced
⅛	teaspoon red pepper flakes
5	ounces baby arugula, cut into ½-inch strips
¼	cup oil-packed sun-dried tomatoes, minced
8	large eggs
½	teaspoon salt
⅛	teaspoon ground black pepper
2	tablespoons unsalted butter
3	ounces provolone cheese, shredded (¾ cup)

1. Heat the oil in a 12-inch nonstick skillet over medium-high heat until shimmering. Add the onion and red pepper flakes and cook until softened, about 5 minutes. Stir in the arugula and sun-dried tomatoes and cook until the arugula begins to wilt, about 1 minute. Transfer the mixture to a plate and set aside. Wipe out the skillet with a wad of paper towels.

2. Whisk the eggs, salt, and pepper together until combined. Add the butter to the skillet and melt over medium heat.

3. Add the eggs and arugula mixture to the skillet and cook, stirring gently in a circular motion, until the mixture is slightly thickened, about 1 minute. Following the illustrations on page 260, use a rubber spatula to pull the cooked edges of egg toward the center of the pan, tilting the pan so the uncooked egg runs to the cleared edge of the pan. Repeat until the bottom of the omelet is just set but the top is still runny, about 1 minute.

4. Cover the skillet, reduce the heat to low, and cook until the top of the omelet begins to set but is still moist, about 5 minutes. Remove the pan from the heat. Sprinkle the cheese evenly over the eggs, cover, and let sit until the cheese partially melts, about 1 minute.

5. Slide half of the omelet onto a serving platter or cutting board using a rubber spatula, then tilt the skillet so the remaining omelet flips over onto itself, forming a half-moon shape. Cut into wedges and serve immediately.

THICK AND HEARTY FRITTATA

A FRITTATA HAS ALL THE GOOD CHARACteristics of an omelet—a quick and easy eggs-for-dinner-meal that can be almost infinitely varied just by changing the fillings used—but without the finicky cooking technique. Like our family-sized omelets (see pages 259–261), a single frittata can feed a family of four, and because frittatas incorporate more filling than omelets, they offer a more substantial option. When it comes to cooking, frittatas are more forgiving than their omelet cousins, but they are certainly not foolproof. Tough, rubbery, dry frittatas are an all-too-common outcome, so we set out to create a recipe that yielded a perfect frittata every time, one that was firm yet moist, with a pleasing balance of egg to filling and a supportive, browned exterior.

We knew from our previous tests in this chapter that some fillings would add moisture, particularly vegetables, so these ingredients would need to be sautéed before being combined with the eggs. To keep the procedure simple, we sautéed them in the same pan that we would use to cook the frittata. Doing so enabled us to simply pour the beaten eggs over the sautéed filling and proceed. We found that 12 eggs mixed with 3 cups of cooked vegetables and/or meat provided the best balance of filling to eggs and did a good job serving four to six people for dinner. Any more than those amounts caused the frittata to cook unevenly; any less and the frittata lacked substance.

Once the eggs are added to the skillet, the cooking methods we found in our research go in one of three directions: cooking the frittata fully on the stovetop, cooking it fully in the oven, or starting it on the stovetop and finishing it in the oven. We first tried cooking our frittata fully on the stovetop, but no matter what we did, varying both time and temperature, the underside always ended up tough and overcooked. Cooking the frittata fully in the oven proved problematic as well. Again, we tried cooking at different temperatures and for different lengths of time, but the results were either too dry or unevenly cooked. A combination of stovetop and oven showed the most promise. We began by cooking the frittata almost fully on top of the stove and then slid the skillet in the oven to finish up. We learned quickly during the stovetop stage that dumping the eggs in the skillet and leaving them be wasn't acceptable—the results were unevenly cooked and rubbery. Stirring the eggs on the stovetop until large curds began forming solved the problem; it evenly distributed the eggs as they began cooking, leading to more tender eggs and a frittata that was properly cooked throughout. We discovered that for even cooking it was also important to make sure the eggs were set on the bottom before they left the stovetop.

Now we just had to iron out the details of the oven stage. Knowing from previous egg recipe tests that residual heat can be a key player in perfectly cooked eggs, we pulled our skillet from the oven when the eggs were still slightly wet and runny, so that the residual heat would just cook them through. The last remaining problem was that the top of our frittata didn't show the browning that is the trademark of a good frittata. Modifying our stovetop to oven method slightly, we tried finishing the frittata under the broiler. This worked best of all. The resulting frittata was evenly cooked, lightly browned, and firm without being too dry—exactly what we had been seeking. (It's worthwhile to note you shouldn't walk away from the broiler, since some cook quicker than others.)

As for the pan size, we tried making 12-egg frittatas in skillets measuring 10 inches and 12 inches (the volume of eggs automatically excluded an 8-inch skillet). Tasters were split down the middle with regard to thickness, but the majority liked the increased amount of browning gained by using the 12-inch skillet. We then tried making frittatas in both a traditional pan and a nonstick pan. While we were able to produce satisfactory frittatas in both pans, we had to use a lot more oil in the traditional pan to prevent sticking, making the resulting frittata slightly greasy. The 12-inch nonstick skillet was deemed the winner. Because the frittata is slid under the high heat of the broiler, it's important that the nonstick skillet be ovensafe.

With our method down pat, we finessed the fillings. First we tested a number of cheeses. Parmesan was too dry, but Gruyère, goat cheese, and fontina all worked well; cubing the cheese (or crumbling, in the case of goat cheese) rather than shredding added a nice change in texture. Looking to our scrambled egg testing (see page 254), we also tried adding half-and-half to the eggs before pouring them in the skillet. Though not traditional for a frittata, it lent a nice touch of creaminess so we kept it in. We tried adding various meats and vegetables and came up with myriad combinations. Asparagus, ham, and Gruyère formed a winning variation, as did leek, prosciutto, and goat cheese. Tasters also enjoyed the earthy combination of broccoli rabe and sun-dried tomatoes with buttery, nutty fontina.

Regardless of which add-in ingredients we used, we found it important to cut them into small pieces and precook most of them (vegetables in particular) in the skillet before adding the eggs. Doing so drove off moisture, which would have otherwise made for a soggy frittata. After whisking the eggs together, we precooked the vegetables, then poured the eggs over the top and let the mixture cook for a few minutes before moving it to the oven. In less than 10 minutes we had a perfectly puffed and browned frittata.

One last frittata asset worth noting: they do not have to be eaten hot. They can be served at room temperature or even cold, so timing isn't an issue, as it is with omelets.

INGREDIENTS: Gruyère Cheese

Authentic versions of Gruyère, made in both Switzerland and France (the French cheese is called Gruyère de Comté), are crafted from raw cow's milk and aged for the better part of a year in government-designated regions. Meanwhile, we have found that domestic cheeses that are labeled "Gruyère" actually bear little resemblance to the real thing. Made from pasteurized cow's milk, they are aged for fewer months and have a rubbery texture and bland flavor. In fact, in a blind taste test of nine brands, tasters overwhelmingly panned the two domestic versions, likening one (from Boar's Head) to "plastic." Imported Gruyères, on the other hand, received raves. The top picks in the lineup were both reserve cheeses, aged 10 or more months to develop stronger flavor: Emmi Le Gruyère Reserve and a Gruyère Salé from a Boston-area cheese shop. The top pick, the Swiss-produced Emmi Le Gruyère Reserve, was described as "grassy," "salty," and "nicely dry" and won favor with most tasters, especially when melted.

Asparagus, Ham, and Gruyère Frittata
SERVES 4 TO 6

Although we prefer the strong flavor of Gruyère in this recipe, you can substitute Swiss if desired. Because broilers vary so much in intensity, watch the frittata carefully as it cooks.

12	large eggs
3	tablespoons half-and-half
½	teaspoon salt
¼	teaspoon ground black pepper
3	ounces Gruyère cheese, cut into ¼-inch cubes
2	teaspoons olive oil
½	pound asparagus (½ bunch), tough ends trimmed (see the illustration on page 92) and sliced thin on the bias
4	ounces thick-sliced deli ham, chopped small
1	medium shallot, minced (about 3 tablespoons)

1. Adjust an oven rack about 5 inches from the broiler element and heat the broiler. Whisk the eggs, half-and-half, salt, and pepper together, then stir in the cheese.

2. Heat the oil in a 12-inch ovensafe nonstick skillet over medium heat until shimmering. Add the asparagus and cook until lightly browned and crisp-tender, 2 to 4 minutes. Stir in the ham and shallot and cook until the shallot softens, about 2 minutes.

3. Add the egg mixture to the skillet and cook, using a rubber spatula to stir and scrape the bottom of the skillet, until large curds form and the spatula begins to leave a wake but the eggs are still very wet, about 2 minutes. Shake the skillet to distribute the eggs evenly and continue to cook without stirring to set the bottom, about 30 seconds.

4. Slide the skillet under the broiler and cook

until the surface is puffed and spotty brown, yet the center remains slightly wet and runny when cut into with a paring knife, 3 to 4 minutes.

5. Remove the skillet from the broiler and let stand until the eggs in the middle are just set, about 5 minutes. Use a rubber spatula to loosen the frittata from the skillet, then slide onto a cutting board, slice into wedges, and serve.

> VARIATIONS
Leek, Prosciutto, and Goat Cheese Frittata
Thinly sliced deli ham can be substituted for the prosciutto. Because broilers vary so much in intensity, watch the frittata carefully as it cooks.

12	large eggs
3	tablespoons half-and-half
	Salt
¼	teaspoon ground black pepper
3	ounces thinly sliced prosciutto, chopped coarse
¼	cup minced fresh basil
2	ounces goat cheese, crumbled (½ cup)
2	tablespoons unsalted butter
2	medium leeks, white and light green parts only, halved lengthwise, sliced thin crosswise, and rinsed thoroughly

1. Adjust an oven rack about 5 inches from the broiler element and heat the broiler. Whisk the eggs, half-and-half, ½ teaspoon salt, and pepper together, then stir in the prosciutto, basil, and half of the goat cheese.

2. Melt the butter in a 12-inch ovensafe nonstick skillet over medium heat. Add the leeks and a pinch salt, cover, reduce the heat to low, and cook, stirring occasionally, until softened, 8 to 10 minutes.

3. Uncover the skillet, add the egg mixture, and cook, using a rubber spatula to stir and scrape the bottom of the skillet, until large curds form and the spatula begins to leave a wake but the eggs are still very wet, about 2 minutes. Shake the skillet to distribute the eggs evenly and continue to cook without stirring to set the bottom, about 30 seconds.

4. Dot the remaining goat cheese evenly over the eggs. Slide the skillet under the broiler and cook until the surface is puffed and spotty brown, yet the center remains slightly wet and runny when cut into with a paring knife, 3 to 4 minutes.

5. Remove the skillet from the broiler and let stand until the eggs in the middle are just set, about 5 minutes. Use a rubber spatula to loosen the frittata from the skillet, then slide onto a cutting board, slice into wedges, and serve.

Broccoli Rabe, Sun-Dried Tomato, and Fontina Frittata
Be sure to use oil-packed sun-dried tomatoes here or the tomatoes will remain tough and chewy in the frittata. Because broilers vary so much in intensity, watch the frittata carefully as it cooks.

12	large eggs
3	tablespoons half-and-half
	Salt
¼	teaspoon ground black pepper
3	ounces Italian fontina cheese, cut into ¼-inch cubes
¼	cup oil-packed sun-dried tomatoes, minced
2	teaspoons olive oil
8	ounces broccoli rabe, trimmed and cut into 1-inch pieces
1	medium garlic clove, minced or pressed through a garlic press (about 1 teaspoon)
⅛	teaspoon red pepper flakes

1. Adjust an oven rack about 5 inches from the broiler element and heat the broiler. Whisk the eggs, half-and-half, ½ teaspoon salt, and pepper together, then stir in the fontina and sun-dried tomatoes.

2. Heat the oil in a 12-inch ovensafe nonstick skillet over medium heat until shimmering. Add the broccoli rabe and a pinch salt and cook until just beginning to brown and soften, 6 to 8 minutes. Add the garlic and red pepper flakes and cook until fragrant, about 30 seconds.

3. Add the egg mixture to the skillet and cook, using a rubber spatula to stir and scrape the bottom of the skillet, until large curds form and the spatula begins to leave a wake but the eggs are still very

wet, about 2 minutes. Shake the skillet to distribute the eggs evenly and continue to cook without stirring to set the bottom, about 30 seconds.

4. Slide the skillet under the broiler and cook until the surface is puffed and spotty brown, yet the center remains slightly wet and runny when cut into with a paring knife, 3 to 4 minutes.

5. Remove the skillet from the broiler and let stand until the eggs in the middle are just set, about 5 minutes. Use a rubber spatula to loosen the frittata from the skillet, then slide onto a cutting board, slice into wedges, and serve.

SPANISH TORTILLA

EGGS AND POTATOES ARE NEARLY EVER-present kitchen staples, but we wanted to go beyond just eggs and hash browns. To find our jumping-off point, we began by researching recipes from around the world that brought our two key ingredients together into a single, flavorful dish. Given the mildness of both, their combination creates an ideal palette for introducing flavor, so it wasn't surprising that the variations we found were numerous. But one recipe seemed to come up more than the others: Spanish tortilla.

Traditionally, a Spanish tortilla is made by slow cooking potatoes and onions in ample olive oil, which gives the dish both flavor and moisture, then adding beaten eggs. The whole mixture coalesces into a savory, velvety cake somewhat like a frittata, but with an emphasis on deep potato flavor. Because of its popularity and simplicity, Spanish tortilla seemed like a good foundation on which to build a skillet potato and egg recipe; we could then change the flavors to suit our tastes.

Overall, we wanted our potato and egg dish to be firm enough to cut into wedges but still tender. In our initial recipe tests, we encountered both dry and greasy versions, so our two primary goals were to nail down the technique and to quantify the amount of oil required. We started with the potatoes.

Starchy, creamy potatoes would be key; we narrowed our testing down to russets and Yukon Golds. Though they share many common traits, the russets ended up edging out the Yukon Golds with their creamier texture. Traditionally, Spanish tortilla recipes call for thinly sliced potatoes, but we found it easier to manage ½-inch pieces. We cooked the potatoes in the microwave until they were just beginning to get tender, which not only sped up the cooking process but also made them light and fluffy on the inside. Then we finished them in the skillet, where they picked up a nice, light browning on the exterior. Most recipes include onions, cooked along with the potatoes. Yellow Spanish onions, a common choice, worked well in our recipe.

We would rely on olive oil to lend the potatoes both flavor and texture. Many recipes for Spanish tortilla start by frying the potatoes and onions in up to 2 cups of olive oil. This amount seemed excessive to us, but we decided to try it anyway. Our hunch was confirmed when we found ourselves pouring off excess oil from our finished dish. Testing lesser amounts, we determined that ¼ cup was just enough to cook the potatoes and onions and add the right amount of richness and flavor.

Once the potatoes and onions were done, all we needed to do was add beaten eggs to the pan and finish up the cooking. At this point, we had two options. One was to finish the tortilla on the stovetop, but doing so would require flipping the eggs and potatoes to cook the top, a step we felt was cumbersome. So we turned to the second option, a technique we use for frittatas—cooking on the stovetop just until the eggs are set, then transferring the skillet to the oven to finish cooking the eggs through. We tried this method, and once the eggs had puffed and started to pull away from the sides of the skillet, we knew the tortilla was close to ready. To make sure it didn't overcook, at this point we pulled it from the oven and let it sit for five minutes to finish cooking from the residual heat.

Tasters enjoyed our Spanish tortilla served hot, room temperature, and cold, so serving temperature is not an issue. We found that accompanying it with a dollop of smoky-sweet roasted red pepper aioli (see page 266) added a nice touch of complexity.

With our master tortilla recipe determined, we could then easily swap flavors in and out to create a couple of variations. A hearty combination of tomatoes, onions, peppers, and ham was a big hit with tasters, and they raved about the Indian-spiced variation with curry, mustard seeds, and fresh cilantro.

Spanish Egg and Potato Tortilla

SERVES 4 TO 6

In a pinch, Yukon Gold potatoes can be substituted for the russets. Make sure to use a 10-inch ovensafe nonstick skillet.

10	large eggs
	Salt and ground black pepper
1	pound russet potatoes (about 2 medium), peeled and cut into ½-inch pieces
5	tablespoons olive oil
1	medium onion, minced
1	recipe Roasted Red Pepper Aioli (see recipe at right)

1. Adjust an oven rack to the middle position and heat the oven to 450 degrees. Whisk the eggs, ¼ teaspoon salt, and ¼ teaspoon pepper together and set aside.

2. Toss the potatoes with 1 tablespoon of the oil, ¼ teaspoon salt, and a pinch pepper in a microwave-safe bowl. Cover the bowl and microwave on high until the potatoes begin to soften, 5 to 7 minutes, stirring the potatoes halfway through cooking. Drain the potatoes well.

3. Heat the remaining ¼ cup oil in a 10-inch ovensafe nonstick skillet over medium heat until shimmering. Add the drained potatoes, onion, and ¼ teaspoon salt. Cover and cook, stirring occasionally, until the potatoes and onion are lightly browned and soft, about 8 minutes.

4. Uncover the skillet, gently stir in the eggs until combined, and cook until the eggs begin to set on the bottom, about 1 minute. Transfer the skillet to the oven and bake until the top is puffed and the edges have pulled away slightly from the sides of the pan, 7 to 9 minutes.

5. Let the tortilla cool in the pan for 5 minutes to set. Use a rubber spatula to loosen the tortilla from the skillet, then slide onto a cutting board, slice into wedges, and serve with the aioli.

Roasted Red Pepper Aioli

MAKES ABOUT 1¼ CUPS

In Spanish tapas bars, it's not uncommon to find a creamy, potatoey wedge of tortilla served along with a small dollop of aioli—the Provençal version of mayonnaise made with olive oil and fresh garlic. To give our aioli a bit of a Spanish flair, we added roasted red peppers; their roasty-sweet flavor adds a good amount of complexity and depth. This finished sauce contains raw eggs. If you do not have regular olive oil, use a blend of equal parts extra-virgin olive oil and vegetable oil—using all extra-virgin olive oil will make the aioli taste too bitter. The aioli can be refrigerated in an airtight container for up to 3 days.

2	large egg yolks
1	tablespoon fresh lemon juice
1	medium garlic clove, minced or pressed through a garlic press (about 1 teaspoon)
⅛	teaspoon sugar
	Salt and ground black pepper
	Pinch cayenne pepper
¾	cup olive oil (see note)
2	medium jarred roasted red peppers, rinsed, patted dry, and chopped (½ cup)

1. Process the yolks, lemon juice, garlic, sugar, ¼ teaspoon salt, a pinch black pepper, and cayenne together in a food processor until combined, about 10 seconds. With the machine running, gradually add the oil in a slow, steady stream, about 30 seconds.

2. Scrape down the sides of the bowl with a rubber spatula. Add the peppers and continue to process until smooth, about 1 minute. Season with salt and pepper to taste and serve.

INGREDIENTS:
Jarred Roasted Red Peppers

To find the best-tasting jarred roasted red peppers, we sampled eight supermarket brands: three used domestically grown peppers, while the rest were products of Spain, Greece, or Turkey. Tasted plain, we preferred firmer-textured, smokier, sweeter peppers in strong yet simple brines of salt and water. Peppers packed in brines that contained garlic, vinegar, olive oil, and grape must—characteristic of most of the European peppers—received lower ratings. While these extra ingredients provided "interesting" and "lively" flavor profiles, they often masked the authentic red pepper flavor and smoky notes that tasters preferred, particularly when they contained vinegar. Overly plain peppers had another problem: the two blandest brands were noted as being "slimy." They earned our lowest scores.

Our favorite was domestically grown Dunbar's Sweet Roasted Peppers. Sweet with a hint of smokiness, this brand showcased mild, pure red pepper flavor, with a balanced brine of salt and water.

THE BEST JARRED ROASTED RED PEPPERS

"Authentic," and "not overbearing," the flavor of these red peppers was the "perfect balance of smoky and sweet." Tasters liked their "firm and crisp" texture.

DUNBAR'S

➤ VARIATIONS
Tortilla with Tomatoes, Peppers, and Ham
This recipe was developed using thick-sliced deli ham, but a ham steak also works well.

10	large eggs
2	tablespoons minced fresh parsley leaves
	Salt and ground black pepper
¾	pound russet potatoes (about 1 large), peeled and cut into ½-inch pieces
5	tablespoons olive oil
1	red bell pepper, stemmed, seeded, and cut into ¼-inch pieces
2	plum tomatoes, cut into ½-inch pieces
1	medium onion, minced
⅛	teaspoon red pepper flakes
2	ounces thick-sliced deli ham, cut into ½-inch pieces
2	medium garlic cloves, minced or pressed through a garlic press (about 2 teaspoons)

1. Adjust an oven rack to the middle position and heat the oven to 450 degrees. Whisk the eggs, parsley, ¼ teaspoon salt, and ¼ teaspoon pepper together and set aside.

2. Toss the potatoes with 1 tablespoon of the oil, ¼ teaspoon salt, and a pinch pepper in a microwave-safe bowl. Cover the bowl and microwave on high until the potatoes begin to soften, 5 to 7 minutes, stirring the potatoes halfway through cooking. Drain the potatoes well.

3. Heat the remaining ¼ cup oil in a 10-inch ovensafe nonstick skillet over medium heat until shimmering. Add the drained potatoes, bell pepper, tomatoes, onion, red pepper flakes, and ¼ teaspoon salt. Cover and cook, stirring occasionally, until the vegetables are lightly browned and soft, about 8 minutes.

4. Uncover the skillet, stir in the ham and garlic, and cook until fragrant, about 1 minute. Gently stir in the eggs until combined and cook until the eggs begin to set on the bottom, about 1 minute. Transfer the skillet to the oven and bake until the top is puffed and the edges have pulled away slightly from the sides of the pan, 7 to 9 minutes.

5. Let the tortilla cool in the pan for 5 minutes to set. Use a rubber spatula to loosen the tortilla from the skillet, then slide onto a cutting board, slice into wedges, and serve.

Indian-Spiced Tortilla
Penzeys Sweet Curry Powder is our favorite; however, any brand of curry powder will work fine here. Serve with a jarred mango chutney.

10	large eggs
2	scallions, sliced thin
2	tablespoons minced fresh cilantro leaves
	Salt and ground black pepper
1	pound russet potatoes (about 2 medium), peeled and cut into ½-inch pieces
5	tablespoons olive oil

I   medium onion, minced

I   teaspoon curry powder

I   teaspoon whole mustard seeds

1. Adjust an oven rack to the middle position and heat the oven to 450 degrees. Whisk the eggs, scallions, cilantro, ¼ teaspoon salt, and ¼ teaspoon pepper together and set aside.

2. Toss the potatoes with 1 tablespoon of the oil, ¼ teaspoon salt, and a pinch pepper in a microwave-safe bowl. Cover the bowl and microwave on high until the potatoes begin to soften, 5 to 7 minutes, stirring the potatoes halfway through cooking. Drain the potatoes well.

3. Heat the remaining ¼ cup oil in a 10-inch ovensafe nonstick skillet over medium heat until shimmering. Add the drained potatoes, onion, curry powder, mustard seeds, and ¼ teaspoon salt. Cover and cook, stirring occasionally, until the potatoes and onion are lightly browned and soft, about 8 minutes.

4. Uncover the skillet, gently stir in the eggs until combined, and cook until the eggs begin to set on the bottom, about 1 minute. Transfer the skillet to the oven and bake until the top is puffed and the edges have pulled away slightly from the sides of the pan, 7 to 9 minutes.

5. Let the tortilla cool in the pan for 5 minutes to set. Use a rubber spatula to loosen the tortilla from the skillet, then slide onto a cutting board, slice into wedges, and serve.

INGREDIENTS: Curry Powder

Though blends can vary dramatically, curry powders come in two basic styles—mild or sweet and a hotter version called Madras. The former combines as many as 20 different ground spices, herbs, and seeds. We tasted six curry powders—mixed into rice pilaf and in our vegetable curry. The result? Our favorite is Penzeys Sweet Curry Powder, though Durkee Curry Powder came in a close second.

THE BEST CURRY POWDER

Neither too sweet nor too hot, this blend set the standard in our tasting for a balanced yet complex curry powder.

PENZEYS

CORNED BEEF HASH

IN THE EARLY DAYS OF AMERICAN INGENUITY and frugality, New Englanders utilized leftovers from the previous night's boiled dinner to make corned beef hash for the next morning's breakfast. Meat, potatoes, carrots, and sometimes cabbage would be fried up in a skillet and capped with eggs. It was a hearty, simple, one-pan entrée that seemed like a perfect candidate for this book. But recipes for traditional corned beef hash are few and far between, as if to say making it should be common sense. The few recipes we did come across produced starchy, one-dimensional hashes that were light on flavor. The door was open for us to create a corned beef hash for the twenty-first century, one that was flavorful and easy to prepare, with fresh ingredients (since most of us don't have the required leftovers lying around).

Meat and potatoes, though accented by flavorings and bound by stock or cream, are the heart and soul of this dish. Choosing the right potatoes was easy. Texture being foremost, we knew we wanted starchy potatoes that would retain some character but would soften and crumble about the edges to help bind the hash together. We quickly ruled out anything waxy, such as red potatoes, because they would remain too firm. Russets were our top choice. We opted to speed things along by parcooking the potatoes in the microwave. Once the potatoes were just starting to become tender, we moved them to the skillet.

Next, the meat. While leftover beef from a boiled dinner is traditional, we know most people wouldn't want to wait to have such leftovers on hand. We tested chunks of corned beef, thinking they would be most authentic and similar to cutting up a day-old roast, but they were chewy and unappetizing. In the end, we found that deli-style corned beef worked best. We first tested a basic recipe with our deli meat minced into ¼-inch pieces, but the resulting hash had barely-there meat dust that was hardly noticeable in the final dish. The next time around we cut our thinly sliced corned beef into ½-inch squares. These pieces proved the most tender and were large enough to hold up. We stirred them in toward the end to ensure that the meat would not dry out.

When it came to vegetables other than potatoes, we quickly ruled out everything but onions. Carrots may be traditional, but tasters agreed that their sweetness compromised the simplicity of the hash. Onions, on the other hand, added characteristic body and roundness that supported the meat and potatoes rather than detracting from them. We liked them best when cooked slow and steady until lightly browned. Garlic and thyme also earned spots in our hash; we added them to the skillet after the onions were browned. The garlic sharpened the dish and a small amount of thyme added an earthiness that set off the beef.

Although the potatoes were loosely binding the mixture, most hash recipes call for either stock or cream to hold everything together more firmly. We made a batch with each, adding the potatoes and liquid to the browned aromatics, and found that we preferred the cream for its richness. A little hot pepper sauce added with the cream brought a touch of spice to the dish.

The flavors of our hash were coming together, and the addition of bacon, cooked with the onion, boosted the hash's meaty flavor and contributed a delicate smokiness. Cutting the bacon slightly smaller than the corned beef allowed the beef to take center stage while the bacon played a supporting role. We cooked the bacon with the onion in the skillet first, creating a flavorful foundation for our hash.

After cooking several batches of hash at varying temperatures and times, we discovered that about 10 minutes at medium-high was the key to getting just the right golden crust of browned meat and potatoes that deepened the overall flavor. Meanwhile, we found two modes of thought among recipes when it came to handling the crust: Some preserved the crust in one piece, cooking both sides by flipping the hash or sliding it onto a plate and inverting it back into the skillet; other recipes suggested breaking up the crust and folding it back into the hash. After trying both styles, tasters preferred the latter, feeling that it had a better overall flavor. (And it's a lot easier than trying to flip a single mound of heavy, unwieldy hash.) We lightly packed the hash into the skillet with the back of a spatula, allowed the bottom to crisp up, and then

folded it over the top and repeated the process several times. With this technique, we were able to evenly distribute the crisp browned bits.

Tasters agreed that the eggs served with hash needed to be just barely set, so that the yolks were still runny and could moisten the potatoes. Poaching is the easiest technique for preserving a lightly cooked yolk, and we found that we could make hash a one-pot meal by "poaching" the eggs in the pan with the hash. Once we had browned the hash, we simply nestled the eggs into indentations in the hash, covered the pan, and cooked them over low heat. The results were perfect: eggs with bright, runny yolks conveniently set in the hash, ready to be served.

Corned Beef Hash
SERVES 4

You will need a 12-inch skillet with a tight-fitting lid for this recipe. A well-seasoned cast-iron skillet is traditional, but we prefer a nonstick skillet—the nonstick surface leaves little chance of anything sticking and burning. Our favorite tool for flipping the hash is a stiff plastic spatula.

2	pounds russet potatoes (about 4 medium), peeled and cut into ½-inch pieces
I	tablespoon olive oil
	Salt and ground black pepper
4	ounces (about 4 slices) bacon, cut into ¼-inch pieces
I	medium onion, minced
2	medium garlic cloves, minced or pressed through a garlic press (about 2 teaspoons)
½	teaspoon minced fresh thyme leaves
⅓	cup heavy cream
¼	teaspoon hot sauce
12	ounces thinly sliced corned beef, cut into ½-inch pieces
4	large eggs

1. Toss the potatoes with the oil, ½ teaspoon salt, and ¼ teaspoon pepper in a microwave-safe bowl. Cover the bowl and microwave on high until the potatoes begin to soften, 7 to 10 minutes, stirring the potatoes halfway through cooking. Drain the potatoes well.

2. Cook the bacon in a 12-inch nonstick skillet over medium-high heat until the fat begins to render, about 2 minutes. Stir in the onion and cook until softened and lightly browned, about 8 minutes.

3. Stir in the garlic and thyme and cook until fragrant, about 30 seconds. Stir in the drained potatoes, cream, and hot sauce. Using the back of a spatula, gently pack the potatoes into the pan and cook undisturbed for 2 minutes. Flip the hash, one portion at a time, and lightly repack it into the pan. Repeat the flipping process every few minutes until the potatoes are nicely browned, 6 to 8 minutes.

4. Stir in the corned beef and lightly repack the hash into the pan. Make four shallow wells (about 2 inches wide) in the surface of the hash.

5. Crack 1 egg into each indentation and sprinkle with salt and pepper. Reduce the heat to medium-low, cover, and continue to cook until the eggs are just set, about 5 minutes. Serve immediately.

➤ VARIATION

Ham and Sweet Potato Hash

Be sure to substitute sweet potatoes for just half of the potatoes here. If you try to replace all of the potatoes with sweet potatoes, the hash will have a very soft, mushy consistency.

Follow the recipe for Corned Beef Hash, substituting 1 pound sweet potatoes (about 2 small), peeled and cut into ½-inch pieces, for 1 pound of the russet potatoes and 12 ounces thinly sliced deli ham, cut into ½-inch pieces, for the corned beef.

EGG, SAUSAGE, AND PEPPER SUPPER

AFTER GETTING SUCH GREAT REVIEWS FROM tasters on our Indian-Spiced Tortilla (page 267), we were inspired to create another internationally influenced hearty egg dish. We decided that the full-flavored one-pot meal called *chackchouka*, found in the Middle East and parts of North Africa, would be a good place to start. Typically for this dish, a sauce is built by simmering onions, garlic, peppers, tomatoes, and fresh chiles until they are soft and their flavors have blended together, then eggs are added and lightly poached in the mixture. When done well, the eggs are a soft, creamy counterpoint that perfectly tempers the spiciness of the sauce. Chackchouka is usually served as a light meal or appetizer alongside a stack of warm pita bread, but we wanted our skillet version to have a bit more heft. We settled on the addition of sausage, as it would pair well with the dish's traditional ingredients and would be able to push this recipe into the supper category. With our main components decided, we pulled out our skillet and got to work.

We started with the basic elements of the sauce: onion, garlic, bell peppers, and tomatoes. Once the vegetables were sautéed, tasters found they liked the textural contrast of thin slices of pepper over chopped. A hefty shot of garlic added a pungent bite that also got the thumbs up.

While the onion, garlic, and bell pepper were fairly straightforward, the choice of tomatoes was up for discussion. We sautéed our way through a few simple sauces, trying out various types of tomatoes, both canned and fresh. Among the fresh tomatoes, we tested diminutive cherry and oblong plum tomatoes, as well as beefsteak. The tart flavor of cherry tomatoes held the most promise, but tasters couldn't get past the amount of skin and seeds in the sauce, so they were dropped from the running. The plum tomatoes had slightly more complexity than the beefsteak tomatoes and a more compact, less watery texture. But, despite their advantage over the other tomatoes, they still yielded a watery sauce.

We hoped canned tomatoes would give us a deeper tomato flavor and better texture than the fresh. Pureed tomatoes were too thin and smooth, while whole tomatoes lacked fresh flavor and had to be chopped to an appropriate size so they wouldn't dominate the sauce. Diced tomatoes were slightly firmer than the whole tomatoes, and they were chunky without overtaking the other ingredients. Tasters also preferred the brighter flavor and convenience that the diced tomatoes offered. We opted not to drain them, instead using the juice in the can as a good base for our sauce. (For more on diced tomatoes, see page 81.)

With the basics for the sauce under our belt, we next looked to the fresh chile component. We tested a number of fresh chiles found in our local supermarket—poblanos, jalapeños, habaneros—but none of them seemed right. Without access to the bounty of complexly flavored fresh chiles available in the Middle East and North Africa, we were forced to head to our pantry to see if there was a dried chile or combination of spices we could use as a substitute. Ancho and chipotle chiles, two of the more common dried chiles available in supermarkets, seemed out of place, giving the sauce a Mexican feel. Chili powder was in the running for a while, until tasters tried a mix of cumin and cayenne. Together, these commonplace spices found in most cupboards added the exotic complexity, depth, and moderate spiciness we were after.

The last detail of our sauce was the sausage. After trying grocery store staples such as kielbasa and Italian sausage with poor results, we turned our attention to chorizo. Cut into ¼-inch slices, it offered a pleasing textural contrast, and tasters liked its sweet-smoky flavor. Cooking the sausage in the skillet first allowed us to prepare our sauce in the rendered fat left behind, giving the dish an extra boost of flavor.

With the sauce finished and the chorizo stirred in, we turned to the eggs. Following tradition, we poached them right in the sauce, which not only saved us from dirtying another pan, but also gave the eggs' flavor a boost. Following the method used in our Corned Beef Hash recipe (page 269), we scooped out four small wells in the sauce (each about two inches wide) and cracked an egg into each, then fit a lid over the top for even cooking. After five minutes, the golden, runny yolks looked right, but we didn't like that the edges of the whites were disrupted from the bubbling sauce. Lowering the heat from medium to medium-low solved the frayed-edge problem, and the cooked eggs could be easily scooped with the sauce to the plate. After sprinkling on a bit of minced cilantro for freshness and color, we took one bite and knew we had finally achieved the look and spicy-creamy pairing that we were after.

Egg, Sausage, and Pepper Supper
SERVES 4

For more color, use a mix of different colors of bell peppers. Serve with warm pita bread or slices of toast.

2	tablespoons olive oil
8	ounces chorizo sausage, split in half and cut into ¼-inch slices
1	medium onion, minced
	Salt
2	large bell peppers, stemmed, seeded, and sliced into ¼-inch strips
4	medium garlic cloves, minced or pressed through a garlic press (about 4 teaspoons)
1	(14.5-ounce) can diced tomatoes
1	teaspoon ground cumin
¼	teaspoon cayenne pepper
4	large eggs
	Ground black pepper
2	tablespoons minced fresh cilantro

1. Heat 1 tablespoon of the oil in a 12-inch nonstick skillet over medium-high heat until shimmering. Add the chorizo and cook until lightly browned and the fat has rendered, 3 to 5 minutes. Transfer to a small bowl and set aside.

2. Add the remaining tablespoon oil to the skillet and heat over medium-high heat until shimmering. Add the onion and ¼ teaspoon salt and cook until the onion begins to soften, about 3 minutes. Stir in the peppers, cover, and cook until the peppers are soft and lightly browned, about 10 minutes.

3. Uncover the skillet, stir in the garlic, and cook until fragrant, about 30 seconds. Stir in the tomatoes with their juice, cumin, and cayenne. Reduce the heat to medium and cook until the sauce is slightly thickened and the flavors have melded, about 5 minutes. Stir in the cooked chorizo.

4. Make four shallow wells (about 2 inches wide) in the surface of the sauce. Crack 1 egg into each indentation and sprinkle with salt and pepper. Reduce the heat to medium-low, cover, and continue to cook until the eggs are just set, about 5 minutes. Sprinkle with cilantro and serve immediately.

STRATA

STRATA IN ITS MOST BASIC FORM IS A LAY-
ered brunch casserole of day-old bread, eggs, cheese,
and milk. The result is a hearty, savory bread pudding that can feed a crowd for breakfast or brunch.
Typically, strata is prepared hours in advance, if
not the night before serving, to give the dry bread
enough time to soak up the custard; it then bakes
for an hour or so before serving. We were after a
simplified skillet strata, one that would deliver the
same cheesy richness as a layered casserole but could
be made on the fly, with little advance planning
aside from the trip to the grocery store.

We quickly discovered this skillet method was
not without issues. Many of the stratas we sampled
were simply too rich, with a belly-busting over-
abundance of custard. On the other end of the
spectrum, stratas with the bread dominating or
calling attention to itself were equally unappealing.

And then there were the fillings. Many of the stratas we tried suffered simply from largesse, adding as
many fillings as could be squeezed in. This every-
thing-but-the-kitchen-sink approach led to wet,
sagging, overworked stratas. What we were after
was a skillet strata with a balance between bread
and custard, and with a restrained filling of only
a few components chosen to accent the leading
ingredients, not overwhelm them. We also wanted
a cohesive casserole rather than a bunch of stray
ingredients cooked together in a skillet. To come
up with our recipe, all the principal parts—custard,
bread, and fillings, and how and when they were
assembled and cooked—were subject to review.

Bread is the foundation of strata. Though sliced
white sandwich bread was specified in most recipes, we saw numerous others—Italian, French,
sourdough, multigrain, rye, pumpernickel, chal-
lah, focaccia, even hamburger and hot dog buns—

INGREDIENTS: White Sandwich Bread

With all the hype about artisanal bread, the sliced stuff in the
plastic bags doesn't get much attention these days, but it should.
Not only is it a regular in many households for the obvious
lunchtime use, but it also proved the best choice for making our
skillet strata (see pages 273–274). So we gathered eight leading
brands of white sandwich bread, in country styles with larger
slices whenever possible, and held a blind tasting.

For our first test, tasters sampled the bread plain. Because
some of the breads are not available in larger slices, we cut the
samples into pieces so tasters would focus on taste and texture,
not size. Tasters weren't fooled. They gave top marks to the
hearty texture of Arnold Country Classics and Pepperidge
Farm Farmhouse. These brands also have larger-than-usual
slices—½ ounce each versus 1 ounce for the competition.

Tasters detected big flavor differences, too. Top-rated
Arnold and Pepperidge Farm were deemed the "sweetest"
breads in the lineup. There were many complaints about "sour"
and "off-" notes in the lower-rated brands; it turns out that some
of these brands contain vinegar (an ingredient often added to
increase shelf life). Lower-rated breads also contain almost
twice as many ingredients as our top-rated breads, with many
more additives and preservatives, which may also explain the
unpleasant aftertaste.

We also had tasters try the breads in grilled cheese sandwiches and prepared as croutons seasoned only with olive oil and
salt. Though there was no clear winner in the case of the grilled
cheeses, there were two clear top picks in the crouton tasting:
once again, Arnold and Pepperidge Farm swept the tasting.

We recommend Arnold Country Classics and Pepperidge
Farm Farmhouse. Their hearty texture and slightly sweet (not
sour) flavor put them a cut above the competition.

THE BEST WHITE SANDWICH BREADS

ARNOLD   PEPPERIDGE FARM

Tasters described Arnold Country Classics White as "what
I expect from sandwich bread." Others agreed, praising its
"perfect structure" and "subtle sweetness." Our other top pick,
Pepperidge Farm Farmhouse Hearty White, was deemed "well
balanced," and "likeable," with a "familiar" taste that was "not
overly sweet—just enough."

called for in one case or another. We tried them all, but tasters preferred supermarket sliced white sandwich bread for its neutral flavor and convenience. There were no objections to the crust, so we left it on; keeping it helped our bread hold up throughout the cooking process. We learned, too, that the texture of toasted fresh bread was preferable to that of stale bread; toasting the bread prevented it from turning to mush by the end of cooking and gave the strata structure. All we had to do was cut fresh bread into 1-inch squares and toast it in the skillet.

We then turned our attention to the tender custard that binds the bread. Recipes commonly call for low-fat milk, whole milk, or half-and-half, though sometimes we saw heavy cream (usually in combination with another dairy liquid). We tried each one of these alone and in every conceivable combination, and most tasters preferred whole milk on its own for a balanced but not overwhelming richness. In a battery of custard tests, tasters' preferences were divided between mixtures with equal parts milk and egg and those with twice as much milk as egg. In the end, adding just a little extra milk to a 50–50 mixture—six eggs to 1½ cups of milk—made everyone happy.

Next we looked to balancing the amount of bread with our custard base. We found that five slices of bread was just right, giving us the perfect balance between crusty exterior and soft custardy interior. This amount also fit perfectly in our 10-inch skillet.

Though our basic strata was very good, we knew the flavorings and fillings could catapult it to glory. Sautéed onion, a traditional strata inclusion, beat out shallots and garlic. Though another common strata flavoring, white wine, showed promise because it lightened the flavor of the dish, it also imparted a booziness that was out of place, so we took it out of the running. A full cup of cheddar cheese mixed into the eggs added sharpness, and fresh thyme lent a nice herbal note.

After sautéing the onions and toasting the bread in our skillet, we folded in the custard-cheese mixture off the heat and moved the skillet to the oven.

Finishing up in the oven helped produce a delicate, souffléed texture, and we found that increasing the baking temperature from the frequently recommended 350 degrees to 425 degrees produced a more evenly cooked strata. Cooking until the top was crisp and golden brown was another common directive, but we found that doing so usually led to an overcooked interior, leaving the strata too firm, even a bit rubbery. So we tried removing the strata from the oven when the top was just beginning to brown and the center and edges were barely puffed and still slightly loose when the pan was gently jiggled. We wondered if the strata was cooked through, but after a mere five-minute rest, our strata was not only cool enough to eat without burning our mouths, but the center had finished cooking from residual heat, reaching that perfectly set, supple strata texture.

❧

Cheddar and Thyme Strata

SERVES 4 TO 6

Do not trim the crusts from the bread or the strata will be dense and eggy. Using a 10-inch skillet is crucial to the thickness and texture of this dish.

6	large eggs
1½	cups whole milk
1	teaspoon minced fresh thyme leaves
	Ground black pepper
4	ounces cheddar cheese, shredded (1 cup)
4	tablespoons (½ stick) unsalted butter
1	medium onion, minced
½	teaspoon salt
5	slices high-quality white sandwich bread, cut into 1-inch squares

1. Adjust an oven rack to the middle position and heat the oven to 425 degrees. Whisk the eggs, milk, thyme, and ¼ teaspoon pepper together, then stir in the cheese and set aside.

2. Melt the butter in a 10-inch ovensafe nonstick skillet over medium-high heat. Add the onion and salt and cook until the onion is softened and lightly browned, about 6 minutes.

3. Add the bread and, using a rubber spatula, carefully fold the bread into the onion mixture until evenly coated. Cook the bread, folding occasionally, until lightly toasted, about 3 minutes.

4. Off the heat, fold in the egg mixture until slightly thickened and well combined with the bread. Gently press on the top of the strata to help it soak up the egg mixture. Transfer the skillet to the oven and bake until the edges and center are puffed and the edges have pulled away slightly from the sides of the pan, about 12 minutes. Let rest for 5 minutes before serving.

➤ VARIATIONS

Bacon and Pepper Jack Strata

Follow the recipe for Cheddar and Thyme Strata, substituting 4 ounces (about 4 slices) bacon, chopped fine, for the butter. Cook the bacon in the skillet over medium-high heat until the fat begins to render, about 2 minutes, before adding the onion in step 2. Omit the thyme. Substitute 4 ounces pepper Jack cheese, shredded (1 cup), for the cheddar and sprinkle with 2 scallions, sliced thin, before serving.

Sausage and Gruyère Strata

Follow the recipe for Cheddar and Thyme Strata, reducing the butter to 1 tablespoon and adding 8 ounces raw, crumbled breakfast sausage to the skillet with the onion in step 2. Substitute 4 ounces Gruyère or Swiss cheese, shredded (1 cup), for the cheddar.

Spinach and Gouda Strata

Removing the excess moisture from the spinach is crucial here. After thawing the spinach in the microwave, wrap it in a clean kitchen towel and squeeze out as much liquid as possible.

Follow the recipe for Strata with Cheddar and Thyme, stirring 2 medium garlic cloves, minced or pressed through a garlic press (about 2 teaspoons), into the skillet after the bread has toasted in step 3 and cook until fragrant, about 30 seconds. Stir 1 (10-ounce) package frozen chopped spinach, thawed and squeezed dry, into the skillet with the eggs in step 4. Substitute 4 ounces smoked Gouda cheese, shredded (1 cup), for the cheddar.

POPOVER CASSEROLE

WHETHER SERVED AS HOME FRIES OR HASH browns, the dense texture and earthy flavor of potatoes is a perfect complement to rich, creamy eggs. We had already come up with winning skillet recipes that capitalized on the affinity the two have for one another (see our tortilla recipes, pages 266–267, and Corned Beef Hash, page 269), but there was still plenty of room for creativity. Few recipes in our research caught our attention, that is until we came across impossible pie. Impossible pie was popularized back in the 1970s by the folks at Betty Crocker. The idea is to pour a thinned-out biscuit batter (made with Bisquick, milk, and eggs) on top of some filling ingredients in a pie plate; the batter sinks to the bottom of the dish and "impossibly" forms its own crust when baked. But after trying several versions of this recipe, we found them impossibly heavy and dense. However, the concept caused a spark: The edges of impossible pie were puffed and crisp, reminding everyone in the test kitchen of a supersized popover. Popovers, in a way, seem to do the impossible, as the heat of the oven transforms their humble ingredients—eggs, milk, flour, salt, and butter—into the culinary equivalent of a hot air balloon. They are crisp and golden brown on the outside, tender and moist inside. Could we employ our skillet to make a potato and egg casserole held together with light, fluffy popover batter? We traded in the popover pan for a 10-inch nonstick skillet and went to the kitchen to find out.

The batter was easiest. We used a standard popover recipe—two eggs, 1 cup each of milk and flour, and 1 tablespoon of melted butter—which conveniently fit into a 10-inch skillet with enough room for additional ingredients. The simple addition of scallions gave our batter a touch of freshness and color. After mixing the batter together and setting it aside, we quickly moved on to the casserole's filling. We decided that sausage would be a logical match with the potatoes and would make the dish into a hearty one-pan meal. For simplicity, we limited our testing to ground bulk breakfast sausage and diced links; tasters unanimously preferred the ground sausage.

Next, we considered the potatoes, which turned out to need a bit more attention. Hoping to save time, we first tested frozen hash browns, both shredded and diced. Even when precooked and crisped, the shredded hash browns were lost in the batter and didn't contribute much of anything. Diced hash browns had better texture, but they still had that stale freezer taste. Switching to diced fresh potatoes was a big improvement. Tasters preferred the flavor and texture of russets over Yukon Gold and Red Bliss potatoes, and parcooking the potatoes in the microwave while our sausage was browning in the skillet gave them a head start and left their interiors fluffy. We added the potatoes to the skillet with the sausage to finish cooking and to pick up more savory flavor, then we poured the batter over the mixture and moved the skillet to the oven.

Popovers are usually cooked at 450 degrees, a temperature that provides the necessary heat to turn the moisture in the batter to steam, which in turn is what makes the popovers rise and expand. Because we weren't sure how the added ingredients would affect the final results, we started our testing at a cautious 400 degrees. When our casserole emerged, the flavors were spot on, but things weren't looking quite right. The popover part didn't have the dramatic rise we'd expected nor did it brown as much as we would have liked. So we jumped up to the 450-degree mark. That adjustment gave us the browning and rise we were after. Sprinkling cheese on top of the casserole before it went into the oven further encouraged a well-browned top and added a nice counterpoint of flavor to our sausage and potatoes. Thanks to our nonstick skillet, we were able to remove the casserole from the skillet with ease, exposing a beautifully browned bottom crust. One bite told us our recipe for Popover Casserole was, in fact, impossibly delicious.

EQUIPMENT: Heatproof Rubber Spatulas

We evaluated 10 heatproof rubber (or silicone) spatulas, all dishwasher-safe, running each through nine tests, including lifting omelets, scraping the bowl of a food processor, hand-mixing nuts and other ingredients into stiff cookie dough, folding whipped egg whites into cake batter, making a pan sauce, and stirring risotto. We also simmered the spatulas in a pot of tomato-curry sauce for an hour to see if they would stain and absorb odors, and we ran them through the dishwasher twice to see if they would come through clean and odor-free. We tested their heat-safe claims, trying to melt them in a cast-iron skillet as hot as we could get it—up to 674 degrees Fahrenheit. Finally, we asked a variety of test cooks to weigh in on the spatulas' comfort and performance.

Our favorite was the Rubbermaid Professional 13½-Inch Heat Resistant Scraper. This was a practical, no-nonsense spatula that aced every cooking test, with a great balance of flexibility and firmness for both the head and the handle. The head did become slightly discolored by the turmeric in the curry test, and if we were going to quibble, the handle, while providing a great grip, could be a bit cushier. But all around, a terrific choice for nearly any job in the kitchen. We also heated it beyond its top recommended temperature and saw no sign of damage.

We also highly recommend the Tovolo Silicone Spatula, our best buy. This sleek spatula has curves in all the right places. It may look like it's just going to be decorative—until you use it. It passed every performance test, scraping, stirring, folding, and sautéing like a champ. It also withstood our attempts to stain and melt it. The Tovolo's good looks and nice price make it hard to resist, but, in the end, the larger overall size and sturdiness of the Rubbermaid won our highest accolades.

THE BEST HEATPROOF RUBBER SPATULAS

RUBBERMAID   TOVOLO

The practical, no-nonsense Rubbermaid Professional 13½-Inch Heat Resistant Scraper ($18.99) aced every test, while the Tovolo Silicone Spatula ($8.99), with curves in all the right places, proved itself a great buy.

Sausage and Potato Popover Casserole

SERVES 6

We developed this recipe using breakfast sausage, but sweet or hot Italian sausage, removed from its casing, also works well. Make sure to use a 10-inch ovensafe non-stick skillet for this recipe.

12	ounces russet potatoes (about 1 large), peeled and cut into ½-inch pieces
2	tablespoons vegetable oil
	Salt and ground black pepper
2	large eggs
1	cup whole milk
1	tablespoon unsalted butter, melted
1	cup (5 ounces) unbleached all-purpose flour
2	scallions, sliced thin
12	ounces bulk pork sausage
1	ounce Parmesan cheese, grated (½ cup)

1. Adjust an oven rack to the upper-middle position and heat the oven to 450 degrees.

2. Toss the potatoes with 1 tablespoon of the oil, ¼ teaspoon salt, and a pinch pepper in a microwave-safe bowl. Cover the bowl and microwave on high until the potatoes begin to soften, 5 to 7 minutes, stirring the potatoes halfway through cooking. Drain the potatoes well.

3. Meanwhile, whisk the eggs, milk, butter, ½ teaspoon salt, and ⅛ teaspoon pepper together in a large bowl. Stir in the flour and scallions until just incorporated but still a bit lumpy and set aside.

4. Heat the remaining tablespoon oil in a 10-inch ovensafe nonstick skillet over medium-high heat until shimmering. Add the sausage and cook, breaking it up with a wooden spoon, until the meat is no longer pink, about 5 minutes. Add the drained potatoes, cover, and cook, stirring occasionally, until the potatoes are lightly browned and soft, about 8 minutes.

5. Uncover the skillet, pour the egg mixture evenly over the top, and sprinkle with the cheese. Bake until puffed and golden, 25 to 30 minutes.

6. Transfer the skillet to a wire rack and let cool for 5 minutes. Use a rubber spatula to loosen the casserole from the skillet, then slide onto a cutting board, slice into wedges, and serve.

➤ VARIATION

Ham and Cheese Popover Casserole

Use either thick-sliced deli ham or a ham steak here.

Follow the recipe for Sausage and Potato Popover Casserole, substituting 12 ounces thick-sliced deli ham, cut into ½-inch pieces, for the sausage and 2 ounces sharp cheddar cheese, shredded (½ cup), for the Parmesan. Add the ham to the skillet with the potatoes in step 4 and cook as directed until the potatoes are soft before continuing with step 5.

Tex-Mex Popover Casserole

Follow the recipe for Sausage and Potato Popover Casserole, substituting 12 ounces chorizo, cut into ½-inch pieces, for the sausage and 2 ounces pepper Jack cheese, shredded (½ cup), for the Parmesan. Add the chorizo and 1 red bell pepper, stemmed, seeded, and cut into ¼-inch pieces, to the skillet with the potatoes in step 4 and cook as directed until the potatoes are soft before continuing with step 5.

8

VEGETABLES AND SIDES

VEGETABLES AND SIDES

PREPARING VEGETABLES AND OTHER SIDE dishes should be quick and easy—no one wants to labor over a side dish when there is the main course to tend to. By using our skillet for all the recipes in this chapter, we aimed to keep them simple and on the stovetop, since we know that all too often there is a roast or a casserole in the oven.

The benefits of using a skillet are many—it provides a surface area big enough to cook a large quantity of food, it can be used to brown or toast anything from broccoli to orzo, and its sloped sides allow for quick evaporation when we want to sauté or steam green beans or spinach. Our versatile skillet also helps us cut back on the multiple pots, pans, and baking dishes necessary to cook vegetables and other side dishes. And, we find when we use a skillet, what comes out of it is cooked well. When you're boiling or steaming a head of broccoli in a covered pot, it's easy to forget about it—out of sight, out of mind. But with a skillet, everything is out in the open and easy to keep tabs on.

This chapter includes a variety of vegetable recipes, all with their own tricks to make the most of the skillet. We took the term "pan-roasting" literally, and roasted vegetables in our skillet on the stovetop instead of on a baking sheet in the oven; this helped us cut down the cooking time without cutting down on flavor. For our Pan-Roasted Asparagus (page 281), we cooked the asparagus, covered, with oil and a little butter, which released just enough steam for the asparagus to cook through. After a few extra minutes of cooking uncovered, the asparagus was golden brown and crisp on just one side, creating the perfect textural contrast. Tender greens are another good candidate for skillet cookery, but they all too often become a soggy, dull mess. To get excess liquid out of baby spinach, we microwaved the spinach first, then drained, chopped, and drained it again before we sautéed it with garlic for our Sautéed Spinach with Garlic and Lemon (page 298)—sogginess solved.

Pleased with our vegetable dishes, we felt the need to satisfy our starch cravings. Starting with the much-loved spud, we found the best way to make pan-roasted potatoes that were perfectly crispy outside yet soft and creamy inside was to parcook them in the microwave before adding them to the hot

pan. This step preserved the moist interior, while heat from the skillet made the skin crispy. Orzo and couscous also made our list of indispensable side dishes, and toasting these pastas before cooking them deepened their basic flavors. Both are quick cooking and have simple flavors that make them the ideal match to a variety of main dishes.

The recipes in this chapter showcase our preferred skillet techniques and offer up plenty of flavor. You'll never be stuck in a rut again when it comes to vegetables and side dishes, whether they are for Tuesday night's dinner or a holiday meal.

PAN-ROASTED ASPARAGUS

WE LOVE THE CARAMELIZED FLAVOR OF grilled asparagus, but there are plenty of rainy nights when asparagus sits in the back of the fridge, begging to be cooked. Rather than waste time heating a finicky broiler, we hoped that a simple stovetop method might deliver crisp, nicely browned spears. We found several promising recipes, but the results were disappointing. In most cases, the spears were indeed browned but also limp, greasy, and shriveled. Equally daunting were the logistics of cooking enough asparagus to feed more than just two people. All the recipes we consulted suggested laying the spears out in a single layer, then individually rotating them to ensure even browning. This seemed like a lot of fuss for one measly bunch of asparagus, which, with these restrictions, was all we could fit into a 12-inch skillet.

We began our tests with different sizes of spears. As in grilling, the thinner spears would have to be eliminated; they overcooked so quickly that there was no way to get a proper sear. Selecting thicker spears helped to solve this problem, but we were still a long way from getting them to brown properly. Over moderate heat, the spears took so long to develop a crisp, browned exterior that they overcooked. But cranking up the burner was not a good alternative—the spears skipped brown altogether and went straight to spotty and blackened.

We wondered if parcooking the asparagus first—a common cooking method to keep vegetables looking vibrant—would enhance browning. We tried searing some asparagus spears that had been quickly blanched in boiling water. Sure enough, they quickly developed a crisp, golden brown crust. Blanching the asparagus spears releases sugars in their cell walls, sugars which are then able to brown in the skillet. We got the texture we were looking for, but were reluctant to call for the extra step. Could simply covering the pan at the start of the cooking to retain evaporated moisture have the same effect?

We cooked two more batches, covering the skillets for the first five minutes and adding a few tablespoons of water to one of them. The batch with water was definitely steamed, but the extra moisture inhibited its browning after we removed the lid. The asparagus in the other skillet, which had contained nothing besides olive oil, steamed very little. When we replaced the oil with butter, however, the small amount of moisture in the butter (while olive oil is 100 percent fat, butter is roughly 20 percent water) was enough to start steaming the asparagus, which then began to release its own moisture. The asparagus was bright green and just barely softened. We sought to retain both the flavor of the olive oil and the steam created by the butter, so we used a combination of the two.

Once the lid was removed, however, it was a race against the clock to try to get all the spears turned and evenly browned before they overcooked and turned limp. Even with very thick asparagus, it was a race we almost always lost. But we made a fortunate discovery. Citing the pleasing contrast of textures, tasters actually preferred the spears that were browned on one side only and remained bright green on the other—and these half-browned spears never went limp.

We noticed that by arranging the spears so that half of them pointed in one direction and the other half pointed in the opposite direction, we were able to improve the level of browning on the one side. Now just an occasional toss was enough to ensure that all the spears became partially browned. With just a light seasoning of salt and pepper, our asparagus was crisp, green, and delicious.

Pan-Roasted Asparagus
SERVES 4 TO 6

This recipe works best with asparagus that is at least ½ inch thick near the base. Do not use pencil-thin asparagus because it cannot withstand the heat and will overcook too easily. Either a traditional or a nonstick 12-inch skillet will work fine for this recipe.

I   tablespoon olive oil
I   tablespoon unsalted butter
2   pounds thick asparagus (about 2 bunches, see note), tough ends trimmed (see the illustration on page 92)
    Salt and ground black pepper
I   lemon, cut into wedges, for serving

1. Heat the oil and butter in a 12-inch skillet over medium-high heat until the oil is shimmering and the butter has melted. Add half of the asparagus to the skillet with tips pointed in one direction and the remaining spears with tips pointed in the opposite direction. Sprinkle with ¼ teaspoon salt. Using tongs, distribute the spears in an even layer (the spears will not quite fit into a single layer).

2. Cover and cook until the spears are bright green and still crisp, about 5 minutes. Uncover, increase the heat to high, and continue to cook until the spears are tender and well browned along one side, 5 to 7 minutes, using tongs to move spears from the center of the pan to the edge of the pan to ensure all are browned.

3. Season with salt and pepper to taste, transfer to a serving dish, and serve with the lemon wedges.

➤ VARIATIONS

Pan-Roasted Asparagus with Toasted Garlic and Parmesan
Cook 3 medium garlic cloves, sliced thin, in 2 tablespoons olive oil in the skillet over medium heat until crisp and golden, about 5 minutes. Transfer the garlic to a paper towel–lined plate; set aside. Follow the recipe for Pan-Roasted Asparagus, omitting the oil and adding the butter to the oil left in the skillet from cooking the garlic. Sprinkle the toasted garlic

and 2 tablespoons grated Parmesan cheese over the asparagus before serving.

Pan-Roasted Asparagus with Warm Orange-Almond Vinaigrette

Toast ¼ cup slivered almonds in 2 tablespoons olive oil in the skillet over medium heat until golden, about 5 minutes. Stir in ½ cup juice from 1 orange and 1 teaspoon minced fresh thyme, increase the heat to medium-high, and simmer until thickened, about 4 minutes. Off the heat, stir in 2 tablespoons minced shallot and 2 tablespoons sherry vinegar and season with salt and pepper to taste. Transfer the vinaigrette to a small bowl and wipe out the skillet with a wad of paper towels. Follow the recipe for Pan-Roasted Asparagus, tossing the cooked asparagus with the vinaigrette before serving.

PAN-ROASTED BROCCOLI

STEAMING BROCCOLI OFTEN RESULTS IN mushy, drab stalks and waterlogged florets. The color fades to an unappealing military green and the broccoli itself needs more than just a pat of butter to improve the flavor. To get away from this cafeteria classic, we turned to pan-roasting to revive our broccoli in the skillet. This method, unlike steaming broccoli with just water, would also let us incorporate different flavors into the finished dish. The dry pan and high heat would improve our chances for rich, caramelized bites of broccoli, but we'd have to be careful not to let the florets and stems dry out.

In researching recipes for pan-roasted broccoli, we found that many cooks either blanch or steam the broccoli first, then add it to a hot pan to finish it off. Blanching produced soggy florets that absorbed too much water, but steaming proved a much better method, producing crisp, bright green florets. We wanted to find out if steaming then pan-roasting would be the secret to succulent skillet-cooked broccoli.

We already knew that it takes only seconds for vibrant and crisp broccoli to morph into a dull, soft mess. When broccoli is cooked for just a few minutes too long, the chlorophyll breaks down, causing the broccoli to lose color and texture. In addition, all vegetables contain acids that leach out during cooking and create an acidic environment, further contributing to the breakdown of the chlorophyll. We'd have to look out for overcooking our broccoli, and make sure we kept an eye on its time in the skillet.

The first step was to transform a head of broccoli into pieces that would cook evenly by trimming the florets into small pieces and the stalks into oblong coins. We steamed the pieces briefly with just a bit of water until a fork inserted met with some resistance, then set them aside and heated a tablespoon of oil in the skillet. We added the steamed pieces back in an even layer, hoping the heat would promote caramelization and the oil would keep the broccoli from drying out. But it quickly became clear that some moist heat (steam) was needed if the broccoli was to cook through without burning or drying out.

What if we reversed the method from the recipes we had found in our research, and browned the broccoli first to partially cook it, then steamed it? We prepared another bunch of broccoli and began by sautéing the stems and florets. Once the pieces began to brown, we added a splash of water and a pinch of salt and covered the skillet to let the pieces steam. When the broccoli turned bright green, we removed the lid and let the excess moisture evaporate. Because the hardier stems take longer to cook than the delicate florets, we found that adding the stems first, and tossing in the florets two minutes later, kept the florets from overcooking and going limp.

After spending just 10 minutes at the stove, we had broccoli with bright green florets and toasty-brown stems that was tasty enough to be eaten as is, but we couldn't pass up the chance to add some assertive flavorings. We started off with a simple garlicky version, finished with a lemon browned butter. Next we opted for a spicy version with Asian flavors, and finally—unable to resist a good cheese sauce—we paired the broccoli with creamy, melted Gruyère.

Garlicky Pan-Roasted Broccoli with Lemon Browned Butter

SERVES 4

Make sure to watch the butter closely as it browns in step 3; it can go from nutty brown to black and burnt in a matter of seconds. Either a traditional or a nonstick 12-inch skillet will work fine for this recipe.

2	tablespoons vegetable or olive oil
1	large bunch broccoli (about 1½ pounds), florets and stems separated, florets cut into bite-sized pieces, stems trimmed, peeled, and sliced ¼ inch thick on the bias (see the illustrations on page 284)
	Salt
3	tablespoons water
4	tablespoons (½ stick) unsalted butter
1	small shallot, minced (about 1½ tablespoons)
2	medium garlic cloves, minced or pressed through a garlic press (about 2 teaspoons)
	Ground black pepper
1½	teaspoons juice from 1 lemon
½	teaspoon minced fresh thyme leaves

1. Heat the oil in a 12-inch skillet over medium-high heat until just smoking. Add the broccoli stems and ¼ teaspoon salt and cook, without stirring, until browned on the bottoms, about 2 minutes. Stir in the florets and continue to cook, without stirring, until the bottoms of the florets begin to brown, 1 to 2 minutes longer.

2. Add the water, cover, and cook until the broccoli is bright green but still crisp, about 2 minutes. Uncover and continue to cook until the water has evaporated, the broccoli stems are tender, and the florets are crisp-tender, about 2 minutes longer. Transfer the broccoli to a bowl.

3. Melt the butter in the skillet over medium-high heat and continue to cook, swirling occasionally, until the butter is browned and releases a nutty aroma, about 1½ minutes.

4. Off the heat, stir in the shallot, garlic, ¼ teaspoon salt, and ⅛ teaspoon pepper until fragrant, about 1 minute. Stir in the lemon juice and thyme. Return the broccoli to the skillet and toss to coat with the browned butter. Season with salt and pepper to taste, transfer to a serving dish, and serve.

➤ VARIATIONS

Pan-Roasted Broccoli with Spicy Southeast Asian Flavors

Don't confuse Asian chili sauce with Asian chili-garlic paste, which has a stronger, spicier flavor. Either a traditional or a nonstick 12-inch skillet will work fine for this recipe.

1	tablespoon creamy peanut butter
1	tablespoon hoisin sauce
2	teaspoons juice from 1 lime
2	medium garlic cloves, minced or pressed through a garlic press (about 2 teaspoons)
1	teaspoon light or dark brown sugar
¾	teaspoon Asian chili sauce
2	tablespoons vegetable oil
1	large bunch broccoli (about 1½ pounds), florets and stems separated, florets cut into bite-sized pieces, stems trimmed, peeled, and sliced ¼ inch thick on the bias (see the illustrations on page 284)
	Salt
3	tablespoons water
¼	cup chopped fresh basil leaves
	Ground black pepper
2	tablespoons chopped roasted unsalted peanuts

1. Combine the peanut butter, hoisin, lime juice, garlic, sugar, and chili sauce in a medium bowl and set aside.

2. Heat the oil in a 12-inch skillet over medium-high heat until just smoking. Add the broccoli stems and ¼ teaspoon salt and cook, without stirring, until browned on the bottoms, about 2 minutes. Stir in the florets and continue to cook, without stirring, until the bottoms of the florets begin to brown, 1 to 2 minutes longer.

3. Add the water, cover, and cook until the broccoli is bright green but still crisp, about 2 minutes. Uncover and continue to cook until the water has evaporated, the broccoli stems are tender, and the florets are crisp-tender, about 2 minutes longer.

PREPARING BROCCOLI

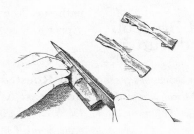

1. Place the head of broccoli upside down on a cutting board and, using a large knife, trim off the florets very close to their heads. Cut the florets into bite-sized pieces.

2. Place the stalk on the cutting board and square it off with the knife, removing the tough, outer ⅛-inch peel.

3. Cut the peeled stalk on the bias into ¼-inch-thick slices.

4. Stir in the peanut butter mixture and basil and toss until the broccoli is evenly coated and heated through, about 30 seconds. Season with salt and pepper to taste and transfer to a serving dish. Sprinkle with the chopped peanuts and serve.

Pan-Roasted Broccoli with Creamy Gruyère Sauce

Either a traditional or a nonstick 12-inch skillet will work fine for this recipe.

2	tablespoons vegetable oil
1	large bunch broccoli (about 1½ pounds), florets and stems separated, florets cut into bite-sized pieces, stems trimmed, peeled, and sliced ¼ inch thick on the bias (see the illustrations above)
	Salt
3	tablespoons water
1	tablespoon unsalted butter
1	medium shallot, peeled and sliced into thin rings
½	cup heavy cream
½	teaspoon Dijon mustard
½	teaspoon dry sherry
	Pinch cayenne pepper
1	ounce Gruyère cheese, finely grated (¼ cup)
1	teaspoon juice from 1 lemon
	Ground black pepper

1. Heat the oil in a 12-inch skillet over medium-high heat until just smoking. Add the broccoli stems and ¼ teaspoon salt and cook, without stirring, until browned on the bottoms, about 2 minutes. Stir in the florets and continue to cook, without stirring, until the bottoms of the florets begin to brown, 1 to 2 minutes longer.

2. Add the water, cover, and cook until the broccoli is bright green but still crisp, about 2 minutes. Uncover and continue to cook until the water has evaporated, the broccoli stems are tender, and the florets are crisp-tender, about 2 minutes longer. Transfer the broccoli to a bowl.

3. Melt the butter in the skillet over medium heat. Add the shallot and cook until golden and softened, about 2 minutes. Stir in the cream, mustard, sherry, cayenne, and ⅛ teaspoon salt. Increase the heat to medium-high and cook until the mixture bubbles and thickens, about 1 minute.

4. Off the heat, stir in 3 tablespoons of the cheese and the lemon juice until the sauce is smooth. Return the broccoli to the skillet and toss to coat with the cheese sauce. Season with salt and pepper to taste and transfer to a serving dish. Sprinkle with the remaining 1 tablespoon cheese and serve.

GLAZED CARROTS

GLAZING CARROTS IS ARGUABLY THE EASIEST and most popular way to prepare them. However, all too often, glazed carrots are an awful, saccharine-sweet nightmare, adrift in a sea of syrup. They're either limp and soggy from overcooking or raw and fibrous from undercooking. The recipes we tried for glazed carrots, many of which are hopelessly dated, never delivered what we hoped for: tender, well-seasoned carrots with a glossy, bright glaze. We headed into the kitchen with piles of carrots and our skillet, looking to rejuvenate this sad side dish.

We began by preparing the carrots for cooking. Matchstick pieces were out from the get-go as we were looking for simplicity, not to improve our knife skills. Instead, we peeled regular bagged carrots and cut them on the bias into handsome oval pieces.

Most recipes suggest that the carrots need to be steamed, parboiled, or blanched prior to glazing, resulting in a battery of dirtied utensils. We opted for a different style of cooking and put the carrots, along with ½ cup water, in a 12-inch skillet, then added some salt and 1 tablespoon sugar for flavor, covered the skillet, and simmered it. Mission accomplished—the carrots were cooked through without much ado. But they were severely lacking in flavor.

We looked at the two main components that would instill flavor in our carrots: the cooking liquid and the sweetener. We swapped out the water for wine, but this move turned our carrots sour and astringent. Next we tried chicken broth—the broth lent the carrots a savory backbone and full, round flavor. As for the sugar, we substituted more compelling sweeteners, without much luck. Maple syrup proved to be too assertive, while honey imparted a floral flavor. We stood by clean, pure, easy-to-measure granulated sugar, satisfied with the chicken broth and sugar combination.

Finally, we moved on to finessing the glaze, which was still thin and watery. When the carrots had simmered for a few minutes and were just on the verge of becoming tender, we lifted the lid from the skillet, stepped up the heat, and let the liquid reduce. To encourage glaze formation and increase the sweetness slightly, we added butter and 2 more tablespoons sugar. All of this resulted in a light, clingy glaze that with a few more minutes of high-heat cooking took on a pale amber hue and a light caramel flavor.

A squirt of fresh lemon juice gave the dish sparkle, and a twist or two of freshly ground black pepper provided depth. Now inspired, we created two unconventional variations—one with chopped bacon and pecans and another with dried cranberries. We were surprised, as were our tasters, that glazed carrots could be this good and this easy.

Lemony Glazed Carrots
SERVES 4

Either a traditional or a nonstick 12-inch skillet will work fine for this recipe.

1½	pounds carrots, peeled and sliced ¼ inch thick on the bias (see the illustration on page 286)
½	cup low-sodium chicken broth
3	tablespoons sugar
	Salt
1	tablespoon unsalted butter
2	teaspoons juice from 1 lemon
	Ground black pepper

1. Bring the carrots, broth, 1 tablespoon of the sugar, and ½ teaspoon salt to a simmer in a 12-inch skillet over medium-high heat. Cover, reduce the heat to medium, and cook until the carrots are almost tender, about 5 minutes.

2. Uncover, increase the heat to high, and simmer rapidly until the liquid measures about 2 tablespoons, 2 to 3 minutes.

3. Stir in the butter and remaining 2 tablespoons sugar and continue to cook, stirring often, until the carrots are completely tender and the sauce is light golden and has thickened to a glaze, 3 to 4 minutes. Off the heat, stir in the lemon juice and season with salt and pepper to taste. Transfer to a serving dish and serve.

➤ VARIATIONS

Glazed Carrots with Orange and Cranberries

Follow the recipe for Lemony Glazed Carrots, omitting the tablespoon of sugar in step 1 and reducing the amount of low-sodium chicken broth to ¼ cup. Add ½ teaspoon grated zest and ¼ cup juice from 1 orange, and ¼ cup dried cranberries to the skillet with the carrots in step 1. Omit the lemon juice in step 3.

Glazed Carrots with Bacon and Pecans

Granulated sugar works best in our traditional glazed carrots, but in this variation light brown sugar was the best choice. Its rich caramel flavor goes well with the bacon and pecans.

Cook 3 ounces (about 3 slices) bacon, chopped coarse, in the skillet over medium-high heat until crisp, about 5 minutes. Transfer the bacon to a paper towel–lined plate and pour off all but 1 tablespoon of the bacon fat left in the pan. Add the pecans to the skillet and toast over medium heat until fragrant, about 4 minutes; transfer to the plate with the bacon. Follow the recipe for Lemony Glazed Carrots, substituting light brown sugar for the granulated sugar and adding ½ teaspoon minced fresh thyme leaves to the pan with the butter. Sprinkle the carrots with the bacon and pecans before serving.

PAN-ROASTED CARROTS AND PARSNIPS

TOASTY AND CARAMELIZED ON THE OUTSIDE and tender and moist on the inside, roasted root vegetables are a mainstay on many fall dinner and holiday tables. But unless you are lucky enough to have two ovens, cooking your bird and roasting a pan full of root vegetables tends to be a logistical nightmare. Could we find a way to create such a dish on the stovetop, using just a skillet? It was easy enough to find recipes for pan-roasted vegetables—the hard part started when we tried making them.

Many recipes began with carrots and cooked them in combination with other root vegetables such as parsnips, rutabagas, and turnips in oil over medium or high heat, covered, to simulate oven-roasting. These recipes produced scorched exteriors and underdone centers. Other recipes first steamed the vegetables, then sautéed them in butter or oil for a roasted color, but the tender vegetables fell apart by the end of cooking. Skillet in hand, we were determined to figure out a way to make the perfect oven-roasted vegetables without using an oven.

Our first step was to whittle down our vegetable choices. We landed on carrots and parsnips for three reasons: Their similar shape makes them easier to prep; they cook at about the same rate; and most important, their flavors work well together. We started out with a pound of each, then peeled

them and sliced them on the bias for an elegant presentation.

We knew that we would have to cook these vegetables in fat to caramelize them, so we tested both butter and oil as the fat component. The butter burned easily, even when used in conjunction with some oil, because we were cooking the vegetables over medium-high heat for almost 15 minutes and butter has a lower smoke point than oil. Starting again with just vegetable oil, we browned the carrots and parsnips, then turned down the heat and covered the pan so they could steam and cook through. This gave us evenly browned, tender vegetables, but by the time they were tender, they were also dry and wrinkled. To rectify the moisture loss, we added ¾ cup water to the pan before covering it, which created a gentle steaming effect. We had achieved our goal of nicely browned, tender vegetables, but their flavor seemed a little flat.

Some recipes add sugar to enhance the natural sweetness of the vegetables, but adding sugar when we were sautéing the carrots and parsnips just made a scorched mess of the pan. We had better results by dissolving just a teaspoon of granulated sugar (and ½ teaspoon of salt) in the water before adding it to the pan. A few turns of the pepper mill and a sprinkling of fresh parsley added to the cooked vegetables rounded out the flavors.

Our simple stovetop method provided ample opportunity to introduce new flavors to carrots

SLICING CARROTS AND PARSNIPS ON THE BIAS

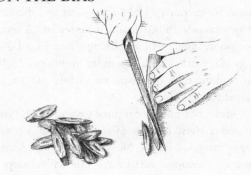

For an elegant presentation, slice the carrots or parsnips on the bias into approximately 2-inch-long rounds that are the desired thickness.

and parsnips. We developed a variation using apple cider, maple syrup, and rosemary and another with orange juice, honey, and thyme.

Pan-Roasted Carrots and Parsnips
SERVES 4 TO 6

Look for parsnips no wider than 1 inch; larger parsnips can have unpalatably tough, fibrous cores. Provided the total weight is 2 pounds, any combination of carrots and parsnips can be used here. Either a traditional or a nonstick 12-inch skillet will work fine for this recipe.

3   tablespoons vegetable oil
1   pound carrots, peeled and sliced ½ inch thick on the bias (see the illustration on page 286)
1   pound parsnips, peeled and sliced ½ inch thick on the bias (see the illustration on page 286)
¾   cup warm water
1   teaspoon sugar
    Salt
1   tablespoon minced fresh parsley leaves
    Ground black pepper

1. Heat the oil in a 12-inch skillet over medium-high heat until shimmering. Add the carrots and parsnips and cook, stirring occasionally, until golden brown, 12 to 14 minutes.

2. Whisk the water, sugar, and ½ teaspoon salt together in a small bowl until the sugar dissolves, then add to the skillet. Cover, reduce the heat to medium-low, and cook, stirring occasionally, until the vegetables are completely tender and the liquid has evaporated, 12 to 14 minutes.

3. Off the heat, stir in the parsley and season with salt and pepper to taste. Transfer to a serving dish and serve.

➤ VARIATIONS

Maple-Rosemary Pan-Roasted Carrots and Parsnips

Follow the recipe for Pan-Roasted Carrots and Parsnips, substituting ¾ cup apple cider for the water, 1 tablespoon maple syrup for the sugar, and ½ teaspoon minced fresh rosemary for the parsley.

Honey-Orange Pan-Roasted Carrots and Parsnips

Follow the recipe for Pan-Roasted Carrots and Parsnips, substituting ¾ cup orange juice for the water, 1 tablespoon honey for the sugar, and ½ teaspoon minced fresh thyme leaves for the parsley.

BRAISED CAULIFLOWER

MANY OF US IN THE TEST KITCHEN GREW UP eating soggy, overcooked cauliflower cloaked in a thick layer of congealed neon-orange cheese sauce. Some of us ate the cheesy sauce, but no one remembers liking—or even eating—the cauliflower. But cauliflower doesn't have to be prepared this way. When properly cooked and imaginatively flavored, cauliflower can be nutty and slightly sweet, and it's the perfect side dish for a simple pot roast or sautéed chicken breast.

When we stopped shuddering at the thought of that awful cheese sauce, we realized it had acted to disguise the true flavor of the cauliflower. What we wanted was to bring out the flavor of the vegetable. We knew that braising cauliflower (cooking it covered with a small amount of liquid) would help develop the flavor of the finished dish because porous vegetables, such as cauliflower, absorb liquid—and flavor—during cooking.

But we quickly learned that simply braising this dense vegetable, with no precooking at all, took too long. Also, it required close monitoring; we had to stand over the stove to make sure the cauliflower did not overcook and become waterlogged. Would steaming or sautéing the cauliflower first help to jump-start the cooking process? After several tests, we found that partially cooking the cauliflower by steaming then braising it resulted in a lackluster, flat-tasting side dish with no nuttiness or oomph.

We tried another path and sautéed the cauliflower on medium-high heat, then added some chicken broth and covered the skillet to braise it until tender. Finally, we had the texture we were after, and the naturally mild flavors of the cauliflower were intensified as well. Not only did the cauliflower absorb the flavors from the braising liquid, but the browned cauliflower also tasted wonderfully nutty and earthy.

To boost the flavor even further, we replaced some of the chicken broth with white wine and added a tablespoon of garlic and a pinch of red pepper flakes to the skillet before braising the cauliflower.

There was still one nagging problem—because we were cooking the cauliflower for almost 15 minutes, it began to release unpleasant sulfur-containing compounds. To avoid this problem, we found it best to cut the cauliflower into bite-sized pieces (about 1 inch) that cook uniformly and quickly. We also liked the fact that the cut surface of the florets lay flat in the sauté pan. The cut surfaces browned beautifully and the sweetness of the florets was well pronounced.

With our basic method down, we took things a step further and came up with two variations— one with the tangy flavors of capers and anchovies, and another with curry powder. Cauliflower will never be boring—or artificially orange—again.

Braised Cauliflower with Garlic and White Wine

SERVES 4

For the best texture and flavor, make sure to brown the cauliflower well in step 2. Either a traditional or a nonstick 12-inch skillet will work fine for this recipe.

3   tablespoons plus I teaspoon olive oil
3   medium garlic cloves, minced or pressed through a garlic press (about I tablespoon)
⅛   teaspoon red pepper flakes
I   medium head cauliflower (about 2½ pounds), trimmed, cored, and cut into bite-sized florets
     Salt
⅓   cup dry white wine
⅓   cup low-sodium chicken broth
2   tablespoons minced fresh parsley leaves
     Ground black pepper

1. Combine 1 teaspoon of the oil, the garlic, and red pepper flakes in a small bowl.

2. Heat the remaining 3 tablespoons of the oil in a 12-inch skillet over medium-high heat until shimmering. Add the cauliflower and ¼ teaspoon

salt and cook, stirring occasionally, until the florets are golden brown, 7 to 9 minutes.

3. Clear the center of the skillet, add the garlic mixture, and cook, mashing the mixture into the pan, until fragrant, 15 to 30 seconds. Stir the garlic mixture into the cauliflower.

4. Add the wine and broth, cover, and cook until the cauliflower is crisp-tender, 4 to 5 minutes. Off the heat, stir in the parsley and season with salt and pepper to taste. Transfer to a serving dish and serve.

➤ VARIATIONS

Braised Cauliflower with Capers and Anchovies

Follow the recipe for Braised Cauliflower with Garlic and White Wine, adding 2 medium anchovy fillets, rinsed and minced to a paste, and 1 tablespoon capers, rinsed, with the garlic in step 1. Stir in 1 tablespoon juice from 1 lemon with the parsley.

Braised Curried Cauliflower

Follow the recipe for Braised Cauliflower with Garlic and White Wine, substituting ½ cup water for the wine, ⅓ cup plain yogurt for the chicken broth, and 2 tablespoons minced fresh cilantro leaves for the parsley. Add 2 teaspoons curry powder with the garlic in step 1 and stir in 1 tablespoon juice from 1 lime with the cilantro.

SAUTÉED CORN

WHEN SUMMER ARRIVES, FARM STAND SIGNS spring up everywhere, announcing the arrival of fresh-picked corn. Boiling corn on the cob is probably the most popular way to cook fresh corn, but eating off the cob can be messy. We wanted an alternative—a simple skillet sauté that would bring out the sweetness of the corn and maintain its crisp crunch, while also being worthy of appearing on a dinner party menu.

First we checked out the varieties of corn available at the supermarket. Remember those old-fashioned nonhybrid varieties of corn, advertised on

REMOVING KERNELS FROM CORN COBS

Hold the ear of corn on its end inside a large, wide bowl and use a paring knife to cut off the kernels.

homey farm stand signs? Those kinds of corn can be nearly impossible to find at the local market. The sweetness and fresh flavor of these old-time varieties was short-lived, and corn has since been crossbred to make for sweeter ears that have a longer hold on their fresh flavor and tender texture. Of the commonly available hybrid types, the supersweet variety is the one you'll most likely find at your supermarket during the off-season; it has a relatively slow conversion of sugar to starch after being picked, making for a longer shelf life. And while we prefer to use fresh corn for sautéing, we know it can be tough to find in the dead of winter (the test kitchen is located in New England, after all), so we set out to develop a recipe for both fresh corn—be it supersweet or any other variety—and its frozen cousin.

We started with preparing the corn. To remove kernels from the cob, we found it best to place the ear of corn on its end in a large bowl and cut the kernels off with a paring knife (see the illustration above). This way the kernels end up in a confined space, rather than all over the floor and counter. After a couple of tests, we discovered that frozen corn was best sautéed just out of the package—no special treatment necessary.

With our kernels ready to go, they needed only a brief sauté in a hot skillet to bring out their sweet flavor and crisp texture. Thinking back to summery afternoons full of buttered corn on the cob, we added butter to our skillet and let it melt, then stirred in a little shallot and garlic. These

aromatics enhanced the sweetness of the corn, which only needed about two minutes to cook though. Our tasters liked the corn to have a nice crunch to it, so we kept the cooking time brief; but feel free to adjust the time depending on your desired texture.

A teaspoon of minced fresh thyme finished off the dish, making it a perfect accompaniment to any summertime meal. A few flavor variations including cherry tomatoes, bacon, scallions, fennel, and tarragon transformed our corn kernels into a side fit for company.

Sautéed Corn with Thyme and Shallot
SERVES 4

We prefer fresh corn in this recipe, but you can use frozen corn instead. Fresh corn may take a little longer to cook than frozen, depending on how crunchy you like your corn. If you are using frozen corn, do not thaw it before adding it to the pan. Either a traditional or a nonstick 12-inch skillet will work fine for this recipe.

- 2   tablespoons unsalted butter
- 1   medium shallot, minced (about 3 tablespoons)
       Salt
- 1   medium garlic clove, minced or pressed through a garlic press (about 1 teaspoon)
- 4   ears corn, husk and silk removed, kernels cut from the cob (see the illustration above), or 3 cups frozen corn
- 1   teaspoon minced fresh thyme leaves
       Ground black pepper

1. Melt the butter in a 12-inch skillet over medium heat. Add the shallot and ¼ teaspoon salt and cook until softened, about 2 minutes. Stir in the garlic and cook until fragrant, about 30 seconds.

2. Increase the heat to high, stir in the corn, and cook, stirring often, until heated through but still crunchy, 2 to 4 minutes. Off the heat, stir in the thyme and season with salt and pepper to taste. Transfer to a serving dish and serve.

Sautéed Corn with Cherry Tomatoes and Basil

Follow the recipe for Sautéed Corn with Thyme and Shallot, substituting 2 tablespoons extra-virgin olive oil for the butter; heat the oil over medium heat until shimmering in step 1. Substitute 1 teaspoon chopped fresh basil leaves for the thyme and stir in 8 ounces cherry tomatoes, halved, with the basil.

Sautéed Corn with Bacon and Scallions

Cook 6 ounces (about 6 slices) bacon, chopped coarse, in the skillet over medium-high heat until crisp, about 5 minutes. Transfer the bacon to a paper towel–lined plate and pour off all but 2 tablespoons of the bacon fat left in the pan. Follow the recipe for Sautéed Corn with Thyme and Shallot, substituting the bacon fat for the butter. Omit the thyme and sprinkle with the bacon and 3 scallions, thinly sliced, before serving.

Sautéed Corn with Fennel, Tomatoes, and Tarragon

Follow the recipe for Sautéed Corn with Thyme and Shallot, adding 1 medium fennel bulb, halved, cored, and sliced thin (see the illustrations on page 307) with the shallot; cook until softened, about 5 minutes. Substitute 1 tablespoon minced fresh tarragon leaves for the thyme and stir in 8 ounces cherry tomatoes, halved, with the tarragon.

SAUTÉED GREEN BEANS

THE STANDARD TECHNIQUE FOR MOST sautéed green bean recipes goes something like this: parboil, shock in ice water, dry with towels, and finally sauté. We have always appreciated this technique because it allows you to do most of the prep work ahead of time. But on weekday evenings, we want something a little more streamlined that doesn't involve two pots, a colander, and an ice-bath. How could we make lightly browned, crisp-tender, fresh-tasting beans, with only one pan?

We first tried sautéing the beans in a skillet with oil without parboiling them. Big mistake. The dry heat took too long to penetrate the beans, so that by the time they were tender and cooked, their exteriors were blackened—similar to Chinese stir-fried green beans. Not bad, but not exactly fresh tasting either.

Our next thought was to try a variation on parboiling. We threw the beans and a small amount of water into a cold pan, covered it, and brought it to a simmer. Once the beans were almost cooked, we removed the lid and added a little oil to sauté the beans until they were browned. Unfortunately, in the time it took for the water to evaporate, the beans had become limp and overcooked and still needed more time to brown.

Seeing some promise in the tender green beans from our first test, we decided to sauté the beans first, then steam them. We sautéed the beans briefly until they were spotty brown but not yet cooked through, then added ¼ cup water to the pan and covered it. When the water hit the hot skillet, it turned into steam. Covering the pan captured the steam and quickly cooked the beans. Once they were cooked, we removed the lid and let the excess moisture evaporate. These beans were cooked through yet still crisp, but now the flavor needed work. Adding water to the skillet had washed away some of the caramelized flavor that we had developed, making our beans taste more like ordinary steamed beans.

Instead of steaming the beans, covered, to the point where they were almost fully cooked, we found it better to slightly undercook them and then blast the heat once the lid was removed. This quickly evaporated what little water was left in the pan and allowed us to promote additional caramelization before the beans were fully cooked. We also found that adding a tablespoon of butter to the skillet after the water evaporated deepened the flavor profile and further aided in browning. We used softened butter, which was quick to melt and browned faster than cold butter.

To pump up the flavor just a bit more, we mixed garlic and thyme into the butter before adding it to the beans. After a couple of minutes, our beans were delicious and crisp. A touch of lemon juice added off the heat upped the freshness of our new side dish.

For more exotic and dressed up green bean dishes, we added smoked paprika and slivered almonds for an easy but elegant alternative, and Asian chili-garlic paste for beans with a spicy kick.

Sautéed Green Beans with Garlic and Herbs

SERVES 4

This recipe yields beans that are crisp-tender. If you prefer beans that are a little softer or you are using large, tough beans, increase the amount of water by a tablespoon and cook, covered, for an extra minute. Either a traditional or a nonstick 12-inch skillet will work fine for this recipe.

1	tablespoon unsalted butter, softened
3	medium garlic cloves, minced or pressed through a garlic press (about 1 tablespoon)
1	teaspoon minced fresh thyme leaves
1	teaspoon olive oil
1	pound green beans, ends trimmed (see the illustration on page 235) and cut on the bias into 2-inch lengths
	Salt and ground black pepper
¼	cup water
2	teaspoons juice from 1 lemon
1	tablespoon minced fresh parsley leaves

1. Combine the butter, garlic, and thyme in a small bowl and set aside. Heat the oil in a 12-inch skillet over medium heat until just smoking. Add the beans, ¼ teaspoon salt, and ⅛ teaspoon pepper and cook, stirring occasionally, until spotty brown, 4 to 6 minutes.

2. Add the water, cover, and cook until the beans are bright green and still crisp, about 2 minutes. Uncover, increase the heat to high, and cook until the water evaporates, 30 to 60 seconds.

3. Add the butter mixture and continue to cook, stirring often, until the beans are crisp-tender, lightly browned, and beginning to wrinkle, 1 to 3 minutes longer. Off the heat, stir in the lemon juice and parsley and season with salt and pepper to taste. Transfer the green beans to a serving bowl and serve.

➤ VARIATIONS

Sautéed Green Beans with Smoked Paprika and Almonds

Follow the recipe for Sautéed Green Beans with Garlic and Herbs, omitting the thyme and parsley. Add ¼ teaspoon smoked paprika to the softened butter mixture in step 1. Sprinkle ¼ cup slivered almonds, toasted, over the beans before serving.

Spicy Sautéed Green Beans

Don't confuse Asian chili-garlic paste with Asian chili sauce, which has a milder flavor.

Combine 1 tablespoon Asian chili-garlic paste, 1 teaspoon toasted sesame oil, and 1 teaspoon minced or grated fresh ginger in a small bowl. Follow the recipe for Sautéed Green Beans with Garlic and Herbs, substituting the chili-garlic paste mixture for the softened butter mixture and 2 teaspoons vegetable oil for the olive oil. Omit the lemon juice and parsley and sprinkle with 2 teaspoons toasted sesame seeds before serving.

BUTTERY PEAS

FROZEN PEAS DEFINITELY GIVE THEIR FRESHER kin a run for their money. Not only are they more convenient than fresh peas, but they often taste better, consistently cooking up more tender and sweeter. We wanted to come up with a quick skillet recipe for buttered peas that played up these attributes while maintaining their bright green color and sweet, fresh flavor. But first, we wondered why it was that we preferred frozen to fresh—a preference that seemed to defy logic.

We looked to the frozen food industry for some answers. Despite their long history—green peas are one of the oldest vegetables known to man—peas have a relatively short shelf life and are incredibly delicate. Green peas lose a good amount of their nutrients within a day of being picked and, like corn, their sugar quickly converts into starch. This fast deterioration is why most peas found at the grocery store in the produce section taste starchy and bland. These peas might be several days old, depending on where they came from and how long they were there. Frozen peas, on the other hand, are picked, cleaned, sorted, and frozen just after harvest, which helps to preserve their sweetness and flavor when they are at their peak.

Frozen peas, in fact, may just be the perfect vegetable. Not only are they inexpensive, but they require no washing, stemming, or chopping, and they cook in a matter of minutes. We found that the key to cooking frozen peas was to ignore the instructions printed on the package. There is no need to cook them in water—all that does is wash away the fresh, sweet pea flavor.

Instead, we found it was far better to sauté them—still frozen—in butter with a shallot, garlic, and some sugar. The richness of butter plays well against their sweet, refreshing flavor and 2 teaspoons of sugar highlights that sweetness. Tasters liked the addition of sautéed shallot and garlic, which deepened the overall flavor of the finished dish. We found that thawing the peas before cooking them was unnecessary—the little bit of moisture still stuck to them from the freezer helps by providing a bit of steam when the peas are cooking.

Our peas were bright green, sweet, and incredibly easy to make. They were also easy to match with other ingredients, including mint, pearl onions, tarragon, and bacon. Although we created only a handful of variations, we're fairly confident that these little green orbs taste good with just about anything.

Buttery Peas with Thyme
SERVES 4
Either a traditional or a nonstick 12-inch skillet will work fine for this recipe.

- 2 tablespoons unsalted butter
- 1 medium shallot, minced (about 3 tablespoons)
- 2 teaspoons sugar
  Salt
- 1 medium garlic clove, minced or pressed through a garlic press (about 1 teaspoon)
- 3 cups frozen peas
- 1 teaspoon minced fresh thyme leaves
  Ground black pepper

1. Melt the butter in a 12-inch skillet over medium-high heat. Add the shallot, sugar, and ¼ teaspoon salt and cook until softened, about 2 minutes. Stir in the garlic and cook until fragrant, about 30 seconds.

2. Stir in the peas and cook, stirring often, until just heated through, about 2 minutes. Off the heat, stir in the thyme and season with salt and pepper to taste. Transfer to a serving dish and serve.

➤ VARIATIONS
Buttery Peas with Feta and Mint
Follow the recipe for Buttery Peas with Thyme, substituting 1 tablespoon minced fresh mint leaves for the thyme. Crumble 3 ounces feta cheese (about ¾ cup) over the peas before serving.

Buttery Peas with Bacon
Cook 6 ounces (about 6 slices) bacon, chopped coarse, in the skillet over medium-high until crisp, about 5 minutes. Transfer the bacon to a paper towel–lined plate and pour off all but 2 tablespoons of the bacon fat left in the pan. Follow the recipe for Buttery Peas with Thyme, substituting the bacon fat for the butter. Stir in the bacon and 2 teaspoons sherry vinegar with the thyme.

Buttery Peas with Pearl Onions and Lemon
Follow the recipe for Buttery Peas with Thyme, omitting the shallot and garlic. After melting the butter, add 1 cup frozen pearl onions, 2 teaspoons sugar, ¼ teaspoon salt, and ½ cup water to the skillet. Cover the pan and cook, shaking occasionally, until the onions are tender, about 5 minutes. Uncover the pan and simmer until the water has evaporated and the onions have browned, about 5 minutes, then add the frozen peas and cook as directed in step 2. Stir in 2 teaspoons juice from 1 lemon with the thyme.

Buttery Peas with Tarragon Cream
Follow the recipe for Buttery Peas with Thyme, substituting 1 tablespoon minced fresh tarragon leaves for the thyme. Before adding the peas to the skillet, pour ½ cup heavy cream into the pan, bring to a simmer, and cook until thickened.

PAN-ROASTED POTATOES

POTATOES ARE ARGUABLY THE MOST POPULAR side dish in the world. Just think about the myriad ways they can be prepared: fried, baked, boiled, mashed, and roasted, not to mention the various permutations of these methods. We have our favorite potato dishes (french fries, anyone?), but we think it's important to have other recipes in your arsenal, for when you want a break in the routine. Pan-roasted potatoes—with an extra-crisp exterior and moist and creamy interior—are a great way to mix it up, and they are a speedy side dish, ready to hit the table in just minutes. Some nights there's no time to wait for the oven, so skillet-roasting is a natural substitute. With our mouths already watering in anticipation, we decided to do a bit of research into pan-roasted potatoes and get cooking.

Some recipes we unearthed required peeling and cutting the potatoes, while others left the skin on or used whole potatoes. Olive oil, vegetable oil, butter, and clarified butter were all suggested, as were various methods to facilitate crisping and cooking. So we got out our peeler and started cooking. The result? Six batches of stovetop-roasted potatoes that failed to impress. Uneven cooking, browned but soft exteriors, pale exteriors, dry insides, and greasy outsides were just a few of the problems. We wanted to know what had gone wrong with our half-dozen plates of disappointing spuds.

Initial tests taught us some important lessons. If the potatoes were to brown evenly and not stick, they would have to cook in a single layer in a nonstick skillet. We also noted that the best browning occurred when the potatoes were left undisturbed before turning. We liked Red Bliss potatoes for this recipe; with a low starch and high moisture content, they roast well since they already contain some moisture and don't absorb more liquid when cooking. They keep their shape well and stay moist inside, while the outside becomes brown and crusty. Tasters preferred the appearance, texture, and flavor of potatoes cooked with the skin on, so we put the peeler aside. Medium potatoes (lemon-sized) were best, as they offered two cut sides for crisping and one beautifully rounded side.

As we proceeded, we found that our biggest challenge was getting the interiors to cook through completely within the time it took for the exteriors to crisp and brown. Of the recipes we came across, some parcooked the potatoes first while others did not, and we wondered if precooking the potatoes might help. We tested three methods: parboiling, steaming, and microwaving. Parboiling produced potatoes that were cooked through, but slightly mushy, and the outsides did not brown well. Steaming and microwaving produced similar results, but microwaving proved to be the winning method—fewer pots and pans, less time, and just that much easier. We tossed the potatoes with a touch of olive oil, to prevent them from drying out, and microwaved them for 10 minutes, which proved the right length of time to render the potatoes soft, but not so soft they lost their shape.

Olive oil was also the best choice for browning the potatoes. Butter burned too easily, and vegetable oil lacked flavor. Two tablespoons of oil was the right amount to pan-roast our microwaved potatoes. We cooked them for five minutes, stirred them so the other side of each wedge could brown, and let them roast another five minutes. A sprinkling of salt and pepper, added just before serving, had a big impact, providing nice hits of flavor on the crisp exterior.

With a great crust, a moist interior, and a nicely salted outer layer, these skillet-roasted potatoes were ready to move into the weekly lineup.

Pan-Roasted Potatoes

SERVES 4

We prefer to use small or medium potatoes (1½ to 3 inches in diameter) here because they are easier to cut into uniform pieces; cut small potatoes in half and medium potatoes into quarters that measure roughly 1 inch. Regardless of what size potatoes you use, be sure to cut them into uniform wedges to ensure even cooking and browning.

2   pounds small or medium Red Bliss potatoes (6 to 12 potatoes), scrubbed and cut into 1-inch wedges (see note)
3   tablespoons olive oil
    Salt and ground black pepper

1. Toss the potatoes with 1 tablespoon of the oil, ¼ teaspoon salt, and a pinch pepper in a microwave-safe bowl. Microwave on high, uncovered, until the potatoes soften but still hold their shape, about 10 minutes, gently stirring twice during cooking. Drain the potatoes thoroughly.

2. Heat the remaining 2 tablespoons oil in a 12-inch nonstick skillet over medium-high heat until shimmering. Add the potatoes cut side down in a single layer and cook until golden brown on one side, 5 to 7 minutes.

3. Gently stir the potatoes, rearrange in a single layer, and cook until tender and deep golden brown on a second side, 5 to 7 minutes longer. Season with salt and pepper to taste, transfer to a serving dish, and serve.

➤ VARIATIONS

Pan-Roasted Potatoes with Lemon and Chives

Follow the recipe for Pan-Roasted Potatoes, tossing the potatoes with 2 tablespoons minced fresh chives and 2 teaspoons grated zest from 1 lemon before serving.

Pan-Roasted Potatoes with Southwestern Spices

Combine ½ teaspoon chili powder, ½ teaspoon sweet paprika, ¼ teaspoon ground cumin, and ⅛ teaspoon cayenne pepper in a small bowl. Follow the recipe for Pan-Roasted Potatoes, substituting a pinch of the chili mixture for the black pepper in step 1. Add the remaining spice mixture to the potatoes after they have browned in step 3 and continue to cook until the spices are fragrant, about 30 seconds.

Pan-Roasted Potatoes with Garlic and Rosemary

Combine 1 teaspoon olive oil, 2 garlic cloves, minced or pressed through a garlic press (about 2 teaspoons), and 2 teaspoons minced fresh rosemary leaves in a small bowl. Follow the recipe for Pan-Roasted Potatoes, clearing the center of the skillet after cooking the potatoes on the second side in step 3. Add the garlic mixture to the clearing and cook, mashing the mixture into the pan, until fragrant, 15 to 30 seconds, then stir it into the potatoes.

POTATO RÖSTI

NOTHING GETS YOU GOING IN THE MORNING like a big plate of hash browns—grated potatoes, simply seasoned with salt and pepper and fried in loads of butter. If you're in the mood for breakfast at supper, and you've already eaten your weekly quota of dinnertime eggs and cereal, you can always make a satisfying meal of potato rösti—a heartier and more grown-up version of hash browns.

This Swiss potato cake boasts a crunchy, crisp exterior and a tender, creamy interior tasting of earthy potatoes and, of course, rich butter. Since this skillet side pairs well with anything or works as a standalone dinner, we had to include it in this chapter. We started to research rösti recipes, and found that many followed a pretty basic protocol: Pat the grated potatoes dry with paper towels, season with salt and pepper, pack into a well-buttered nonstick skillet, fry over medium heat until browned, and flip to cook the second side. Where hash browns are sometimes served still in shreds, potato rösti is always flipped and fried as a cake, and served in elegant slices. With our final vision of rösti in mind, we headed into the kitchen.

Almost every recipe we came across recommended using either starchy russets or Yukon Golds. We tested these varieties, along with Red Bliss potatoes and all-purpose potatoes. The high-moisture Red Bliss variety made a rösti with a mushy, granular texture that fell apart in the pan. All-purpose potatoes turned out an okay rösti, but ultimately the Yukons won out for their buttery flavor and sunny complexion.

We now looked at the amount and kind of fat used to cook the potatoes. Recipes almost universally favored butter, though a few used oil or lard. We tried all three, and nothing could touch the flavor or rich browning contributed by butter. For an exterior that was crisp but not greasy, we eventually settled on 4 tablespoons of butter—two for each side of the rösti.

The interior texture of the potatoes still needed a hand—it was gummy and dense from not being fully cooked on the inside by the time the exterior was just right. We had been cooking the potatoes uncovered, but a few recipes recommended covering the grated potatoes as they cooked. We thought this would trap moisture and make the potato cake even more gluey than it already was, but just the opposite occurred. When we cooked a batch covered for part of the time the potatoes were surprisingly light, as if the moist heat cooked them through more fully than did dry heat alone. After a few more batches, we found that cooking the cake for six minutes covered, then another few minutes uncovered (until the bottom was a deep golden brown) before it was flipped over, yielded the best results yet. Another tip, packing the potatoes gently into a cake shape, rather than packing them tightly into the pan, helped steam escape and upped the lightness of the dish.

We were satisfied with the texture and ready to move on when we came across an odd step in one of the research recipes—rinsing the grated potatoes in cold water before squeezing them out and cooking them in the skillet. Wouldn't the potatoes absorb the water and become even wetter, effectively negating the squeezing? The proof, however, was in the rösti: rinsed, dried potatoes yielded the best cake yet: lighter, drier, and without a hint of gumminess. Rinsing, it seems, removed excess starch; squeezing removed the moisture. It was the combination of moisture and starch that was causing the gumminess, and we had now eliminated both. To supplement some of the lost starch that was imperative for keeping the cake bound together, we tossed the rinsed, squeezed-dry grated potato with a teaspoon of cornstarch.

We tried our recipe again, and once we removed the lid and gave the skillet a shake, the strands of potato were stuck together in an airy nest—we hadn't even touched them with a spatula. We finished cooking the cake, flipping it to the second side to brown for five more minutes, and our rösti was dreamy: a caramel-gold crust, creamy, just cooked-through interior, and airy, light texture that was perfectly sliceable.

Potato Rösti
SERVES 4

We prefer to shred the potatoes using the large shredding disk of a food processor. You can use a box grater to shred the potatoes, but they should be cut lengthwise, so you are left with long shreds. It is important to squeeze the potatoes as dry as possible in step 1 to ensure a crisp exterior. Serve with a dollop of sour cream.

1½	pounds Yukon Gold or russet potatoes (3 to 4 medium), peeled and shredded (see note)
1	teaspoon cornstarch
½	teaspoon salt
¼	teaspoon ground black pepper
4	tablespoons (½ stick) unsalted butter

1. Place the potatoes in a large bowl, fill with cold water, and swirl to remove excess starch. Drain the potatoes into a strainer. Working in two batches,

FLIPPING POTATO RÖSTI

1. Shake the skillet to loosen the rösti, then slide it onto a large plate.

2. Cover the rösti with a second plate, then invert the rösti so that the browned side is facing up.

3. Melt the remaining butter in the skillet and slide the rösti, browned side facing up, back into the skillet and continue to cook on the second side.

wrap the potatoes in a clean kitchen towel, squeeze out the excess liquid, and transfer the potatoes to a dry bowl.

2. Sprinkle the cornstarch, salt, and pepper over the potatoes and gently toss until thoroughly incorporated. Melt 2 tablespoons of the butter in a 12-inch nonstick skillet over medium heat. Add the potato mixture and spread it into an even layer. Cover and cook for 6 minutes.

3. Uncover and use a spatula to gently press the potatoes down to form a compact, round cake. Continue to cook, uncovered, occasionally pressing on the potatoes to shape into a uniform round cake, until the bottom is deep golden brown, about 2 minutes longer. Following the illustrations on page 295, slide the rösti onto a large plate.

4. Melt the remaining 2 tablespoons butter in the skillet. Invert the rösti onto a second plate and slide it back into the skillet, browned side facing up. Continue to cook, uncovered and occasionally pressing down on the cake, until the bottom is well browned, 5 to 7 minutes.

5. Remove the pan from the heat and allow the rösti to cool in the pan for 5 minutes. Slide the rösti onto a carving board, cut into 4 wedges, and serve.

RATATOUILLE

RATATOUILLE, FEATURING EGGPLANT, ZUC-chini, pepper, tomatoes, and fresh herbs, may be a rustic dish, but that doesn't mean it's simple to prepare. Judging from the numerous bad versions we've had, ratatouille is not an easy dish to get right. The bad ones are a soggy mess of vegetables indistinguishable in taste and texture, often sitting in a watery tomato bath. But the good ones more than make up the difference—the flavors of a well-made ratatouille are light and multilayered; each vegetable can be tasted independently, its flavor heightened by the presence of the others.

The name ratatouille is derived from the French *touiller,* meaning "to stir"—a possible warning of the work involved in the classical French preparation, where each vegetable is sautéed separately and combined at the last minute. This method, although time-consuming, lends itself perfectly to skillet cookery. But considering all the chopping and prep work involved in making this dish, we thought we could at least simplify and speed up the cooking process. We've seen recipes that make ratatouille by tossing all the ingredients together in one pot, slowly stewing them till tender. We were skeptical that these vegetables would retain their individual character, but there was only one way to find out.

Before we began cooking, we prepared the vegetables. We kept the usual main ingredients—eggplant, zucchini, onion, bell peppers, and tomatoes—in our recipe. To keep some contrast in texture, we sliced the onions and peppers into strips and cut the zucchini and eggplant into 1-inch cubes, leaving the skin on. Fresh, ripe tomatoes would be ideal, but outside the peak summer months, they have little flavor and poor texture. Because they are picked at the height of the season, canned diced tomatoes are guaranteed to be ripe and sweet (see page 81 for our favorite brand of canned diced tomatoes).

With our key players in place, we could now address cooking technique. Despite our skepticism, we thought it made sense to start with the simplest method first—the one-pot version that stewed everything together. We sweated the onions and peppers, then tossed in the rest of the vegetables and simmered on the stove until tender. Our low expectations were fulfilled: the resulting product was mushy, soupy, and one-dimensional. We knew the eggplant and zucchini were the two parties guilty for releasing much of the liquid that led to this dish's soupiness. Browning them before the vegetables were combined, we thought, would help reduce this liquid and, at the same time, help develop additional flavor in the pan.

Returning to the stove, we sautéed the eggplant and zucchini, separately, in a large skillet with olive oil. Eggplant is often salted and set aside to release liquid before cooking, but the prospect of tacking an extra half-hour onto our overall cooking time wasn't really appealing. Instead, we thought that using relatively high heat to brown the eggplant and the zucchini on the stovetop could both evaporate the juices and concentrate the vegetables' flavor. Since we weren't looking to cook them through but just sear the outside, it only took about 5 minutes each on medium-high heat to get a good browning. We had heard the urban legend about the heavy amounts of oil that eggplant can absorb while sautéing, but found that 1 tablespoon of oil per batch was sufficient, provided we used a nonstick skillet and didn't stir too often.

Our next step was to sauté the onions and peppers together until golden brown. We covered them for the first 10 minutes so they would release excess liquid, then cooked them another 5 minutes uncovered. Garlic and fresh thyme were added to the skillet for flavor. Then we gently folded in the tomatoes, zucchini, and eggplant, turned down the heat, and let the vegetables simmer together, covered, until just saucy. We found that uncovering the skillet for the final 10 minutes of cooking allowed the juices to reduce and thicken to just the right consistency. The vegetables were cooked through but still retained their shape.

This ratatouille was a vast improvement on the soupy mess we'd made earlier. And despite the etymology of the dish, very little stirring was actually required; in fact, the less we stirred, the better. We had finally achieved a medley of vegetables with distinct textures and flavors that were in harmony but still retained their own voice.

Ratatouille

SERVES 4 TO 6

Using fresh herbs is important here; 2 teaspoons minced rosemary can be substituted for the thyme. Do not peel the eggplant as the skin helps the eggplant hold together during cooking. It is important to cook the eggplant and zucchini (in batches) until they are brown, but to stir them as little as possible to prevent them from turning mushy.

¼   cup olive oil
1   medium eggplant (about 1 pound), cut into 1-inch pieces (see note)
2   medium zucchini (about 1 pound), cut into 1-inch pieces
1   medium onion, halved and sliced ¼ inch thick
1   red bell pepper, stemmed, seeded, and sliced into ¼-inch strips
     Salt

2   medium garlic cloves, minced or pressed through a garlic press (about 2 teaspoons)
2   teaspoons minced fresh thyme leaves
1   (14.5-ounce) can diced tomatoes
2   tablespoons chopped fresh basil or minced fresh parsley leaves
     Ground black pepper

1. Heat 1 tablespoon of the oil in a 12-inch nonstick skillet over medium-high until shimmering. Add the eggplant and cook, stirring occasionally, until browned, 5 to 7 minutes. Transfer the eggplant to a medium bowl. Repeat with 1 tablespoon more oil and the zucchini; transfer to the bowl with the eggplant.

2. Heat the remaining 2 tablespoons oil in the skillet over medium-low heat until shimmering. Add the onion, bell pepper, and ½ teaspoon salt, cover, and cook, stirring occasionally, until the vegetables are softened and have released their liquid, about 10 minutes. Uncover, increase the heat to medium, and cook, stirring occasionally, until the onion is golden brown, 5 to 10 minutes longer.

3. Stir in the garlic and thyme and cook until fragrant, about 30 seconds. Add the tomatoes with their juice, scraping up any browned bits. Gently stir in the browned eggplant and zucchini and bring to a simmer. Cover, turn the heat to medium-low, and cook for 5 minutes until saucy.

4. Uncover and continue to cook until the ratatouille is thickened but the vegetables still retain their shape, about 10 minutes longer. Gently stir in the basil and season with salt and pepper to taste. Transfer to a serving dish and serve.

SAUTÉED SPINACH

IN THE TEST KITCHEN, WE'VE ALWAYS reserved delicate baby spinach for salads, turning to bigger, mature flat-leaf spinach for cooking. The reason? Tender young baby spinach releases a lot of liquid when it hits a hot pan, and it turns into a waterlogged, mushy mess. But given how convenient baby spinach is (no stems to remove or grit to rinse out), we thought it was time to give cooking it another try.

In the past, we've solved the water problem of mature spinach by wilting it first in a pan, squeezing it with tongs in a colander to remove liquid, and then returning it to the skillet. But this tactic failed miserably when we tried it with the more delicate baby spinach. As soon as the pressed spinach was put back in the pan, it exuded even more juices, which watered down the other ingredients in the skillet.

What if we microwaved the spinach? After all, that's the suggestion offered on the back of the spinach bag. We placed the leaves in a large glass bowl and covered it with a plate. After six minutes, the spinach was warm but still not sufficiently wilted. While we were loath to do it, we thought adding just a little water to the bowl might help speed things up. Eureka! After three minutes, the spinach had softened and shrunk to half its size, thanks to the release of a great deal of liquid. Yet a nagging problem remained: How would we extract all the liquid from the leaves of spinach? We pressed the spinach against the inside of a colander, but that couldn't remove enough of the liquid without ruining its tissue-like texture.

A colleague told us about a recipe that called for precooking the spinach before sautéing, and chopping the wilted spinach as a way to remove liquid. Taking up a new batch of spinach, we microwaved, pressed, and then roughly chopped it on a cutting board. Not only was the mushy texture gone, but the chopping had released even more of the excess water.

With victory in sight, we threw the greens back in the colander for a second squeeze. This chopped and double-pressed spinach needed only a couple minutes in the skillet and a little seasoning before it was just right. We enhanced the freshness of the spinach with lemon juice and added red pepper flakes for some bite. Now our greens were tender, sweet, and flavorful.

Paired with almonds and raisins, or pecans and feta, our sautéed spinach was elevated from lowly salad green to delicious and fresh side dish, ready to take its place next to the main course.

Sautéed Spinach with Garlic and Lemon
SERVES 4

If you don't have a microwave-safe bowl large enough to accommodate the entire amount of spinach, cook it in a smaller bowl in two batches, reducing the amount of water to 2 tablespoons per batch and the cooking time for each batch to about 1½ minutes. Either a traditional or a nonstick 12-inch skillet will work fine for this recipe.

3   (6-ounce) bags baby spinach (about 16 cups)
¼   cup water
2   tablespoons plus 2 teaspoons extra-virgin olive oil
4   medium garlic cloves, peeled and sliced thin crosswise
¼   teaspoon red pepper flakes
    Salt
2   teaspoons juice from 1 lemon
    Ground black pepper

1. Place the spinach and water in a large microwave-safe bowl. Cover the bowl and microwave on high power until the spinach is wilted and has decreased in volume by half, 3 to 4 minutes. Using potholders, remove the bowl from the microwave and keep covered for 1 minute.

2. Carefully uncover the spinach and transfer it to a colander set in the sink. Using the back of a rubber spatula, gently press the spinach against the colander to release the excess liquid. Transfer the spinach to a cutting board and roughly chop. Return the spinach to the colander and press a second time.

3. Heat 2 tablespoons of the oil in a 12-inch skillet over medium-high heat, add the garlic and red pepper flakes and cook, stirring constantly, until the garlic is light golden and beginning to sizzle, 2 to 3 minutes. Add the drained spinach and ¼ teaspoon salt, toss with tongs to coat with the oil, and cook until uniformly wilted and glossy green, about 2 minutes.

4. Off the heat, stir in the lemon juice and season with salt and pepper to taste. Transfer to

a serving dish, drizzle with the remaining 2 teaspoons oil, and serve.

➤ VARIATIONS

Sautéed Spinach with Almonds and Golden Raisins

Follow the recipe for Sautéed Spinach with Garlic and Lemon, adding ½ cup golden raisins with the garlic and red pepper flakes in step 3. Substitute 2 teaspoons sherry vinegar for the lemon juice and stir in ⅓ cup slivered almonds, toasted, with the vinegar in step 4.

Sautéed Spinach with Pecans and Feta

Follow the recipe for Sautéed Spinach with Garlic and Lemon, omitting the red pepper flakes. Substitute 3 large shallots, sliced thin crosswise (about 1 cup), for the garlic and 2 teaspoons red wine vinegar for the lemon juice. Sprinkle ⅓ cup pecans, toasted, and 1½ ounces feta cheese, crumbled (about ¼ cup), over the spinach before serving.

SAUTÉED SWISS CHARD

LEAFY GREENS FALL INTO TWO DISTINCT categories—tender and mild flavored, and tough and assertively flavored—each of which should be handled quite differently. Swiss chard belongs in the tender category, along with spinach and beet greens, all of which taste of the earth and minerals but are still rather delicate. Having already satisfied our spinach craving (see page 298 for our Sautéed Spinach with Garlic and Lemon), we moved on to Swiss chard to create a skillet dish that would bring out its earthy flavor, but not compromise its texture.

There are two main varieties of chard available at the supermarket—green chard, which has medium to dark green leaves with thick white stalks, and red or rhubarb chard with brilliant red stalks, which is most similar to beet greens (not much of a stretch, considering chard is related to beets). Either one will work well here, but the rhubarb chard has

SEPARATING CHARD STEMS AND LEAVES

Hold each leaf at the base of the stem over a bowl filled with water. Use a sharp knife to slash the leafy portion from either side of the thick stem. This technique also works well with kale and collard and mustard greens.

a stronger flavor than the green chard. Both the chard stems and leaves are delicious cooked; there's no need to discard the tougher stems, as some cooks do. To prepare chard, we cut the leaves from the stems (see the illustration above) and set them aside for the time being, since the leaves and stems cook at different rates.

We considered preparation methods—steaming or sautéing were the most skillet-friendly options. We tried steaming the chard first, stems then leaves, but the greens were mushy. Clearly, these tender greens, with their high moisture content, did not need extra liquid added to the pan. We turned to our other idea—sautéing.

We heated 2 tablespoons of olive oil, which tasters preferred over butter with the meaty flavor of the chard, and added the chopped stems to the skillet first since they take a little more time to cook. In just five minutes, the stems had softened. We tossed in the chopped leaves, covered the pan, and let the greens wilt and become tender. Another five minutes passed, and the greens were just right. We took a shortcut by not fully drying the leaves after washing them, and this omission paid off—slightly dried, damp greens added just enough moisture to ensure the greens were perfectly tender.

Our sautéed chard was tender and meaty, but the flavor needed a kick. We tried again, this time adding a chopped onion to the skillet with the stems; the onion lent a sweet flavor and balanced the slightly more assertive and bitter taste of the chard. We normally favor the addition of garlic and lemon juice to sautéed greens, and this proved no exception. A handful of chopped thyme and final drizzle of olive oil was all this dish needed to become a new weeknight favorite.

For some Mediterranean flair, we created a variation with canned chickpeas and a pinch of saffron, which gave the chard a deeper flavor and made this a heartier side dish.

Sautéed Swiss Chard
SERVES 4

Don't dry the chard greens completely after washing; a little extra water clinging to the leaves will help them wilt when cooking in step 2. Either a traditional or a nonstick 12-inch skillet will work fine for this recipe.

3   tablespoons extra-virgin olive oil
1   small onion, minced
1   large bunch Swiss chard (about 1 pound),
    stems and leaves separated (see the
    illustration on page 299), stems chopped
    medium and leaves sliced ½ inch thick
    Salt
2   medium garlic cloves, minced or pressed
    through a garlic press (about 2 teaspoons)
2   teaspoons minced fresh thyme leaves
2   teaspoons juice from 1 lemon
    Ground black pepper

1. Heat 2 tablespoons of the oil in a 12-inch skillet over medium heat until shimmering. Add the onion, chard stems, and ¼ teaspoon salt and cook, stirring often, until softened and beginning to brown, 5 to 7 minutes.

2. Stir in the garlic and thyme and cook until fragrant, about 30 seconds. Stir in the chard leaves, cover, and cook until the chard is wilted and tender, about 5 minutes.

3. Off the heat, stir in the lemon juice and season with salt and pepper to taste. Transfer to a serving dish, drizzle with the remaining 1 tablespoon oil, and serve.

➤ VARIATION
Sautéed Swiss Chard with Chickpeas and Saffron
Follow the recipe for Sautéed Swiss Chard, substituting a pinch of saffron for the thyme and 2 teaspoons sherry vinegar for the lemon juice. Stir in 1 (14-ounce) can chickpeas, rinsed and drained, with the chard leaves in step 2. Increase the amount of drizzling oil to 2 tablespoons in step 3.

SAUTÉED CHERRY TOMATOES

MOST COOKS DON'T EVEN THINK ABOUT cooking cherry tomatoes, reserving them for use in salads or on a crudités platter as a ready and willing partner for ranch dip. But the truth is that when sautéed, these miniature tomatoes make a fresh-tasting and easy side dish all year long. Cherry tomatoes have a sweetness all their own and release a juicy goodness with every single bite. We wanted to explore this simple yet delicious side, which is a natural for skillet cooking.

When shopping for cherry tomatoes, we look for plump tomatoes with smooth skins—signs that the tomatoes are fully ripe. Cherry tomatoes contain a lot of liquid, so we knew they had to be cooked as quickly as possible, otherwise they would soften and fall apart. Our large skillet was perfect for this task, as it allowed the tomatoes to cook in a single layer. We turned the heat to medium-high—this would speed up the cooking time—and added a tablespoon of olive oil to the pan. We halved our cherry tomatoes and dropped them in the skillet, already reaching for our forks.

Unfortunately, we still had some work to do. Our first batch of cherry tomatoes lost its sweetness and acquired a bitter flavor. We thought a dash of added sugar could help, so we sprinkled 2 teaspoons of sugar, and a dash of salt, over another batch of tomatoes before they went into the pan. The sugar helped with caramelization and balanced the acidity in the tomatoes. We were almost there, but the sautéed tomatoes lacked seasoning.

After sautéing the tomatoes for a minute, we added a teaspoon of minced garlic to the skillet and cooked the tomatoes another 30 seconds. At this point, they were ready to come off the heat, and had a bright, garlicky bite. We stirred in a hefty amount of chopped basil—this added the flavor we were looking for. The fresh herb complemented the sweetness of the tomatoes, and a grind of black pepper added a nice contrast. These tomatoes were succulent, sweet, and satisfying. And they could be ready in under five minutes, any time of the year.

For another, equally speedy, side dish, we added anchovies and capers; they offer a briny contrast to the tomatoes' sweetness in an Italian-inspired variation.

Sautéed Cherry Tomatoes
SERVES 4

Don't toss the tomatoes with the sugar and salt ahead of time or you will draw out their juices and make them overly soft. If the cherry tomatoes are especially sweet, you may want to reduce or omit the sugar. Either a traditional or a nonstick 12-inch skillet will work fine for this recipe.

- 1 tablespoon extra-virgin olive oil
- 2 pints cherry tomatoes (about 1½ pounds), halved
- 2 teaspoons sugar
  Salt
- 1 medium garlic clove, minced or pressed through a garlic press (about 1 teaspoon)
- 2 tablespoons chopped fresh basil leaves
  Ground black pepper

1. Heat the oil in a 12-inch skillet over medium-high heat until shimmering. Toss the tomatoes with the sugar and ¼ teaspoon salt, then add to the skillet and cook, stirring often, for 1 minute. Stir in the garlic and cook until fragrant, about 30 seconds.

2. Off the heat, stir in the basil and season with salt and pepper to taste. Transfer to a serving dish and serve.

➤ VARIATION
Sautéed Cherry Tomatoes with Capers and Anchovies

Don't toss the tomatoes with the sugar and salt ahead of time or you will draw out their juices and make them overly soft. If the cherry tomatoes are especially sweet, you may want to reduce or omit the sugar. Either a traditional or a nonstick 12-inch skillet will work fine for this recipe.

- 2 medium anchovy fillets, rinsed and minced
- 1 tablespoon extra-virgin olive oil
- 2 pints cherry tomatoes (about 1½ pounds), halved
- 2 teaspoons sugar
  Salt
- 2 tablespoons capers, rinsed
- 2 medium garlic cloves, minced or pressed through a garlic press (about 2 teaspoons)
- 2 tablespoons minced fresh parsley leaves
  Ground black pepper

1. Cook the anchovies in the oil in a 12-inch skillet over medium-high heat, stirring constantly, until they begin to sizzle, 1 to 2 minutes. Toss the tomatoes with the sugar and ¼ teaspoon salt, then add to the skillet and cook, stirring often, for 1 minute. Stir in the capers and garlic and cook until fragrant, about 30 seconds.

2. Off the heat, stir in the parsley and season with salt and pepper to taste. Transfer to a serving dish and serve.

SAUTÉED ZUCCHINI

WITH THE FIRST BUDS THAT POP UP FROM the still-frozen ground in spring, we inevitably start to daydream about the long summer days and nights ahead, full of ripe, garden-fresh vegetables. Many favorites, like tomatoes, have countless preparation options and can be added to just about any dish, but what about the humble zucchini? We usually resort to stuffing these summer darlings with a mixture of meat, vegetables, and cheese, or layering them in a baked casserole, but then they completely lose their flavor and texture. Surely, we thought, there must be more we can do to retain the earthy flavor of this vegetable and keep it crisp—and we were certain our trusty skillet could help.

Thinking about how to make the best use of our skillet and its wide surface area, we hit on the idea of shredding the zucchini, so there was more of the vegetable in contact with the skillet. This would retain the flavor of the vegetable while allowing us to add other flavors. The hidden bonus of cooking these slivers was that we would need to stand in front of the stovetop for a lot less time, and we wouldn't even have to turn on the oven. We set out to develop this speedy recipe and looked back to our previous experiences cooking zucchini.

The biggest problem that confronts the cook when preparing zucchini is its wateriness. This vegetable is about 95 percent water and becomes soupy if just thrown into a hot pan. If zucchini cooks in its own juices, it will steam, not brown—and because it is fairly bland, zucchini really benefits from browning. Clearly, some of the water must be removed before sautéing.

The first precautions against wateriness must take place when you're selecting zucchini—size and firmness are the most important factors. After extensive testing, we found that smaller zucchini are more flavorful and less watery. Smaller zucchini also have fewer seeds. Look for zucchini no larger than 8 ounces and preferably just 6 ounces each. Huge zucchini might look impressive in the garden, but they will only cause headaches in the kitchen. Also, look for zucchini with tiny prickly hairs around the stem end; the hairs are a sign of freshness.

Even small zucchini have a fairly high amount of moisture, which should be removed. Many sources recommend salting sliced zucchini before cooking it. We tested salting to draw off some water and found that sliced and salted zucchini sheds about 20 percent of its weight after sitting for 30 minutes. But given that we had set out to come up with a quick side dish recipe, we wanted to develop a faster method for removing excess water. We tried shredding the zucchini on the large holes of a box grater, tossing the shredded zucchini with the salt to drain in a fine-mesh strainer for 10 minutes, and then squeezing

---

EQUIPMENT: Box Graters

Thanks to packaged grated cheeses and bagged hash browns, box graters have been steadily losing their appeal, but we think they still have their place in the kitchen. True, food processors may shred pounds of cheese or vegetables more swiftly, but dragging one out of the cabinet to grate half a cube of mozzarella seems silly. Surely, the handy box grater could excel as a pinch hitter. To find out, we tested eight graters, grating raw potatoes and mozzarella and Parmesan cheeses on each of them.

When it came to bells and whistles on these graters, nonskid bases and plastic measuring cup attachments were the main differentiating factors. Nonskid bases on Anolon's Box Grater, KitchenAid's KG300 Box Grater, and OXO's Good Grips Box Grater, while not an unwelcome feature, only marginally improved the graters' stability. Besides, once the measuring cup attachments were in place, these rubber bases were irrelevant.

The principle feature that significantly distinguished one grater from another was blade quality. Six of the eight graters, including Cuisipro's excessively comprehensive 6-Sided Grater,

featured traditionally deep punctures—fine for semisoft cheeses and softer vegetables, but no match for the shallower, razor-sharp edges on Microplane's 34005 Better Box Grater. Dry Parmesan shreds, which occasionally chipped and flaked on the other models, fell lithely from these exceptionally sharp blades. However, Microplane's unusually short (under five inches) shredding plane disqualified it from the top ranks.

Meanwhile, with its sharp blades and clear, marked container, the OXO delivered on all fronts, and its low price tag—prices of tested graters went all the way up to $25—made it a smart choice as well.

THE BEST BOX GRATER

An all-around good tool, our winning box grater, the OXO Good Grips Box Grater ($14.99), features sharp blades, a slim body, and a labeled container for easy storage.

OXO GOOD GRIPS

out the excess water by hand. This removed a good amount of water, but we had even more luck when we wrapped the drained shreds in a kitchen towel and then squeezed them until dry. Because shredded zucchini has so much more surface area than sliced zucchini, and the towel could absorb more released water, this method worked like magic.

With the shredded zucchini ready to sauté, we heated some olive oil in the skillet. Unlike butter, the olive oil imparted a rich, savory flavor that we liked paired with the zucchini. A few cloves of minced garlic elevated the flavor from bland and dull to bright and robust. In just minutes, the zucchini was browned and still had some bite to it. A handful of fresh parsley only enhanced the sweet, fresh flavors of our zucchini.

This side dish was a totally new take on one of our favorite summer vegetables. And we were able to reinvent zucchini yet again with two new variations, both of which use tangy ingredients (chives in one, anchovies in the other) to create a nice contrast with the summer-fresh zucchini.

Sautéed Shredded Zucchini

SERVES 4

If you like, replace one of the zucchini with two medium carrots that have been peeled and shredded on the large holes of a box grater—there's no need to squeeze the carrots dry.

1½	pounds zucchini (about 3 medium), trimmed
	Salt
3	tablespoons extra-virgin olive oil
3	medium garlic cloves, minced or pressed through a garlic press (about 1 tablespoon)
2	tablespoons minced fresh parsley
	Ground black pepper

1. Following the illustrations at right, shred the zucchini on the large holes of a box grater or in a food processor fitted with the shredding disk. Toss the shredded zucchini with 1 teaspoon salt and let it drain in a fine-mesh strainer set over a bowl for 10 minutes. Wrap the zucchini in a clean kitchen towel and squeeze out the excess liquid.

2. Heat the oil in a 12-inch nonstick skillet over medium-high heat until shimmering. Add

the zucchini and garlic and cook, stirring occasionally, until tender, about 7 minutes. Stir in the parsley and season with salt and pepper to taste. Serve immediately.

➤ VARIATIONS
Sautéed Shredded Zucchini with Sweet Corn and Chives
This recipe also works with frozen corn; just defrost the corn and add it during the last minute or two of the cooking time. See the illustration on page 289 for removing the kernels from fresh corn.

1½	pounds zucchini (about 3 medium), trimmed
	Salt
3	tablespoons unsalted butter
1	medium shallot, minced
2	medium ears sweet corn, husk and silk removed, kernels cut from the cob (about 1¼ cups; see the illustration on page 289)
1	tablespoon minced fresh chives
	Ground black pepper

SHREDDING AND DRAINING ZUCCHINI

1. Shred the trimmed zucchini on the large holes of a box grater or in a food processor fitted with the shredding disk.

2. After salting and draining the zucchini, wrap it in a clean kitchen towel and squeeze out the excess liquid. Proceed with the recipe.

1. Following the illustrations on page 303, shred the zucchini on the large holes of a box grater or in a food processor fitted with the shredding disk. Toss the shredded zucchini with 1 teaspoon salt and let it drain in a fine-mesh strainer set over a bowl for 10 minutes. Wrap the zucchini in a clean kitchen towel and squeeze out the excess liquid.

2. Heat the butter in a 12-inch nonstick skillet over medium-high heat. When the foaming subsides, add the shallot and cook, stirring occasionally, until soft, 2 to 3 minutes. Add the zucchini and corn and cook, stirring occasionally, until tender, about 7 minutes. Stir in the chives and season with salt and pepper to taste. Serve immediately.

Spicy Sautéed Shredded Zucchini with Anchovies

Anchovies bring a deep, salty flavor without any hint of fishiness to this dish.

1½	pounds zucchini (about 3 medium), trimmed
	Salt
3	tablespoons extra-virgin olive oil
3	medium garlic cloves, minced or pressed through a garlic press (about 1 tablespoon)
2	medium anchovy fillets, rinsed and minced
¼	teaspoon red pepper flakes
	Ground black pepper

1. Following the illustrations on page 303, shred the zucchini on the large holes of a box grater or in a food processor fitted with the shredding disk. Toss the shredded zucchini with 1 teaspoon salt and let it drain in a fine-mesh strainer set over a bowl for 10 minutes. Wrap the zucchini in a clean kitchen towel and squeeze out the excess liquid.

2. Heat the oil in a 12-inch nonstick skillet over medium-high heat until shimmering. Add the garlic, anchovies, and red pepper flakes and cook, mashing the anchovies into the oil, until fragrant, about 30 seconds. Add the zucchini and cook, stirring occasionally, until tender, about 7 minutes. Season with salt and pepper to taste. Serve immediately.

ZUCCHINI FRITTERS

WE HAD PREVIOUSLY COME ACROSS THE IDEA of zucchini fritters—battered and fried shredded zucchini—and thought they would be the natural extension of our Sautéed Shredded Zucchini side dish (page 303). Fritters, we surmised, would be another interesting, not-so-basic option, and a nice complement to our skillet sides. While cooks in the Mediterranean and Middle East seem to have mastered making this side dish, we knew we'd have to look out for the zucchini's high moisture content to make sure we didn't end up with soggy, bland fritters. We wanted crisp, highly seasoned fritters and would have to find a way to get rid of the excess water.

We researched several recipes and found only small differences in the ingredient lists and techniques. All the recipes called for some sort of binder—usually eggs, a starch, or a combination of the two—and seasonings. According to some recipes, salting and draining the zucchini before combining them with the other fritter ingredients was a vital step. Also, although all the recipes cooked the fritters in a skillet, they called for different amounts of oil.

We wanted to find out if the same technique we had used to remove excess moisture from our sautéed shredded zucchini would be sufficient here, or if we would need to find an even better way to absorb the water from our zucchini. Since we would be pan-frying, not sautéing, the zucchini, it was imperative that it be bone-dry. A quick trial of preparing fritters from two different batches of shredded zucchini—one tossed with salt and set aside to drain for 10 minutes, as in our sautéed zucchini recipe, and another simply salted and set on paper towels to absorb excess water—gave us our answer. The salted and drained zucchini made for the better fritter, resulting in crisp and dry fritters. The fritters made from the second method were almost as good, but not quite as dry. We decided that salting the zucchini for 10 minutes and setting it in a strainer so the liquid could drain off, rather than be absorbed by paper towels, was the most effective way to remove moisture. After the time was up, we placed the zucchini on a clean kitchen towel, rolled it up, and gave it a quick squeeze to get every last drop of water out.

Next, we tested various binders, including all-purpose flour, potato starch, and cornstarch, both with and without egg. Our tasters far preferred the consistent, unified texture of the fritters made with egg. As for the starch, the differences were noticeable but minimal, so we chose flour because it's what most cooks tend to have on hand.

As for seasoning, we looked to the traditional recipes for clues. All of them called for onions or scallions—our tasters preferred the more delicate flavor of scallions. Dill was also common, and we liked the freshness it added to the fritters. Last, we added crumbled feta cheese to give every bite of crispy zucchini fritter a pocket of creamy and salty feta.

Now we were ready to fry. Making enough fritters to serve four to six people required cooking them in two batches. We found that 2 tablespoons of batter created the right size fritter, and 3 tablespoons of oil was just the right amount to fry our first batch, which was done in about 5 minutes. Using less oil than this amount caused the fritters to cook unevenly and burn. We wiped the used oil from our skillet and added fresh oil to the pan for batch two. (If we skipped this step, the burnt bits from the first batch of fritters stuck to the second batch.)

The first batch was kept warm in the oven while we fried up the second and got ready to sample our fritters. They were outstanding—perfectly crisp (with nary a hint of sogginess!), well seasoned, and had a tangy bite from the feta.

Zucchini Fritters

MAKES ABOUT 12 FRITTERS, SERVES 4 TO 6

Be sure to squeeze the zucchini until it is completely dry, or the fritters will fall apart in the skillet. Don't let the squeeze-dried zucchini sit on its own for too long or it will turn brown. These fritters are great warm or at room temperature.

1	pound zucchini (about 2 medium), trimmed
1	teaspoon salt
8	ounces feta cheese, crumbled (about 2 cups)
2	scallions, minced
2	tablespoons minced fresh dill
2	large eggs, lightly beaten
1	medium garlic clove, minced or pressed through a garlic press (about 1 teaspoon)
¼	teaspoon ground black pepper
¼	cup unbleached all-purpose flour
6	tablespoons olive oil
1	lemon, cut into wedges, for serving

1. Adjust an oven rack to the middle position and heat the oven to 200 degrees. Following the illustrations on page 303, shred the zucchini on the large holes of a box grater or in a food processor fitted with the shredding disk. Toss the shredded zucchini with the salt and let it drain in a fine-mesh strainer set over a bowl for 10 minutes. Wrap the zucchini in a clean kitchen towel and squeeze out the excess liquid.

2. Combine the dried zucchini, feta, scallions, dill, eggs, garlic, and pepper together in a medium bowl. Sprinkle the flour over the mixture and toss until uniformly incorporated.

3. Heat 3 tablespoons of the oil in a 12-inch nonstick skillet over medium heat until shimmering. Drop 2-tablespoon-sized portions of the batter into the pan, then use the back of a spoon to press the batter into 2-inch-wide fritters (you should fit about 6 fritters in the pan at a time). Fry until golden brown on both sides, 2 to 3 minutes per side.

4. Transfer the fritters to a paper towel–lined baking sheet and place in the oven to keep warm. Wipe the skillet clean with a wad of paper towels. Return the skillet to medium heat, add the remaining 3 tablespoons oil, and repeat with the remaining batter. Serve warm or at room temperature with the lemon wedges.

Toasted Orzo

ORZO, LIKE COUSCOUS, IS A SMALL PASTA that is sometimes treated like a grain. Shaped like a flat grain of rice, orzo can be used to produce many a side dish, since it can fill the role of either grain or pasta. Lots of ingredients pair nicely with its compact, even shape, but we especially like matching bright, Mediterranean flavors to orzo.

The basic concept of this side dish is similar to rice pilaf—sauté aromatics, toast the orzo, and simmer in liquid until tender. But our pasta would need a bit more care and attention than basic rice or pilaf. So we started our testing by figuring out how long to toast the orzo for the best flavor and texture, and then looked at how much liquid would be needed to cook the orzo to an al dente texture.

After toasting orzo to shades varying from pale yellow to golden brown, we found that the darker the orzo, the richer the flavor (shy of burning it, of course). Well-browned orzo possessed a full, nutty flavor that tasters favored over that of more lightly toasted orzo. The key was timing—we opted for medium heat, which produced golden orzo in about five minutes, though it did require diligent stirring and a watchful eye to prevent scorching.

White rice requires around 1½ times its volume in liquid to cook, but we didn't know if this ratio would work for orzo. First, we tried cooking 1 pound of orzo (2½ cups) in 6 cups chicken broth, but the result was extraordinarily soupy. We then tried just 3 cups broth, but the orzo was chalky and undercooked. Four cups came closer to the mark, and an additional ⅔ cup proved perfect; the orzo plumped to a tender yet firm consistency, somewhere between that of pasta and rice. Chicken broth added a more desirable flavor than that of beef broth or water. We replaced part of the broth with vermouth and tasters liked the result. One nagging problem remained—our 12-inch skillet was a bit too full. We cut the liquid and pasta amounts in half, and found cooking the orzo much more manageable; furthermore, it fed six people perfectly as a side dish.

With our orzo toasted and the liquid-to-pasta ratio settled, we worked on our cooking method. We tried cooking the orzo as we might a traditional risotto, by adding the liquid a little at a time until it was absorbed, but found this time-consuming technique unnecessary, as was a low, covered simmer, the standard when making rice. The easiest way proved the best. Once the broth came to a boil in the skillet, we reduced the heat to medium-low and left the orzo uncovered until done—it took a mere 10 minutes.

For flavor, we decided simple was best; sautéed onion and garlic formed the base, and grated Parmesan cheese, stirred in once the orzo was cooked, gave the pasta a silky feel. We included frozen peas at the last minute for a springtime touch. They needed only two minutes of ambient heat to warm through.

Our orzo was perfectly cooked—with just a slight al dente bite—and had a garden-fresh tone from the peas. For two options, we added oil-cured olives for a robust, briny flavor and bacon for a crisp bite.

Toasted Orzo with Peas and Parmesan
SERVES 6

Be careful when adding the broth to the pan, because it will create a lot of steam.

2	tablespoons unsalted butter
1	small onion, minced
	Salt
2	medium garlic cloves, minced or pressed through a garlic press (about 2 teaspoons)
1¼	cups orzo
2	cups low-sodium chicken broth
⅓	cup vermouth or dry white wine
1	cup frozen peas, thawed
1	ounce Parmesan cheese, grated (1 cup)
2	tablespoons fresh minced parsley leaves
	Ground black pepper
1	lemon, cut into wedges, for serving

1. Melt the butter in a 12-inch nonstick skillet over medium heat. Add the onion and ¾ teaspoon salt and cook, stirring often, until softened, 5 to 7 minutes. Stir in the garlic and cook until fragrant, about 30 seconds. Stir in the orzo and cook, stirring often, until most of the grains are golden, about 5 minutes.

2. Stir in the broth and vermouth, being careful of the steam. Bring to a boil, then reduce the heat to medium-low and simmer, stirring occasionally, until all of the liquid has been absorbed and the orzo is tender, 10 to 12 minutes.

3. Off the heat, stir in the peas, Parmesan, and parsley and let sit until the peas are warmed through, about 2 minutes. Season with salt and pepper to taste and serve with the lemon wedges.

➤ VARIATIONS

Toasted Orzo with Fennel, Olives, and Cilantro

See the illustrations below on how to prepare fennel for this recipe.

Follow the recipe for Toasted Orzo with Peas and Parmesan, adding 1 small fennel bulb (about 9 ounces), trimmed of stems, cored, and cut into ¼-inch dice, and ¾ teaspoon fennel seeds, with the onion; cook until softened, 7 to 10 minutes. Substitute ½ cup oil-cured olives, pitted and coarsely chopped, for the peas and 2 tablespoons minced fresh cilantro leaves for the parsley.

Toasted Orzo with Bacon, Scallions, and Peas

Cook 4 ounces (about 4 slices) bacon, chopped coarse, in the skillet over medium-high heat until crisp, about 5 minutes. Transfer the bacon to a paper towel–lined plate, leaving the bacon fat in the skillet. Follow the recipe for Toasted Orzo with Peas and Parmesan, substituting the bacon fat for the butter. Substitute 3 scallions, sliced thin on the bias, for the parsley and sprinkle with the bacon before serving.

COUSCOUS

COUSCOUS MAY LOOK LIKE A GRAIN, BUT IT'S really a tiny pasta. Made from semolina flour, the individual grains are formed by rolling the flour with lightly salted water into little balls; these are then steamed and dried for long term storage. This Middle Eastern and North African food has gained in popularity in the United States and become a ubiquitous stand-in for starchy sides like white rice or noodles. We've had couscous at lots of restaurants, but it frequently falls flat, with a bland flavor and heavy, clumpy texture. We wanted to come up with the best way to make light, fluffy, and savory couscous at home, to serve alongside an array of dishes.

The most common and easiest way to cook couscous is in a saucepan, soaking the dried couscous in boiling hot water or broth until it's tender and ready to eat. The traditional cooking method uses a couscoussière, which is basically a stockpot fitted with a small-holed colander, with the couscous sitting in the colander and plumping in steam rising from the stock or soup at the bottom. We put away the saucepan and fancy equipment, knowing we could replicate this cooking method with our skillet, which offers a wide surface area, perfect for holding a lot of liquid to steam the grains of couscous.

We started out with the streamlined method of boiling liquid and soaking the couscous in it until tender, but discovered one big downside—the couscous tends to clump into tight balls. We found that

TRIMMING AND CORING FENNEL

1. Cut off the stems and feathery fronds. (The fronds can be saved and minced for a garnish.)

2. Trim a very thin slice from the base and remove any tough or blemished outer layers from the bulb.

3. Cut the bulb in half through the base. Use a small, sharp knife to remove the pyramid-shaped core, then cut as directed in the recipe.

the addition of a little oil or butter to the hydrating liquid helped but didn't completely rectify the situation. Borrowing a technique from our Toasted Orzo with Peas and Parmesan (page 306), we tried toasting the raw couscous in a little butter before adding the liquid. In the skillet, the couscous was able to brown quickly and evenly due to the large cooking surface. The resulting cooked couscous was our best batch yet; the grains were discrete and the flavor nutty.

With our couscous plumped and smooth, we were ready to address the couscous flavorings. Although it's not traditional to add aromatics to plain couscous, we had already heated the skillet, so why not do a little sautéing while we were at it? Just one small onion sautéed in butter lent the couscous both sweetness and a subtle sharpness. Garlic seemed too harsh and out of place.

For liquid, water was the easiest choice, but it made for a bland couscous, even with the onion. We then tried chicken broth, but it was too strong; the chicken flavor overpowered the mild couscous. A combination of chicken broth and water, however, worked fine, giving the couscous body and a pleasant richness. For a final touch, we chose to add a little lemon juice, which sharpened the seasonings.

We liked the simplicity of the dish—it was the perfect neutral match to a host of flavors—but some tasters wanted to jazz it up a bit, so without altering our basic recipe too much, we added toasted sliced almonds and a pinch of saffron for an alluring golden hue and distinct aroma in one variation. Lemon zest and fresh basil brought a bright tone to another couscous dish.

Basic Couscous

SERVES 6 TO 8

Be sure to use a fork to fluff the grains in step 4; a spoon or spatula will turn its light texture mushy. Specialty markets may carry couscous of varying sizes (such as large Israeli-style couscous), but stick to the basic fine-grained variety, as the other sizes require different cooking methods.

4	tablespoons (½ stick) unsalted butter
2	cups couscous
I	small onion, minced
	Salt
2	cups water
I ¾	cups low-sodium chicken broth
I ½	teaspoons juice from I lemon
	Ground black pepper

1. Melt 2 tablespoons of the butter in a 12-inch nonstick skillet over medium-high heat. Add the couscous and cook, stirring often, until some grains are just beginning to brown, about 3 minutes. Transfer the couscous to a large bowl.

2. Melt the remaining 2 tablespoons butter in the skillet over medium heat. Add the onion and ¾ teaspoon salt and cook, stirring occasionally, until softened, 5 to 7 minutes. Stir in the water and broth and bring to a boil.

3. Pour the boiling liquid over the toasted couscous, cover tightly with plastic wrap, and let sit until the couscous is tender, about 12 minutes.

4. Remove the plastic wrap, fluff the couscous with a fork, and gently stir in the lemon juice. Season with salt and pepper to taste and serve.

➤ VARIATIONS

Couscous with Lemon and Herbs

Follow the recipe for Basic Couscous, adding ½ teaspoon grated zest from 1 lemon with the broth in step 2. Stir in ⅓ cup minced fresh basil or parsley leaves with the lemon juice in step 4.

Saffron Couscous with Almonds and Raisins

Serve with our Sautéed Chicken Breasts (page 6) or Sautéed Chicken Cutlets (page 7).

Follow the recipe for Basic Couscous, adding ¾ cup raisins and a pinch saffron threads, crumbled, with the onion in step 2. Stir in ¾ cup sliced almonds, toasted, with the lemon juice in step 4.

9
DESSERTS

DESSERTS

WHETHER YOU'RE ENTERTAINING FRIENDS on a leisurely weekend or a busy weeknight, it's nice to have some dessert recipes in your repertoire that can be whipped up at the last minute—no fussy preparation or hours of chilling (or baking) required. And confining desserts to the skillet is our newly found secret for turning out appealingly rustic yet company-worthy desserts that come together in no time. In fact, many of these are meant to go directly from the stovetop or oven to the table—no waiting required.

For these recipes, we worked to present a range of desserts that are easy, quick, and more foolproof than their complicated originals. Our Skillet-Roasted Pears (page 321) and Tarte Tatin (page 324), already well-established skillet favorites, were natural choices for this book. Others, like our Rustic Blueberry Pie (page 318) and Lemon Soufflé (page 332), benefited from a skillet makeover because the level of difficulty or the time required to make them was reduced, bringing dessert to the table in record time.

That's not to say that reengineering these recipes for the skillet was easy. In fact, especially with our fruit desserts, this process was fraught with challenges. For example, in several recipes, we made a fruit filling right in the skillet, before topping it with crust and baking it in the oven. While this method might seem simple at first glance, it was actually made more difficult by the inherent juiciness of the fruit. We had to make sure that we didn't cook the fillings too much, or they would overcook in the oven and turn to mush. On the flip side, we had to make sure that the fruit fillings cooked down just enough to keep our desserts full and juicy, not dried out and bland. For our Cherry Cobbler (page 313), we opted to use jarred cherries, guaranteeing a consistent amount of juiciness in the fruit. This worked splendidly; our cobbler is juicy *and* foolproof. Using jarred or frozen fruits has the added benefit of increased availability, allowing cherry cobbler to be a year-round treat, not just a seasonal indulgence.

After perfecting our fruit fillings, we polished up the toppings. With many of our traditional crisps and cobblers, we parbake the toppings, which ensures that they stay crisp throughout cooking. But for our skillet versions, we wanted to eliminate the need for separate baking times for the biscuits and other toppings—not to mention all the extra pans and bowls this requires. The solution? For our Peach Crisp (page 316), we toasted the topping in stages and then set it aside before using the skillet to make the filling. To fix cobbles that were overbaked on top but gummy underneath, we simply made them smaller; the mini cobbles on our Cherry Cobbler cook through quickly and are perfectly crisp. We employed a simpler solution for our blueberry pie, cutting 2-inch long slits in the crust to allow enough steam to escape, thereby keeping our top crust crisp.

Decidedly rustic, nearly all the desserts in this chapter have a homey charm and can be simply scooped into bowls. That said, our skillet Lemon Soufflé (page 332) has the same rise and ethereal texture of its French precursor—minus all the fuss. You may have the impression that this classic French dessert is impossibly hard to make and have thought you would never attempt one. But our skillet soufflé, which doesn't seem like a natural for the stovetop, actually turned out to be easier and more delicious than the classic version. We found that, unlike the traditional baked fruit desserts, the soufflé needed a more concentrated heat to rise properly, therefore making the skillet the perfect baking dish to get the right height and texture. We also nixed the step of making a fussy base (usually a cooked sauce) and instead used our hot skillet to activate the whipped egg white batter for that essential soufflé rise.

Our handy skillet, which took the place of everything from a pie plate to a soufflé dish, was key to helping us create these best recipes. Now, with so many easy weeknight recipes available, you can spend your evenings enjoying dessert instead of making it.

CHERRY COBBLER

A FLEET OF TENDER BISCUITS ON A SEA OF sweet, saucy cherries, a good cherry cobbler can hold its own against other fruit desserts, especially because this down-to-earth dessert comes together in just a couple of quick steps and can be dished up right away, ready to be devoured with a scoop of vanilla ice cream. The filling is traditionally cooked on the stovetop, which means this simple dish was easy to make—and bake—in our skillet.

First we had to decide on the perfect cherries for this cobbler. Sour cherries were the obvious choice, as they have sufficient acidity to cook up well and become truly flavorful with a touch of sugar and some heat. Sweet cherries, like Bing cherries, are better for snacking because they lose their flavor when cooked. Since fresh sour cherries have such a short season, we knew that using jarred or canned sour cherries would be easier— they're always in season and already pitted, plus they're usually packed in a juice that can be used to flavor the sauce.

We tested several canned and jarred varieties, and found jarred Morello cherries to be the best; they were plump, meaty, and tart, right out of the jar. To make the sauce, we drained two 24-ounce jars of Morello cherries, reserved the juice, and set the cherries aside for the time being. We had 2 cups of juice, which we would thicken to form the base of our rich, saucy cobbler. Three tablespoons of cornstarch seemed like it would do the trick, so we added this amount to the juice in the skillet. For sweetness, we found that ¾ to 1 cup of sugar was the right amount, depending on the brand and sweetness level of the cherries. To heighten the cherry flavor, we also added some vanilla extract, then cooked the mixture until it had thickened. Off the heat, we stirred in the cherries. Since jarred (and canned) cherries have been processed, they are already cooked, so the less heat they're exposed to thereafter the better. By fully cooking the sauce on the stove prior to adding the cherries, we could also lessen the baking time—the sauce wouldn't have to cook in the oven—ensuring that the topping wouldn't burn.

INGREDIENTS: Baking Powder and Baking Soda

Cookies, cakes, muffins, and biscuits, including the mini cobbles in our Cherry Cobbler, get their rise from chemical leaveners— baking soda and baking powder—rather than yeast. Chemical leaveners react with acids to produce carbon dioxide, the gas that causes these baked goods to rise. So, what's the real difference between baking soda and baking powder?

To do its work, baking soda relies on an acid in the recipe, provided by ingredients such as buttermilk (in our Cherry Cobbler), sour cream, or yogurt. It's important to use the right amount of baking soda called for—use too much and it won't be neutralized by the acid, making for a metallic-tasting, coarse-crumbed cake.

Baking powder is actually nothing more than baking soda (about one-quarter to one-third of the total makeup) mixed with a dry acid and double-dried cornstarch. The cornstarch absorbs moisture and keeps the baking soda and dry acid apart during storage, preventing premature production of the gas. When baking powder becomes wet, the acid comes into contact with the baking soda, producing carbon dioxide. Most commercial baking powders are "double-acting." In other words, they contain two kinds of acids—one that produces a carbon dioxide reaction at room temperature and one that responds only to heat. (Baking soda, on the other hand, is "single-acting.")

We have tested and tasted the four largest national brands of baking powder and found little difference in action or flavor. (There's only one widely available brand of baking soda.) Each baking powder we tested worked well, and any differences in flavor were virtually undetectable. The only thing to keep in mind with baking powder is freshness; old baking powder will yield squat biscuits and flat cakes. To prevent disappointment in your baked goods, write the date you open your baking powder right on the can and discard it after six months.

Moving on to the cobbles, we knew we wanted them to be light but browned and crisp. We omitted the eggs, which we've learned can give biscuits a dense texture, and added buttermilk for the opposite effect, creating biscuits that are light and tender. We tested several biscuit variations and settled on a fairly standard mix of all-purpose flour, butter, baking powder and soda, sugar, salt, and buttermilk.

Our biggest question was how to cook the biscuit dough evenly without burning it. We started out by dropping heaping spoonfuls of dough over the cooked cherry filling, instead of the more time-consuming method of rolling out the dough and cutting out biscuits. Although this technique was promising and gave our cobbler a rustic look, we found the large drops of dough took too long to bake through, and the undersides remained raw and gummy. For the next test, we traded in the large spoon for a teaspoon and dropped small scoops of biscuit dough evenly over the fruit for a truly cobbled effect. These mini-cobbles worked perfectly and cooked through in just half an hour without issue—no soggy bottoms here. To give the topping a bit more oomph, we sprinkled turbinado sugar over the tops before baking. This gave our biscuits a crispy texture that contrasted nicely against the softened cherries and sweet sauce.

With our topping perfected and our juicy cherry filling hot and bubbling, we let the finished cobbler sit for a short time before we dug in. The biscuits were brown and crisp, and the cherry filling was just right, somewhere between sweet and tart. Our Cherry Cobbler was ready in minutes and, since we used jarred cherries, it could satisfy our down-home dessert cravings any time of the year.

To dress up this dessert for company, we created two slightly more sophisticated versions—one with almond extract and toasted sliced almonds and a second with the lush flavors of cinnamon and red wine.

Cherry Cobbler

SERVES 6

Trader Joe's is our favorite brand of jarred Morello cherries to use here, but if you can't find it, other brands of jarred or canned Morello cherries in juice will work fine. The amount of sugar you use will depend on the sweetness of your cherries; if they are very sweet, use the smaller amount of sugar given. We prefer the crunchy texture of turbinado sugar sprinkled over the biscuits before baking, but regular granulated sugar can be substituted.

BISCUIT TOPPING

1½	cups (7½ ounces) unbleached all-purpose flour
5	tablespoons granulated sugar
1½	teaspoons baking powder
¼	teaspoon baking soda
¼	teaspoon salt
¾	cup buttermilk
4	tablespoons (½ stick) unsalted butter, melted and cooled

CHERRY FILLING

¾–1	cup (5¼ to 7 ounces) granulated sugar
3	tablespoons cornstarch
	Pinch salt
2	(24-ounce) jars Morello cherries, drained (about 4 cups cherries), with 2 cups juice reserved
½	teaspoon vanilla extract
2	tablespoons turbinado sugar (see note)

1. FOR THE BISCUIT TOPPING: Adjust an oven rack to the middle position and heat the oven to 400 degrees. Whisk the flour, granulated sugar, baking powder, baking soda, and salt together in a medium bowl. Stir in the buttermilk and melted butter until a dough forms. Cover and set aside until needed.

2. FOR THE CHERRY FILLING: Whisk the granulated sugar, cornstarch, and salt together in a 12-inch ovenproof skillet. Whisk in the reserved cherry juice

and vanilla. Set the skillet over medium-high heat and cook, whisking frequently, until the mixture simmers and is slightly thickened, about 5 minutes. Off the heat, stir in the cherries.

3. Using a spoon, scoop and drop 1-inch pieces of the dough, spaced about ½ inch apart, over the cherry filling in the skillet, then sprinkle with the turbinado sugar. Transfer the skillet to the oven and bake the cobbler until the biscuits are golden brown and the filling is thick and glossy, 25 to 30 minutes.

4. Using a potholder (the skillet handle will be hot), remove the skillet from the oven. Let the cobbler cool in the skillet for at least 15 minutes before serving.

➤ VARIATIONS
Cherry-Almond Cobbler
Follow the recipe for Cherry Cobbler, substituting ½ teaspoon almond extract for the vanilla. Sprinkle ¼ cup sliced almonds, toasted, over the top before serving.

Cherry, Red Wine, and Cinnamon Cobbler
Follow the recipe for Cherry Cobbler, substituting 1 cup dry red wine for 1 cup of the reserved jarred cherry juice. Add 1 cinnamon stick to the skillet with the cherry juice in step 2; remove and discard the cinnamon stick when stirring in the cherries.

PEACH CRISP

PEACH CRISP SHOULD TASTE LIKE SUMMER, with juicy ripe peaches and a buttery, nutty topping. But all too often, the peaches are mushy and saccharine-sweet, and the topping is sandy and flavorless. Where do these recipes go so wrong? There's a fundamental problem with peach crisp: the peaches.

Few fruits are as inconsistent in texture and juiciness as the peach. Unripe peaches take forever to cook through and usually produce a chokingly dry crisp devoid of flavor; at the other extreme,

very ripe peaches overcook easily and produce a soupy mess with a soggy topping. Some recipes try to address these problems by specifying the ripeness level of the peaches or adjusting the amount of thickener to suit the fruit's ripeness (and juiciness). Sadly, other recipes drain away some of the peach's juices before cooking them. All of these solutions, however, have obvious drawbacks. We wanted an easy, anytime peach crisp that would highlight the natural, fragrant flavors of peaches, without making a trip to every supermarket in town looking for the perfect peaches, guessing at the right amount of thickener, or sending any of the precious, flavorful peach juices down the drain.

With a skillet in hand, we wondered if we couldn't solve many of the peach filling issues by using the direct heat of the stovetop. Our theory was that we could cook the peaches in the skillet to release and reduce their juices to a thick, glossy sauce. After the peach juices had been reduced to a sauce, we would then sprinkle the crumble topping evenly over the filling and finish baking the crisp in the oven.

This idea, however, flopped—the natural juices never really thickened, although they did give the peaches a nice, glossy coating. The peach flavor, though, was terrific, with a perfumed, concentrated taste. Our theory wasn't perfect, but we were clearly onto something worth pursuing.

Switching gears, we realized that adding a little thickener to the skillet would be necessary to help the peach juices thicken into a sauce. We jump-started the release of juices by cooking the peaches in a covered skillet first, then tried adding three separate thickeners: flour, tapioca, and cornstarch. Flour tasted too starchy and tapioca left odd white bits floating in the sauce, but the cornstarch worked like a charm, producing a glossy, light sauce with no aftertaste or funny texture.

Up until now, we had been faithfully peeling, pitting, and slicing fresh peaches, but since some peaches are juicier than others, we found that there wasn't one set amount of cornstarch that could accommodate both drier peaches and juicier peaches. We wondered if using frozen sliced peaches could help us standardize the amount of juice that the peaches released during cooking, and therefore help us nail down the amount of cornstarch required, making our recipe more foolproof.

After just one test, we found ourselves fully convinced that frozen peaches far surpassed fresh peaches as the base of our crisp. Not only do they release a reliable amount of juice, but they are always available, perfectly ripe, and prep-time free—ideal for our anytime skillet peach crisp. Also, we noted that the same covered cooking method we used for fresh peaches worked perfectly with the frozen peaches. And, as a bonus, we found there was no reason to thaw the frozen peaches before cooking them. After just about 10 minutes in the covered skillet, the frozen

peaches thawed and softened, leaving us with plenty of juice for a nice sauce. For this simple skillet dessert, it was clear that fresh peaches were out and frozen peaches were in.

Our peaches were sweet and softened, and they needed just a couple of flavor enhancements—we added a touch of sugar, lemon juice to bring out the sweet-tart taste of the fruit, and salt to define the flavors. With the filling finessed, it was time to test crisp toppings.

We tried baking the peaches with a variety of options, including a spiced streusel mixture, an oat-almond mixture, and a simple, buttery bread crumb mixture. The streusel-like topping tasted great, but it tended to melt into the juicy peach filling rather than bake into crisp bits on top. Tasters also liked the nutty flavor of the oat-almond

INGREDIENTS: Vanilla Ice Cream

The perfect complement to hot, bubbly cobblers and crisps, vanilla ice cream has universal appeal. But in spite of its simplicity, we're often stumped when selecting ice cream at the supermarket. There are tons of brands to choose from, and they all have different ingredients—many of them difficult to pronounce. To find out which brand was best, we tasted 18 varieties, including 10 French-style (with egg yolks) and eight regular (yolkless) vanilla ice creams.

As varied as the ice creams looked on paper, the side-by-side comparison was striking. Some were fluffy and light; others were dense and rich. A few had assertive vanilla notes that reminded tasters of "frozen, boozy eggnog." Several ice creams, on the other hand, seemed to be lacking in vanilla flavor altogether. We examined the labels, thinking the various ingredients might have something to do with these differences.

We learned that high fat content and egg yolks can give ice cream a rich, creamy texture, but the use of stabilizers and emulsifiers (like carob bean gum, carrageenan, and mono- and diglycerides) can also go a long way toward enhancing the texture. Not surprisingly, the ice creams in our lineup that got the lowest scores for texture had a low fat content and no egg yolks, stabilizers, or emulsifiers.

But ice cream is more than just creamy—there's the flavor to think about too. Flavor is generally contributed by vanilla beans, imitation vanilla extract, or compounds derived from natural vanilla extract. Our top two ice creams, which scored high for both creamy texture and flavor, use natural vanilla compounds. For a smooth, subtle, and balanced vanilla ice cream, Turkey Hill Vanilla Bean is our top choice, while the second-place Edy's Dreamery Vanilla has a creamy texture and stronger vanilla flavor than Turkey Hill.

THE BEST VANILLA ICE CREAM

TURKEY HILL   EDY'S DREAMERY

Turkey Hill All Natural Flavor Vanilla Bean ice cream has a very clean flavor and creamy texture, while Edy's Dreamery was praised for being "ultra-creamy" with a strong vanilla flavor.

topping, but they hated the raw flavor and texture of the oats. And while the buttery bread crumb topping had a nice crisp texture and buttery flavor, it was just too boring.

Putting the best aspects of these three toppings together, we combined a mixture of sugar and butter, sliced almonds, and bread crumbs. Our first attempt at this topping was a bit of a dud, failing to toast up sufficiently in the oven before the peaches overcooked. For a second attempt, we gave the topping a quick toast in the skillet before cooking the peaches. This worked better, but we found that the sugar-butter mixture, nuts, and bread crumbs didn't toast or caramelize at the same rate, so the final topping was unevenly crisp when it came out of the oven. Giving the topping one more shot, we tried staggering the addition of ingredients for toasting. We added the nuts to the skillet first because they would need the most time in the pan, then stirred in butter and bread crumbs, and finally added the sugar and more butter, along with cinnamon and nutmeg, to the center of the skillet.

We found two easy ways to guarantee a richly caramelized and crispier topping. First, we substituted light brown sugar for some of the white sugar. Second, we mixed the brown sugar into the butter right in the middle of the skillet—there was no need to dirty an additional bowl to mix the two ingredients in advance. This butter–brown sugar mixture melted and turned bubbly, coating the almonds and bread crumbs and making for a crispy, caramelized topping.

At this point, we realized we had unwittingly engineered the recipe so that the topping could be made and emerge from the skillet first, with the crisp texture and deeply caramelized flavor you'd find on a finished crisp, after which the peach filling could be cooked to the perfect softened and saucy consistency—and it all happened on the stovetop. Why bother, then, putting it into the oven at all? Simply sprinkling the topping over the cooked peaches in the skillet was the best plan yet, and tasters didn't even notice that the crisp was unbaked—they were too busy eating.

Peach Crisp
SERVES 6

Do not thaw the peaches before cooking. If, however, your peaches are frozen into a solid block, thaw them slightly to separate them before cooking. Serve with vanilla ice cream.

TOPPING

2	slices high-quality white sandwich bread, torn into large pieces
½	cup sliced almonds
4	tablespoons (½ stick) unsalted butter
¼	cup packed (1¾ ounces) light brown sugar
¼	teaspoon ground cinnamon
⅛	teaspoon ground nutmeg
⅛	teaspoon salt

FILLING

2	pounds frozen peaches (see note)
⅓	cup (2⅓ ounces) granulated sugar
2	tablespoons unsalted butter
⅛	teaspoon salt
4	teaspoons juice from 1 lemon
2	teaspoons cornstarch

1. FOR THE TOPPING: Pulse the bread in a food processor to coarse crumbs, 3 to 5 pulses; set aside. Toast the almonds in a 12-inch nonstick skillet over medium heat until golden, 3 to 5 minutes. Stir in 1 tablespoon of the butter until melted. Stir in the bread crumbs and continue to cook, stirring constantly, until the crumbs are golden, 3 to 5 minutes (the smaller crumbs will brown more quickly).

2. Turn the heat to low. Clear the center of the skillet and add the remaining 3 tablespoons butter, the brown sugar, cinnamon, nutmeg, and salt to the clearing. Cook, mashing the butter into the sugar, until melted and bubbly. Stir the sugar mixture into the almonds and bread crumbs and continue to cook, stirring constantly, until the mixture is thoroughly coated and well toasted, 1 to 3 minutes longer. Spread the mixture out over a large plate to cool.

3. **FOR THE FILLING:** Wipe out the skillet with a wad of paper towels. Add the frozen peaches, granulated sugar, butter, and salt to the skillet, cover, and cook over medium-high heat until the peaches are thawed and have released their juices, 8 to 12 minutes. Reduce the heat to medium-low and continue to cook, covered, until the peaches are soft when poked with a fork, 8 to 12 minutes longer.

4. Whisk the lemon juice and cornstarch together to dissolve the cornstarch, then stir the mixture quickly into the cooked peaches. Continue to cook, stirring constantly, until the liquid has thickened, about 1 minute. Off the heat, sprinkle the topping over the peaches and serve.

➤ VARIATIONS

Peach-Ginger Crisp

Follow the recipe for Peach Crisp, adding 2 tablespoons finely chopped crystallized ginger to the skillet with the peaches in step 3.

Peach, Cardamom, and Pistachio Crisp

Follow the recipe for Peach Crisp, substituting ½ cup shelled pistachio nuts, chopped coarse, for the almonds and adding ½ teaspoon ground cardamom to the skillet with the peaches in step 3.

BLUEBERRY PIE

WE LOVE A GOOD, OLD-FASHIONED BLUE-berry pie made with ripe berries, picked at their peak. Summer pies are irresistible, and blueberry pie is especially tempting, with its golden crust and dripping blueberry juice. We think everyone should have a great recipe for this classic American dessert in their arsenal, so we set out to make the perfect one—in a skillet no less. But blueberry pies can be rife with problems; because the berries are so juicy, the filling can become waterlogged and flavorless, making the pie difficult to cut into. By using our skillet, we hoped to make an easy scoop-and-go pie with just a top crust, eliminating the usually wet bottom crust.

To get started, we assembled a classic blueberry pie filling in the skillet, using 6 cups of fresh blueberries, sugar, a little cornstarch, and some flavorings, then topped it with a crust and baked it in a moderately hot oven. Not too surprisingly, this version wasn't perfect, but the method was indeed as promising as we had hoped. The crust baked to a brown, crisp shell in just 30 minutes, but the blueberry filling still tasted fairly raw—only a few of the berries had burst open to release their juices and dissolve the sugar and cornstarch. Considering that a traditional blueberry pie usually takes almost an hour to bake, these findings weren't too far off base. But at least we got the ratio of berries to crust right, and now we knew the blueberries had to cook down a bit in the skillet before we could add the crust and bake our pie.

Next, we tried mixing the filling ingredients right in the skillet and simmering them on the stovetop before laying on the crust. This worked better than our first attempt, but the pie filling was way too thick and had a jammy flavor by the time the crust was fully baked. Tasters wanted a berry filling with fresher flavors and the textural contrast of both cooked-down berries and whole berries. With this in mind, we experimented further and found the solution by cooking a third of the berries and mashing them to help release their juices, then folding in the rest of the berries before topping the filling with pastry. This two-step method produced the ideal combination of textures and blueberry flavor in the final pie. We also got the consistency we were after because we stirred in a small amount of cornstarch before folding in the raw berries.

Now we had to adjust the sweetness level and overall flavor of the filling. We liked the clean, neutral flavor of regular white granulated sugar with the blueberries, and found that ¾ cup sugar was the right amount to prevent the filling from being cloyingly sweet or not sweet enough. Blueberries and lemon are a natural combination, and a little zest and juice enhanced the flavor of the berries. We also added a dash of vanilla to further complement the fruit's flavor. Finally, we found that 2 tablespoons of butter, cut into small bits and scattered over the filling just before placing the pastry, gave the finished pie a lushness that everyone enjoyed. It was time to prepare our top crust.

We had several pie crust recipes in our archives to work from, but we opted for a single pie crust made with both vegetable shortening and butter—from past experience, we had learned that using both kinds of fat yields a tasty and flaky crust. We pulsed the shortening and butter into a mixture of flour, sugar, and salt, and used ice water as the liquid to bring the ingredients together. By pressing the ice water gently into the dough, we minimized the

risk of overworking it, so it would still be flaky and tender when baked.

To make this pie easy to assemble, we simply rolled the dough out into a round and gently laid it over the blueberry filling right in the skillet for a rustic presentation. We found it crucial to cut several vent holes in the dough to allow the steam from the berries to escape during baking, or else the crust became quite soggy.

We tested a range of baking temperatures and times, and we found that a 400-degree oven—and just 30 minutes—produced the best crust and gave the whole berries in the filling enough time to heat through. Served straight from the skillet, this was blueberry pie bliss.

TOPPING BLUEBERRY PIE IN A SKILLET

1. Roll the dough gently around a rolling pin, and unroll it over the blueberry filling in the skillet.

2. With a sharp knife, gently cut six vent holes around the center of the pie. The vent holes should be about 2 inches long and ⅛ inch wide.

Rustic Blueberry Pie

SERVES 6

We prefer using fresh blueberries here, but 6 cups of frozen blueberries, thawed, can be substituted. If using frozen berries, don't mash them in step 3. If the dough is very firm, let it sit on the counter to soften slightly for about 10 minutes before rolling out in step 5. Store-bought pie dough can be substituted for the crust if desired.

CRUST

1¼	cups (6¼ ounces) unbleached all-purpose flour, plus extra for the work surface
1	tablespoon sugar
½	teaspoon salt
3	tablespoons vegetable shortening, cut into ½-inch pieces and chilled
5	tablespoons unsalted butter, cut into ¼-inch pieces and chilled
4–6	tablespoons ice water

BLUEBERRY FILLING

6	cups fresh blueberries (see note)
2	tablespoons juice from 1 lemon
2	tablespoons water
3	tablespoons cornstarch
1	teaspoon grated zest from 1 lemon

¾ cup (5¼ ounces) sugar
½ teaspoon vanilla extract
Pinch salt
2 tablespoons unsalted butter, cut into ¼-inch pieces

1. FOR THE CRUST: Pulse the flour, sugar, and salt together in a food processor to combine. Sprinkle the shortening over the top and pulse until the mixture has the texture of coarse sand, about 10 pulses. Sprinkle the butter over the top and pulse until the mixture resembles coarse crumbs with butter bits no larger than small peas, about 10 pulses. Transfer the mixture to a medium bowl.

2. Sprinkle 4 tablespoons of the ice water over the mixture and fold to incorporate with a rubber spatula. Press down on the dough with the broad side of the spatula until the dough sticks together, adding the remaining 2 tablespoons ice water as needed if the dough does not come together. Turn the dough out onto a work surface and flatten into

a 4-inch disk. Wrap the dough in plastic wrap and refrigerate for at least 30 minutes, or up to 2 days.

3. FOR THE BLUEBERRY FILLING: Adjust an oven rack to the middle position and heat the oven to 400 degrees. Cook 2 cups of the berries in a 12-inch ovenproof skillet over medium heat, mashing the berries with a potato masher, until the mixture is hot, thickened, and measures 1 cup, about 8 minutes. Remove from the heat.

4. Whisk the lemon juice, water, and cornstarch together to dissolve the cornstarch, then stir into the cooked blueberries. Stir in the remaining 4 cups blueberries, lemon zest, sugar, vanilla, and salt and sprinkle the butter over the top.

5. Roll the dough out on a lightly floured work surface into an 11-inch round. Following the illustrations on page 318, loosely roll the dough around the rolling pin, then gently unroll it over the blueberry filling in the skillet. Use a sharp knife to cut six vent holes in the dough. Transfer the skillet to the oven and bake the pie until the

INGREDIENTS: Frozen Blueberries

Our Rustic Blueberry Pie (page 318) is full of juicy, tender blueberries, but what if it's the middle of winter and there are no fresh blueberries to be had? You could try buying a pint of fresh berries from South America, but the high price tends to make blueberry pie an expensive endeavor in December. Walking down the frozen foods aisle at our local supermarket, we surveyed a few bags of frozen berries and wondered how they would fare cooked up. Noting that both cultivated and wild blueberries are available frozen, we picked up a couple bags of each—along with a fresh pint from Chile—and headed back to the kitchen to test them out.

Compared with cultivated berries, the smaller wild berries are just better—they're more intense in color, firmer in texture, and more sweet and tangy in flavor. So we weren't exactly shocked when Wyman's Frozen Wild Blueberries swept the tastings. But we were a bit surprised that they surpassed the imported fresh berries in our tests.

A dive into the berry-packing process gave us the answer to why the frozen wild berries outranked the fresh berries. To help them survive transport, the imported berries are picked before they have a chance to fully ripen. As a result, they are often tart and not so flavorful. Frozen berries, on the other hand, have been picked at their peak of perfect ripeness and are then individually quick frozen at -20 degrees. This quick freezing preserves their sweetness, letting us enjoy them—and blueberry pie—year-round, and at a price just about anyone can afford.

THE BEST FROZEN BLUEBERRIES

Wyman's Frozen Wild Blueberries had a pleasing balance of sweetness and tanginess and a clean, fresh berry finish that won tasters over.

WYMAN'S

crust is golden brown and the juices are bubbling, 30 to 40 minutes.

6. Using a potholder (the skillet handle will be hot), remove the skillet from the oven. Let the pie cool in the skillet for at least 15 minutes before serving.

➤ VARIATIONS

Blueberry-Raspberry Pie

Follow the recipe for Rustic Blueberry Pie, substituting 1 cup fresh raspberries for the blueberries in step 3, and 1 cup fresh raspberries for the blueberries in step 4.

Blueberry-Nectarine Pie

Follow the recipe for Rustic Blueberry Pie, substituting 4 nectarines peeled, pitted, and cut into ½-inch wedges, for 2 cups of the blueberries in step 4.

SKILLET-ROASTED PEARS

PEARS TASTE GREAT SIMPLY EATEN OUT OF hand or with a pungent cheese, but they are also excellent when cooked, because they hold their shape and texture well. Unfortunately, this often-overlooked fruit tends to take a back seat in the dessert world, frequently passed over for more colorful berries or reliable apples. We wanted to give the juicy, sweet pear the attention it deserves by developing an uncomplicated recipe for skillet-roasted pears that would allow the inherent flavor of the fruit to shine through.

But first, we had to select our pears. We immediately narrowed it down to the readily available varieties—Bosc, Anjou, Comice, and Bartlett—and cooked several of each to discern flavor differences among the cooked fruit. The Anjou and Comice pears developed a rather ordinary and mild flavor once cooked. The Bartlett and Bosc varieties fared much better; tasters liked both the sweet, slightly spicy Bosc and the floral Bartlett, which grows sweeter with cooking.

In the test kitchen, we have experience cooking pears at different levels of ripeness. Perfectly ripe pears aren't the best choice for cooking because the already-soft flesh quickly becomes mushy and mealy when heated. Rock-hard pears, however, aren't a great option either, because they never attain a tender texture no matter how long they are cooked. Moderately firm pears, on the other hand, are perfect to work with. They can withstand enough heat to allow them to cook up tender, just to the point where they give slightly when pressed with a finger. With slightly firm pears in hand, it was time to start cooking.

We were ready to roast our pears, but we wondered about incorporating other flavors with a skillet-made sauce. Caramel complements pears nicely because it brings an otherwise absent richness to a sweet fruit dish. We decided to roast our pears until soft and golden, and create a caramel sauce that would cling to the fruit. To be more efficient, we would cook the pears right in the caramel sauce instead of cooking them in separate pans.

Making caramel can be a daunting task for many home cooks, but it's really nothing more than heating sugar until it melts and becomes a thick liquid. It's easy to do, although many recipes do require the use of a candy thermometer to monitor the temperature changes and various stages of the caramel. For our caramel sauce, we simplified the process by cutting out the candy thermometer—we would look for visual clues to tell us when the sauce was done—and using our skillet, not a saucepan, to make it. We brought a mixture of water and sugar to a boil over high heat until the sugar had completely dissolved; this took only a couple of minutes, and the sauce was now hot and bubbling (be careful around this hot mixture).

With our caramel on its way, we added three halved pears (the best cut for an elegant presentation) to the skillet and let them cook in the slowly browning caramel. To prevent the pears from drying out, we kept the lid on the skillet to retain evaporating moisture. After 15 minutes, the pears were almost tender, with a hint of resistance when a fork was inserted. The last thing we wanted was overcooked, mushy pears, so we moved the halves to a wire rack set over a baking sheet to drain while we finished the caramel sauce.

For a perfectly gooey consistency and rich caramel flavor, we added heavy cream to the sauce and shook the pan over medium heat until the sauce was smooth and had developed a deep caramel color. A dash of salt enhanced the flavor. Ready to plate our dessert, we reached for the pears, but they had turned unappetizingly sticky from being cooked in what was basically sugar candy (our pre-cream caramel sauce). We tried the recipe again, this time stirring the cream into the skillet around the pears as they finished caramelizing, transforming the sticky sugar syrup into a smooth sauce that slid right off the pears. We let the pears drain for a few minutes before serving, then drizzled them with the caramel sauce.

Instead of laying our pear halves flat on the plate, we trimmed the bottoms of the pears before cooking them, so that they would stand upright on the plate. Our roasted pears were now so expertly presented, we were almost reluctant to bite into them, but watching caramel roll down the side of a pear quickly relieved us of our restraint. One bite told us we had done right by these pears—they were sweet and juicy and perfectly balanced by the luxurious caramel.

Skillet-Roasted Pears with Caramel Sauce

SERVES 6

This dish is quite rich, so figure on serving just half a pear per person. For the best texture, try to buy pears that are neither fully ripe nor rock hard; choose those that yield just slightly when pressed. Trimming ¼ inch off the bottom of each pear half allows them to stand up straight when serving, making for a beautiful presentation.

3   medium, ripe but firm Bosc or Bartlett pears (about 8 ounces each)
⅓   cup water
⅔   cup (4⅔ ounces) sugar
⅔   cup heavy cream
   Salt

1. Line a large rimmed baking sheet with aluminum foil (for easy cleanup), set a wire rack inside the prepared baking sheet, and set aside. Halve and core the pears, following the illustrations below. Trim ¼ inch off the bottom of each pear half.

CORING PEARS

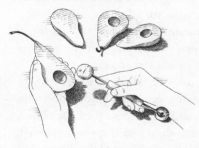

1. Using a melon baller or teaspoon measuring spoon, scoop out the seed and core in the center of each pear half.

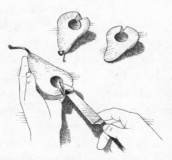

2. Using the tip of a paring knife, cut out the blossom end (bottom) of each pear half.

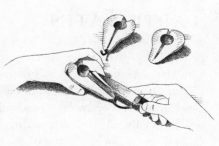

3. Remove the thin fibrous core and stem by making a V-shaped incision along both sides of the core, leaving the stem attached if desired for presentation.

2. Add the water to a 12-inch nonstick skillet, then pour the sugar into the center of the pan, being careful to not let it hit the sides of the pan. Gently stir the sugar with a clean spatula to moisten it thoroughly. Bring to a boil over high heat and cook, stirring occasionally, until the sugar has dissolved completely and the liquid is bubbling, about 2 minutes.

3. Add the pears to the skillet, cut side down, cover, reduce the heat to medium-high, and cook until the pears are almost tender and a fork inserted into the center of the pears meets slight resistance, 13 to 15 minutes, reducing the heat as needed to prevent the caramel from getting too dark.

4. Uncover, reduce the heat to medium, and cook until the sauce is golden brown and the cut sides of the pears are beginning to brown, 3 to 5 minutes. Pour the heavy cream around the pears and cook, shaking the pan until the sauce is a smooth, deep caramel color and the cut sides of the pears are golden brown, 3 to 5 minutes.

5. Off the heat, transfer the pears, cut side up, to the prepared wire rack and cool slightly. Season the sauce left in the pan with salt to taste, then transfer it to a small bowl. Carefully (the pears will still be hot) stand each pear half upright on individual plates or a serving platter, drizzle with the caramel sauce, and serve.

TARTE TATIN

IN OUR OPINION, THERE IS PERHAPS NO better skillet-based apple dessert than tarte Tatin. This classic French dessert was invented accidentally at l'Hôtel Tatin in the Loire Valley of France. The inn was run by two sisters, and the elder one was especially talented at cooking, but she was easily distracted by the bustle of the kitchen. One day, she mistakenly placed her tart upside down in the pan; she decided to salvage the tart after it was baked by flipping it right side up. The results were amazing—buttery pastry, a sweet caramel sauce, and luscious baked apples.

Nowadays, this dessert is usually made for special occasions that call for something more elegant than cake and ice cream. While it takes a bit of time and attention, tarte Tatin is rather simple to make—and bake—in a skillet. The apples are neatly arranged in the pan, heated until soft in a butter and sugar mixture that caramelizes into a rich syrup, then covered with pastry and baked. We were ready to start baking, but first looked into our recipe archives for more information.

When tarte Tatin first came to this country, all sorts of different recipes for it appeared. Some were based on traditional French formulas, but others were highly Americanized. The latter, generally speaking, simply do not work. The unsuccessful recipes vary, but most of them exhibit one of two serious flaws. One of these mistakes is using sliced or chopped apples, which make a wet, loose tart that sprawls and collapses when inverted. The second common error in Americanized recipes is the decision to caramelize the apples on top of the stove after the tart has been completely baked. Caramelizing a fully baked tart is simply impossible. If the tart turns out juicy, it will not caramelize at all, and if it bakes up dry, it will burn. And you won't even know which disaster is about to befall you because you cannot see what the apples are doing underneath the crust.

We resolved not to make these same mistakes and forged ahead with our caramel sauce, which we would make right in the skillet. We combined butter and sugar and cooked it for a couple minutes until it began to turn lightly golden—any longer and the caramel might burn in the time it took for the apples to cook. With the caramel ready, it was time to add the apples.

First we had to select the right variety. Many recipes recommend Golden Delicious, and one recipe we came across specified Red Delicious, because of its pretty elongated shape when sliced. We tested both Golden and Red Delicious, as well as Granny Smith, Gala, and Fuji apples. The results were surprising—we had expected most of the apples to fall apart, but all held their shape quite well. Flavor, unfortunately, was another story. The

Golden Delicious apples were barely acceptable, and most of the others were completely tasteless. We tried adding lemon juice to augment the flavor of the insipid apples, but this didn't work. Granny Smiths ended up as the best choice, since they have their own flavor even before being cooked.

While tarte Tatin is typically made with apple quarters, we encountered some recipes that called for apple halves. When made with apple quarters, tarte Tatin can sometimes seem a little light on fruit because the apples lose their juices and shrink when caramelized. We experimented with halved apples, but had trouble getting the caramel to penetrate all the way through such large pieces of apple. When we cooked the halves longer to remedy this problem, we ended up with another snag—the apples were pulpy and mushy, and there seemed to be too much fruit in relation to crust.

In the end, we abandoned the apple halves, but these tests proved useful since they gave us an idea of how to refine the original method using quarters. When we tried using halved apples for the tart, we had rested the apples on their outer peeled surface so that the full cut inside surface faced up—leaving wasted empty space along the apple's curved outer peel that could be filled with more fruit. Apple quarters, by contrast, tend to flop over onto a cut side. We reasoned that if we tipped each apple quarter onto its cut edge and held it there while we laid the next quarter in place, we could fit more fruit in the skillet. It turned out that we were able to cram an entire extra apple into the skillet this way, with very good results. To caramelize the other side of the apple quarters, we flipped them over by spearing them with the tip of a paring knife after a few minutes of cooking. Even though the caramelized sides of the apples were soft, the side facing up remained firm enough not to tear when we did this. A nonstick skillet helped prevent the quarters from sticking.

Finally, we tended to the crust, which had to be durable enough to be flipped over after baking. We made a tart dough with flour, butter, sugar, and an egg. Using an egg in the crust made it stronger, and the sugar added more flavor, but it also made the pastry dough sticky and crumbly because the sugar binds the little bits of butter together in the dough, creating small crunchy bits. We switched out the granulated sugar for confectioners' sugar, which disappeared into the dough and sweetened it without causing any problems. With our pastry dough mixed, we rolled it out into a 14-inch circle and refrigerated it on a baking sheet until needed. When our apples were cooked, we simply slid the circle of dough off the baking sheet and onto the skillet. Twenty minutes in a 425-degree oven was enough to brown the pastry, which was now superbly flaky.

After allowing the skillet to cool briefly, we embarked upon the last major step of our Tarte Tatin—flipping it over—to give it its trademark

EQUIPMENT: Apple Corers

When you're ready to get cooking and make Tarte Tatin, you don't want prep work to slow you down. Rather than slicing an apple into quarters and then removing the core and seeds from each piece, we'd rather reach for an apple corer, which takes care of the core in one fell swoop. A good apple corer should work fast and eliminate the core neatly. We tested five models and found out the task wasn't always so cut and dried.

Narrow blade diameters—less than ¾ inch—on two models, the Henckels Twin Cuisine Apple Corer and Messermeister's Serrated Apple Corer, struggled to break through the firmer flesh on Granny Smith apples and forced us to poke and prod the core with the sharp metal teeth. The relatively stubby—3½ inches or less—metal tubes on the Henckels corer and the Leifheit Hinged Apple Corer came up short when asked to plow through large apples. We had much better results with the sharp OXO Good Grips Corer, which testers liked for its effectiveness and comfortable grip.

THE BEST APPLE CORER
OXO Good Grips Corer ($8.95) has the trademark "good grip" and very sharp teeth.

OXO

PREPARING TARTE TATIN

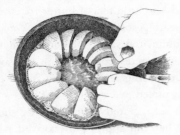

1. Off the heat, place the first apple quarter cut side down, with an end touching the skillet wall. Continue to arrange the apples, lifting each quarter on its edge and placing the next apple quarter on its edge, so that the apples stand straight up on a cut edge. Fill the skillet middle with the remaining quarters, halved if necessary.

2. Cook the apples as directed, then remove the skillet from the heat and, using a paring knife, turn the apples onto their uncaramelized sides halfway through cooking. Continue cooking as directed.

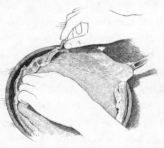

3. Off the heat, slide the prepared dough off the baking sheet over the skillet and, taking care not to burn your fingers, tuck the dough edges gently up against the skillet wall. Bake and cool as directed.

4. Place a heatproof serving platter over the skillet and hold it tightly against the skillet. Invert the skillet and platter and set the platter on the counter. Lift the skillet up off the platter, leaving the tart behind.

upside-down presentation. Using a paring knife, we separated the tart from the inside edge of the skillet, and then held a platter over the top of the skillet and flipped it over to ease the tart out onto the platter.

Our Tarte Tatin was flawless and had a great caramelized flavor, but some whipped cream helped cut through its richness. Now our dessert had everything going for it—a flaky crust and a rich, caramelized apple filling, with a creamy garnish that lightened and balanced the dish.

Tarte Tatin
SERVES 6

Make sure that the caramel doesn't get too brown before adding the apples in step 5; it should be just golden. If the dough is very firm, let it sit on the counter to soften slightly for about 10 minutes before rolling out in step 3. Be sure to let the tart rest for 30 minutes before serving, or it will likely break into pieces when you unmold it.

TART DOUGH

- 1⅓ cups (6⅔ ounces) unbleached all-purpose flour, plus extra for the work surface
- ¼ cup (1 ounce) confectioners' sugar
- ½ teaspoon salt
- 8 tablespoons (1 stick) unsalted butter, cut into ¼-inch pieces and chilled
- 1 large egg, lightly beaten

APPLES

- 8 tablespoons (1 stick) unsalted butter
- ¾ cup (5¼ ounces) granulated sugar
- 5 large Granny Smith apples (about 2½ pounds), peeled, cored, and quartered

TOPPING

- 1 cup heavy cream, chilled
- ½ cup sour cream, chilled

1. FOR THE TART DOUGH: Pulse the flour, confectioners' sugar, and salt together in a food processor until combined. Sprinkle the butter over the top and pulse until the mixture resembles coarse cornmeal, about 15 pulses. With the machine running,

add the egg through the feed tube and continue to process until the dough just comes together around the processor blade, about 12 seconds.

2. Turn the dough out onto a work surface and flatten into a 6-inch disk. Wrap the dough in plastic wrap and refrigerate for at least 1 hour, or up to 2 days.

3. Roll the dough out on a lightly floured work surface into a 14-inch circle. Slide the dough onto a lightly floured rimless (or inverted) baking sheet, cover with plastic wrap, and refrigerate until needed.

4. FOR THE APPLES: Adjust an oven rack to the upper-middle position and heat the oven to 425 degrees. Melt the butter in a heavy-bottomed 12-inch nonstick skillet over medium-high heat. Stir in the granulated sugar and cook until the foaming subsides and the mixture is light golden, 2 to 4 minutes.

5. Following the illustrations on page 324, and off the heat, arrange the apples around the edge of the skillet, lifting them on their edges so that they stand up, being careful not to burn your fingers. Arrange the remaining apples in the middle of the skillet. Cook the apples over medium heat until they are lightly golden and the caramel is darkly colored, about 6 minutes, turning the apples over halfway through cooking.

6. Off the heat, slide the chilled dough over the apples in the skillet. Being careful not to burn your fingers, fold back the edge of the dough so that it fits snugly into the skillet. Transfer the skillet to the oven and bake the tart until the crust is golden brown, about 20 minutes, rotating it halfway through baking.

7. FOR THE TOPPING: Using an electric mixer, whip the heavy cream and sour cream together on medium-high speed until the mixture thickens and forms soft peaks, about 1 minute. Refrigerate until needed.

8. Using a potholder (the skillet handle will be hot), remove the skillet from the oven. Let the tart cool in the skillet for 30 minutes. Run a small knife around the edge, place an inverted serving platter (or cutting board) over the top and gently flip the tart onto the platter, using mitts or kitchen towels if the skillet is still hot. Scrape out

any apples that stick to the skillet and put them back into place on the tart. Slice the tart into wedges, dollop with the topping, and serve.

➤ VARIATION
Apricot Tarte Tatin
Follow the recipe for Tarte Tatin, substituting 9 fresh apricots (about 1½ pounds), pitted and halved, for the apples. In step 5, lay the apricot halves, cut side down, flat in the skillet and cook over medium-high heat until golden on both sides, about 3 minutes, turning the apricots over halfway through cooking. Once browned, lay the dough over the apricots (now facing cut side up) and bake as directed.

GERMAN APPLE PANCAKE

THIS QUICK DESSERT, ALSO REFERRED TO AS a Dutch baby, is a crisp, puffy skillet-baked pancake packed with caramelized apples. We've sampled it at many a pancake house, when we've succeeded at justifying a sweet treat for breakfast, but few German apple pancakes actually have the crisp top, rich cake, and well-caramelized apples that are the hallmark of this dessert when done right. With a 10-inch ovenproof skillet in hand—just the right size to make this appealing dessert for four—we decided to rescue this (Dutch) baby and restore the German apple pancake to its original fluffy yet crispy finish.

The traditional batter for this dish more closely resembles a thin crêpe batter than a thick pancake batter—which is probably why it works so well as a dessert. The batter is a loose mixture of eggs, milk or cream, flour, and a pinch of salt. The secret to perfecting this batter is balancing the amount of egg with the milk or cream. Many of the batters we tested yielded pancakes that were way too eggy. Tasters agreed that two eggs were enough for structure and flavor; three eggs made a dense, gummy pancake.

As for the dairy component of the batter, we tried milk, cream, and half-and-half. Milk alone made for a flavorless pancake dominated by the eggs. Cream produced an over-the-top rich pancake that almost resembled custard in texture. Half-and-half proved a great compromise between milk and cream, giving the pancake body and depth without being overly rich.

To round out the pancake's flavors, we added salt, vanilla extract, and a small amount of granulated sugar. The apples would provide sweetness in the pancake, but a tablespoon of sugar helped the flavors meld.

We moved on to the apples, which we wanted well-caramelized but with some bite for contrast against the soft and creamy pancake. We liked firm Granny Smith apples, which we also used in our Tarte Tatin (page 324), because they stand up well to cooking and we knew their tartness would keep the dish from becoming too sweet.

Starting with the simplest method, we tried cooking the apples in some butter in a nonstick skillet until they turned golden brown and their natural sugars caramelized. Our first few attempts were frustrating—over medium heat, the apples morphed into chunky applesauce before they caramelized; over high heat, they scorched before their sugars browned. We then tried adding sugar to the apples in the skillet, hoping to start the caramelization process. Unfortunately, our apples

were slightly overcooked by the time the sugars had caramelized. When we switched to light brown sugar, the technique worked beautifully; the apple slices were golden and still had some bite. We realized early on the importance of cutting the apples into even slices, otherwise they cooked unevenly and the smaller pieces burned quickly.

Now that we'd brought the right flavoring elements together, we focused on our cooking method. Unlike stovetop pancakes, which use chemical leaveners to promote height, oven-baked pancakes rely on heat and eggs for rising power. The pancake gets its first burst of heat from the hot skillet, then the heat from the oven takes over the rest of the cooking. In our tests, a very hot oven—500 degrees—guaranteed a dramatic rise and golden crust, but it failed to fully cook the pancake's interior. Leaving the pancake in the oven for more time to bake through at this high temperature caused the crust to burn, so to remedy the problem we tried starting the pancake at a high temperature and quickly reduced the heat to finish cooking. We discovered that if the oven temperature is brought too low, the pancake needs to bake too long and the exterior dries out by the time the interior is set. After several tests, we found it best to preheat the oven to 500 degrees, then lower the temperature to 425 degrees when

PREPARING GERMAN APPLE PANCAKE

1. Pour the batter around the edge of the pan, then over the apples.

2. Loosen the edge of the pancake with a heatproof spatula.

3. Invert the pancake onto a large plate or serving platter.

the pancake goes into the oven. With our apples already in the skillet, we poured the batter over them and around the edges of the skillet so the pancake would puff up.

Straight from the oven and with a sprinkling of confectioners' sugar, German apple pancake is quite dramatic and will certainly impress your dining companions. Just make sure to speed it to the table—the pancake sinks within a couple of minutes.

German Apple Pancake
SERVES 4

Be ready to serve the pancake as soon as it comes out of the oven as its puffy texture sinks within just a few minutes. Using a 10-inch skillet is essential to getting the right texture and height in the pancake. Serve with vanilla ice cream.

¾	cup half-and-half
2	large eggs
1	tablespoon granulated sugar
1	teaspoon vanilla extract
½	teaspoon salt
½	cup (2½ ounces) unbleached all-purpose flour
1	tablespoon unsalted butter
3	medium Granny Smith apples (about 1¼ pounds), peeled, cored, and cut into ¼-inch slices
¼	cup packed (1¾ ounces) light brown sugar
2	tablespoons confectioners' sugar

1. Adjust an oven rack to the middle position and heat the oven to 500 degrees. Process the half-and-half, eggs, granulated sugar, vanilla, and salt together in a food processor (or blender) until well combined, about 15 seconds. Add the flour and continue to process until thoroughly mixed and free of lumps, about 30 seconds.

2. Melt the butter in a 10-inch ovenproof nonstick skillet over medium-high heat. Add the apples and sprinkle with the brown sugar. Cook,

stirring occasionally, until the apples brown lightly, about 5 minutes. Continue to cook over medium-high heat, stirring constantly, until the apples are golden brown, 4 to 5 minutes.

3. Off the heat, quickly pour the batter around the edge of the pan, then over the apples following the illustrations on page 326. Immediately transfer the skillet to the oven, reduce the oven temperature to 425 degrees, and bake until browned and puffed, 15 to 17 minutes.

4. Using a potholder (the skillet handle will be hot), remove the skillet from the oven. With a heatproof spatula, loosen the edge of the pancake. Invert the pancake onto a serving platter, dust it with the confectioners' sugar, and serve immediately.

HOT FUDGE PUDDING CAKE

THIS DECADENT DISH IS A RICH CHOCOLATE cake coated by warm, gooey chocolate sauce. It might not win awards for looks, considering its lumps and bumps, but it's incredibly satisfying and practically the definition of "comfort food." Even the few non-chocoholics we know melt at its aroma and richness.

This incredible dessert is made by baking both the cake and sauce at the same time in the same dish, so we thought we could make this scoop-and-serve dessert even easier than it already is by using a skillet to assemble the batter, bake the cake, and serve the finished dessert—saving us from cleaning at least a few of the extra bowls and baking dishes that are usually required to make this chocolaty indulgence.

First, we looked at how this dessert works. Flour, eggs, milk, cocoa powder, butter, and baking powder are combined to make a brownie-style batter, which then goes into a baking dish and is sprinkled with sugar and cocoa powder. Then things start to get weird: Hot water is poured on top, and the whole mess goes into the oven. With baking, however, the picture improves—the cake rises to the surface, and the water sinks to the bottom, mixing with the sugar and cocoa powder to form hot fudge. Odd, maybe; good, definitely. With an idea of pudding cake mechanics, we were ready to start testing.

INGREDIENTS: Dark Chocolate

Nowadays, picking out a chocolate for baking is a complex task—there are several choices at the supermarket, and dozens more at boutique markets. You could spend forever poring over the labels, comparing cacao percentages and locations of origin. Put into play the varying prices—anywhere from 44 cents per ounce to several times that amount—and it's a wonder the baking aisle isn't full of confused shoppers scratching their heads.

To find out if any of these differences really mattered, we tested chocolates containing roughly 60 percent cacao—the type that most recipes calling for dark chocolate have been developed to use. Chocolates were tasted plain, in chocolate pots de crème, and baked into brownies.

Much to our surprise, tasters preferred chocolates with a lower amount of fat and a moderate amount of sugar. Overall, we liked the dark chocolates that achieved the best balance of the three major components—cocoa butter, cocoa solids, and sugar. Callebaut Intense Dark Chocolate L-60-40NV was favored for its rich chocolate flavor, moderate sugar, and cocoa solids, and comparatively low fat. Ghirardelli's Bittersweet Chocolate Baking Bar came in a close second, praised for its "smoky," "fruity" notes.

THE BEST DARK CHOCOLATE

Callebaut Intense Dark Chocolate L-60-40NV boasts "dark and earthy" tones with a "rich cocoa flavor." The runner-up, Ghirardelli Bittersweet Chocolate Baking Bar, was praised by tasters as a "creamy, rich, glossy" chocolate.

CALLEBAUT

GHIRARDELLI

We gathered a few recipes and began baking. Sadly, all were disappointing. Instead of deep and chocolaty, the cakes tasted dull and mild. Instead of gooey and spoonable, the sauce was dry or overly soupy, dominating the baking dish and obscuring the cake. Certainly, we could do better.

Learning from the mistakes these recipes made, we focused first on pumping up the chocolate flavor, which we suspected was absent because most recipes called for cocoa powder, not chocolate. Using both would solve the problem, so we started playing around with various amounts of the two ingredients. After a bit of trial and error, we eventually settled on 2 ounces of bittersweet chocolate and ⅓ cup of Dutch-processed cocoa powder, which has a smoother, fuller flavor than natural cocoa powder, to give our cake the full, rich flavor we sought. With any less chocolate, the flavor was too faint; with more chocolate, the cake became too rich and its texture sodden. To prevent the chocolate from burning, we melted it right in the skillet over low heat with the cocoa powder and some butter. We mixed in salt and vanilla to heighten the chocolate flavor, and sugar to counter the bitterness of the cocoa powder and sweeten the overall flavor.

The next issue to settle was how many— if any—eggs to use. We had encountered a few eggless pudding cakes; these were mushy and crumbly, and the cake and hot fudge seemed to morph together into a sad, boring lump. Pudding cakes made with one or two eggs were dry and slightly rubbery. We tried the middle ground, and added just one yolk to the chocolate mixture— the resulting cake had the texture of a brownie, with a nice, formidable crumb. To retain moisture in the cake, we added a small amount of milk with the egg yolk. A modest amount of flour (we used ¾ cup) also helped to keep the interior from drying out.

For the cake's height, we relied on baking powder. One recipe called for a hefty 2 tablespoons—"chemical warfare" was one taster's term for this pudding cake—but we found that a fraction of that (2 teaspoons) worked just fine. With our cake base in place, it was time to get the sauce going.

To make the fudgy sauce, we started with an equal amount of cocoa powder and granulated sugar, sprinkling the mixture over our batter. This baked up into a cake with a sticky, toffee-like crust with one-dimensional sweetness. To get a deeper, fuller flavor, we replaced some of the granulated sugar with brown sugar. This worked like magic.

Now, we got to the odd step of pouring hot water on top of the batter to create the luscious sauce. After several tests, we determined that 1½ cups of water gave us an ample amount of sauce with the right consistency, neither too thick nor too thin. Taking a hint from a few of the recipes we'd found, we swapped out the water for coffee—a logical move, since chocolate and coffee are perfect partners, both with rich and complex undertones.

With our batter sugared and covered with coffee, we moved the skillet to a 325-degree oven for

35 minutes. Baking the cake slowly at a low temperature promoted a nice crust and a silky sauce. When the timer went off, we had a surefire hit on our hands. Loaded with sumptuous chocolate sauce and rich, fudgy cake, our Hot Fudge Pudding Cake was a guilty pleasure if there ever was one.

Hot Fudge Pudding Cake
SERVES 6 TO 8

This recipe requires 1½ cups weak coffee; use either 1 cup coffee diluted with ½ cup water or 1½ cups water mixed with 2 teaspoons instant espresso or instant coffee. Using a 10-inch skillet is essential to getting the right texture and consistency.

6	tablespoons (¾ stick) unsalted butter, cut into 6 pieces
2	ounces bittersweet or semisweet chocolate, chopped coarse
⅔	cup (2 ounces) Dutch-processed cocoa powder
¾	cup (3¾ ounces) unbleached all-purpose flour
2	teaspoons baking powder
¼	teaspoon salt
⅓	cup packed (2⅓ ounces) light brown sugar
1	cup (7 ounces) granulated sugar
⅓	cup whole milk
1	tablespoon vanilla extract
1	large egg yolk
1½	cups weak coffee (see note)

1. Adjust an oven rack to the middle position and heat the oven to 325 degrees. Melt the butter, chocolate, and ⅓ cup of the cocoa together in a 10-inch ovenproof skillet over low heat, stirring often, until smooth, 1 to 3 minutes. Set aside to cool slightly.

2. In a small bowl, whisk the flour, baking powder, and salt together. In a separate small bowl, whisk the brown sugar, remaining ⅓ cup cocoa, and ⅓ cup of the granulated sugar together, breaking

Whipped Cream
MAKES ABOUT 2 CUPS

For lightly sweetened whipped cream, reduce the sugar to 1½ teaspoons. On very hot days, chill the bowl and beaters before whipping. Dollop this whipped cream on bowls of our Hot Fudge Pudding Cake.

1 cup heavy cream, chilled
1 tablespoon sugar
1 teaspoon vanilla extract

Using an electric mixer, whip the cream, sugar, and vanilla together in a large bowl on medium-low speed until frothy, about 1 minute. Increase the mixer speed to high and continue to whip until the cream forms soft peaks, 1 to 3 minutes.

up any large clumps with your fingers.

3. Whisk the remaining ⅔ cup granulated sugar, the milk, vanilla, and egg yolk into the cooled chocolate mixture in the skillet. Whisk in the flour mixture, until just combined. Sprinkle the brown sugar mixture evenly over the top, covering the entire surface of the batter. Pour the coffee gently over the brown sugar mixture.

4. Transfer the skillet to the oven and bake the cake until puffed and bubbling and just beginning to pull away from the sides of the skillet, rotating the skillet halfway through baking, about 35 minutes.

5. Using a potholder (the skillet handle will be hot), remove the skillet from the oven. Let the cake cool in the skillet for at least 20 minutes before serving.

SIMPLE SOUFFLÉ

MANY HOME COOKS HAVE NEVER MADE A soufflé, relegating it to the category of "restaurant desserts" that are impossibly difficult to make. While soufflés can be finicky and fussy, requiring stiffly beaten egg whites and a clean bowl (more on this later), they are not nearly as daunting as people think. And, for the chef, it is a rewarding exercise; serving a soufflé for dessert guarantees complete admiration from fellow diners, since the soufflé's airy, foamy texture is in a realm all its own.

We decided the misunderstood soufflé would be a nice addition to our skillet desserts chapter, and wanted to show that it can actually be quite easy to master. We hypothesized that the skillet would help make our soufflé foolproof, because we could utilize heat from the stovetop to activate the batter and ensure a tall, sturdy rise from our egg whites, instead of baking the batter for almost half an hour, as many recipes do. We also thought we could streamline the process and find a much simpler way than the traditional French method to make our soufflé.

In classical French cooking, soufflés are made with either a *béchamel* base (a classic French sauce made from butter, flour, and milk) or a *bouillie* base (a paste made from flour and milk) mixed in to help stabilize the whipped egg whites. But we thought we could eliminate the fussy step of making a béchamel or bouillie, and instead make a simpler base and utilize our skillet and the direct heat of the stovetop to cook and stabilize the egg whites in the batter. We pitted three skillet soufflés—one with béchamel, one with bouillie, and one with raw whipped egg yolks as the base—against one another to see if we were right. Lemon, a common dessert soufflé variation, was the flavor we wanted because the bright, citrus notes burst through the eggy base especially well.

Giving all three soufflés a head start on the stovetop, we found our theory worked out just as we had hoped. Sure, the béchamel- and bouillie-based soufflés tasted fine, but the soufflé with a whipped egg yolk base was far easier to make—we didn't have to cook anything in advance—and boasted a cleaner, fresher lemon flavor. Theory confirmed, we began to tweak the ratio of soufflé batter ingredients in search of the ultimate skillet soufflé texture.

We started with the eggs, which give the soufflé its delicate and lofty texture, using a simple ingredient list—egg whites, egg yolks, and sugar. To determine the proper ratio of egg whites to egg yolks, we tried four variations, whipping whites and yolks separately, then folding the egg whites into the whipped yolk base. We found that too many egg whites resulted in a foamy but stiff soufflé. Eventually we hit on using an equal amount of yolks and whites—five of each—for a supremely rich and creamy soufflé.

The technique used to beat the egg whites is crucial to a successful soufflé—its structure comes solely from the aerated eggs. The objective is to create a strong, stable foam that rises well and doesn't collapse during either folding or baking. We knew that adding sugar to the whites during beating would result in stable whites that would be more resilient when it came time to fold them into the yolks, and the soufflé would be less apt to fall quickly after baking. We made sure our mixing bowl was clean—a bowl with even the tiniest speck of oil or dirt can prevent the whites from rising well—and began whipping our whites, adding sugar at various intervals. Most of the sugar, it turned out, should be added not at the outset of whipping but after the whites break up and become foamy. We also learned that the sugar must be added gradually instead of all at once; dumping in the sugar all at one time produced a soufflé with an uneven, shorter rise and an overly sweet taste. Adding an acid (we used cream of tartar) to the whites as they were whipped also helped them build to a sturdy texture and retain their shape.

At this point, our soufflé was slightly foamier than we wanted. Having tinkered with our egg whites already, we looked to make a few adjustments to our whipped yolk base. We followed the lead of many classic soufflé recipes and added some flour. Two tablespoons turned our foamy soufflé creamy—exactly the texture we were looking for.

We had the great texture of a first-class soufflé, but now had to work on the flavor. A good lemon soufflé should burst with bright, citrus flavors, instead of being overly eggy. We wanted a clean, natural lemon flavor, so we decided against lemon oil and lemon extract, which left harsh, artificial notes behind. In place of the oil and extract, we added a mixture of lemon juice and lemon zest. Starting out with a mere 2 tablespoons of juice and 1 teaspoon zest whipped in with the yolks, we felt that the lemon flavor was hardly present. More zest wasn't the answer, as increased amounts simply added an unwelcome bitter flavor. We upped the lemon juice to ⅓ cup; now we were happy with the lemony flavor and zing.

With our whites sturdily whipped and the egg yolk base brightly flavored, we folded the whites gently into the yolks, being careful not to overmix and deflate the whites. We poured the entire batter into a buttered 10-inch skillet (our soufflé rose

better and had a creamier center in the smaller skillet) and let it cook for a couple minutes over medium-low heat until just set around the edges and on the bottom, setting up the base for the soufflé to rise in the oven. As a bonus, the direct heat on the bottom of the skillet gave the finished soufflé a great crust that tasters loved.

Almost there, we moved the soufflé into the oven to finish cooking. Although we had been

EQUIPMENT: Rasp Graters

To grate raw vegetables or big hunks of cheese, we rely on our sturdy, stand-up box grater. But for zesting a lemon or grating chocolate, we turn to the compact rasp grater. A good grater should be efficient and easy to use, and this one takes up almost zero storage space. To find out which rasp grater performed best, we tested four models currently on the market.

We concluded that success is dependent on a combination of sharp grating teeth and a comfortable handle or grip. In our tests, we encountered flimsy, weak teeth, uncomfortable handles, and incisor-like teeth that ripped through our lemon straight down to the pith. The one that came out on top was the Microplane 8.5-Inch Grater/Zester. Shaped like a ruler, but with lots and lots of tiny, sharp teeth, the Microplane can grate cheese, zest, chocolate, and whole nutmegs smoothly and almost effortlessly. The black plastic handle, which we found more comfortable than any of the others, also earned high praise.

So for grating an endless amount of mozzarella, the box grater is the way to go. But for zesting a lemon or finely grating bittersweet chocolate to make our soufflé recipes, get out the masterful Microplane.

THE BEST RASP GRATER
The Microplane 8.5-inch Grater/Zester ($12.95) has very sharp teeth and a solid handle, which together make grating chocolate and citrus zest a breeze.

MICROPLANE

using a 350-degree oven with decent success up to this point, we wondered if either a higher or lower temperature would work even better. Lower oven temperatures produced heavy, dense soufflés, but a slightly higher temperature of 375 degrees produced a more dramatic rise and sharper contrast between the cooked exterior and the creamy interior.

We expected the soufflé to be done quickly, and started checking on it after seven minutes—just one extra minute in the oven makes all the difference between a perfectly cooked soufflé and one that's overdone. Looking through the oven window, we saw that the top was lightly golden—just right. We dipped into the soufflé with our spoons and found it was perfectly lemony, creamy and moist in the middle, and firm around the outside—another skillet success.

Lemon Soufflé

SERVES 6

Don't open the oven door during the first 7 minutes of baking, but do check the soufflé regularly for doneness during the final few minutes in the oven. Be ready to serve the soufflé immediately after removing it from the oven. Using a 10-inch traditional (not nonstick) skillet is essential to getting the right texture and height in the soufflé.

5	large eggs, separated
¼	teaspoon cream of tartar
⅔	cup (4⅔ ounces) granulated sugar
⅛	teaspoon salt
⅓	cup juice from 2 to 3 lemons
1	teaspoon grated zest from 1 lemon
2	tablespoons unbleached all-purpose flour
1	tablespoon unsalted butter
	Confectioners' sugar, for dusting

1. Adjust an oven rack to the middle position and heat the oven to 375 degrees. Using an electric mixer, whip the egg whites and cream of tartar together on medium-low speed until foamy, about 1 minute. Slowly add ⅓ cup of the granulated sugar and the salt, then increase the mixer speed to medium-high, and continue to whip until stiff peaks form, 3 to 5 minutes. Gently transfer the whites to a clean bowl and set aside.

2. Using an electric mixer (no need to wash the mixing bowl), whip the yolks and the remaining ⅓ cup sugar together on medium-high speed until pale and thick, about 1 minute. Whip in the lemon juice, zest, and flour until incorporated, about 30 seconds.

3. Fold one-quarter of the whipped egg whites into the yolk mixture until almost no white streaks remain. Gently fold in the remaining egg whites until just incorporated.

4. Melt the butter in a 10-inch ovenproof skillet over medium-low heat. Swirl the pan to coat it evenly with the melted butter, then gently scrape the soufflé batter into the skillet and cook until the edges begin to set and bubble slightly, about 2 minutes.

5. Transfer the skillet to the oven and bake the soufflé until puffed, the center jiggles slightly when shaken, and the surface is golden, 7 to 11 minutes. Using a potholder (the skillet handle will be hot), remove the skillet from the oven. Dust the soufflé with the confectioners' sugar and serve immediately.

➤ VARIATION

Chocolate-Orange Soufflé

Grating the chocolate fine is key here; we find it easiest to use either a rasp grater or the fine holes of a box grater.

Follow the recipe for Lemon Soufflé, substituting 1 tablespoon grated zest from 1 orange for the lemon zest, and ⅓ cup orange juice for the lemon juice. Gently fold 1 ounce finely grated bittersweet chocolate (about ½ cup) into the soufflé batter after incorporating all of the whites in step 3.

INDEX

INDEX

A NOTE ON CONVERSIONS

A Note on Conversions

SOME SAY COOKING IS A SCIENCE AND AN art. We would say that geography has a hand in it, too. Flour milled in the United Kingdom and elsewhere will feel and taste different from flour milled in the United States. So we cannot promise that the loaf of bread you bake in Canada or England will taste the same as a loaf baked in the States, but we can offer guidelines for converting weights and measures. We also recommend that you rely on your instincts when making our recipes. Refer to the visual cues provided. If the bread dough hasn't "come together in a ball," as described, you may need to add more flour—even if the recipe doesn't tell you so. You be the judge. To find this information online, visit our Web site at www.cooksillustrated.com and type "conversion chart" in the search box.

The recipes in this book were developed using standard U.S. measures following U.S. government guidelines. The charts below offer equivalents for U.S., metric, and Imperial (U.K.) measures. All conversions are approximate and have been rounded up or down to the nearest whole number.

EXAMPLE:

1 teaspoon	=	4.9292 milliliters, rounded up to 5 milliliters
1 ounce	=	28.3495 grams, rounded down to 28 grams

Volume Conversions

U.S.	METRIC
1 teaspoon	5 milliliters
2 teaspoons	10 milliliters
1 tablespoon	15 milliliters
2 tablespoons	30 milliliters
¼ cup	59 milliliters
⅓ cup	79 milliliters
½ cup	118 milliliters
¾ cup	177 milliliters
1 cup	237 milliliters
1¼ cups	296 milliliters
1½ cups	355 milliliters
2 cups	473 milliliters
2½ cups	592 milliliters
3 cups	710 milliliters
4 cups (1 quart)	0.946 liter
1.06 quarts	1 liter
4 quarts (1 gallon)	3.8 liters

Weight Conversions

OUNCES	GRAMS
½	14
¾	21
1	28
1½	43
2	57
2½	71
3	85
3½	99
4	113
4½	128
5	142
6	170
7	198
8	227
9	255
10	283
12	340
16 (1 pound)	454

Conversions for Ingredients Commonly Used in Baking

Baking is an exacting science. Because measuring by weight is far more accurate than measuring by volume, and thus more likely to achieve reliable results, in our recipes we provide ounce measures in addition to cup measures for many ingredients. Refer to the chart below to convert these measures into grams.

INGREDIENT	OUNCES	GRAMS
1 cup all-purpose flour*	5	142
1 cup whole wheat flour	5½	156
1 cup granulated (white) sugar	7	198
1 cup packed brown sugar (light or dark)	7	198
1 cup confectioners' sugar	4	113
1 cup cocoa powder	3	85
Butter†		
4 tablespoons (½ stick, or ¼ cup)	2	57
8 tablespoons (1 stick, or ½ cup)	4	113
16 tablespoons (2 sticks, or 1 cup)	8	227

* U.S. all-purpose flour, the most frequently used flour in this book, does not contain leaveners, as some European flours do. These leavened flours are called self-rising or self-raising. If you are using self-rising flour, take this into consideration before adding leavening to a recipe.

† In the United States, butter is sold both salted and unsalted. We generally recommend unsalted butter. If you are using salted butter, take this into consideration before adding salt to a recipe.

Oven Temperatures

FAHRENHEIT	CELSIUS	GAS MARK (IMPERIAL)
225	105	¼
250	120	½
275	130	1
300	150	2
325	165	3
350	180	4
375	190	5
400	200	6
425	220	7
450	230	8
475	245	9

Converting Temperatures from an Instant-Read Thermometer

We include doneness temperatures in many of our recipes, such as those for poultry, meat, and bread. We recommend an instant-read thermometer for the job. Refer to the table above to convert Fahrenheit degrees to Celsius. Or, for temperatures not represented in the chart, use this simple formula:

Subtract 32 degrees from the Fahrenheit reading, then divide the result by 1.8 to find the Celsius reading.

EXAMPLE:

"Roast until the juices run clear when the chicken is cut with a paring knife or the thickest part of the breast registers 160 degrees on an instant-read thermometer." To convert:

160°F − 32 = 128°
128° ÷ 1.8 = 71°C (rounded down from 71.11)